THIRTEENTH EDITION

EARLY CHILDHOOD EDUCATION TODAY

GEORGE S. MORRISON

University of North Texas

PEARSON

Boston   Columbus   Indianapolis   New York   San Francisco   Upper Saddle River
Amsterdam   Cape Town   Dubai   London   Madrid   Milan   Munich   Paris   Montréal   Toronto
Delhi   Mexico City   São Paulo   Sydney   Hong Kong   Seoul   Singapore   Taipei   Tokyo

Vice President and Editorial Director: Jeffery W. Johnston
Senior Acquisitions Editor: Julie Peters
Senior Development Editor: Christina Robb
Editorial Assistant: Andrea Hall
Senior Marketing Manager: Krista Clark
Senior Project Manager: Laura Messerly
Senior Operations Supervisor: Michelle Klein
Senior Art Director: Diane C. Lorenzo
Cover and Text Designer: Candace Rowley
Photo Researcher: Jorgensen Fernandez

Permissions Administrator: Tania Zamora
Cover Image: Corbis
Media Producer: Allison Longley
Media Project Manager: Noelle Chun
Full-Service Project Management: Thistle Hill Publishing Services, LLC
Composition: S4Carlisle Publishing Services
Printer/Binder: Courier Kendallville
Cover Printer: Lehigh/Phoenix Color
Text Font: ITC Garamond Std, 10/12

Credits and acknowledgments for materials borrowed from other sources and reproduced, with permission, in this text appear on the appropriate pages within text.

Every effort has been made to provide accurate and current Internet information in this text. However, the Internet and information posted on it are constantly changing, so it is inevitable that some of the Internet addresses listed in this text will change.

Photo Credits: Photo credits appear on page 577, which constitutes a continuation of this copyright page.

Library of Congress Cataloging-in-Publication Data

Morrison, George S.
  Early childhood education today/George S. Morrison, University of North Texas.—Thirteenth edition.
    pages cm
  Includes bibliographical references and index.
  ISBN-13: 978-0-13-343650-1 (hardcover)
  ISBN-10: 0-13-343650-0 (hardcover)
  1. Early childhood education—United States.   I. Title.
  LB1139.25.M66 2014
  372.21—dc23

2013043931

10 9 8 7 6 5 4 3 2 1

ISBN 10:   0-13-343650-0
ISBN 13: 978-0-13-343650-1

To
BETTY JANE
**whose life is full of grace and who
lives the true meaning of love every day.**

GEORGE S. MORRISON is professor of early childhood education at the University of North Texas where he teaches early childhood education and development to undergraduates and mentors masters and doctoral students. He is an experienced teacher and principal in the public schools.

Professor Morrison's accomplishments include a Distinguished Academic Service Award from the Pennsylvania Department of Education, Outstanding Service and Teaching Awards from Florida International University, and the College of Education Faculty Teaching Excellence Award at the University of North Texas. His books include *Early Childhood Education Today*; *Fundamentals of Early Childhood Education*, Seventh Edition; and *Teaching in America*, Fifth Edition. Professor Morrison has also written books about the education and development of infants, toddlers, and preschoolers; child development; the contemporary curriculum; and parent/family/community involvement.

Dr. Morrison is a popular author, speaker, and presenter. He is Senior Contributing Editor for the *Public School Montessorian*. His research and presentations focus on the globalization of early childhood education, the influence of contemporary educational reforms on education, and the application of best practices to early childhood education. Professor Morrison also lectures and gives keynote addresses on early childhood education and development in Thailand, Taiwan, China, South Korea, and the Philippines.

Professor Morrison with mentor teacher Wendy Schwind, intern Meagan Brewer, and children at Caprock Elementary, Keller (TX) ISD. Professor Morrison regularly supervises student interns from the University of North Texas and participates in various school-based activities.

PREFACE

Changes are sweeping across the early childhood landscape, transforming our profession before our eyes! These changes create exciting possibilities for you and all early childhood professionals. We discuss these changes in every chapter of *Early Childhood Education Today*, which is designed to keep you current and on the cutting edge of early childhood teaching practice.

Changes in early childhood education and development bring both opportunities and challenges. Opportunities are endless for you to participate in the ongoing re-creation of the early childhood profession. In fact, creating and re-creating the early childhood profession is one of your constant professional roles. This means you have to create and constantly re-create *yourself* as an early childhood professional. *Early Childhood Education Today* helps you achieve this professional goal. The challenges involved in reforming the profession include collaboration, hard work, and constant dedication to achieving high-quality education for *all* children. I hope you will take full advantage of these opportunities to help all children learn the knowledge and skills they need to succeed in school and life. I believe how you and I respond to the opportunities we have in front of us today will determine the future of early childhood education. This text helps you learn what it takes to understand and teach young children and how to provide them the support they and their families need and deserve.

NEW TO THIS EDITION

Of the many changes in the new edition, I am perhaps most excited to introduce you to a new version of *Early Childhood Education Today*—the new eText. The eText is an affordable, interactive version of the print text that includes many new and exciting features in every chapter, such as chapter-opening links to specific NAEYC standards that correlate with the chapter, interactive Observe and Reflect exercises that provide video illustrations of chapter content, interactive Reflect and Apply exercises that prompt you to apply what you've just read by suggesting a solution for a challenging situation typically encountered in early childhood settings, and interactive Check Your Understanding features that help you determine whether you understand fundamental concepts covered in the chapter or need a review. (See the Text Features section for additional new features.)

To learn more about the enhanced Pearson eText, go to www.pearsonhighered.com/etextbooks.

In addition to the new eText, in the thirteenth edition, you can expect the following:

- Increased focus on *practical and applicable content,* which provides you with instructional practices you can take into the classroom. Every chapter specifically outlines and identifies through *Implications for Teaching* headings what teachers can do in their classrooms to help children learn and grow.

- Seven new *Voice from the Field* and *Voice from the Field: Competency Builder* features.

- A refocused emphasis on the *professional goals and responsibilities* of early childhood teachers today. Every chapter focuses on the *contemporary societal and educational issues* that influence what teachers teach and how they teach and the professional practices teachers need to be successful.

- An expanded discussion of *teaching with standards*, including state standards, Common Core State Standards, and professional organization standards. Teaching today is truly standard-based, and this new edition provides you with an understanding of how important standards are in today's classroom.

- An increased emphasis on how teachers can incorporate *culturally appropriate and respectful practices* into their teaching and learning.

- An expanded discussion of the integration of *technology* through teaching and learning. This expanded discussion is demonstrated by more examples of how teachers use technology to teach and by a new 5E lesson plan specifically designed around teaching with technology.

- An expanded discussion with many examples of the teacher's role in observation and assessment of children's learning and how to use observation and *assessment* to enhance instructional practices.

- New *Ethical Dilemmas* at the end of the chapters which involve you in issues and dilemmas from contemporary classrooms.

THEMES OF THIS BOOK

Early Childhood Education Today, Thirteenth Edition, integrates thirteen critical themes that are foundational to the field today.

1. The importance of *children's literacy development*. As more school districts move toward complying with legislation that requires children to read on grade level by grade 3, you must know how to promote children's reading achievement so that all children can learn and be successful.

2. The growing number of *diverse children* in America's classrooms today and implications of this demographic shift for your teaching and learning.

3. The importance of *developmentally appropriate practices (DAP)* and the application of these practices to all aspects of early childhood programs and classroom activities. With today's emphasis on academic achievement, this text anchors your professional practice in DAP, beginning in Chapter 1.

4. The effects of the Great Recession on children and their families. More children and families have slipped below the *poverty* line. Many of your children will come to school unprepared to meet the challenges of preschool or kindergarten. This text helps you educate all children and close the achievement gaps that exist between children in poverty and their more economically advantaged peers.

5. The integration of the fields of *special education* and early childhood education. Increasingly, special education practices are influencing early childhood practices. This text helps you understand the integration of the two fields and how this integration provides enhanced opportunities for you and the children you teach.

6. The *inclusive classroom* movement. You will teach in an inclusive classroom. This text prepares you to be an inclusive teacher of all young children regardless of disability, in the least restrictive environment possible.

7. *School readiness*. How to help families get their children ready for school and how to promote children's school readiness is at the forefront of issues facing society today. This text provides you with helpful information, ideas, and strategies that enable you to close the readiness gaps that exist across ethnic, gender, linguistic, and socioeconomic backgrounds.

8. The emphasis on *teacher accountability for student achievement*. Today, early childhood teachers—indeed, all teachers—are accountable for how, what, and to what extent children learn. This text helps you meet this challenge confidently and boldly; it provides you with step-by-step strategies for helping all children learn in developmentally appropriate ways.

9. The integration of *STEM* (science, technology, engineering, and mathematics) subjects into the curriculum. STEM subjects are considered to be of great importance by the nation's business leaders and constitute the foundation for providing a well-trained and educated workforce.

10. A renewed emphasis on providing for *children's mental health*. With the shootings at Sandy Hook Elementary School and other violent tragedies around the nation, society is demanding that the nation's schools provide for children's healthy social and emotional development.

11. The use of *technology* to support children's learning. Contemporary teachers are savvy users of technology to promote children's learning and their own professional development. This text helps you gain the technological skills you need to teach in today's classroom. Practicing teachers provide you practical technological examples for how to use technology to support teaching and learning in *Voices from the Field* as well as in Chapter 13.

12. *Ongoing professional development.* As an early childhood professional, you will be constantly challenged to create and re-create yourself as society and professional practices change. *Early Childhood Education Today* helps you be the professional you need to be by explaining the competencies you'll need in the classroom today. See Seventeen Competencies for Becoming a Professional in Chapter 1 (Figure 1.6), which can guide your development.

13. *Guiding children's behavior* and promoting children's ability to be responsible for their own behavior.

TEXT FEATURES

The thirteenth edition of *Early Childhood Education Today* includes numerous features designed to illustrate developmentally appropriate practice and provide a framework for you to reflect on and apply the chapter content. Here are a few things to look for:

A new modular chapter organization built around critical learning outcomes and aligned to professional standards

- **NEW CHAPTER-OPENING LEARNING OUTCOMES.** Clarifying exactly what you will learn in the chapter, these learning outcomes align with the major text sections of the chapter. In the eText, you can click on the learning outcome to be taken directly to the relevant section of the chapter.

LEARNING OUTCOMES

1. Explain what kindergarten is like today.
2. Describe high-quality environments for kindergarten children.
3. List the physical, social-emotional, and cognitive characteristics of kindergartners.
4. Explain what the kindergarten curriculum is like.
5. List the ways in which you can accommodate diverse kindergarten learners.

- **CORRELATION TO NAEYC STANDARDS FOR PROFESSIONAL PREPARATION PROGRAMS.** In the eText, new chapter-opening links correlate the chapter to the specific National Association for the Education of Young Children (NAEYC) standards covered, helping you become familiar with these important standards for knowledge and practice.

Features contributed by early childhood educators that demonstrate authentic developmentally appropriate practices from around the country

- **VOICE FROM THE FIELD.** Teachers' authentic voices play a major role in illustrating authentic practices. Voice from the Field features enable practicing teachers to explain to you their philosophies, beliefs, and program practices. These teachers mentor you as they relate how they practice early childhood education. Among the contributors are professionals who are Teachers of the Year, have received prestigious awards, and have national board certification.

- **VOICE FROM THE FIELD: COMPETENCY BUILDER.** The Voice from the Field features that are labeled as Competency Builders are designed to build your competence and confidence in performing essential teaching tasks, step by step.

VOICE FROM THE FIELD

COMPETENCY BUILDER

Using Blocks to Help Preschoolers Build Mathematical Skills

Froebel, the father of kindergarten, introduced blocks to the early childhood curriculum with his creation of gifts. Froebel developed these materials to facilitate children's creativity and provide opportunities for them to construct geometric forms. Many preschool classrooms today have a block center or area dedicated to block play. These play areas include a variety of blocks that vary in size, shape, color, and texture. When children have time to explore and experiment with these resources, they have the opportunity to develop the foundation for mathematical concepts related to algebra, geometry, and measurement.

When including blocks in the early childhood mathematics classroom, consider the following ideas.

STEP 1 **Use a Variety of Instructional Approaches**
- Give children time to explore freely with blocks during center time as well as other times during the day. Providing opportunities for free play allows children to develop various intuitive geometric concepts and problem-solving skills while tapping into their innate mathematical interest about the world around them.
- Informally guide children's individual block play to help them connect prior learning experiences or deepen their understanding of a concept. Pose questions about the children's play to provoke mathematical conversations. For example, when a child sorts blocks into different groups, ask the child about these groupings with questions such as:
  - Why did you put these blocks together?
  - What other blocks could you put into this group?
  - What is the name of this group?
- Use blocks in small group or whole group instruction to introduce or review mathematical concepts such as counting or identifying various shapes.

STEP 2 **Provide Children with Different Types of Blocks to Explore**
Incorporate a variety of manipulatives—including different types of blocks—for young children to use in the preschool classroom. Providing these materials will allow children to explore mathematical concepts such as sorting, patterns, measurement, and geometry. The accompanying table lists some of the common types of blocks used in preschool classrooms and some of the mathematical concepts children develop when using these materials.

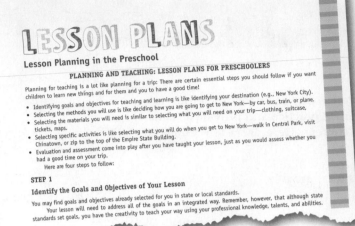

LESSON PLANS

Lesson Planning in the Preschool

PLANNING AND TEACHING: LESSON PLANS FOR PRESCHOOLERS

Planning for teaching is a lot like planning for a trip: There are certain essential steps you should follow if you want children to learn new things and for them and you to have a good time!

- Identifying goals and objectives for teaching and learning is like identifying your destination (e.g., New York City).
- Selecting the methods you will use is like deciding how you are going to get to New York—by car, bus, train, or plane.
- Selecting the materials you will need is similar to selecting what you will need on your trip—clothing, suitcase, tickets, maps.
- Selecting specific activities is like selecting what you will do when you get to New York—walk in Central Park, visit Chinatown, or zip to the top of the Empire State Building.
- Evaluation and assessment come into play after you have taught your lesson, just as you would assess whether you had a good time on your trip.
  Here are four steps to follow:

STEP 1

Identify the Goals and Objectives of Your Lesson

You may find goals and objectives already selected for you in state or local standards.
      Your lesson will need to address all of the goals in an integrated way. Remember, however, that although state standards set goals, you have the creativity to teach your way using your professional knowledge, talents, and abilities.

- **LESSON PLANS.** Planning for teaching and learning constitutes an important dimension of your role as a professional. This is especially true today, with the emphasis on ensuring that children learn what is mandated by state standards. The lesson plans in this text, found in chapters 9–13, follow the 5E Model (engage, explore, explain, extend, and evaluate). They enable you to look over the shoulder of experienced teachers and observe how they plans for instruction. These award-winning teachers share with you plans to ensure that their children learn important knowledge and skills.

Features that show you real children and early childhood settings in action.

- **NEW VIDEO EXAMPLES.** In each chapter at least one video is included that illustrates text concepts and provides a window into the real world of teaching young children.

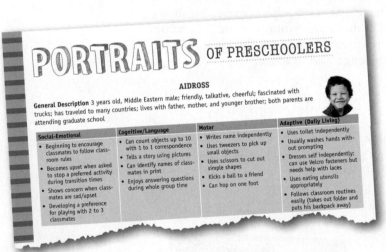

PORTRAITS OF PRESCHOOLERS

AIDROSS

General Description 3 years old, Middle Eastern male; friendly, talkative, cheerful; fascinated with trucks; has traveled to many countries; lives with father, mother, and younger brother; both parents are attending graduate school

Social-Emotional	Cognitive/Language	Motor	Adaptive (Daily Living)
• Beginning to encourage classmates to follow classroom rules • Becomes upset when asked to stop a preferred activity during transition times • Shows concern when classmates are sad/upset • Developing a preference for playing with 2 to 3 classmates	• Can count objects up to 10 with 1 to 1 correspondence • Tells a story using pictures • Can identify names of classmates in print • Enjoys answering questions during whole group time	• Writes name independently • Uses tweezers to pick up small objects • Uses scissors to cut out simple shapes • Kicks a ball to a friend • Can hop on one foot	• Uses toilet independently • Usually washes hands without prompting • Dresses self independently; can use Velcro fasteners but needs help with laces • Uses eating utensils appropriately • Follows classroom routines easily (takes out folder and puts his backpack away)

- **PORTRAITS OF CHILDREN.** In a text about children, it is sometimes easy to think about them in the abstract. The Portraits of Children found in Chapters 9 through 12 are designed to ensure that you consider children as individuals as we discuss how to teach them. The features present authentic portraits of real children from all cultures and backgrounds, enrolled in real child care, preschool, and primary-grade programs across the United States. Each portrait includes developmental information across four domains: social-emotional, cognitive, motor, and adaptive (daily living). Accompanying questions challenge you to think and reflect about how you would provide for these children's educational and social needs if they were in your classroom.

Activities and features that help you assess and apply your understanding. New interactive features in the eText require a higher level of engagement with text concepts.

L: Listen and learn. The child's previous teachers, therapists, and parents have a wealth of child-specific, relevant information that includes strategies or adaptations that have previously been successful. Having a collaborative dialogue also allows you to share the services and supports available at your school. For example, a parent might tell you that a child uses modified scissors when cutting or enjoys social praise.

Check Your Understanding: Programs

- **NEW CHECK YOUR UNDERSTANDING EXERCISES.** These interactive eText exercises present you with a scenario and a set of response options. Feedback on your answers will help you determine whether you understand fundamental concepts covered in the chapter or need a review.

- **NEW REFLECT AND APPLY EXERCISES.** These eText exercises present you with challenging situations and ask you to apply text content to propose a solution. Feedback is provided so that you can compare your response with that of an experienced teacher.

> Some teachers use technology to develop digital portfolios, which can stand alone or supplement the traditional portfolio. Digital portfolios include books and journals that children keep on computers and then illustrate with digital cameras. However, it is important to remember that portfolios are only one part of children's assessment.
>
> **Reflect and Apply:** Portfolio

- **NEW OBSERVE AND ANALYZE EXERCISES.** These video-based eText exercises present you with a video illustrating child growth and development, teaching, and/or learning in action. An open-ended question asks you to examine the video critically and respond using evidence from the video and your understanding of chapter concepts. Feedback is provided for support or to compare your answer with that of an experienced teacher. Examples include meeting the needs of English language learners and supporting early literacy.

> knowledge or experiences to math, motivates students to explore, and supports memorization. Another way to appeal to different learning modalities in math is to use manipulatives. When children can count beans, coins, and pattern blocks, they are able to understand concepts more readily, which boosts self-esteem and confidence in their math capabilities.
>
> ▶ **Observe and Analyze**

Chapter-ending *Activities for Professional Development.*

- **ETHICAL DILEMMAS.** As an early childhood professional you will inevitably face difficult choices in your career that require you to have a solid understanding of ethical responsibility and best practices. To that end, each chapter includes an ethical dilemma based on facts, current issues, and real-life situations faced by early childhood professionals today. They present difficult decisions early childhood professionals have to make. These ethical dilemmas help you build a better understanding of what it means to think like a professional and to respond appropriately in complicated and potentially compromising situations.

- **ACTIVITIES TO APPLY WHAT YOU HAVE LEARNED.** Here we revisit the chapter-opening learning outcomes and provide one activity per learning outcome to help you assess your content knowledge and/or apply your understanding of that content. For each set of questions, one has been labeled a "key assessment," meaning that it is designed around a critical concept in the chapter. For these assessments, a rubric is provided to help guide your work (and to help your instructor evaluate it).

- **GLOSSARY TERMS AND DEFINITIONS.** Keeping track of important key terms is a problem often associated with reading and studying. Key terms and concepts are defined in the text as they are presented and are also placed in page margins. In this way, you have immediate access to them for reflection and review, and they maximize your study time by helping you retain essential knowledge. A glossary of terms at the end of the book incorporates all of the definitions and terms found in the margin notes, providing a quick reference for study and reflection. In the eText, you can simply click on the key term in the text and the definition will pop up for you.

SUPPLEMENTS TO THE TEXT

The supplements for the thirteenth edition are revised, upgraded, and available for instructors to download on www.pearsonhighered.com/educators. Instructors enter the author or title of this book, select this particular edition of the book, and then click on the "Resources" tab to log in and download textbook supplements.

INSTRUCTOR'S RESOURCE MANUAL (0-13-355282-9) This manual contains chapter overviews and activity ideas to enhance chapter concepts.

TEST BANK (0-13-355283-7) The Test Bank includes a variety of test items, including multiple choice, true/false, and short answer items.

TESTGEN COMPUTERIZED TEST BANK (0-13-355281-0) TestGen is a powerful assessment generation program available exclusively from Pearson that helps instructors easily create quizzes and exams. You install TestGen on your personal computer (Windows or Macintosh) and create your own exams for print or online use. It contains a set of test items organized by chapter, based on this textbook's contents. The items are the same as those in the Test Bank. The tests can be downloaded in a variety of learning management system formats.

POWERPOINT SLIDES (0-13-355284-5) PowerPoint slides highlight key concepts and strategies in each chapter and enhance lectures and discussions.

ACKNOWLEDGMENTS

In the course of my teaching, service, consulting, and writing, I meet and talk with many early childhood professionals who are deeply dedicated to doing their best for young children and their families. I am always touched, heartened, and encouraged by the openness, honesty, and unselfish sharing of ideas that characterize my professional colleagues. I thank all the individuals who contributed to the Voice from the Field features and other program descriptions. They are all credited for sharing their personal accounts of their lives, their children's lives, and their programs.

I am blessed to work with my colleagues at Pearson. My editor, Julie Peters, is bright, savvy, and always relentless in her efforts to make *Early Childhood Education Today* the best. Julie continues to be a constant source of creative and exciting ideas. Development Editor Christie Robb is a pleasure to work with. Christie is focused on providing a high-quality textbook for the early childhood profession. For every step in the writing, editing, and publishing process, Christie centered our attention on getting the job done. Project Managers Laura Messerly and Angela Williams Urquhart (Thistle Hill Publishing Services) are very attentive to detail and make sure every part of the production process is done right and that we meet all production deadlines.

I want to especially thank my outstanding student assistant Cassandra Cardwell. Cassie participated in the revision of *Early Childhood Education Today*, Thirteenth Edition, from the beginning and has been indispensable in assisting with the research and the many details necessary to publish a high-quality textbook. Cassie brought her outstanding organizational skills, intellect, and professionalism to the revision process. I am grateful and thankful to her for this. I would also like to thank student researchers Dylan Lee, Jerrica Anderson, and Amanda Bower for their help and support.

Finally, I want to thank the reviewers: Sabine Gerhardt, University of Akron; Kathleen Head, Lorain County Community College; Robin Johns, Ashland Community and Technical College; Tara Mathien, Harper College; and Elvia Rivero, Oxnard College.

BRIEF CONTENTS

CONTENTS

Federal and State Governments:
Supporting Children's Success 204

PART 4
Teaching Today's Young Children: Linking Development and Learning

Infants and Toddlers:
Foundation Years for Learning 234

15

Multiculturalism:
Living and Learning in a Diverse Society 434

16

Children with Diverse Needs:
Appropriate Education for All 456

17 Parents, Families, and the Community:
Building Partnerships for Student Success 496

SPECIAL FEATURES

*Voice from the Field: Competency Builders outline specific steps, strategies, or guidelines to guide early childhood professionals as they develop competencies or skills in these areas.

THIRTEENTH EDITION

EARLY CHILDHOOD EDUCATION TODAY

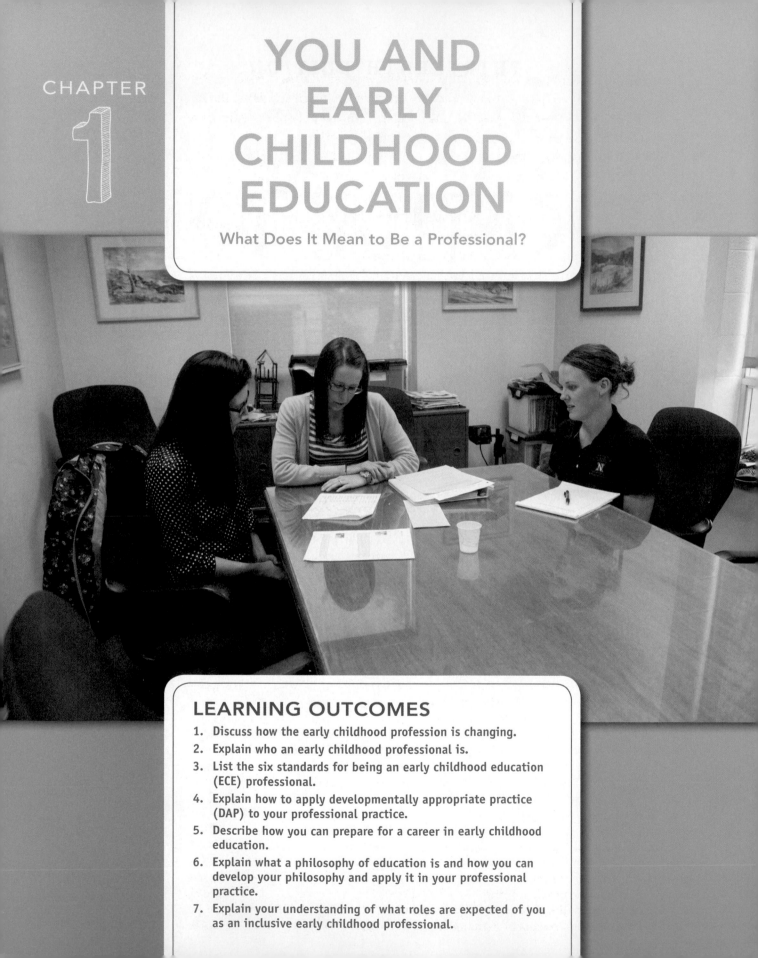

YOU AND EARLY CHILDHOOD EDUCATION

What Does It Mean to Be a Professional?

LEARNING OUTCOMES

1. Discuss how the early childhood profession is changing.
2. Explain who an early childhood professional is.
3. List the six standards for being an early childhood education (ECE) professional.
4. Explain how to apply developmentally appropriate practice (DAP) to your professional practice.
5. Describe how you can prepare for a career in early childhood education.
6. Explain what a philosophy of education is and how you can develop your philosophy and apply it in your professional practice.
7. Explain your understanding of what roles are expected of you as an inclusive early childhood professional.

EVER since she was in high school, Renee Comacho wanted to teach young children. Not just any children, but children with disabilities. During her junior year, Renee joined a summer volunteer intern program at her local child care center that had five children with disabilities. She really enjoyed working with them! That experience got her hooked on early childhood special education! Today, Renee teaches K–3 in a public early childhood center of two hundred children that includes children with many kinds of disabilities. Renee is working on her master's degree and wants to earn National Board Certification as an exceptional needs specialist. Renee works with teams of teachers and they are always learning how to accommodate lessons and activities to assure that they are meeting the needs of all children—especially those with disabilities. At the beginning of this school year, they all participated in training about how to accommodate the curriculum and classroom environments to support learning. They also learned how to involve families of children with disabilities. Renee and her colleagues have high expectations for all the children, so they want to make sure they do the best they can for them. As you can tell, Renee is excited about teaching and wants the best for her children. I hope you feel the same way!

CHANGES IN THE EARLY CHILDHOOD PROFESSION

This is a wonderful time to be a member of the early childhood education profession. The field of **early childhood education**, which includes knowledge of how children from birth to age eight grow, develop, and learn, has changed more in the last ten years than in the previous fifty years, and more changes are on the way! Why is early childhood education undergoing dramatic transformation and reform?

CHANGES IN EARLY CHILDHOOD EDUCATION. First, there is a tremendous increase in scientific knowledge about how young children grow, develop, and learn. This new knowledge helps parents and teachers view young children as being extremely capable and naturally eager to learn at very young ages. Second, all across the United States, educators have developed research-based programs and curricula that enable children to learn literally from the beginning of life. Third, influential research, such as the HighScope Perry Preschool Project, validates the fact that high-quality education in the early years has positive and lasting benefits for children throughout their lives.[1] Additional research from the Abecedarian Project and the Chicago Parent-Child Centers (CPCs) demonstrate the long- and short-term benefits of quality early education and child care, particularly for children who come from low-income families.[2] The way children are reared and educated in the early formative years makes a significant difference in the way they develop and learn. When families, teachers, and other caring adults get it right from the start of children's lives, all of society reaps big dividends. Fourth, more than 75 percent of all four-year-olds attend some kind of preschool program, and more than 1.3 million children attend state-funded preschool education.[3] The demand for teachers for these children, as well as ongoing public and professional interest, will continue to focus attention on the early years and the importance they play in lifelong education. Finally, politicians are rediscovering young children. During the Great Recession of 2007–2010 and the years following, politicians either eliminated or reduced funding for preschool programs. Now, thanks in part to President Obama's call for universal preschool in his 2013 State

early childhood education
The growth, development, and education of children birth through age eight.

of the Union Address, all seems to be changing, with more states joining the federal government in allocating more funding for preschools.

As a result of all these changes, the field of early childhood education is entering a new era, which requires well-educated early childhood professionals who are up-to-date on current methods, who are willing to develop new and improved programs for children and families, and who will advocate for best practices for all young children. Ongoing change and how you can respond to it is one of the themes of the early childhood profession and this book.

WHO IS AN EARLY CHILDHOOD PROFESSIONAL?

Like Renee, you are preparing to be a highly qualified and effective early childhood professional, who teaches children from birth to age eight. You are going to work with families and the community to bring high-quality education and services to all children. How would you explain the term *early childhood professional* to others? What does *professional* mean?

Early childhood professionals promote child development and learning; build family and community relationships; observe, document, and assess to support young children and families; promote positive teaching and learning for young children; and identify with and conduct themselves as members of the early childhood profession.

early childhood professional An educator who successfully teaches all children, promotes high personal standards, and continually expands his or her skills and knowledge.

You are preparing to be an **early childhood professional**—that is, a person who successfully teaches all children (birth to age eight), promotes high personal and professional standards, and continually expands your skills and knowledge. You will teach all children and develop supportive relationships with them to help ensure that each child can achieve and be successful. For example, National Teacher of the Year Rebecca Mieliwoki promotes high-quality teaching based on her belief that students learn best when they have the most enthusiastic, engaged teachers possible.[4]

Professionals promote high standards for themselves, their colleagues, and their students. They are multidimensional people who use their many talents to enrich the lives of children and families.

Early childhood professionals constantly change in response to new jobs created by the expanding field of early childhood education. They continually improve their skills and knowledge. You can expect that you will participate in many professional development activities, will be constantly involved in new programs and practices, and will have opportunities to engage in new and different roles as a professional.

THE SIX STANDARDS OF PROFESSIONAL DEVELOPMENT

Being a professional goes beyond academic degrees and experiences. High-quality professionalism in early childhood education has six integrated standards, all of which are important and necessary dimensions of your professional experience. These are located at the beginning of each chapter. Figure 1.1, "The Six NAEYC Standards for Early Childhood Professional Practice," shows how each of these standards plays a powerful role in determining who and what a professional is and how professionals implement practice in early childhood classrooms. Let's review each of these standards and see how you can apply them to your professional practice. In the video, George S. Morrison, EdD, Professor of Early Childhood Education at the University of North Texas, discusses the NAEYC Professional Development Standards. Professor Morrison clearly identifies how and why these standards are important for your professional development. As you observe, make sure that you clearly understand each standard and how you can begin to apply them to your ongoing professional development.

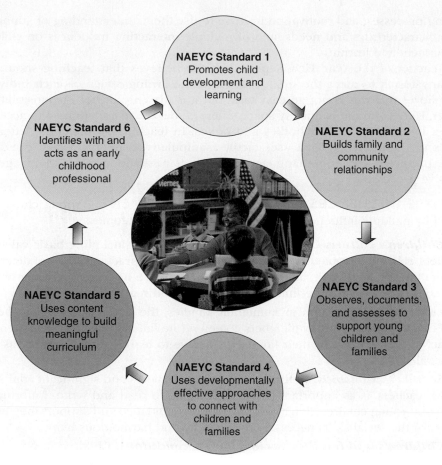

FIGURE 1.1 | Six NAEYC Standards for Early Childhood Professional Preparation Programs

These standards of professional preparation provide guidelines for what you should know and be able to do in your lifelong career as an early childhood professional.

Source: National Association for the Education of Young Children, NAEYC Standards for Early Childhood Professional Preparation Programs, July 2009.

STANDARD 1: PROMOTING CHILD DEVELOPMENT AND LEARNING

CHILD DEVELOPMENT. As an early childhood professional you will need to understand child development and learning and how to promote them. **Child development** is the stages of physical, social, mental, and linguistic growth that occur from birth through age eight. Learning how to do this includes knowledge and understanding of young children's characteristics and needs and the multiple influences on children's development and learning.

Knowledge of child development is fundamental for all early childhood educators regardless of their roles or the ages of the children they teach. It enables an educator to confidently implement developmentally appropriate practices with all children. All early childhood professionals "base their practice on sound knowledge and understanding of young children's characteristics and needs. This foundation encompasses multiple, interrelated areas of children's development and learning—including physical, cognitive, social, emotional, language, and aesthetic domains; play, activity, and

child development
The stages of physical, social, mental, and linguistic growth that occur from birth through age eight years.

learning processes; and motivation to learn to use their understanding of young children's characteristics and needs, and of multiple interacting influences on children's development and learning."[5]

Teacher of the Year Tina Repetti-Renzullo believes that teaching should take on many forms to meet the unique needs and learning styles of each individual. She believes that this is not an easy task, but it is the core of her responsibility as a teacher. Her classroom is a lively space where students are encouraged to access the content by employing their bodies and brains. In teaching students the letters and sounds of the alphabet, Tina uses tactile manipulatives, poetry, visual cues, song, dance, puppetry, and home language as much as possible in order to engage their cognitive processes.[6]

MULTIPLE INFLUENCES AND CHILD DEVELOPMENT. Young children are shaped by multiple influences that determine their life outcomes:

culture A group's way of life, including basic values, beliefs, religion, language, clothing, food, and various practices.

- *Children's culture.* Culture is a group's way of life, including basic values, beliefs, religion, language, clothing, food, and various practices. Culture determines the foods children eat, the kind of care they receive or do not receive from their parents, and helps determine how they view and react to the world.
- *Language.* Quite often in immigrant families, the burden of helping the non-English-speaking family members communicate falls on the child. Children often act as interpreters for their families and have to learn to communicate as a survival skill.
- *Social relationships.* Getting along with one's peers and significant adults, such as teachers, is as important a skill as learning to read and write. Unfortunately, many young children don't have the parental guidance and support they need to learn the social skills necessary for peaceful and harmonious living.
- *Children's and families' socioeconomic conditions.* Children in poverty represent 24 percent of the total population.[7] Research clearly shows that children in poverty do not do well in school and life. This means that you will teach children in poverty, and as a professional you will be responsible for their learning, growth, and development.
- *Children with disabilities.* It is estimated that 13 percent of all children in public schools have a disability of some kind.[8] There is every reason to believe that this number will increase as methods for diagnoses increase. Children come to child care, preschool, and grades K–3 with many physical, behavioral, and learning disabilities. As an early childhood professional, you will care for and educate children with physical, behavioral, and learning disabilities.

EARLY CHILDHOOD AND SPECIAL EDUCATION AND YOU

CHILDREN WITH DISABILITIES. As more children with disabilities are included in the regular classroom, early childhood and special education are blending and integrating. For example, kindergarten teacher Julie Sanders has in her classroom a child with autism and a child with attention deficit hyperactivity disorder (ADHD). As a result, she applies knowledge of typical and atypical child development. As a teacher of young children, you will more than likely have at least one child with a disability in your classroom. Consequently, it is important that you, like Julie, know the developmental characteristics of children with disabilities as well as typically developing children.

Throughout this text, you will find specific ideas and skills for accommodating children with disabilities.

Just as the NAEYC has standards for professional development, so too does the Division of Early Childhood (DEC) of the Council for Exceptional Children. These professional standards guide the preparation of teachers who are preparing to be early childhood special education teachers. These standards apply to you for two reasons: First, you will be teaching in an **inclusive classroom**, a regular classroom in which children with disabilities are included. The inclusive classroom is the "new normal" for teachers today. Second, you must know typical and atypical child growth and development and how to provide developmentally appropriate teaching and learning for children with disabilities in your classroom. You can access DEC's professional standards at the DEC website.

Knowledge of individual children, combined with knowledge of child growth and development, enables you to provide care and education that is developmentally appropriate for each child. **Developmentally Appropriate Practice**, or DAP, means basing your teaching on how children grow and develop, and DAP is the recommended teaching practice of the early childhood profession. You can access the NAEYC's Position Statement on Developmentally Appropriate Practice in Early Childhood Programs at the NAEYC website.

Melanie Park, the 2012 Indiana Teacher of the Year, connects with each of her students individually in order to motivate them to learn and to differentiate instruction. She helps students set reading goals, create data portfolios, and chart their own reading growth. Her superintendent believes that Melanie views herself as an academic trainer whose primary mission is to relate, motivate, and differentiate instruction for her students. She has an exceptional ability to achieve this mission by using her life experiences and learned abilities as a professional educator to connect with the learning needs of her students.[9]

DEVELOPMENTALLY APPROPRIATE APPROACHES. Knowledge of child development provides the foundation for you to conduct **developmentally appropriate practices (DAP)**. With your understanding of child development you will be able to select essential curricula and instructional approaches with confidence. All early childhood professionals use their understanding of child development as the foundation for their work with young children.

Teachers such as Steven Hokama, from Mililani-Ike Elementary School in Hawaii, understand that they must teach the whole child. Hokama believes that every student can learn, should experience success, and have fun as he develops the "whole" child—physically, mentally, and socially. In teaching physical education, Hokama has found ways to encourage cognitive and emotional development and teamwork while students improve motor skills and physical endurance.[10]

We discuss DAP in more detail throughout this book. These ideas and specific strategies for implementing DAP serve as your road map for teaching. As you read about DAP suggestions, consider how you can begin now to apply them in your professional practice.

Culturally Appropriate Practice. **Developmentally and culturally responsive practice (DCRP)** includes being sensitive to and responding to children's cultural and ethnic backgrounds and needs. The United States is a nation of diverse people, and this diversity will increase. Children in every early childhood program represent this diversity. When children enter schools and programs, they do not leave their uniqueness, gender, culture, socioeconomic status, and race at the classroom door. Children bring themselves and their backgrounds to early childhood programs. As part of your professional practice you will embrace, value, and incorporate **culturally appropriate practice** into your teaching. Learning how to teach children of all cultures is an important part of your professional role.

---

inclusive classroom
A regular classroom in which children with disabilities are included.

developmentally appropriate practice (DAP) Practice based on how children grow and develop and on individual and cultural differences.

developmentally and culturally responsive practice (DCRP) Teaching based on the ability to respond appropriately to children's and families' developmental, cultural, and ethnic backgrounds and needs.

culturally appropriate practice An approach to education based on the premise that all peoples in the United States should receive proportional attention in the curriculum.

individual cultural
identity Learning about
the self.

Critical goals for developing cultural identity include developing in children an **individual cultural identity** that involves learning about the self—"who am I?" They also involve learning about the culture of which the child is a part and how the child relates to and functions in that culture. For this reason, you should provide activities and an environmental context in which children can learn about their cultures, identify with them, and feel comfortable about being a part of them.

IMPLICATIONS FOR TEACHING

- ***Evaluate your classroom environment and instructional materials to determine if they are appropriate for culturally appropriate practice.*** Make sure your books, fiction and nonfiction, represent children of all races and cultures. In my visits to early childhood classrooms, I observe many that are "cluttered," meaning they contain too many materials that do not contribute to a multicultural learning environment. Include photos and representations from all cultures in your classroom.

- ***Redesign your classroom.*** For example, you may decide to add a literacy center that encourages children to read and write about multicultural themes. Remember that children need the time, opportunity, and materials required to read and write about a wide range of multicultural topics. Make sure you provide children with books relating to gender, culture, and ethnic themes.

- ***Evaluate your current curriculum and approaches to diversity.*** Review your curriculum to see how it is supporting multicultural approaches. Learning experiences should be relevant to your students, their community, and their families' cultures. When you are diversifying your curriculum, consider two categories: how you teach and what you teach.

- ***Make sure all children are accepted and valued.*** For example, develop plans for ensuring that children of all cultures and genders are included in play groups and activities. Anne Borys, a physical therapist from Drexel University, suggests that teachers promote disability awareness and acceptance in childhood by having a "disability for a day" in your classroom. Have children wear mittens and attempt to button their shirt, play with play dough with rubber bands on fingers, and put Vaseline on plastic glasses to help your inclusive classroom gain awareness and understanding of children who have disabilities.[11]

The United States is a pluralistic society and will continue to be a nation of diverse cultures and ethnic backgrounds. It is important for you to promote racial and cultural awareness and to help children live in harmony with others.

- ***Reflect on your interaction with all children.*** You may unknowingly give more attention to boys than to girls. Also, you may overlook some important environmental accommodations that can support the learning of children with disabilities. How do you interact with children of different cultures? With children who have disabilities?

- ***Include multicultural activities in your lesson plans.*** Intentional planning helps ensure that you include a full range of antibias activities in your program. Intentional multicultural planning also helps you integrate multicultural activities into your curriculum for meeting national, state, and local learning standards.

- ***Work with families to incorporate your multicultural curriculum.*** Remember, families are valuable resources in helping you achieve your goals. One way to connect with parents is to send home a survey to learn more about your students' ethnic and cultural backgrounds so that you can incorporate them into your classroom's instructional activities.

Implementing a multicultural education will not be easy and will require a lot of hard work and effort on your part. However, this is what teaching and being a professional is about. You owe it to yourself, your children, and the profession to conduct programs that enable all children to live and learn in them.

KNOWLEDGE OF INDIVIDUAL CHILDREN. Knowledge and understanding of young children's characteristics and needs enables you to develop and implement meaningful learning experiences that promote learning for all children. Say, for example, you were a beginning teacher with several English language learners or ELLs (also referred to as Dual Language Learners or DLLs) in your class. You would want to know how ELLs learn best and how to teach them so they learn at high levels. Effective pedagogical approaches include using developmentally appropriate practices, selecting and using culturally appropriate learning materials, promoting children's oral language and communication, supporting child-initiated learning, guiding children's learning and behavior, promoting responsive relationships, establishing and using learning centers, using play as a foundation for children's learning, and using technology as a teaching and learning tool. These are all topics you will want to study and reflect on as you prepare to be an early childhood professional.

The featured Voice from the Field that follows, "Tools for Teaching Tolerance to Young Children," shares some important suggestions to guide you in making sure your professional practice is multicultural. This Voice from the Field is also a Competency Builder. Competency Builders are features designed to help you increase your teaching competence and performance in specific professional areas. By completing the Competency Builder activities, you enhance your professional development and contribute to your qualifications as a high-quality and highly effective teacher.

CREATING HEALTHY, RESPECTFUL, SUPPORTIVE, AND CHALLENGING LEARNING ENVIRONMENTS. Children are healthier, happier, and more achievement oriented when they are cared for and taught in enriched environments. To attain this goal for all children, provide them with environments that are healthy, respectful, supportive, and challenging.

- **Healthy environments:** *Provide for children's physical and psychological health, safety, and sense of security.* For example, the Austin Eco School in Austin, Texas, creates an environment for its students where they can learn and play in an environment that is free from chemical toxins typically found in cleansers, paint, and flooring.[12]

More and more, parents look for child care centers and schools that make efforts to be environmentally safe and friendly. Many early childhood programs use eco-friendly diapers, nontoxic paints and pest control, and organic baby foods.[13]

- **Respectful environments:** *Show respect for each individual child and for the child's culture, home language, individual abilities or disabilities, family context, and community.* Meredith Abbott, a teacher of the year, believes that outstanding teachers provide a structured, safe environment where students feel they can experiment without the threat of ridicule or disappointment. She also believes that students feel safest when they can trust their teacher. Therefore, she takes the time to get to know students by building lessons that allow them to share openly and freely. The secret to cracking even the hardest nut is to listen—truly listen—when they open up and share. Meredith empathizes with students, builds trust, and tackles any obstacle they face with fierce tenacity.[14]

Santos Ramirez, a first grader with ataxic cerebral palsy, uses a DynaVox Vmax, an augmentative and alternative communication device that helps children with speech and learning challenges communicate. Santos is in an inclusive classroom with other first graders and enjoys physical education and recess along

healthy environments
Those environments that provide for children's physical and psychological health, safety, and sense of security.

respectful environments
Those environments that show respect for each individual child and for the child's culture, home language, individual abilities or disabilities, family context, and community.

VOICE FROM THE FIELD

COMPETENCY BUILDER

Tools for Teaching Tolerance to Young Children

One of the joys of teaching young children is being surrounded by people full of wonder and who are open to possibility. One important job of a teacher of young children is to keep alive that sense of awe and openness—that spirit of tolerance—to foster the respect for diversity and the awareness of interdependence that will be requisite skills in their twenty-first-century lives. Here are some tools to help you teach tolerance in the early childhood classroom:

STEP 1 Know Yourself

Sounds simple, right? Not always! Remember, you are the adult in the classroom and the children look to you for guidance—let them be guided by someone who has learned to guide him- or herself! Teaching tolerance means facilitating a respect for differences, so understand how your family, your community, and its culture and history are different from and/or similar to the experiences of other children, families, and communities in the United States and across the globe. Become your own subject, examine your own biases and privileges, explore your own experiences of the educational system, and allow it all to guide you to a deeper understanding of and respect for yourself so that you can have a deeper respect for your children.

STEP 2 Know Your Students and Their Families

You can't teach tolerance (or anything else!) to those you don't know! Take the time necessary to learn as much as you can about your students. This includes understanding the histories of the communities from which your students come as well as their home cultures, languages, and values. Creating an authentic connection to a child's family is crucial when working with young children, especially when there are cultural differences between teacher and family. Offer a home visit, learn a few pleasantries in the languages spoken by your students' families, go to the afterschool programs and community centers in the neighborhoods of your students. Demonstrate through action that you have the will to learn about how to be the best teacher you can be for your students.

STEP 3 Get Students Talking

When teachers provide children with opportunities to plan, discuss, investigate, create, and play with one another, ignorance and fear are uprooted and in their place are cultivated tolerance and respect. The routines teachers provide in their classrooms create the framework within which children feel safe to venture beyond their own community and get to know others. Ensure that children have multiple opportunities to authentically engage with one another through interaction protocols such as *Give One Get One* (where children share ideas with several self-selected partners) as well as with partners to whom they are appointed through the use of a partner-of-the-day rotation.

In this way, you establish routines of consistent interaction that build relationship and a genuine sense of community in your classroom.

STEP 4

Remember—Not Better, Not Worse—Just Different

Even our youngest students are aware of human diversity. Children are keen observers of the differences that exist between themselves and their classmates as well as between themselves and you. So, discuss those insights, being certain to frame them as no more or no less than what they are: differences. What better way to facilitate a respect for diversity and an understanding of differences than through high-quality, culturally relevant children's literature! Thoughtfully chosen books provide opportunities to challenge stereotypes; moreover, stories selected with intentionality expand students' knowledge of—or simply introduce them to—the continents and cultures from which their own communities (and those of their classmates) are derived. Great books become open doors through which you and your students can venture into a realm of rich discussions about the interconnectedness of the human experience—an experience that teachers must help students see as one that simply varies from place to place.

STEP 5

Create a Community Circle

Can young children really understand what a community is? When they become involved in building their classroom community and in maintaining its culture, the answer is, "Yes, without a doubt!" Also "without a doubt" is why students need to understand community—to foster the interdependence and respect for diverse perspectives that is critical to responsible citizenship. Create a classroom ritual of a community circle, a space in which children sit facing one another, a space wherein you, the teacher, become an equal participant in constructing this interdependence. Starting each day in community circle, greeting one another by name using the languages spoken at home, allowing a "student of the day" to read a daily affirmation that the community repeats and then briefly discusses are powerful ways to build trust, relationship, and commitment to one another.

Source: Contributed by Robert Sautter, kindergarten teacher at Leonard R. Flynn Elementary, San Francisco, California, and recipient of the Teaching Tolerance Award for Excellence in Culturally Responsive Teaching.

---

with his friends. Santos's teacher, Lisa Hamilton, was initially nervous about having Santos in her class. However, Lisa says Santos won everyone over. He's a regular kid trapped in a body that won't work the way he wants it to. He is capable of the first grade curriculum. He is very intelligent.[15]

- **Supportive environments:** *Believe each child can learn, and help children understand and make meaning of their experiences.* Teachers at Discovery Elementary School in Idaho, encourage and support their students by offering a program that pairs students who have autism with typically developing children. The goal of the program is to "ease autistic students into the traditional classroom and bring the regular school experience to students who spend most of their day in the autistic classroom," says Discovery Principal Ken Marlowe.[16] English language learners are another group that benefit from supportive environments. Pairing ELLs with English-speaking "buddies," constantly recognizing students' abilities and accomplishments; and building positive relationships with ELLs are ways to support students academically and socially.

  supportive environments Those environments in which professionals believe each child can learn, and that help children understand and make meaning of their experiences.

- **Challenging environments:** *Provide achievable and "stretching" experiences for all children.* Environments and experiences should provide opportunities for children to engage in activities that challenge them about how to use play materials in different ways, to solve their own problems and negotiate with others, and to use tools and materials in different ways. A woodworking area for preschoolers would be a good example of this. Play time, especially outdoor play time on well-designed and well-maintained equipment, enables a child to challenge and develop his or her physical abilities and skills.

  challenging environments Those environments that provide achievable and "stretching" experiences for all children.

Early childhood educators are professionals who collaborate and work with families and communities to help children of all backgrounds and abilities learn.

STANDARD 2: BUILDING FAMILY AND COMMUNITY RELATIONSHIPS

Families are an important part of children's lives. Creating a collaborative relationship with your students' families and the community makes sense in order to give your students the best opportunity to succeed. To do this, you need to know about and be respectful of children's families and the communities in which they live.

RESPECTING CHILDREN AND FAMILIES. Saying that you are respectful of children and families is one thing; putting respect into practice means you will use your skills and knowledge of child development and family involvement to make respectfulness a reality.

Implications for Teaching Here are some things you can do to demonstrate your respect for children and their families:

- Plan cooking and other activities in collaboration with parents. Inquire about restricted diets to determine acceptable foods and recipes so all children can participate; have parents advise you about appropriate cultural activities; and ask children what cultural practices they would like to include in classroom activities.
- Validate children's home languages by learning words and teaching them to the other children. For example, when counting the days on the calendar, you can count in English, Spanish, Vietnamese, and so on.[17]
- Keep expectations clear between your students and their families. For example, at the beginning of the school year, kindergarten teacher Rebecca Allen at Wood River Elementary School in Wood River, Nebraska, sends out a newsletter titled the "ABC's of Kindergarten" for parents, which includes information such as attendance, behavior, and classroom expectations, as well as content areas taught and roles of the parent in the classroom. She sends regular newsletters to parents, all of which are on her website for families to download online.[18]
- Isabel Martinez, first grade bilingual teacher and teacher of the year, supports parents by giving them strategies for helping children with their homework, encourages parents to stay in contact with her, and makes home visits when needed. She believes her job is not just to teach children academics, but to teach citizenship as well. She teaches citizenship and character traits, striving to help each child learn to share the concern for the well-being and dignity of others. Isabel believes children must learn to demonstrate loyalty and pride toward their country. Isabel teaches her children to be responsible, respectful, courteous, and honest toward others with whom we share our values and different ways of life.[19]

Learn about families' child-rearing practices and how they handle routines relating to toileting, behavioral problems, and so on. Learning how to build family relationships is an important part of your professional development. Respectful and reciprocal relationships with parents and families empower them to be involved in their children's educations.

STANDARD 3: OBSERVING, DOCUMENTING, AND ASSESSING TO SUPPORT CHILDREN AND FAMILIES

One of your most important responsibilities as an early childhood professional will be to observe, document, and assess children's learning. The outcomes of **assessment,** the cognitive process of collecting information about children's development, learning,

assessment The process of collecting information about children's development, learning, behavior, academic progress, need for special services, and achievement in order to make decisions.

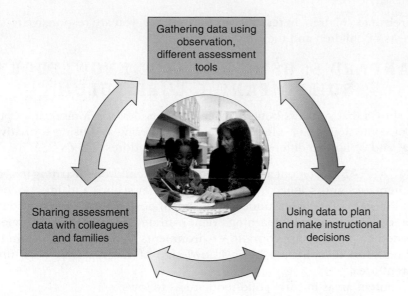

FIGURE 1.2 | The Three-Way Process of Assessment
Today teachers are accountable for what they teach and how they teach it. Observing and assessing provides the data you need to plan for each child.

behavior, academic progress, need for special services, and achievement in order to make decisions, will guide you and will provide you abundant information to share with parents and families. Consider assessment as a three-way process, as shown in Figure 1.2.

One of your main means for gathering information about young children is through observation and documentation, which are two forms of assessment you will use in ongoing, systematic ways. In fact, observation is one of your main means for gathering information about young children.

Through assessment, observation, and documentation practices, you can provide accommodations for children with disabilities and also involve parents in the process. For example, first grade teacher Addie Hare asks parents to fill out a short survey about their children's interests and learning needs. Parents know their children best, and you can learn a lot when you listen to what they have to say. Ask parents what their children like to do outside of school, special accommodations a child may need, and how they would like to be involved. Finish your survey with an open-ended question such as, "Is there anything else you would like me to know?" This often yields helpful information that might not emerge from previous questions.

STANDARD 4: USING DEVELOPMENTALLY EFFECTIVE APPROACHES TO CONNECT WITH CHILDREN AND FAMILIES

As an early childhood professional, you will integrate your understanding of and relationships with children and families; your understanding of developmentally effective approaches to teaching and learning; and your knowledge of content areas to design, implement, and evaluate experiences that promote positive, developmentally appropriate learning for all children.[20] To be a professional in this area, you will also demonstrate positive relationships with children and families. All of education is about relationships: how you relate to your colleagues, how you relate to parents and other family members, and

One of the most important professional classroom skills is the ability to observe and assess children's learning.

responsive relationships
The relationship that exists between yourself, children, and their families in which you are responsive to their needs and interests.

how you relate to children. In **responsive relationships**, you are responsive to the needs and interests of children and their families.

STANDARD 5: USING CONTENT KNOWLEDGE TO BUILD MEANING CURRICULUM

Research shows that students benefit when teachers develop a more in-depth understanding of content areas, of effective means of gathering and using formative assessment data, and of how to differentiate instruction to address needs.[21]

CONTENT AREAS.   Content areas are the basis for children's learning to read, write, learn mathematics and science, and be successful in school and life. Consequently, early childhood professionals understand the importance of each content area in children's development and learning, demonstrate the essential knowledge and skills needed to provide appropriate environments that support learning in each content area, and demonstrate basic knowledge of the research base underlying each content area.[22]

The content areas in early childhood are as follows:

* Language and literacy, which consists of listening, speaking, reading and writing
* Reading, which includes the learning skills necessary for beginning to read and being able to read fluently for meaning. The national goal for reading is for all children to read on grade level by grade three.
* The arts, including music, creative movement, dance, drama, and various forms of art
* Mathematics, the study of numbers, patterns, space, and change
* Science, which involves using observation and experimentation to describe and explain things
* Technology, the application of tools and information to change and modify the natural environment to solve problems and make products
* Engineering, the process of using materials and forces of nature for the benefit of humankind
* Social studies, which involves geography, history, economics, and social relations/civics
* Physical activity and physical education, which includes dance, sports, health, and nutrition

SCIENCE, TECHNOLOGY, ENGINEERING, AND MATHEMATICS (STEM). Today there is a growing emphasis on incorporating engineering and technology content in the school curriculum beginning in preschool. You will hear a lot about STEM throughout your teaching preparation and career. For example, Michelle Shearer, a National Teacher of the Year, is an advocate for STEM education for all K–12 students and successfully reaches those who have been traditionally underrepresented in scientific fields, including students with special needs and those from diverse racial and socioeconomic backgrounds. Her teaching methods rely heavily on real-life applications of scientific concepts.[23]

Much of the content knowledge in pre-K through third grade programs is integrated in state, national, and the common core state standards (CCSS) adopted by forty-five states. However, not all school curricula are specified by or through standards. What gets taught in early childhood programs is also based on children's interests and on the "teachable moment," when classroom, school, and communities lend themselves to teaching ideas, concepts, and skills. How you teach with standards is a result of your professional background and training. This is where Professional Standard 4, Using

Developmentally Effective Approaches to Connect with Children and Families, applies to your teaching in each of the content areas and in your use of instructional processes to teach each area.

Content Knowledge. The knowledge that comes from content areas is known as **content knowledge**. Teachers must understand the content they teach (e.g., math, science, social studies) and what constitutes the essential knowledge and skills of each content area. It is for this reason that state standards are important and helpful; you will want to be familiar with your state standards for each subject and grade level you teach, as well as the state's Common Core State Standards for reading and math.

content knowledge
The content and subjects teachers plan to teach.

Pedagogical Content Knowledge. In addition to knowing content, teachers also must know *how* to teach students so they learn content knowledge. This is called **pedagogical content knowledge**, which is knowing how to teach children so the content knowledge is accessible to them. This means that you must be able to provide appropriate examples and use appropriate strategies to illustrate the content. In addition, you must be able to identify the interests and learning needs of young children so that you can make content knowledge accessible to them. For example, first grade teacher Sarah Becker created a Blooming Earth Garden, an outdoor classroom that provides an exciting hands-on learning experience across all grade levels and covers several school curriculum areas such as science, writing, math, and art. Students study the importance of Illinois prairies, documenting and photographing, and by the end of the year are able to identify the differences between living and nonliving things and have an increased understanding of plant and animal growth.[24]

pedagogical content knowledge The teaching skills teachers need to help all children learn.

Second grade students at Robert E. Clow Elementary School in Naperville, Illinois, learn social studies by building a model community resembling their city out of cardboard and shoe boxes. The students learn how to use map grids and keys and use the telephone book to look up addresses and descriptions of actual landmarks in Naperville, such as the town hall, stores, and roads.[25]

Pedagogical Knowledge. A third type of knowledge, general **pedagogical knowledge**, involves how to effectively teach and facilitate learning regardless of the content area. This knowledge involves considering school, family, community contexts, and children's prior experiences to develop meaningful learning experiences. It also involves reflecting on teaching practice and includes a variety of ideas, methods, and technologies to help each child learn. For example, second grade teacher Lauren Smith has her children use iPads for writing and illustrating stories. Students publish their work on a student-created website that allows them to share their writing with students from all over the world. Publishing their writing facilitates discussions across many contexts and content areas and creates a meaningful learning experience for her students.

pedagogical knowledge The ability to apply pedagogical and content knowledge to develop meaningful learning experiences for children.

Knowledge of Learners and Learning. Finally, high-quality teachers know and understand the students they teach. This is called **knowledge of learners and learning**.[26]

Third grade teacher Sarah Hennessey, a North Carolina Teacher of the Year, is constantly aware that words, deeds, and actions create memories in her students' minds. She knows firsthand how powerful a teacher's influence and example are on children.

knowledge of learners and learning Understanding students and how they learn (DAP); managing classroom environments and guiding children.

Robert Stephenson, third grade teacher and Michigan Teacher of the Year, knows it is important to treat each child with respect and dignity, to accept each child with understanding, and to have faith in his or her abilities. He also wants to help students learn to value themselves, value others, and develop a love and enthusiasm for learning. He believes in connecting with individual children and challenging them to reach their highest potential.[27]

collaborative planning
A type of planning used by groups of teachers at the grade levels or across grade levels to plan curriculum daily, weekly, and monthly. Also called *team planning*.

reflective practice
The active process of thinking before teaching, during teaching, and after teaching in order to make decisions about how to plan, assess, and teach.

COLLABORATIVE PLANNING.   Today's teachers engage in **collaborative planning**. They meet collaboratively in grade level teams and across grade level teams in order to examine student data and to plan and develop instructional strategies. Collaborative teams also incorporate and align their curricula with local and state standards and state Common Core State Standards.

REFLECTIVE PRACTICE.   Building a meaningful curriculum for young children also involves reflective practice. **Reflective practice** helps you think about how children learn and enables you to make decisions about how best to support their development and learning. Thinking about learning and understanding how children learn makes it easier for you to improve your teaching effectiveness, student learning, and professional satisfaction. In addition, thinking about learning and thinking about teaching are part of your reflective practice. Reflective practice involves deliberate and careful consideration about the children you teach, the theories on which you base your teaching, how you teach, what children learn, and how you will teach in the future. Although solitary reflection is useful, the power of reflective practice is more fully realized when you engage in such practice with your mentor teacher in collaborative planning. The reflective teacher is a thoughtful teacher. Reflective practice involves the three steps shown in Figure 1.3.

Check Your Understanding: Standard 5

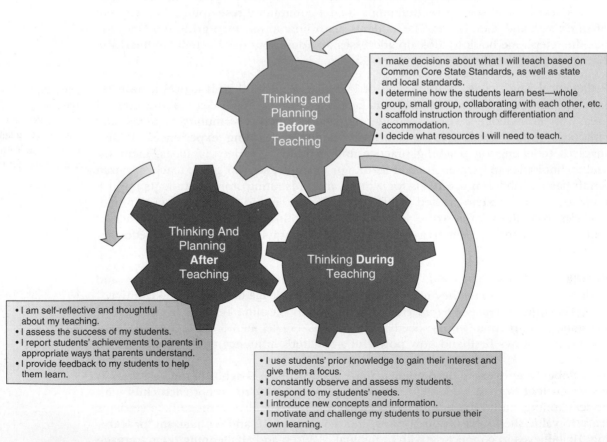

FIGURE 1.3 | The Cycle of Reflective Practice: Thinking, Planning, and Deciding

STANDARD 6: BECOMING A PROFESSIONAL

Early childhood professionals conduct themselves as professionals and identify with their profession.[28] When you identify with and are involved in your profession, you can proudly proclaim that you are a teacher of young children. Being a professional means that you (1) know about and engage in ethical practice; (2) engage in continuous lifelong learning and professional development; (3) collaborate with colleagues, parents, families, and community partners; (4) engage in reflective practice; and (5) advocate on behalf of children, families, and the profession.[29] These competencies represent the heart and soul of professional practice.

CONTINUOUS AND LIFELONG PROFESSIONAL DEVELOPMENT OPPORTUNITIES.

A professional is never a "finished" product; you are always involved in **professional development**, a process of studying, learning, changing, and becoming more professional. Professional development involves participation in training and education beyond the minimum needed for your current position. You will also want to consider your career objectives and the qualifications you might need for positions of increasing responsibility. Today, more teachers are also getting certified in special education and teaching ELLs. In fact, many students complete these certifications before they graduate.

professional development A process of studying, learning, changing, and becoming more professional.

PROFESSIONAL LEARNING COMMUNITIES.

As previously discussed, you, your colleagues, and your administrators will engage in collaborative planning in which you develop curricula and instructional processes. This process is often accomplished through a **professional learning community (PLC)**, a team of early childhood professionals working collaboratively to improve teaching and learning. Professional learning communities support a school culture that recognizes and capitalizes on the collective strengths and talents of the staff. They are designed to increase student achievement by creating a school culture focused on learning.

professional learning community (PLC) A team of early childhood professionals working collaboratively to improve teaching and learning.

For example, all teachers in Northfield Public School District in Northfield, Maine, participate in weekly PLC meetings with colleagues who share the same students and/or subject matter. They use their district curriculum and all existing student data to determine: what knowledge and skills they expect students to learn, how they will know if students meet the desired objectives, how they will respond when students have difficulty achieving the desired objectives and when students have already met the desired objectives, and how they can use student data and work samples to better inform their practice and communicate with parents.[30]

Peer Coaching.

I'll bet all of you had experience with coaches—Little League, soccer, softball, or whatever other sport you participated in. Coaches provide invaluable assistance and support. They help guide, direct, model, and encourage others to use their talents and abilities. Just as coaches play an invaluable role in the field of sports, coaches also play an important role in teaching and learning. **Peer coaching** is a process whereby teachers agree to learn from each other through observation, interaction, and discussions. In peer coaching, teachers work in pairs with each other to observe and identify areas in which they would like to improve. Peer coaching is powerful and enables you to grow and develop as you collaborate with your colleagues.

peer coaching A process whereby teachers agree to learn from each other through observation, interaction, and discussions.

Mentoring.

Mentoring is the process in which an experienced and highly qualified teacher works with a novice or beginning teacher to help the new teacher be successful. More than likely, as a beginning teacher, you will be assigned to a mentor teacher who will act as a leader, guide, sponsor, and role model for you. Generally, the mentor teacher works with the new early childhood professional during the first year of teaching.

mentoring The process in which an experienced and highly qualified teacher works with a novice or beginning teacher to help the new teacher be successful.

Just in Time Professional Development. Even though some professional development occurs grade-wide and school-wide, often teachers need help implementing instructional strategies in their classrooms. Increasing numbers of school districts provide "just in time," teacher-specific staff development. For example, when first-year teacher Ashley Higgins had difficultly implementing guided reading in her first grade classroom, instructional specialist Amanda Murphy worked with Ashley in her classroom to develop the skills to implement guided reading.

ENGAGING IN ETHICAL PRACTICE.   Ethical conduct—the exercise of responsible behavior with children, families, colleagues, and community and society—enables you to engage confidently in exemplary professional practice. The profession of early childhood education has a set of ethical standards to guide your thinking and behavior. NAEYC has developed the Code of Ethical Conduct and a Statement of Commitment, which can be reviewed by going to the NAEYC website.

You can begin now to incorporate professional ethical practices into your interactions with children and colleagues. To stimulate your thinking, the Activities for Professional Development section at the end of this and every chapter includes an ethical dilemma.

In each case, the ethical dilemma is a situation that a teacher, groups of teachers, and administrators face in making decisions when there is not always an easy or "right" answer.

As you reflect on and respond to the dilemmas, use the NAEYC Code of Ethical Conduct as a valuable guide and resource.

COLLABORATING WITH PARENTS, FAMILIES, AND COMMUNITY PARTNERS. Part of becoming a professional, involves gaining experience with parents, families, and the community. These experiences allow you to gain a better understanding of the complex characteristics of families and communities as well as to begin to create respectful, reciprocal relationships that support and empower families. Parents, families, and the community are essential partners in the process of schooling. Knowing how to collaborate effectively with these key partners will serve you well throughout your career.

 Observe and Analyze

ADVOCACY.   Advocacy is the act of pleading the issues impacting children and families to the profession and the public and engaging in strategies designed to improve the life outcomes of children and families. Advocates move beyond their day-to-day professional responsibilities and work collaboratively to help others. Children and families today need teachers who understand their needs and who will work to improve the health, education, and well-being of all young children. You and other early childhood professionals are in a unique position to know and understand children and their needs and to make a difference in their lives by collaborating with their parents.

Kindergarten teacher Kristi Luetjen, a Connecticut Teacher of the Year, moves fluidly in and out of special education and is praised for integrating students with special needs into her classroom. She dedicates herself to improving the services for kindergartners with special needs. She blends the lines of regular and special education and created a new co-teaching model that incorporates yoga practice with the curriculum to create a yoga program for kindergartners. Luetjen is grateful for the opportunity to continue to advocate for her youngest students, her students with disabilities, and the general importance of a kindergarten education.[31]

There is no shortage of issues to advocate for in the lives of children and families. Some of the issues in need of strong advocates involve providing high-quality

---

ethical conduct
Responsible behavior toward students and parents that allows you to be considered a professional.

advocacy The act of engaging in strategies designed to improve the circumstances of children and families. Advocates move beyond their day-to-day professional responsibilities and work collaboratively to help others.

programs for all children, reducing and preventing child abuse and neglect, closing the achievement gap between socioeconomic and racial groups, and providing good health and nutrition for each child. You must become actively engaged to change policies and procedures that negatively impact children. The following are some of the ways in which you can advocate for children and families:

- *Join an early childhood professional organization that advocates for children and families.* Organizations such as NAEYC, the Association for Childhood Education International (ACEI), Children's Defense Fund (CDF), and the Council for Exceptional Children (CEC) have local affiliates at colleges and universities and in many cities and towns, and they are very active in advocating for young children. You can serve on a committee or be involved in some other way.

- *Volunteer in community activities that support children and families.* Donate to an organization that helps children and families and volunteer your time at a local event that helps children get ready for school. For example, the Georgia Justice Project hosts its annual "Back-2-School" event to help their clients prepare for the first day of school. The community of Atlanta, Georgia, supplies families with backpacks, school supplies, and health and dental screenings.

  Early childhood major Chris Sayen, through his college, volunteers in a program called Success for Life Through Reading. Chris reads books to children in child care programs serving children from low-income families. Chris also helps raise funds to purchase new books for the children.

- *Investigate the issues that face children and families today.* Read the news and become informed about relevant issues. For example, subscribe to *Early Childhood News* and receive a biweekly electronic newsletter from a group that informs you of news affecting children aged birth through eight years and their families; news updates are automatically sent on current issues. Then, share the news with colleagues, family, and friends.

- *Seek opportunities to share your knowledge of young children and the issues that face children and families.* Inform others about the needs of young children by speaking with groups. For example, volunteer to meet with a group of parents at a local child care program to help them learn how to share storybooks with their young children, or meet with a local civic group that maintains the community park to discuss appropriate equipment for younger children. Identify a specific concern you have for children and families, and talk to others about that issue. For example, if you are concerned about the number of children who do not have adequate health care, learn the facts about the issue in your community, and then talk to people you know about ways to solve that problem. Begin with your own circle of influence: your colleagues, friends, family members, and other social groups of which you are a member.

- *Enlist the support of others.* Contact others to help you disseminate information about an issue. For example, enlist the help of your local Parent-Teacher Association in a letter-writing effort to inform town leaders about the need for safety improvements at the local playground.

- *Be persistent.* Identify an issue you are passionate about, and find a way to make a difference. There are many ways to advocate for children and families. Change takes time!

Within your own program or classroom, you will face many issues that should inspire you to advocate for your children and their families.

Reflect and Apply: Advocacy

Caring and Kindness Are Keys to the Profession

"Kind hearts, the garden; Kind thoughts, the root; Kind words, the blossoms; Kind deeds, the fruit." If we think of our classrooms as gardens, then teachers are the master gardeners. Not only do we need to plant academic seeds of many varieties; we need to plant the seeds of kindness and caring, as well. Our actions and our attitudes define who we are. Kindness and caring are not skills; they are attitudes. As teachers, we need to be the essence of kindness and caring. We must cultivate our students to bloom into the loveliest of flowers, and it starts with the attitude and the actions of the teacher. We believe that students who can express kindness are happier and more productive in the classroom.

We are instructors in a team classroom: forty students and two teachers. Every student in our classroom knows that he or she is loved and accepted, and every student in our classroom knows that he or she is accountable for his or her attitudes and actions. We promote a simple, yet positive behavior plan for our classroom: be safe, be respectful, be responsible. We also believe in task-oriented consequences, rather than time-oriented consequences. For example, if a child says something unkind to another student, resulting in hurt feelings, a letter/picture of apology is a better choice than missing five minutes of playtime.

At the beginning of the school year, we read the book, *Have You Filled a Bucket Today? A Guide to Happiness for Kids*, by Carol McCloud. This book encourages positive behavior through love, kindness and appreciation. The premise of the book is that everyone in the world carries an invisible bucket. The bucket has only one purpose, and it is to hold good thoughts and feelings about yourself; but you need other people to fill your bucket. So when you smile, show love to someone, say or do a kind deed, you are being a bucket filler. But you can also dip into someone's bucket and take out some happiness when your words and actions are inappropriate. Every morning, during our morning meeting, we encourage our students to be bucket fillers, not bucket dippers. We encourage our students to say, "Thank you for filling my bucket!" when an act of kindness is shown, or "You dipped into my bucket" when hurtful words or actions are not acceptable.

To promote our action plan of kindness, each student decorates his or her own bucket, including a self-portrait to be displayed year-long in our classroom (see photo). We often refer to our bulletin board when issues arise in our classroom. Our "visible buckets" remind us of the importance of being kind at school, on the playground, in the cafeteria, on the bus. Our "invisible buckets" travel everywhere with us, reminding us that we can make a difference through kindness and caring wherever we are!

We can also promote kindness and caring though community service. Each month, we "fill the buckets of others" in our school or community with acts of kindness. Recently, we made an American flag from chain-links and presented it to our local firefighters and police officers

Elizabeth

as a way of saying thank you for keeping our school safe (see photo). There are so many ways that "wee hands can do big deeds."

Most important, we need to teach our students to be kind and caring through example. Our students learn from our actions and our attitudes. Every teacher has a garden, and your garden will have a variety of plants. How you choose to cultivate your garden will determine its beauty. Choose to cultivate kindness and caring in your classroom.

Source: Contributed by Christa Pehrson and Vicki Sheffler, 2002 USA Today, First-Team Teachers, Amos K. Hutchinson Elementary School, Greensburg, Pennsylvania.

PROFESSIONAL DISPOSITIONS

In addition to the six professional standards discussed in this chapter, professional dispositions play an important role in ensuring that you will be a well-rounded and highly qualified professional. **Professional dispositions** are the values, commitments, attitudes, and professional ethics that influence behaviors toward students, families, colleagues, and communities and affect student learning, motivation, and development, as well your own professional growth. Dispositions are guided by beliefs and attitudes related to values such as caring, fairness, honesty, and responsibility. For example, they might include a belief that all students can learn, a vision of high and challenging standards for all children, or a commitment to a safe and supportive learning environment. We have already discussed other dispositions, such as ethical practice, collaborating with colleagues and families, and reflective practice. Many programs that prepare professionals for the early childhood profession have a set of dispositions that are important for professional practice.

The Voice from the Field feature, "Caring and Kindness Are Keys to the Profession," illustrates the importance of caring and kindness and provides many examples that you can use in your classroom.

professional dispositions The values, commitments, and professional ethics that influence behaviors toward students, families, colleagues, and communities and affect student learning, motivation, and development, as well as the educator's own professional growth.

CARING: THE MOST IMPORTANT DISPOSITION For every early childhood professional, *caring* is the most important of all the professional dispositions. Professionals care about children; they accept and respect all children and their cultural and socioeconomic backgrounds. As a professional, you will work in classrooms, programs, and other settings where things do not always go smoothly; for example, children will not always learn ably and well, and they will not always be clean and free from illness and hunger. Children's and their parents' backgrounds and ways of life will not always be the same as yours. Caring means you will lose sleep trying to find a way to help a child learn to read, and you will spend long hours planning and gathering materials. Caring also means you will not leave your intelligence, enthusiasm, and other talents at home but will bring them into the center, the classroom, administration offices, boards of directors' meetings, and wherever else you can make a difference in the lives of children and their families. The theme of caring should run deep in your professional preparation and in your teaching.

DAP AND THE EARLY CHILDHOOD EDUCATION PROFESSIONAL

The NAEYC's Position Statement on Developmentally Appropriate Practice (DAP) on the NAEYC's website represents a commitment to promote excellence in the constantly evolving field of early childhood education and early childhood special education. The position statement provides a framework for best practices rooted in numerous research studies on child development and learning, which promotes each child's optimal learning and development. There are three knowledge bases that form the core considerations of DAP. Figure 1.4 further clarifies these dimensions and how they are related. These are as follows:

> ***Knowledge of Social and Cultural Contexts in Which Children Live.*** Values, expectations, and behavioral and linguistic conventions shape children's lives at home and in their communities. Teachers must strive to understand these contexts to ensure that learning experiences in the program or school are meaningful, relevant, and respectful for each child and family.

FIGURE 1.4 | Core Considerations in Developmentally Appropriate Practice

Knowledge of Social and Cultural Contexts in Which Children Live

The values, expectations, and behavioral and linguistic conventions that shape children's lives at home and in their communities that practitioners must strive to understand in order to ensure that learning experiences in the program or school are meaningful, relevant, and respectful for each child and family.

Knowledge of Child Development

Knowledge of age-related characteristics that permit general predictions about what experiences are likely to best promote children's learning and development.

Knowledge of the Child as an Individual

What practitioners learn about each child that has implications for how best to adapt and be responsive to that individual variation.

Knowledge of Child Development. Knowledge of age-related characteristics that permit general predictions about what experiences are likely to best promote children's learning and development.

Knowledge of the Child, as an Individual. What practitioners learn about each child that has implications for how best to adapt and be responsive to that individual variation.

The NAEYC Position Statement on Developmentally Appropriate Practice (DAP) is clear about what constitutes DAP:

- Developmentally appropriate practice requires both meeting children where they are—which means that teachers must get to know them well—and enabling them to reach goals that are both challenging and achievable.

- All teaching practices should be (a) appropriate to children's age and developmental status, (b) attuned to children as unique individuals, and (c) responsive to the social and cultural contexts in which children live.

- Developmentally appropriate practice does not mean making things easier for children. Rather, it means ensuring that goals and experiences are suited to children's learning and development and challenging enough to promote their progress and interest.[32]

PATHWAYS TO PROFESSIONAL DEVELOPMENT

The educational dimension of professionalism involves knowing about and demonstrating essential knowledge of the profession and professional practice. This knowledge includes the history and ethics of the profession, understanding how children develop and learn, and keeping up-to-date on public issues that influence early childhood and the profession.

Training and certification are major challenges facing all areas of the early childhood profession and those who care for and teach young children. Training and certification requirements vary from state to state, and more states are tightening personnel standards for child care, preschool, kindergarten, and primary-grade professionals.

Many states have career ladders that specify the requirements for progressing from one level of professionalism to the next. For example, Figure 1.5 outlines a career pyramid of professional development. What two things do you find most informative about this career pyramid? How can you use the pyramid to enhance your professional development?

THE CDA PROGRAM

The **Child Development Associate (CDA)** National Credentialing Program is a competency-based assessment system that offers early childhood professionals the opportunity to develop and demonstrate competence in their work with children aged five years and younger. Since its inception in 1975, the CDA program has provided a nationally recognized system that has stimulated early childhood training and education opportunities for teachers of young children in every state in the country and on military bases worldwide. The credential is recognized nationwide in state regulations for licensed child care and preschool programs as a qualification for teachers, directors, and/or family child care providers. The standards for performance this program has established are used as a basis for professional development in the field.

child development associate (CDA) An individual who has successfully completed the CDA assessment process and has been awarded the CDA credential. CDAs are able to meet the specific needs of children and work with parents and other adults to nurture children's physical, social, emotional, and intellectual growth in a child development framework.

Advanced Level and Degrees—MS, MA, PhD, EdD

Traditional:
- Teacher educator at a two-year college or four-year university
- Child development specialist
- Children guidance specialist
- Research/writer
- Early intervention
- Family education

Related with further education/training/certifications:
- Social worker
- Teacher/administration/special educator in a public elementary school
- Librarian
- Pediatric therapist-occupational and physical
- Child life specialist in a hospital
- Speech and hearing pathologist
- Dietitian for children
- Counselor
- Child psychologist
- Psychiatrist
- Recreation supervisor
- Dental hygienist
- Child care center or playground/recreation center designer
- Probation officer
- County extension educator with 4-H
- Adoption specialist
- "Friend of Court" counselor
- Faith-based community coordinator and educator
- Infant/child mental health specialist

Baccalaureate Level—Bachelors of Science (BS), Bachelors of Arts (BA), & Bachelors of Education (BEd)

Traditional:
- Early childhood teacher in public school, Head Start or child care settings
- Special education teacher
- Family child care home provider
- Nanny
- Administrator in a Head Start program, child care center
- Child care center director with the department of defense
- Parent/family educator
- Family advocate
- Director of school-age (out of school time) program

Related with some positions requiring additional coursework at the baccalaureate level which will be in a field other than early childhood:
- Recreation director/worker/leader
- Adult educator
- Children's librarian
- Teacher of ELL and ESOL
- Music teacher, musician/entertainer for children
- Recreation camp director
- Camp counselor/scouts camp ranger
- Domestic violence prevention and education
- Childbirth educator
- Gymnastic or dance teacher
- Pediatric nurse aide
- Faith community coordinator and educator
- Foster care services

Associate Level—Associate of Arts (AA), Associate of Science (AS), & Associate of Applied Science (AAS)

Traditional:
- Head Start–Early Head Start teacher
- Child care teacher
- Family child care home provider
- Nanny
- Child care center director
- School-age provider
- Para-professional assistant
- Parent educator

Related in addition to those listed at the core level:
- Family and human services worker
- Entertainer for children at theme restaurants, parks or parties
- Social service aide
- Youth services
- Playground monitor
- Physical therapy assistant
- Faith community coordinators for families and children

National Credential Level—Child Development Associate (CDA) and Certified Child Care Professional (CCP)

Traditional:
- Head Start teacher (CDA required)
- Child care teacher-master teacher
- Family childhood care home provider
- Teacher assistant in public school classroom (additional college hours required)
- Child care center director
- Home visitor
- Nursing home aide/worker
- Nanny

Basic Level—Positions may require education and training depending on the position

Traditional:
- Child care teaching assistant
- Family child care home provider
- Head Start teacher assistant
- Nanny
- Foster parent
- Church nursery attendant
- Volunteer in public/private school setting

Related positions which involve working with children in settings other than a child care center, family child care home, Head Start, or public school program may require specialized pre-service training:
- Recreation center assistant
- Camp counselor
- Special needs child care assistant
- Cook's aide, camp cook, Head Start or child care center cook

FIGURE 1.5 | Early Childhood Professional Development Career Pyramid

The CDA program offers credentials to caregivers in four types of settings: (1) center-based programs for preschoolers, (2) center-based programs for infants/toddlers, (3) family child care homes, and (4) home visitor programs.

Evidence of ability is collected from a variety of sources, including firsthand observational evidence of the CDA candidate's performance with children and families. This evidence is weighed against national standards. The CDA national office sets the standards for competent performance and monitors this assessment process so it is uniform throughout the country.

ASSOCIATE DEGREE PROGRAMS

Many community colleges provide training in early childhood education to qualify recipients to be **child care** aides, primary child care providers, and assistant teachers. Associate degree programs provide a foundation for knowledge in child development and working with children and families. These programs usually last two years and can provide the following early childhood education career opportunities: child care instructor, director, owner, director of a family day home, or manager of a corporate child care facility.[33]

child care Comprehensive care and education of young children outside their homes.

BACCALAUREATE DEGREE PROGRAMS

These programs provide more extensive knowledge on early childhood education and work to ensure their students or candidates have mastered the six professional preparation competencies, with differences expected in depth and breadth of competencies for the bachelor's level. The ages and grades to which the certification applies vary from state to state. Four-year colleges provide programs that may result in early childhood teacher certification. Some states have separate teacher certification for **pre-kindergarten** and grades K–3 and grades 4–6. In other states, early childhood and elementary teacher certification are combined in a K–6 program. This is the way it is at the author's university, the University of North Texas.

pre-kindergarten A class or program preceding kindergarten for children usually from three to four years old.

ALTERNATIVE CERTIFICATION PROGRAMS

Many professionals enter the teaching profession after they have a baccalaureate degree in another field such as finance, psychology, biology, or English. These individuals don't need another bachelor's degree. They need the pedagogical knowledge and skills necessary to be a highly effective teacher. To fulfill this need for a different pathway to the teaching profession, many states, school districts, and private agencies offer alternative certification programs. **Alternative certification** is an alternative process to teacher certification through which an individual who already has at least a bachelor's degree can obtain certification to teach without necessarily having to go back to college and complete a college-based teacher education program. These alternative teacher-training programs are sponsored by colleges of education, state departments of education, and for-profit agencies.

alternative certification Teacher certification through which an individual who already has at least a bachelor's degree can obtain certification to teach.

MASTER'S DEGREE PROGRAMS

Depending on the state, individuals may gain initial early childhood certification at the master's degree level. Many colleges and universities offer master's programs for people who want to qualify as program directors or assistant directors or who may want to pursue a career in teaching. Linda Smerge graduated with bachelor's and master's degrees in elementary education from Northern Illinois University, as well as a juris doctorate. She taught second grade and kindergarten before practicing transactional law for thirteen years in Chicago. Smerge felt the calling to return to the classroom and satisfy her desire to work with young children. Now Smerge is an Illinois Teacher of the Year!

Gay Barnes, 2012 Alabama state Teacher of the Year has taught for twenty-one years and obtained a bachelor of arts degree from the University of Alabama and a doctorate in literacy and reading. Gay is in charge of knowing her students as individual learners, knowing what they need to learn and how to plan and teach lessons that will take them to the next level of their learning.[34]

Check Your Understanding: NAEYC Standards

WHAT ARE NEW ROLES FOR EARLY CHILDHOOD PROFESSIONALS TODAY?

The role of the early childhood professional today is radically different from what it was even two or three years ago. Although the goals of professionalism and the characteristics of the highly effective professional remain the same, responsibilities, expectations, and roles have changed and will continue to change. Here are some of these new roles of the contemporary early childhood professional:

- *Teacher as an instructional leader.* Teachers have always been responsible for classroom and program instruction, but this role is now reemphasized and given a much more prominent place in what early childhood teachers do, such as planning for what children will learn, guiding and teaching so that children learn, assessing what children learn, and arranging the classroom environment so that children learn. The professional learning community we previously discussed will play a more prominent role throughout your teaching career to refine and focus your role as an instructional leader.

- *Teacher of Common Core State Standards, state, district, and program goals and standards.* Common Core State Standards and state standards provide a framework for what teachers should be teaching and students should be learning.

- *Teachers with intention.* Intentional teaching occurs when teachers teach for a purpose, are clear about what they teach, and teach so that children learn specific knowledge and skills. In this context, teachers spend more time during the day planning activities that involve the children in active learning while making a conscious effort to be more involved in each child's learning process. Intentional teaching to standards can and should occur in a child-centered approach for specified times and purposes throughout the school day.

- *Teacher who maximizes instructional time.* Teachers are expected to maximize the full length of instructional time with activities and content that provide students with valuable learning experiences every day. Teachers emphasize engaging children in learning activities, spend more time on instruction, actively involve themselves in children's learning, and increase the amount of time spent on learning.

- *Teacher of performance-based accountability for learning.* Teachers today are far more accountable for children's learning. Previously, the emphasis was on the process of schooling; teachers were able to explain their role as "I taught Mario how to...." Today the emphasis is on "What did Mario learn?" and "Did Mario learn what he needs to know and do to perform at or above grade level?"

- ***Teacher of literacy and reading.*** Although the teaching of reading has always been a responsibility of early childhood professionals, this role has greatly expanded. Today, every early childhood teacher is now a teacher of literacy and reading. As more states and districts focus on having all children read on grade level by grade three, the effective teaching of reading is assuming a more prominent role.

- ***Teacher who integrates technology into teaching and learning.*** As our children become more technologically savvy, so do teachers. Today's generation of children prefer to learn with technology. Teachers must integrate it into all instructional activities.

- ***Teacher of twenty-first century skills.*** The role of the contemporary teacher to be able to improve and advance students' knowledge of twenty-first century skills is becoming more and more important in early childhood education. Teachers are expected to be advocates of these special skills and to integrate them into their teaching. The Partnership for 21st Century Skills (P21) says the following: "As the United States continues to compete in a global economy that demands innovation, P21 and its members provide tools and resources to help the U.S. education system keep up by fusing the 3Rs and 4Cs (Critical thinking and problem solving, Communication, Collaboration, and Creativity and innovation). While leading districts and schools are already doing this, P21 advocates for local, state and federal policies that support this approach for every school."[35]

- ***Teacher in the inclusive classroom.*** Teaching in an inclusive classroom offers many new opportunities for you and your students. With the fields of early childhood and early childhood special education merging together, there is a greater demand for all teachers to have knowledge and skills for how to teach in inclusive classrooms. This may at first seem challenging for some teachers. However, with collaborative teamwork, this experience can be very successful for all involved. Teacher of the year Laura Ditman teaches second grade. When she began her teaching career three years ago, she did not expect she would have three children in her classroom with disabilities. Laura is fortunate to have the help and support of her principal and special education personnel as she meets the demands of teaching two children with learning disabilities and a third with attention deficit hyperactivity disorder (ADHD). Laura believes all children can be successful and welcomes diversity in her classroom. She adapts the curriculum and designs instructional strategies to meet each student's needs. Laura thinks the inclusive classroom is the best way to teach all children.

As the field of early childhood education continues to change, the details of your role as an early childhood professional will continue to be refined. You will want to devote the time and energy necessary to keep yourself in the forefront of your field. Figure 1.6 contains a developmental checklist for becoming a professional. Complete this checklist now, and review it throughout your teaching career to further refine your professional teaching role.

Daniel Leija, known as "Dan Dan the Science Man" and a fifth grade teacher at Esparza Elementary School, is a Texas Teacher of the year. Every Monday, Daniel conducts televised science experiments to the whole campus as one way to help bridge the gap between concepts and real world application. As a thirteen-year veteran of early childhood education, Leija has written an essay about what it means to be a teacher and to be passionate about early childhood education. His ideals (see p. 30) can guide your teaching, too!

NAEYC Standard	Desired Professional Goals
Standard 1	**Promoting Child Development and Learning** I use my understanding of young children's characteristics and needs, and of multiple interacting influences on children's development and learning, to create environments that are healthy, respectful, supportive, and challenging for each child.
Standard 1	**Delivering Education and Child Care** I am familiar with a variety of models and approaches for delivering education and child care, and I use this knowledge to deliver education and child care in a safe, healthy learning environment.
Standard 1	**Guiding Behavior** I understand the principles and importance of behavior guidance. I guide children to be peaceful, cooperative, and in control of their behavior.
Standard 1	**Theories of Early Childhood Education** I understand the principles of each major theory of educating young children. The approach I use is consistent with my beliefs about how children learn.
Standard 2	**Building Family and Community Relationships** I know about, understand, and value the importance and complex characteristics of children's families and communities. I use this understanding to create respectful, reciprocal relationships that support and empower families, and to involve all families in their children's development and learning.
Standard 3	**Observing, Documenting, and Assessing to Support Young Children and Families** I know about and understand the goals, benefits, and uses of assessment. I know about and use systematic observations, documentation, and other effective assessment strategies in a responsible way, in partnership with families and other professionals, to positively influence the development of every child.
Standard 4	**Using Developmentally Effective Approaches to Connect with Children and Families** I understand and use positive relationships and supportive interactions as the foundation for my work with young children and families. I know, understand, and use a wide array of developmentally appropriate approaches, instructional strategies, and tools to connect with children and families and positively influence each child's development and learning.
Standard 4	**Educating Diverse Students** I understand that all children are individuals with unique strengths and challenges. I embrace these differences, work to fulfill special needs, and promote tolerance and inclusion in my classroom. I value and respect the dignity of all children.
Standard 4	**Developmentally Appropriate Practice** I understand children's developmental stages and growth from birth through age eight, and use this knowledge to implement developmentally appropriate practice. I do all I can to advance the physical, intellectual, social, and emotional development of the children in my care to their full potential.
Standard 4	**Technology** I am technologically literate and integrate technology into my classroom to help all children learn.
Standard 5	**Using Content Knowledge to Build Meaningful Curriculum** I understand the importance of developmental domains and academic (or content) disciplines in early childhood curriculum. I know the essential concepts, inquiry tools, and structure of content areas, including academic subjects, and can identify resources to deepen my understanding. I use my own knowledge and other resources to design, implement, and evaluate meaningful, challenging curricula that promote comprehensive developmental and learning outcomes for every young child.
Standard 6	**Becoming a Professional** I identify and conduct myself as a member of the early childhood profession. I know and use ethical guidelines and other professional standards related to early childhood practice. I am a continuous, collaborative learner who demonstrates knowledgeable, reflective, and critical perspectives on my work, making informed decisions that integrate knowledge from a variety of sources. I am an informed advocate for sound educational practices and policies.
Standard 6	**Ongoing Professional Development** I have a professional career plan for the next year. I engage in study and training programs to improve my knowledge and competence, belong to a professional organization, and have earned or am working on a degree or credential (CDA, AA, BS, or BA). I strive for positive, collaborative relationships with my colleagues and employer.
Standard 6	**Philosophy of Teaching** I have thought about and written my philosophy of teaching and caring for young children. My actions are consistent with this philosophy.
Standard 6	**Keeping Current in an Age of Change** I am familiar with the profession's contemporary development, and I understand current issues in society and trends in the field. I am willing to change my ideas, thinking, and practices based on study, new information, and the advice of colleagues and professionals.
Standard 6	**Professional Dispositions** I work with students, families, and communities in ways that reflect the dispositions expected of professional educators as delineated in professional, state, and institutional standards. I recognize when my own dispositions may need to be adjusted and am able to develop plans to do so.
Standard 6	**Historical Knowledge** I am familiar with my profession's history, and I use my knowledge of the past to inform my practice.

Note: These professional development outcomes are consistent with the core values of the NAEYC and the competencies of the CDA.

FIGURE 1.6 | Seventeen Competencies for Becoming a Professional: A Professional Development Checklist

Level of Accomplishment? (Circle One)	If High, Provide Evidence of Accomplishment	If Needs Improvement, Specify Action Plan for Accomplishment	Target Date of Completion of Accomplishment	See the following for more information on how to meet the desired professional outcomes
High Needs Improvement				Chapters 1, 5, 6, 7, 8, 9, 10, 11, 12, 14, 15, and 16
High Needs Improvement				Chapters 3, 5, 6, 7, 8, 9, 10, 11, 12, 14, 15, and 16
High Needs Improvement				Chapter 14
High Needs Improvement				Chapters 4 and 5
High Needs Improvement				Chapters 1 and 17
High Needs Improvement				Chapters 3 and 16
High Needs Improvement				Chapters 1, 3, 5, 6, 7, 8, 9, 10, 11, 12, 14, 15, 16, and 17
High Needs Improvement				Chapters 1, 2, 5, 6, 7, 8, 9, 10, 11, 12, 14, 15, and 16
High Needs Improvement				Chapters 1, 2, 3, 5, 6, 7, 8, 9, 10, 11, 12, 13, 14, 15, 16, and 17
High Needs Improvement				Chapter 13
High Needs Improvement				Chapters 3, 5, 6, 7, 9, 10, 11, 12, 13, 15, and 16
High Needs Improvement				Chapter 1, all Ethical Dilemma features, and all Voice from the Field features
High Needs Improvement				Chapter 1 and all Ethical Dilemma features
High Needs Improvement				Chapter 1, all Ethical Dilemma features, and all Voice from the Field features
High Needs Improvement				All chapters
High Needs Improvement				Chapter 1, all Ethical Dilemma features, and all Voice from the Field features
High Needs Improvement				Chapters 4 and 5

I AM A TEACHER

- "I am a teacher. I have answered my nation's call to redefine the future. I have been entrusted to nurture and develop our country's most precious resource . . . our children.

- I am a coach, mentor, counselor, and friend, fully prepared to take the necessary steps to make each student's dream become a reality. I will never waver from my course.

- I am a professional, the descendant of a proud and honorable heritage. I hold myself to a higher standard because I am accountable to our nation, my community, the students, and myself. I will always conduct myself in a manner that will bring credit to my field. I actively seek ways to sharpen my skills through continuing education and collaboration with my colleagues.

- I am a partner. I work together with the community, business organizations, support agencies, administration, and parents to ensure each student receives the quality education that many seek and relatively few realize. My classroom door is always open for my students and all who wish to catch a glimpse of how tomorrow's leaders are being prepared.

- I am a shepherd. I openly reach out to and guide each student who passes through my door; rich, poor, privileged, or disadvantaged. I nurture and encourage each student to achieve [his or her] full potential. My students will overcome life's obstacles to become successful.

- I am an advocate. I encourage my students to take risks, think outside the box, and always dream big. I help my students learn to be humble winners, gracious losers, and work together as a team to achieve their goals."

- I am a confidant. I offer counsel to students who have nowhere else to turn in times of personal crisis. I offer the support, guidance, and encouragement my students need to pilot them through their hour of darkness. I will never jeopardize that bond of trust. I gladly take on each of these roles to ensure my students have the tools they need to be successful in an ever-changing world."

DEVELOPING A PHILOSOPHY OF EDUCATION

philosophy of education
A set of beliefs about how children develop and learn and what and how they should be taught.

Professional practice entails teaching with and from a philosophy of education, which acts as a guidepost to help you support your teaching on what you believe about children.

A **philosophy of education** is a set of beliefs about how children develop and learn; what children should know, learn, and do; and how to best teach young children. Your philosophy of education is based in part on your philosophy of life. What you believe about yourself, about others, and about life determines your philosophy of education. For example, we previously talked about caring. If you care about others, chances are you will be a caring person for your children. We know that when teachers care about and have high expectations for their children, then children achieve at higher levels. Core beliefs and values about education and teaching include what you believe about children, what you think are the purposes of education, how you view the teacher's role, and what you think you should know and be able to do.

In summary, your philosophy of education guides and directs your daily teaching. As you reflect on your philosophy of education, think about what makes it special. What are some critical elements that you can incorporate into yours? The following guidelines will help you develop your philosophy of education.

READ

Read widely in textbooks, journals, and on the Web to get ideas and points of view. For example, these are some of the short philosophies of education from teachers of the year in Lee County, North Carolina:

Lisa Howard, second grade teacher: Lisa believes that the goal of education is to provide students with the tools necessary to achieve success. Through guidance and nurturing, teachers can empower students to become positive contributors to our society.

Candace Bloedorn, third grade teacher: Candace believes that every child has the ability to learn. As an educator, She hopes to create an environment where children are able to take risks, make mistakes, and learn from them. Candace inspires and motivates her twenty-first-century learners by incorporating technology and providing instruction that is meaningful and hands-on.

Donna Thomas, first grade teacher: Donna believes every child is unique and special. Her role is to facilitate learning while guiding students toward self-discovery in an environment that is conducive to positive physical, social, cognitive, and emotional growth in an accepting, caring, supportive, and safe environment that encourages every child to reach his/her fullest potential.[36]

The Activities for Professional Development section at the end of this chapter will also help you get started.

REFLECT

As you continue to study early childhood education, make notes and reflect about your philosophy of education. The following prompts will help you get started:

- I believe the purposes of education are . . . .
- I believe that children learn best when they are taught under certain conditions and in certain ways. Some of these are . . . .
- The curriculum—all of the activities and experiences—of my classroom should include certain "basics" that contribute to children's social, emotional, intellectual, and physical development. These basics include . . . .
- Children learn best in an environment that promotes learning. Features of a good learning environment are . . . .
- All children have certain needs that must be met if they are to grow and learn at their best. Some of these basic needs are . . . .
- I would meet these needs by . . . .
- A teacher should have certain qualities and behave in certain ways. Qualities I think important for teaching are . . . .

In addition, reflect on this philosophy statement of a teacher of the year as a context for expanding and enriching your philosophy.

- First grade teacher Corey Haughton teaches her students how to teach themselves and gives them the necessary tools for becoming lifelong learners. Corey believes that when children love learning, they will love coming to school; they will love to study; they will ultimately love their work; they will learn to love, understand, and appreciate their family; they will learn to love, understand, and appreciate their community; and they will learn to love, understand and appreciate who they are, why they are here, and what they should be doing. Furthermore,

The future of early childhood education holds many opportunities and exciting changes for you. It is important for you to keep up with the changing times and to align your teaching with current practices and new ideas.

Corey believes education should build good, inquisitive people not skilled test takers. Corey intends to help create thousands of little questioning minds who want to know how everything works, why it should work, and how to do it better.[37]

DISCUSS

Discuss with successful teachers and other educators their philosophies and practices. The personal accounts in the Voice From the Field boxes in this chapter are evidence that a philosophy can help you be a successful, effective teacher. They also serve as an opportunity to "talk" with successful professionals and understand how they translate theory into practice. Join or create an on-line discussion group to share your thoughts and ideas about teaching. For example, *Third Grade Teachers* is a free, interactive website for third grade teachers and support staff that enables users to blog, chat, post photos, and collaborate with other teachers across the world to exchange ideas, activities, and resources.[38]

WRITE AND SHARE

Once you have thought about your philosophy of education, write a draft and have others read it. Writing and sharing helps you to clarify your ideas and redefine your thoughts because your philosophy should be understandable to others (although they do not necessarily have to agree with you).

EVALUATE

Finally, evaluate your philosophy using this checklist:
- Does my philosophy accurately relate my beliefs about teaching? Have I been honest with myself?
- Is it understandable to me and others?
- Do I clearly state what I believe are the key essentials of teaching?
- Do I clearly state what I consider to be the essentials that children should learn?
- Does it provide practical guidance for my teaching?
- Are my ideas consistent with one another?
- Does what I believe make good sense to me and others?

First grade teacher Callie Smith constantly evaluates and revises her philosophy of education. Her teaching philosophy varies from year to year, incorporating new research-based strategies. Overall, the main idea of her philosophy stays the same: that children are individuals that should be taught according to their personal learning styles and needs and that she must teach the *whole child*.

Now finalize your draft into a polished copy. A well-thought-out philosophy will be like a compass throughout your career. You will modify your philosophy throughout your career, but it will be your global positioning system and serve to point you in the right direction and keep you focused on doing your best for children.

ACCOMMODATING DIVERSE LEARNERS

When you consider the makeup of pre-K–3 classrooms today, every classroom is an inclusion classroom. Teachers have always taught to all kinds of children with diverse needs. For example, in most classrooms you will find children of different developmental levels and capacities; different races and ethnicities; diverse religions and cultural beliefs and backgrounds; with different fears, hopes, and dreams; with diverse strengths and differences; different health levels and health-specific needs; with different family configurations; with different income levels; and with different learning styles and needs. In addition, all children, by the time they come to you, have a history of experiences, of feelings, pains and triumphs, all of which you have to consider as you plan and teach. As an early childhood professional you will be responsible for accommodating the naturally occurring diversity of your classroom.

The DEC and the NAEYC have issued a joint statement of inclusion and inclusionary practices. They define inclusion as education that

> embodies the values, policies, and practices that support the right of every infant and young child and his or her family, regardless of ability, to participate in a broad range of activities and contexts as full members of families, communities, and society. The desired results of inclusive experiences for children with and without disabilities and their families include a sense of belonging and membership, positive social relationships and friendships, and development and learning to reach their full potential. The defining features of inclusion that can be used to identify high quality early childhood programs and services are access, participation, and supports.[39]

True inclusion, as the NAEYC and the DEC defines it, involves providing for the needs of all children of different abilities, ranging from the developmental to the social, from the academic to emotional and behavioral. To do so, the NAEYC and DEC recommend that you and your early childhood programs do the following:

1. *Create high expectations for every child to reach his or her full potential.* A commitment to early childhood inclusion involves high expectations for each child, regardless of ability.

2. *Develop a program philosophy on inclusion.* Programs need a philosophy on inclusion as a part of their broader program mission statement to ensure that teachers and staff operate under a similar set of assumptions, values, and beliefs about the most effective ways to support infants and young children with disabilities and their families.

3. *Establish a system of services and supports.* A system of services and supports for children with disabilities and their families should respond to the needs and characteristics of children with varying types of disabilities and levels of severity, including children who are at risk for disabilities.[40]

As an early childhood professional, you have a unique role in making inclusive education a reality by promoting inclusiveness in all aspects of children's lives, giving each child a chance to thrive and succeed in school and in life.

ACTIVITIES FOR PROFESSIONAL DEVELOPMENT

ETHICAL DILEMMA

"MY PRINCIPAL REWARDS HER FAVORITE TEACHERS . . ."

First-year kindergarten teacher Emily Wittmer is happy in her classroom teaching. She loves her children and enjoys helping them learn and grow. However, she is having second thoughts about whether or not she wants to continue teaching at her school next year. The problem is that Emily's principal, Kelli Morton, has her favorite teachers and involves them, and only them, in school-based decisions. For example, last week Kelli and five of her favorite teachers went off campus for a day-long retreat to develop plans for new school programs. Several days later at a faculty meeting, Kelli announced that "she and her faculty representatives set goals for the rest of the school year." Emily thinks that this process is unfair and she is upset that only the principal's favorites get to make any decisions.

What should Emily do? Should Emily schedule a meeting with her principal and tell her that she does not approve of how decisions are made—possibly risking her career as a kindergarten teacher? Or, should Emily keep quiet and do nothing? Or, should Emily inquire about procedures for making a transfer to another school? What do you recommend that Emily do?

ACTIVITIES TO APPLY WHAT YOU LEARNED

1. Read and reflect again on the material presented at the beginning of the chapter about the five reasons change is sweeping across the early childhood profession. Which one of these reasons is most important to the profession? Why? Add a sixth reason you can identify for why and how the profession is changing. Be sure to give several clear reasons for your sixth example. Share this information with your colleagues on your class discussion board.

2. You can learn a great deal about what is involved in being a high-quality early childhood educator by reading the biographies of National Teachers of the Year. Go to the website for the Council of Chief State School Officers to read the biographies of national and state teachers of the year. Make a list of the characteristics and dispositions that you think make them effective teachers. From your list, choose three characteristics/dispositions and tell how you will incorporate them into your professional development plan. Post your ideas on your class discussion board or blog and ask for your classmates' comments and feedback.

3. **KEY ASSESSMENT:** Develop a computer-based professional resource portfolio/folder. Your professional resource portfolio includes your philosophy of education, lesson plan ideas, reflections, book lists, DVDs, websites, and classroom resources that will help you as a beginning teacher. Use the six NAEYC Standards for Professional Preparation Programs, to organize your professional resource portfolio to authenticate how you are meeting the six standards. Use the rubric provided to guide your work.

4. Access the NAEYC website and review the developmentally appropriate practice position statement. Give three specific examples of how you will apply DAP to your teaching so that children learn at high levels. Use the professional development checklist in Figure 1.6 and a daily/monthly planner to develop your professional development plan for the next year. First, list your career development goals and then, on a monthly basis, specify activities, events, and other ways that you will achieve these goals. For example, in addition to attending classes at a local community college, Rosa Vasquez plans to read a book a month on a topic related to teaching.

5. Part of becoming a professional includes mapping out your career pathway. Use PowerPoint to state your goals for becoming a professional. For example, do you want to become a teacher assistant, a classroom teacher, a principal, a special educator? Tell what professional roles you aspire to and the professional development you will involve yourself in to achieve your pathway goals. Ask your professor if you can share your PowerPoint presentation with your class as part of the discussion of this chapter.

6. Review your teaching philosophy draft. Evaluate your strengths and areas in which you hope to improve. As you review your professional teaching philosophy statement, reflect on the examples from teachers of the year and others you read about in the chapter. What were some of the qualities you admire about Renee? What are the qualities that make her a professional? What dimensions of Renee's background can you apply to your professional development?

7. Interview three teachers of inclusive classrooms and gather this information. (a) Why do the teachers think inclusive education is an important part of education today? (b) What do the teachers believe is their most important role as an inclusive teacher? (c) Ask teachers for suggestions on how you can become a high-quality inclusive teacher. Use the information from your interviews to inform and modify as appropriate, your professional development plan.

LINKING TO LEARNING

The following agencies and programs, which can be located easily online, provide additional information about topics discussed in this chapter.

Division for Early Childhood (DEC) Professional Standards

A division of the Council for Exceptional Children that promotes policies and advances evidence-based practices that support families and enhance the optimal development of young children who have or are at risk for developmental delays and disabilities.

Children's Defense Fund

Provides research and persistent advocacy for children's rights on issues including poverty, discrimination, and gun violence to ensure every child a healthy, fair, and safe start in life and successful passage to adulthood with the help of caring families and communities.

Council for Early Childhood Professional Recognition

Offers a nationally recognized, competency-based child development associate credential that provides training, assessment, and certification of child care professionals; also offers bilingual specialization.

Council for Exceptional Children (CEC)

Offers a variety of information regarding children with disabilities and serves as an advocate for these exceptional children. Also acts as the largest international professional organization dedicated to improving the educational success of individuals with disabilities and/or gifts and talents.

National Association for the Education of Young Children

Publishes brochures, posters, videotapes, books, and journals discussing teaching and program ideas, ways to improve parent-teacher relations, and resources for students about safety, language arts, and learning. Offers training opportunities through national, state, and local affiliate groups.

Third Grade Teachers

A free, interactive website for third grade teachers and support staff that enables users to blog, chat, post photos, and collaborate with other teachers across the world to exchange ideas, activities, and resources.

CHAPTER 2

CURRENT ISSUES: IMPLICATIONS for TEACHING and LEARNING

Contemporary Influences on Children and Families

LEARNING OUTCOMES

1. List the current public policy and issues in early childhood education.
2. Explain how you can prevent violence and bullying.
3. Identify ways you can provide for cultural diversity.
4. Explain how you can accommodate diverse learners in your classroom.
5. List hot topics in early childhood education and explain what they mean to you and your teaching.

IN this chapter we discuss public policy and current issues as they influence early childhood education. At no time in U.S. history has there been so much interest and involvement by early childhood professionals in the development and implementation of public policy. **Public policy** refers to the proposed or actual actions of government and nongovernmental organizations (NGOs) to address and solve social issues. It includes such things as laws; federal, state, and local government guidelines; position statements of professional organizations such as NAEYC; and court decisions. Public policy also involves the analysis and discussion of governmental decisions.

President Obama's universal preschool agenda, the federal government's current initiative to reform Head Start, and state legislators' proposals to fail children who don't read on grade level at the end of third grade are contemporary examples of public policy in action. Public policy influences education in every way from funding, to what children should know and be able to do (think Common Core State Standards), to what constitutes a high-quality early childhood program and teacher. Be assured that as an early childhood teacher you will be involved in and affected by public policy.

CONTEMPORARY ISSUES: CHILDREN, FAMILIES AND YOU

Contemporary issues affect how you provide for children's development, education, and care. They influence every dimension of practice from how we teach children to read, to the health care we provide, to special education services, to the quality of our teaching. We cannot ignore issues of education or pretend they do not exist. We must be part of the solution to make it possible for each child to achieve his or her full potential. Education today is very political, and politicians look to early childhood professionals to help develop educational solutions to social problems.

The *2013 State of America's Children Report* by the Children's Defense Fund, shows that the number of children who live in poverty in America is on the increase. Since 2000, the number of children living in poverty has increased by four million. The number of children who fell into poverty between 2008 and 2009 was the largest single-year increase ever recorded. **Poverty** is the condition of having insufficient income to support a minimum standard of living. One out of nine (or 8.1 million) American children is living with an unemployed parent. Children whose parents are unemployed are at increased risk for experiencing poverty, homelessness, and child abuse. It is almost a given in early childhood education that low socioeconomic status, unhealthy lifestyles, and family circumstances are major contributors to poor school achievement and life outcomes.[1] As a result, a number of social issues facing children today put their chances for learning and success at risk.

Check Your Understanding: Public Policy

CHILDREN OF THE GREAT RECESSION: THE GAPS

Throughout the course of their in-school and out-of-school lives, children's successes and achievement are greatly influenced by their family's socioeconomic status (SES). SES consists of three broad but interrelated measures: parents' education levels, parents' employment status, and family income. These three measures, acting individually and as an integrated whole, influence (1) how children are reared, (2) family–child

public policy All the plans that local, state, and national governmental and nongovernmental organizations have for implementing their goals.

poverty The condition of having insufficient income to support a minimum standard of living.

interactions, (3) home environments and the extent to which they do or do not support language development and learning, (4) the kind and amount of discipline used, and (5) the kind and extent of future plans involving children's education and employment.

THE CURRENT SES STATUS OF CHILDREN AND FAMILIES.   The headlines say it all: "Poverty Rate Hits 18-Year High as Median Income Falls." Forty-six million people live in poverty: That's 15.1 percent of the population! Twenty-one percent of young children live in poor families. Currently, the federal poverty level is $23,550 for a family of four.[2] This provides an idea of the circumstances that poor children and their families face. When I ask my university students to consider whether or not they could—or would want to—live as a part of a family of four where the income is less than $23,550, not one student answers affirmatively. No one wants to be poor, but we have many children and families who are. We should not bestow the label of poor or the conditions that go with being poor on any of our nation's children. Socioeconomic status creates gaps between children of low socioeconomic homes and their middle- to high-income classmates.

ACHIEVEMENT GAPS

Perhaps the most devastating of all achievement gaps are those related to pervasive poverty. The achievement gaps among students of different income levels are severe. Compared to their peers from higher-income families, infants and toddlers from low-income families score lower on cognitive assessments, are less likely to be in excellent or very good health, and are less likely to receive positive behavior ratings at both 9 and 24 months old. Impoverished students are roughly two years of learning behind the average financially better-off student of the same age. The income achievement gap appears early and persists over the lifetime of a student.[3]

achievement gaps The difference in performance between low-income and minority students, students of different genders, and students with different levels of maternal education, compared to that of their peers.

Achievement gaps are the difference in performance between low-income and minority students, students of different genders, and students with different levels of maternal education, compared to that of their peers. Traditionally, low-income and minority children have not performed as well as their peers have on tests.[4] Therefore, lower test scores for Latinos, blacks, and low-income students equals less school funding, which equals the perpetuation of the achievement gap.[5]

The achievement gap also influences individual outcomes. There is a demonstrable link between early performance in school and subsequent rates of high school graduation, college attendance and completion, and ultimately earnings. The less education children have, the more likely they are to be incarcerated, a smoker, obese, uninsured, and to not vote.[6]

MATERNAL EDUCATION ACHIEVEMENT GAP.   The causes of achievement gaps go beyond family income. Maternal education plays a significant role, too. Compared to infants whose mothers have a BA degree or higher, infants and toddlers whose mothers have less than a high school diploma score lower on both cognitive and behavioral measures. They are also less likely to be in excellent or very good health and are less likely to have secure attachments to their mothers.[7] So, with regard to public policy, encouraging all girls to graduate from high school would be a start in the right direction.

Because school achievement gaps are linked to socioeconomic status and family income and wealth, we can say that the achievement gaps that are recognizable at children's entry to preschool begin before they come to school. Merely providing programs to prevent and reduce achievement gaps on children's entry to school is not sufficient. We must provide, beginning at birth, programs for parents, families, and children with the knowledge and skills equivalent to what middle- and upper-income families provide their children.

The Kindergarten Achievement Gap

In the opening pages of the third edition of NAEYC's *Developmentally Appropriate Practice: Serving Children from Age Birth–8*, the authors discuss the early childhood achievement gap as one of the critical issues faced by children and early childhood professionals. Here is what they say:

> All families, educators, and the larger society hope that all children will achieve in school and go on to lead satisfying and productive lives, but that optimistic future is not equally likely for all of the nation's school children. Most disturbing, low income and African American and Hispanic students lag significantly behind their peers on standardized comparisons of academic achievement throughout the school years, and they experience more difficulties while in the school setting.[*]

The achievement gap between students of various races, cultures, and socioeconomic backgrounds is a serious issue that all of us as early childhood educators must address. Many children come to school already behind their more advantaged counterparts because they are not prepared to meet the demands of contemporary schooling. For example, children from low-income families are already well behind children in the highest socioeconomic groups.

The extent and seriousness of the achievement gap is further illustrated in the results of a survey of Michigan kindergarten teachers.

- Thirty-two percent of kindergarten teachers were not satisfied with the abilities of their kindergarten students when they started school, with an additional 50 percent being only somewhat satisfied.
- According to the teachers, only 65 percent of children entered kindergarten classrooms ready to learn the curriculum.
- Eighty-six percent of teachers reported that students who are behind academically at kindergarten entrance have an impact on their teachers' ability to effectively provide instruction to the rest of the class.[†]

Awareness of the extent of the problem is only one part of our efforts to reduce and eliminate achievement gaps. Taking effective action is the other part of the solution. Here are some things for which you can advocate:

- The opportunity for all children, but particularly children from low-income backgrounds and ELLs, to participate in preschool programs. There is a growing consensus that providing universal preschool will help all children socially and academically as they continue through the elementary grades.
- High-quality preschool and other early education programs for all children. Unfortunately, not all children have high-quality programs available to them; this is particularly true for students from low-income families.
- "Ready schools and ready communities" means that the schools children attend and the communities they live in are united in their efforts to provide the health, nutrition, and educational experiences all children need in order to be successful in school and life. Ready schools are those that have strong leadership, have continuity between early child care and education, promote smooth transitions between home and school, and are committed to the success of every child as well as every teacher and adult who interacts with children at school. Ready communities provide neighborhoods that are safe; have high-quality schools; have safe homes free of lead paint; and have amenities such as parks, playgrounds, and libraries.[‡]

In addition, there are many specific things that preschool and kindergarten teachers can do to help children catch up with their more advantaged peers. Children need specific language and literacy skills such as oral language, vocabulary, listening comprehension, and print awareness skills to be successful. Intentional teaching of these skills will go a long way to help eliminate the achievement gap.

[*]Carol Copple and Sue Bredekamp, *Developmentally Appropriate Practice in Early Childhood Programs: Serving Children from Birth Through Age 8,* 3rd ed. (Washington, DC: National Association for the Education of Young Children, 2009), 8.

[†]Lansing, MI, Early Childhood Investment Corporation. *A Summary of Michigan Kindergarten Teachers' Beliefs About the School Readiness of Kindergarten Children and Other Issues Related to School Readiness,* August 2009; accessed on August 24, 2013, at http://www.researchconnections.org/childcare/resources/12681.

[‡]Wisconsin Council on Children and Families, "Ready Kids, Ready Schools and Ready Communities," February 23, 2012; accessed on January 11, 2014, at www.wccf.org/?s=ready+kids%2c+ready+school+and+ready+communities.

This Voice from the Field illustrates the extent of the ways that the achievement gaps begin before children enter school.

Reflect and Apply: Poverty

GENDER ACHIEVEMENT GAP. There has long been a prevailing idea that science-, math-, and athletic-based classes are considered to be "masculine" subjects. Teachers, parents, and students all hold this belief. The idea that when girls excel at math, it is due to hard work, and that when boys excel at math, it is due to natural talent, still persists. Teachers are reported to show preferential treatment to boys in math classes.[8] As a result, there is a high participation gap in math and science subjects between genders. The math achievement gap between girls and boys remains. This has created a shortage of girls in science, technology, engineering, and math (STEM) classes and later on in scientific career fields (which produce more income than do female-dominated fields).[9]

Another gender gap involves black males. For black boys, the gender gap relating to achievement is severe. As early as nine months of age, there are differences between black males and their white counterparts in cognitive and language development.[10] By grade four, only 12 percent of black males in large city schools are proficient in reading.[11] Public policy measures to counter the black male achievement gap should include such initiatives as working with parents and families to eliminate chaotic home lives that lead to behavioral and social problems and providing health and social services to young parents and their children. In addition, a seamless system of pre-K–3 education could do wonders to support school readiness and provide black children the cognitive and behavioral skills necessary for ongoing school success.

HIGH QUALITY TEACHERS. In addition, research informs us that teacher expertise has a direct correlation to high student performance and eliminating achievement gaps. Students who have highly effective teachers three years in a row score as much as 50 percent higher on achievement tests than do those who have ineffective teachers for three years in a row.[12] Effective teachers know the content they are teaching, engage students in learning, and challenge them to greater accomplishments. Yet, frequently schools that serve low-income children often have the least-qualified and least-effective teachers.[13] Thus, putting highly effective teachers in schools serving low-income and black children would be another way to eliminate the achievement gap that separates black boys from higher achievements and opportunities.

Implications for Teaching. Here are some things you could do to close the achievement gaps.

- Accept all children. We casually say that teachers should accept all children, but it is true that acceptance and respect are the foundation for all teacher–student relationships. When children know that they are loved, respected, and accepted by the teacher, then they are more likely to engage and be involved.
- Create classroom environments that are safe and trusting. The living environment of many children of poverty is one of high stress. Create a climate in your classroom in which children feel safe and comfortable and in which they can focus on being a student learner.
- Attune yourself to the vast array of needs that children of poverty bring to your classroom. The social world that many children of poverty live in dictates how they behave and act, so the more you know about the homes, cultures, and backgrounds that children come from, the more sensitive you can be to meet their needs.
- Work with parents and families to find out about children's home lives. Many children of poverty lack the home support they need for learning. Help parents learn how to encourage their children to learn. Work with parents to provide learning materials in the home, such as books to read.
- Be accessible to parents at a variety of times before and after school. Many children's parents work multiple and varied shifts. Parent–teacher conferences

need to be rescheduled to help meet the needs of the parents as well as the students.

- Work with parents to encourage that their children attend school regularly. If children are not in school, they cannot learn. Regular school attendance supports learning.

- Advocate for readiness programs for young children that provide them with skills they need to enter school so that they are successful.

- Have high expectations for all students. Low socioeconomic status does not mean that you should have low expectations for children. Quite, the contrary! All children need teachers who have high expectations for them. This is especially true of children from low socioeconomic status backgrounds. High expectations increase children's self-image, which leads to higher achievement.

- Help ensure the learning success of each child. Provide children with the individual instructional attention they need to master basic academic skills, particularly reading and mathematics. Increasingly, school districts are failing children who do not read on level at the end of the third grade. One of your goals is to make sure that children learn to read and write well and on grade level to avoid future failure and school dropout.

- **Differentiate** (teach in response to the diverse needs of students so that all students within a classroom can learn effectively regardless of differences in ability) instruction so all children learn. Angelica L. Jordan, Department of Defense Education Activity (DoDEA) Teacher of the Year, believes that effective teachers spend time building relationships with students, parents, colleagues, and administrators. When she knows a student's likes, dislikes, and interests, she can differentiate lessons.[14]

differentiate To teach in response to the diverse needs of students so that all students within a classroom can learn effectively regardless of differences in ability.

FAMILY ISSUES

A primary goal of early childhood education is to meet children's needs in culturally and developmentally appropriate ways. Early childhood professionals agree that a good way to meet the needs of children is through their families, whatever their family unit may be. Family-centered practice is one of the cornerstone features of early childhood education and early childhood special education. This follows the fundamental notion that children's development is influenced by their environment: their family, teachers, school, town, media, governmental systems, and so on.[15] Review Figure 2.1, which shows the potential benefits of working with children and their families.

BENEFITS OF FAMILY-CENTERED PROGRAMS.   Providing for children's needs through and within the family system makes sense for a number of reasons. First, helping families function better means that everyone stands to benefit. When the other people in the family unit—mother, father, grandparents, and relatives—function better, children in the family function better, too.

Second, professionals frequently need to address family problems and issues to help children effectively. For example, helping parents gain access to adequate, affordable health care means that the whole family, including the children, will be healthier. And when children are healthy, they achieve more.[16]

Third, early childhood professionals can do many things concurrently with children and their families that benefit both. Literacy is a good example. Early childhood professionals take a family approach to helping children, their parents, and other family members learn to read, write, speak, and listen. Teaching parents to read helps them understand the importance of supporting their children in the learning process.

Fourth, addressing the needs of children and their families as a whole (i.e., the holistic approach to education and the delivery of services) enables early childhood professionals and others to address a range of social concerns simultaneously. Programs that provide education and support for literacy, health care, nutrition,

FIGURE 2.1 | A Model
for Meeting the Needs
of Children and Families

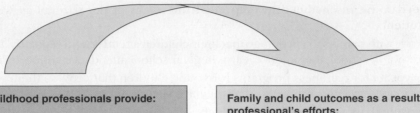

Early childhood professionals provide:

- Parent education to help parents learn basic child-rearing knowledge and skills
- Literacy programs to help children
- Readiness activities and programs designed to get children ready for school
- Family referrals to community agencies that can provide help (e.g., the Special Supplement Nutrition Program for Women, Infants, and Children or WIC, a preventative health and nutrition program that promotes optimal growth and development)
- Assistance with problems of daily living

Family and child outcomes as a result of professional's efforts:

- Less family and child stress
- Healthier families and children
- More involvement of families in their children's education
- Increased school achievement and success
- Reduced child abuse and neglect
- A better quality of life for children and families

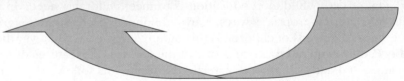

obesity prevention, healthy living, abuse prevention, and parenting are examples of this family-centered approach. A major trend in early childhood education is that professionals are expanding the family-centered approach to meeting the needs of children and families.

Thus, keeping children healthy becomes an important aspect of early childhood programs. In addition to nutrition and health information children can use at home, early childhood professionals can include daily activities in the classroom to support healthy lifestyles.

CHANGING FAMILY UNITS.   Families are in a continual state of change as a result of social issues and changing times. Even the definition of what a family is varies as society changes. Consider the following ways families are changing:

1. *Structure.* Families now include arrangements other than that of the traditional nuclear family:
   - Single-parent families, headed by mothers or fathers
   - Stepfamilies, including individuals related by either marriage or adoption
   - Heterosexual, gay, or lesbian partners living together with children
   - Extended families, which may include grandparents, uncles, aunts, other relatives, and individuals not related by kinship

2. **Roles.** As families change, so do the roles of parents, family members, and others:

- More parents work and have less time for their children and family affairs.
- Working parents combine the roles of parents and employees. The number of hats that parents wear will increase as families change.
- Grandparents and non–family members must learn new parenting roles.

As families continue to change, you and other early childhood professionals must develop creative ways to provide services to children and families of all kinds.

When families are involved in their children's education, everyone benefits. What are some culturally appropriate ways you can reach out to the families of the children in your care?

Working Parents. More and more families find that both parents must work to make ends meet. Reasons for more women working include decline in male earnings; the growth of single parent families; and the increase in women's educational levels. As a result of the Great Recession, more women entered the work force than ever before.

An increasing percentage of women—68 percent with children under age six—are currently employed, thereby creating a greater need for early childhood programs.[17] This demand focuses increased attention on early childhood programs and encourages early childhood professionals to meet working parents' needs. You can help working parents by effectively communicating with them and providing ways for them to be connected to their children's learning.

Collaborating with Families. Early childhood professionals agree that a good way to meet the needs of children is through their families, whatever the family units may be. As families change, early childhood professionals have to develop new and different ways of meeting parents' and children's needs. Providing for children's needs through and within the family system makes sense for a number of reasons:

- The family system has the primary responsibility for meeting children's many needs. Parents are children's first teachers, and the experiences and guidance they do or do not provide shapes their children for life. It is in the family that basic values, literacy skills, and approaches to learning are set and reinforced. This is why it is important to work with families and help them get a good start on parenting. For example, teachers can encourage parent phone calls or plan regular conferences to promote family collaboration.[18]
- Teachers frequently need to address family problems and issues simultaneously as they help children. For example, working with family services agencies to help parents access adequate, affordable health care means that the whole family, including children, will be healthier.
- Early childhood professionals can work with children and their families and benefit both. Family literacy is a good example. Helping children, their parents, and other family members learn to read and write helps the whole family. Many early childhood programs have literacy programs for parents and children. For example, the Toyota Family Literacy Program (TFLP) partners with the National Center for Family Literacy and addresses the growing needs of Hispanic and other immigrant families by increasing English language and literacy skills for adults while also supporting parents' involvement in their children's education.[19] Families matter in the education and development of children. Working with parents becomes a win–win proposition for everyone. You are the key to making family-centered education work.

Fathers and Early Childhood. Fathers are rediscovering the joys of parenting and working with young children, and early childhood education is discovering fathers! Men are now playing a more active role in providing basic care, love, and nurturance to their children. Fathers are more concerned about their role and their participation in family events before, during, and after the birth of their children than they were in previous generations. Fathers want to be involved in the whole process of child rearing.

An increasing number of fathers—3.4 percent of all dads or 176,000—are full-time stay-at-home dads.[20] Kindergarten teacher Lauren Gonzales's husband is a full-time stay-at-home dad. He bathes, feeds, diapers, and cares for their three-month-old child. He also helps his nine-year-old stepdaughter with homework and takes her to extra-curricular activities. And fathers are receiving some of the employment benefits that have traditionally gone only to women, such as paternity leaves, flexible work schedules, and sick leave for family illness.

Many men feel unprepared for fatherhood, and as result, early childhood programs and agencies such as hospitals and community colleges are providing courses and seminars to introduce fathers to the joys, rewards, and responsibilities of fathering.

Single Parent Families. An important part of your professional preparation is to develop the knowledge and skills necessary for collaborating with single-parent families. The number of one-parent families continues to increase. In 2013, 40.8 percent of all births were to single women.[21]

People become single parents for a number of reasons: About 36 percent of all marriages end in divorce,[22] and some parents, including a growing number of college-educated women, are single parents by choice. In addition, liberalized adoption procedures, artificial insemination, surrogate childbearing, and increasing public support for single parents make this lifestyle an attractive option for some individuals. The reality is that more women are choosing to bear children without marrying.

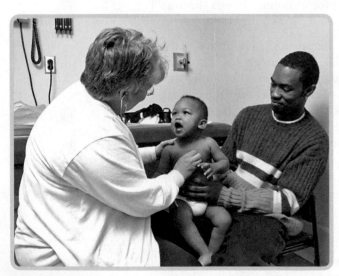

Readiness includes physical growth and general health, such as being well-rested, well-fed, and properly immunized. How does children's health status affect their readiness for learning?

No matter how people become single parents, they have tremendous implications for early childhood professionals. In response to growing single parenthood, early childhood programs are developing curricula to help children and their single parents. In addition to needing assistance with child care, single parents frequently seek help in child rearing, especially in regard to parenting practices. At Maplebrook Elementary School in Naperville, Illinois, early childhood professionals conduct seminars to help parents gain skills that will maximize children's learning and social growth.[23] In seminars parents learn things such as how to praise, how to disapprove, time-out procedures for misbehavior, and how to set up special incentive systems for motivating cooperative behavior.[24] How well early childhood professionals meet the needs of single parents can make a difference in how successful single parents are in providing for the needs of their children and other family members. Thus your support of single parents can impact how well their children progress in your programs and classroom.

WELLNESS AND HEALTHY LIVING.   As you know, when you feel good, life goes much better. The same is true for children and their families. Poor health and unhealthy living conditions are major contributors to poor school achievement and life outcomes. A number of health issues facing children today put their chances for learning and success at risk.

Illnesses. When you think of children's illnesses, you probably think of measles, chicken pox, and strep throat. Actually, dental caries (cavities), asthma, lead poisoning, obesity, and diabetes are the leading childhood diseases.

Watch the following **video** to see how two teachers respond to children's symptoms of illness. Notice in particular how each teacher responds. Reflect on which teacher responds most appropriately to each illness.

Dental Caries. Dental caries (tooth decay) remains the most prevalent chronic disease in both children and adults, even though it is largely preventable. Forty-two percent of children two to eleven have had dental caries in their primary teeth, and 23 percent have untreated dental caries. Black and Hispanic children and those living in families with lower incomes suffer from twice as much tooth decay as do their more affluent peers, and they are less likely to have health insurance. Providing children the dental health they need should be a huge priority for society and the early childhood profession. Dental caries leads to children being less ready to learn and results in diminished productivity in the classroom. Tooth decay causes pain and infection, leading to impaired chewing, speech, and facial expression, in addition to a loss in self-esteem.[25] Children with dental health problems show poor academic performance. They are distracted by pain and often have behavioral problems. As well, tooth decay leads to a lack of attendance in school, with fifty-one million school hours lost to dental-related illness each year.[26]

Implications for Teaching. Some things you can do to promote children's dental health include the following:

- Provide parents with information about the importance of toothbrushing and flossing. Some parents are surprised to learn that toothbrushing begins with the first tooth!
- Remind children of the importance of brushing and flossing by engaging them in reading stories, dramatic play, and other activities.
- Encourage parents to cut back on and reduce the amount of carbonated beverages and candy that their children consume.
- Provide time in the daily schedule for children to brush and floss their teeth, especially after meals and snacks. Many early childhood programs, including Head Start, do this.
- Invite dental hygienists to present programs on the dos and don'ts of good dental health.

Asthma. **Asthma**, a chronic inflammatory disorder of the airways, is also one of the most prevalent childhood illnesses in the United States. An estimated 7.1 million children under the age of eighteen suffer from asthma; 4.1 million children suffer from an asthma attack or episode every year.[27] Asthma is caused in part by poor air quality, dust, mold, animal fur and dander, allergens from cockroaches and rodent feces, and strong fumes. Many of these causes are found in poor and low-quality housing.

In your role as advocate, you can work with the American Lung Association, which has two initiatives designed to help children with asthma. One program is the Asthma Friendly School Initiative (AFSI). The other is the Kids with Asthma Bill of Rights, designed to help children with asthma talk to their parents and teachers about asthma management.

asthma A chronic inflammatory disorder of the airways; one of the most prevalent childhood illnesses in the United States.

You will want to reduce asthma-causing conditions in your early childhood program and work with parents to reduce the causes of asthma in their homes.

Implications for Teaching. In your school environment, here are some things you can do to reduce asthma:

- Prohibit smoking around children.
- Keep your classroom and center clean and free of mold. Mold is a frequent trigger of asthma attacks.
- Reduce or eliminate carpeting.
- Have children sleep on mats or cots rather than on the floor.
- Regularly change air conditioner filters.
- Wipe down all classroom surfaces each day.
- Use nontoxic and odor-free pest-control products.
- Work with parents to ensure that their children are getting appropriate asthma medication.

Lead Poisoning. Lead poisoning is also a serious childhood disease. The Centers for Disease Control and Prevention (CDC) estimate that approximately 535,000 U.S. children aged one to five years have elevated blood lead levels and that 3 percent of the nation's children have lead levels that pose a risk to their health.[28] Lead enters the body through inhalation and ingestion. These children are at risk for low IQs, short attention spans, reading and learning disabilities, hyperactivity, and behavioral problems. A major source of lead poisoning is from old lead-based paint in many older homes and apartments; most homes built before 1978 have lead-based paint in them. The federal government banned the use of lead in paint in 1978, but because paint with lead has a sweet taste that children like, it is not uncommon for them to eat chips of paint and to scratch a tooth on window sills.[29] Across the United States, many homes are near the sites of former lead factories. The soil in these areas is so contaminated with lead that it poses grave risks to the children who play in it—yet many do. Young children are especially vulnerable because they put many things in their mouths and crawl on floors.

Implications for Teaching

- Your primary roles in the prevention of lead poisoning in children are awareness and education.
- Make parents aware of the danger of lead poisoning in their children. Agencies such as the CDC provide flyers and brochures about the dangers of and prevention of lead poisoning. In addition, in October of each year, the CDC sponsors a National Lead Poisoning Prevention Week.
- Advise parents to have their children tested for lead as part of a periodic health examination.
- Alert parents to the recall of any toys with paint that may contain excess amounts of lead.

Diabetes. **Diabetes**, a chronic condition that affects how the body metabolizes sugar, is fast becoming one of the most common childhood diseases.[30] There are two types of diabetes in children. Type 1 diabetes is usually diagnosed in children and young adults and was previously known as juvenile diabetes. In Type 1 diabetes, the body does not produce insulin.[31] In Type 2 diabetes, the body produces insufficient amounts

diabetes A chronic condition that affects how the body metabolizes sugar; one of the most common childhood diseases.

of insulin, or the body adequately uses the insulin that is produced. The increase in Type 2 diabetes in children is alarming because it is usually an adult disease, more frequently diagnosed beginning in middle adulthood. Reasons for the increase in Type 2 diabetes include increasing childhood obesity, poor eating habits, and an emphasis on high calorie and sugary foods and drinks. Preventive measures for Type 2 diabetes go hand in hand with efforts to reduce childhood obesity—stressing healthy diets and regular (daily) exercise.[32]

Implications for Teaching. Again, your primary role in helping to prevent childhood diabetes is to raise awareness of the problem and to provide parents with information about diabetes and how to prevent it.

- Alert parents to the growing numbers of children with diabetes. This is a first step in prevention. Some parents may not know what diabetes is or they may think of it as only an adult disease.
- Advise parents about the risk for their children of sugary drinks, high-calorie foods, and overeating. Nutrition education can be a primary way to reduce the number of children with diabetes.

Obesity. Today's generation of young children is often referred to as the "Supersize Generation" because of their **obesity**. In fact, the Supersize Generation is getting younger! The American Heart Association reports that more than nine million children between the ages of six and nineteen years are considered to be overweight; 11.5 percent of children between the ages of six months and twenty-three months are overweight; and nearly 14 percent of preschool children between the ages of two and five years are overweight. Among children ages two to nineteen years, 17.6 percent of American children are overweight.[33] Additionally, the tipping point for early childhood obesity begins in infancy. More and more obesity prevention programs are geared toward infants and toddlers.[34]

obesity A medical condition in which excess body fat has stored to the amount that it may have an adverse effect on health, leading to reduced life expectancy and/or increased health problems.

In addition, new waves of research report the relationship of obesity to other diseases and health problems, especially later in life. Excess weight in childhood and adolescence predicts weight problems in adults. Overweight children, ages ten to fourteen, with at least one overweight or obese parent, are reported to have an 80 percent likelihood of being overweight into adulthood.[35] Research reveals that children who are substantially overweight throughout much of their childhood and adolescence have a higher incidence of depression than do those who aren't overweight. There are several significant findings related to this research. First, a link was shown between obesity and psychiatric disorders. Second, researchers found that boys were at greater risk than girls for weight-related depression.[36]

The dramatic rise in obesity is due to a combination of factors, including less physical activity and more fat and calorie intake. More children spend more time in front of televisions and computer screens, and fewer schools mandate physical education. Also, restaurant promotions to "supersize" meals encourage high-fat and high-calorie diets. Studies suggest that a ban on fast-food advertisements on television, especially those targeting young children, could reduce the number of overweight children by as much as 18 percent. Although it is unlikely that such a ban will ever materialize, these studies demonstrate how advertising food and childhood obesity are linked.[37]

As the rate of obesity in American children continues to rise, it is especially important for you to keep yourself healthy and to model healthy habits for the children you teach to ensure that they have a good role model as encouragement to develop healthy nutritional habits.

FIGURE 2.2 |
Choosemyplate.gov
The MyPlate icon is intended to prompt consumers to think about how to build a healthy plate at mealtimes. It also provides a means to combat childhood obesity.

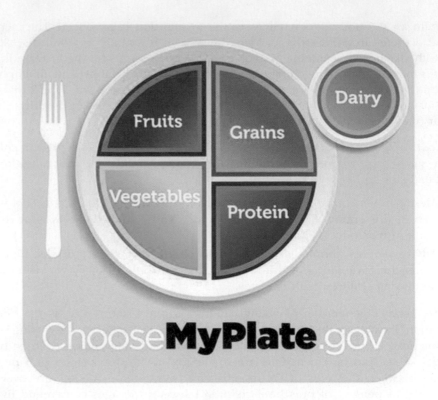

Implications for Teaching. Here are some ways you can help children and parents win the obesity war:

- *Provide parents with information about nutrition.* What children eat—or don't eat—plays a major role in how they grow, develop, and learn. Diet also plays a powerful role in whether or not children engage in classroom activities with energy and enthusiasm. For example, send home copies of MyPlate for Kids (see Figure 2.2). You can log on to MyPlate for Kids and individualize a food "plate" for each of your children. You can also send this information home to parents and share with them how to access and use the MyPlate nutrition guide in order to serve healthy meals to their families.

- *Encourage your children to eat breakfast and encourage parents to provide breakfast for their children.* Also, investigate your school's lunch and breakfast programs. If your program does not serve breakfast to children, you can advocate for such a program for children whose families' incomes make them eligible for federal- and state-supported nutrition programs. Research is very clear that serving breakfast to children who do not get it elsewhere significantly improves their cognitive abilities; this enables them to be more alert, pay better attention, and do better in terms of reading, math, and on standardized test scores.[38]

- *Counsel parents to pull the plug on the television.* TV watching at mealtime is associated with obesity because children are more likely to eat fast foods such as pizza and salty snack foods while they watch TV. Also, children who watch a lot of television tend to be less physically active, and inactivity tends to promote weight gain.[39]

- *Cook with children and talk about foods and their nutritional values.* Cooking activities are also a good way to eat and talk about new foods. Cooking and other nutrition-related activities are ideal ways to integrate math, science, literacy, art, music, and other content areas.

- *Integrate literacy and nutritional activities.* Reading and discussing labels is a good way to encourage children to be aware of and think about nutritional information. For example, calories provide energy; too much fat and sugar are not good for us; and protein is important, especially in the morning.[40]

- *Provide opportunities for physical exercise and physical activities every day.* For their part, schools are fighting the obesity war in the following ways:

  - Banning the sale of sodas and candy bars in school vending machines during lunch hours.[41]

  - Teaching about and encouraging healthier lifestyles in and out of school.

  - Including salad bars as part of their cafeterias. For example, in California, the Riverside Unified School District Farm to School Program is a program designed to promote healthy eating in children by increasing the availability of fruits and vegetables in school lunches and providing nutrition education to increase knowledge of and improve attitudes toward eating a variety of locally grown produce.[42]

  - Banning bake sales and other fundraising activities involving non-nutritious foods; banning cupcakes and other sweets at class birthday parties; and urging the use of healthier snack choices for homeroom celebrations.[43]

  - Restoring recess and physical education to the elementary school curriculum.

  - Working with parents to help them get their children to be more active and to eat healthier foods at home.

Involving children in nutritional and cooking activities is an excellent way to promote literacy development and build a strong foundation for good nutritional habits.

 Observe and Analyze

LET'S MOVE. The First Lady's Let's Move! project is a federal program that encourages healthy living. Let's Move! is a comprehensive initiative launched by First Lady Michelle Obama, dedicated to solving the challenge of childhood obesity within a generation, so that children born today will grow up healthier and able to pursue their dreams. Combining comprehensive strategies with common sense, Let's Move! aims to put children on the path to a healthy future during their earliest months and years by giving parents helpful information and by doing the following:

- Fostering environments that support healthy choices
- Providing healthier foods in our schools
- Ensuring that every family has access to healthy, affordable food
- Helping kids become more physically active

The goal of this program is to reduce childhood obesity from 20 percent to 5 percent by 2030.

Gender and Obesity. Have you ever heard an adult say, "Boys are just more active than girls; they need more time to run and play outdoors" or "The girls are content to play inside; it's the boys who have to get out on the playground"? Knowledgeable preschool and primary teachers know that vigorous physical activity is very important for girls as well as for boys. Both girls and boys need and deserve plenty of time to be physically active indoors and out. Improved aerobic endurance, muscular strength, motor coordination, and growth stimulation of the heart, lungs, and other vital organs are among the benefits of physical activity for all children. Giving equal opportunity to girls and boys—starting in preschool—is what Title IX of the Education Amendments of 1972 is all about.

Physical activity, for both genders, helps build and maintain healthy muscles, bones, and joints; increases the body's infection-fighting white blood cells and germ-fighting antibodies; helps control weight; and reduces the risk of developing such illnesses as diabetes, heart disease, and many types of cancer.

PREVENTING VIOLENCE, BULLYING, AND ABUSE

Every day, news reports are full of graphic accounts of how children are abused, abandoned, neglected, bullied, and treated inhumanely. Taken collectively, these acts seriously threaten the safety, health, and well-being of the nation's children.

VIOLENCE

Violence pervades American society. From television to video games to domestic violence, children are exposed to high doses of undesirable behavior. Children experience violence, both directly and indirectly, in these ways:

- Every day in the United States, 10 young children are murdered, 16 killed in firearm accidents, and 8,042 are reported as physically abused.[44]
- Over three million children per year witness domestic violence in their homes.[45]
- Children in poverty are 22 times more likely to be physically abused and 60 more times likely to die from the abuse than those in the middle class.[46]
- By the time they reach middle school, children will have watched 100,000 acts of violence through television, including 8,000 depictions of murder.[47]
- On average, school-aged children play video games fifty-three minutes per day; 49 percent of video games feature serious violence, and 40 percent show violence in a comic way.[48]

Research shows that violent behavior is learned and that it is learned early.[49] Your students' brains are remarkably **plastic**, or capable of being molded or adapted to conditions; the neurons are still arranging and rearranging connections. Brain plasticity usually works to children's advantage, because it enables them to learn and develop in spite of poor influences, allowing us to redirect neural pathways away from violence and toward amiable and peaceful conflict resolution. However, when children are routinely and repeatedly exposed to violence, their emotions, cognition, and behavior become centered on themes of aggression and violence.

plastic Capable of being molded or adapted to conditions.

Increasing acts of violence lead to proposals for how to provide violence-free homes and educational environments; how to teach children to get along nonviolently with others, such as by using puppets to discuss feelings with younger children or by role-playing and discussing appropriate ways to behave on the playground with older children; and how to reduce violence on television, in the movies, and in video games.[50] Advocating for reducing violence on television, for example, in turn leads to discussions for ways to limit children's television viewing. Such proposals include "pulling the plug" on television; using the V-chip included in every TV, which enables parents to block out programs with violent content; boycotting companies whose advertisements support programs with violent content; and limiting violence shown during prime-time viewing hours for children.

IMPLICATIONS FOR TEACHING. Here are some other steps you can take to prevent or reduce violence in children's lives:

- Show children photographs of the facial expressions of children and adults. Have the children identify various emotions; discuss appropriate and inappropriate responses to these emotions.
- Have children role-play how to respond appropriately to various emotions.
- Discuss with your students their behavior and the clear logical consequences of that behavior.
- Have children involved in disagreements discuss with one another the feelings that caused their actions and think about how they could have done things differently.
- Discuss violence openly in your classroom. Be honest about the repercussions of violence. Focus on the pain and humiliation it causes. For example, if you are reading a book in class in which the characters engage in violence, discuss how the victim felt, what the character could have done differently, and what they themselves would have done in the same situation.
- Send home information about media violence and encourage parents to monitor and limit screen time.

BULLYING

All across the country, state legislatures have passed laws requiring schools to implement anti-bullying programs. In response, school activists have developed proactive programs such as that at Kate Schenck Elementary School in San Antonio, Texas. Each morning the children take an anti-bullying pledge, and each Thursday the children wear anti-bullying T-shirts, both shown in Figure 2.3. The student council of Kate Schenck was instrumental in developing the pledge and designing the T-shirt.

Programs to prevent and curb **bullying** are another example of how educators are combating the effects of violence on children. Although in the past bullying has been dismissed as "normal" or "kids' play," this is no longer the case because bullying is related to personal and school violence. Bullying includes teasing, slapping, hitting, pushing, unwanted touching, taking personal belongings, name-calling, and making sexual comments and insults about looks, behavior, or culture.

bullying Teasing, slapping, hitting, pushing, unwanted touching, taking personal belongings, name-calling, and making sexual comments and insults about looks, behavior, or culture.

IMPLICATIONS FOR TEACHING. Here are some things you can do to help prevent bullying in your classroom:

- Talk to children individually and in groups when you see them engage in hurtful behavior. For instance: "Chad, how do you think Brad felt when you pushed him out of the way?"

front   back

- Be constantly alert to any signs of bullying behavior in your classroom and inter-vene immediately.
- Teach cooperative and helpful behavior, courtesy, and respect. Much of what children do, they model from others' behaviors. When you provide examples of courteous and respectful behavior in your classroom it sets a good example for children.
- Have children work together on a project. Then, have the students talk about how they got along and worked together.
- Make children and others in your classroom feel welcome and important.
- Talk to parents and help them understand your desire to stop bullying and to have a bully-free classroom.
- Conduct a workshop for parents on anti-bullying behavior and for signs of bullying.
- Report bullying to your principal! Remember that if you are aware of bullying behavior and do nothing about it, then you have not done your job of protecting and advocating for every child.
- Teach your students the "talk, walk, and squawk" method (or some other method your school uses) in response to bullying. Role-play and practice this technique in class:
  - *Talk:* Encourage your students to stand up for themselves verbally: "Leave me alone" or "You don't scare me" are some choices. Have children practice these responses in a calm and assertive voice.
  - *Walk:* Teach your students to walk away, but not to run away. If students run away, it is likely to increase the intensity of the bullying.
  - *Squawk:* The last step is to tell a teacher. Teachers can then take steps to halt the bullying behavior.[51]
- Keep parents informed of their child's interactions with violence in school. If a child is a bully or is being bullied, tell the parents so that you and they can col-laborate to remediate the situation.

- Read books about bullying. You can read books about bullying to and with your children during story time, group reading lessons, guided reading, and shared reading. You can also send books home for parents to read with their children. The following are some books you might want to read:

  - *The Juice Box Bully* by Bob Sornson, Maria Dismondy and Kim Shaw. Have you ever seen a bully in action and done nothing about it? The kids at Pete's new school get involved instead of being bystanders. When Pete begins to behave badly, his classmates teach him about "The Promise." Will Pete decide to shed his bullying ways and make "The Promise"?

  - *The Savvy Cyber Kids: Defeat of the Cyber Bully* by Ben Halpert and Taylor Southerland. While playing an online game, CyberPrincess and CyberThunder encounter a cyber-bully. Throughout the book, Tony and Emma learn strategies on how to appropriately respond to a bully online.

  - *Confessions of a Former Bully* by Trudy Ludwig and Beth Adams. After Katie gets caught teasing a schoolmate, she's told to meet with Mrs. Petrowski, the school counselor, so she can make right her wrong and learn to be a better friend. Bothered at first, it doesn't take long before Katie realizes that bullying has hurt not only the people around her, but her too.

  - *Jungle Bullies* by Steven Kroll and Vincent Nguyen. No one in the jungle will share. Elephant orders Hippo out of the pond; in turn Hippo orders Lion out of the path; Lion orders Leopard out of the grass; and Leopard orders Monkey off the branch of the tree. But Monkey's Mama has some very good advice for standing up for himself and teaching others how to share.

  - *Bullies Never Win* by Margery Cuyler and Arthur Howard. When the class bully, Brenda Bailey, makes fun of Jessica's skinny legs and her boyish lunch box, Jessica doesn't know what to do. She doesn't want to be a tattletale, but she also wants the bullying to stop. Can Jessica find the courage to stand up for herself?

Cyberbullying. The wide-spread use of the Internet, iPhones, texting devices, and social networking sites has led to the development of a new type of bullying: cyberbullying. **Cyberbullying** is the threat, stalking, harassment, torment, and humiliation of one child by another through cell phones, MySpace, Facebook, Twitter, chat rooms, blogs, texting, and picture messaging. Cyberbullying is often anonymous and sometimes occurs between cliques and a single victim. Cyberbullying occurs in females more frequently than males.[52]

Examples of cyberbullying include the following:

- Sydney sent Emily an e-mail that said she was fat, stupid, and ugly.

- Mia Photoshopped Gina's face onto a naked picture and posted it on MySpace.

- Kiera posted a note in a popular after-school study group chat that Shawna was the biggest blank in the third grade.

- Verbally abusing another person during an online game.

- Stealing another person's password and pretending to be that person in a chat room.

Implications for Teaching. Here are some ways to help prevent cyberbullying:

- Tell children of the consequences of forwarding any type of electronic message.

- Discuss with children the dangers involved in posting and sharing their personal information online and through social media.

- Advise students that if they think they are being cyberbullied they should log-off, report the incident to their teachers and parents, and change privacy settings on social networking sites.

> **cyberbullying** The threat, stalking, harassment, torment, and humiliation of one child by another through cell phones, MySpace, Facebook, Twitter, chat rooms, blogs, texting, and picture messaging.

Because most cyberbullying takes place outside the classroom, parents must take time to educate children about it. Here are more steps that parents can take to prevent cyberbullying in their own homes.

- Understand what cyberbullying is and how technology can be used to bully others.
- Contact the Internet service provider to see what parental controls are offered.
- Monitor what children are doing.
- Talk to children about online activity they are engaging in.
- Notify school officials if there is an incident that involves the school.
- Save all harassing messages so they can be reported.
- Keep computers in a common area.
- Look for signs that children may be a victim of cyberbullying.[53]

Being aware of the different ways that you can prevent cyberbullying will help you become more knowledgeable about the ways you can avoid this type of behavior in your classrooms. When you are alert for signs of cyberbullying, then you can lessen the likelihood that children will be the victims of the electronic age version of the playground bully.

PROVIDING FOR CULTURAL DIVERSITY

Changing demographics are changing the United States and U.S. public schools. These changes mean that more students will require special education, English as a Second Language education, and other special services. Issues of culture and diversity shape instruction and curriculum. Changing demographics also have tremendous implications for how you teach and how your children learn.

CHANGING DEMOGRAPHICS

Minority children are in most of the nation's school districts. Projections are that by 2050, minorities will constitute more than 47 percent of the American population.[54] The population of young children in the United States reflects the population at large and thus represents a number of different cultures and ethnicities. The New Majority Minorities are primarily Hispanic and Asian. Thus, many cities and school districts have populations that express great ethnic diversity, including Asian Americans, Native Americans, African Americans, and Hispanic Americans. Across the United States, seismic demographic changes herald how diverse populations are transforming regional geographic areas, states, school districts, and schools.

The South has become the first region in the country in which more than half of public school students are poor. Additionally, more than half of students in the South and Southwest are members of minorities (Arizona, 56 percent; California, 71 percent; Florida, 54 percent; Georgia, 54 percent; Louisiana, 51 percent; Mississippi, 54 percent; Nevada, 57 percent; New Mexico, 70 percent; and Texas, 65 percent). This shift is fueled by an influx of Latinos and other ethnic groups, the return of African Americans to the South, and higher birth rates among African American and Latino families. The numbers also herald the future of the United States as a whole because minority students are expected to exceed 50 percent of public school enrollment by 2020 and the numbers of students poor enough to qualify for free or reduced-price lunches continues to rise.[55] The constantly changing population demographics mean teachers have to understand diversity and embrace it in their classroom. The nation's schools have to do a better job of educating minorities. You can design your classroom and teaching to address issues relating to the needs of diverse populations and groups.

THINKING AND ACTING MULTICULTURALLY

As an early childhood professional, keep in mind that you are the key to the classroom environment that promotes **cultural competency** for all children. Cultural competence involves knowledge of other cultures and an ability to confidently interact with people of other cultures.

cultural competency
Involves knowledge of other cultures and an ability to confidently interact with people of other cultures.

IMPLICATIONS FOR TEACHING

- *Recognize that all children are unique.* Children have special talents, abilities, and styles of learning and relating to others. Make your classroom a place in which children are comfortable being who they are. Always value uniqueness and diversity.

- *Get to know, appreciate, and respect the cultural backgrounds of your children.* Visit families and community neighborhoods to learn more about cultures and religion and the ways of life they engender. Children are rooted in their families' culture and the family structure is the basis of the child's culture.

- *Use authentic situations to provide for cultural learning and understanding.* For example, a field trip to a culturally diverse neighborhood of your city or town provides children an opportunity for understanding firsthand many of the details about how people live. Such an experience provides wonderful opportunities for involving children in writing, cooking, reading, and dramatic play activities. What about setting up a market in the classroom?

- *Use authentic assessment activities to assess fully children's learning and growth.* Portfolios are ideal for assessing children's learning in nonbiased and culturally sensitive ways.

- *Infuse culture into your lesson planning, teaching, and caregiving and make it a foundation for learning.* Use all subject areas—math, science, language arts, literacy, music, art, and social studies—to relate culture to children's lives and cultural backgrounds. This approach makes students feel good about their backgrounds, cultures, families, and experiences.

- *Be a role model by accepting, appreciating, and respecting other languages and cultures.* In other words, infuse multiculturalism into your personal and professional lives.

- *Be knowledgeable about, proud of, and secure in your own culture.* Children will ask about you, and you should be prepared to share your cultural background with them.

It is up to you to help your children to accept and respect all people and their cultures.

CULTURAL AWARENESS.
Cultural awareness is the appreciation for and understanding of people's cultures, socioeconomic status, and gender. It includes understanding one's own culture. Cultural awareness programs and activities focus on other cultures while making children aware of the content, nature, and richness of their own. Learning about other cultures concurrently with their own culture enables children to integrate commonalities and appreciate differences without inferring inferiority or superiority of one or the other. Promoting cultural awareness in an early childhood program has implications far beyond your school, classroom, and program. Culture influences and affects work habits, interpersonal relations, and a child's general outlook on life. Being a culturally aware teacher means that you are sensitive to the socioeconomic backgrounds of children and families. For example, we know that low family socioeconomic status tends to dampen children's school achievement. The same is true with children's school achievement and level of maternal education. Research

cultural awareness
The appreciation for and understanding of people's cultures, socioeconomic status, and gender; includes understanding one's own culture.

shows that children that have educated parents enter school with a higher level of academic skills and continue to perform better than other children.[56] By learning about family background you can provide children from diverse backgrounds the extra help they may need to be successful in school.

Early childhood professionals must take these influences into consideration when designing curriculum and instructional processes for the impressionable children they teach. One way to accomplish the primary goal of cultural infusion and awareness—to positively change the lives of children and their families—is to infuse acceptance of diversity in early childhood activities and practices. Children must be culturally competent. They need to develop proficiency to respond respectfully and effectively to diverse cultures.[57]

USING APPROPRIATE INSTRUCTIONAL MATERIALS.   Carefully selected and appropriate instructional materials support children's cultural awareness. What does this mean? Here are some suggestions for achieving the goal of promoting cultural awareness.

- *Multicultural literature.* Choose literature that embraces similarities and welcomes differences regarding how children and families live their whole lives.
- *Themes.* Early childhood professionals may select and teach thematic units that help strengthen children's understanding of themselves, their culture, and the cultures of others. Here are some appropriate theme topics, all of which are appropriate for meeting various state standards and the standards of the National Council for the Social Studies (NCSS):
  - Getting to know myself, getting to know others
  - What is special about you and me?
  - Growing up in the city
  - Tell me about Africa (or South America, China, etc.)
- *Personal accomplishments.* Add to classroom activities, as appropriate, the accomplishments of people from different cultural groups, women of all cultures, and individuals with disabilities.

TEACHING ENGLISH LANGUAGE LEARNERS.   You will teach children from different cultures whose first language is not English. Educating students with diverse backgrounds and individual needs makes for a challenging and rewarding career. Learning how to constantly improve your responses to children's needs and improve learning environments and curricula will be one of your ongoing professional responsibilities. Given the high number of students from diverse backgrounds, today it is more important than ever that educators be aware of cultural differences. Lack of knowledge of these differences can lead to the overrepresentation of students from diverse backgrounds in special education programs.[58] The accompanying Voice from the Field, "How to Help English Language Learners Succeed," provides you with seven strategies for becoming a successful teacher of linguistically and culturally diverse children (see p. 58).

GREEN SCHOOLS AND GREEN CURRICULA

All across the United States, schools are going green. Green schools are those in which the building creates a healthy environment conducive to learning while saving energy, resources, and money.[59] Green schools and curricula are a response to eco-issues around the world and represent ways to save energy, conserve resources, infuse curricula with environmental education, build school gardens, and offer more healthy school lunches.

GREEN CURRICULA. Green schools are only one part of contemporary eco-friendly initiatives. Making the school curriculum greener is the other part. More schools and teachers are teaching children and their families about the environment and how to preserve it and about the benefits of green living. At the University City Children's Center in St. Louis, Missouri, preschool children have a garden bed in which they raise vegetables that become part of their school lunches.[60] Child care programs are turning to eco-friendly diapers, organic baby foods, odor-free, zero-VOC (volatile organic compounds) paints, and the use of nontoxic techniques to control pests.

Just as saving the environment permeates all of our daily lives, so too is the eco-movement becoming an essential part of the schools and the curriculum.

As schools and curricula go "green," you will want to involve your children in activities that help them learn about and preserve their environment, as well as how to incorporate green living into their classrooms and homes.

ACCOMMODATING DIVERSE LEARNERS

Now that you have read about public policy and current issues affecting young children today, let's look at one issue that has many policy implications as well as one about which many early childhood teachers have questions: *inclusion*, typically defined as educating children with and without disabilities in the same classroom. While the Division for Early Childhood (DEC) of the Council for Exceptional Children (CEC) and the National Association for the Education of Young Children (NAEYC) have identified inclusion as the preferred service delivery option for young children with special needs, there is no agreed-on model for developing and delivering these services. A classroom template for inclusion is not available, but it is essential that teachers believe that preparing all children to function in society is best achieved by creating environments that include children with varying abilities and disabilities and backgrounds.

Once teachers support the philosophy of inclusion, they must be able to plan for and provide for the needs of the diverse children in their classroom. Creating a successful inclusive environment requires a well-planned and well-organized classroom. Teachers who plan and evaluate the different aspects of the classroom setting can construct classrooms that meet the needs of all students. You will gradually gain the skills, awareness, and disposition to do this. The following list provides some examples of ways to create, implement, evaluate, and modify classrooms so that optimal learning conditions are created for all students:

- *Classroom schedule.* A consistent schedule helps students feel secure and adds to the predictability of the environment. A visual schedule that is reviewed orally every day benefits all children. In addition, some students will need their own individual schedules, particularly if their day includes therapists who provide services for them.
- *Routines.* Routines for different times of the day and scheduling a particular activity at the same time every day or on the same day every week is beneficial for students who need the stability of knowing what their day will entail.
- *Classroom curriculum.* Classroom curriculum that is appropriate for all children does not mean each child will do the same things every day. The curriculum must include activities that can be modified and adapted to meet the needs of each child.

How to Help English Language Learners Succeed

My ongoing attempt to learn Spanish provides me with a lot of empathy for English language learners! Perhaps you have had the same experience that I have of frustration with comprehension, pronunciation, and understandable communication. English language learners (ELLs) face these same problems. Many come from low socioeconomic backgrounds. Others come to this country lacking many of the early literacy and learning opportunities we take for granted.

Picture yourself in this classroom. Which of the activities suggested here would you select to help your students learn English?

INCREASING NUMBERS

Many school districts across the country have seen their numbers of ELLs skyrocket. For example, in 2013 the Texas Education Agency reported there were 838,000 ELLs in K–12 programs throughout the state. Over 120 languages were represented, 90 percent were Spanish speakers. Prominent languages other than Spanish were Korean, Vietnamese, Urdu, and Arabic.*

The chances are great that you will have ELLs in your classroom wherever you choose to teach.

STRATEGY 1

Develop Content Around a Theme
The repetition of vocabulary and concepts reinforces language and ideas and gives ELLs better access to content.

- Provide a word wall or word bank for students to display the vocabulary associated with the theme being studied. Use pictures to explain vocabulary whenever possible.
- Provide a variety of reading, writing, listening, and speaking experiences around the theme.

- Include higher-order thinking skills, such as evaluating, synthesizing, and application for children to think about and problem-solve.

STRATEGY 2

Use Visual Aids and Hands-On Activities in Your Instruction
Children retain information better when you involve their senses in learning.

- Rely on visual cues (pictures, etc.) as frequently as possible.
- Have students create flash cards for key vocabulary words. Be sure to include enough time in your lessons so that students can use their vocabulary words.
- Encourage students to use computer programs and books with CDs or DVDs.
- Use rubrics (scoring and performance guides) with pictures to help students learn what is expected of them.
- Use visual aids and hands-on activities in your instruction. ELLs benefit from illustrations, manipulatives, and real experiences that provide clues to meaning and support their language development.
- Engage children in learning activities they enjoy. Create opportunities for children to talk about things that they find interesting, motivating, and exciting. If you scaffold and build their academic language, they will learn English and grow academically too.

STRATEGY 3

Use Routines to Reinforce Language
Use routines in your classroom. Repetition allows students to tie language to what's happening around them. Routines also increase children's comfort level when learning a new language because they can know what to expect. Language acquisition is easier in low-stress environments. For example, start your school day with a morning routine that includes counting the children present, noting the day of the month, talking about the weather, etc.

- Use daily reading with pictures, gestures, and a dramatic voice to help convey meaning.
- Provide "scripts," instructions for a set of actions, by tying language to content instead of simply trying to teach language in isolation. For example,

engage children in role play in which they act out common activities such as lining up or going to the cafeteria, recess, or the zoo. Teach useful language frames such as, "Can you help me find the bathroom?"

- Remember that there is a distinction between the language children use on the playground and academic language—the language they need to succeed with tasks they encounter in school. Teachers need to consciously and carefully scaffold academic language. For example, before you ask children to retell a story, teach words such as *first*, *then*, and *after*.

STRATEGY 4
Engage English Language Learners with English Speakers
Cooperative learning groups composed of children with mixed language abilities give students a meaningful context for using English.

- Use cooperative learning. Cooperative learning groups usually assist children of different achievement levels; in this case, ELLs need English-speaking role models to help them learn English. Language learning requires interaction. You want to get your students talking. **Cooperative learning** creates a context for students to converse about meaningful ideas. Pairs work too. Pair ELLs with English speakers in a variety of activities. Small groups (four or less) and pairs promote interaction. Remember, learning is social. Good language learning environments are not quiet and involve student interaction!

- Make language learning fun. Children don't learn language because they think they want a career in international marketing. They learn language because they want to talk, make friends, and do the things that children do.

Classroom activities such as those suggested here can help English language learners gain important skills.

STRATEGY 5
Allow Students to Use Nonverbal Responses
Permit students to demonstrate their knowledge and comprehension in alternative ways. For example, one teacher asks her children to hold up cardboard "lollipops" (green or red side forward) to indicate a yes or no answer to a question.

- Allow students to draw pictures to demonstrate their understanding. They can explain about their picture to a small group. Remember, a picture is worth 1,000 words!

- Don't correct all nonstandard responses. It's better to get students talking; they acquire accepted forms of language usage and communication through regular use and practice. You can always paraphrase a student's answer to model Standard English.

STRATEGY 6
Use Technology
You can use technology to scaffold language development of ELLs. Technology is student centered and gives students some control over their own learning. Focus on technological tools and activities. For example, do the following:

- Use iPods as voice recorders so children can hear themselves read and talk. When students are able to record and hear themselves read and talk, they become more engaged and motivated to learn English.

- English language development teacher Amanda Currey believes an array of technology helps engage students and provides the structured one-on-one English practice they need, and that software, online tools, and other technologies help students hone basic language skills they can later apply in authentic social settings. Amanda uses technology to mix things up, capture students' attention, and engage them in a way traditional classroom instruction doesn't.

STRATEGY 7
Respect, Preserve, and Honor Children's Culture
Encourage students to preserve their cultural identity as they are learning English.

- Have children show their countries of origin on a world map, then talk and write about it.

*L. Ayala, Texas Education Agency, *2010 Texas Assessment Conference ELL Student Assessment Update*; accessed on January 11, 2014, from www.texaspolicy.com/center/education-policy/blog/english-language-learning-population-growing-texas-schools.

cooperative learning groups A context that allows English language learners to converse about meaningful ideas.

skill deficit When a child has not learned how to perform a particular skill or behavior.

- *Classroom management.* Teachers must support and encourage appropriate behavior, prevent inappropriate behavior, and guide or redirect misbehavior when it does occur. In the inclusive classroom, you can achieve this goal by creating a positive management plan that addresses skill deficits. A **skill deficit** is the result when a child has not learned how to perform a particular skill or behavior. For example, a child with a disability may have a social skill deficit associated with making friends and gaining popularity. Motivational deficits involve the unwillingness or lack of cooperation of children to perform a skill they possess, either entirely or at an appropriate level. For example, some children may be reluctant or hesitant to engage in an activity because of their disability. In contrast, some children may lack motivational self-control and be aggressive and intrusive to others.

- *Grouping.* The inclusive classroom can include heterogeneous and homogeneous grouping, depending on the activity. Teachers must have explicit individual behavioral and academic expectations for each child depending on his or her needs.

- *Physical arrangement.* In the early childhood classroom, the four-desk cluster provides the most opportunities for students with disabilities to be included in the classroom. Teachers can move efficiently from child to child, and socialization, cooperation, and group work are optimized.

- *Rules.* Rules should be stated positively, be limited in number, observable, measurable, and applied to behavior only. Rules should not address academic or homework issues that could unfairly impact students with disabilities or who are linguistically diverse.

- *Transitions.* Strategies that support smooth transitions between activities include verbal cues (e.g., "Five minutes before clean-up"); visual cues (e.g., picture schedules); auditory cues (e.g., timers); and praise after successful transitions.

Teachers who actively prepare for all students are better able to provide accommodations, support, and instruction where needed. Organizations such as DEC, CEC, and NAEYC are excellent sources for position papers, instructional resources, and other documents that will assist you with teaching in the inclusive classroom.

HOT TOPICS IN EARLY CHILDHOOD EDUCATION

Issues facing early childhood education today are many and varied and have considerable consequences, both positive and negative, for young children. The following "hot topics" are building across the profession.

- *The globalization of early childhood education.* Countries around the world are using early childhood education as a foundation by which to muscle their way into the top tier of world economic influence. Nowhere is this more evident than in Asia. Early childhood education has emerged as a tool of economic competitiveness.[61] This helps explain, in part, why there is so much state and federal emphasis on universal preschool and other issues facing young children and their families.

- *The politicization of early childhood education.* There has been a dramatic increase in state and federal involvement in the education of young children, for reasons discussed above. President Obama and his administration have initiated numerous programs to provide funding to improve early education learning. Once again, early childhood, especially preschool, is in the political spotlight and will remain there for the next decade.

- *Emphasis on science, technology, engineering, and math (STEM).* Children need an education with a foundation in STEM areas so that they are prepared to both work and live in the twenty-first century.[62] There is a particular emphasis on how to involve girls in the STEM areas and to interest them in careers in the sciences.

- *Alignment of the public schools and early childhood programs.* The alignment of public schools with early childhood programs is becoming increasingly popular. Some think it makes sense to put the responsibility for educating and caring for the nation's children under the sponsorship of one agency—the public schools. For their part, public school teachers and the unions that represent them are anxious to bring early childhood programs within the structure of the public school system. However, a growing vocal minority views federal funding of preschool programs as a movement to "standardize childhood." They argue that with federal funding comes federal control and a standardized one-size-fits-all approach to preschool education. This tension between local and federal funding and control of early childhood education will continue to give both sides opportunities to advocate for which approach they think best meets the needs of children and families.

  It seems inevitable that the presence of public schools in early childhood education will continue to expand. Given that so many public schools offer programs for three- and four-year-olds, can public school programs for infants and toddlers be far behind?

- *The use of research results to inform and guide program and classroom practice.* Another name for this research emphasis is *evidence-based* or *research-based practice*. You can use research results as part of your advocacy agenda. For example, research that shows the benefits and lifelong value of children's participation in early childhood programs enables you to advocate for additional high-quality programs. The application of research to practice is one of the hallmarks of the "new" early childhood education.

- *Whole-child education.* There is definitely a trend toward rethinking what is an appropriate education for all children. There has been a tendency, in many sectors, to look at education as consisting of primarily achievement as measured by test scores. Now, more people are coming to support what early childhood educators have always known and held dear: We must educate the whole child in all developmental dimensions—physical, social, emotional, cognitive, linguistic, and spiritual!

- *Child-centered education.* This movement is closely aligned with the "whole child" movement. It is designed to make children the center of the educational process—not teachers, not the curriculum, not tests, but children. This seems like such an obvious idea, but unfortunately the public, and quite often the profession, loses sight of the fact that education is—and should be—about the children. Everything else should be designed to make their educational experience meaningful.

- *Children's mental/social/emotional/behavioral health and well-being.* The Sandy Hook shooting, in which twenty children and six adults were killed, focused the nation's attention once again on the role mental health plays in the decisions and actions of children and adults. Early childhood professionals are now focusing on how to support the positive mental health of infants and toddlers as the foundation for life-long positive mental health. You will be involved in programs and efforts to help prevent behaviors that lead to violence and criminal behavior.

- *Universal preschool.* President Obama's call for universal preschool for the nation's four- to five-year-old children is a game changer for early childhood education. Not only will more children than ever before enroll in preschool, but also the demand for preschool teachers will dramatically increase. I think the future of early childhood is being defined by how the nation responds to the president's call for preschool funding.

- *Highly effective teachers and teaching.* A highly effective teaching force is essential for implementing the universal preschool initiative. This means that there will be more of a professional effort to recruit and educate high-quality teachers for the teaching profession. Colleges of education are in the process of revamping their teacher training programs to meet the demand for teachers who are highly qualified and who can help children achieve to the highest levels.

- *Teaching English learners (ELLs).* As the nation's school population becomes more diverse, there is more demand for teachers who are willing and able to teach English learners. You will want to consider earning a bilingual certificate or endorsement along with your standard teaching certificate. Many colleges of education are making this possible for their students. At the same time, increasing numbers of school districts are demanding such training before they hire new teachers.

- *Technology integration.* The integration of technology into the teaching and learning process is a powerful theme running through all of education today, pre-K–12. Learning how to use technology to help children learn and how to involve children in the use of technology to ensure their learning is an essential teacher role today. You have no choice but to learn to confidently integrate technology into children's learning.

This is a great time for early childhood education and a wonderful time to be a teacher of young children. The numerous changes in the field and the compelling issues that accompany them provide many opportunities for you to become even more professional and for all children to gain the knowledge and skills necessary for success in school and life.

ACTIVITIES FOR PROFESSIONAL DEVELOPMENT

ETHICAL DILEMMA

"MY CHILD'S NOT DANGEROUS!"

Zachary Christie, a six-year-old, was suspended for forty-five days after he was found with a camping utensil that was ruled a weapon. Zachary got the camping utensil after joining Boy Scouts and was excited to use it at lunch, using it as a spoon, fork, and knife.

Local school districts' zero tolerance policy restricts students from bringing weapons to school. Regardless of Zachary's intent, school officials proclaimed that they had to penalize him because bringing knives to school is against school policy. There is a growing debate over whether or not zero tolerance policies have gone too far. Although Zachary may not have intended to harm anyone, administrators argue that it is hard to distinguish between pranks, innocent mistakes, and serious threats. To ensure the safety of all children they must adhere to strict rules. Zachary's mom started a website to gain support and persuade others that "he is not some sort of threat to his classmates." So, what do you think?

Do you think that the zero tolerance policies are too strict? Or, should administrators have the final say and make decisions on a case-by-case basis? Do you agree with the decision to suspend Zachary from school? What should Zachary's mom do? What would you do with Zachary?

ACTIVITIES TO APPLY WHAT YOU LEARNED

1. **KEY ASSESSMENT:** Academic achievement gaps between poor children and their middle- and upper-income classmates is a serious issue in early childhood today. Think about and identify three things you can do to help close achievement gaps in your classroom. Log on to Facebook and share with your classmates by creating an online blog. Ask for their ideas for how they would close the gaps. Take a look at the number of people that have viewed your blog and read their comments. What do their comments tell you? Use the rubric provided to guide your work.

2. Conduct an Internet search of school-based bully prevention programs and identify the best features. From these best features develop a PowerPoint presentation titled "Best Practices for Bully Prevention in Early Childhood Programs." Ask your teacher if you can make a presentation to your class.

3. Many young children live in diverse families. Conduct online research about the challenges of providing for different types of families. Think about diverse families, the challenges families face, and what you can do as an early childhood professional to support contemporary families. Log on to Twitter and share with a small group of classmates your findings through Twitter's online website.

4. How can you create and modify classrooms to accommodate diverse learners? Go online and find ways teachers in inclusive classrooms accommodate their diverse learners. Next, discuss your findings with classmates in a chat room. Finally, develop a list of ways you will support students with disabilities in your classroom.

5. Think about the hot topics discussed in this text. Which hot topic do you think is the most important? Why? Log on to Facebook and share your ideas by posting a note. Tag your classmates to get their feedback.

LINKING TO LEARNING

The following agencies and programs, which can be located easily online, provide additional information about topics discussed in this chapter.

Annie E. Casey Foundation
Presents the latest information on issues affecting America's disadvantaged children; a friendly, newly updated resource.

Council for Exceptional Children (CEC)
A national organization dedicated to improving educational outcomes for individuals with exceptionalities, students with disabilities, and/or the gifted.

The Division for Early Childhood (DEC)
A division of the Council for Exceptional Children that promotes policies and advances evidence-based practices that support families and enhance the optimal development of young children who have or are at risk for developmental delays and disabilities.

U.S. Department of Agriculture—Choose My Plate
Provides useful information on current nutrition guidelines, including MyPlate, which promotes a healthy diet.

Zero to Three
Promotes the healthy development of the nation's infants and toddlers by supporting and strengthening families, communities, and those who work on their behalf.

USA Today—Ghost Factories
Collection of comprehensive investigative reports on contaminated soil and the effects of children's play in these contaminated areas.

Child Welfare Information Gateway
A service of the Administration for Children and Families, U.S. Department of Health and Human Services, which helps coordinate and develop programs and policies concerning child abuse and neglect.

Childhelp USA
Handles crisis calls and provides information and referrals to every county in the United States; hotline 1-800-422-4453 or 4-A-CHILD.

Let's Move
A national initiative founded and run by First Lady Michelle Obama to bring awareness and dramatic change to obesity within one generation.

OBSERVATION and ASSESSMENT for TEACHING and LEARNING

Effective Teaching Through Appropriate Evaluation

LEARNING OUTCOMES

1. Explain what assessment is and why it is important.
2. List the purposes of assessment.
3. Describe the importance of observation to the early childhood professional.
4. List some major ways to assess children's school readiness and learning.
5. Explain some critical issues concerning assessment.

TEACHERS use assessments every day, and each teacher uses assessments differently. First grade teacher Katie Sandifer uses assessments in different ways to help improve student learning. She uses performance-based assessments that are fun for the students, such as playing *Jeopardy, Who Wants to Be a Millionaire, Deal or No Deal*, and other games with them. The children really enjoy it and learn a lot while they 'play.' These are wonderful ways to assess, especially when you have a SMART Board.[1] Kindergarten teacher Michaele Bachman acknowledges that some schools include preliminary formal assessments for incoming kindergarten students. . . . However, her own preference is to refrain from putting barely five-year-olds through additional performance stress.[2] Instead, Michaele uses observational assessments to get to know her students. She writes down thoughts and observations about each of the children as they familiarize themselves with their environment. These observations include: *What is the child's size, and how does she/he use physical space? Does the child squint, or say 'huh' or ask for directions to be repeated again? Does the student only demonstrate parallel play? Does the child recognize and choose to acknowledge and cooperate with transitions? Is the student a watcher or a do-er? A little of both? How long does it take him/her to come out of a comfortable shell?*[3]

Teachers' minutes, hours, and days are filled with such assessment questions and decisions. Assessment is continuous. Questions abound: "What is Jeremy ready for now?" "What can I tell Maria's parents about her language development?" "The activity I used in the large-group time yesterday didn't seem to work well. What can I do differently?" Appropriate assessment can help you find the answers to these and many other questions about how to teach, how to assess, and what is best for each child.

WHAT IS ASSESSMENT?

Teaching without assessment is like driving without headlights. Teaching in the dark does not benefit you or your children. Assessment casts light on what children know and can do. It is an invaluable tool to guide your teaching and your students' learning.

Your children's lives, both in and out of school, are influenced by your assessment and the assessment of others. As an early childhood professional, assessment influences your professional life and is a vital part of your professional practice. Developmentally appropriate and effective assessment is one of your most important responsibilities.

Assessment is the ongoing, continuous process of collecting, gathering, and documenting information about children's development, learning, health, behavior, academic progress, need for special services, and achievement in order to make informed decisions about how to best educate them. Teachers and early childhood programs use assessment results for children's benefit by making sound decisions regarding teaching and program improvement.

Figure 3.1 outlines the purposes of assessment. Student assessment occurs primarily through observation, performance-based assessment with commercial and teacher-made tests, and evaluation of students' portfolios and work samples. You will use all three of these assessment procedures to inform your teaching so you can help all children be successful.

FIGURE 3.1 | Purposes of Assessment

For Children, Assessment:

- Identifies what they know
- Identifies their special needs
- Determines their appropriate placement
- Refers them and their families for additional services to programs and agencies

For Families, Assessment:

- Provides information about their children's progress and learning
- Relates school activities to home activities and experiences to promote at-home learning
- Enables teachers and families to work collaboratively to benefit children and family members

For Teachers, Assessment:

- Informs lesson and activity plans and establishes goals
- Creates new classroom arrangements
- Selects materials
- Monitors and improves the teaching–learning process
- Groups for instruction

For Early Childhood Programs, Assessment:

- Informs policy decisions regarding what is and is not appropriate for children
- Determines how well and to what extent programs and services children receive are beneficial and appropriate
- Aligns curriculum and teaching with children's needs

For the Public, Assessment:

- Informs them of children's achievement
- Provides information relating to students' school-wide achievements
- Provides a basis for public policy (e.g., legislation, recommendations, and position statements)

DEVELOPMENTALLY APPROPRIATE ASSESSMENT

assessment The process of collecting information about children's development, learning, behavior, academic progress, need for special services, and attainment of grade level goals in order to make decisions.

Early childhood professionals use assessment in developmentally appropriate ways to make many important decisions about their teaching and children's learning. You can develop a broad background of information about developmentally appropriate assessment by reviewing the Early Childhood Curriculum, Assessment, and Program Evaluation Position Statement of the National Association for the Education of Young Children (NAEYC) and the National Association of Early Childhood Specialists in State Departments of Education (NAECS/SDE) on their websites. This important document provides you with many essential guidelines to follow as you assess young children.

Ensuring that your assessment practices are developmentally appropriate is challenging because children develop and learn in ways that are unique to them and their specific cultural and linguistic backgrounds. You not only need to consider such factors as children's age and development, but also how well they speak English. Developmentally appropriate assessment is ongoing, intentional, used to make appropriate instructional decisions—appropriate for children's developmental levels.

DEVELOPMENTALLY APPROPRIATE CLASSROOM ASSESSMENT

Selecting appropriate assessment methods and instruments is an important part of the assessment process. You will know that the assessment practices and tools that you are using are appropriate when you use the following information:

FORMATIVE ASSESSMENT

In the classroom, you will be using assessment on a regular, daily basis. **Formative assessment** is the ongoing process of gathering data on students over the school year. Formative assessments are incorporated into your classroom practices and are a part of your instructional process. They provide information to inform you about what is needed to adjust your teaching and learning to your children's achievement. Through the use of formative assessment, you are consistently monitoring over the school year the progress of children as they learn outcomes of local, state, and common core state standards.

This video depicts a teacher and student involved in formative assessment of reading comprehension and fluency. Pay particular attention to the teacher with a handheld device to assess how she interacts with the student, what kind of formative assessment she provides, and how she uses assessment to determine what she wants the student to do.

formative assessment
The ongoing process of gathering data on students over the school year.

INFORMAL ASSESSMENT

Any assessment that obtains information that can be used to make judgments about children's learning behavior and characteristics or programs using means other than standardized tests is considered to be *informal* because it is not "standardized" or entails standard guidelines for administration and use. Formative assessments are considered to be the most *authentic*, or truest, means of evaluating children's actual learning and the instructional activities in which they are involved. The terms *informal assessments*, *formative assessments*, and *authentic assessments* are often used interchangeably.

AUTHENTIC ASSESSMENT

Figure 3.2 outlines characteristics of authentic formative assessment. As you examine these characteristics, think about how you will apply them to your professional practice. Following the authentic assessment strategies shown in Figure 3.2 will help ensure the information you gather will be useful and appropriate for all children. Authentic assessment relies heavily on informal procedures. Observations, checklists, and portfolios are just some of the informal methods of authentic assessment available to early childhood educators, as discussed in the following sections. *Informal screening* is what you and other professionals do when you gather information to make decisions about small-group placements, instructional levels, and so forth.

PERFORMANCE-BASED ASSESSMENT.   Part of authentic assessment includes *performance-based assessment*. In performance-based assessment, children *demonstrate* by doing what they know and are able to do. Authentic assessments are particularly useful when teaching children who are from diverse backgrounds as well as for children with disabilities because you can gain a good picture of what they can do. For example, second grade teacher Robert Brooks uses authentic assessment in his inclusion classroom, particularly at the beginning of the school year, to determine

FIGURE 3.2 |
Characteristics of
Authentic Assessment

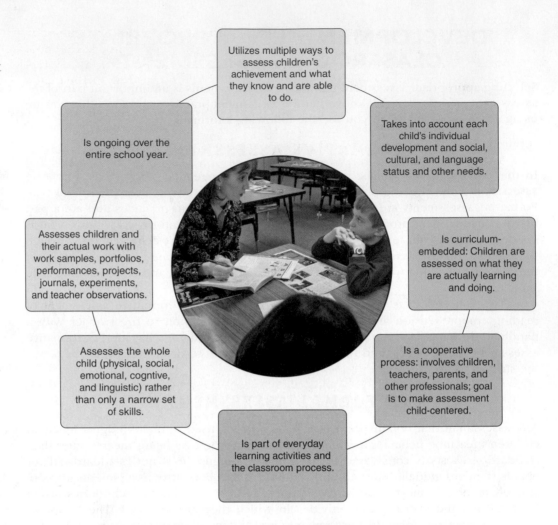

Utilizes multiple ways to assess children's achievement and what they know and are able to do.

Takes into account each child's individual development and social, cultural, and language status and other needs.

Is ongoing over the entire school year.

Assesses children and their actual work with work samples, portfolios, performances, projects, journals, experiments, and teacher observations.

Is curriculum-embedded: Children are assessed on what they are actually learning and doing.

Assesses the whole child (physical, social, emotional, cogntive, and linguistic) rather than only a narrow set of skills.

Is a cooperative process: involves children, teachers, parents, and other professionals; goal is to make assessment child-centered.

Is part of everyday learning activities and the classroom process.

what each of his students is capable of doing. From there, he designs activities and sets goals for each individual student. First grade teacher Marisa Cortez uses authentic assessments to keep track of her students' progress. If her assessment shows that a student is falling behind, she individualizes the material, re-teaches, and provides more one-on-one attention.

AUTHENTIC ASSESSMENT GUIDELINES.   Here are some guidelines to follow as you authentically assess young children:

- *Assess children based on their actual work.* Use work samples, exhibitions, performances, learning logs, journals, projects, presentations, experiments, and teacher observations.
- *Assess children based on what they are actually doing in and through the curriculum.* For example, children demonstrate skills, behaviors, and concepts as evidence of their learning.
- *Assess what each individual child can do.* Evaluate what each child is learning, rather than comparing one child with another or one group of children with another.
- *Make assessment part of the learning process.* Encourage children to show what they know through presentations and participation.

- *Learn about the whole child.* Make the assessment process an opportunity to learn more than just a child's acquisition of a narrow set of skills. Learn about many of the children's domains of development, such as their social development, as they work with other children to solve a math problem, or their emotional development as they analyze a story.
- *Involve children and parents in a collaborative assessment process.* Authentic assessment is child centered.
- *Provide ongoing assessment over the entire year.* Assess children continually throughout the year, not just at the end of a grading period or at the end of the year.
- *Use developmentally appropriate assessments and techniques.* Assessment procedures are most authentic and results are most accurate when assessments and techniques are developmentally appropriate.

METHODS OF AUTHENTIC ASSESSMENT

Authentic assessment plays a major role in helping you understand what students can do and what they have learned. Table 3.1 provides a list of the different types of informal, authentic assessments that you can use in your classroom practice.

OBSERVATION. Early childhood professionals recognize that children are more than that which is measured by any particular standardized test. Observation is an authentic means of learning about children—what they know and are able to do, especially as it occurs in more naturalistic settings such as classrooms, child care centers, playgrounds, and homes—and it is the most widely used method of assessment. **Observation** is the intentional, systematic act of looking at the behavior of a child or children in a particular setting, program, or situation. Observation is sometimes referred to as "kid-watching" and is an excellent way to find out about children's behaviors and learning.

Anecdotal records, running records, event sampling, time sampling, rating scales, and checklists are all excellent assessment tools used to authentically observe children and record observations for assessment purposes.

observation Observation is the intentional, systematic act of looking at the behavior of a child in a particular setting, program, or situation.

ANECDOTAL RECORDS. Teachers use an **anecdotal record** to write down brief reports of a student's behavior and what they see and hear. Marisa Rodriguez likes to use anecdotal records in her kindergarten classroom because they provide insight into a particular behavior and give a basis for planning a specific teaching strategy. In order for an anecdotal record to be considered authentic, Marisa knows to record only observed facts, not her inferences or opinions. For example, she records where and when a behavior occurred and who said what to whom. Figure 3.3 is an example of an anecdotal record. As you can see in Figure 3.3, Marisa does not record her opinions about Amy's behavior. You can tell she isn't recording her opinions or inferences because she does not use phrases such as "she seems to," "she liked/disliked," "she felt," "she understands," or "she can't." Instead, Marisa reports only what she sees and hears.

Marisa uses the anecdotal record to gain insight about Amy's strengths and weaknesses. Marisa infers that Amy has a strong basis for language acquisition, likes to be challenged, isn't afraid to get messy, and isn't turned off by the texture of shaving cream. Marisa also notices that Amy shows a lot of interest in farm animals and decides that using animals as a means of gaining Amy's interest and participation may be helpful in lessons that Amy finds difficult. Based on this assessment, Marisa decides

anecdotal record A brief written recording of student behavior that includes only what a teacher sees or hears, not what he or she thinks or infers.

TABLE 3.1 | Methods of Authentic Assessment

Method	Purpose	Guidelines
Observation Kid-watching—looking at children in a systematic way	Enables teachers to identify children's behaviors, document performance, and make decisions	Plan for observation and be clear about the purposes of the observation.
Anecdotal record Gives a brief written description of student behavior at one time	Provides insight into a particular behavior and a basis for planning a specific teaching strategy	Record only what is observed or heard; should deal with the facts and should include the setting (e.g., where the behavior occurs) and what was said and done.
Running record Focuses on a sequence of events that occurs over time	Helps obtain a more detailed insight into behavior over a period of time	Maintain objectivity and try to include as much detail as possible.
Event sampling Focuses on a particular behavior during a particular event (e.g., behavior at lunchtime, behavior on the playground, behavior in a reading group)	Helps identify behaviors during a particular event over time	Identify a target behavior to be observed during particular times (e.g., fighting during transition activities).
Time sampling Record particular events or behaviors at specific time intervals (e.g., five minutes, ten minutes)	Helps identify when a particular child demonstrates a particular behavior; helps answer the question, "Does the child do something all the time or just at certain times and events?"	Observe only during the time period specified.
Rating scale Contains a list of descriptors for a set of behaviors	Enables teachers to record data when they are observed	Make sure that key descriptors and the rating scale are appropriate for what is being observed.
Checklist A list of behaviors identifying children's skills and knowledge	Enables teachers to observe and easily check off what children know and are able to do	Make sure that the checklist includes behaviors that are important for the program and for learning (e.g., counts from 1 to 10, hops on one foot).
Work sample Piece of children's work that demonstrates what they know and are able to do	Provides a concrete example of learning; can show growth and achievement over time	Make sure that the work sample demonstrates what children know and are able to do. Let children help select the items they want to use as examples of their learning.
Portfolio Collection of children's work samples and other products	Provides documentation of a child's achievement in specific areas over time; can include test scores, writing work samples, videotapes, etc.	Make sure the portfolio is not a dumpster but a thoughtful collection of materials that documents learning over time.

TABLE 3.1 | Methods of Authentic Assessment *(continued)*

Method	Purpose	Guidelines
Interview Engaging children in discussion through questions	Allows children to explain behavior, work samples, or particular answers	Ask questions at all levels of Bloom's taxonomy (see Figure 3.13) in order to gain insight into children's learning.
Rubric Scoring guides that differentiate among levels of performance	Enables teachers to assess performance based on preestablished criteria, makes teachers' expectations clear, and enables children to participate in evaluation of own work	Provide children with models or examples of each level of work and encourage them to revise their work according to the rubric assessment. Give children opportunities to contribute to the rubric criteria.

. . . Today we had a lesson on letter recognition. I had the children write their abc's with their fingers in shaving cream on their desks. Amy started immediately and wanted to start spelling whole words. She spelled Cat, Dog, and Cow on her own. Once she had written the abc's several times and the words she already knew, she began to ask for other words to spell. We talked about how to spell Mom, Dad, and Rob, her brother's name. She asked three or four times, "Ms. R, Ms. R, how do you spell farm?" from across the room. When I was helping another student, she fidgeted and raised her voice to get my attention. At one point she grabbed me by the hand to lead me to her table and wanted to know how to spell House . . .

FIGURE 3.3 | Excerpt of an Anecdotal Record

An anecdotal record, as the name implies, is a short account of a behavior. An anecdotal record enables you to evaluate progress and then plan for appropriate instruction that meets the needs of a particular student. An anecdote enables you to have concrete information on which you can develop your strategy for instructional and behavioral improvement.

to teach Amy with a lot of hands-on activities that are on or slightly above her level of knowledge so that Amy stays interested and challenged. Marisa also uses the anecdotal record to inform her opinion that Amy feels a need for a lot of individual attention. Marisa will help her learn to wait her turn and raise her hand.

RUNNING RECORD. We refer to a **running record** as a detailed narrative of a child's behavior that focuses on a sequence of events that occur over a period of time. Anna Beatty uses running records frequently in her kindergarten classroom to assess her students' social skills. Running records are useful in assessing more abstract behaviors and skills because they help obtain a more detailed insight into behavior in general, rather than specific events such as those in the anecdotal record. When using running records, Anna maintains objectivity and includes as much detail as possible. Running records should include objective observations, and unlike anecdotal records, they provide Anna an opportunity to write down her comments concerning the sequence of events. Figure 3.4 is an example of a running record Anna kept in her classroom.

As you can see in Figure 3.4, Anna objectively records what each child says while focusing on Ali's behavior. She separately records her own ideas and questions about Ali's social skills. Using both her observations and her comments, Anna can infer a lot

running record A detailed narrative of a child's behavior that focuses on a sequence of events that occur over a period of time. Includes both factual observations and teacher's inferences.

Teacher _Anna Beatty_
Student _Ali R._
Age _5_
School _Reed Elementary_
Date _04/08/2014_
Time _10:00am – 10:20am_

Observations	Comments
Ali is playing the block center with Jake and Travis. Ali has surrounded himself with the blocks and begins stacking them. The blocks are about waist high. Jake is playing with cars with Travis.	Ali has spent a lot of time building with the blocks and is very careful about stacking them just right. But he seems to be looking at Jake and Travis a lot.
A: "I'm building a fort!" J: "That doesn't look like a fort." A: "It's a fort; I made it to be a fort." T: "I think it's a garage for our cars!"	Travis and Jake play together a lot. It doesn't look like Ali knows how to join them. Maybe that's why Ali told them it was a fort?
Travis and Jake start to push their cars along Ali's fort. Ali keeps stacking blocks.	Ali definitely doesn't look like he likes them putting cars on his fort. What will he do?
A: "I said it's a fort. I built it so I get to pick. It's a fort, not a garage." T: "Why can't it be a garage?" A: "I don't have a car." Ali pauses. Then says, "If you let me be the red car, the fort can be a garage. It can be a garage first, then a fort!"	Shows good compromising skills! The red car is a favorite of most of the boys. Good way to get what he wants and still get to play with J & T.
Jake gives Ali the red convertible car and they start to zoom the cars all over the "garage."	
J: "Let's add a ramp." A: "That's a good idea. Put it here."	Pretty flexible of Ali to let J & T change his fort. Another good play skill.

about Ali's social skills, his problem-solving capabilities, and even his fine motor skills. For example, she can infer that Ali is flexible in his play schemes, that he knows how and when to compromise, and that he has the fine motor skills to build intricate systems with the blocks. From here, she can design instruction. She pairs Ali with a more rigid classmate to help the classmate become more flexible and to help Ali continue practicing his compromising skills.

EVENT SAMPLING.   Dustin Kramer often uses event sampling as a method to informally but authentically assess his first graders. **Event sampling**—a form of assessment that systematically observes a specific behavior during a particular period of time—allows Dustin to identify students' behaviors, document their performance, and then make decisions about teaching methods, lesson plans, partner groupings, and such. Use event sampling clearly and purposefully. In order for event sampling to be an authentic assessment you must repeat it several times. For example, during math time, which follows physical education (P.E.), Dustin realizes that Keith has difficulty paying attention to directions, and he tends to be rowdy and to distract other students.

Dustin decides to use the ABC observation system during the forty-five-minute period to observe Keith for a week.

Figure 3.5 shows an example of an ABC observation system. The A (antecedent) column, or the precursor to a behavior, enables Dustin to watch for what happens *before* Keith's distracting behavior begins. Does Keith seem to enjoy P.E.? Is he readily a part of P.E. teams, or is he picked last? Does Keith get along with the coach? How does Keith look: happy, grumpy, sweaty? Dustin then documents his observations in the A column. The B (behavior) column allows Dustin to target the behavior that he wants to assess—in this case, Keith's distractibility and disruptiveness. What exactly is Keith doing? Talking, fidgeting, fighting, joking? Is he involving other students? Does the behavior occur at the beginning of the lesson when Dustin gives verbal information, or at the end when Keith is expected to work independently? Was math a group effort today or an individual project? Whatever it is, Dustin writes the behavior down in the B column. The C (consequences) column, or the results of the behavior, helps Dustin to understand what Keith gets out of his behavior. Is Keith getting peer recognition, more individual attention? Is the lesson disrupted and thus less time is spent on math?

Teacher: D. Kramer
Student: Keith C.
Grade: 1st
School: Dupont Elementary
Date: 10-17-14

A	B	C
	Tuesday	
1:15 pm: Keith just finished P.E. He looks a little upset. Ask if he's ok. I ask class to get out pencils and look at the board.	1:20 pm: Keith fidgets a little but is mostly calm, says he's fine.	1:22 pm: Lessons continued.
1:24 pm: Told class we would do a group project with cubes first, then they will work individually.	1:27 pm: Keith fidgets and scoots around in his chair. Some classmates giggle & turn to watch, others ignore.	1:28 pm: I ignore it, hand out Rubik cubes to groups.
1:33 pm: Keith stopped fidgeting; I show class how to count by 5s with Rubik cubes.	1:40 pm: Keith participates with group, seems to enjoy.	1:42 pm: Tell class only a few more minutes with the group before we move on to individual work.
1:43 pm: Told class to clean up cubes and start own work.	1:44 pm: Keith plays with blocks, tossing them in the air, throwing at friends.	1:46 pm: Ask Keith to clean up, classmates laugh with Keith.
1:50 pm: Asked Keith to clean up, he is still playing with cubes.	1:55 pm: Keith making silly faces at me and classmates, playing with blocks.	1:57 pm: Take the cubes away and give Keith a warning.
1:59 pm: Gave Keith warning, worksheet, but realize we're out of time, class will be late for art.	2:01 pm: Assign Keith the worksheet for homework.	2:02 pm: Keith lines up for art without a problem, walks quietly in the hallway on way to art.

FIGURE 3.5 | Example of Event Sampling Using the ABC Method
The intended use of event sampling is to identify a pattern in a child's behavior over time. Through event sampling you are able to identify problems and start to focus on solutions that will create desired behavior and keep the child on a positive pathway of success.

What happens after math? Is the following activity difficult for Keith, or does Keith settle into the activity easily? This time Dustin writes his observations in the C column.

Dustin systematically monitors Keith for a week during the forty-five minutes of math. As Figure 3.5 shows, Dustin is careful to document the time and the nature of the ABC observations. After a week of observations, Dustin looks for a pattern in Keith's behavior. He realizes that Keith is calmer and paying attention at the beginning of math, but when the class generally works independently, Keith becomes increasingly disruptive. Keith is often so disruptive that the class runs out of time to do the independent work, and Keith has extra homework as a result. Dustin decides to talk to Coach Culp about Keith's behavior in P.E. Coach Culp reports that some of the students had teased Keith about asking for "so much" help with his math work and that Keith seemed embarrassed. Dustin uses this information to ask himself more questions. If Keith needs more help on individual work, does that mean that he doesn't understand the instructions? Is Dustin relying too much on verbal teaching instead of differentiating the information in a lot of different ways? Does Keith need more one-on-one attention in math? But, how to keep the other kids from teasing Keith? How does Keith learn best? Isn't Keith a *tactile* (hands-on or concrete) learner?

Using the Results of ABC Observations. As a result of these explorations, Dustin uses the event-sampling information to tailor his teaching methods to Keith's needs; he makes sure to encourage and praise students who ask questions, and he provides Keith individual directions on individual work to build his confidence and competency. For example, Dustin gives directions to the class as a whole first and then slowly gives them again to Keith. He stops frequently to make sure Keith follows them. Dustin makes sure to incorporate as many tactile exercises in math lessons as possible so that Keith can use his hands to better understand math concepts. Also, Dustin starts giving high-fives to students when they ask questions or for help and uses encouraging phrases such as, "Wow, what a great question," and "Asking questions means you really care about learning."

time sampling Authentic means to assess children that involves focusing on a particular behavior over a continuous period of time.

TIME SAMPLING.   Another authentic means to assess children that involves focusing on a particular behavior over a continuous period of time is called **time sampling**. For example, Charlotte Lu wants to know if her first grade student Amanda is as distractible as she thinks Amanda is. Charlotte decides to use time sampling to determine how on-task or off-task Amanda is during center time. She and Benjamin Woods, her teaching assistant, first sit down together to determine what exactly on-task behavior looks like and what off-task behavior looks like. Then they both observe Amanda during center time and specifically watch for the previously specified behavior, such as wandering around the room or staring into space. Afterward, Charlotte and Benjamin compare their samples to determine how often they agree on Amanda's behavior. Figure 3.6 is the time sample Charlotte and Benjamin used.

From their sample (shown in Figure 3.6), Charlotte and Benjamin can see that they agreed that Amanda was off task 7 out of 10 minutes of center time. Their collaboration established a mutually agreed-upon means of observing and collecting data. It also prevented sampling bias by getting more than one opinion. For more reliable results, as with event sampling, Charlotte and Benjamin should repeat their time sampling several more times. To gain an even more accurate picture of Amanda's behavior, Charlotte and Benjamin should take time samples of Amanda in various settings. For example, they should assess Amanda not just in centers, but during reading lessons, library time, P.E., math lessons, and so on.

Charlotte and Benjamin know the more data they have about Amanda's behavior, the more they can use their assessment to teach to her needs. If they find that Amanda is off task only during centers, they may decide to change the way the centers are structured, rearrange Amanda's group, or institute a pictorial schedule to help keep

Charlotte Lu—Teacher			
Event	time	On task	Off Task
Center time	10:01 am	✔	
	10:02 am	✔	
	10:03 am		✔
	10:04 am		✔
	10:05 am		✔
	10:06 am	✔	
	10:07 am		✔
	10:08 am		✔
	10:09 am		✔
	10:10 am		✔
		Total: 3	Total: 7

Benjamin Woods—Para-Educator			
Event	time	On task	Off Task
Center time	10:01 am	✔	
	10:02 am	✔	
	10:03 am	✔	
	10:04 am		✔
	10:05 am		✔
	10:06 am	✔	
	10:07 am		✔
	10:08 am		✔
	10:09 am		✔
	10:10 am		✔
		Total: 4	Total: 6

FIGURE 3.6 |
Example of a Time Sample
Time sampling is a very useful way for you to collect observation data when you need information about children's achievement in behavior over a period of time. Time sampling can provide you with a useful "snap shot" of children, and they serve as useful information for you to share with parents as well.

her on task. However, if Charlotte and Benjamin find from their multiple samples that Amanda is in fact off task for most of the day across multiple settings and situations and that her off-task behavior is detrimental to her social and academic growth, they may decide to refer Amanda to the district special education services or to recommend to Amanda's parents that they seek an evaluation from her pediatrician for possible developmental, neurological, or cognitive delays or deficits.

RATING SCALE. Rating scales are usually numeric scales that contain a list of descriptors for a set of behaviors or goals. They usually begin with the phrase, "On a scale of (a number) to (a number), you rate the (behavior) as. . . ." Rating scales enable teachers to record data when behaviors are observed. When using rating scales, make sure that the key descriptors and the rating scales are appropriate for what is being observed.

rating scales Usually numeric scales that contain a list of descriptors for a set of behaviors or goals.

Rating scales are one of my favorite means of authentic assessment. They enable teachers to gather data quickly. You should develop rating scales for all instructional activities and have them with you while you teach. In this way, your rating scale is embedded in the instructional process.

Teacher: _Bess Stensel_

Student: _Rebecca M., Pre-k_

School: _Stephen F. Austin Elementary School_

Date: _11-10-14_

Skill Set	No Mastery		Developing Mastery		Full Mastery
Demonstrates knowledge that print carries a message in a book	1	2	3	4	⑤
Orally retells a story	1	2	③	4	5
Listens with interest and comprehension when a story is read aloud	1	2	3	④	5
Sequences the events of a story in proper order	1	2	3	④	5
Answers questions concerning the meaning of a story	1	2	3	4	⑤

Bess Stensel uses rating scales in her preschool classroom to gain a broad picture of her students' development. Figure 3.7 is an example of a rating scale that Bess uses to gauge the degree of Rebecca's language development. As the figure shows, Bess is not only able to assess the appearance of a skill set, but also the *degree* to which it is present. From her rating scale, Bess concludes that Rebecca has gained some mastery, if not full mastery, in most areas of early literacy skills, but that she still is developing her skills in orally retelling information. Now that she has assessed Rebecca, Bess can plan for how to provide for her needs in reading and language skills.

checklists Lists of behaviors identifying children's skills and knowledge.

CHECKLIST.   An excellent and powerful tool for observing and gathering information about a wide range of student abilities in all settings is the checklist. **Checklists** are lists of behaviors identifying children's skills and knowledge and can be used as a regular part of your teaching on a wide variety of topics and subjects. Some checklists, such as those in Figure 3.8 and Figure 3.9, are cognitive or social; others can help you assess behaviors, traits, skills, and abilities. In addition, using the same checklists over a period of time enables you to evaluate progress and achievement. Figure 3.10 is a checklist for assessing children in inclusive classrooms and can be used as a template or model to make other checklists. How could you modify Figure 3.10 to assess children's technology use and skills in your classroom?

Keep in mind that many skills or behaviors assessed by checklists may have a cultural or religious connotation. You should take cultural factors into context when using any form of assessment. For example, in Figure 3.8, one item denoting proper social development is eye contact. Whereas in the United States eye contact is considered a demonstration of respect and engagement, this is not true for all people. In some Eastern cultures such as South Korea and China, children are taught to show respect to adults by refraining from making eye contact. In the United States, not making eye contact is often a cause for concern as it may indicate developmental delays. As a result, you may be tempted to considerer some children as lagging developmentally when in fact they are trying to show you respect according to their cultural norms.

Social-Emotional Checklist First Grade		
Social Behavioral Skills	**Yes(Y)/No(N)**	**Date**
Student is able to ask for what he/she needs and wants from caregivers.	Y	11-05-14
Student is able to follow directions and general expectations of caregivers.	Y	11-05-14
Student has good eye contact with peers.	Y	11-05-14
Student is able to express feelings appropriately to peers.	N	11-05-14
Student is able to share and interact cooperatively with peers.	N	11-05-14
Student is able to start conversations with peers.	Y	11-05-14
Student is able to ask questions of peers.	Y	11-05-14
Student is able to listen to peers.	N	11-05-14
Student is able to ignore peers when he/she should.	Y	11-05-14
Student is not passive with peers.	Y	11-05-14
Student is not aggressive with peers.	Y	11-05-14
Social and General Problem-Solving Skills	**Yes(Y)/No(N)**	**Date**
Student thinks about what he/she is doing.	Y	11-05-14
Student understands the consequences of behavior.	Y	11-05-14
Student behavior is goal oriented.	N	11-05-14
Student is aware when he/she is having a problem.	Y	11-05-14
Student learns from past mistakes and does not repeat them.	Y	11-05-14
Student uses good strategies to solve problems.	Y	11-05-14
Student knows when he/she is having a social problem.	Y	11-05-14
Student is knowledgeable of how he/she affects others.	Y	11-05-14
Student uses appropriate strategies to solve interpersonal difficulties.	N	11-05-14
Student uses nonaggressive solutions to solve disagreements with others.	Y	11-05-14
Emotional Well-Being and Level of Self-Esteem	**Yes(Y)/No(N)**	**Date**
Student acknowledges his/her own feelings.	Y	11-05-14
Student expresses feelings in appropriate ways.	N	11-05-14
Student is able to tell others about his/her concerns/troubles.	Y	11-05-14
Student thinks and verbalizes positive thoughts about self and others.	Y	11-05-14
Student seems to like him/herself (can identify positive self qualities).	Y	11-05-14
Student focuses on positive things and manages negative things.	Y	11-05-14
Student is able to take responsibility for achievements and mistakes.	Y	11-05-14

Source: From Child Care Resource & Referral of Central Iowa, www.centraliowachildcare.org/healthconsulting/schoolagescreentoolkg.pdf. Used with permission.

FIGURE 3.8 | Example of a Social-Emotional Developmental Checklist
Social and emotional learning are important factors to incorporate into your teaching. Checklists such as this one help you keep track of how each child is participating and growing in his or her social and emotional development.

FIGURE 3.9 |
Example of a Cognitive Developmental Checklist, Age Four to Five Years

Today, with the emphasis on the Common Core State Standards and children's achievements, it is essential for teachers to gather data about children's achievement and their ability to perform certain tasks. Before, during, and after their teaching many teachers have short, concise checklists such as this one with them at all times to assist them in making decisions about grouping, differentiation, and other strategies for helping children achieve.

✔ Can correctly name several colors (4+)

✔ Tries to solve problems from a single point of view

✗ Follows three-part commands   *Will provide differentiated activities for working on three.*

✔ Recalls parts of a story

✔ Understands the concepts of "same" and "different"

✔ Engages in fantasy play

✔ Can count 10 or more objects *Is up to 13!*

✔ Better understands the concept of time

✔ Knows about things used every day in the home (money, food, appliances)

Sources: www.cdc.gov/ncbddd/actearly/interactive/milestones/cognitive_5years.html; www.cdc.gov/ncbddd/actearly/interactive/milestones/cognitive_4years.html

FIGURE 3.10 |
Example of an Inclusion Classroom Checklist

As stated throughout this text, we don't teach standards, we teach children. It is important for teachers to teach the whole child. You will be teaching in inclusive classrooms, and you will need to adjust your curriculum to teach children with disabilities. Observational checklists such as this one help keep track of how the children are learning and their individual needs.

Teacher: *Graciela Gomez*   School: *Mission Hill Elementary*

Student: *Tenisha B.*   Class: *First grade*

Number of children in class: *16*   Number of children with disabilities in class: *1*

Date: *09-08-14*   Types of disability: *Tenisha has moderate cerebral palsy (CB), and must use a wheelchair.*

Physical Features of the Classroom

1. Are all areas of the classroom accessible to children with disabilities?

    No, Tenisha cannot access the library/literacy center.

2. Are learning materials and equipment accessible for all children?

    There is not enough room for Tenisha to manipulate her wheelchair past the easel and the shelf with art materials.

3. Are work and play areas separated to minimize distractions?

    Yes, but pathways are too narrow for Tenisha's wheelchair.

4. Are special tables or chairs necessary to accommodate children's disabilities?

    Tenisha has a large work board/table that attaches to her wheelchair.

Academic Features of the Classroom

1. What special accommodations are necessary to help children with disabilities achieve state and local standards?

    I need to check on this.

2. Are principles of developmentally appropriate practice applied to all children, including those with disabilities?

   Yes.

3. Is there a wide range of classroom literature on all kinds of disabilities?

   I have a few books but not enough. I would like more.

Classroom Interaction

1. Are children with disabilities included in cooperative work projects?

   I will work on this next week.

2. Do children without disabilities interact positively with children with disabilities?

   Tenisha is a very sociable person. Students interact well with her. Tenisha could not reach the crayons by herself, so she asked Billy for help. She and Billy seem to get along well.

Play Routines

1. Are children with disabilities able to participate in all classroom and grade-level activities?

   I need to talk with the P.E. teacher. I also need to observe Tenisha during lunch and recess to see if she is involved in play and social activities during these times.

Conclusions

1. *I need to rearrange my classroom to make sure that Tenisha has access to all learning centers and materials.*

2. *The children are not as helpful to Tenisha as I want them to be.*

3. *The classroom library/lit center needs more books relating to children with disabilities.*

4. *There are a lot of questions I don't have the answer to at this time (i.e., meeting state standards).*

5. *I need to include more group work and cooperative activities in my planning.*

Recommendations

1. *I will ask a custodian to help me move a heavy bookshelf. I can move and rearrange the other things. I'll give the new arrangement a trial run and see how it works for all the children.*

2. *In our daily class meetings, I will talk about helpful behaviors and helping others.*

   a. *We can read books about helping.*

   b. *I plan to start a class buddy system; I can pair Tenisha and Billy!*

3. *In my lesson plans, I need to include activities for learning helpful behaviors.*

4. *I will search for books about children with disabilities.*

   a. *I'll consult with the school librarian.*

   b. *I'll talk to my grade-level leader and ask for money for books.*

5. *I will talk with the director of special education about meeting state standards. Tenisha is very smart so I don't anticipate any problems.*

6. *I will develop a lesson involving group work and projects. I will include Tenisha and observe the children's interactions.*

7. *I will observe Tenisha at lunch and during recess.*

Therefore, you should be careful to use checklists, and indeed all forms of assessment, within the larger context of a student's religious, cultural, and ethnic background. Here are some other things for you to keep in mind when making and using checklists:

- Each checklist should contain the qualities, skills, behaviors, and other information you want to observe. In other words, tailor each checklist to a specific situation.
- File all checklists in students' folders to track their progress and for future reference and use.
- Use checklists as a basis for conferences with children and parents.
- Use the information from checklists to plan for small-group and individual instruction.

work sample, or student artifact An example of children's work that demonstrates what they know and are able to do. Such examples are used as evidence to assess student abilities. Work samples can be physical or electronic and come in many different forms.

performance assessment The ongoing process of gathering information about students during learning and teaching. Also called informal assessment, formative assessment, and authentic assessment.

WORK SAMPLE.   A **work sample**, or a **student artifact**, is an example of a child's work that demonstrates what the child knows and is able to do, and it is used as evidence to assess a student's abilities. Work samples are often used to document a child's accomplishments and achievements. Work samples can be physical or electronic and come in many different forms. Oregon's work-sampling system consists of three components: (1) multiple-choice tests, (2) performance assessments, and (3) classroom work samples. **Performance assessment** is the ongoing process of gathering information about students during learning and teaching. It is also called informal assessment, formative assessment, and authentic assessment.

Figure 3.11 demonstrates second-grader Jackson's ability to write a prompt (to write about what he is thankful for), and his ability to use English language conventions such as beginning a sentence with a capital letter. Examples of artifacts like Jackson's are artwork; paper documents such as written work; electronic documents and electronic images; DVD recordings or excerpts of daily behavior; photographs of projects; voice recordings of oral skills (i.e., reading, speaking, singing); video recordings of

FIGURE 3.11 |
Example of a
Work Sample

 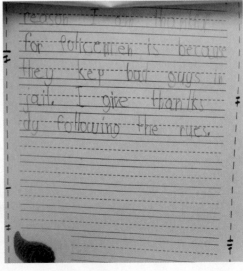

performances (i.e., sports, musical, theatrical); scanned images of three-dimensional or large-scale art; and multimedia projects or web pages exploring curriculum topics, current events, or social problems.

PORTFOLIOS.   Today, many teachers use **portfolios**—a compilation of children's work samples, products, and teacher observations collected over time that attest to what children are able to do—as a basis for authentic assessment.

Portfolios are used for several purposes:

- To provide a record of each student's process of learning
- To support learning
- To encourage children to do their best work
- To guide instruction

Portfolio entries should meet the following criteria:

- They should reflect students' cognitive, social, emotional, and physical development.
- They should provide a visual record of a student's process of learning over time.
- They should encourage input from students, teachers, and parents.

Examples of what to put in portfolios vary, but they should include the several types of artifacts and work samples discussed above. The following are items many teachers include in a portfolio:

- Writing samples
- Math problem-solving activities
- Science journals and drawing of scientific experiments
- Art/drawing samples

Each teacher compiles a portfolio differently. Jonathon Barrio lets his third grade students put their best work in their portfolios, whereas Megan LeBlanc decides with her second graders what will be included.

Implications for Teaching. Here are steps to follow for developing and using portfolios:

Step 1: ***Determine the purpose of your classroom portfolios.*** Why do you want to develop and use portfolios? Here are some reasons:

    a. Develop a record of student achievement through performance-based assessment.

    b. Provide parents with authentic examples of student work progress.

Step 2: ***Align portfolio samples with state and Common Core State Standards.***

    a. Label work samples according to a state standard(s). This enables you and the children to document when and how the child met the standard(s).

Step 3: ***Create a table of contents for the portfolio.***

    a. Use a checklist format. This helps keep track of what is in the portfolio and ensures that you and the children include important samples that document learning outcomes.

Step 4: ***Include your assessment of the children's progress and achievement with each work sample.***

portfolio A compilation of children's work samples, products, and teacher observations collected over time.

Step 5: ***Use the portfolio.*** The portfolio is neither a dumpster nor a storage closet. It is the assessment/documentation phase of the teaching/learning process. Some portfolio uses include the following:

a. As a basis for parent/teacher/student conferences. Portfolios let you and the children review with parents and other family members what children have learned and what they are able to do.

b. As an ongoing means to encourage teacher/student review, reflection, and planning

Also, websites such as TeacherVision and books such as *Developing Portfolios in Education: A Guide to Reflection, Inquiry, and Assessment* by Johnson et al. (2010) and *The Portfolio Connection: Student Work Linked to Standards* by Belgrad et al. (2008) may be helpful to you in designing and implementing portfolios as a means of authentic assessment in your early childhood classrooms.

Some teachers use technology to develop digital portfolios, which can stand alone or supplement the traditional portfolio. Digital portfolios include books and journals that children keep on computers and then illustrate with digital cameras. However, it is important to remember that portfolios are only one part of children's assessment.

Reflect and Apply: Portfolio

interview A common way that observers and researchers engage children in discussion through questions to obtain information.

INTERVIEW.   An **interview** is a common way for observers and teachers to engage children in discussions using questions to obtain information. Carla Silliman likes to use interviews in her second grade classroom because it allows her students to explain their own behavior, work samples, and particular answers. Interviewing gives an eyewitness account of obtaining information and can describe more visible information otherwise not shown through written records such as portfolios or checklists. Figure 3.12 is an excerpt of Carla's interview with Jorge.

When Carla uses interviewing as a form of assessment, she makes sure to use the hierarchy of questions in Bloom's taxonomy to gain further insight into children's learning. **Bloom's taxonomy** refers to a classification of different objectives that educators set for students in three domains: affective, psychomotor, and cognitive (see Figure 3.13). Within the taxonomy, learning at higher levels is dependent on having mastered foundational knowledge and skills at lower levels (i.e., you must be able to add and subtract before you can multiply or divide). For example, Carla assessed Jorge's knowledge, the first level of the cognitive domain, by using questions such as, "What happened in the story?" In her interview, Carla can see that Jorge has mastered the second level, comprehension, because he can summarize the main ideas of the story. She can also see that he has mastered application, the third level, because he solved his problem of not knowing what "unique" meant and synthesized it into his understanding of the content of the story. Carla moved onto the fourth level, analysis, by asking questions such as, "Why do you think . . . ?"

Bloom's taxonomy Refers to a classification of different objectives that educators set for students in three domains: affective, psychomotor, and cognitive. Within the taxonomy, learning at higher levels is dependent on having mastered foundational knowledge and skills at lower levels of skills.

As a result of her interview with Jorge and her use of Bloom's taxonomy, Carla sees that Jorge meets several standards set forth in the Texas English Language Arts and Reading Grade 2 Standards. For example, Carla can tell that Jorge can listen critically to interpret and evaluate language and that he can use vocabulary to clearly describe ideas and feelings. She is also pleased to see that Jorge discusses the meaning of words to develop his vocabulary, and that he successfully uses problem-solving skills and reference tools to enhance his knowledge and comprehension. From her interview, Carla is able to assess Jorge's reading comprehension, vocabulary growth, and overall literacy fluency.[4]

Teacher: Carla Silliman

School: Dewberry Elementary

Student: Jorge V.

Grade: 2nd

Date: 10-27-14

CS: Jorge, do you remember the "Yellow School Bus" story we read on Wednesday?

JV : Yeah, they took the bus to Antarctica.

CS: Who all went to Antarctica in the story?

JV : Well, the Friz, and Arnold, and Ralphie . . . Dorothy Ann, Carlos, and Phoebe. And the uncle. Phoebe's uncle went on this trip too.

CS: That's right, Jorge. Can you tell me what happened in the story?

JV : Well, like, the school bus turns into a ship and they go to Antarctica. And it's really cold, right?

at penguins and they all complained about how bad it smelled.

CS: Mmhmm, then what happened next?

JV: Oh! Phoebe's uncle accidentally turns some of the kids into penguins. Some of the kids thought it was cool and some of them were afraid. Ralphie was afraid. He's always the one that's afraid. That'd be so cool to turn into a penguin. I'd be one of those giant penguins. Well, then they all go swim in the ocean. Penguins fly in the ocean but not in the air.

CS: Why do you think that's important?

JV: Most birds fly in the air. But in class we talked about how penguins can't fly because their feathers are made differently. Regular birds' feathers are, like, empty, hollow. But penguins are too heavy and they have all this extra fat on them. But penguins are special. I mean, unique, because they swim like they're flying. They're special that way. And remember, you said that that made penguins unique, and I said I didn't know what unique meant so I used the dictionary to look it up. So yeah, but anyway, penguins swim so fast they can get away from sea lions and stuff.

CS: So penguins are unique. Tell me, why do you think Ralphie was afraid when they got turned into penguins?

JV: I don't know. Well, maybe because it was an accident. Or, maybe he was nervous. Um, I think maybe he was afraid he couldn't turn back into a kid again . . .

FIGURE 3.12 | Excerpt of an Interview Assessment

I'm sure that you have heard and watched interviews of celebrities and others. An interview is an excellent way to gather information that you might not be able to gather with paper and pencil or work samples. Interviewing children about their achievements, behaviors, and attitudes enables you to learn more about them and provides you with much useful information to guide your teaching.

rubric Scoring guide that differentiates among levels of performance.

RUBRIC. A **rubric** is a performance and scoring guide that differentiates among levels of performance. Conventional rubrics use a range of three or more levels—for example, beginning, developing, and proficient. Each of the levels contains specific, measurable performance characteristics, such as "makes few/occasional/frequent spelling errors." Figure 3.14 provides you with an example of a rubric and shows different categories of performance levels.

Checklists, which provide specific steps for completing tasks to the highest level, are similar to rubrics.[5]

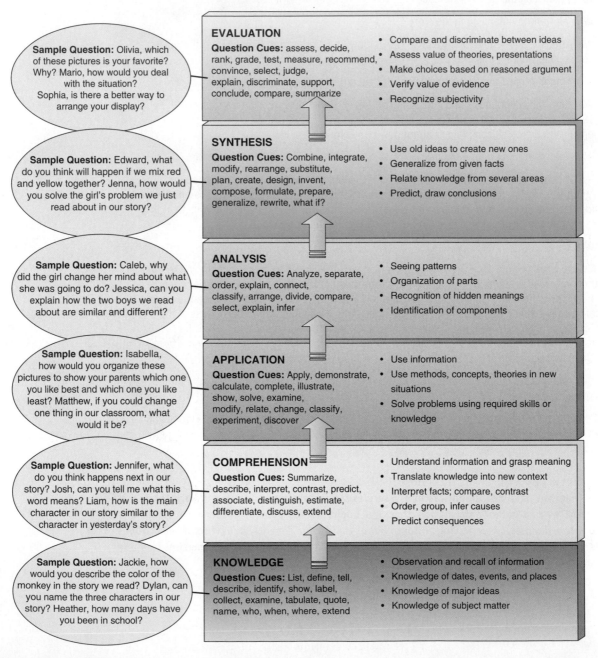

FIGURE 3.13 | Applying Bloom's Taxonomy to Early Childhood Classrooms

FIGURE 3.14 |
Example of Rubric

Conventions	Punctuation	Capitalization	Word Use	Ideas
My letters are written clearly. ✔	I use a period at the end of each sentence. ✔	I use both capital and lowercase letters. ✔	I use synonyms for words I write a lot. ✔	I describe where my story takes place. ✔
I leave white spaces between my words. ✔	I use a question mark at the end of each question. ✗	I use a capital letter to start the names of people, pets, and places. ✔	I use new spelling words. ✔	I describe what characters feel. ✔
My sentences go from left to right. ✔	I use an exclamation point at the end of an exclamation. ✔	I use a capital letter to start the first word of a sentence. ✔	I use the right action word form with my nouns. ✗	My story has a beginning, middle, and end. ✔

Rubrics have a number of purposes:

- To enable teachers to assess performance based on preestablished criteria
- To make teachers' expectations clear
- To enable children to participate in the evaluation of their own work
- To enable children to distinguish between levels of performance and to strive to do their best

To use rubrics effectively in your classroom, provide children with models or examples of each level of work and encourage them to revise their work according to the rubric assessment. You should also give children opportunities to contribute to the rubric criteria.

First grade teacher Emily Cherry, for example, created a writing rubric for her students. She believes that her students will gain a beginning understanding of what is expected of them in a clear and concise manner. Figure 3.14 is an example of a writing rubric for Charlie, a student in Emily's class.

Note how each example can be checked against the rubric by the student. This involves the student in the informal assessment process. Rubrics allow children to know what is generally expected of them and help them complete a specific piece of work. By adapting the rubric for writing, the child's progress is acknowledged. Over several weeks, as Charlie improved in his writing, Emily created rubrics that became more specific and more challenging so that she could assess how Charlie performed as expectations rose.

Check Your Understanding: Checklist/Rubric

THE POWER OF OBSERVATION

As we discussed above, observation is one of the most widely used methods of assessment.[6] Table 3.1 provided information on and guidelines for observation and other informal methods of authentic assessment.

PURPOSES OF OBSERVATION

Observation is designed to gather information on which to base decisions, make recommendations, develop curriculum, plan for teaching, select activities and learning strategies, and assess children's growth, development, and learning. When professionals and parents look at children, sometimes they do not really see or concern themselves with what the children are doing or why, as long as they are safe and orderly. Consequently, the significance and importance of critical behaviors may go undetected if observation is done casually and is limited to unsystematic looking.

Systematic observation has these specific purposes.

- *To determine the cognitive, linguistic, social, emotional, and physical development of children.* Using a developmental checklist is one way you can systematically observe and chart the development of children.
- *To identify children's interests and learning styles.* Today, teachers are very interested in developing learning activities, materials, and classroom centers based on children's interests, preferences, and learning styles.
- *To plan.* The professional practice of teaching requires daily ongoing planning. Observation provides useful, authentic, and solid information that enables you to plan intentionally for activities rather than to make decisions with little or no information.
- *To meet the needs of individual children.* Meeting the needs of individual children is an important part of teaching and learning. For example, a child may be advanced cognitively but be overly aggressive and lacking the social skills necessary to play cooperatively and interact with others. Through observation, you can gather information to develop a plan to help that child learn how to play with others.
- *To determine progress.* Systematic observation, over time, provides a rich and valuable source of information about how individuals and groups of children are progressing in their learning and behavior.

- *To provide information to parents.* Teachers report to and have conferences with parents on an ongoing basis. Observational information, along with other information, such as test results and child work samples, provides a fuller and more complete picture of individual children.
- *To provide professional insight.* Observational information helps professionals learn more about themselves and what to do to help children.

Observing children at play enables teachers to learn about children's developmental levels, social skills, and peer interactions. How might you use such information to plan play-based activities?

ADVANTAGES OF INTENTIONAL, SYSTEMATIC OBSERVATION

There are a number of advantages to gathering data through observation. Observation does the following:

- *Enables teachers to collect information that they might not otherwise gather through other sources.* Many of the causes and consequences of children's behavior can be assessed only through observation and not through formal standardized tests, questioning, or parent and child interviews.
- *Is ideally suited to learning more about children in play settings.* Observation affords the opportunity to note a child's social behavior in a play group and

discern how cooperatively he or she interacts with peers. Observing a child at play gives a wealth of information about developmental levels, social skills, and what a child is or is not learning in play settings.

- *Reveals a lot about children's prosocial behavior and peer interactions.* It helps you plan for appropriate and inclusive activities to promote the social growth of young children. Additionally, your observations can serve as the basis for developing multicultural activities to benefit all children.

- *Is a useful accompaniment to other assessments for children who may not typically respond.* For some students with certain disabilities, observation is used to support or refute the results of other assessment measures. These children may have a limited capability for the appropriate response or they may fatigue quickly. This fatigue may cause them to not complete the assessment, and their scores are affected.

- *Provides a basis for assessment of what children are developmentally able to do.* Many learning skills are developed sequentially, such as the refinement of large-motor skills before small-motor skills. Through observation, you can determine if children's abilities are within a normal range of growth and development.

- *Is useful to assess children's performance over time.* Documentation of daily, weekly, and monthly observations of children's behaviors and learning provides a database for the cumulative evaluation of each child's achievement and development.

- *Provides concrete information for use in reporting to and conferencing with parents.* Increasingly, reports to parents involve professionals' observations and children's work samples so that parents and educators can collaborate to determine how to help children develop cognitively, socially, emotionally, and physically.

Intentional observation is a useful, informative, and powerful means of guiding teaching and helping to ensure the learning of all children.

The following Voice from the Field, "How to Evaluate Environments for Young Children," is a Competency Builder that will help you learn how to observe in a classroom setting and use your observations as a basis for making decisions about how to structure your classroom to benefit young children.

STEPS FOR CONDUCTING OBSERVATIONS

Four steps are involved in the process of systematic, purposeful observation.

STEP 1: PLAN FOR THE OBSERVATION.   Planning is an important part of the observation process; everything you do should be planned in advance of the observation. A good guide to follow in planning is to ask *who, what, when, where,* and *how* you will observe.

Setting goals for observation is also an important part of the planning process. Goals allow you to reflect on why you want to observe and thus direct your efforts to what you will observe. Your goal might include observing the physical classroom environment for effectiveness, social interactions, or improvements to children's learning activities. Stating a goal focuses your attention on the purpose of your observation. For example, to focus on providing an inclusive classroom or program and fully including an exceptional child, your goals might read like this:

Goal 1: To determine what modifications are necessary in the classroom to provide Tenisha and her wheelchair access to all parts of the classroom

Goal 2: To assess the kinds of prosocial behavior other children display to Tenisha while they interact in the classroom

How to Evaluate Environments for Young Children

One of your roles as an early childhood professional is to create and maintain environments that are healthy, respectful, supportive, and challenging for all young children. This Competency Builder will help you achieve this goal, which is part of Standard 1 of NAEYC's Standards for Professional Development. In addition, you will learn to assess and evaluate environmental strengths and weaknesses and to reflect and make decisions for improvement and changes.

STEP 1 **Plan for the Observation**
- Decide what you will observe, how you will observe, and where you will observe. In our case, we are observing environmental features of classrooms and child care centers.
- Write your goals for observation. Our goals for observing environments are to do the following:
  - Assess the features of environments that contribute to their being healthy, respectful, supportive, and challenging for each child.
  - Make recommendations for what features of environments do not contribute to these criteria.
  - Make recommendations for what to include in environments so that they do meet these criteria.
- Select your observation tool. For our observation, a checklist will achieve our goals and provide the data necessary to make conclusions and recommendations. Our checklist is as follows:

Healthy
- Does this environment provide for children's physical and psychological health?
- Does this environment provide for children's safety?
- Does this environment provide children with a sense of security?

Respectful and Supportive
- Does this environment show respect for each individual child's:
- culture
- home language
- individual abilities or disabilities
- family context
- community?

- Do the professionals in this environment believe each child can learn?
- Do the professionals in this environment help children understand and make meaning of their experiences?

CHALLENGING
- Does this environment provide achievable expectations?
- Does this environment encourage children to try to new things?

STEP 2 **Conduct the Observation**
- As you conduct your observation, look for each of the items on your checklist. As you go through the checklist, take notes about what you are seeing and ask yourself specific questions so that you will be prepared to make recommendations in the steps that follow. Examples of specific questions concerning healthy environments might include:
- What are three characteristics of this environment that would make it safe, healthy, and supportive for children?
- What environmental features promote children's physical and psychological security?
- What evidence is there that this is conducting healthy environment practices?
- In addition, as you observe, you should ask yourself the following about respectful and supportive environments:
  - Is the teacher using positive interactions with the children?
  - Does the teacher show interest in children's ideas and activities?
  - Is the teacher supporting children's learning?
  - What evidence is there that the teacher is supporting learning and wants children to succeed?
  - What background evidence can you identify in the classroom that would lead you to believe that this classroom environment is/is not respectful and supportive?
- Observe for the following when assessing how challenging the environment is:
  - What evidence is there that this environment contains materials that would provide challenging activities for the children?
  - What evidence do you observe that the children are being challenged to succeed in their learning?
  - What evidence do you observe that individual children are being challenged to learn?

STEP 3 Interpret the Data
- Review your goals for observing.
- Look at the observation data as a whole. Place your observation in the context of all that you know about young children and all that you know about healthy, respectful, supportive, and challenging environments.
- Reflect on your observation and look for patterns.
- Make decisions about what actions you want to pursue based on your conclusions from the data.
- Your decision-making process can include consulting with other colleagues and professionals. Who are some people who could coach and mentor you in observing and developing environments that are healthy, respectful, supportive, and challenging?

STEP 4 Implement a Plan
- Make recommendations for what needs to be included to make the environment healthier, supportive, respectful, and challenging.
- Make recommendations for what needs to be removed from the environment for it to be more healthy, supportive, respectful, and challenging.
- Make recommendations for what needs to continue for the environment to meet these criteria.
- Take action based on your interpretation of the data.

Planning also involves selecting the type of observational tool you will use—one that will meet your goal for observing. To assess the physical modifications necessary to accommodate Tenisha and to examine students' social interactions with her, you might select an observational tool similar to the checklist in Figure 3.10. Review that figure to see how the teacher, Graciela Gomez, used the checklist to achieve goals 1 and 2 above.

STEP 2: CONDUCT THE OBSERVATION. While conducting your observation, it is imperative that you be objective, specific, and as thorough as possible. There are many ways to record your observations, including taking notes, using a checklist or a tally sheet, making a sketch of an indoor or outdoor environment, and making a video or an audio recording. Here are some suggestions for collecting observation data:

- Record information on self-stick notes, which are easily transferred to student files and folders.
- Use a clipboard to hold a checklist and other forms to record data as you observe.
- Take photographs of children's accomplishments or infants' milestones. Take other photos of room arrangements (such as play areas, storage, and circle time area), children's interactions, teacher-child interactions, and student artifacts. Digital camera images are easily manipulated and transferred to student files.
- Use technology whenever possible. For example, a laptop loaded with student files makes it easier to record, store, and manage data after an observation session. In addition, video cameras are a good way to capture certain events and activities.

STEP 3: INTERPRET THE DATA. All observations should result in some kind of **interpretation**. Interpreting data includes drawing conclusions about what you have observed and making recommendations for the actions you will take based on what you have observed. This serves several important functions. First, interpretation enables you to use your professional knowledge to make sense of what you have seen. Second, interpretation can help you learn to anticipate behaviors associated with normal growth and development and to recognize what is not representative of appropriate growth, development, and learning for each child. Third, interpretation provides direction for the implementation or modification of programs and curriculum. Review again the observational checklist in Figure 3.10, and note the teacher's interpretation of data—that is, her conclusions and recommendations.

interpretation Forming a conclusion based on observational and assessment data with the intent of planning and improving teaching and learning.

89

implementation
Committing to a certain action based on interpretations of observational data.

STEP 4: IMPLEMENT A PLAN.   The **implementation** phase is the time that you act on the results or the findings of your observation. For example, although Tenisha's behavior is appropriate for her, the other children can benefit from activities designed to help them recognize and respond to the needs of others. In addition, the physical environment of the classroom requires the rearrangement of furniture to make spaces more accessible for Tenisha. Implementing—doing something with the results of your observations—is the most important part of the process.

ASSESSMENT FOR SCHOOL READINESS

Because of federal mandates and state laws, many school districts formally assess children in some manner before or at the time of their entrance into school. Table 3.2 shows formal methods of assessment. Some type of screening occurs at the time of kindergarten entrance to evaluate learning readiness. Unfortunately, children are often classified on the basis of how well they perform on these early screenings. When assessment is appropriate and the results are used to design developmentally appropriate instruction, assessment is valuable and worthwhile.

summative assessments
Those assessments given periodically to determine at a particular point in time what students know and are able to do. Examples of summative assessments include state, end of year, and end of grading period assessments.

Formal methods of assessment that involve the use of standardized tests with set procedures and instructions for administration and have been normalized, meaning it is possible to compare a child's score with the scores of a group of children who have already taken the same exam, are called **summative assessments**. Summative assessments are given periodically to determine what students do and do not know at particular points in time.[7] Examples of summative assessments are state assessments, such as the State of Texas Assessment of Academic Readiness (STAAR) test, the Florida Comprehensive Assessment Test (FCAT), and the Oklahoma Core Curriculum Test (OCCT), and district benchmark or interim assessments, such as the Early Literacy Inventory and the DIBELS (Dynamic Indicators of Basic Early Literacy Skills). Summative assessments are most often used for accountability for schools, such as making Adequate Yearly Progress (AYP), a measurement mandated by No Child Left Behind.[8] Next we discuss screening procedures, which are also a type of summative assessment.

> **Check Your Understanding: Formative/Summative**

SCREENING

screening A type of summative assessment that gives a broad picture of what children know and are able to do, as well as their physical health and emotional status.

Screening is designed to provide a glimpse of a child's overall developmental state in all domains—social, physical, emotional, and cognitive abilities—or in one particular domain, that is, health status, language development, etc. Screening results are used to make initial decisions about placement, instructional level and grouping, and referral to other programs or agencies. Screening usually occurs during the initial entry of a child into a program. Ongoing screening can also take place three or four times over the course of the program year. Again, this ongoing screening provides information for placement and instructional grouping. Screening data are also used to make decisions about a child exiting a program such as speech therapy. School districts and other programs such as Head Start (HS) and Early Head Start (EHS) have regulations that specify that children will be screened on their initial entry to a grade, program, or service.

Screening gives you and other school personnel a broad picture of what children know and are able to do, as well as their physical and emotional status. As gross indicators of children's abilities, screening procedures provide much useful information for decisions about placement for initial instruction, referral to other agencies, and additional testing that may be necessary to pinpoint a learning or health problem. In special education, screening measures are used to determine if further, more in-depth

TABLE 3.2 | Examples of Formal Measures of Assessment Used in Early Childhood Education

Assessment Instrument	Age/Grade Level	Purpose
Ages and Stages Questionnaires, 3rd ed. (ASQ-3)	Birth to 5 years	Provides developmental and social-emotional screening for children; looks at the child's developmental delays and educates parents about developmental milestones
Early Childhood Environment Rating Scale Revised (ECERS-R)	Ages 2½ to 5 years	Assesses the space and furnishings, personal care routines, language-reasoning, activities, interactions, program structure, and parents and staff of group programs
Early Literacy Inventory (ELI)	Kindergarten through third grade	Assesses writing level, phonemic awareness, rhyming, syllable segmentation, concepts about print, letter/sound identification, sight word identification
Dynamic Indicators of Basic Early Literacy Skills (DIEBLS)	Kindergarten through sixth grade	Assesses three of the five big ideas of early literacy: phonological awareness, alphabetic principle, and fluency with connected text
BRIGANCE® Screens and Inventories	Prekindergarten to grade nine	Obtains a broad sampling of children's skills and behaviors to determine initial placement, plan appropriate instruction, and comply with mandated testing requirements
Developmental Indicators for the Assessment of Learning, 4th ed. (DIAL-4)	Ages 3 to 6 years	Identifies children who may have special educational needs
Preschool Child Observation Record, 2nd ed.	Ages 2½ to 6 years	Measures children's progress in all early childhood programs

assessment measures and techniques are needed to make final determinations about student placement.

Many school districts conduct comprehensive screening programs for children entering preschool and kindergarten. For example, in Colorado, vision and hearing screenings must be provided to all children in kindergarten.[9] In addition, each school district must assess the reading readiness or literacy reading comprehension level of each pupil enrolled in kindergarten.[10] These screening programs are conducted in one day or over several days. Data for each child are usually evaluated by a team of professionals who make instructional placement recommendations and, when appropriate, suggest additional testing and make referrals to other agencies for assistance.

Screening programs can involve the following:

- Interviewing parents to gather information about their children's health, learning patterns, learning achievements, personal habits, and special problems
- Conducting health screenings, including a physical examination, a health history, and a blood sample for analysis
- Conducting vision, hearing, and speech screenings
- Collecting and analyzing data from former programs and teachers, such as preschools, Head Start, and child care programs
- Administering a cognitive and/or behavioral screening instrument such as those shown in Table 3.2

Many school districts conduct a comprehensive screening for children entering kindergarten, which may include assessment of readiness skills, vision, hearing, and speech.

Increasing numbers of states are adapting and mandating screens for all their children. The Brigance K & 1 Screen III is used to screen all Kentucky kindergarteners in the first weeks of school. In fact, most school districts administer a screening instrument at the beginning of the school year to establish a base line of achievement for each child. This base line forms the basis for initial instruction and grouping.

COMMUNICATING WITH PARENTS. Although the screening process itself is important, just as important is communicating the results to parents and families. Parents are more likely to accept information when they have good communication with the person doing the screening. For example, Head Start, in its ongoing partnerships with families, uses family conferences as an opportunity to communicate screening and assessment results to parents in a manner that recognizes the child's strengths while systematically responding when a concern warrants it.[11]

SCREENING INSTRUMENTS. Screening instruments provide information for grouping and planning instructional strategies. Most can be administered by people who do not have specialized training. However, some instruments require administration by someone who is specifically trained to administer assessment instruments, such as a psychologist. Parent volunteers often help administer screening instruments, many of which are administered in about thirty minutes. See Table 3.2 for examples of these screening instruments.

In addition to participating in the formal assessment of young children, you will have many opportunities to engage in informal assessment of children with disabilities in your classroom. For example, some children with disabilities such as dyslexia may also have attention-deficit disorder (ADD). Also, some children with disabilities, though certainly not all, may exhibit behavioral problems in addition to their particular disability. Learning how to assess children's behavior so that you may provide appropriate intervention is one of your key roles.

WHAT ARE CRITICAL ASSESSMENT ISSUES?

In early childhood education, essential questions surround what constitutes appropriate and inappropriate practice and what is best for children and families. Assessment is no exception.

ASSESSMENT AND ACCOUNTABILITY

There is a tremendous emphasis on assessment and the use of summative test results by educators, and politicians use tests to measure achievement in order to compare children, programs, school districts, and countries. In other words, this emphasis will likely continue for a number of reasons. First, the public, including politicians and legislatures, sees assessment as a means of making schools and teachers accountable for teaching all children so that they achieve at or above grade level. Second, assessment is seen as playing a critical role in improving education: Assessment results are used to make decisions about how the curriculum and instructional practices can increase achievement. As long as there is a public desire to improve teaching and achievement, we will continue to see an emphasis on the use of assessment for accountability purposes.

BLURRING THE LINE BETWEEN ASSESSMENT AND TEACHING. As an early childhood professional you are constantly multitasking. You are simultaneously assessing and teaching children. But many believe that the emphasis on assessment leads to "teaching to the test." This leads to children knowing how to fill in a bubble in a scantron sheet, but not necessarily *really understand* the material. Many fear that the emphasis on accountability is creating an educational culture that puts test scores ahead of intellectual growth.

PERFORMANCE-BASED PAY. Many school districts give their teachers extra compensation or bonuses if their schools meet certain student achievement goals. Such plans are based on measuring student achievement with standardized tests, and this means more testing for students of all ages. Performance-based pay programs may not be popular with all teachers, but they are a part of many districts' pay plans and are growing in popularity.

STANDARDS AND TESTING. Although there is no national curriculum in the United States, states are required to develop standards in order to receive federal assistance. Standardized tests are the main means of determining if schools are meeting state standards, federal guidelines, and the Common Core state standards.

State Standards. Each state determines what is taught in its public schools. For example, in the state of Texas, the Texas Essential Knowledge and Skills (TEKS) are those sets of knowledge and skills that the state has determined are essential for each student to know and do. Each grade level has a specific set of TEKS for each content area, ranging from technology and science to literature, art, and physical education. The state's standardized test, the STAAR (State of Texas Assessment of Academic Readiness), is based on the TEKS. The state of Texas requires that its textbooks teach the TEKS as well, which means that the major textbook publishers tailor their content for Texas, in many cases creating textbooks that are different from those purchased by the other states. As a result, the curriculum in Texas is heavily dependent upon the TEKS because the TEKS builds on skills established in the preschool and kindergarten and throughout the high school years. Now would be a good time for you to learn about procedures of standardized testing and how standardized testing affects the curriculum in your state.

HIGH-STAKES TESTING. **High-stakes testing** occurs when standardized tests are used to make important and often life-influencing decisions about children. Standardized tests have specific and standardized content, administration, and scoring procedures, and norms for interpreting scores. High-stakes outcomes include decisions about whether to admit children into programs (e.g., kindergarten), whether children will have to attend summer school, and whether children will be retained or promoted. Generally, the early childhood profession is opposed to high-stakes testing for children through grade three. Take, for example, kindergarten teacher Kelly Aldo, who believes we are testing children so much that she barely has time to teach the curriculum.[12] This sums up how many early childhood teachers feel!

> **high-stakes testing** An assessment test used to either admit children into programs or promote them from one grade to the next.

Despite early childhood professionals' opposition, as part of the accountability movement, many politicians and school administrators view high-stakes testing as a means of making sure that children learn and that promotions from one grade to another are based on achievement. Many school critics maintain that in the pre-K and primary grades there is too much social promotion—that is, passing children from grade to grade merely to enable students to keep pace with their age peers.

PUBLIC CONCERNS. A growing number of states now require children to pass a reading test at the end of third grade or be held back from fourth grade. Thirteen states have adopted laws that require schools to identify, intervene, and in many cases, retain students who fail a reading proficiency test by the end of third grade.

What all of this means is that there is pressure for teachers to teach every child, regardless of socioeconomic status, culture, gender, or race, how to read on grade level by the end of third grade, as measured by a standardized test.

Proponents of these pass-or-fail initiatives say that they are necessary in order to promote higher standards, end social promotion, and help decrease the school drop-out rate. On the other hand, opponents of the "third grade rule" claim that grade failure does a disservice to children and actually promotes school dropout. For their part, schools are teaching reading earlier, beginning in preschool; providing help for struggling readers earlier; reinstating remedial programs; and assigning poor readers to summer school.

With so much emphasis on tests, it is understandable that the issue of testing and assessment raises many concerns on the part of teachers, parents, and the public. Some argue that testing reduces teaching and learning to the lowest common denominator—teaching children what they need to know to get the right answers. Many early childhood professionals believe that standardized tests do not measure children's thinking, problem-solving ability, creativity, or responsibility for their own learning. Furthermore, critics believe that group-administered, objectively scored, skills-focused tests—which dominate much of U.S. education—do not support(indeed, may undermine) many of the curricular reforms taking place today.

As an early childhood professional, part of your responsibility is to be an advocate for the appropriate use of assessment (see the Ethical Dilemma at the end of this text). You will make ongoing, daily decisions about how best to assess your children and how best to use assessment results.

ASSESSMENT OF CHILDREN WITH DISABILITIES

As an early childhood professional, you will have many opportunities to assess or participate in the assessment of young children with disabilities. Assessment is a pivotal event for families and their children because assessment results are used to include or exclude children from specialized intervention that can change their developmental and academic destinies.[13]

Let's look at assessment considerations for students with special needs and English language learners (ELLs). The Individuals with Disabilities Education Act (IDEA) mandates that children with disabilities be included in statewide and district-wide assessments unless alternate assessments are more appropriate. For many students with disabilities, participation in classroom, district, or state assessments will not necessitate any changes in the way in which teachers administer assessments. Assessment and evaluation for children with special needs must be fair and equitable for all children, and teachers must adhere to the mandates required by IDEA, as follows:

- Be administered in the child's native language or other mode of communication.
- Be validated for the purpose for which they are being used.
- Be administered by trained personnel in conformance with instructions from the test publisher.
- Not be used as the only basis of special education eligibility.
- Provide information about the students' educational needs, not simply intelligence.

In addition, here you have learned about the various ways teachers assess children that go beyond state, district, or standardized tests. Children, both with and without disabilities, will require accommodations to those assessments and the more informal assessments given by classroom teachers. These accommodations do not change the content of the test but usually fall into one of five categories. Using these accommodations will help you and other teachers equitably assess all children:

1. *Format Accommodations:* The assessment directions or content are altered to include visual (such as large print), tactile (such as Braille or raised print), or

auditory (such as an audio recording) presentations, depending on the needs of the child.

2. ***Response Accommodations:*** Children can respond in different ways, such as using an assistive communication device, typing, sign language, or pointing.

3. ***Setting Accommodations:*** The location of an assessment is changed so that it is free from distractions and other interruptions. For example, a child might be moved to a room that is quiet or that has fewer children moving about.

4. ***Timing Accommodations:*** These accommodations change the allowable length of the testing time and provide students with the time and breaks they need.

5. ***Scheduling Accommodations:*** These accommodations may change the particular time of day, day of the week, or number of days an assessment is given.

REPORTING TO AND COMMUNICATING WITH FAMILIES

Part of your responsibility as a professional is to report to families about the growth, development, and achievement of their children. Communicating with parents and families is one of the most important jobs of the early childhood professional. The following guidelines will help you meet the important responsibility of reporting assessment information to family members:

- ***Be honest and realistic.*** Too often, we do not want to hurt parents' feelings, so we sugarcoat what we are reporting. However, families need our honest assessments about their children and what they know, are able to do, and will be able to do.

- ***Communicate clearly.*** What we communicate to families must make sense to them; they have to understand what we are saying. Reporting to families often has to be a combination of written (in their language) and oral communication. Use a translator when necessary, and be sure to have someone who is fluent in the other language to check and double-check any written translations for cultural errors and grammatical mistakes.

- ***Share student work samples and portfolios.*** Documentation of student progress is a concrete, tangible way to report and share information with family members.

- ***Provide ideas and information to help them assist in their children's learning.*** Remember that you and the families are partners in helping children be successful in school and life.

Observe and Analyze

HOW YOUNG IS TOO YOUNG?

There are many issues involved in testing young children. For example, one report cautions early childhood professionals about testing young children and the misuse of those test results.

All assessments, and particularly assessments for accountability, must be used carefully and appropriately if they are to resolve, and not create, educational problems. Assessment of young children poses greater challenges than people generally realize. The first five years of life are a time of incredible growth and learning, but the course of development is uneven and sporadic. The status of a child's development as of any given day can change very rapidly. Consequently, assessment results—in particular, standardized test scores that reflect a given point in time—can easily misrepresent children's learning.[14]

Using Technology to Assess Children

In the early 1970s, Intel developed the first microprocessor, and personal computers (PCs) were born. By the twenty-first century, the Internet and the World Wide Web had exploded onto the scene, and the Internet became the world's largest database. In 2008, the National Center for Education Statistics reported that 100 percent of all schools had computers and the student-to-computer ratio was at an all-time low of 3:1.

This technological revolution provides early childhood teachers with tools to more effectively and efficiently assess young children in a formative way. Teachers can quickly and efficiently assess a child's literacy, phonological awareness, vocabulary, and math development using a netbook, notebook, Apple iPad, Apple iPod Touch, or laptop. Consider the following scenario:

It's September and Tracy Richard is ready to begin assessing her four-year-old pre-K children. They have been in school for one month, and the children are comfortable in their new surroundings. Tracy is anxious to see what the children in her class know about letters, vocabulary, math, and phonological awareness. This beginning-of-the-year assessment will provide her with a benchmark and enable her to modify her instruction to better meet her children's needs. Tracy grabs her netbook, reminds her assistant that she will be in the conference room next door, and calls Cassie, the first child that she will assess.

Together, Tracy and Cassie walk to the conference room chattering about the "games" they will play on the "little computer." The room is set up so that there is a small table and two child-size chairs. Tracy sits next to Cassie, places the netbook where they both can see the screen, and begins the letter assessment. One by one, letters appear on the netbook screen, and Cassie quickly names them. Tracy easily scores each answer by discreetly tapping the arrows on the keyboard. Sixty seconds later the letter knowledge assessment is complete! Tracy walks Cassie back to the classroom and repeats the process with the other children. After she has assessed each child's letter knowledge, she will systematically work through the remaining parts of the assessment. The entire assessment would take Tracy less than 20 minutes to complete with each child.

Tracy gets the netbook back out and connects it to the Internet in her classroom. She clicks on the "sync" icon on the desktop and quickly her assessments synchronize with a secure server. In just a few seconds, she has a report on how well each of her children know the letters of the alphabet. She will have a class report as well as a report on each individual child. Tracy assesses which children have an emerging understanding of letters, and she will know exactly which children to whom she will need to provide additional assistance. Tracy now has the information she needs to plan her instruction in the weeks to come.

Mobile-to-Web technology allows teachers now to quickly and accurately assess children at multiple checkpoints throughout the year. HTML5 technology (the assessment process) is simplified by allowing the teacher to assess information off-line. Teachers can administer assessments outside the classroom in environments that are more conducive for assessment.

There are many benefits for early childhood teachers who assess children using one of the many, readily available mobile-to-Web assessment tools currently on the market. The benefits of technology-based assessment over traditional assessment methods include the following:

- More accurate assessment results
- Less time spent preparing materials for assessment
- Less time spent in administering the actual assessment, which results in more time devoted to teaching in the classroom
- More cost-effective
- More flexibility to choose the appropriate setting for the assessment
- Immediate feedback
- Results are easy-to-interpret and share with administrators and parents
- Results enable teachers to differentiate instruction with greater ease

Tracy Richard is part of a generation that has never been without technology. She understands and values its early childhood applications. The result is that she is able to deliver instruction to her children that will have a positive impact on student achievement.

Source: Contributed by Cheri Sherley, The University of Texas Health Science Center at Houston's Children's Learning Institute.

ACCOMMODATING DIVERSE LEARNERS

Although not speaking English is not a disability, like children with disabilities, English language learners (ELLs) are often at a disadvantage when it comes to testing. It is a troubling fact that ELLs' academic performance is well below that of their peers and that ELLs have excessively high dropout rates.[15] Contributing to the difficulty many ELLs face in reaching achievement performance scores comparable to those of non-ELLs is that assessing students in English is required by law, and as a result, assessments are often not authentic.[16]

Report assessment findings accurately and honestly to parents. How can such communication build trust? What are other advantages of honest, open communication?

ELLS AND ASSESSMENT ISSUES. Assessments are often inauthentic for many reasons. First, ELLs are expected to master content in English before they have reached a certain level of English proficiency. For example, Marisol is expected to read and write in English even though she only understands and speaks Spanish.[17] Second, each state (and frequently several districts) has divergent policies concerning ELLs.[18] As a result, the accommodations ELLs receive often vary from school to school, district to district, and state to state. Third, standards for what ELLs should know are not matched with a corresponding test.[19] In other words, ELLs are held accountable to one set of standards, like those specified in accommodating for level of language, but then are assessed with a test that is normalized for children who are fluent speakers of English. When it comes to ELLs, the standards are not standardized! This contributes to the difficulty ELLs face when it comes to accurate and authentic assessments, equal education, and chances to succeed in an educational setting.

CULTURAL ISSUES AND ACCOMMODATION. In addition to issues of alignment of standards with assessments, ELLs may also have cultural differences that make achievement difficult. For example, the activities and learning behaviors fostered in U.S. schools are often based on individual achievement and behavior, whereas many ELLs come from schools in which the desired achievement and behaviors are based on a collectivistic perspective.[20] For example, in the United States, the phrase "Pull yourself up by your own bootstraps" is indicative of American culture, emphasizing personal achievement without help from others; but in some other countries, the phrase might better be applied as "You help me, I'll help you, and we'll both benefit." In such cultures, individual accomplishment is not as important as the group equally achieving or benefiting. As a result, children from a different cultural background may not understand the importance placed on their own academic achievement because they are used to thinking about themselves as a member of the greater whole. Also, while U.S. schooling encourages creativity, problem-solving, and analysis, schooling in other cultures often emphasizes recitation and rote memorization.[21] Furthermore, academic communication in speech and writing in U.S. schools is mostly linear; we tell stories in a straight line, with a beginning, middle, and end, but in some other cultures it is often circular or digressive.[22] For example, conversations in other cultures may not be straightforward but instead circle around a topic in order to emphasize its importance or make a point. The pattern of communicating is different, and as a result, translations from other languages into English often don't make sense or they appear to be disjointed. With such barriers, it is no wonder that ELLs are struggling in areas of academic performance achievement!

GUIDELINES FOR ELL SUCCESS. To help ELLs in your classroom, consider the following:

- Review the standards and assessments used to determine ELL achievement performance in your state. Do the standards and assessments align? If they do not, become an advocate for your students. For more information, go to the World-Class Instructional Design and Assessment Consortium (WIDA) website, as well as the Center for Research on Education, Diversity, and Excellence.

- Use a variety of assessment types and techniques. We have already discussed how standardized tests are often not accurate representations of what ELLs know and can do. Therefore, a diverse array of assessments is especially important in order for you to get an accurate picture of your students' progress, knowledge, and abilities. Portfolios are particularly helpful to achieve this goal because they include work samples collected over time. Interviews also increase language fluency and teacher-student relationships.

- Make sure your ELLs receive a high-quality education so that they can perform their best on assessments. For example do the following:

    - In addition to the traditional American education emphasis on individual learning and achievement, include plenty of activities such as group projects and group discussions to appeal to many ELLs' preference for working with others.

    - Encourage ELLs to use memorization and recitations because these are the more common learning modes in many of their cultures. At the same time, also teach creative thinking, problem solving, and analysis.

    - Get to know your ELLs well. The more you know about your students and the more you are involved in their lives, the better you can teach to their needs. Conduct home visits, talk with providers, and talk with your students.

Today there is a great deal of emphasis on accountability. Teachers are asked to be accountable to parents, legislators, and the public. Providing for and conducting developmentally appropriate assessment of young children and their programs is one of the best ways for you to be accountable for what you do. Conducting an appropriate assessment not only makes you accountable to parents and the public, but it also enables you to be accountable to young children. You have accepted a sacred trust and have dedicated your life to helping children learn and develop. Effective assessment practices will help you achieve this goal.

ACTIVITIES FOR PROFESSIONAL DEVELOPMENT

ETHICAL DILEMMA

"TO TEST OR NOT TO TEST?"

Recently, a school district suspended two special education teachers without pay for refusing to give a state-mandated test to children with cognitive disabilities. Third grade teachers, Janice Morris and Sally Sutton were concerned about the authenticity and appropriateness of a grade-level-based test that their students had already failed the previous semester. Janice and Sally agreed to parents' request that their students not be tested. They also believed the test was not in the best interests of the children. Both teachers maintain they have high expectations for their children, but when a test is inappropriate to children's needs, it is wrong to administer it. Janice and Sally think the test was a one-size-fits-all assessment. The parents are very supportive of Sally and Janice's actions, saying, "They stood up for our children and what's best for them." The school district's superintendent maintains that although he understood the teachers' position, they should have administered the test because it is state mandated.[23]

What do you think? Do you agree with Janice and Sally, or do you agree with the superintendent? Should Janice and Sally have administered the test because it is the law, even though they believed that it was unethical for them to do so? What would you have done?

ACTIVITIES TO APPLY WHAT YOU LEARNED

1. Write a journal or a blog entry stating three reasons about how and why authentic assessment is important for you as a classroom teacher. How is assessment important for your children? Post your answers to your class discussion board for comments.

2. **KEY ASSESSMENT:** Formative (authentic) assessment is a daily part of the teacher's tool bag of instructional activities. Refer to Table 3.1 and choose a method of assessment and describe how you would use it to gather data on children's achievement in reading, math, and science.

   Reading: Method of assessment and how you would use it:

   Math: Method of assessment and how you would use it:

   Science: Method of assessment and how you would use it:

   Share your results with your classmates with PowerPoint, Prezi, or another technology-based method. Use the **rubric** provided to guide your work.

3. Observation is an important professional skill. For example, you can use observation to learn more about three- and four-year-old children's toy preferences. Using ideas from this text, develop an observation form and write guidelines for how you would collect data about preschool children's toy preferences. Share this information with two or three of your classmates and ask for their feedback.

4. Of the various screening methods for kindergarten readiness described in this text, which one would you choose? Why? Now ask a classroom teacher for his/her preferred method of screening. What have you learned from how you said you would screen and how the teacher said she/he would screen?

5. There are many critical issues associated with the testing and assessment of young children. Which three issues do you think are the most critical for children? Why? What can you and your colleagues do to help reduce some of the pressure placed on children as a result of testing? Share your opinions online with your classmates.

LINKING TO LEARNING

The following agencies and programs, which can be located easily online, provide additional information about topics discussed in this chapter.

ARCNet
This website is for anyone interested in the world of assessment.

Assessing Young Children's Progress Appropriately
Here you will find another good source for looking at critical issues relating to the appropriate assessment of children's progress.

A Guide to the Developmentally Appropriate Assessment of Young Children
This guide to the developmentally appropriate assessment of young children provides useful information about the appropriate uses of assessment and assessment results.

Linking Assessment and Teaching in the Critical Early Years
These are excellent sources for additional information about assessment through documentation and about linking assessment and teaching.

National Association of Early Childhood Specialists in State Departments of Education (NAECS/SDE)
NAECS/SDE is a national organization for state education agency staff and others interested in the field of early childhood education from infancy through the primary grades.

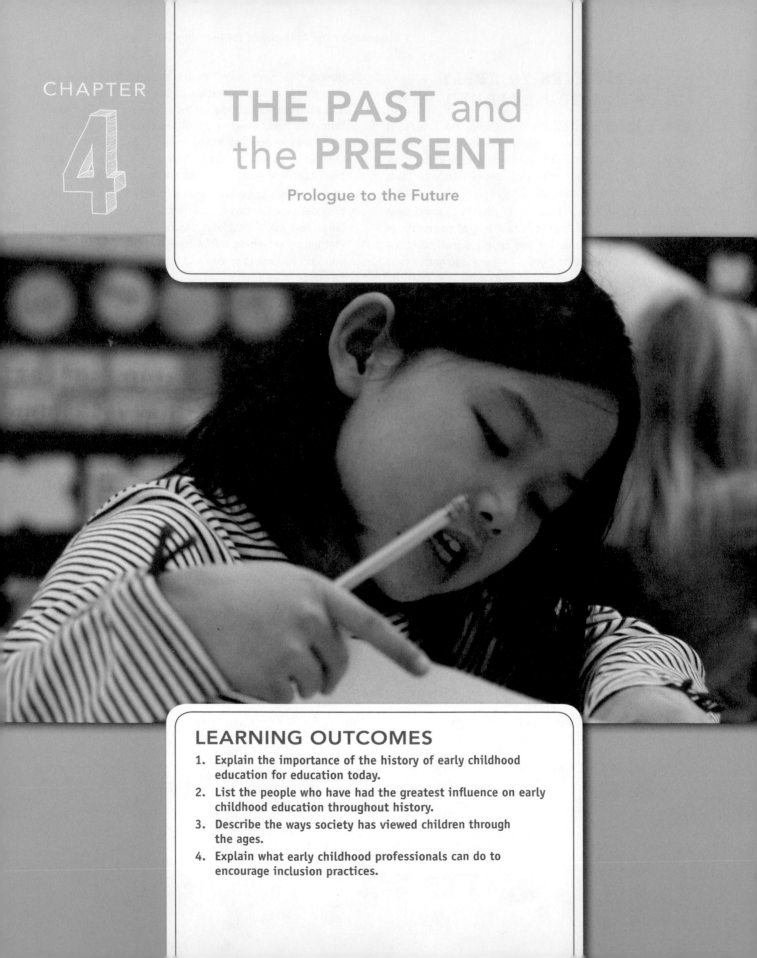

THE PAST and the PRESENT

Prologue to the Future

LEARNING OUTCOMES

1. Explain the importance of the history of early childhood education for education today.
2. List the people who have had the greatest influence on early childhood education throughout history.
3. Describe the ways society has viewed children through the ages.
4. Explain what early childhood professionals can do to encourage inclusion practices.

WHY IS THE PAST IMPORTANT?

When we read of the hopes, ideas, and accomplishments of people whom those in our profession judge famous, we realize that many of today's ideas are built on those of the past. There are at least five reasons to know about the ideas and theories of great educators who have influenced and continue to influence the field of early childhood education.

NAEYC STANDARDS

REBIRTH OF IDEAS

Old ideas and theories are often reborn. Good ideas and practices persist over time and are recycled through educational thought and practices in ten- to twenty-year periods. For example, many education initiatives that started in the 1980s and the 1990s are widely implemented today. The public concern over the condition and quality of education of the 1980s and 1990s has matured into today's current full-fledged accountability movement. This is reflected in the state standards, the adoption of the national Common Core State Standards (CCSS) and pay-for-performance measures, all designed to improve education in the United States and raise the achievement levels of U.S. children.

However, old ideas and practices seldom get recycled in exactly their previous form; they are changed and modified as necessary for contemporary society and to fit current beliefs. However, when you know about former ideas and practices, you can more easily recognize how they are recycled today. This knowledge enables you to be an active participant in the process of recycling best practices and ideas of previous years and applying them to contemporary practice. And, you can more fully appreciate this recycling if you understand the roots of the early education profession. Take a moment to review and reflect on Table 4.1, Contributions of Famous Individuals to Early Childhood Education. It will help you understand how ideas about early childhood education have been revived and reused through the years.

BUILDING THE DREAM—AGAIN

Many of today's early childhood practices have their roots in the past. In this sense, building the dream seems like a never-ending process. For example, the idea of universal preschool in the United States has been around since 1830, when the Infant School Society of Boston submitted a petition to incorporate infant schools into the Boston Public Schools.[1]

We are *still* trying to implement universal preschool education. This dream of universal preschool for all four-year-old children was rekindled by President Obama's call to the states to partnership with the federal government in funding it. We have inherited the ideas and visions of a long line of early childhood educators, which we use as a base to build meaningful teaching careers and programs for children and their families. You are both a builder of dreams and an implementer of dreams as you join the ranks of educators in the early childhood profession.

IMPLEMENTING CURRENT PRACTICE

Understanding the ideas of early educators helps you implement current teaching strategies, whatever they may be. For instance, Rousseau, Froebel, and Montessori all believed children should be taught with dignity and respect. This attitude toward children is essential to an understanding of good educational practice and contributes to good teaching and quality programs. You and any program you are involved in should include respect for children and families—among many other dispositions—as one of your core values.

TABLE 4.1 | Contributions of Famous Individuals to Early Childhood Education

Individual and Dates	Major Contributions	Influences on Modern Education
Martin Luther (1483–1546)	• Translated the Bible from Latin to vernacular language, allowing people to be educated in their own language • Advocated establishing schools to teach children how to read	• Universal education • Public support of education • Teaching of reading to all children • Adult literacy
John Comenius (1592–1670)	• Wrote *Orbis Pictus,* the first picture book for children • Thought early experiences formed what a child would be like • Said education should occur through the senses	• Early learning helps determine school and life success • Sensory experiences support and promote learning • Believed teaching/learning should progress from easy to difficult
John Locke (1632–1704)	• Said children are born as blank tablets or *tabula rasa* • Believed children's experiences determine who they are • Experiences are the basis of all learning	• Learning should begin early. • Children learn what they are taught—teachers literally make children • It is possible to rear children to think and act as society wants them to
Jean-Jacques Rousseau (1712–1778)	• Advocated natural approaches to child rearing • Felt that children's natures unfold as a result of maturation according to an innate timetable	• Natural approaches to education work best (e.g., nature play, authentic assessment, and environmental studies)
Johann Pestalozzi (1746–1827)	• Advocated that education should follow the course of nature • Believed all education is based on sensory impressions • Promoted the idea that mothers could best teach children	• Family-centered approaches to early childhood education • Home schooling • Education through the senses • Laid the basis for discovery learning • Believed in the idea that when children can represent their experiences through drawing, writing, etc., then learning really occurs
Robert Owen (1771–1858)	• Held that environment determines children's beliefs, behaviors, and achievements • Believed society can shape children's character • Taught that education can help build a new society	• Importance of infant programs • Education can counteract children's poor environment • Early childhood education can reform society
Friedrich Froebel (1782–1852)	• Believed children develop through "unfolding" • Compared children to growing plants • Founded the kindergarten, or the "Garden of Children" • Developed "gifts" and "occupations" to help young children learn • Believed children can and should learn through play	• Teacher's role is similar to that of a gardener • Children should have specific materials to learn concepts and skills • Learning occurs through play

TABLE 4.1 | Contributions of Famous Individuals to Early Childhood Education *(continued)*

Individual and Dates	Major Contributions	Influences on Modern Education
Maria Montessori (1870–1952)	• The Montessori method for educating young children • All knowledge comes intrinsically from sensory experiences. • Learning materials to meet the needs of young children • Sensory-based materials that are self-correcting • Prepared environments are essential for learning. • Respect for children is the foundation of teaching.	• Large number of public and private Montessori schools that emphasize her approach, methods, and materials • Renewed emphasis on preparing environment to support and promote children's learning • Teacher training programs to train Montessori teachers
John Dewey (1859–1952)	• Progressive education movement • Children's interests form the basis of the curriculum. • Educate children for today—not tomorrow.	• Child-centered education • Curriculum based on children's interests • Discovery learning
Jean Piaget (1896–1980)	• Theory of cognitive development based on ages and stages • Children are "little scientists" and literally develop their own intelligence. • Mental and physical activities are important for cognitive development. • Project approach to learning	• Constructivist approaches to early childhood education • Matching education to children's stages of cognitive development • Active involvement of children in learning activities
Lev Vygotsky (1896–1934)	• Sociocultural theory, which emphasizes importance of inter-personal relationships in social and cognitive development • Concept of zone of proximal development—children can learn more with the help of a more competent person • Communication between teachers and children can act as a means of scaffolding to higher levels of learning.	• Use of scaffolding techniques to help children learn • Use of cooperative learning and other forms of social learning
Abraham Maslow (1908–1970)	• Theory of self-actualization based on needs motivation • Human development is a process of meeting basic needs throughout life. • Humanistic psychology	• Importance of meeting basic needs before cognitive learning can occur • Teachers develop programs to meet children's basic needs. • Growth of the self-esteem movement • Emphasis on providing safety, security, love, and affection for all children

(Continued)

TABLE 4.1 | Contributions of Famous Individuals to Early Childhood Education *(continued)*

Individual and Dates	Major Contributions	Influences on Modern Education
Erik Erikson (1902–1994)	• Theory of psychosocial development—cognitive development occurs in conjunction with social development • Life is a series of eight stages, with each stage representing a critical period in social development. • How parents and teachers interact with and care for children helps determine their emotional and cognitive development.	• Play supports children's social and cognitive development. • The emotional plays as great a role as the cognitive in development. • All children need predictable, consistent love, care, and education.
Urie Bronfenbrenner (1917–2005)	• Ecological systems theory views the child as developing within a system of relationships. • Five interrelating systems—microsystem, mesosystem, exosystem, macrosystem, and chronosystem—have a powerful impact on development. • Each system influences and is influenced by the other. • Development is influenced by children and their environments.	• Teachers are more aware of how different environments shape children's lives in different ways. • Parents and educators strive to provide positive influences in each system and minimize or eliminate negative influences. • Teachers and parents recognize that children's development depends on children's natures and their environments.
Howard Gardner (b. 1943)	• Theory of multiple intelligences • Intelligence consists of nine abilities. • Intelligence is not a single broad ability, but rather a set of abilities.	• Teachers develop programs and curricula to match children's particular intelligences. • Teachers individualize curricula and approaches to children's intelligences. • More awareness and attention to multiple ways in which children learn and think

EMPOWERING PROFESSIONALS

Theories about how young children grow, develop, and learn shape educational and child-rearing practices. Studying the beliefs of the great educators helps parents, you, and all early childhood professionals clarify what to do and gives insight into educational practice. In this sense, knowing about theories liberates the uninformed from ignorance and empowers you and other professionals to educate all the children of the United States. Those who understand historical ideas and theories are able to confidently implement developmentally appropriate practices.

INSPIRING PROFESSIONALS

Exploring, analyzing, and discovering the roots of early childhood education inspires professionals. Recurring rediscovery forces professionals to contrast current practices with that which others advocated for in past generations. Examining sources of beliefs helps clarify modern practice, and reading about and studying others' ideas make us rethink our own beliefs and positions. Knowledge of the great educators and their beliefs helps keep us current. When you pause long enough to listen to what they have to say, you frequently find a new insight or idea that will motivate you to continue your quest to be the best you can be.

HISTORY AND HISTORICAL FIGURES

The contributors to the American education system are many and distinguished. In the following text, you will read about some of the most notable contributors to the field of education as we know it today. As you read, consider how the contributions of the past play a part in the work you will do in the early childhood education field today. Take a moment to reflect again on Table 4.1. As you read, refer to the Appendix and you will be able to trace how historical figures and important moments in education have influenced one another and how events from the distant past influence us even today. As you read, you should be wondering, "How will I contribute to the field? How will I continue or influence and modify the ideas of the founders of the field?"

1500–1700: THE FOUNDATIONS

The primary focus of the Protestant Reformation in Europe was religious. However, other far-reaching effects were secular. Two of these effects involved *universal education*, or education for all, and *literacy*, both of which are very much in the forefront of educational practice today. In addition, the advent of the printing press made the written word accessible to a wide population, making literacy education more necessary on a larger scale than ever before.

MARTIN LUTHER.   The question of what to teach is an issue in any educational endeavor. Does society create schools and then decide what to teach, or do the needs of society determine what schools it will establish to meet desired goals? This is a question early childhood professionals wrestle with today. In the case of sixteenth-century European education, Martin Luther (1483–1546) emphasized the necessity of establishing schools to teach children to read. Prior to the Reformation, most of the people who could read were clergy members, not the general populace. Luther replaced the authority of the hierarchy of the Catholic Church with the authority of the Bible in his landmark *Ninety-Five Theses*. He believed that individuals were free to work out their own salvation through the scriptures. This meant that people had to learn to read so that they could access the Bible.

This concept marked the real beginning of teaching and learning in people's native languages, or vernacular, as opposed to Latin, the official language of the Catholic Church. After Luther translated the Bible into German, other translations followed, finally making the Bible available to people in their own languages. In this way, the Protestant Reformation encouraged and supported popular universal education and learning to read.

Another outcome of the Reformation was that religious denominations developed their own schools to preserve their faith. Today, many churches, synagogues, and mosques operate child care and pre-K–12 programs. A growing number of parents who want early childhood programs that support their religious values, beliefs, and culture enroll their children in programs operated by religious organizations. For example, 80 percent of the nation's private schools are religiously affiliated, and over four million K–12 students are currently enrolled in religious schools.[2]

JOHN AMOS COMENIUS.   Born in Moravia, then a province of the Czech Republic, John Amos Comenius (1592–1670) became a Moravian minister. He spent his life serving as a bishop, teaching school, and writing textbooks. Of his many writings, those that have received the most attention are *The Great Didactic* and *Orbis Pictus (The World in Pictures)*, considered the first picture book for children.

Orbis Pictus (The World in Pictures) Considered the first picture book for children.

Comenius believed that humans are born in the image of God. Therefore, each individual has an obligation and duty to be educated to the fullest extent of his or her abilities so as to fulfill this God-like image. Because so much depends on education, as far as Comenius was concerned, it should begin in the early years.[3]

Comenius also believed that education should follow the order of nature, which implies a timetable for growth and learning. Early childhood professionals should observe this pattern to avoid forcing learning before children are ready.

Sensory Education. Comenius also thought that learning is best achieved when the senses are involved and that **sensory education** forms the basis for all learning. Comenius said the golden rule of teaching should be to place everything before the senses—for example, that children should not be taught the names of objects apart from the objects themselves or pictures of the objects. *Orbis Pictus* helped children learn the names of things and concepts as they appeared during Comenius's time, through pictures and words. Comenius's emphasis on the concrete and the sensory is a pedagogical principle early childhood professionals still try to fully grasp and implement. Many contemporary programs, especially Montessori programs, stress sensory learning.

JOHN LOCKE.   The English philosopher John Locke (1632–1704) popularized the *tabula rasa*, or **blank tablet**, view of children in his work *Essay Concerning Human Understanding*. More precisely, Locke developed the theory of and laid the foundation for **environmentalism**—the belief that the environment, not innate characteristics, determines what children will become. The extent of Locke's influence on modern early childhood education and practice is unappreciated by many who daily implement practices based on his theories.

Locke's assumption in regard to human learning and nature was that there are no innate ideas. This belief gave rise to his theory of the mind as a blank tablet. By this, Locke meant that the environment and experiences literally form the mind. This belief is clearly reflected in modern educational programs that encourage and promote early education as a means of overcoming or compensating for a poor or disadvantaged environment. Based partly on the idea that all children are born with the same general capacity for mental development and learning, these programs assume that differences in learning, achievement, and behavior are attributable to environmental factors, such as home and family conditions, socioeconomic context, early education, and experiences. Programs of early schooling, especially the current ongoing efforts for public schooling for three- and four-year-olds, work on the premise that some children don't have the readiness experiences necessary for kindergarten and first grade and are at risk for failure in school and life.

1700–1850: FROM NATURALISM TO THE KINDERGARTEN

The foundation laid by philosophers such as Luther and Locke paved the way for others to focus on education as a humanistic imperative. With this foundation, the world of education was able to evolve with the sometimes revolutionary ideas of Rousseau, Wollstonecraft, Owen, and Froebel.

JEAN-JACQUES ROUSSEAU.   Best remembered by educators for his book *Émile*, in which Jean-Jacques Rousseau (1712–1778) raises a hypothetical child from birth to adolescence, Rousseau's theories were radical for his time. The opening lines of *Émile* set the tone not only for Rousseau's educational views, but also for many of his political ideas as well: "God makes all things good; man meddles with them and they become evil."[4]

Naturalism.   Rousseau advocated a return to nature and an approach to educating children called **naturalism**. To Rousseau, naturalism meant abandoning society's artificiality and

---

sensory education Learning experiences involving the five senses: seeing, touching, hearing, tasting, and smelling.

blank tablet The belief that at birth the mind is blank and that experiences create the mind.

environmentalism The theory that the environment, rather than heredity, exerts the primary influence on intellectual growth and cultural development.

Émile Jean-Jacques Rousseau's famous book that outlines his ideas about how children should be reared.

naturalism Education that follows the natural development of children and does not force the educational process on them.

pretentiousness. A naturalistic education permits growth without undue interference or restrictions. Rousseau would probably argue against such modern practices as dress codes, compulsory attendance, frequent and standardized testing, and ability grouping on the grounds that they are "unnatural." On the other hand, more early childhood programs are incorporating outdoor activities, nature education, and gardening as ways of getting children involved in more natural approaches to education. We will discuss Rousseau's influence on environmental education later in this text.

American education tends to emphasize ideas associated with naturalism. For example, family grouping seeks to create a more natural, family-like atmosphere in schools and classrooms; literacy programs emphasize literature from the natural environment (e.g., using menus to show children how reading is important in their everyday lives); and conflict resolution programs teach children how to get along with others.

Rousseau maintained that a natural education encourages spontaneity and inquisitiveness. What should families and teachers do to provide experiences in which children can develop their natural abilities?

According to Rousseau, natural education promotes and encourages qualities such as happiness, spontaneity, and the inquisitiveness associated with childhood. Rousseau felt that Émile's education occurred through three sources: nature, people, and things.

Unfolding. Rousseau believed that although parents and others have control over education that comes from social and sensory experiences, they have no control over children's natural growth. In essence, this is the principle of **unfolding**, in which the nature of children—what they are to be—develops as a result of maturation according to their innate developmental schedules. We should observe the child's growth and provide experiences at appropriate times. Some educators interpret this as a *laissez-faire*, or "let alone," approach to parenting and education. However, understanding unfolding is also important to our understanding of developmentally appropriate practice.

unfolding Process by which the nature of children—what they are to be—develops as a result of maturation according to their innate developmental schedules.

The belief in unfolding can be seen today in high-stakes testing. With the trend toward testing children at younger and younger ages, even in preschool, there is a heightened concern about the developmental appropriateness of such practices. Many critics say that kindergarten is a time of developmental fluctuation, not just between children, but on a daily basis in an individual child, and that high-stakes tests are therefore inappropriate. As a result, proponents of developmental unfolding are in a deadlock with proponents of testing for accountability.

Another example of the use of unfolding in today's education scene is *redshirting*, the act of holding a "young" five-year-old back from entering kindergarten for a year so that he or she is more developmentally capable to meet the demands of the increased rigor of school. Redshirting is becoming ever more popular.[5] Parents who hold back their children hope that the extra year will give their children an opportunity to further *unfold* and perform to higher standards when they do enter school.

Rousseau established a way of thinking about young children that is reflected in the educational practice of Pestalozzi and Froebel. Rousseau's concept of natural unfolding echoes Comenius's concept of naturalness and appears in current programs that stress children's readiness as a factor in learning. Jean Piaget's cognitive developmental stages also reinforce Rousseau's thinking about the importance of natural development.

JOHANN HEINRICH PESTALOZZI.   Impressed by Rousseau's back-to-nature concepts, Johann Heinrich Pestalozzi (1746–1827) purchased a farm and started a school called Neuhof. There Pestalozzi developed his ideas about the integration of home life, vocational education, and education for reading and writing.

Rousseau's influence is most apparent in Pestalozzi's belief that education should follow children's natural development. Pestalozzi reared his only son, Jean-Jacques, using *Émile* as a guide and on harmonizing nature and educational practices.

Object Lessons. Pestalozzi believed that all education is based on sensory impressions and that through the proper sensory experiences, children can achieve their natural potential. This belief led to his development of object lessons. As the name implies, Pestalozzi thought the best way to learn many concepts was through manipulatives—counting, measuring, feeling, touching. Pestalozzi believed the best teachers were those who teach children, not subjects. He also believed in multiage grouping.[6]

MARY WOLLSTONECRAFT.   In 1787, Mary Wollstonecraft (1759–1797), a British philosopher and early feminist, published *Thoughts on the Education of Daughters: With Reflections on Female Conduct in the More Important Duties of Life.* With this work, published in the wake of the Declaration of Independence and the French Revolution, Wollstonecraft became one of the first philosophers to extend the burgeoning ideals of equality and independence to women through education. Wollstonecraft emphasized education as a means to better society. In *Thoughts on the Education of Daughters,* Wollstonecraft offered advice on female education as well as basic child-rearing instructions, such as how to care for babies. Wollstonecraft was significantly influenced by Locke's *Some Thoughts Concerning Education* and Rousseau's *Émile.* Wollstonecraft followed Locke's example in emphasizing a parent-directed domestic education and built on Rousseau's beliefs in natural abilities.

Later, Wollstonecraft published *A Vindication of the Rights of Woman: With Strictures on Political and Moral Subjects,* in which she responded to those educational and political theorists of the eighteenth century who argued against educating women. In the eighteenth century, it was argued by most European educational philosophers that women were incapable of thinking clearly because they were too susceptible to following their feelings rather than rationality. Wollstonecraft, along with other reformers, maintained that women were capable of rational thought and deserved to be educated. In *A Vindication of the Rights of Woman,* she argued that women ought to have an education because they are essential to the nation as educators of its children. Wollstonecraft's work is essential because it was one of the first arguments for truly educating all people, an idea that we are still very much influenced by and are striving toward today. In addition, she paved the way for women to become educators, not only of their own children, but of other children as well.

ROBERT OWEN.   Quite often, people who affect the course of educational thought and practice are also visionaries in political and social affairs. Robert Owen (1771–1858) was no exception. Owen's influences on education resulted from his entrepreneurial activities associated with New Lanark, Scotland, a model mill town he managed. Owen was an environmentalist—that is, he believed that the environment in which children are reared is the main factor contributing to their beliefs, behavior, and achievement. Consequently, he maintained that society and persons acting in the best interests of society can shape children's individual characters.

He also was a **utopian**, believing that by controlling the circumstances and consequent outcomes of child rearing, it was possible to build a new and perhaps more perfect society. Such a deterministic view of child rearing and education pushes free will to the background and makes environmental conditions the dominant force in directing and determining human behavior. Owen believed that good traits were instilled at an early age and that children's behavior was influenced primarily by the environment.

utopian The belief that by controlling circumstances and consequent outcomes of child rearing, it is possible to build a new and more perfect society.

Infant Schools. To implement his beliefs, Owen opened an infant school in 1816 at New Lanark, designed to provide care for about a hundred children ages eighteen months to ten years while their parents worked in his cotton mills. This led to the opening of the first infant school in London in 1818. Because part of Owen's motivation for opening the infant schools was to get children away from their uneducated parents, he also opened a night school for his workers to provide them an education and transform them into "rational beings."

Although we tend to think that early education for children from low-income families began with Head Start in 1965, Owen's infant school came more than a hundred years before. Owen's legacy also lives on in the infant schools and kindergartens of England. In addition, during World War II, as an extension of Owen's ideas, the Kaiser Company built shipyard child care centers for working mothers in Richmond, California, and Portland, Oregon. These were twenty-four-hour child care centers and served nearly 4,000 children.[7]

Owen believed that infant schools were an ideal way to provide for the needs of young children while their families worked. What are some issues facing early childhood professionals today as they try to provide quality infant care for working families?

FRIEDRICH WILHELM FROEBEL. Friedrich Wilhelm Froebel (1782–1852) devoted his life to developing a system for educating young children. Whereas Pestalozzi, a contemporary with whom he studied and worked, advocated a system for teaching, Froebel developed a curriculum and educational methodology. In the process, Froebel earned the distinction of being called the *Father of Kindergarten*.

Froebel's primary contributions to educational thought and practice are in the areas of learning, curriculum, methodology, and teacher training. His concept of children and how they learn is based in part on the idea of unfolding. According to Froebel, the educator's role, whether parent or teacher, is to observe this natural unfolding and provide activities that will enable children to learn what they are ready to learn when they are ready to learn it. The teacher's role is to help children develop their inherent qualities for learning. In this sense, the teacher is a designer of experiences and activities.

Kindergarten. Consistent with his idea of unfolding, Froebel compared the child to a seed that is planted, germinates, brings forth a new shoot, and grows from a young, tender plant to a mature, fruit-producing one. In so doing, he likened the role of educator to that of gardener. In his **kindergarten**, or *garden of children*, he envisioned children being educated in close harmony with their own nature and the nature of the universe. Children unfold their uniqueness in play, and it is in learning through play that Froebel makes one of his greatest contributions to the early childhood curriculum.

In 1876, a model kindergarten was on display in the first World's Fair in the United States in Fairmount Park, Pennsylvania. Ruth Burrit, a member of the Froebel Society of Boston, was the teacher and demonstrator in the Kindergarten Cottage that was a live exhibit of Froebelian kindergarten principles. Three days a week, Burrit explained and demonstrated the system to visitors to the fair as a group of orphans followed a typical kindergarten routine including games, singing, playing, and manipulating Froebel's gifts.[8] From there, parents and teachers alike took Froebel's ideas, and his gifts, back with them to their homes and schools and applied them to their lives and teaching.

kindergarten The name Friedrich Froebel gave to his system of education for children ages three through six; means "garden of children."

Gifts and Occupations. Froebel knew from experience that unstructured play doesn't work and that children left to their own devices may not learn much. Without guidance, direction, and a prepared environment in which to learn, there was a real possibility that little or the wrong kind of learning would occur. According to Froebel, the teacher is responsible for guidance and direction so children can become creative, contributing members of society, a value all early childhood teachers today should embrace. Today there is an emphasis on teachers being instructional leaders and intentional teachers.

As a result, Froebel developed a systematic, planned curriculum for the education of young children. Gifts, occupations, songs, and educational games were its basis. **Froebel's gifts** were objects for children to handle and explore with a teacher's supervision and guidance. Figure 4.1 identifies all ten gifts. The children formed impressions about the shapes and materials, relating them to mathematics, design

Froebel's gifts Ten sets of learning materials designed to help children learn through play and manipulation.

Gift 1:
Six colored balls of soft yarn or wool

Gift 2:
Wooden sphere, cylinder, and cube

Gift 3:
Eight cubes, presented together as a cube

Gift 4:
Eight rectangular pieces, presented as a cube

Gift 5:
Twenty-one cubes, six half-cubes, and twelve quarter-cubes

Gift 6:
Twenty-four rectangular pieces, six columns, and twelve caps

Gift 7:
Parquetry tablets derived from the surfaces of the gifts, including squares, equilateral triangles, right triangles, and obtuse triangles

Gift 8:
Straight sticks of wood, plastic, or metal in various lengths, plus rings and half-rings of various diameters made from wood, plastic, or metal

Gift 9:
Small points in various colors made of plastic, paper, or wood

Gift 10:
Materials that utilize rods and connectors, similar to Tinker Toys

FIGURE 4.1 | Froebel's Gifts
Froebel's concept of learning through play remains one of the basic principles of early childhood practice.
Source: Used by permission of Scott Bultman, Froebel Foundation USA, www.froebelfoundation.org.

(symmetry), and their own life experiences. Froebel himself named only the first six materials as gifts; his followers have since included other materials that Froebel used in his kindergarten.

Currently, there are ten sets of learning materials, or gifts, designed to help children learn through play and manipulation. The first six gifts are meant to represent solid forms, gift seven represents surfaces, gift eight represents line, gift nine represents the point, and gift ten completes the cycle with the use of point and line to represent the framework of solid forms.

Froebel's most well-known gift, the second, consists of a cube, a cylinder, and a sphere, all able to be suspended in such a way that children can examine their different properties by rotating, spinning, and touching. The sphere, because of its symmetry, has only one loop hole by which it is to be suspended. But the cube and the cylinder have multiple loop holes so that children can suspend the solids in different ways and examine the complexity of these seemingly simple shapes.

A significant idea behind the gifts is the importance for developing children's minds for examining things around them in a free but structured manner. It is not difficult to imagine three- or four-year-olds playing with the wooden solids and learning from their play. Froebel's traditional gifts are still used throughout preschools and kindergartens throughout the world. In fact, can you even imagine a young child's classroom without a block center or manipulatives? Over the years, Froebel's gifts have given rise to an entire modern toy industry. Consider Lincoln Logs; oversized, large cardboard building blocks; 3-D puzzles and alphabet sets; construction sets; Rainbow Building Blocks, and Modern City wooden building blocks: The list goes on!

In addition to his gifts, Froebel used **occupations**, which provide materials for craft activities, such as drawing, paper weaving, folding paper, modeling with clay, and sewing. These activities were intended to be extensions of the gifts and would enable children to create and explore different materials.

occupations Materials designed to engage children in learning activities.

Father of the Kindergarten. Froebel was the first educator to develop a planned, systematic program for educating young children. He envisioned the kindergarten as a place where children could and would learn through play. The idea that children could learn through play was as radical in Froebel's time as the idea that children don't need to play in order to learn is radical today.

Froebel's supporters imported his ideas and kindergarten program, virtually intact, into the United States in the last half of the nineteenth century. Even though Froebel's ideas seem perfectly acceptable today, they were not acceptable then to those who subscribed to the notion of early education. Especially innovative and hard to accept was the idea that learning could be child centered, based on play and children's interests. Most European and American schools were subject oriented and emphasized basic skills. In addition, Froebel was the first to advocate a communal education for young children outside the home. Until Froebel, most young children were educated in the home by their mothers. The idea of educating children as a group in a special place outside the home was revolutionary.

1850–1950: FROM A GARDEN OF CHILDREN TO THE CHILDREN'S HOUSE

Contemporary early childhood programs have their roots in the past and continue to be influenced by twentieth- and twenty-first-century people and their ideas. For example, contrary to the popular perception that contemporary environmentalism is a recent grassroots movement, "going green" has long been a part of the evolution of education. In addition, environmentalism as we know it can, in part, be traced back to Rousseau and his belief in going "back to nature."

MARGARETHE SCHURZ.   Margarethe Schurz (1833–1876) established the first kindergarten in the United States. After attending lectures in Germany on Froebelian principles, she returned to the United States and in 1856 opened her kindergarten in Watertown, Wisconsin. Schurz's program was conducted in German, as were many of the new kindergarten programs of the time. Schurz was instrumental in converting Elizabeth Peabody to the Froebelian kindergarten system.

ELIZABETH PEABODY.   Elizabeth Peabody (1804–1894) opened the first English-speaking kindergarten in the United States in Boston in 1860. She and her sister, Mary Mann, also published *Kindergarten Guide*. Peabody realized almost immediately that she lacked the necessary education to implement Froebel's ideas, so she visited kindergartens in Germany and then returned to the United States to popularize Froebel's methods. Peabody is credited as being kindergarten's main promoter in the United States.

SUSAN BLOW.   The first public kindergarten was founded in St. Louis, Missouri, in 1873 by Susan E. Blow (1843–1916) with the cooperation of the St. Louis superintendent of schools, William T. Harris. Endorsement of the kindergarten program by a public school system did much to increase its popularity and spread the Froebelian influence within early childhood education. Harris, who later became the U.S. Commissioner of Education, encouraged support for Froebel's ideas and methods.

PATTY SMITH HILL.   The kindergarten movement in the United States was not without growing pains. Over a period of time, the kindergarten program, at first ahead of its time, became rigid and teacher centered rather than child centered. By the beginning of the twentieth century, many kindergarten leaders thought that programs and training should be open to experimentation and innovation rather than rigidly tied to Froebel's ideas. Susan Blow was the chief defender of the Froebelian approach. In the more moderate camp was Patty Smith Hill (1868–1946), who thought that kindergarten should remain faithful to Froebel's ideas but nevertheless be open to innovation. She believed that to survive, the kindergarten movement had to move into the twentieth century, and she was able to convince many of her colleagues of the value of kindergarten reform. More than anyone else, Hill is responsible for the kindergarten as we know it today.

JOHN DEWEY.   John Dewey (1859–1952) was very influential regarding the course of education in the United States. Through his positions as professor of philosophy at the University of Chicago and Columbia University and his extensive writing, such as *My Pedagogical Creed*, Dewey redirected the course of education in the United States.

progressivism Dewey's theory of education that emphasizes the importance of focusing on the needs and interests of children rather than teachers.

Dewey's theory of schooling, called **progressivism**, emphasizes children and their interests rather than subject matter. From this emphasis come the terms *child-centered curriculum* and *child-centered schools*. The progressive education philosophy maintains that schools should prepare children for the realities of today rather than for some vague future time. As expressed by Dewey in *My Pedagogical Creed*, "Education, therefore, is a process of living and not a preparation for future living."[9] Thus, out of daily life should come the activities in which children learn about life and the skills necessary for living.

In a classroom based on Dewey's ideas, children are involved in physical activities, hands-on learning, intellectual pursuits, and social interaction. The growing child learns to use tools and materials to construct things. Dewey felt that an ideal expression for this interest was daily home and work occupations such as cooking and carpentry. Dewey also believed that social interactions with children and adults are encouraged in a democratically run classroom.

MARIA MONTESSORI.   Maria Montessori (1870–1952) devoted her life to developing an educational system that has influenced virtually all early childhood programs. She chose medicine as her career and became the first woman in Italy to earn a medical degree. She was then appointed assistant instructor in the psychiatric clinic of the University of Rome, where her work brought her into contact with children who were believed to be mentally retarded and had been committed to insane asylums.

Montessori soon became interested in educational solutions for problems such as deafness, paralysis, and "idiocy." Montessori said she differed from her colleagues in that she instinctively felt that mental deficiency was more of an educational problem than a medical one.[10]

In 1906 Montessori was invited by the director general of the Roman Association for Good Building to organize schools for the young children of the families who occupied the tenement houses constructed by the association. In the first school, named Casa dei Bambini, or **Children's House**, she tested her ideas and gained insights into children and teaching that led to the perfection of her system.

Children's House
Montessori's first school especially designed to implement her ideas.

In 1915 at the Panama Pacific International Exposition in San Francisco, California, Montessori installed a "glass classroom" to showcase her new educational methodology. Three of the room walls had large windows that enabled fairgoers to observe the Montessori classroom in action. In this glass classroom, thirty children between the ages of two and six, who had never attended school, were taught by lead teacher Helen Parkhurst who would later found the Dalton School in New York. (See Linking to Learning at the end of the chapter.) The glass classroom was a huge success and helped spread the Montessori method throughout the United States.[11]

THE MCMILLAN SISTERS.   In the 1900s, President Theodore Roosevelt advanced environmentalism when he advocated for responsible use and conservation of the environment. In 1914, the McMillan sisters, Rachel and Margaret, built on the foundation of Rousseau, Thoreau, and Roosevelt and incorporated environmentalism into the education of young children by opening an **open-air nursery school** and training center in Peckham, England. The McMillan sisters believed in a method of education in which young children could explore their imaginations, develop their sensory and perceptual faculties, and care for gardens and pets. The first open-air nursery is recognized as a milestone in the history of the early years of education and in environmental education.

open-air nursery school School established by the McMillan sisters, who believed in education where young children could explore their imaginations, develop their sensory and perceptual faculties, and care for gardens and pets.

A modern and innovative equivalent to the McMillans' nursery is an educational approach to outdoor play and learning called *Forest Schools*. The idea, inspired by the open-air nursery, originated in Scandinavia, where it is now embedded into practice, especially in the early years of education. British educators also became interested in the model and have for some time created similar experiences in their own education systems. The **Forest Schools** pedagogy is based on the belief that by participating in engaging, motivating, and achievable tasks and activities in a woodland environment, each child has an opportunity to develop intrinsic motivation and sound emotional and social skills.[12]

forest schools Programs with the belief that by participating in engaging, motivating, and achievable tasks and activities in a woodland environment, each child has an opportunity to develop intrinsic motivation and sound emotional and social skills.

1950–1962: FROM POLITICS TO EDUCATION

After the World Wars, education in the United States became much more influenced by political and social trends than by individuals. With the advent of mass communication through radio and television, education became a movement motivated by large groups of people rather than single influential individuals. As such, it is important to understand that education always occurs within a social and political context and is often a direct outgrowth of social and political trends. The purposes of education, how we view children, and how we teach them are all influenced by what is going on in the world around us. Social and political trends of the last fifty years have created an educational culture that influenced your education and will influence you as a teacher.

EDUCATION AS NATIONAL DEFENSE.   After the end of World War II in 1945, the United States and the Soviet Union became embroiled in a heated competition consisting of a nuclear arms race, a race to be first in space, and a race for world dominance. Out of this Cold War came *Sputnik*.

Sputnik The world's first satellite.

National Defense Education Act (NDEA) Provided federal funding for science, technology, engineering, math (STEM), and foreign language education and is considered by many to be the beginning of federal standards in education.

Sputnik.   In 1957, The Soviet Union launched *Sputnik*, the world's first satellite. *Sputnik* sparked a nationwide fear of Soviet dominion, the spread of communism, and the fall of the United States as a world power. In response to this national fear, Congress passed the **National Defense Education Act (NDEA)** of 1958. NDEA's founding idea was that the best defense is a good (educational) offense. NDEA provided federal funding for science, technology, engineering, mathematics (STEM), and foreign language education and is considered by many to be the beginning of federal standards in education.

The launch of *Sputnik* is important to you today because the current emphasis on STEM, was born out of the race for world superiority. It resulted in amazing scientific discoveries that impact how we think about education and teaching children. Today, the worldwide race for scientific, technological, engineering, and mathematic superiority continues. The idea is that education is a nationalistic imperative and that its role is to keep America strong in a competing world and stable and prosperous at home.

Twenty-First Century Skills.   The race for superiority on a global scale is also continued today by the emphasis on teaching and encouraging twenty-first-century skills. Essentially, twenty-first-century skills are those that are necessary for working and living in a technological environment and a rapidly changing global society. These skills include core subjects such as language arts, mathematics, science, global awareness, and financial literacy, but they also emphasize learning and invocation skills such as creativity, innovation, critical thinking, and problem solving. Other twenty-first-century skills are information, media, and technology skills and life and career skills such as taking initiative and self-direction.[13]

1962–THE PRESENT: FROM CIVIL RIGHTS TO THE EDUCATION OF TODAY

In the 1960s, the Civil Rights Movement permanently altered the course of education as we know it today. With the civil rights movement, the federal government became ever more involved in ensuring education for all and in altering the environments of education as a whole.

ENVIRONMENTALISM.   Modern environmentalism is largely a product of the social movements of the 1960s and 1970s and the progressive politics of the federal government at the time. In 1962, Rachel Carson published *Silent Spring*, which described and decried the environmental impacts of the spraying of DDT, a pesticide used on crops. Following the widespread popularity of *Silent Spring* between 1963 and 1968, President Johnson signed into law almost three hundred conservation and beautification measures that were supported by more than $12 billion in authorized funds. In 1969, the first Earth Day revealed the environment to be a potent political issue and one of importance to schools and children around the world.

Civil Rights Act of 1964 Legislation that prohibits discrimination on the basis of race, color, religion, sex, or national origin; includes a provision that protects the constitutional rights of individuals in public facilities, including public education.

Environmentalism continues strong in the homes and classrooms of today. Some might say environmentalism is stronger than ever because it is now a part of the curriculum for many schools and thus has the potential to grow and effect change on a national level from the ground up, or rather, from the child up. Based on the environmental movement, eco-issues around the world, and the McMillans' pioneering efforts, schools in the United States are responding by going green! Going green in the school setting represents an attempt to save energy, conserve resources, infuse curricula with environmental education and awareness, build school gardens, and offer more healthy school lunches. Green schools are those in which the building creates a healthy environment conducive to learning while saving energy, resources, and money.

EDUCATION AS EQUALIZER. In the 1960s, society began to stress civil rights, and the education system played a large part in ensuring equality for everyone. The **Civil Rights Act of 1964** included a provision that protects the constitutional rights of individuals in public facilities, including public education. Congress amended the Civil Rights Act in 1972. The most famous of these amendments is Title IX. The education amendments of the Civil Rights Act are now called The Equal Opportunity in Education Act.

Head Start addresses systemic poverty in the United States. It provides comprehensive education, health, nutrition, and parent involvement services to low-income children and their families.

THE ECONOMIC OPPORTUNITY ACT. A part of President Lyndon B. Johnson's war on poverty was the **Economic Opportunity Act of 1964 (EOA)**. The EOA implemented several social programs to promote the health, education, and general welfare of people with low socioeconomic status and was designed to put them to work. Most of the initiatives in the act have since been modified, weakened, or altogether rolled back, but remaining programs include Head Start, Early Head Start, and the Job Corps.

The EOA provided for the beginning of Head Start in 1965. The EOA was later updated as The Head Start Act of 1981. **Head Start** (HS) is one of the longest-running programs to address systemic poverty in the United States. Its programs include Early Head Start (EHS), Family and Community Partnerships, Migrant and Seasonal Head Start, and American Indian–Alaska Native Head Start.

ELEMENTARY SECONDARY EDUCATION ACT. In 1965, Congress passed the **Elementary Secondary Education Act (ESEA)**, which served to more fully fund primary and secondary education. At the time, ESEA prohibited the establishment of a national curriculum. Implementing a national curriculum continues to be a hot debate topic today and is gaining full steam, as demonstrated by the adoption of the Common Core State Standards. As one editorial commented, the "common standards mean teaching to the best global standards of the twenty-first century."[14] Opponents of a national curriculum and national standards argue that the federal government is exceeding its authority and eroding state sovereignty.

The ESEA of 1965 provided monies to help educate children from low-income families. This portion of the ESEA is known as **Title I**. Eligibility for Title I funds is based on the number of children eligible for free or reduced-price school lunches. Schools with Title I funds have at least 40 percent of their students on free or reduced-price school lunches.[15] Eligibility for free or reduced school lunches for the 2012–2013 school year is based on family income. Texas children in a family of four with an income of less than $42,643 qualify for reduced lunches whereas children in a family of four and an income less than $29,965 qualify for free lunch.[16] Schools use funds to provide additional academic support and learning opportunities so that low-income children can master challenging curricula and meet state standards in core academic subjects. For example, funds support extra instruction in reading and mathematics, as well as special preschool, after-school, and summer programs to extend and reinforce the regular school curriculum. More than thirty thousand schools use Title I funds for the whole school, and at last count, Title I served more than seventeen million children. Of these students, approximately 60 percent were in

Economic Opportunity Act of 1964 (EOA) Implemented several social programs to promote the health, education, and general welfare of people of low socioeconomic status and was designed to put them to work.

Head Start One of the longest-running programs in the United States to address systemic poverty and education for young children and their families.

Elementary Secondary Education Act (ESEA) Designed to more fully fund primary and secondary education.

Title I Provided monies to help educate children from low-income families under the Elementary Secondary Education Act.

kindergarten through fifth grade. Therefore, it is likely that you will teach children served by Title I and teach at a Title I school.[17]

No Child Left Behind
The current reauthorization of ESEA; provides federal funding for schools that accrue high test scores and meet adequate yearly progress (AYP).

NO CHILD LEFT BEHIND.   The current reauthorization of ESEA is the No Child Left Behind Act of 2001. The **No Child Left Behind Act (NCLB)** continues the standards movement established by the National Defense Education Act and emphasizes accountability through testing. After NCLB was passed, all fifty states developed standards for what children should know and be able to do at each grade level across the curriculum. NCLB provides federal funding for schools that accrue high test scores and meet adequate yearly progress (AYP), an accountability measurement.

Opponents of NCLB and the accountability movement argue that it relies too heavily on standardized testing rather than authentic means of assessment. Although the law is still in effect, many states have applied for and have been approved for waivers from its requirements, including the requirement of AYP and that all children be proficient in reading and math by 2014. These waivers allow states to focus their efforts on the bottom 5 percent of their schools and to consider multiple forms of assessment and teacher evaluation, instead of merely standardized testing.[18]

Education of All Handicapped Children Act (EAHC) Mandated that in order to receive federal funds, states must develop and implement policies that assure a Free Appropriate Public Education (FAPE) for all children with disabilities.

THE EDUCATION OF ALL HANDICAPPED CHILDREN ACT.   In 1975, Congress passed Public Law 94-142, the **Education of All Handicapped Children Act (EAHC)**. The EAHC mandated that in order to receive federal funds, states must develop and implement policies that ensure a Free Appropriate Public Education (FAPE) for all children with disabilities.

Individuals with Disabilities Education Act (IDEA) The current reauthorization of the Education of All Handicapped Children Act; provides for inclusion, universal design, response to instruction, and differentiated instruction.

THE INDIVIDUALS WITH DISABILITIES EDUCATION ACT.   In 1990, the Education of All Handicapped Children Act was reauthorized and renamed the **Individuals with Disabilities Education Act (IDEA)**. The IDEA was reauthorized again in 1997 and 2004 and is still in effect today. The IDEA provides for inclusion, **universal design (UD)** (a broad-spectrum solution that produces buildings, products, and environments that are usable and effective for everyone, not just people with disabilities); **response to instruction (RTI)** (a multi-tiered approach to the early identification and support of students with learning and behavior needs); and **differentiated instruction (DI)** (an approach that enables teachers to plan strategically to meet the needs of every student in order to teach to the needs of each child and allow for diversity in the classroom). IDEA was the foundation for the integration and blending of early childhood education and early childhood special education. Today, every early childhood teacher is a special education teacher.

universal design (UD) A broad-spectrum solution that produces buildings, products, and environments that are usable and effective for everyone, not just people with disabilities.

response to instruction (RTI) A multitiered approach to the early identification and support of students with learning and behavior needs.

Observe and Analyze

differentiated instruction (DI) An approach that enables teachers to plan strategically to meet the needs of every student in order to teach to the needs of each child and allow for diversity in the classroom.

Providing equal education for all of the country's children continues to be one of the larger purposes of federally funded education. However, as our following discussion on the views of children shows, we are still fighting the battle of equality in the education system.

NATIONAL COMMISSION ON EXCELLENCE IN EDUCATION AND DEVELOPMENTALLY APPROPRIATE PRACTICE.   An emphasis on developmentally appropriate practice emerged in the 1980s as the nation became alarmed at the state of education. The alarm arose when the National Commission on Excellence in Education published a federal report in 1983 titled *A Nation at Risk*. The report found that students in the United States were not studying the right subjects, working hard enough, or learning enough; that teachers were ill prepared; and the schools suffered from slack and uneven standards. The emphasis on developmentally appropriate practice (DAP) arose partially in response to *A Nation at Risk* to counterbalance the claim that "America will soon be engulfed by a rising tide of mediocrity in elementary and secondary schools" and the fear that "our social structure will crack, our culture erode, our economy totter, and our national defenses weaken."[19]

Since then, education reform has become a permanent item on the national agenda, and DAP has emerged as the center of good educational practices. DAP consists of four essentials: (1) DAP requires meeting children where they are so that they can reach their goals; (2) DAP is also appropriate to age and development and is responsive to various social and cultural contexts of children's lives; (3) DAP is not only appropriate to age and development, but also challenges and promotes children's growth as members of a larger society; (4) DAP is based on knowledge—research and systematic observation—not assumptions. For the education field to meet these four essentials of DAP, it must incorporate essentials of learning, teaching, and families.[20]

Check Your Understanding: Laws

VIEWS OF CHILDREN THROUGH THE AGES

How we think about children determines how we rear them and how society responds to their needs. As you read here about how society views children, try to clarify what you believe, and change your beliefs when appropriate. Also, identify social, environmental, and political factors that tend to support each particular view. Sometimes views overlap, so it is possible to integrate ideas from several perspectives into your own particular view of children.

MINIATURE ADULTS

Childhood as we know it has not always been considered a distinct period of life. During medieval times, the notion of childhood did not exist; little distinction was made between children and adults. This concept of **children as miniature adults** was logical for the time and conditions of medieval Europe. Economic conditions did not allow a long childhood dependency. The only characteristics that separated children from adults were size and age. Children were expected to act as adults in every way, and they did so.[21]

children as miniature adults Belief that children are similar to adults and should be treated as such.

In many respects, twenty-first-century society is no different. Children are still viewed and treated as adults. Concern is growing that childhood as we knew or remembered it is disappearing. Children are viewed as pseudoadults; they dress like adults, in designer clothes and expensive footwear designed especially for them. Children as young as four years old are frequenting boutiques where they are pampered with manicures, pedicures, and the latest hair and clothing styles. Reality television shows, such as TLC's *Toddlers and Tiaras*, highlights children competing for beauty pageant prizes while wearing excessive amounts of make-up and highly sexualized and expensive clothing. Children are forced to grow up too fast, too soon.[22] Early childhood educators must help families hold on to their better instincts and let children be children, not little adults.

Encouraging children to act like adults and hurrying them toward adulthood causes conflicts between capabilities and expectations, particularly when parents and others demand adult-like behavior from children and set unrealistic expectations for them.

SINFUL CHILDREN

Based primarily on the religious belief of original sin, the view of the **child as sinful** was widely accepted in the fourteenth through the eighteenth centuries, particularly

child as sinful View that children are basically sinful, need supervision and control, and should be taught to be obedient.

in colonial North America during the Puritan era of the sixteenth and seventeenth centuries. Misbehavior was a sign of this inherent sin. Those who sought to correct misbehavior forced children to behave and used physical punishment whenever necessary. Misbehavior was taken as proof of the devil's influence, and "beating the devil out" of the child was an acceptable solution.[23]

This view of inherent sinfulness persists, manifested in the belief that children need to be controlled through strict supervision and insistence on unquestioning obedience to and respect for adults. Many private and parochial or religious schools emphasize respect, obedience, and correct behavior, responding to parents' hopes of rearing children who are less susceptible to the temptations of crime, drugs, and declining moral values. Many Christian religious conservatives advocate a biblical approach to child rearing, encouraging parents to raise their children to obey them. Thus, disobedience is still viewed as sinful, and obedience is promoted, in part through strict discipline and when deemed necessary, through physical punishment.

BLANK TABLETS

children as blank tablets View that presupposes no innate genetic code or inborn traits exist and that the sum of what a child becomes depends on the nature and quality of experience.

Earlier we discussed John Locke's belief that children were born into the world as *tabulae rasae*, or blank tablets.[24] Locke believed that children's experiences determined what they learned and, consequently, what they became. The **children as blank tablets** view presupposes no innate genetic code or inborn traits—that is, children are born with no predisposition toward any behavior except that which is characteristic of human beings. The sum of what a child becomes depends on the nature and quality of experience; in other words, environment is the primary determinant.

The blank tablet view has several implications for teaching and child rearing. If children are seen as empty vessels to be filled, the teacher's job is to fill them—to present knowledge without regard to needs, interests, or readiness for learning. What is important is that children learn what is taught. Children become what adults make of them.

GROWING PLANTS

children as growing plants View of children popularized by Froebel, which equates children to plants and teachers and parents to gardeners.

A perennially popular view of children, which dates back to Rousseau and Froebel, considers **children as growing plants**, with teachers and parents performing the role of gardeners. This is why Froebel named his program *kindergarten*—garden of children. Classrooms and homes are gardens in which children grow and mature in harmony with their natural growth patterns. As children grow and mature, they unfold, much as a flower blooms under the proper conditions. In other words, what children become results from natural growth and a nurturing environment. Two key ingredients of this natural unfolding are play and readiness. The content and process of learning are included in play, and materials and activities are designed to promote play. Children become ready for learning through maturation and play. Lack of readiness to learn indicates that children have not sufficiently matured and the natural process of unfolding has not occurred.

PROPERTY

children as property Belief that children are literally the property of their parents.

The view of **children as property** has persisted throughout history. Its foundation is that children are the property of their parents or institutions. This view is justified in part by the idea that, as creators of children, parents have a right to them and their labors; parents have broad authority and jurisdiction over their children. Interestingly, few laws interfere with the right of parents to control their children's lives, although this situation is changing somewhat as children are given more rights as courts protect and extend children's rights.

Although difficult to enforce, laws protect children from physical and emotional abuse. In addition, where there are compulsory attendance laws, parents must send their children to school. Generally, however, parents have a free hand in dealing with their children. Legislatures and courts are reluctant to interfere in what is considered a sacrosanct parent–child relationship. A widely publicized Supreme Court decision, *Troxel v. Granville*, reaffirmed this right and declared that parents have a "fundamental right to make decisions concerning the care, custody, and control" of their children.[25] Parents are generally free to exercise full authority over their children; within certain broad limits, most parents feel their children are theirs to do with as they please.

INVESTMENTS IN THE FUTURE

Closely associated with the notion of children as property is the view that children represent future wealth or potential for parents and the nation. Since medieval times, people have viewed child rearing as an investment in their future. Many parents assume (not always consciously) that, when they are no longer able to work or must retire, their children will be there to provide for them.

This view of **children as investments**, particularly in their parents' future, is being dramatically played out in contemporary society as more middle-aged adults are caring for their own aging and ill parents. Also, as a result of the Great Recession of 2007–2012, many parents have found that the investment they thought they were making in their children's education is reversed, and many children move back home with their parents after college. As of 2012, as many as 85 percent of college graduates will move back home with their families at some point.[26]

children as investments
View that investing in the care and education of children reaps future benefits for parents and society.

Over the last several decades, some U.S. social policies have been based on the view that children are future investments for society in general. Many programs are built on the underlying assumption that preventing problems in childhood leads to more productive adulthood. And many federal programs, such as Head Start, are based on the idea of conserving one of the country's greatest resources—its children.

Check Your Understanding: Beliefs

NATIVE AMERICAN EDUCATION. For several centuries, Native American children were not seen as part of this nation's great resource, and their appropriate education was given little attention. Today, however, attitudes are changing, and programs focus on providing high-quality education for Native American children. One such program in California, Project Nee-Sim-Pom, which is a collaborative effort that acknowledges the importance of the entire "family"—including home, school, and community—to the academic success of American Indian children.[27] There are several such projects in the United States today.

Federally funded programs, such as Project BabyFACE, send parent educators into Native American homes with preschoolers every other week to help families better understand early child development and learning. These parent educators come from the communities in which they work and are currently working with more than seven hundred families in rural, tribal communities spanning from Arizona to North Carolina. Their work is very hands-on and labor intensive, and it focuses on helping families support healthy development in their young children.[28]

AFRICAN AMERICAN EDUCATION. As with Native Americans, African Americans have a long history of unequal early childhood education. In 1896, the case of **Plessy v. Ferguson** established the "separate but equal" doctrine.[29] This doctrine determined that as long as the opportunities and accommodations were equal for both races, segregating people in public places, including schools, was lawful. This ruling

Plessy v. Ferguson Court ruling that established the "separate but equal" doctrine, which determined that as long as the opportunities and accommodations were equal for both races, that segregating people in public places, including schools, was lawful.

legitimized a legal tradition in which the races were kept separated under the pretense of equality. However, education, as well as many other opportunities, was not equal.

The 1954 case **Brown v. Board of Education** overturned the *Plessy v. Ferguson* ruling and paved the way for the civil rights movement and the integration of schools and other public places. The *Brown v. Board* ruling states:

> Segregation of children in public schools solely on the basis of race deprives children of the minority group of equal educational opportunities, even though the physical facilities and other "tangible" factors may be equal. The "separate but equal" doctrine adopted in *Plessy v. Ferguson* has no place in the field of public education.[30]

However, even since *Brown v. Board* and the civil rights movement, education of African American and other minority children remains unequal. Poor and minority students tend to have less access to the most effective, experienced teachers with knowledge in their content field.[31] Many of the nation's public schools today have a minority majority; minorities are rapidly emerging as the majority of public school students.[32] Schools that are minority heavy and of lower income remain highly unequal in terms of funding, qualified teachers, and curriculum. As a result, Latinos and African Americans are actually more segregated today than they were during the civil rights movement.[33]

This inequality shows up in test scores. For example, on the 2013 National Assessment of Educational Progress, or NAEP, minority students have lower reading and mathematics achievement scores than do Caucasian children.[34] This is due in large part to the history of unequal education and opportunities, testing bias, cultural bias, and other sociocultural factors. This has a profound effect on children and our country. Research shows that the underutilization of human potential reflected in the achievement gap is very costly. In fact, the existing achievement gaps impose the economic equivalent of a permanent national recession.[35]

GENDER AND EDUCATION.   Discrimination on the basis of gender persisted long after it was illegal on the basis of race or ethnicity. **Title IX** of the Education Amendments of 1972 stated that:

> No person in the United States shall, on the basis of sex, be excluded from participation in, be denied the benefits of, or be subjected to discrimination under any program or activity receiving federal financial assistance.[36]

However, even with Title IX in place, research indicates that the genders are still not equal in education. For example, there are still gaps in the test scores in areas of math and science between girls and boys,[37] and there is a shortage of girls in certain science-, technology-, engineering-, and math-related (STEM-related) classes and career fields.[38] Research shows that in countries with high levels of gender equality, like Iceland, Sweden, and the UK, the math gender gap is significantly smaller, has disappeared entirely, or is even reversed.[39] Countries with low levels of gender equality have larger gender gaps in mathematics.[40] Gender inequality has a direct effect on the performance of children, and gender inequality still persists in the United States, with negative effects for all our children.

CHILDREN WITH DISABILITIES.   Attempting to improve the lives of those with differences is relatively new in the United States and other countries. It has not always been a U.S. priority to accommodate differences. People with mental impairments were put in group homes, out of the public eye, and often abused. Deaf and mute children were often considered "idiots" and not worth teaching. Most communities did not have schools for children with disabilities, so if parents wanted their children with disabilities to be educated, they often had to send their children away to live in state-run (and often unregulated) group homes.[41]

Brown v. Board of Education Court ruling that stated, "Segregation of children in public schools solely on the basis of race deprives children of the minority group of equal educational opportunities, even though the physical facilities and other 'tangible' factors may be equal. The 'separate but equal' doctrine adopted in *Plessy v. Ferguson* has no place in the field of public education."

Title IX Amended the Constitution to state, "No person in the United States shall, on the basis of sex, be excluded from participation in, be denied the benefits of, or be subjected to discrimination under any program or activity receiving federal financial assistance."

The history of disabilities education has been one mostly of exclusion and separation. In attempts to address individual children's needs, separate educations were considered to be best practice. It was not until the Education for All Handicapped Children Act of 1975 that the trend slowly began to reverse.[42] This act required local education authorities to provide educational services within the community, which allowed children with disabilities to remain living with their families.[43]

Although the Education for All Handicapped Children Act might be considered the beginning of the inclusion movement, and children with disabilities were finally provided access to schools within their districts, this still created two educational tracks—one for nondisabled children and a second for children with disabilities. It was not until 1990, when the law was reauthorized and renamed the Individuals with Disabilities Education Act, that support and related services were provided for the education of children with disabilities in their general education settings.[44] Even more recently, inclusionary classroom practices, medication, and various therapies are the latest developments in attempts to address and accommodate children's different needs and to incorporate and accept children with disabilities into the educational mainstream.

However, even with these accommodations, many children still fall through the cracks. Just as the racial/ethnic achievement gap produces national economic consequences so does the gap between children with disabilities and those without disabilities. For example, while nationally the unemployment rate is 8.4 percent, more than 13 percent of individuals with disabilities are unemployed.[45] In addition, the myth persists that people with disabilities are unable to work or are inadequate workers, but most people with disabilities are able and willing to work just as hard and efficiently as their peers without disabilities.[46] Clearly, the United States still has much to do to ensure that we educate all children to their fullest capacity.

The Individuals with Disabilities Education Act (IDEA) supports and provides services for the education of children who have disabilities in a general education setting. What can teachers and families do to ensure children benefit from IDEA as much as possible?

child centered Term meaning that every child is a unique and special individual; that all children have a right to an education that helps them grow and develop to their fullest; that children are active participants in their own education and development; and teachers should consider children's ideas, preferences, learning styles, and interests in planning for and implementing instructional practices.

A RETURN ON INVESTMENT. Head Start and child intervention programs are products of the view that children are investments in the future. This is a human capital, or investment, rationale for child care, preschools, and other services. Research about the HighScope Perry Preschool program is frequently cited to demonstrate how high-quality preschool programs save taxpayers money. The latest HighScope preschool research study reports that for each dollar invested, $17.07 is returned to taxpayers. This monetary return results from students who attend high-quality preschools being involved in less crime, staying in school longer, and paying higher taxes as adults.[47]

Child-Centered Education. As the public increasingly reexamines its views of children and comes to see children as a return on investment, educators are responding by implementing more child-centered approaches. **Child centered** is a term that means every child is a unique and special individual; all children have a right to an education that helps them grow and develop to their fullest; children are active participants in their own education and development; and that teachers should consider children's ideas, preferences, learning styles, and interests in planning for and implementing instructional practices. The Voice from the Field, "How to Teach in a Child-Centered Program," describes a real-life program and includes guidelines for involving children

VOICE FROM THE FIELD

COMPETENCY BUILDER

How to Teach in a Child-Centered Program

The City and Country School, founded by Caroline Pratt in 1914, believes an educator's greatest challenge isn't to teach children, but rather to create an environment that keeps their inherent curiosity intact. The C&C classroom serves as an ideal place for children to explore, experiment, learn, and grow, both as individuals and as a group.

In the partnership of learning among children and teachers, community is lived through purposeful experiences that foster responsibility, cooperation, active participation, care and respect—qualities necessary to the life of a democratic society.

Lower School classrooms are equipped with ample space and an abundant supply of carefully chosen, open-ended materials, including blocks, paint, clay, paper, wood, sand, and water. These materials, along with teachers who expertly guide their use, promote children's active involvement and independence while also inspiring creativity and cooperation. Children use the materials to explore, experiment, and in the process, build a foundation in the academic disciplines of social studies, reading, writing, math, and science. As the children move through the Lower School, academic skills are taught more formally. Systematic teaching of reading begins in Kindergarten.

GUIDELINE 1: Arrange the Classroom to Support Child-Centered Learning

Example: C&C teachers, rather than filling the room with teacher-driven materials, display the work and current interests of the children, such as child-created murals that may depict their social studies. Furthermore, the design of the room provides materials and space that allow children to experiment with sand and water; research their interests with books; and recreate their learning through blocks, clay, woodshop materials, artwork, writing, and dramatic play.

GUIDELINE 2: Provide Easily Accessible Materials and Supplies

Example: The classrooms at C&C are simple in design, with child-accessible shelves filled with clearly labeled and organized open-ended materials and tools. The children keep their spaces orderly, and are responsible for classroom tasks, such as distributing snack and cleaning tables. In this and other ways, the children have ownership of their space.

GUIDELINE 3: Provide Opportunities for Children to Move Around and Engage in Active Learning

Example: Woodworking, block, and dramatic play offer children opportunities to use their bodies and minds. For example, beginning with four year olds, children start working with real woodworking tools in their classroom. If they want a boat or a car to use in their play, they can create one. By trusting children to achieve their visions in such a substantial way, they gain a tremendous sense of autonomy, accomplishment, and respect. Furthermore, children at C&C are not restricted to sitting at a desk or table as they find a comfortable way to work.

GUIDELINE 4: Provide Materials and Space for Focused Hands-On Activities

Example: As social studies topics are explored in-depth, children engage in active learning by first exploring their ideas through research, such as trips, and then reconstruct their knowledge in a number of ways. For example, as six year olds learn about transportation, they may visit Grand Central Station where they use research logs to take notes of their observations (in pictures or writing); they later might create books based on their research and then plan, build, and accessorize a large-scale Grand Central Station and railroads with blocks and art materials.

GUIDELINE 5: Arrange Furniture so that Children can Work and Play Together

Example: Tables and workspaces are provided so children can work together, side by side, and across from one another, rather than in desks and rows. C&C classrooms also provide ample open space for children to work with blocks and on large-scale group work, such as murals.

GUIDELINE 6: Support Cooperative Learning

Example: Our youngest children share materials, space, and group responsibilities. When children ages four and older recreate their research and interests in blocks or plays, they share and discuss what they've learned as a group, then plan the layout and design, or scripts and sets, together as a whole group, and work on smaller, discrete tasks in small groups. In this way, the goals of the whole group are achieved in a variety of social configurations and contexts for democratic decision-making.

GUIDELINE 7
Provide for Individual Differences and Individualized Instruction

Example: After studying the operations of a restaurant, the six-year-old children plan the opening of a real restaurant in the classroom.

They can work on areas of specific interest to them, such as cooking, menu creation, organizing the space, practicing communicating with their customers, and writing down orders, thus allowing each child to take ownership of his or her learning. Teachers work alongside the child and challenge each child to explore their strengths and take time to work on areas where they are less experienced.

GUIDELINE 8
Provide Ample Time for Children to Engage in Cooperative Activities

Example: As eight year olds learn multiplication tables, they are also working on opening the school post office. In order to quickly tally orders, they must know their multiplication tables. This real-world need for a rote skill solidifies the knowledge in a concrete activity, while group-mates are relying on them to keep the post office running smoothly. The motivation to learn the math facts is intrinsic to the group's need and to the job at hand.

City and Country School remains committed to its founding principles and continues to promote and exemplify progressive education.

Source: Contributed by Jennifer Moran, Director of Publications and Archives, City and Country School, New York, NY.

in active learning. After you read the feature article, consider how you could apply the eight guidelines to your work with young children. It can be a valuable tool to help you assess whether programs support child-centered learning. The Whole Child Initiative, put forth by the Association for Supervision and Curriculum Development (ASCD), promotes child-centered practices because they will lead to children who are healthy, safe, engaged, supported, and challenged in their education. We redefine what a successful learner is and how we measure success by keeping in mind these guiding principles about child-centered education:[48]

In this video observe how the teacher teaches and interacts with the child in a very child-centered way.

Implications for Teaching

- All children have a right to an education that helps them grow and develop to their fullest. This basic premise is at the heart of our understanding of child-centered education. Base your daily interactions with children on the fundamental question, "Am I teaching and supporting each child in his/her growth and development across all domains—social, emotional, physical, linguistic, and intellectual?" Such teaching is at the heart of developmentally appropriate practice.

- Every child is a unique and special individual. Consequently, teach individual children and be respectful of and account for their individual uniqueness of age, gender, culture, temperament, and learning style.

- Children are active participants in their own education and development. This means that they should be mentally involved and physically active in learning what they need to know and do.

- Consider children's ideas, preferences, learning styles, and interests in your planning for and implementation of instructional practices.

Child-centered education has been an important foundation of early childhood education since the time of Froebel. As a professional, you will want to make your teaching and practice child centered. In addition, you will want to advocate for the inherent right of every child to a child-centered education.

All great educators have believed in the basic goodness of children; the teacher is to provide the environment for this goodness to manifest itself. A central theme of

Luther, Comenius, Pestalozzi, Froebel, Montessori, and Dewey is that we must do our work as educators well, and we must really care about those whom we have been called to serve. This indeed is the essence of child-centered education.

Reflect and Apply: Child Centered

ACCOMMODATING DIVERSE LEARNERS

In this text, we have discussed some of the ways in which society's views of children affect the education they receive. Throughout U.S. history, concepts of children as a whole, and of subgroups based on individual differences such as race, culture, and disability status, in particular, have kept many children from receiving their rightful education. In the past, exclusionary practices were formal. Today, exclusionary practices are not socially accepted, yet in many ways they still persist and affect children's education as revealed by the achievement and gender gaps we previously discussed.

Inclusion practices are considered by many to be in the best interest of children both with and without developmental disabilities. **Inclusion** is generally defined as educating typically developing students in the same classroom as students who have various disabilities. Although inclusion has been identified as the preferred method of delivering services to children with special needs by the Division for Early Childhood of the Council for Exceptional Children and the National Association for the Education of Young Children, teachers and policy makers have yet to determine a universal model for delivering inclusive services.

Here is something you should consider: Inclusion is not just a school issue; it extends to the communities in which children and their families live. This means that you must consider not only the varying abilities and disabilities of your students, but also the context in which they occur on a larger societal level. Children's differences exist not only in the classroom, but also in their homes and communities. This means that children's disabilities occur within the context of various cultures, religions, ethnicities, and socioeconomic backgrounds. As a result, like any other classroom, diversity is as much a consideration as the abilities and disabilities of your students. You should support and nourish diversity in the inclusive classroom.

You may be faced with parents and possibly other teachers who are uncomfortable with inclusion practices. "I know Ella needs to be in the classroom, too," Kathy Mason, a mother of a typically developing kindergartener, says of her daughter's classmate, Olivia, who has autism. "But, sometimes I really think that she disrupts the classroom and my daughter's education gets interrupted. My daughter's education shouldn't be put in jeopardy just because Olivia has autism." As a teacher, it can be difficult juggling the needs of typically developing children and children with learning differences, especially when parents are not supportive or may have concerns about the quality of their children's education. But inclusion teacher Brandy Hightower maintains that the children in her classroom benefit from inclusion. "Olivia has really improved. She used to have meltdowns almost every day. In the beginning, it was really difficult—it took a lot of work on my part, but I think it's paying off. Olivia is learning and is a part of the group. She's getting the education and the peer interaction she deserves. But the others are doing well, too. At first, the other students weren't sure about Olivia. But now Olivia is a part of the group, and I've really noticed that the other kids are much more responsive and respectful of differences. I think this arrangement has improved education for everyone—not just Olivia."

inclusion Generally defined as educating typically developing students in the same classroom as students who have various disabilities.

IMPLICATIONS FOR TEACHING

How can you make inclusion work in your classroom? Here are some pointers from Brandy:

- Inclusive classrooms don't exist in isolation; cooperation is key. Adults—teachers, parents, administrators, and other professionals—must collaborate to train one another, plan, support, and respond to challenges.

- Get the parents involved. Inclusion cannot occur just in the classroom. If a concerned parent either explicitly or implicitly discourages the inclusion of a child into the classroom, her attitude will likely be picked up by her daughter and may be reflected in the classroom. Inclusion, like all social movements, starts at home.

  - At the beginning of the year, invite the parents of your classroom to a meeting and encourage the parents of children with differences to discuss their story. What has it been like for Olivia? What have been her struggles and triumphs? What are Olivia's gifts that make her special? The more parents can identify with Olivia as a child and with her parents as advocates, the more they can empathize and approach inclusion as a positive experience.

  - Assure your parents that you consider the needs of all of the children to be of equal and paramount importance. Your goal is to make the school year beneficial and positive for everyone. Encourage parents to come to you with their concerns or questions and remember to respect their roles as parents.

  - The process of building an inclusion experience may be rocky at times. Ask for patience and support, and be up-front about your needs as a teacher. Do you want volunteers or parent aides? Let the parents know. Frustration on the parents' part is likely to come from a sense of powerlessness or inactivity. If you let parents know that you not only value their concerns and time, but would value their help, input, and contributions, the road will be much smoother.

  - Tell parents that you have a zero-tolerance policy when it comes to bullying and teasing. Ask that they help to carry over this policy in their homes.

- The inclusive classroom is a starting point for children, not something they have to earn. Remember, each child has the right to an equal education. This means that if a child lacks certain skill sets, like toilet training, has a communication deficit, or has difficulty transitioning, the program needs to accommodate the child; the child does not accommodate the program. Inclusion classrooms are a place in which children are encouraged, and when necessary, helped, to participate.

- Support inclusion in your classroom in these ways:

  - Arrange the classroom in a way that is accessible to a student like Olivia. Make sure that his or her schedule is individualized, visual, and easily accessible. Be sure to provide a quiet place where he or she can recuperate from meltdowns or sensory overload.

  - On the first day of class, have students sit in a circle and share about themselves. Let children tell their classmates their names, where they are from, something they are good at and something that is difficult for them. This sharing establishes from the beginning a positive sense of differences and similarities.

ACTIVITIES FOR PROFESSIONAL DEVELOPMENT

ETHICAL DILEMMA

"WHY DON'T MY KIDS GET THEIR FAIR SHARE?"

Latisha is a novice first grade teacher in Rocky Springs School District. Her class of twenty-eight children includes fifteen Hispanic students, nine African American students, and four Vietnamese students. Latisha's room is sparsely furnished, many of the tables and chairs need repair, and the classroom library of thirty-seven books is old and worn. Last week, at an orientation for pre-K–3 teachers held across town at the new Valley View Ranch elementary school, Latisha learned that the students there are 90 percent white and class size averages nineteen. A tour of the classrooms revealed the latest in furniture, learning materials, and technology, with well-stocked classroom libraries. Latisha has read the latest research about how school districts invest fewer dollars in resources in poorer neighborhoods. She is very concerned about the unequal distribution of resources in the school district, and she knows her children are not getting their fair share.

What should Latisha do? Should she just keep quiet and hope things get better? Should she advocate for her students by using Facebook to organize a group of her colleagues who share her concerns? Should Latisha start a blog about the unequal distribution of resources in the district to raise support for her views? Or, should Latisha take some other course of action? What should Latisha do? What would you do?

ACTIVITIES TO APPLY WHAT YOU LEARNED

1. We say that one reason that knowing about the past is important is because it informs current practices. Identify three current educational practices and for each one describe how they are related to past practices and ideas. One example could be the use of child-centered practices to help all children learn. Share your conclusions with your classmates on your online discussion board.

2. **KEY ASSESSMENT:** Write a brief historical summary of the major ideas of five educational pioneers you read about in this text. You are limited to fifty words for each person and are to write as though you were the historical figure. For example, for Locke: "At birth the mind is a blank slate and experiences are important for making impressions on the mind. I believe learning occurs best through the senses. A proper education begins early in life, and hands-on experiences are an important part of education." Use PowerPoint to post your summaries to your class discussion board. Use the rubric provided to guide your work.

3. If you were to choose only one of the views of children discussed in this chapter to describe today's children, which one would it be? Explain in a 250-word essay your reasons for your choice. Post your essay to your class bulletin board and invite comments.

4. Think about and reflect on your attitudes toward the inclusive classroom. How will your attitudes influence how you will teach? Now reflect on what you will need to do to prepare yourself for teaching in your inclusive classroom. Make a prioritized list of the things you will have to do. Now state how you will implement your plan. Share your plan with your professor and ask for feedback.

LINKING TO LEARNING

The following agencies and programs, which can be located easily online, provide additional information about topics discussed in this chapter.

Friedrich Wilhelm Froebel
Biography and bibliography of the father of the kindergarten.

John Locke
The Internet Encyclopedia of Philosophy's entry on John Locke, including his writings and a list of sources.

Martin Luther
Provides links to many of Luther's writings online.

Maria Montessori
Historical perspective of her life and teaching methods.

Robert Owen
A bibliography of writings by Robert Owen.

Jean Heinrich Pestalozzi
A page about Pestalozzi similar to that about Rousseau.

Jean-Jacques Rousseau
Contains a brief statement on education by Rousseau and links to other Rousseau sites.

Dalton School
A private school that focuses on meeting the needs of a very diverse student population.

City and Country School
A co-educational progressive school that welcomes ages two through thirteen.

CHAPTER

5

THEORIES APPLIED to TEACHING and LEARNING

Foundations for Practice

LEARNING OUTCOMES

1. Explain Piaget's theory of cognitive development.
2. Describe Vygotsky's sociocultural theory and how you can apply it.
3. Explain how Gardner's theory of multiple intelligences contributes to early childhood education.
4. Explain behaviorism and how to apply it to your teaching.
5. Describe Erikson's stages of psychosocial development and their implications for teaching.
6. Explain Maslow's theory of self-actualization/human motivation.
7. Explain Bronfenbrenner's ecological theory of human development.

HERE we discuss the pioneering work of theorists who have contributed to our knowledge and understanding of how children learn, grow, and develop cognitively, behaviorally, and socially. Theorists Jean Piaget and Lev Vygotsky laid the foundation for the practice of *constructivism*, which is based on the theory that children construct their own knowledge and that their knowledge is unique for each child. We also discuss the multiple intelligences theory of Howard Gardner, which maintains that intelligence based on IQ is much too limiting and that children possess many different intelligences; the psychosocial theory of Erik Erikson, which explains how children develop socially and emotionally; the basic needs theory of Abraham Maslow, which stresses the role of basic needs in learning; the cultural context theory of Urie Bronfenbrenner, which encourages us to consider how environments influence children's development; and the behaviorist approaches to learning of B.F. Skinner and Albert Bandura, which emphasize the roles of stimulus-response behavior and observation in children's learning.

Teaching without an understanding of the various theories and an understanding of how children learn and develop is like driving off the highway with no idea of where you are going. Theories guide and direct us on the roadways of teaching. Sure, off-roading can be good weekend fun, but when you are serious about where you want to go, you can't beat an interstate highway! The same is true of using theories to guide your professional practice. A **theory** is a statement of principles and ideas used to explain how things happen. In our case, theories explain how children learn and develop.

Theories explain how children grow and change physically, socially, emotionally, and intellectually over time. The theories of Jean Piaget and Erik Erikson are age related or stage related because they describe what children are able to do, cognitively and socioemotionally, as they grow and mature.

Understanding and using learning and developmental theories are an important part of your professional practice for these reasons.

- *Guidance.* Theories help you understand how, why, where, and when learning occurs. As a result, they guide you in developing programs for children that support and enhance their learning. For example, knowledge about how children learn directly influences classroom arrangements and the early childhood curriculum—what you teach; and how to teach. For example, developmentally appropriate practice (DAP) and other teaching approaches stress the importance of matching children's developmental stages with instructional practices. Developing programs and curriculum is an important part of your professional practice.

- *Evaluation.* Evaluation of children's development and learning is another important job of all teachers. Theories describe behaviors and identify what children are able to do at certain ages. You can use this information to evaluate children's learning and plan for teaching.

- *Decision-making.* Early childhood teachers make decisions every day about their instructional practices. Many ongoing decisions involve matching what and how you teach to each child's unique developmental characteristics.

- *Communication.* Theories enable you to explain to others, especially parents and families, the complex process of learning and what you and they can expect of children. Communicating with parents and others with clarity and understanding about how children learn is one of the most important jobs for all early

theory A set of
explanations of how
children develop and learn.

childhood professionals. To do this, you need to know the theories that explain children's growth, development, and learning.

Keep in mind these reasons for why theories are an important part of your professional practice as we take an in-depth look at learning and behavioral theories.

PIAGET AND CONSTRUCTIVIST LEARNING THEORY

Jean Piaget's (1896–1980) learning theory is about cognitive development; it explains how children think, understand, and learn. His theory is basically a logico-mathematical theory; that is, cognitive development is perceived as consisting primarily of logical and mathematical abilities, such as numeration, seriation, classification, and temporal (time) relationships.

In addition, Piaget, along with John Dewey and Lev Vygotsky, laid the foundation for constructivism, a cognitive theory of development and learning.

constructivism Theory that
emphasizes the active role
of children in developing
their understanding and
learning.

Constructivism is the cognitive process by which children organize, structure, and restructure their experiences. This is an ongoing lifelong process in which existing schemes of thought are modified and enriched through interaction with the physical and social world. The *constructivist approach* supports the belief that children actively seek knowledge; it explains children's cognitive development, provides guidance for how and what to teach, and provides direction for how to arrange learning environments. Active involvement is basic to Piaget's cognitive theory. Piaget believed that through direct experiences with the physical world children develop intelligence.

Generally, the term *intelligence* suggests intelligence quotient, or IQ—that which is measured on an intelligence test. But this is not what Piaget means by intelligence. Instead, intelligence is the cognitive, or mental, process by which children acquire knowledge; in this sense, intelligence is "to know." It is synonymous with "thinking" in that it involves the use of mental operations to mentally and physically interact with the environment.

In addition, constructivist teachers build on their children's past knowledge and experiences to guide their teaching. For example, children bring many kinds of musical experiences—singing, dancing—with them to preschool. You can have children sing the ABC song to help them learn the alphabet and have them clap the syllables in their name, for example, La (clap) shan (clap) dra (clap). Other basic concepts of Piaget's theory of cognitive development include *active learning*, *adaptation*, *schemes*, *assimilation*, and *accommodation*.

ACTIVE LEARNING

active learning The view
that children develop
knowledge and learn
by being physically and
mentally engaged in
learning activities.

Active learning is an essential part of constructivism. Active learning means that children construct knowledge through physical and mental activity and that they are actively involved in problem-setting and problem-solving activities.

Think for a minute about what would happen if you gave six-month-old Emily some blocks. What would she try to do with them? More than likely, she would put them in her mouth; she would try to eat the blocks. But if you gave blocks to Emily's three-year-old sister Madeleine, she would try to stack them. Both Emily and Madeleine want to be actively involved with things and people as active learners. Children are naturally curious and want to seek out information that helps them make sense of it. Very young children do this by experimenting with everything in their environment. This is why providing an enriched environment of learning materials is so important in the home and classroom. Active involvement comes naturally for all children and is an essential part of how they learn.

ADAPTATION

The adaptive process operates at the cognitive level much as it does at the physical level. A newborn's intelligence is expressed through reflexive motor actions such as sucking, grasping, head turning, and swallowing. Children develop their intelligence through this process of **adaptation** to the environment through reflexive actions.[1] Piaget uses adaptation in the same sense that you and I use *learning* and *development*. Children develop and learn (adapt) in response to their environments.

Through interactions with their environment, children organize sensations and experiences. The quality of the environment and the nature of children's experiences play a major role in the development of their intelligence.

SCHEMES.   **Schemes** refer to organized units of knowledge that children develop through the adaptation process. Infants use their reflexive actions such as sucking and grasping to build their concepts and understanding of the world. Think of schemes as children's thoughts and actions that result from their experiences. Children mentally organize their experiences beginning at birth. Their schemes change as they develop and have new experiences. At birth, children's schemes are reflexive schemes. They are sensorimotor-based schemes, such as sucking, grasping, and gross motor activities. Schemes drive development and learning. A child interprets or understands new experiences with the schemes he or she has.

In the process of developing new schemes, Piaget ascribed primary importance to physical activity. Physical activity leads to mental stimulus, which in turn leads to mental activity. There is not a clear line between physical and mental activity in infancy and early childhood. Piaget stressed that physical activity plays an important role in children's development of schemes. Physical activity leads to mental stimulus, which in turn leads to mental activity. This is why early childhood teachers provide active learning by arranging classrooms to allow children to explore with a wide variety of learning materials. Consequently, early childhood teachers provide for active learning by arranging classrooms to allow children to explore and interact with people and objects.

ASSIMILATION AND ACCOMMODATION.   Assimilation and accommodation are mental processes by which children change old schemes and develop new schemes. **Assimilation** is the taking in of sensory data through experiences and impressions and incorporating this information into existing knowledge (schemes). Assimilation then is using an existing scheme to deal with a new object or situation. Through assimilation, children use old methods or experiences to understand and make sense of new information and experiences. Emily used assimilation when she put a block in her mouth and ended up sucking on it. The block was fine for sucking, but not for eating. When Emily encountered a new toy, she responded to it with her existing scheme of exploring something new by using her existing scheme of "putting it in mouth and sucking." When Emily's mom put food a spoon and tried to feed Emily for the first time, Emily "ate" by sucking. She applied her sucking scheme to the act of eating food.

Accommodation is the process by which children change their way of thinking, behaving, or believing to come into accord with reality. Accommodation involves changing old methods to adjust to new situations. Whereas Emily tried to eat the blocks, Madeleine wanted to stack them. Through accommodation she had learned not to try to eat them. Madeline accommodated and developed a new scheme for dealing with blocks that includes "stacking." Bobby, who is familiar with kittens because he has several cats at home, may, when he sees a dog for the first time, call it a kitty. He has assimilated dog into his organization of kitty. However, Bobby must change (i.e., accommodate) his model of what constitutes "kittyness" to exclude dogs. He will start to construct, or build, a scheme for dog and thus what "dogness" represents.[2] The twin processes of assimilation and accommodation, viewed as an integrated and

adaptation The process of building schemes through interaction with the environment. Consists of two complementary processes—assimilation and accommodation.

schemes Organized units of knowledge.

assimilation The process of fitting new information into existing schemes.

accommodation Changing or altering existing schemes or creating new ones in response to new information.

Adaptation Process

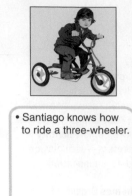

Disequilibrium

- Santiago rides a bicycle with training wheels for the first time.
- Santiago uses the motor process knowledge of a three-wheeler to fit the motor process needed to ride an upright bicycle with training wheels.

- Santiago's dad removes his training wheels.
- Santiago cannot assimilate his old motor process of riding a bicycle with training wheels to the motor process needs of a regular bicycle.
- Santiago falls off the bicycle.

- Santiago knows how to ride a three-wheeler.

- Santiago uses his old scheme of riding a three-wheeler and modifies it to fit the motor process needs of riding a bicycle with training wheels.
- Santiago becomes proficient at riding with training wheels.

- Santiago builds on his knowledge of riding a three-wheeler and a bicycle with training wheels.
- Santiago modifies his knowledge by gaining new experience without training wheels.
- Santiago has accommodated new knowledge and can now ride a regular bicycle with ease.

Initial Scheme

Assimilation

Accommodation

FIGURE 5.1 | Assimilation and Accommodation

functioning whole, constitutes adaptation. Figure 5.1 demonstrates the assimilation and accommodation process as Santiago learns to ride a bike. After reviewing this figure, see if you understand this concept in "Check Your Understanding: Assimilation and Accommodation" in the pop-up feature.

Check Your Understanding: Assimilation and Accommodation

equilibrium A balance between existing and new schemes, developed through assimilation and accommodation of new information.

EQUILIBRIUM.   **Equilibrium** is the balance between assimilation and accommo-dation. Children assimilate, or fit, new data into their already-existing knowledge (i.e., scheme) of reality and the world. If the new data can be immediately assimilated, then equilibrium occurs. However, if children are unable to assimilate the new data easily, they try to accommodate their way of thinking, acting, or perceiving to account for the new data and restore equilibrium to their intellectual system. Assimilation and accommodation work together creating a balance between the child's existing schemes and advancing his or her adaptation or learning through new experiences. When a child's schemes are appropriate (at that moment) for dealing with experiences, then equilibrium occurs. However, when the child cannot fit new experience into his or her existing schemes (assimilation), the child will try to restore equilibrium by incorporating the new experience and modifying existing schemes (accommodation). When Emily is first given food from a spoon, she accommodates or changes her scheme of sucking to include eating food from a spoon.

Children have difficulty with assimilation and accommodation when new experiences are radically different from their past experiences. For this reason Piaget insisted that new experiences must have a connection to previous experiences. It is imperative that you learn and understand as much as possible about the children you teach—their culture, family, and community—so that you can tap into and build on their past experiences.

PIAGET'S STAGES OF INTELLECTUAL DEVELOPMENT

Piaget contended that developmental stages are the same for all children, including the atypical child, and that all children progress through each stage in the same order. Thus, the sequence of growth through the developmental stages does not vary, even though the ages at which progression occurs do vary. Figure 5.2 summarizes Piaget's first three developmental stages and provides examples of stage-related characteristics.

The process of development from stage to stage is gradual and continual and occurs over a period of time as a result of maturation and experiences. No simple sets of exercises will cause children to move up the developmental ladder. Rather, ongoing developmentally appropriate activities lead to conceptual understanding.

SENSORIMOTOR STAGE.   Piaget's first stage, the **sensorimotor stage**, begins at birth and lasts about two years. During this period, children use their senses and motor reflexes—seeing, sucking, grasping—to build their knowledge of the world and to develop intellectually. Reflexive actions help children construct a mental scheme of what is suckable, for example, and what is not (i.e., what can fit into the mouth and what cannot) and what sensations (e.g., warm and cold) occur by sucking. Children use the grasping reflex in much the same way to build schemes of what can and cannot be grasped. Through these innate sensory and reflexive actions, they develop an increasingly complex and individualized hierarchy of schemes. What children become, physically and intellectually, is related to these sensorimotor functions and interactions.

During the sensorimotor period, children:

- Are dependent on and use their innate reflexive actions
- Develop initial object permanency (the idea that objects can exist without being seen, heard, or touched)
- Are egocentric, whereby they see themselves as the center of the world and believe events are caused by them

sensorimotor stage The stage during which children learn through the senses and motor activities.

I. The Sensorimotor Stage

Appropriate Age:
Birth to about 2 years

Characteristics:
Children use their innate sensorimotor systems of sucking, grasping, and gross-body activities to build schemes. They begin to develop object permanency and "think" with their senses and their innate reflexive actions. In addition, children "solve" problems by playing with toys and using everyday "tools" such as spoons to learn to feed themselves.

II. The Preoperational Stage

Appropriate Age:
2 to 7 years

Characteristics:
Children depend on concrete representations and "think" with concrete materials. They use the world of here and now as a frame of reference. Children in this stage enjoy accelerated language development. They are very egocentric in thought and action and therefore tend to internalize events. Children think everything has a reason or purpose. Children are perceptually bound and therefore make judgments based primarily on how things look.

III. The Concrete Operations Stage

Appropriate Age:
7 to 12 years

Characteristics:
Children are able to reverse their thought processes and conserve and understand numbers. Children depend on how things look for decision-making, but they are less egocentric. They begin to structure time and space and to think logically. In this stage, children can apply logic to concrete situations.

FIGURE 5.2 | Piaget's Stages of Cognitive Development

- Are dependent on concrete representations (i.e., things) rather than symbols (i.e., words, pictures) for information
- Become by the end of the second year, less reliant on sensorimotor reflexive actions and begin to use symbols for things that are not present

Teachers' Role in Sensorimotor Stage. During the sensorimotor period, teachers respond to and match their caregiving and teaching to children when they do the following:

- Provide interactive toys, such as rattles, mobiles, and pound-a-peg
- Provide many and varied multisensory materials to promote investigation and sensory involvement, including household items such as pots, pans, and spoons
- Provide environments in which infants and toddlers can crawl and explore, keeping infants out of their cribs, seats, swings, and playpens as much as safely possible
- Play hide-and-seek games that involve looking for hidden objects
- Provide rich language environments that include talking and singing and encouraging infants and toddlers to interact with people and objects

preoperational stage
The stage of cognitive development in which young children are capable of mental representations.

PREOPERATIONAL STAGE. Piaget's second stage, the **preoperational stage**, begins at age two and ends at approximately seven years old. These years are at the center stage of early childhood education.

Representation. During the preoperational stage, a child's major accomplishment is the ability to use symbols to represent objects and events—symbols such as language, pictures, picture books, maps, drawings, and make-believe play. At about age two years, children's ability to use language rapidly accelerates, and at about age three years they begin to understand that a picture of a house, for example, stands for a house in the real world. This ability to think symbolically, to visualize things mentally, opens many opportunities for children to develop cognitively and increases their knowledge of their environment.

Children in the preoperational stage make judgments based on how things look. When they look at an object that has multiple characteristics—such as a big, round, yellow crayon—they see whichever of those qualities first catches their eye. Thus their knowledge is based mainly on what they are able to see, simply because they do not yet have *operational* intelligence, or the ability to think logically.

Conservation. The absence of operations makes it impossible for preoperational children to *conserve*, or determine that the quantity of an object does not change simply because a transformation occurs in its physical appearance. For example, if you show preoperational children two identical rows of coins (see Figure 5.3) and ask whether each row has the same number of coins, the children will answer "yes." If you then space out the coins in one row and ask whether the two rows still have the same number of coins, they will reply that more coins are in one row because it's longer. These children are basing their judgment on what they see—namely, the spatial extension of one row beyond the other row. This example also illustrates that preoperational children are not able to *reverse* thought or action, which requires mentally putting the row back to its original length. Figure 5.3 shows other examples of conservation tasks.

In addition, preoperational children believe and act as though everything happens for a specific reason or purpose. This explains children's constant and recurring questions about why things happen and how things work.

▶ Observe and Analyze

Conservation Task	Original Representation	Transformation	Preoperational Children's Responses
Number	"Are there the same number of pennies in each row?"	"Now are there the same number in each row or does one row have more?"	Original Representation: "Yes, the rows are the same." Transformation: "The longer row has more."
Length	"Is each line just as long as the other?"	"Now are the two lines equal in length or is one longer?"	Original Representation: "Yes, they are the same." Transformation: "The one on top is longer."
Mass	"Is there the same amount of clay in each ball?"	"Now does each piece have the same amount of clay or does one have more?"	Original Representation: "Yes, they are the same." Transformation: "The longer ball has more clay."
Liquid	"Is there the same amount of water in each glass?"	"Now does each glass have the same amount of water or does one have more?"	Original Representation: "There is the same amount in each glass." Transformation: "The tall glass has more."

FIGURE 5.3 | Piagetian Conservation Tasks

Egocentrism. Preoperational children believe that everyone thinks as they think and act as they do for the same reasons. They have a hard time putting themselves in another's place, and it is difficult for them to be sympathetic and empathetic. The way preoperational children talk reflects their *egocentrism*. For example, in explaining about his dog running away, three-year-old Matt might say something like this: "And we couldn't find him . . . and my dad he looked . . . and we were glad." Matt assumes you have the same point of view he does and know the whole story. The details are missing for you, not for Matt.

Self-Talk. Young children's egocentrism also helps explain why they tend to talk at each other rather than with each other and why they talk to themselves. Perhaps you have observed a four-year-old busily engrossed in putting a puzzle together and saying to herself, "Which piece comes next?" Children use this **self-talk**, which Piaget called *egocentric speech*, to guide their thinking and actions. Egocentrism, quite simply, is a fact of cognitive development in the early childhood years.

self-talk Speech directed to oneself that helps guide one's behavior.

Teachers' Role in Preoperational Stage. During the preoperational period of development, teachers provide the following:

- Toys and materials for pretend play, to help children to learn through imagining and doing
- Building blocks of many kinds, to create a foundation for mathematical concepts, such as classifying, seriating, spatial relationships, and to develop children's visual and motor skills

- Materials for arts and crafts
- Many and varied kinds of concrete manipulatives, such as puzzles, and craft materials to support children's active learning
- Ongoing developmentally appropriate language opportunities involving speaking, listening, reading, and writing to develop skills necessary for reading

concrete operations stage
The stage of cognitive development during which children's thought is logical and can organize concrete experiences.

CONCRETE OPERATIONS STAGE.   Piaget's third stage of cognitive development is the **concrete operations stage**. Children in this stage, from about age seven to about age twelve, begin to use mental images and symbols during their thinking and can reverse operations.

Children in the concrete operational stage begin to understand that change in physical appearance does not necessarily change quality or quantity. They also begin to reverse thought processes, going back and undoing a mental action just accomplished. Other mental operations are also typical of this stage:

- *One-to-one correspondence.* This is the basis for counting and matching objects. Concrete operational children have mastered the ability, for example, to give one cookie to each classmate and a pencil to each member of their work group.

classification Refers to putting like things together and naming the group, such as big bears, little bears; shiny shells, dull shells; round buttons, square buttons; or smooth rocks, rough rocks.

- *Classification of objects, events, and time according to certain characteristics.* **Classification** refers to putting like things together and naming the group, such as animal classification, for example, mammal, amphibian; shiny shells, dull shells; round buttons, square buttons; or smooth rocks, rough rocks. Classification schemes are important for young children because they are central to scientific thinking. Rocks, sea shells, birds, seeds, and just about everything in nature has a classification system.[3]
- *Classification involving multiple properties.* Multiple classifications occur when a child can classify objects on the basis of more than one property, such as color and size; shape and size; and shape and color; or shape, color and size.
- *Class inclusive operations.* Class inclusion is a form of classification. For example, if children in this stage are shown five apples, five oranges, and five lemons and asked whether there are more apples or fruit, they are able to respond with "fruit."

The concrete stage does not represent a period into which children suddenly emerge after having been preoperational.

Teachers' Role in Concrete Operations Stage. During the concrete operations stage, teachers should do the following:

- Use props and visual aids and give students a chance to manipulate and test objects to help them think through hands-on learning
- Make sure presentations and readings are brief and well organized
- Use familiar examples to explain more complex ideas
- Give opportunities to classify and group objects and ideas on increasingly complex levels
- Provide opportunities for role taking, problem solving, and self-reflection

DEVELOPMENTALLY APPROPRIATE PRACTICE

The National Association for the Education of Young Children believes, as Piaget believed, that children are thinking, moving, feeling, and interacting human beings.[4] As such, developmentally appropriate practice involves considering and fostering children's cognitive development. Piaget believed development occurred in stages and the

NAEYC supports this belief, that development proceeds toward greater complexity, self-regulation, and symbolic or representational capacities. Developmentally appropriate teaching involves reaching children at their developmental level, or stage, while challenging them to grow, and when ready, to continuously advance to their next stage of development.

VYGOTSKY AND SOCIOCULTURAL THEORY

Lev Vygotsky (1896–1934), a contemporary of Piaget, exerts an ongoing influence on the practices of early childhood professionals. Vygotsky believed that children's cognitive, linguistic, and social development is supported by and enhanced through social interaction. This view is the opposite of the Piagetian perspective, which sees children as much more solitary developers of their own intelligence and language. Learning occurs best in children when they interact with peers and teachers in an environment that is collaborative. Vygotsky further believed that beginning at birth, children seek out adults for social interaction and that development occurs through these ongoing interactions with caregivers and teachers.

ZONE OF PROXIMAL DEVELOPMENT

One of Vygotsky's most important concepts is the **zone of proximal development (ZPD)**. Vygotsky said that the ZPD is an area of development into which each child can be led as a result of interactions with a more competent partner, either adult or peer. The ZPD is the difference between what a child can accomplish independently and what he or she can achieve in collaboration with another, more competent person. Consequently, for Vygotsky, social interaction results in learning. Vygotsky maintained the ZPD is created as a result of social interaction.

zone of proximal development (ZPD) The range of tasks that are too difficult to master alone but that can be learned with guidance and assistance.

The zone of proximal development represents the range of tasks that children cannot do independently but can do with the help of a more competent person—teacher, adult, peer, brother, sister, parent, etc. Tasks below the ZPD, children can learn independently. Tasks, concepts, ideas, and information above the ZPD, children are not yet able to learn, even with help. Children can master tasks slightly above their abilities with the help of others. For all children, the zone is constantly shifting upward to higher levels of performance and accomplishments with the guided help of others. Figure 5.4 conceptually illustrates the ZPD functions.

In addition, Vygotsky believed that learning and development constitute a dynamic and interactive process. In other words, learning drives or leads development. The experiences children have influence their development. For this reason it is important for teachers and parents to provide high-quality learning experiences for all children. In addition, part of your role is to create zones of proximal development for each child by creating environments in which children can learn new behaviors and skills in collaboration with others. Watch this video to see how an early child educator helps a child to work in her zone of proximal development while completing a puzzle.

SOCIAL INTERACTIONS. Social interaction among students and between teachers and students promotes learning. When you provide opportunities for children to socially engage in small groups, you support thinking and interaction.

For example, after teaching a unit on jungle creatures, first grade teacher Amanda Le divides her class into small groups and asks them to discuss which reptile, the

FIGURE 5.4 | Zone of Proximal Development

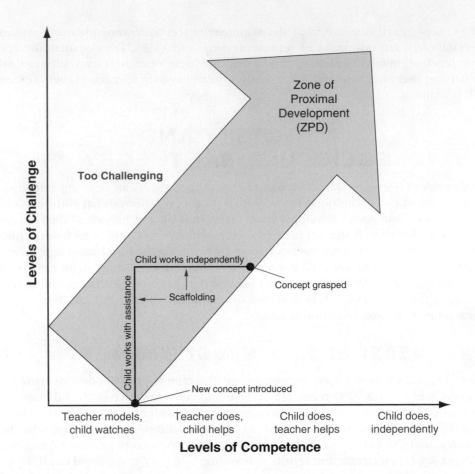

three-horned chameleon or leaf-tailed gecko, had the best camouflage abilities and why. As she moves about the classroom, she hears children shouting out their answers to one another. "But why?" she gently reminds them, and soon the children are debating. Amy says, "I think the gecko is the best 'cause he looks just like a leaf and wood." "But the chameleon can change into *any* color!" Jorge objects. "Yeah, but it turns black if it gets scared or mad; all a predator would have to do was sneak up on him and then you'd see it right away," Amy argues. Jorge purses his lips, thinking, and says, "Yeah . . . that's true. But if the gecko sat on a green leaf you could see it. His camouflage wouldn't work then!" Amy looks stumped and then says triumphantly, "Yeah, but the chameleon's got those horns! He'd beat up your gecko!"

From this example, you can see how Amanda facilitates opportunities for students to share their viewpoints, discuss, and teach one another and learn from each other. These social interactions promote true critical thinking and learning; they also promote children's social and communication skills.

SCAFFOLDING

Vygotsky believed that communication or dialogue between teachers and children is very important; it becomes a means of helping children develop new concepts and think their way to higher-level concepts. Assistance in the ZPD is called **scaffolding** and is a major component of teaching; it enables children to complete tasks they could not complete independently. When adults assist toddlers in learning to walk, they are scaffolding them from not being able to walk to walking. Teachers guide and support children's language learning by building on what those children are already able to do

scaffolding The process of providing various types of support, guidance, or direction during the course of an activity.

and moving them to a higher level of language use. For example, kindergarten teacher Amy Jordan reviews the concept of nouns with her class, something they learned last week. Then she tells them about verbs. She brings out a stack of magazines and asks them to look for action word pictures. She motivates them by using their pictures to create a collage to hang in the hallway. As the children apply what they already know about nouns, they expand their knowledge to include verbs. Next week, Amy plans to start working on sentence structure!

Reflect and Apply: Vygotsky

DIFFERENT LEVELS OF SUPPORT.   Scaffolding is a gradual process of providing different levels of support during the course of an activity. At the beginning of a new task, scaffolding should be concrete and visible; Vygotskian theory maintains that learning begins with the concrete and moves to the abstract. As a child masters the task, the teacher slowly withdraws her scaffolding support. Thus, scaffolding builds on children's strengths and enables them to grow cognitively and become independent learners. Figure 5.5 gives you specific steps to scaffold children's learning.

TEACHER-CHILD DIALOGUE.   Communication and dialogue between teachers and children is very important. You can use dialogue to scaffold children's learning and to promote self-talk as a means of helping children scaffold their own learning. The following example of working a puzzle gives you insight regarding how to use dialogue to scaffold learning.

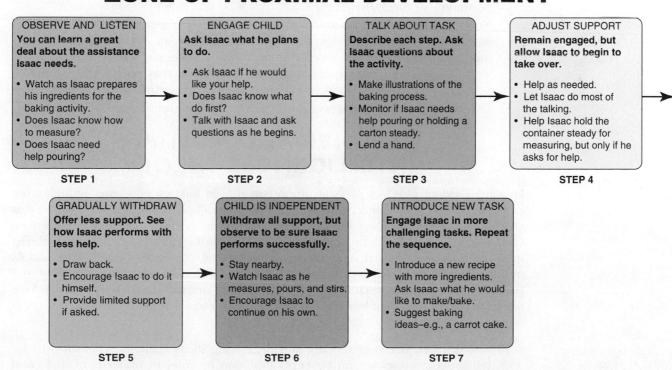

ZONE OF PROXIMAL DEVELOPMENT

OBSERVE AND LISTEN	ENGAGE CHILD	TALK ABOUT TASK	ADJUST SUPPORT
You can learn a great deal about the assistance Isaac needs.	**Ask Isaac what he plans to do.**	**Describe each step. Ask Isaac questions about the activity.**	**Remain engaged, but allow Isaac to begin to take over.**
• Watch as Isaac prepares his ingredients for the baking activity. • Does Isaac know how to measure? • Does Isaac need help pouring?	• Ask Isaac if he would like your help. • Does Isaac know what do first? • Talk with Isaac and ask questions as he begins.	• Make illustrations of the baking process. • Monitor if Isaac needs help pouring or holding a carton steady. • Lend a hand.	• Help as needed. • Let Isaac do most of the talking. • Help Isaac hold the container steady for measuring, but only if he asks for help.
STEP 1	**STEP 2**	**STEP 3**	**STEP 4**

GRADUALLY WITHDRAW	CHILD IS INDEPENDENT	INTRODUCE NEW TASK
Offer less support. See how Isaac performs with less help.	**Withdraw all support, but observe to be sure Isaac performs successfully.**	**Engage Isaac in more challenging tasks. Repeat the sequence.**
• Draw back. • Encourage Isaac to do it himself. • Provide limited support if asked.	• Stay nearby. • Watch Isaac as he measures, pours, and stirs. • Encourage Isaac to continue on his own.	• Introduce a new recipe with more ingredients. Ask Isaac what he would like to make/bake. • Suggest baking ideas–e.g., a carrot cake.
STEP 5	**STEP 6**	**STEP 7**

FIGURE 5.5 | Scaffolding a Baking Lesson Through the Zone of Proximal Development

Scaffolding Example—Working a Puzzle. Emma picks a puzzle to work and dumps the pieces out. She randomly picks up a piece and moves it around inside the frame. She tries another. Look at her face: Is she smiling or showing signs of stress? Is she talking to herself?

Perhaps Emma needs a puzzle with fewer pieces. If so, you can offer her one. But from prior observation, you may know she just needs a little assistance. Try sitting with Emma and suggesting that you will help. Start by turning all the pieces right side up. As you do this, talk about the pieces you see: This one is red with a little green, this one has a straight edge, and this one is curved. Move your finger along the edge.

Ask Emma whether she can find a straight edge on the side of the puzzle and then whether she can find a piece with a straight edge that matches the color. Ask what hints the pieces give her. Repeat with several other pieces. Then pause to give Emma the opportunity to try one on her own. As she does, describe what she is doing and the position, shape, and color of the piece. Demonstrate turning a piece in different directions while saying, "I'll try turning it another way." (If you just say, "Turn the piece," she will most likely turn it upside down.) By listening to you verbalize and by repeating the verbalizing, Emma is learning to self-talk—that is, to talk herself through a task. By practicing this private speech, children realize they can answer their own questions and regulate their own behavior. When the puzzle is complete, offer Emma another of similar difficulty and encourage her to try it on her own while you stay nearby to offer assistance as needed, allowing her to take the lead.[5]

IMPLICATIONS FOR TEACHING.   These are basic constructivist concepts you can use to guide your professional practice. In the constructivist classroom young children:

- Are unique individuals who construct their own knowledge based on what they already know and on the developmentally appropriate activities teachers involve them in.
- Are active agents who problem-solve and think for themselves. Children want to do things for themselves.
- Need experiences with people, places, and things as a framework for the construction of their knowledge. Social interactions are an essential part of learning, as are unique experiences and appropriate materials. Children need social interactions with peers, teachers and other adults as they collaborate, complete projects, problem-solve, and engage in cooperative learning.
- Learn best through experiences and activities that they initiate and find interesting.

GARDNER AND MULTIPLE INTELLIGENCES THEORY

Howard Gardner (1943–) plays an important role in helping educators rethink what constitutes basic intelligence. Gardner's theory of *multiple intelligences* proposes that children are smart in many ways. Gardner has identified nine different intelligences: visual/spatial, verbal/linguistic, mathematical/logical, bodily/kinesthetic, musical/rhythmic, intrapersonal, interpersonal, naturalistic, and existential. His view of intelligence and its multiple components will undoubtedly continue to influence educational thought and practice. Following are the characteristics for each of Gardner's nine intelligences and the teacher's role in providing learning opportunities for each of these intelligences.

Characteristics

Visual/spatial. Learning visually and organizing ideas spatially. This form of intelligence requires seeing concepts in action in order to understand them and includes the ability to "see" things in one's mind in planning to create a product or solve a problem.

Verbal/linguistic. Learning through the spoken and written word. This intelligence was always valued in the traditional classroom and in traditional assessments of intelligence and achievement.

Mathematical/logical. Learning through reasoning and problem solving. It is highly valued in the traditional classroom, where students were asked to adapt to logically sequenced delivery of instruction.

Bodily/kinesthetic. Learning through interaction with one's environment. This intelligence is not just the domain of "overly active" learners. It promotes understanding through concrete experiences.

Musical/rhythmic. Learning through patterns, rhythms, and music. This form of intelligence includes not only auditory abilities, but also the identification of patterns using all the senses.

Interpersonal. Learning through interaction with others. This intelligence is not the domain of children who are simply "talkative" or "overly social." It promotes collaboration and working cooperatively with others.

Existential. Children who learn in the context of where humankind stands in the "big" picture of existence. They ask, "Why are we here?" and "What is my role in my family, school, and community?" This intelligence is seen in the discipline of philosophy.

Intrapersonal. Learning through feelings, values, and attitudes. This is a decidedly affective component of learning through which students place value on what they learn and take ownership for their learning.

Naturalist. Learning through classification, categories, and hierarchies. The naturalist intelligence picks up on subtle differences in meaning. It is not simply the study of nature; it can be used in all areas of study.

Teacher's Role

Visual/spatial. Provide a visually stimulating environment, work with manipulatives, use technologies such as KidPix or SMART Boards.

Verbal/linguistic. Introduce new vocabulary, provide opportunities for speaking in front of class, incorporate drama in classroom.

Mathematical/logical. Present objectives at the beginning of an activity to provide structure, encourage debates, incorporate puzzles into learning centers.

Bodily/kinesthetic. Provide hands on learning centers, offer experiences in movement to rhythm and music, allow opportunities for building and taking apart.

Musical/rhythmic. Work with pattern blocks, have students move to rhythm, have students listen to music while working.

Interpersonal. Allow interaction among students during learning tasks, include group work tasks, form cooperative groups so that each member has an assigned role.

Existential. Offer an overview before starting new instruction; discuss how topics are important to the classroom, school, and community; bring in resource people or offer additional perspectives on a topic.

Intrapersonal. Differentiate instruction, provide activities that offer learner choices, have students set goals for themselves in the classroom, include daily journal writing.

Naturalist. Use graphic organizers, provide sorting and grouping tasks, build portfolios of student work.

BEHAVIORISM AND BEHAVIORAL THEORIES

At Sweetwater Elementary, second grader Rudy Reynoso looks forward to flying his good behavior kite on the classroom bulletin board. Every time his teacher recognizes his good behavior, such as finishing his work on time or helping his friends in the lunchroom, Rudy gets to move his kite up to the next level. After ten moves, Rudy is eligible for a good behavior reward such as picking out a prize from the school store or extra time with one of the classroom iPads.

Reward systems such as the one that Rudy's teacher uses are popular in early childhood education today and are based on **behaviorism**, a learning theory that promotes learning through rewards and punishment. All classroom teachers use rewards and punishment as a means of encouraging children to follow rules, pay attention, and do their best work with the goal of learning the skills and knowledge expected for their grade level. In addition, teachers use rewards and punishment to guide hard-to-manage children with behaviors such as lack of motivation, aggression, bullying, and not staying on task. It is hard to imagine that a classroom exists today in which a behaviorist approach of some kind is not intentionally or unintentionally used.

In addition, special educators use behaviorist approaches to plan and implement their instructional practices in working with children with disabilities. One of the results of integrating the fields of early childhood special education and early childhood education is the integration of behaviorist ideas and practices into early childhood education. Because all early childhood classrooms are inclusive classrooms with children of varying abilities and disabilities, it makes sense for all teachers to use behaviorist practices to help each and every child learn.

Behavioral learning theories, theories that explain how children learn cognitively, socially, and behaviorally, play down the roles of biology and maturation in learning. Instead, they stress the experiences that children have and the role of the environment in determining these experiences. For behaviorists, critical factors in learning are the environmental opportunities to learn and the rewards and punishments teachers and parents use to support and encourage children's behavior. For behaviorists, change in behavior is a function of learning, not age or mental schemes or psychosocial stages.

BEHAVIORIST FOUNDATIONS.   Behaviorism began with the work of primarily three people: Ivan Pavlov, J.B. Watson, and Edward Thorndike.

Ivan Pavlov (1849–1936) was interested in how biological events such as digestion relate to changes in the environment. The application of this interest to learning was truly revolutionary. Pavlov knew that a hungry dog salivates when presented with food. This food is the *unconditioned stimulus* and the salivation is the *unconditioned response*. Pavlov conditioned (trained) a dog's salivary response by providing food simultaneously with the ringing of a bell. After several repetitions, Pavlov could merely ring a bell and the dog salivated. This process of conditioning a response is called **classical conditioning**. The process sounds familiar doesn't it? How is your life influenced by conditioned responses? Do you salivate or "get hungry" at the sight or smell of freshly baked cookies or pizza? I do!

J.B. Watson (1878–1958) is considered the founder of behaviorism. Important concepts for Watson were **stimulus**, an event that activates behavior, and **response**, an act that is an observable reaction to a stimulus. Stimulus-response pairs or connections resulting in new behaviors are at the heart of behavioral theory.

Edward Thorndike (1874–1949) popularized **reinforcement theory**, the belief that consequences strengthen behavior. Thorndike believed people do things that bring them pleasure and avoid doing things that bring them pain. This is not a new idea for us. Thorndike stated what today seems fairly obvious, namely that the consequences of

behaviorism A learning theory based on the idea that behaviors are learned through rewards and punishment; popular in early childhood education today.

behavioral learning theories Theories that explain how children learn cognitively, socially and behaviorally that play down the roles of biology and maturation in learning.

classical conditioning Association of automatic responses with new stimuli.

stimulus An event that activates behavior.

response An observable reaction to a stimulus.

reinforcement theory The belief that consequences strengthen behavior.

a particular response will be continued and therefore learned. What happens to a child following a behavior helps determine whether or not he will continue to act in the same manner. When Charlie cries and his mother gives a cookie, he will likely learn to use crying as a means of getting cookies. Pleasurable responses increase tendencies to act; unpleasant consequences decrease tendencies to act. As you know from your own experiences, you don't usually do something in order to see how painful it is.

SKINNER AND OPERANT CONDITIONING. B.F. Skinner (1904–1990) is the modern day popularizer of behaviorism. He did more than any other individual to spread the behaviorist theory by applying behaviorist ideas to educational practices. One of Skinner's major contributions is the process of **operant conditioning**, which is learning in which voluntary behavior is strengthened or weakened by consequences or antecedents—events that precede an action. Operant conditioning describes the process of learning that occurs when responses are followed by reinforcers. The term *operant* means that children operate or act in and on the environment. As a result of this operation or interaction, certain behaviors are reinforced and learning results. Whereas Pavlov *created* a new stimulus-response relation, in operant conditioning an already existing response is strengthened or weakened. A child makes a response, and the response is reinforced and conditioned.

> **operant conditioning**
> Learning in which voluntary behavior is strengthened or weakened by consequences or antecedents—events that precede an action.

For example, Melody Jacobs wants her eighteen-month-old son, J.P., to learn names for things. She shows J.P. many toys while saying their names. One day, much to Melody's delight, J.P. says "ball." She profusely praises J.P. "Great, fantastic, good for you, J.P.! You know the name for 'ball.'" Consequently, when J.P. plays with his toys and touches, picks up, or otherwise interacts with a ball and says "ball," Melody praises him. It is precisely in this manner that behaviorists believe J.P. learns language and other behaviors as well. Your life and the lives of children are full of other such examples.

BANDURA AND SOCIAL LEARNING THEORY

Albert Bandura (1925–) has extended behaviorist beliefs to include his **social learning theory**. Bandura believes observational learning can also be used to explain how children learn and that children play a significant role in the development of their behaviors. Bandura believes learning occurs primarily through modeling, observation, vicarious experiences, and self-regulation.

> **social learning theory**
> Developed by Albert Bandura to explain how children learn and gain new information by observing others.

Bandura suggests there are four processes involved in modeling:

- *Attention to people.* Attention to people is based on their engaging qualities, their particular behaviors, and a child's frame of reference. Sports figures, pop culture celebrities, and cartoon characters, in particular, are a popular source of role models for children.

- *Selecting behaviors to reproduce.* Selecting what behaviors to reproduce is largely a matter of what children value or what they see others, whom they admire, valuing. Behaviors that bring pleasure will more likely be modeled, whereas if a child sees a peer being punished for a particular behavior, he or she is less likely to model that behavior.

- *Remembering the observed behaviors.* Remembering occurs through recalling the observed because if a child does not remember a behavior, she or he will not be influenced by it.

- *Reproducing what was observed.* Reproduction is more than a process of "monkey see, monkey do." Replication occurs best when a child has the necessary skills to perform the behavior and an opportunity to practice. Musical instruments and sports activities come quickly to mind.

Social learning theorists believe that a child does not have to directly observe a behavior to model it, but that vicarious experiences experienced through books and the media also serve as models for behavior.

IMPLICATIONS FOR TEACHING.   The following are basic principles that make behaviorism unique and distinctive as compared to other theories.

- The environment is everything. Experiences come from environmental stimuli. In the nature/nurture versus heredity/environment controversy, behaviors are environmentally oriented and emphasize the role of the environment in controlling and determining behavior.
- Observable behaviors are what is important, not what children think. Actions speak louder than words!
- The principles of learning hold true for children of all ages, races, cultures, and abilities. For behaviorists, experiences, especially the right ones, are the gold standard of learning.
- Learning is gradual and continuous, not stage-related. Behaviorists see learning and development as an incremental sequence of specific conditioned behaviors.

ACCOMMODATING DIVERSE LEARNERS

Here we have talked about using constructivism to structure learning for children from all walks of life. But what will you do when a student's behaviors are preventing you from using tried-and-true theories of learning? After all, a child whose behavior is out of control cannot learn. One way to effectively and (relatively) quickly modify behavior is to use **applied behavior analysis (ABA)**. ABA is the application of behavioral learning principles to change behavior. Behavioral learning theory states that all behavior is motivated by a purpose and is learned through systematic reinforcement. In other words, when behavior is rewarded, it continues; but when behavior is not rewarded or is ignored, the behavior will stop. For example, a child who wants a candy bar in the grocery store has *learned* that screaming, crying, and kicking in the candy aisle will get him or her what she wants. The mother *reinforces* that behavior by giving the child a candy bar to stop the tantrum. If the mother had ignored the tantrum or removed the child from the store instead of reinforcing the behavior, would the behavior continue? Probably not.

applied behavior analysis (ABA) A technique based on the learning theory of behaviorism, which states that all behavior is motivated by a purpose and is learned through systematic reinforcement.

APPLYING ABA

You can apply ABA to your classroom to accommodate a variety of behavioral disturbances. Let's consider Robert, a five-year-old whom protective services removed from his home last year because his parents were physically abusive. Robert has learned from his parents to solve his problems by hitting. For example, if he is trying to get your attention and you don't provide it right away, he hits you. This pattern of behavior seriously affects Robert's learning and social development and it also affects you!

Using ABA, there are two ways you can modify Robert's behavior: positive reinforcement and negative reinforcement. **Positive reinforcement** is adding something to promote or diminish a behavior, such as giving a high-five for a job well done. **Negative reinforcement** is taking away something to promote or diminish a behavior, such as removing your attention from someone (ignoring them). To choose which kind of reinforcement to use, you have to know what is meaningful to Robert. For example, providing Robert positive reinforcement in the form of a sticker when Robert doesn't care anything about stickers will not reinforce appropriate behavior. Instead, for a child such as Robert who has had nothing but negative and painful

positive reinforcement Adding something to promote or diminish a behavior, such as giving a high-five for a job well done.

negative reinforcement Taking away something to promote or diminish a behavior, such as removing your attention from someone (ignoring them).

relationships, social interactions that are positive, consistent, and satisfying may be very rewarding.

You decide to use both positive and negative reinforcement. You will ignore Robert when he hits you and reward him when he uses his words. At the beginning of the day you pull Robert aside and tell him, "I know that it's hard for you to remember to use your words and wait to get my attention. But if you hit me instead of using your words, I'm not going to listen to you. If you use your words, you will earn story time with me at the end of the day."

After lunch, Robert is frustrated and he has not gotten your attention; he forgets the plan and hits you. You ignore him. You give him no other reaction and continue to focus on the other children. Remember, consistency is the only way to make ABA techniques work. With ABA, it is important to have a plan for your intervention and to *follow it every time*. It is likely that after Robert hits you and gets no response, he will hit you again, harder. His behavior will likely escalate because it is the only behavior he has learned.

If you break down, turn around, and shout, "STOP!" you have positively reinforced his behavior by giving him a reaction and your attention. It is not the kind of reaction or the attention he wants, but it is still a reaction, and at this point, for Robert, a negative reaction is better than no reaction or attention at all. In this way, you are teaching him that his behavior is *working*. If you continue to ignore his behavior, and it does not work, Robert will be forced to learn a new behavior to meet his needs because the old behavior is not working.

When Robert does not hit you, immediately and consistently provide positive reinforcement. Genuine verbal encouragement, high-fives, and hugs are all positive reinforcements. At the end of the day, make sure to have the special story time between the two of you as planned. In this way, you are teaching Robert that there are other ways of getting attention. Robert can get nurturing and meaningful attention by following the rules, waiting patiently, and using his words.

You have to develop and modify your plan to fit the child. For example, going all day without hitting you may be impossible for Robert because the behavior is so ingrained in him. Instead of rewarding him at the end of the day, break the day into smaller, more manageable segments. In other words, if Robert has not hit you in one hour, reinforce his accomplishment with five minutes of special Robert and Teacher time. You can also help Robert develop patience by reassuring him that you aware of his needs without giving him overt attention with nonverbal clues, such as a wink to communicate, "I'm thinking about you;" holding up a finger as if to say, "I hear you, but I need a minute to finish with someone else;" or even a gentle hand on the shoulder to communicate closeness and responsiveness along with his need to wait patiently. As Robert develops new skills and begins to phase out his hitting behavior because it isn't working, you can extend the time for his behavioral expectations, pushing back the reinforcement period to two hours, then three, and eventually the whole day. Changing children's behavior can be difficult, but it is worth it! And, in Robert's case, you put theory into action.

ERIKSON AND PSYCHOSOCIAL DEVELOPMENT

Erik H. Erikson (1902–1994) developed his *psychosocial development* theory based on the premise that cognitive and social development occur hand in hand and cannot be separated. According to Erikson, children's personalities and social skills grow and develop within the context of society and in response to its demands, expectations, values, and social institutions, such as families, schools, and child care programs. Parents and teachers are key parts of these environments and therefore play a powerful role in helping or hindering children in their personality and cognitive development. For example, school-aged children must deal with the demands of learning new skills or risk a crisis of *industry*—the ability to do, be involved, be competent, and to achieve—versus *inferiority*, marked by failure and feelings of incompetence. Many of the cases of school violence in the news today are connected to children who feel inferior and unappreciated and who lack the social skills to get along with their classmates.[6] Table 5.1 outlines Erikson's stages of psychosocial development and identifies children's characteristics for each of the four stages. Review and reflect on Erickson's psychosocial stages and then read below how you can help children achieve the mastery of the challenges for each stage.

IMPLICATIONS FOR TEACHING

Stage 1   ***Basic trust versus mistrust:*** Birth to 18 months, teachers meet children's needs when they do the following:
- Meet children's needs with consistency and continuity.
- Identify and take care of basic needs such as diapering and feeding.

TABLE 5.1 | Erikson's Stages

Stage	Description	Characteristics
Basic Trust Versus Mistrust: Birth to 18 months	Children learn to trust or mistrust their environment and their caregivers. Trust develops when children's needs are met consistently, predictably, and lovingly. Children then view the world as safe and dependable.	Infants learn to trust or mistrust that others will care for their basic needs; learn how to get their needs met (smiling, laughing, crying, etc.); and develop attachments that are either secure or insecure.
Autonomy Versus Shame and Doubt: 18 months to 3 years	Children want to do things for themselves. Given adequate opportunities, they learn independence and competence. Inadequate opportunities and professional overprotection result in self-doubt and poor achievement; children come to feel ashamed of their abilities.	Toddlers learn to be self-sufficient or to doubt their abilities in activities such as toileting, feeding, walking, and talking. Children either learn to trust themselves and their relationships or learn to doubt others and themselves.
Initiative Versus Guilt: 3 to 5 years	Children need opportunities to respond with initiative to activities and tasks, which gives them a sense of purposefulness and accomplishment. Children feel guilty if they are discouraged or prohibited from initiating activities and are overly restricted in attempts to do things on their own.	Preschoolers sometimes overstep the limits set by parents and feel guilty. They seek and respond to opportunities to explore, learn, experiment, and experience new things. As a result, children begin to gain a sense of a success and failure.
Industry Versus Inferiority: 5 to 8 years	Children display an industrious attitude and want to be productive. They want to build things, discover, manipulate objects, and find out how things work. They also want recognition for their productivity. Feelings of inferiority result when children are criticized or belittled or have few opportunities for productivity.	Primary age children actively and busily learn to be competent and productive or inferior and unable to do things well. Children need to feel they are capable and equal to peers to avoid inferiority.

- Hold babies when feeding them to promote attachment and develop trust.
- Socialize through smiling, talking, and singing and other forms of communication.
- Be attentive and respond to infants' cues and comfort infants when they are in distress.

Stage 2 *Autonomy versus shame and doubt:* 18 months to 3 years, teachers should do the following:

- Encourage children to do what they are capable of doing.
- Do not shame children for any behavior.
- Do not use harsh punishment or discipline.
- Provide for safe exploration of classrooms and outdoor areas.

Stage 3 *Initiative versus guilt:* 3 to 5 years, teachers should do the following:

- Observe children and follow their interests.
- Encourage children to engage in many activities.
- Provide environments in which children can explore.
- Promote language development.
- Provide each child with the opportunity to succeed.

Stage 4 *Industry versus inferiority:* 5 to 8 years, teachers should do the following:

- Help children win recognition and learn confidence by making things. See the accompanying photo of children engaged in a wood-working project.
- Help ensure that children are successful in literacy skills and learning to read.
- Provide support for students who seem confused or discouraged.

Check Your Understanding: Erikson

MASLOW AND SELF-ACTUALIZATION THEORY

Abraham Maslow (1890–1970) developed a theory of human motivation called *self-actualization*. His theory is based on the satisfaction of human needs, and he identified self-actualization, or self-fulfillment, as the highest human need. However, Maslow said that children and adults cannot achieve self-fulfillment until other basic needs are satisfied. Maslow identified these essential human needs:

- Life essentials, such as food and water
- Safety and security
- Belonging and love
- Achievement and prestige
- Aesthetic needs

hierarchy of needs
Maslow's theory that basic needs must be satisfied before higher-level needs can be satisfied.

Maslow maintained that everyone has these basic needs, regardless of race, gender, sexual orientation, socioeconomic status, or age. The satisfaction of basic needs is essential for children to function well and to achieve all they are capable of achieving. Figure 5.6 depicts Maslow's **hierarchy of needs**. As you review and reflect on it, identify ways you can help children meet their needs.

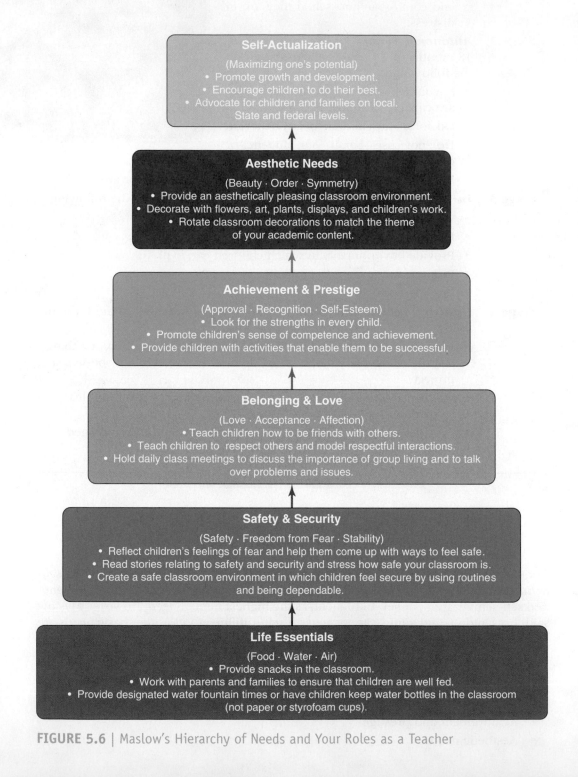

Self-Actualization
(Maximizing one's potential)
• Promote growth and development.
• Encourage children to do their best.
• Advocate for children and families on local.
State and federal levels.

Aesthetic Needs
(Beauty · Order · Symmetry)
• Provide an aesthetically pleasing classroom environment.
• Decorate with flowers, art, plants, displays, and children's work.
• Rotate classroom decorations to match the theme
of your academic content.

Achievement & Prestige
(Approval · Recognition · Self-Esteem)
• Look for the strengths in every child.
• Promote children's sense of competence and achievement.
• Provide children with activities that enable them to be successful.

Belonging & Love
(Love · Acceptance · Affection)
• Teach children how to be friends with others.
• Teach children to respect others and model respectful interactions.
• Hold daily class meetings to discuss the importance of group living and to talk
over problems and issues.

Safety & Security
(Safety · Freedom from Fear · Stability)
• Reflect children's feelings of fear and help them come up with ways to feel safe.
• Read stories relating to safety and security and stress how safe your classroom is.
• Create a safe classroom environment in which children feel secure by using routines
and being dependable.

Life Essentials
(Food · Water · Air)
• Provide snacks in the classroom.
• Work with parents and families to ensure that children are well fed.
• Provide designated water fountain times or have children keep water bottles in the classroom
(not paper or styrofoam cups).

FIGURE 5.6 | Maslow's Hierarchy of Needs and Your Roles as a Teacher

LIFE ESSENTIALS

Just as water is essential for proper brain functions,[7] the same is true of food and nourishment.[8] We know that when children are hungry, they perform poorly in school. Thus children who begin school without eating breakfast, don't have a healthy lunch, or eat improperly at home don't achieve as well as they should and experience difficulty concentrating on their school activities. They can even drop in IQ![9] Additionally, obesity, malnutrition, and diabetes also come from improper nutrition. For these reasons, many early childhood programs provide children with breakfast, lunch, and snacks throughout the day.[10] For some children with disabilities or other health impairments that affect their ability to ingest or digest food, these conditions may also impact their performance in school.

The state of children's nutrition today has caused growing concern on a national level. The statistics are shocking: More than 16 percent of children and adolescents in the United States are overweight,[11] and nearly 16 percent of households with children are food insecure, meaning parents and their children went hungry one or more times sometime during the year.[12] For many children, both obese and food insecure, the National School Lunch Program (NSLP), a federally assisted meal program, provides the only nutritionally balanced meals children eat each school day. Currently the USDA provides meals to over 30 million students each school day, with 17.5 million students receiving free or reduced-price meals each day at school.[13]

SAFETY AND SECURITY

Safety and security needs play an important role in children's lives. When children think that their teachers do not like them or they are fearful of what their teachers or other students may say about them, then they are deprived of a basic need. As a consequence, they do not do well in school, and they become fearful in their relationships with others. Classrooms that have routines and predictability provide children with a greater sense of security.[14] For some children who live in abusive homes and impoverished neighborhoods, their ability to learn and achieve in school may also be affected.

BELONGING AND LOVE

Children need to be loved and feel that they belong in their home and in school in order to thrive and develop. All children have a need for affection that you can help satisfy through smiles, hugs, eye contact, and nearness. For example, in my work with three- and four-year-old children, many want to sit close to me and want me to put my arms around them. They are seeking love and are looking to their teachers and me to satisfy this basic need. Affection plays an important part of children's lives.

Think for a minute about your social relations with others. How others treat you affects you emotionally, physically, and cognitively. The same is true for the children you teach. How you relate to them really matters and affects how well they achieve and behave.

TEACHER–CHILD INTERACTION. Researchers have found that the extent to which children can access the instructional and socialization resources of the classroom environment may be, in part, predicated on teacher–child interactions: "The association between the quality of early teacher–child relationships and later school performance can be both strong and persistent. The association is apparent in both academic and social spheres of school performance."[15]

In addition, teacher–child closeness, such as having an affectionate and warm relationship, reduces the tendency for aggressive behavior. "Closer teacher–child relationships may provide young children with resources (e.g., emotional security, guidance, and aid) that facilitate an 'approach' orientation—as opposed to an 'avoidant' or 'resistant' stance—toward the interpersonal and scholastic demands of the classroom and school."[16] The implication for you is that you need to really care for your children and develop strong and affectionate relationships with them.

In one study regarding teacher–child closeness, females tended to develop higher levels of cooperative participation, school liking, and achievement than did males.[17] This might indicate gender differences in teacher–child relations and suggest that boys are at greater risk of not having a close teacher relationship. Thus, a close teacher–child relationship is particularly important for males, for low-socioeconomic children and minorities, and for all children who might not experience a close relationship with another caring adult. Remember, the caring adult in the classroom is you!

You need to provide a classroom context that is supportive of and responsive to children's social and affectional needs. This, of course, can be a challenging task, but one that is necessary. How we teachers relate to children helps determine their behavioral outcomes now and in the future.

ACHIEVEMENT AND PRESTIGE

Recognition and approval are self-esteem needs that relate to success and accomplishment. Children who are independent, responsible, and who achieve will have high self-esteem. Today, many teachers are concerned about how to enhance children's self-esteem; a key way is through increased achievement.

It is important that you use encouragement to increase achievement rather than rely solely on praise.

First grade teacher Mia Herto says, "I try hard to not use praise phrases like, 'Good job, that's awesome work,' or even, 'I really like that.' Instead I try to encourage kids by saying, 'You worked really hard on that, and I bet you feel proud of yourself, you are trying so hard even though it's really difficult.' It was hard at first! After all, it's instinctual to want to make kids feel good, and we all grew up hearing praise phrases, but I can see a difference in the children's self-confidence already."

AESTHETIC NEEDS

Children enjoy and appreciate beauty. They like to be in classrooms and homes that are physically attractive and pleasant. You can help satisfy children's aesthetic needs by being well dressed and providing a classroom that is pleasant to be in, one that includes plants and flowers, art, and music. For example, second grade teacher Allen Hamilton says, "I always have some flowers or potted plants around the room; it makes it feel homey and the kids like it. They get a charge out of helping care for them and being responsible for the beauty in the classroom. I like having classical music on during the day, too. It encourages children to talk about the music they like, and why they like it. By the end of the semester, I have students bringing in their favorite music. We'll play their music if they can talk with me about why they like it, and not just because it's 'cool'!"

When teachers and parents support children to meet their basic needs, they promote self-actualization. As a result, children have a sense of satisfaction, are enthusiastic, and are eager to learn. Such children want to engage in activities that will lead to higher levels of learning. The Voice from the Field, "Applying Maslow's Hierarchy to a Third Grade Classroom," illustrates how third grade teacher Robert Cote implements Maslow's hierarchy in his classroom.

Applying Maslow's Hierarchy to a Third Grade Classroom

I watch my class of new third graders wander wide-eyed through the hallway of their new school. Last year they were the big kids in their K–2 school. This year will be very different. Can they handle the changes? Will they be ready emotionally to learn what needs to be learned?

Like me, you can apply Abraham Maslow's hierarchy of needs throughout the year and help your children become comfortable, confident learners, willing and able to take the risks necessary to stretch and grow.

PHYSIOLOGICAL NEEDS

I make sure my students know where to put their things in their cubby and desk. We take a tour of the school to find the closest restrooms, cafeteria, main office, and nurse's office. We go over the classroom sign-out process. I explain that I really need to know where they are at all times because I care about them. We talk about snack and lunch and what they can do if they're thirsty. It is impossible to ask a child to pay attention to a math lesson if he or she is worried about going to the restroom or when he or she will be eating lunch.

SAFETY

We also talk about what students can do to help make our classroom a safe and secure place for learning. We talk about "Double D behaviors" (dangerous and destructive) as well as my only nonnegotiable rule: "Hands, feet, and objects to ourselves at all times." We practice the fire drill and lock-down drill procedures. Children's safety needs are related to their physiological needs and are just as important. I've learned students respond well to the structure, and they really want to know they are safe.

BELONGING

Only after we have talked about our basic needs do we talk about how we will learn together as a classroom community. We talk about classroom courtesies and what it means to be part of a group of learners. We set up our first cooperative groups of four, five, or six students. I initially allow students to sit with friends, but I tell them that these groupings change as I get to understand each of their strengths and weaknesses. Each group establishes a group name, and I use this name to recognize good group behaviors or exceptional group thinking throughout the day during team-building activities and classroom lessons.

ESTEEM

Within each cooperative group, students are assigned specific roles they will play or jobs they will do when we engage in group activities such as math problem solving. Roles like time keeper, facilitator, materials handler, recorder, and note taker are important to ensure group success. It is essential early on to help students see the benefits of working together to achieve a common goal. After each group problem-solving activity, I always include a group assessment piece in which students think and talk together about what went well and what didn't. I remind students to keep their comments positive. The goal is to help students build their individual self-esteem while learning and celebrating what they're good at as a group.

SELF-ACTUALIZATION

As my students learn to work together and contribute to each other's success, they begin to become aware of their own strengths and weaknesses. I change the roles and reassign group members from time to time to help bring about continuous improvement as my students work to achieve individual potential. I tell my students that in the real world, we often don't have the luxury of knowing or even liking who we work with. We all need to learn strategies to help us be successful.

Maslow's hierarchy stresses the potential for each individual student to achieve self-actualization. I can see their progress as they learn and become comfortable in each level.

Source: Contributed by Robert Cote, third grade classroom teacher, Jordan Jackson School, Mansfield, Massachusetts.

BRONFENBRENNER AND ECOLOGICAL THEORY

The ecological theory of Urie Bronfenbrenner (1917–2005) looks at children's development within the context of a system of relationships that form their environment. There are five interrelating environmental systems—the microsystem, the mesosystem,

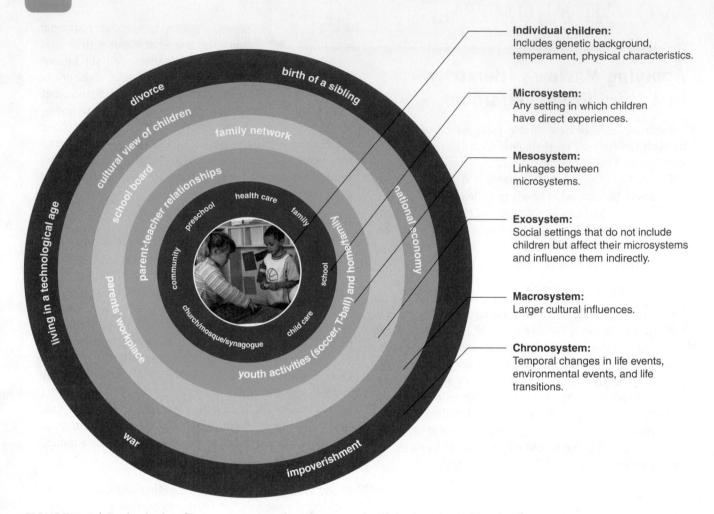

Individual children:
Includes genetic background, temperament, physical characteristics.

Microsystem:
Any setting in which children have direct experiences.

Mesosystem:
Linkages between microsystems.

Exosystem:
Social settings that do not include children but affect their microsystems and influence them indirectly.

Macrosystem:
Larger cultural influences.

Chronosystem:
Temporal changes in life events, environmental events, and life transitions.

FIGURE 5.7 | Ecological Influences on Development

microsystem The environmental settings in which children spend a lot of their time (e.g., children in child care spend about thirty-three hours a week there).

mesosystem Links or interactions between microsystems.

the exosystem, the macrosystem, and the chronosystem. Each system influences and is influenced by the others. Figure 5.7 shows a model of these environmental systems and the ways each influences children's development, learning, and life outcomes.

The **microsystem** encompasses the environments of parents, family, peers, child care, schools, neighborhood, religious groups, playgrounds, community parks, and so forth. The child acts on and influences each of these and is influenced by them. For example, four-year-old April has a physical disability that her child care program accommodates by making the classroom more accessible. Five-year-old Mack's aggressive behavior prompts his teacher to initiate a program of rewards to help him control his behaviors.

The **mesosystem** incorporates linkages or interactions between microsystems. Interactions and influences there relate to all of the environmental influences in the microsystem. For example, the family's support of or lack of attention to literacy influences a child's school performance and ability to learn how to read. Likewise, school support for family literacy influences the extent to which families value literacy and teaches children to value it in their lives. Research is clear that children's academic success is attributable to the amount of talk they hear from their parents and others.[18]

The **exosystem** is the environmental system that encompasses those events with which children do not have direct interaction but that nonetheless influence them. For example, when a local school board enacts a policy that ends social promotion in favor of grade failure, this action can and will influence children's future development. From research, we know that children who are retained suffer academically and developmentally in the long run![19] And when a parent's workplace mandates increased work time (e.g., a ten-hour workday), this may decrease parent–child involvement and have a negative impact on a child's development.

exosystem Environment or setting in which children do not play an active role but that nonetheless influences their development.

The **macrosystem** includes the culture, customs, and values of society in general. How children are viewed, ideas of gender-appropriate behavior, and, for example, an emphasis on funding quality preschool programs or failure to fund preschool programs, are all a part of the macrosystem. For example, as a result of the great recession, many school districts have eliminated or cut back funding for full-day preschool, kindergarten, and other programs that would provide children the services early in life that they need to be successful. In this case, the value of society conflicts with the ability of society to fund and make particular programs a reality, thus potentially affecting children's life outcome. The **chronosystem** consists of environmental influences over time and the ways they impact development and behavior. For example, today's children are very technologically adept and are comfortable using technology for education and entertainment. In addition, the large-scale entry of mothers into the workforce has changed family life and children's developmental outcomes forever. Declarations of war tear families apart for long periods of time, and many children of the Iraq and Afghanistan wars are left without a parent.

macrosystem The broader culture in which children live (e.g., democracy, individual freedom, and religious freedom).

chronosystem The environmental contexts and events that influence children over their lifetimes, such as living in a technological age.

Clearly, as Bronfenbrenner's theory illustrates, there are many influences on children's development. Currently, there is a lot of interest in how these influences shape children's lives and what parents and educators can do to enhance positive influences and minimize or eliminate negative environmental influences and negative social interactions.

ACTIVITIES FOR PROFESSIONAL DEVELOPMENT

ETHICAL DILEMMA

"NOT WITH MY MIKEY!"

On the first day of school, kindergartener Mikey Bodner raised havoc in Michelle Perez's classroom. Mikey hit, pushed, shoved, and shouted at his peers. He was really out of control. Aghast, Michelle immediately knew that she needed to put a behavioral plan together to help Mikey. Working with the school-level special education coordinator, Michelle developed a plan of punishments and rewards that she confidently felt would change Mikey's behavior. Michelle requested a meeting with Mikey's mom to discuss her plan because it also included ideas for how to help Mikey at home. When Michelle discussed the plan with Mikey's mom she was outraged. "What do you mean by this? You are not going to do this behavior reward and punishment kind of stuff with my Mikey! He's a good boy, not a rat in a cage!"

What should Michelle do? Should she try to pacify Mikey's mom and develop a behavioral plan that will satisfy her? Or, should Michelle tell Mikey's mom that she is going to implement the plan without her approval? Or, should Michelle "kick it up" to the district special education administrators and let them worry about it? What should Michelle do? What would you do?

ACTIVITIES TO APPLY WHAT YOU LEARNED

1. Piaget believed old and new experiences needed to be linked in order to maintain equilibrium. What are three ways you can make sure children are not in a constant state of disequilibrium in your classroom? Select a subject area such as math or science and outline a few ways you can connect new subject matter to children's experiences (i.e., the idea of how skip-counting by fives can segue to multiplication). Share your ideas online.

2. Vygotsky's theory states that social interaction is a key process for cognitive development. However, for some children with disabilities, behavioral problems, and those whose home language is other than English, social interactions can be difficult. Conduct an Internet research and make a list of five things you could do to support children's social interactions with others. Share and compare your list with your classmates online.

3. Pick a grade level and think about ways to teach to children's different intelligences. Select two of Gardner's intelligences and outline how you would teach to them in the grade in which you plan to teach. Share your findings with your classmates.

4. Skype with a local school district ABA therapist. Ask for tips on how to effectively incorporate ABA in the classroom. Post your findings to your class discussion board and compare and contrast them with your classmates' findings.

5. Which of Erikson's stages of social development are most important to you? Why? What aspects of Erikson's theory would you suggest are most important for parents? Considering how important it is to keep parents involved in their children's education, create a PowerPoint or Prezi presentation designed to inform parents about Erikson's stages and include tips for how parents can support each stage at home. Post your presentation to the class discussion board.

6. Every day, you may read online or hear in the news about children who are abused and neglected. How does abuse and neglect impact children's development? How could you target their most basic needs in your classroom? Post a link or question about this on some form of social media (Facebook, Twitter, etc.) and ask your friends. What do they suggest?

7. **KEY ASSESSMENT:** Bronfenbrenner's ecological systems theory explains, in part, how children grow and develop. Select one setting for each of the child's ecosystems (microsystem, mesosystem, exosystem, macrosystem, chronosystem), and for each of the ecosystems provide one to two specific interactional influences on children's development and learning. Use a tool such as Prezi, PPT, or other technology to present your findings. Use the rubric provided to guide your work.

LINKING TO LEARNING

The following agencies and programs, which can be located easily online, provide additional information about topics discussed in this chapter.

Building an Understanding of Constructivism

Describes the basic tenets of constructivism and gives a list of resources.

Constructivism and the Five E's

A description of constructivism and the five E's—engage, explore, explain, elaborate, and evaluate.

Jean Piaget and Genetic Epistemology

Detailed description of Piaget's theories concerning genetic epistemology and a QuickTime video clip of Piaget discussing this topic.

Resources for the Constructivist Educator

This group for the Association for Constructivist Teaching provides a rich problem-solving arena that encourages the learner's investigation, invention, and inference.

EARLY CHILDHOOD PROGRAMS

Applying Theories to Practice

LEARNING OUTCOMES

1. Explain why there is a growing demand for quality early childhood education programs.
2. Relate how the Montessori method provides for the needs of young children.
3. List the ways in which the HighScope program model provides for the needs of young children.
4. Explain how the Reggio Emilia approach provides for the needs of young children.
5. Describe how you can use the Project approach to create a unique learning experience for young children.
6. Explain how you can accommodate diverse learners in early childhood programs.

PARENTS

PARENTS want their children to attend high-quality programs that will prepare them for school and provide them with a good start in life. They want to know that their children are being well educated and cared for. Parents want their children to get along with others, be happy, and learn. How best to meet these legitimate parental expectations as well as federal, state, and local expectations is one of the ongoing challenges of early childhood programs and professionals.[1]

NAEYC STANDARDS

DEMAND FOR QUALITY EARLY CHILDHOOD PROGRAMS

The National Association for the Education of Young Children (NAEYC), the nation's largest organization of early childhood educators, accredits over seven thousand early childhood programs serving approximately six hundred thousand children.[2] These programs are only a fraction of the total number of early childhood programs in the United States. Think for a minute about what goes on in these and other programs from day to day. For many children, teachers and staff implement well-thought-out and articulated programs that provide for their growth and development across all the developmental domains—cognitive, linguistic, emotional, social, and physical. In other programs, children are not so fortunate.

With the national spotlight on the importance of the early years, the public is demanding more from early childhood professionals and their programs. On one hand, the public is willing to invest more heavily in early childhood programs, but on the other it is demanding that the early childhood profession and individual programs respond by providing meaningful, high-quality programs.[3] The public wants high-quality early childhood programs that do the following:

- *Help ensure children's early academic and school success.* The public believes that too many children are being left out and left behind. The **achievement gap**—the differences in school achievement between children of different socioeconomic and social groups is a serious national problem. As a result, more resources are being devoted to programs in order to close and erase achievement gaps.[4]

- *Provide for the inclusion of early literacy and reading readiness activities in programs and curricula that enable children to read on grade level in grades one, two, and three.* Early literacy is the key to much of school and life success, and school success begins in preschool and before.[5] Early literacy is everything children know about reading and writing before they can actually read and write. Children develop much of their capacity for learning in the first three years of life. Early childhood programs are challenged to assist parents in laying the foundation for children's early experiences with books and language for success in learning to read.

- *Learning environments that meet the needs of each child.* The public wants its early childhood programs to be inclusive and meet the learning, behavioral, cultural/linguistic, socioeconomic, and disability differences that are reflected in children and families.

- *Promote the national good.* The nation and politicians see the early years as one way to keep America politically and economically strong. In many ways, world leadership begins in the preschool. As a result, the president and other national leaders want to make sure our children are prepared for kindergarten by investing in early childhood education and dramatically expanding programs

achievement gap
The differences in school achievement between children of different socioeconomic and social groups.

to ensure that each child is ready to enter kindergarten.[6] There is a substantial amount of research that shows that a well-educated, high-performing workforce is the key to maintaining the nation's competitive advantage and leadership in the global economy of the twenty-first century.[7] Some of the benefits of investing in early childhood programs are as follows:

- *Contribute positively to today's workforce.* A public investment in early childhood programs allows parents to enter the workforce more easily, decrease their absenteeism, earn higher wages, move between jobs less frequently, and achieve higher productivity.

- *High returns on public investment in early care and education.* Rigorous peer-reviewed longitudinal studies show that high-quality programs offer one of the largest returns on investment of any public spending for economic development. Students who get off to a good start with high-quality early childhood care require fewer additional resources in school, and as adults, draw on fewer social services and pay more in taxes.[8]

MODEL PROGRAMS AND YOU

model early childhood program An exemplary approach to early childhood education that serves as a guide to best practices.

In this chapter we examine and discuss some of the more notable programs for use in early childhood settings designed to address children and family needs. As you read about and reflect on each of these, think about their purposes and curriculum and the ways each tries to meet the needs of children and families. Pause for a minute and review Table 6.1, which outlines and compares four of the **model early childhood programs** discussed in this text: the Montessori method, the HighScope educational model, Reggio Emilia approach, and the Project Approach.

Models are guides that provide us with instructions, ideas, and examples. We use models to guide a lot of what we do in life. We model our lives after others we respect and admire. We adopt the fashions of models in advertisements, and in early childhood education, we model our programs after highly respected models such as Montessori, HighScope, and Reggio Emilia. Even though none of these individual models is a perfect fit for all children, they nonetheless are widely used in the United States and around the world as blueprints to better serve young children and families. In addition,

TABLE 6.1 | Comparing Four Models of Early Childhood Education

Model	Main Features	Teacher's Role
Montessori 	• Theoretical basis is the philosophy and beliefs of Maria Montessori. • Prepared environment supports, invites, and enables learning. • Children educate themselves—self-directed learning. • Sensory materials invite and promote learning. • Has a set curriculum regarding what children should learn. Montessorians try to stay as close to Montessori's ideas as possible. • Children are grouped in multiage environments. • Children learn by manipulating materials and working with others. • Learning takes place through the senses.	• Follows the child's interests and needs. • Prepares an environment that is educationally interesting and safe. • Directs unobtrusively as children individually or in small groups engage in self-directed activity. • Observes, analyzes, and provides materials and activities appropriate for the child's sensitive periods of learning. • Maintains regular communications with the parent.

TABLE 6.1 | Comparing Four Models of Early Childhood Education (*continued*)

Model	Main Features	Teacher's Role
HighScope 	• Theory is based on Piaget, constructivism, Dewey, and Vygotsky. • Plan-do-review is the teaching–learning cycle. • Emergent curriculum is not planned in advance. • Children help determine curriculum. • Key experiences guide the curriculum in promoting children's active learning.	• Plans activities based on children's interests. • Facilitates learning through encouragement. • Engages in positive adult–child interaction strategies.
Reggio Emilia 	• Theory is based on Piaget, constructivism, Vygotsky, and Dewey. • Emergent curriculum is not planned in advance. • Curriculum is based on children's interests and experiences. • Curriculum is project oriented. • Hundred Languages of Children represents the symbolic representation of children's work and learning. • Learning is active. • Atelierista—a special teacher is trained in the arts. • Atelier—an art/design studio is used by children and teachers.	• Works collaboratively with other teachers. • Organizes environments rich in possibilities and provocations. • Acts as recorder for the children, helping them trace and revisit their words and actions.
Project Approach 	• Enables a small group of children to be involved in an investigation or project. • Is an authentic approach to discovery learning. • Can be used by all children including children with disabilities. • Provides a means for integrating concepts and ideas across the curriculum. For example, children use math to measure, conduct research on their topic, and read all kinds of literature (fictional and informational) about their project. • Puts constructivist ideas into action.	• Facilitate projects and investigations that come from children's thinking and ideas. • Enable and support children's behavior and work as they assume responsibility for project activities. • Encourage and support children to make choices and decisions about their project. • Value children's intrinsic motivation to be independent and do good work. • Provide a supportive classroom environment with the necessary and appropriate learning materials including technology. • Provide children with appropriate experiences that extend and enrich their project learning, such as selecting and providing appropriate reading materials, taking children on field trips, inviting outside parents and community members to talk with children about their project, etc.

other programs such as Head Start and Early Head Start and for-profit companies such as Knowledge Learning Corporation, the nation's largest provider of child care, also provide ideas for how to implement high-quality early childhood programs.

As an early childhood teacher, it is important for you to know about various programs for young children. Knowing about programs enables you to talk knowledgeably with colleagues and parents and to critically compare and contrast features of one program with another. As you engage in this reflection and critical analysis you will be able to identify what you think are the strengths and weaknesses of each program and what features of each program you like the best. Knowing about early childhood programs enables you to always be clear about what you believe is best for children and families and to think, talk, and act as a confident professional.

Even though all of the program models we discuss here are unique, at the same time they all have certain similarities. All of them, regardless of their particular philosophical orientation, have as primary goals respect for each child and how to provide the best education for all children.

Here are some critical decisions to make now. First, identify which features of these program models you can and cannot support. Second, decide which of these models and/or features of them you can embrace and incorporate into your own practice. An ongoing rule of the early childhood professional is to decide what you believe is best for children and families before you make decisions about what to teach.

THE MONTESSORI METHOD

Montessori method
A system of early childhood education founded on the ideas and practices of Maria Montessori.

The **Montessori method** continues to be very popular with early childhood professionals and parents in the United States and around the world. The Montessori approach is designed to support the natural development of children in a well-prepared environment. This method is attractive to parents and early childhood professionals for a number of reasons. First, Montessori education has always been identified as a quality program for young children. Second, parents who observe a good Montessori program like what they see: orderliness, independent children, self-directed learning, a calm environment, and children at the center of the learning process. Third, some public schools include Montessori as one of their program options, giving parents choices in the education of their children.

Five basic principles fairly and accurately represent how Montessori educators implement the Montessori method in many kinds of programs across the United States.

RESPECT FOR THE CHILD

Respect for the child is the cornerstone on which all other Montessori principles rest. Montessori believed that we—teachers, parents, and adults—don't respect children. She maintained that we try to force them to follow us without regard to their special needs. Thus, for Montessori and you, respect for children is the foundation—the cornerstone—of teaching children.

You show respect for children when you guide and scaffold their learning, enable them do things and learn for themselves, and differentiate your instruction to their learning and behavioral needs. When you are respectful of children, they are able to develop the skills and abilities necessary for effective learning, autonomy, and positive self-esteem.

THE ABSORBENT MIND

absorbent mind
The idea that the minds of young children are receptive to and capable of learning. The child learns unconsciously by taking in information from the environment.

Montessori believed that children educate themselves by absorbing knowledge directly into their minds. Simply by living, children learn to speak their native language.[9] This is the concept of the **absorbent mind**.

Montessori wanted us to understand that simply by living, children learn from their environment. Children are born to learn, and they are remarkable learning systems. Children learn because they are thinking beings, but what they learn depends greatly on their teachers, experiences, and environments.

Today, as early childhood professionals, we are reemphasizing Montessori's ideas that children are born to learn, are constantly ready to learn, and have the ability to learn.

SENSITIVE PERIODS

Montessori believed there are **sensitive periods** (or critical periods) when children are more susceptible to learning certain behaviors and can learn specific skills more easily.[10] Although all children experience the same sensitive periods (e.g., a sensitive period for writing), the timing varies for each child. One role of the teacher is to use observation to detect times of sensitivity and provide a prepared setting that supports optimum learning.

PREPARED ENVIRONMENT

Montessori believed that children learn best in a **prepared environment**, a place in which children can *do things for themselves*. The prepared environment makes learning materials and experiences available to children in an orderly and organized format. The classrooms that Montessori described are really what educators advocate when they talk about child-centered education and active learning. Freedom is the essential characteristic of the prepared environment. Because children within the environment are free to explore materials of their own choosing, they absorb what they find there. Maria Montessori was a master at creating environments for young children that enabled them to be independent, active, and learn on their own.

In a prepared environment, materials and activities provide for three basic areas of child involvement:

1. Practical life or motor education
2. Sensory materials for training the senses
3. Academic materials for teaching writing, reading, and mathematics

All these activities are taught according to a prescribed procedure.

PRACTICAL LIFE.   The prepared environment supports basic, **practical life** activities, such as walking from place to place in an orderly manner, carrying objects such as trays and chairs, greeting a visitor, and learning self-care skills. For example, *dressing frames* are designed to perfect the motor skills involved in buttoning, zipping, lacing, buckling, and tying. The philosophy for activities such as these is to make children independent and to develop concentration.

Practical life activities are taught through four different types of exercise:

1. *Care of the person:* Activities such as using dressing frames, polishing shoes, and washing hands
2. *Care of the environment:* For example, dusting, polishing a table, and raking leaves
3. *Social relations:* Lessons in grace and courtesy
4. *Analysis and control of movement:* Locomotor activities such as walking and balancing

sensitive periods In the Montessori method, those relatively brief times during which learning is most likely to occur. Also called *critical periods*.

prepared environment A classroom or other space that is arranged and organized to support learning in general and/or special knowledge and skills.

practical life Montessori activities that teach skills related to everyday living.

The Montessori prepared environment makes materials and experiences available for children to explore for themselves. Why is it important to prepare such an organized environment?

sensory materials
Montessori learning materials designed to promote learning through the senses and to train the senses for learning.

SENSORY MATERIALS. The **sensory materials** described in Figure 6.1 are among those found in a typical Montessori classroom. Materials for training and developing the senses have these characteristics:

- *Control of error.* Materials are designed so that children can see whether they make a mistake; for example, a child who does not build the blocks of the pink tower in their proper order does not achieve a tower effect.
- *Isolation of a single quality.* Materials are designed so that other variables are held constant except for the isolated quality or qualities. Therefore, all blocks of the pink tower are pink because size, not color, is the isolated quality.
- *Active involvement.* Materials encourage active involvement rather than the more passive process of looking.

Material	Illustration	Descriptions and Learning Purposes
Pink tower		Ten wooden cubes of the same shape and texture, all pink, the largest of which is 10 centimeters. Each succeeding block is 1 centimeter smaller. Children build a tower beginning with the largest block. (Visual discrimination of dimension)
Brown stairs		Ten wooden blocks, all brown, differing in height and width. Children arrange the blocks next to each other from thickest to thinnest so the blocks resemble a staircase. (Visual discrimination of width and height)
Red rods		Ten rod-shaped pieces of wood, all red, of identical thickness but differing in length from 10 centimeters to 1 meter. The child arranges the rods next to each other from largest to smallest. (Visual discrimination of length)
Cylinder blocks		Four individual wooden blocks that have holes of various sizes and matching cylinders; one block deals with height, one with diameter, and two with the relationship of both variables. Children remove the cylinders in random order, then match each cylinder to the correct hole. (Visual discrimination of size)
Smelling jars		Two identical sets of white opaque glass jars with removable tops through which the child cannot see but through which odors can pass. The teacher places various substances, such as herbs, in the jars, and the child matches the jars according to the smells. (Olfactory discrimination)
Baric tablets		Sets of rectangular pieces of wood that vary according to weight. There are three sets—light, medium, and heavy—which children match according to the weight of the tablets. (Discrimination of weight)
Color tablets		Two identical sets of small rectangular pieces of wood used for matching color or shading. (Discrimination of color and education of the chromatic sense)
Cloth swatches		Two identical swatches of cloth. Children identify them according to touch, first without a blindfold but later using a blindfold. (Sense of touch)
Tonal bells		Two sets of eight bells, alike in shape and size but different in color; one set is white, the other brown. The child matches the bells by tone. (Sound and pitch)
Sound boxes		Two identical sets of cylinders filled with various materials, such as salt and rice. Children match the cylinders according to the sound the fillings make. (Auditory discrimination)
Temperature jugs or thermic bottles		Small metal jugs filled with water of varying temperatures. Children match jugs of the same temperature. (Thermic sense and ability to distinguish between temperatures)

FIGURE 6.1 | Montessori Sensory Materials

- *Attractiveness.* Materials are attractive, with colors and proportions that appeal to children.

  Sensory materials have several purposes:

- To help sharpen children's powers of observation and visual discrimination as readiness for learning to read.
- To increase children's ability to think, a process that depends on the ability to distinguish, classify, and organize.
- To encourage and support children's readiness for writing and reading.

ACADEMIC MATERIALS.   The third area of Montessori materials is more academic. Exercises are presented in a sequence that encourages writing before reading. Reading is therefore an outgrowth of writing. Both processes, however, are introduced so gradually that children are never aware they are learning to write and read until one day they realize they are writing and reading. Describing this phenomenon, Montessori said that children "burst spontaneously" into writing and reading. Thus, Montessori anticipated contemporary educational literacy practices by integrating writing and reading and maintaining that writing lays the foundation for learning to read.

Montessori believed that many children were ready for writing at four years of age. Consequently, children who enter a Montessori system at age three have done most of the sensory exercises by the time they are four. It is not uncommon to see four- and five-year-olds in a Montessori classroom writing and reading.

Following are examples of Montessori materials that promote writing and reading:

- *Ten geometric forms and colored pencils.* These introduce children to the coordination necessary for writing. After selecting a geometric inset, children trace it on paper and fill in the outline with a colored pencil of their choosing.
- *Sandpaper letters.* Each letter of the alphabet is outlined in sandpaper on a card, with vowels in blue and consonants in red. Children see the shape, feel the shape, and hear the sound of the letter, which the teacher repeats when introducing it.
- *Movable alphabet with individual letters.* Consonants are red, vowels are blue. Children learn to put together familiar words, such as *pat* and *rat*.
- *Command cards.* A set of red cards with a single action word printed on each card. Children read the word on the card and do what the word tells them to do (e.g., run, jump).

Please take a moment to watch the following video of a typical Montessori prepared environment.

AUTO-EDUCATION

Montessori named the concept that children are capable of educating themselves **auto-education** (also known as self-education). Children who are actively involved in a prepared environment and who exercise freedom of choice literally educate themselves. Montessori teachers prepare classrooms in which children educate themselves.

auto-education
The idea that children teach themselves through appropriate materials and activities.

THE TEACHER'S ROLE

Montessori believed that it is necessary for the teacher to guide the child without letting him feel her presence too much, so that she may be always ready to supply the desired help, but is never the obstacle between the child and his experience.[11]

The Montessori teacher demonstrates key behaviors to implement this child-centered approach:

- *Make children the center of learning* because the teacher's task is not to talk, but to prepare and arrange a series of lessons in the prepared environment made for the child.[12]

- *Encourage children to learn* by providing freedom for them in the prepared environment.

- *Observe children* so as to prepare the best possible environment, recognizing sensitive periods and diverting inappropriate behavior to meaningful tasks.

- *Introduce learning materials,* demonstrate learning materials, and support children's learning. The teacher introduces learning materials after observing each child.

- *Prepare the learning environment* by ensuring that learning materials are provided in an orderly format and that the materials provide for appropriate experiences for each child.

- *Respect each child* and model ongoing respect for all children and their work.

MONTESSORI AND CONTEMPORARY PRACTICES

The Montessori approach supports many methods of instruction used in contemporary early childhood programs:

active learning
Involvement of the child with materials, activities, and projects in order to learn concepts, knowledge, and skills.

- *Integrated curriculum.* Montessori involves children in actively manipulating concrete materials across the curriculum—writing, reading, science, math, geography, and the arts.

- *Active learning.* Montessori classrooms practice **active learning**, the involvement of children using concrete, manipulative materials to learn concepts, knowledge, and skills.

- *Individualized instruction.* Montessori individualizes learning through children's interactions with the materials as they proceed at their own rates of mastery. Montessori materials are age appropriate for a wide age range of children in mixed-age classrooms.

- *Independence.* The Montessori environment emphasizes respect for children and promotes success, both of which encourage children to be independent.

- *Appropriate assessment.* In a Montessori classroom, observation is the primary means of assessing children's progress, achievement, and behavior. Well-trained Montessori teachers are skilled observers of children and are adept at translating their observations into appropriate ways of guiding, directing, facilitating, and supporting children's active learning.

- *Developmentally appropriate practice.* The concepts and process of developmentally appropriate curricula and practice are foundational in the Montessori method. The Montessori method emphasizes the uniqueness of each child and the importance of independent learning.

You can gain a good understanding of the ebb and flow of life in a Montessori classroom by reading and reflecting on the Voice from the Field, which describes a day at Children's House.

PROVIDING FOR DIVERSITY AND DISABILITY

Montessori education is ideally suited to meet the needs of children from diverse backgrounds, those with disabilities, and those with other special needs, such as giftedness. Montessori believed that all children are intrinsically motivated to learn and that they absorb knowledge when they are provided appropriate environments at appropriate times of development. Thus Montessorians believe in providing for individual differences in enriched environments.

FIGURE 6.2 | Two Examples of Rapidly Growing Apps for the Montessori Method—Letter Tracing and Grouping

MONTESSORI AT THE APPLE STORE

Sandpaper letters and number rods on I-Phone/Pad Apps? Yes, technology is integrating with the 105-year-old Montessori Method! Montessorium is one of the companies that has developed Montessori apps for both the iPad and iPhone (see Figure 6.2).

As you might expect, there are pros and cons for the use of apps in a Montessori setting.

Pros:

1. Apps may help spark a renewed interest in Montessori education by introducing Montessorians to the technological age.
2. The children of today are technologically oriented and want to learn with technology regardless of the program they are in; children should have access to technology and should use technology to learn.

At stake is the Montessori method's ability to change and to use technology to drive that change! I for one believe that apps will play an important role in the future of Montessori education, and if Montessori were alive today, she would be shopping at the Apple Store!

Cons:

1. Apps of a concrete material are not the same as hands-on experience with the material itself. For example, with an app students cannot feel the kinesthetic roughness of the sandpaper letters, and an app for the number rods does not allow children to feel the weight of the rods. Montessori said, "The hand is the tool of the mind."
2. Those who advocate staying "true" to Montessori's ideas and methods believe that deviations from what Montessori taught violate an authentic implementation of her method. Consequently, a virtual representation and application of Montessori's materials would be no substitute for the real thing.

This child is learning independence and active learning—two of the many methods that Montessorian programs use in contemporary early childhood programs. Montessori believed it was important for children to learn the arts as a basis for learning about their world.

Children's House Daily Schedule

This sample schedule is typical of a Montessori program. It is structured to allow for activities in the four main areas of the classroom—practical life, sensoral, math, and language materials—as well as the cultural areas of art, science, geography, and peace, and includes a rest period for the youngest children.

	Classroom Activities	Benefits for Children
8:00–10:45 Work Period	Children spend this uninterrupted time working on individual or small-group activities at a table or on a rug on the floor. Many activities require a lesson from the teacher. Others, such as puzzles, can be used without a lesson. Children who choose an activity that is too difficult for them are offered something that better matches their abilities.	These activities allow children to improve their attention span and concentration skills, small-motor control, eye–hand coordination, attention to detail, perseverance, and the joy of learning. Responsibility for one's own learning is developed as the children make their own choices.
10:45–11:15 Circle Time	This group activity includes calling the roll, a peace ceremony, grace and courtesy lessons, stories, songs, games, or lessons on something new in the classroom. Children help set the tables for lunch, feed the animals, water the plants, and perform other chores.	Whole-group lessons are an important time for children to learn how to take turns, participate appropriately in a larger society, share feelings and ideas, enjoy each other's company in songs and games, and learn respect for others.
11:15–11:45 Outside Play	Climbing on the play apparatus, sand play, and gardening are a few of the activities available on the playground.	Large-motor control, participation in group games, and learning about the wonders of nature take place as the children play outside.
11:45–12:25 Lunchtime	The children wash their hands, wait until all are seated before beginning, concentrate on manners and pleasant conversations at the table, take a taste of everything, pack up leftovers, throw away trash, and remain seated until everyone is finished and excused. After lunch, children help clean the tables and sweep the floor.	Respectful behavior at mealtime is learned through modeling and direction from the teacher. Discussions can include manners, healthy nutrition, and family customs. Cooperation and teamwork are fostered as children help each other clean up and transition to the next activity.
12:25–12:50 Outside Play	Climbing on the play apparatus, sand play, and gardening are again available on the playground.	See earlier outside play.
12:50–3:00 Age-Appropriate Activities	Nappers—Children under the age of four and a half sleep or rest in a small-group setting. Pre-kindergarten—Children between four and a half and five rest quietly for thirty minutes and then join the kindergarten group. Kindergarten—Children who are five years old by September 30 and are ready for the kindergarten experience continue to work on the lessons that were begun in the morning; they also have more extensive lessons in geography, science, art appreciation, writing, and music.	Rest rejuvenates these young children for participation in the remainder of the day. Working alongside kindergartners encourages pre-kindergarten children to emulate their classmates in academic as well as social skills. Kindergarten children benefit from being part of a small group and working to their full potential in any area of their choosing. The joy of learning comes to life as they concentrate on works of intrinsic interest to them.
3:00–3:45 Outside Play	Climbing on the play apparatus, sand play, and gardening are again available on the playground.	See earlier outside play.
3:45–4:00 Group Snack	Children share a snack before starting the afternoon activities.	A snack provides another opportunity to encourage manners and healthy eating.
4:00–5:30 After-School Fun	Activities at this time can include games, art, drama, music, movement, cooking, an educational video, or the continuation of Montessori work begun earlier in the day.	Cooperation, teamwork, and creative expression are fostered as children build self-esteem.
5:30 End of Day	All children should be picked up by this time.	Pick-up time offers the children an opportunity to say good-bye to the teacher and each other. It also gives the teacher a chance to speak briefly with parents.

Source: Contributed by Keturah Collins, owner and director, Children's House Montessori School, Reston, Virginia, www.childrenshouse-montessori.com.

FURTHER THOUGHTS

In many respects, Maria Montessori was a person for all generations who contributed greatly to early childhood programs and practices. Many of her ideas—such as preparing the environment, providing child-sized furniture, promoting active learning and independence, and using multiage/mixed-age grouping—are fully incorporated into early childhood classrooms. As a result, it is easy to take her contributions for granted. We do many things in a Montessorian way without thinking too much about it!

What is important is that early childhood professionals use the best of Montessori for children of the twenty-first century. As with any practice, professionals must adopt approaches to fit the children they are teaching while remaining true to what is best in that approach. Respect for children is never out of date and should be accorded to all children regardless of culture, gender, or socioeconomic background.

Reflect and Apply: Montessori

HIGHSCOPE: A CONSTRUCTIVIST CURRICULUM

The **HighScope educational model**[13] gears curriculum to children's stages of development and promotes constructive processes of learning that broaden children's emerging intellectual and social skills.[14] The HighScope model is based on Piaget's cognitive development theory and fits well with Vygotsky's theory of social development.

HighScope educational model A program for young children based on Piaget's and Vygotsky's ideas.

BASIC PRINCIPLES AND GOALS OF THE HIGHSCOPE CURRICULUM

There are three principles of the HighScope curriculum:

* Active participation of children in choosing, organizing, and evaluating learning activities, which are undertaken with careful teacher observation and guidance in a learning environment with a rich variety of materials located in various classroom learning centers.

* Regular daily planning by the teaching staff in accord with a developmentally based curriculum model and careful child observations.

* Developmentally sequenced goals and materials for children based on HighScope's "key developmental indicators."[15]

The HighScope program strives to develop in children a broad range of skills, including problem solving, interpersonal skills, and communication skills that are essential for successful living in a rapidly changing society. The curriculum encourages student initiative by providing children with materials, equipment, and time to pursue activities they design themselves. At the same time, it provides teachers with a framework for guiding children's independent activities toward sequenced learning goals. The teacher plays a key role in instructional activities by scaffolding (supporting and gently extending) children's knowledge and understanding; selecting appropriate, developmentally sequenced

Notice the facial expressions of these children as they engage in active, hands-on learning with manipulative materials.

material; playing as partners with children and sharing control of the decision-making process; and encouraging children to adopt an active problem-solving approach to learning. This teacher–student interaction—teachers helping students achieve developmentally sequenced goals while also encouraging them to set many of their own goals—uniquely distinguishes the HighScope curriculum from direct instruction and teacher-centered curricula.[16]

FIVE ELEMENTS OF THE HIGHSCOPE CURRICULUM

Professionals who use the HighScope curriculum are fully committed to providing settings in which children actively learn and construct their own knowledge. Teachers create the context for learning by implementing and supporting five essential elements: active learning, classroom arrangement (learning environment), the daily schedule, assessment, and comprehensive curriculum-content.

ACTIVE LEARNING.   Teachers support children's active learning by providing a variety of materials, making plans and reviewing activities with children, carefully observing individual children to determine their interests and abilities, interacting with children to scaffold learning, and leading small- and large-group active learning activities.

CLASSROOM ARRANGEMENT.   The learning environment is divided into well-defined interest centers (for example, art area, book and writing area, block area, house area, toy area, computer area, and outdoor play area) that encourage choice. Interest areas and materials are labeled with symbols, representative objects, letters, and/or words so children can find, use, and return materials and equipment on their own. This encourages development of self-direction and independence and supports children's emerging conceptual understanding of the physical and functional properties used to organize the world.

The teacher selects the centers and activities to use in the classroom based on several considerations:

- Interests of the children (e.g., preschool children are interested in blocks, books, manipulative toys, pretend play, and art)
- Opportunities for children to acquire essential knowledge and skills in all areas of academic, social-emotional, physical, and artistic development
- Sensitivity to the diversity of the children in the classroom including their culture, language, developmental levels, and special needs

Teachers apply these same considerations in designing the outdoor learning environment.

Classroom arrangement is an essential part of professional practice in order to appropriately implement a program's philosophy. This is true for every program with which you may be involved. A well-organized classroom provides a rich context for children's learning.

ASSESSMENT.   Teachers use the Child Observation Record (COR)[17] to record objective anecdotal notes about each child's behavior in every key area of development and periodically score the COR to monitor individual and group progress. Teachers use these observations to scaffold individual learning and to provide materials and activities that support learning in the classroom as a whole. They also share COR observations with parents and discuss how families can extend their children's learning at home. The COR is available in print and online versions; the online version includes a mobile app for entering observational notes.

CURRICULUM/CONTENT. The HighScope educational method is based on **key developmental indicators (KDIs)** in eight curriculum content areas. The KDIs are early childhood milestones that guide teachers as they plan and assess learning experiences and interact with children to support learning.[18] The eight curriculum content areas are approaches to learning; social and emotional development; physical development, health, and well-being; mathematics; creative arts; science and technology; and social studies. You can review all KDIs by accessing the HighScope website.

key developmental indicators (KDIs) Activities that foster developmentally important skills and abilities.

DAILY ROUTINE. HighScope preschool programs follow a predictable sequence of events known as the daily routine. This framework provides for the day's events that support children's security and independence. The daily routine consists of these components:

- *Plan-do-review sequence (planning time, work time, recall time).* The **plan-do-review** sequence is unique to the HighScope curriculum. It includes a ten- to fifteen-minute period during which children plan what they want to do during work time (the area to visit, materials to use, and friends to play with); a forty-five- to sixty-minute work time for children to carry out their plans or shift to new activities that interest them; and another ten- to fifteen-minute period for review and recall. This review permits children to reflect on what they did, how it was done, and what they learned in the process. It brings closure to children's planning and work time activities. Putting their ideas and experiences to words also facilitates children's language development, and it enables children to represent to others their mental schemes.

plan-do-review A sequence in which children, with the help of the teacher, initiate plans for projects or activities, work in learning centers to implement their plans, and then review what they have done with the teacher and their fellow classmates.

- *Small-group time.* During this time, a small group of children meet with an adult to experiment with materials, try out new skills, and solve problems. Adults initiate the activity, but children are free to explore the materials in any ways that interest them.
- *Large-group time.* Large-group time builds a sense of community. All the children and adults in the class come together for movement and music activities, interactive storytelling, and other shared experiences. As with small-group time, adults initiate the activity, but children carry out their own ideas, contribute suggestions, and take turns being the group leader.
- *Outside time.* Children and adults spend at least thirty minutes outside every day, enjoying vigorous play in the fresh air and experiencing nature firsthand.
- *Transition times.* Transitions are the minutes between other activities of the day, as well as arrival and departure times. Teachers intentionally plan transitions to make them active learning experiences and strive to make transitions pass smoothly because they set the stage for the next segment in the day's schedule.
- *Eating and resting times (if applicable).* Meals and snacks allow children to enjoy eating healthy food in a supportive social setting. Rest is for quiet, solitary activities.
- *Adult team planning time.* This time occurs every day in a HighScope program. It can happen during children's nap time, before children arrive, or after they leave. The teaching team meets to discuss their observations of children's developing abilities and interests and plan strategies to scaffold individual and group learning.

ADVANTAGES OF USING HIGHSCOPE. Implementing the HighScope curriculum has several advantages. First, it offers you a method for implementing a constructivist-based program that has its roots in cognitive theory. Second, it is widely popular and has been extensively researched and tested in the United States and other countries.

Third, an extensive network of training and support is provided by the HighScope Foundation. You can learn more about HighScope through its website. Reviewing the website will help you to determine which characteristics of the HighScope program you would like to implement in your classroom and professional development activities.

PROVIDING FOR DIVERSITY AND DISABILITY

The HighScope curriculum is a developmentally appropriate approach that is child centered and promotes active learning. The use of learning centers, active learning, and the plan-do-review cycle, as well as allowing children to progress at their own pace, provides for children's individual and special needs. HighScope teachers emphasize the broad cognitive, social, physical, and creative abilities that are important for each child, instead of focusing on a child's deficits. HighScope teachers identify at what level a child is developmentally and then scaffold (support and gently extend) learning by providing a rich range of experiences appropriate for that level. For example, they would encourage a four-year-old who is functioning at a two-year-old level to express his or her plans by pointing, gesturing, and saying single words, and they would immerse the child in a conversational environment that provides many natural opportunities for using and hearing language.[19] Many early childhood programs for children with special needs incorporate the HighScope approach.

REGGIO EMILIA APPROACH

Reggio Emilia, a city in northern Italy, is widely known for its approach to educating young children.[20] Founded by Loris Malaguzzi (1920–1994), Reggio Emilia sponsors programs for children from three months to six years of age. Certain essential beliefs and practices underlie the **Reggio Emilia approach**. These basic features define the Reggio approach, make it a constructivist program, and enable it to be adapted and implemented in many U.S. early childhood programs. Read the Voice from the Field, "Reggio Emilia," to understand how this model is implemented at the Boulder Journey School on page 174.

Reggio Emilia approach
An approach to education based on the philosophy and practice that children are active constructors of their own knowledge.

BELIEFS ABOUT CHILDREN AND HOW THEY LEARN

As we have discussed, your beliefs about young children determine how you teach them, what kind of programs you provide for them, and your expectations for their learning and development. This is the case with Reggio. Their beliefs drive their program practices.

RESPECT FOR CHILDREN.   Respect for each child is a foundational theme in the Reggio approach. Teachers do not impose adult ideas or daily schedules on children. Rather, the program places each child at the center of learning, and materials used for such learning are child centered and child created.

RELATIONSHIPS.   The Reggio approach focuses on each child and is conducted in relation to the family, other children, teachers, environment of the school, community, and the wider society. Each school is viewed as a system in which all these interconnected relationships are reciprocal, activated, and supported. In other words, as Vygotsky believed, children learn through social interactions. In addition, as Montessori indicated, the environment supports and is important to learning.

When preparing space, teachers offer the possibility for children to be with the teachers and many of the other children, or with just a few of them. Also, children can be alone when they need a little niche to stay by themselves.

Teachers are always aware, however, children learn a great deal in exchanges with their peers, especially when they interact in small groups. Such small groups of two, three, four, or five children provide possibilities for paying attention, listening to each other, developing curiosity and interest, asking questions, and responding. Also, groups provide opportunities for negotiation.

HUNDRED LANGUAGES.   Malaguzzi believed that children use many languages to express themselves.

The hundred languages Malaguzzi was referring to include drawing, building, modeling, sculpturing, discussing, inventing, discovering, and more. However, art and artistic products are the main medium for representing children's thinking. Teachers are encouraged to create environments in which children can literally use all hundred languages to learn. Access the "Hundred Languages" on the Reggio Emilia website.

TIME.   Reggio Emilia teachers believe time is not set by a clock and that continuity is not interrupted by the calendar. Children's own sense of time and their personal rhythms are considered in planning and carrying out activities and projects. The full-day schedule provides sufficient time for being together among peers in an environment that is conducive to getting things done with satisfaction.

Teachers get to know the personal rhythms and learning styles of each child. This is possible in part because children stay with the same teachers and the same peer group for three-year cycles (infancy to three years and three years to six years).

ADULTS' ROLES

In the Reggio approach, adults play a very powerful role in children's lives; children's well-being is connected to the well-being of parents and teachers. One of the essential things you notice from the programs discussed in this text is that high-quality teachers are essential for high-quality programs.

THE TEACHER.   Teachers observe and listen closely to children to know how to plan or proceed with their work. They ask questions and discover children's ideas, hypotheses, and theories. They collaboratively discuss what they have observed and recorded and make flexible plans and preparations. Teachers then enter into dialogues with the children and offer them occasions for discovering and also revisiting and reflecting on experiences, since they consider learning an ongoing process. Teachers are partners with children in a continual process of research and learning.

THE ATELIERISTA.   A teacher trained in the visual arts, the **atelierista**, works closely with teachers and children in every preprimary school and makes visits to the infant/toddler centers. The atelier (the studio area, see page 172) is the focal point for the atelierista and children.

atelierista A teacher trained in the visual arts who works with teachers and children.

PARENTS.   Parents are an essential component of the program and are included in the advisory committee that runs each school. Parents' participation is expected and supported and takes many forms: day-to-day interaction, work in the schools, discussion of educational and psychological issues, special events, excursions, and celebrations.

THE ENVIRONMENT

The infant/toddler centers and school programs are the most visible aspect of the work done by teachers and parents in Reggio Emilia. They convey many messages, of which the most immediate is that this is a place where adults have thought about the quality and the instructive power of space.

THE PHYSICAL SPACE.   The layout of physical space, in addition to welcoming all who enter, fosters encounters, communication, and relationships. The arrangement of structures, objects, and activities encourages choices, problem solving, and discoveries in the process of learning.

The centers and schools using the Reggio Emilia approach are beautiful. Their beauty comes from the message the whole school conveys about children and teachers engaged together in the pleasure of learning. There is attention to detail everywhere: in the color of the walls, the shape of the furniture, the arrangement of simple objects on shelves and tables. Light from the windows and doors shines through transparent collages and weavings made by children. Healthy green plants are everywhere. Behind the shelves displaying shells or other found or made objects are mirrors that reflect the patterns that children and teachers have created.

The environment is also highly personal. For example, a series of small boxes made of white cardboard creates a grid on the wall of a school. On each box the name of a child or a teacher is printed with rubber-stamp letters. These boxes are used for leaving little surprises or messages for one another. Communication is valued and favored at all levels.

The space in the centers and schools of Reggio Emilia is personal in still another way: It is full of the children's own work. Everywhere there are paintings, drawings, paper sculptures, wire constructions, transparent collages coloring the light, and mobiles moving gently overhead. Such things turn up even in unexpected spaces like stairways and bathrooms. Although the work of the children is pleasing to the eye, it is not intended as decoration, but rather to show and document the competence of children, the beauty of their ideas, and the complexity of their learning processes.

atelier A special area or studio for creating projects.

THE ATELIER.   A special workshop or studio, called an **atelier**, is set aside and used by all the children and teachers in the school. It contains a great variety of tools and resource materials, along with records of past projects and experiences.[21]

The activities and projects, however, do not take place only in the atelier. Smaller spaces called mini-ateliers are set up in each classroom. In fact, each classroom becomes an active workshop with children involved with a variety of materials and experiences that they have discussed and chosen with teachers and peers. In the view of Reggio educators, the children's use of many media is not art or a separate part of the curriculum, but rather an inseparable, integral part of the whole cognitive/symbolic expression involved in the process of learning.

Observe and Analyze

PROGRAM PRACTICES

Cooperation is the powerful working mode that makes the achievement of the goals set by Reggio approach educators possible. Teachers work in pairs in each classroom. They see themselves as researchers gathering information about their work with children by means of continual documentation. The strong collegial relationships that are maintained with teachers and staff enable them to engage in collaborative discussion and interpretation of both teachers' and children's work.

DOCUMENTATION. Transcriptions of children's remarks and discussions, photographs of their activity, and representations of their thinking and learning using many media are carefully arranged by the atelierista, along with the other teachers, to document the work and the process of learning. **Documentation** has many functions:

- Making parents aware of children's experiences and maintaining their involvement
- Allowing teachers to understand children better and to evaluate their own work, thus promoting professional growth
- Facilitating communication and exchange of ideas among educators
- Making children aware that their effort is valued
- Creating an archive that traces the history of the school and the pleasure of learning by many children and their teachers

documentation Records of children's work, including videos, photographs, art, work samples, projects, and drawings.

CURRICULUM AND PRACTICES. The curriculum is not established in advance. Teachers express general goals and make hypotheses about what direction activities and projects might take. Based on these discussions, teachers make appropriate preparations for their individualized curriculum. Then, after observing children in action, together teachers compare, discuss, and interpret their observations. Teachers then make choices regarding what to offer and how to sustain the children in their exploration and learning and share those choices with the children. In fact, the curriculum emerges in the process of each activity or project and is flexibly adjusted accordingly through this continuous dialogue among teachers and with children.

FURTHER THOUGHTS. Keep a number of things in mind as you consider the Reggio Emilia approach and how it might relate to your work as an early childhood educator. First, its theoretical base rests within constructivism and shares ideas compatible with those of Piaget, Vygotsky, Dewey, and Gardner, and the process of learning by doing. Second, there is no set curriculum. Rather, the curriculum emerges or springs from children's interests and experiences. This approach is, for many, difficult to implement and does not ensure that children will learn basic academic skills valued by contemporary American society. Third, the Reggio Emilia approach is suited to a particular culture and society. How this approach works, flourishes, and meets the educational needs of children in an Italian village may not necessarily be appropriate for meeting the needs of contemporary American children. The Italian view of education is that it is the responsibility of the state, and the state provides high levels of financial support. Even though education is a state function in the United States, traditionally local community control of education is a powerful and sacred part of American education. The following Voice from the Field feature provides an excellent overview of a Reggio program.

Reflect and Apply: Reggio Emilia

PROVIDING FOR DIVERSITY AND DISABILITY

The Grant Early Childhood Center in Cedar Rapids, Iowa, meets the challenge of inclusion through Prizing Our National Differences (POND), a program based on the Reggio Emilia approach. The POND program includes all children with disabilities as full participants in general education classrooms with their age-appropriate peers. Two

Boulder Journey School: Inspired by Reggio Emilia Educators

Boulder Journey School is a full-day, year-round school that welcomes over 200 children, ages 6 weeks to 6 years, and their families. Beginning in 1995, Boulder Journey School educators have been engaged in a study of the internationally renowned schools for young children in Reggio Emilia, Italy. (For more information about these schools see Linking to Learning at the end of the chapter). Educators in Reggio Emilia illuminate the potential of chil-

dren to actively engage in the co-construction of knowledge, and give visibility to the myriad possibilities for learning that exist when adults honor and respect children as citizens of the present and of the future.

Inspired by the philosophy of education and pedagogy of the schools in Reggio Emilia, at Boulder Journey School we view young children as:

Curious—posing problems and seeking understanding

Capable—asking questions, forming hypotheses and testing theories in an effort to find answers

Competent—sharing their identities and experiences in order to create a culture within the school and within the community in which they reside

Co-constructors of knowledge—collaborating with other children and adults; learning as individuals while contributing to the learning of the group

Creative—not overly attached to traditional culture; comfortable with innovative ways of viewing and interacting with the world

At Boulder Journey School, based on our image of children, we strive to listen to and understand what children have to say about their world, as they perceive it. We maintain that children's voices must be present and central to all aspects of their learning; their ideas, both anticipated and surprising, are invited, acknowledged and respected. As a school community, we support children in constructing, clarifying, deepening, extending, representing, and expressing their ideas by offering abundant materials and experiences and by encouraging the development of long-term investigations. These investigations emanate from and are extended through adults' documented observations of children's questions, thoughts, and actions.

BOULDER JOURNEY SCHOOL: IN PRACTICE

Teachers in a classroom for four-year-olds listened to the children's conversations about the period of time that one of their teachers would be away on maternity leave. Observing and documenting the children's discussions about the concept of time led to the teachers' decision to assess the children's understanding and confusion about the organization of time and about the adult tools that are typically used to map this concept—clocks, schedules, and calendars. As a result of this process, the teachers realized

that calendars typically designed for classrooms are based on adult ideas of what children would find useful. For example, the month of September is often filled with numbered leaves and October with numbered pumpkins. But the children in their class were interested in using the calendar as a tool to track much-anticipated events, such as their birthdays and visits by grandparents—the true purpose of a calendar.

Based on the teachers' documented findings, a question emerged: How can teachers create a tool to support the children's desire to better comprehend and record time? Calendars are based on written words and numbers, but the four-year-old children in this class were still predominantly reading pictures. Initiated by children and with the support of teachers, the children spent much of the year creating and developing their own unique symbol system to record upcoming events on a year-long calendar. This is an excellent example of co-constructivism, as the children realized that the symbols they created required a shared meaning among their classmates, as opposed to having exclusive meaning to the child who created it.

The children's perceptions of time, specifically time as organized by the calendar, documented and interpreted by teachers, led to a long-term investigation not only surrounding the concept of time, but also of the concept of symbols for anticipating and remembering events in time and for communicating these events to others.

Sources: Contributed by Dr. Ellen L. Hall, founder and executive director, and Alison Maher, education director, Boulder Journey School, Boulder, Colorado. Photos courtesy of Boulder Journey School, Boulder, Colorado.

core ingredients of the Reggio approach facilitate successful inclusion at Grant Early Childhood Center:

1. ***Encouraging collaborative relationships.*** For example, children older than five years of age who need special education services are included with kindergarten and first grade classes.

2. ***Constructing effective environments for each child.*** For example, members of Grant's support team include a counselor, speech therapist, occupational therapist, physical therapist, psychologist, resource teacher, nurse, and two Title I teachers. The support team attempts to address the individual needs of students through the PSS (POND Support Sessions) and IDM (Instructional Decision Making) processes to ensure children are getting the proper services needed to succeed.[22]

THE PROJECT APPROACH

The **Project Approach** is another very popular method used in early childhood education. The Reggio Emilia program is an excellent example of the project approach in action.

With the Project Approach, an investigation is undertaken by a small group of children within a class, sometimes by a whole class, and occasionally by an individual child. The key feature of a project is that it is a search for answers to questions about a topic worth learning more about—something the children are interested in.[23]

Projects provide the backbone of the children's and teachers' learning experiences. These projects are based on the strong conviction that learning by doing is of great importance and that to discuss in groups and to revisit ideas and experiences is the premier way of gaining better understanding and learning.

Ideas for projects originate in the experiences of children and teachers as they construct knowledge together. Projects can last from a few days to several months. They may start from a chance event, an idea, or a problem posed by one or more children or from an experience initiated directly by teachers.

The Voice from the Field "How to Use the Project Approach" on pages 176 and 177 is a Competency Builder that shows how you can use projects effectively to involve children in activities that interest them and teach young children traditional academic subjects, such as literacy.

Project Approach
An in-depth investigation of a topic worth learning more about.

Check Your Understanding: Project Approach

ACCOMMODATING DIVERSE LEARNERS

Meet Esmeralda, an energetic and precocious Mexican American four-year-old. She loves to read and play outside with her older brother and with trucks and dolls. But for all of Esmeralda's intrinsic gifts, she faces a great disadvantage because of the achievement gaps that exist in American education today. Research on the achievement gaps reveals that, on average, African American and Latino students are two to three years of learning behind Caucasian students of the same age.[24] Furthermore, in math and reading scores across the fourth and eighth grades, 48 percent of African Americans and 43 percent of Latinos are "below basic," whereas only 17 percent of Caucasians are below basic.[25] These gaps exist in every state and in more pronounced extremes in large urban school districts.[26]

COMPETENCY BUILDER

How to Use the Project Approach

Students in the K–1 classroom at University Primary School in St. Louis, Missouri, begin their day reading a daily sign-in question that is intended to provoke a thoughtful response:

Have you ever eaten the flowers of a plant?
Do you think a van is more like a car or a bus?

Such questions are related to the topic under study and are used to engage children in discussing different views during their whole-group meeting later in the morning.

Opportunities for children to express themselves abound at University Primary School. In addition to an hour of systematic literacy instruction, authentic opportunities to read and write occur throughout the day in the course of the children's regular activities.

INTEGRATING LANGUAGE ARTS WITH THE PROJECT APPROACH

The Project Approach involves students in in-depth investigation of worthy real-world topics: Learning becomes meaningful for them as they pursue answers to their own questions.* Students can carry out specific literacy-related activities in each phase of project investigation:

PHASE 1 Exploring Previous Experiences

- Brainstorm what is already known about a project topic
- Write or dictate stories about memories and experiences
- Categorize and label experiences

Activities you can incorporate into phase 1 that allow children to explore previous experiences are as follows:

- Memory drawings or stories
- Concept webs or maps of student ideas (e.g., Venn diagrams)
- Questionnaires that children develop to ask their peers or parents

PHASE 2 Investigating the Topic

- Write questions, predictions, and hypotheses
- Write questions to ask experts
- Write questionnaires and surveys

- Write thank-you letters to experts
- Record findings
- Record data
- Make all types of lists (what materials need to be collected, what will be shared with others, who will do which tasks)

- Listen to stories and informational texts read aloud
- Read secondary sources to help answer questions
- Compare what was read with what the experts shared

For example, students at the University Primary School work in small groups on subtopics of the larger topic and share what they find with the other students in the class, giving them authentic reasons to express what they have newly learned during phase 2. Fieldwork includes interviewing experts, visiting places of interest, and delving into secondary sources including Internet resources, books, or artifacts.

PHASE 3 Sharing the Project with Parents and Others

- Make charts, displays, and PowerPoint presentations
- Write reports or plays that demonstrate new understanding
- Write invitations to a culminating event
- Host a culminating event as an open house

In phase 3, children share findings with other students and their families. For example, how students at University Primary School have explored music, construction, communication, and measurement through project investigations are described fully on the Primary School website.

Throughout all phases of their project investigation, students have authentic contexts to read, spell, write words, and build their vocabulary. In addition, comparing what they knew with what they have learned from the primary and secondary sources, they develop their analytical thinking and comprehension skills. And they become more fluent readers and writers by using their skills to answer their own questions.

Providing Direct Instruction in Reading and Writing

The five reading components articulated in the No Child Left Behind Act—phonemic awareness, phonics, fluency, vocabulary, and comprehension—are taught throughout the students' day within the context of project investigation and during small-group direct literacy instruction. Direct instruction includes a whole-group meeting during which the teacher reads books aloud (i.e., shared reading) for specific purposes. The teacher may choose to highlight the project topic or specific authors or illustrators or to focus on rhyming words or specific patterns of phonemes.

Following the shared reading time, students engage in writing activities related to the books they heard read aloud. These activities may include literature extensions that encourage students to write creatively. They may write a different ending to a story or write a related story from a different point of view. Students may also write their own stories, using the principles of the writer's workshop, in which students learn to edit and extend their language skills. The teacher may also introduce extended mini-lessons on tools of writing, such as alliteration, similes, metaphors, or syllabic rhythms.

After their noon recess, students choose books to read quietly while the teacher provides individual guided reading. Project-related books may be a popular choice. Students conclude their silent reading with approximately ten minutes to engage in buddy reading. During the buddy reading time, students talk about what they have just read with their buddy and read favorite excerpts of their books to their buddy. This collaboration reinforces comprehension skills and instills the love of literature that motivates all children to read. At University Primary School, students are always improving and using their literacy skills to learn.

*L. G. Katz and S. C. Chard, Engaging Children's Minds: The Project Approach, 2nd ed. (Norwood, NJ: Ablex, 2000).

Source: Contributed by Nancy B. Hertzog, professor, educational psychology, University of Washington, and former director of University Primary School at the University of Illinois.

It is certain you will have children from different backgrounds in your early childhood classroom. You and other early childhood professionals must help close the achievement gap. You have the power to make a difference in children's lives.

CLOSING THE GAPS

The most important thing you can do is be the most effective teacher you can be. You can use effective educational strategies that respond to and are sensitive to the diversity of families and children. You create effective educational strategies when you do the following:

- *Use developmentally appropriate (DAP) practice.* DAP serves as a framework for you to plan the environment and the curriculum. This allows you to create individualized activities and instruction that build on each child's strengths. For children with disabilities of any kind, accommodate and differentiate. For example, because Esmeralda is economically disadvantaged, she may not have had the same resources available to her as her peers to support her development. You may have to spend extra time with Esmeralda to "play catch up," or offer one-on-one time a few days a week before school starts in the morning to ensure she achieves school and state standards.

- *Create accessible physical environments.* Environments that are healthy, safe, respectful, supportive, and challenging support children's independence and interaction and increase achievement. Be familiar with the principles and practices of **universal design (UD)**, the design of products, services, and environments that are usable and accessible for all children. Universal design is intended to make all environments accessible for all people regardless of age, situation, or ability. For example, new paper towel dispensers and faucets that are now common in

universal design (UD)
A broad-spectrum solution that produces buildings, products, and environments that are usable and effective for everyone, not just people with disabilities.

many restrooms and classrooms operate on a motion sensor. This assists young children with mobility or strength issues, and even when they have to hold something in one hand!

You can make environments physically accessible for children by following the principles of UD in these ways:

- **Equitable use.** Make high-quality resources available to all. Ensure that all children have the opportunity and the knowledge to use classroom materials, technology, and networks.

- **Environmental flexibility.** Classrooms and materials should be movable, malleable, and manageable. You should be flexible enough to allow students to rearrange materials, chairs, and so on, if they need to.

- **Simple and intuitive.** Classrooms should be arranged simply enough so that even young children can navigate and understand how things work and where to find and store materials, books, and so on.

- **Perceptible information.** Children should find it easy to look around a classroom and gather the information they need. For example, objects should be clearly labeled and/or color coded. Avoid clutter to prevent confusion, mobility problems, and sensory overload.

- **Tolerance for error.** Physical environments should be forgiving. Materials should be sturdy but not dangerous. For example, do not use a toy chest in your classroom unless it has a lid support to hold the lid open in any position. Make sure the toy box or chest has ventilation holes.

- **Create accessible social environments.** Universal design is intended to make all environments accessible for all people regardless of age, situation, or ability. This pertains to social environments as well as physical environments. You can make environments socially accessible to Esmeralda and others by following the principles of UD.

  - **Cultural inclusiveness.** Include material and subject matter that is culturally inclusive. For example, provide information that goes home in Spanish, study Spanish stories, poetry, and songs as well as other cultural contributions that typically make up the curriculum. Also, ensure that Esmeralda's family is encouraged and supported by the school community. For example, introduce families to one another, encourage parents to join activities, and help to resolve hurdles to their involvement.

  - **Accept all children.** Be sure to remain flexible in your understanding and approach to children from all backgrounds, cultures, languages, and developmental level. Accept children for who they are, but also challenge them to grow. Help classmates develop flexibility through modeling and discussion.

  - **Simple and intuitive.** Follow your gut and listen to what your intuition tells you about a child. For example, if you sense a child is falling behind, has trouble at home, or has difficulties with friends or peers, don't ignore your intuition. Listen to yourself, observe the child closely, and check with the child on a one-to-one basis. Whatever you do, don't just assume the problem will go away on its own. A child who is struggling in one area is usually struggling in another, and often the struggles are connected. Sometimes the simplest or smallest things, like an extra moment of encouragement or even asking the child directly, can brighten a day and improve chances of success.

- *Perceptible information.* Make social expectations and guidelines clear and accessible. Classroom rules should be posted clearly and yours should always be a model for positive social interactions and behavior.
- *Tolerance for error.* Accept mistakes. Children from different cultures and socioeconomic status may have different cultural and educational backgrounds. You may have to help these children play "catch up" so that they can succeed. This means that you need to be patient, encouraging, and tolerant of perspectives and experiences different from your own.
- *Collaborate with other professionals.* Collaboration enables you to develop activities and opportunities designed to promote student success. Collaboration with local agencies and institutions facilitates interactions that benefit children, families, and schools. For example, you can work closely with food banks, local Big Brother Big Sister chapters, libraries, Salvation Army, and others; all of which can be tapped to benefit Esmeralda and other children at your school. In addition, appeal to local advocacy lawyers, pediatricians, psychiatrists, and family counselors to provide pro bono services to children, families, and schools.

Even though the program models discussed here are unique, at the same time they all have certain similarities. All of them, regardless of their particular philosophical orientation, have as their primary goal to provide the best education for all children. Universal design helps achieve this goal.

ACTIVITIES FOR PROFESSIONAL DEVELOPMENT

ETHICAL DILEMMA

"CAVEAT EMPTOR—BUYER BEWARE!"

Victoria Maitland wants only the best for her four-year-old, Kathy. Several months ago, a new Montessori school opened in her town. At the same time, Victoria read an article in the newspaper about how the founders of Google and Amazon are Montessori graduates. Victoria figured if it was good enough for Larry Page, Sergi Brin, and Jeff Bezos, it would certainly be good enough for Kathy. Victoria enrolled Kathy in the newly opened Montessori school. Unfortunately, after six months at the Montessori school, Victoria is disappointed. "It isn't working for Kathy. She seems disinterested and bored. I thought Montessori was going to engage her and make her excited about learning." Last week Victoria talked with the head mistress of the Montessori school and was dismayed to learn that none of the teachers were Montessori certified and that the school was not affiliated with any Montessori association.

What should Victoria do? Should she demand her money back for all of the tuition she has paid for Kathy? Or, should she immediately withdraw Kathy and look for a different Montessori school? Or, should she report the Montessori school to the American Montessori Society and ask them to help her? Or, should Victoria enroll Kathy in the local public preschool? Or, should Victoria stick with this "Montessori" school hoping that things will get better? What should Victoria do? What would you do?

ACTIVITIES TO APPLY WHAT YOU LEARNED

1. The push for high-quality early childhood programs is becoming more prevalent and important worldwide. The New America Foundation in Washington, DC, provides the latest headlines from publications around the country. You can subscribe on their website. Follow the headlines for two weeks. What issues seems the most constant and important? Log on to Twitter and share with your classmates your conclusions.

2. In this text, you read about the Montessori model. Use an online search engine to look up Montessori material websites. Create a list of materials you would buy for inclusion in your pre-K classroom. Share your materials list by making a Wiki and encourage your classmates to comment on your selections.

3. The HighScope program model is widely adopted and impacts the lives of many children. What key components of the model would you incorporate into your classroom? Blog with other classmates and share your ideas.

4. One of the implications the Reggio approach has for all early childhood professionals is how to make all classrooms more aesthetically pleasing. List five things that you and other teachers could do to make your classroom attractive. To get started, go to NEA.org and check out Classroom Beautiful—Jennifer Larson and Classroom Beautiful—Jason Hubler. Share your five suggestions with others on Facebook.

5. **KEY ASSESSMENT:** Preschool teacher Marilyn Griffin's children were experimenting with mixing colors. Suddenly, Kiley screamed, "Mrs. Griffin! My hands are green!" This event led to an ongoing project involving the color green. Identify three other child-centered experiences that could be the catalyst for the project approach in your classroom. Share your ideas with your classmates on your class discussion board. For one of the experiences, (your choice), use the Competency Builder "How to Use the Project Approach" to outline how you would implement it with children. Use the rubric provided to guide your work.

6. Now, and in the years to come, there will be an increased need for teachers who are aware and knowledgeable about inclusive classrooms and how to reach children with special needs. How can you advocate for children with disabilities to get the services they will need in your classroom using the early childhood models you studied here? Share your ideas in an online discussion with your classmates.

LINKING TO LEARNING

The following agencies and programs, which can be located easily online, provide additional information about topics discussed in this chapter.

American Montessori Society

The American Montessori Society serves as a national center for Montessori information, both for its members and for the general public, answering inquiries and facilitating research wherever possible.

International Montessori Society

The International Montessori Society was founded to support the effective application of Montessori principles throughout the world. Through its website you will find a range of programs and services relating to the fundamental principles of (a) observation, (b) individual liberty, and (c) preparation of the environment.

North American Montessori Teachers' Association

This membership organization is open to parents, teachers, and anyone else interested in Montessori education.

ECAP Reggio Emilia Page

This ECAP website contains information and resources related to the approach to early childhood education developed in the preschools of Reggio Emilia, Italy.

Reggio Emilia Approach—The Preschool Child's Languages of Learning

Here you will find information and resources related to the Reggio Emilia approach, history, and learning environment.

Reggio Children

The website Reggio Children contains information and resources related to the approach to early childhood education developed in the preschools of Reggio Emilia, Italy.

HighScope Educational Research Foundation

This is the official site for the HighScope Educational Research Foundation. It provides information on HighScope curriculum, assessment, and research as well as e-tools, lists of trainings and conferences, and an online store for purchasing HighScope classroom materials.

The Project Approach

This group provides information about Project Approach and how you can implement its practices in your classroom. It offers an array of project examples to use for inclusion in the classroom, according to grade level.

Universal Design

The Center for Universal Design (CUD) is a national information, technical assistance, and research center that evaluates, develops, and promotes accessible and universal design.

New America Foundation

The EarlyEd Watch provides information and issues about what's happening in early education.

CHILD CARE

Meeting the Needs of Children and Families

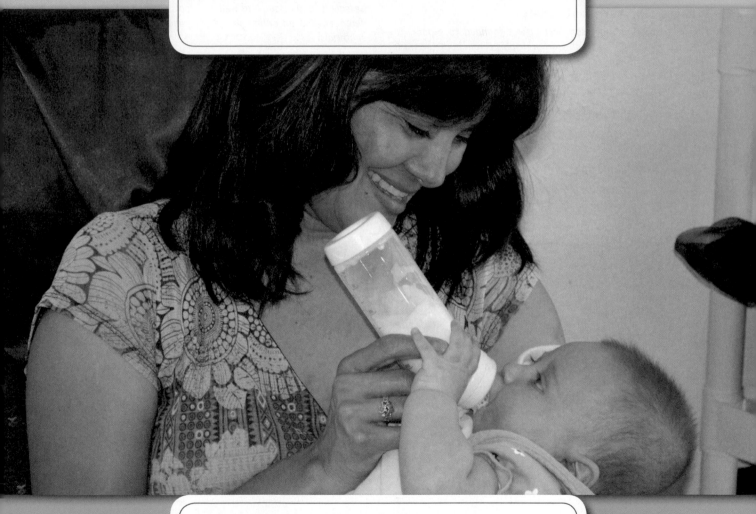

LEARNING OUTCOMES

1. Explain what is happening in the world of child care and why it is significant.
2. Describe the different types of child care that are offered today.
3. Describe the dimensions of high-quality child care.
4. Explain how you can accommodate diverse learners in child care.

THE WORLD OF CHILD CARE

Child care is the comprehensive out-of-home care and education of children that supplements the care and education children receive from their families. Child care programs address a variety of needs. They do the following:

- Provide for children's safety and health needs
- Offer a comprehensive array of services that meet children's physical, social/emotional, and intellectual and language needs
- Incorporate educational and readiness programs and activities that support children's abilities to learn and that prepare them for school
- Collaborate with families and to help them care for and educate their children

Child care has many faces and dimensions. Like the children they serve, child care programs have many similarities and differences; no two are the same. Each program is unique in its location, its teachers and administrators, and the children and families it serves. Parents and other primary caregivers make their decisions about using child care based on its affordability, accessibility, and quality. Consider the following real-life scenarios:

- Maria Gloria is a young single parent with two children ages two and four. Maria works for minimum wage in a local convenience store. "I really can't afford child care, but I have to work. A woman in the apartment three floors up from me keeps my kids and five others while I work. I give her twenty-five dollars a week. It's all I can afford. I'm lucky to have someone to take care of my kids."
- Charlie and Beth Cosdale have jobs that enable them to just get by on their combined incomes. Charlie drops off their children, one-year old Amanda and three-year-old Jesse, at the Children's Barn Child Care Center on his way to work. "It's not the best, but it's about what we can afford. I have to leave twenty minutes early because the child care is out of the way. We're looking for something closer, but we haven't found it yet. With the economy the way it is, we are lucky to have work."
- Seven-year-old Chantel Harris walks home and lets herself into the family apartment after school each day. There is no one else at home. Her mother wishes she had more choices. "I know it isn't the best or safest thing for Chantel to do. I can't afford anyone to take care of her, and the school doesn't offer any kind of programs after school. What am I supposed to do? My cousin's kids have after-school care at their school. Me and my kids, we're stuck."
- Amy Charney is a stay-at-home mom. Three mornings a week she takes her four-year-old daughter, Emily, to a Mothers' Day Out (MDO) program at a local church. "It's a great arrangement and very reasonable, in terms of cost. When Emily is in MDO I volunteer in the community, and still she and I get to do a lot of things together. The staff is great and up-to-date on the latest trends, and I feel Emily is definitely getting ready for school."
- Abby Belanger is an up-and-coming attorney in a prestigious law firm. She is a single mother by choice. Abby's four-year-old daughter, Tiffany, is enrolled in a high-quality, high-end preschool program. "I want Tiffany to have the best, and I can afford the best. I want her to have a good start in life so she can go to whatever schools she wants to attend. Education is important to me."
- Single parent Tamika Barsdale works the 4:30 to 12:30 shift at a local nursing home. It is usually midnight when she picks up her four-year-old daughter Shantel from the ABC child care center that is open twenty-four hours a day. It is one

of the few in the city that does operate twenty-four hours. "A lot of people like me work the late or night shift—a lot," says Tamika. "Where would Shantel and me be without twenty-four hour child care?"

Child care arrangements like these are duplicated countless times every day all across the United States. During the economic crisis that began in 2008 in the United States, many child care centers closed. Parents scrambled to find child care to avoid taking time off from work. Many parents couldn't find child care and were forced to quit their jobs. Think for a moment about the child care arrangements you know about or are involved with. Child care in the United States is often referred to as a patchwork of programs and arrangements of varying costs and quality, combining the good, the bad, and the unavailable. The reality is that America's families need and depend on child care, oftentimes regardless of the cost or quality.

To thrive, children need nurturing families, high-quality early care, and learning experiences. Securing child care is particularly important for working parents with young children. Research shows that child care assistance is positively associated with the long-term employment and financial well-being of parents.[1] In addition, programs that target families with infants and toddlers, such as Early Head Start, improve children's social and cognitive development, and parenting skills.[2]

Part of our job as early childhood professionals is to advocate and work for high-quality, affordable, and accessible child care for all children and families. We will discuss the kind and quality of care children receive outside their homes, which makes a big difference in their lives and the lives of their parents and families. According to the latest U.S. Census Bureau, 7.4 million children under age five are in some form of care other than with their parents while their mothers are working. This is about 68 percent of all young children of working mothers.

- Within this group, 3.5 million children are in organized child care settings, including 2.9 million in child care centers.
- About 910,000 children are cared for primarily by other nonrelatives.
- About 3 million are cared for by relatives other than their parents.
- Over one-quarter of these children are cared for in multiple arrangements.

THE POPULARITY OF CHILD CARE

Child care is a public necessity, is popular, receives much attention, and will continue to be a center of public policy attention for the reasons discussed next.

WORKING PARENTS.   Working parents drive the demand for child care. There are more dual-income families and working single parents today than ever before. For example, 64 percent of mothers with children under six are employed, and it is not uncommon for mothers to return to work as early as six weeks after giving birth.[3] Families are paying on average $11,666 per year for an infant, $6,423 per year for a toddler, and $5,000 per year for a school-aged child in child care, which makes it hard for working parents who are trying to make ends meet in the current economy.[4]

The current unprecedented entry of large numbers of mothers into the workforce has greatly impacted the care and education of children in the early years. The number of working mothers will likely continue to increase and create an even bigger demand for child care. As a result, more parents than ever are balancing work and raising children.

CHILD CARE AND PUBLIC POLICY.   Child care is an important part of this country's solution to the nation's economic and social problems. It is used to address political and social issues and is an essential part of enabling parents to be productively employed.

Politicians also view quality child care as a way of addressing many of the country's social problems through early intervention in children's lives. The reasoning is that if the public provides children with quality programs and experiences early in life, we reduce the possibility that they will need costly social services such as counseling and juvenile detention.

As the demand for child care increases, the challenge for you and other early childhood professionals is clear. You must participate in advocating for and creating quality child care programs that meet the needs of children and families.

PLACEMENT IN CHILD CARE PROGRAMS

Decisions to place children in child care are personal, individual, and complex. We can say with some assurance that because parents work, they place their children in child care. But it could also be the other way around: Because child care is available, some parents choose to work. Decisions relating to child care are not necessarily straight-forward but rather depend on many factors. Consider some of these interesting facts:

- Approximately 2.3 million individuals earn a living caring for and educating children under age five in the United States, of which about 1.2 million are providing child care in formal settings, such as child care centers or family child care homes. The remaining 1.1 million caregivers are paid relatives, friends, or neighbors.[5]
- Children from lower-income families, children whose mothers have less education, and Latino children are significantly less likely than others to attend center-based early care and education programs, even though they are among the groups that consistently show a lack of readiness for school.[6]
- Three- and four-year-old preschoolers in center-based settings are receiving different quality early learning experiences because of quality of caregivers and the setting in which the children are enrolled.[7]
- On average, children under age five of working mothers spend thirty-five hours a week in child care.[8]
- Among low-income children under age five in any type of child care arrangement nationwide, three-quarters are cared for in a home setting.[9]

TYPES OF CHILD CARE PROGRAMS

Child care is offered in many places and by many persons and agencies that provide a variety of services. Of the twelve million children birth to age six, about one-third spends thirty-seven hours a week in multiple child care arrangements.[10] The options for child care are almost endless (see Table 7.1). However, regardless of the kind of child care provided, the issues of *quality, affordability,* and *accessibility* are always part of the child care landscape. For parents of children with disabilities, *inclusivity* is an added dimension to this landscape.

CHILD CARE BY RELATIVES AND FRIENDS

Child care is frequently arranged with family members and friends. Parents handle these arrangements in various ways. In some cases, children are cared for by grand-parents, aunts, uncles, or other relatives. For example, Marie Harvey takes care of her granddaughter while her daughter works. "I'll pitch in wherever it's needed. I truly enjoy taking care of my granddaughter."[11] In addition, approximately 2.5 million—30 percent—of grandparents provide primary child care to the grandchildren who live with them.[12] In Texas 653,556 children live with grandparents (9.5% of all children in the state)[13] and in California 826,037 children live with grandparents (8.9% of the

TABLE 7.1 | Variety of Child Care Programs

Child Care Type	Description
Relatives and friends	Children are cared for by grandparents, aunts, uncles, other relatives, or friends, providing both continuity and stability.
Family	An individual caregiver provides care and education for a small group of children in his or her home.
Intergenerational	Child care programs integrate children and the elderly in an early childhood and adult care facility.
Center-based	Center-based child care is conducted in specially designed and constructed centers, churches, YMCAs and YWCAs, and other such facilities.
Employer-sponsored	To meet the needs of working parents, some employers are providing child care at the work site.
Proprietary	Some child care centers are run by corporations, businesses, or individual proprietors for the purpose of making a profit; these programs often emphasize an educational component.
Before- and after-school	Public schools, center-based programs, community and faith-based agencies, and individuals all offer programs that extend the school day with tutoring, special activities, and a safe space.

children in the state).[14] Many grandparents are taking over the parenting role for their grandchildren because of divorce, child abuse, negligence/abandonment, incarceration, HIV/AIDS, substance abuse, teenage pregnancy, or parental death.[15]

Relative and friend arrangements satisfy parents' needs to have their children cared for by people with similar lifestyles and values. It also meets the needs of working parents to have child care beyond normal working hours and on weekends. Such care may also be less costly, and the caregiver-to-child ratio is low. These types of arrangements allow children to remain in familiar environments with people they know, benefiting from both continuity and stability.

FAMILY CHILD CARE

family child care
Home-based care and education provided by a nonrelative outside the child's home; also known as *family care.*

When home-based care is provided by a nonrelative outside a child's home but in a family setting, it is known as **family child care**, or *family care.* In this arrangement, an individual caregiver provides care and education for a small group of children in the caregiver's home. Nine percent of children under five in child care are in family care.[16] Family child care is the most preferred type of care for young children, especially infants and toddlers.[17] Family child care offers several benefits to parents that are not necessarily available in other early care settings:

- Is often convenient and is close to home or work
- Provides a comfortable homelike environment
- Can provide stability with one consistent caregiver for the children
- Often has a low provider-to-child ratio
- Provides for mixed ages of children in small groups
- Offers flexible days and hours depending on parents' needs
- Provides personal communication between teachers (caregivers) and parents and promotes caring relationships

- Can provide school readiness skills with enriched activities and learning experiences
- May provide an inclusive environment for children with special needs[18]

Child care providers should aspire to provide these services to all children and families.

INTERGENERATIONAL CHILD CARE

Intergenerational refers to the selection and coordination of activities that enrich multiple generations. When older adults tutor young people, they bring critical one-on-one attention to the youths' skill building, while the young people make seniors more comfortable with new technologies. This reciprocity builds mutual respect and a sense of community, providing children and adults with diverse role models. The extraordinary relationships formed last throughout the participants' lives.[19]

Intergenerational child care programs integrate children and the elderly in an early childhood and adult care facility. The elderly derive pleasure and feelings of competence from interacting with children, and young children receive attention and love from older adults. Intergenerational programs blend the best of two worlds: children and the elderly both receive care and attention in a nurturing environment. ONEgeneration in Van Nuys, California, is an intergenerational child care that incorporates senior citizens into its child care programs, which serve children six weeks to six years old. In ONEgeneration, seniors and children work together to help one another. For example, three-year-old Joanna Ray and sixty-one-year-old Keith Mullins work together to stir muffin mix in a bowl. Joanna has not developed the strength and coordination to accomplish this task, whereas Keith's legs became paralyzed after a car accident. They work together to strengthen their skills. Research has found that contact with young children improves adult mood interaction and that children who interact with seniors are more advanced in their social development.[20]

The Voice from the Field feature, "A Spanish Immersion Program," illustrates another multicultural high-quality child care program, where staff and administrators strive to provide children and families with quality, affordable, and accessible child care, while immersing them in English and Spanish.

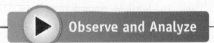
Observe and Analyze

CENTER-BASED CHILD CARE

As the name implies, **center-based child care** is provided to groups of children and families in specially constructed or renovated facilities. Out of 11.3 million children in different childcare arrangements, 15.6 percent of children are cared for in center-based child care centers.[21] For example, KIDCO Child Care Centers in Miami, Florida, operate as a nonprofit corporation out of four renovated warehouses and a former public school. KIDCO Child Care is a year-round early care and education agency that operates from 7:00 a.m. to 6:00 p.m., for 261 days of the year. The centers provide care for 450 children, from birth to age five, who are from primarily moderate and low-income families. Seventy percent of the children come from single parent families with primarily women who need to work in order to raise their children.[22]

Because each state has its own definition of a center-based program, you should research your state's definitions and regulations regarding child care, center care, and other kinds of care. In addition, learn about your state's child care licensing and child-to-staff ratio requirements.

center-based child care
Child care and education provided in a facility other than a home.

EMPLOYER-SPONSORED CHILD CARE

As more parents enter the workforce, child care programs respond with new programs. The Great Recession, which began in 2007, prompted many highly educated women

VOICE FROM THE FIELD

COMPETENCY BUILDER

A Spanish Immersion Program

Bright Years Child Learning Center, in League City, Texas, is designed to provide children with bilingual and biliteral competencies in English and Spanish in a fun, stimulating environment so that they will become world citizens. Our curriculum focuses on Spanish Language Immersion, along with age-appropriate educational growth that will develop emotionally, socially, physically, and academically well-balanced children. Our goal is to prepare our students for their continued education and provide them with the advantages of bilingualism in a global society.

The Spanish Immersion Program is designed for children ages two to twelve years old who have limited or no prior knowledge of Spanish. Children go through their daily schedule of structured learning activities hearing Spanish. In this setting, Spanish is the medium of instruction, and not the subject of instruction, therefore allowing the children to acquire a new language as it is used in context. Through daily exposure, children incorporate core information and are able to process it and comprehend it. The children's ability to accept and understand Spanish comes as they progress through the program. As they become more familiar and comfortable hearing, understanding, and responding in Spanish, it becomes a natural part of their thought process and, eventually, their speaking process.

To reap the full benefits of a Spanish Immersion Program, students need a variety of instructional support to stimulate various learning styles. Visual aids, body language and expression, diverse instructional approaches, and learning opportunities in real-life situations are all important factors in reinforcing the learning.

GUIDELINE 1 — Visual Aids

Incorporate a large variety of visual aids for a successful Spanish immersion program.

- Use prompts, books, puppets, flannel boards, and any other creative learning tools.
- Use students as examples. If you have a child wearing a red T-shirt, use him or her to demonstrate the color red or *rojo*.
- Use flashcards, posters, drawings, and real pictures. If children can relate to it, they will learn it easier.
- Use drawings created by teachers and students.

GUIDELINE 2 — Body Language and Expression

The tone of voice, expression, and physical movement when trying to convey an idea or emotion is also important. For example, if a story is being read about a sad bear, the facial expression and tone should be gloomy and the body posture should be poor when saying *triste* or sad.

- Dramatize the message using nonverbal communication.
- Act out feelings.
- Smiling goes a long way. Students will follow the teacher's joyful and optimistic attitude.

GUIDELINE 3 — Diverse Instructional Approaches

- Repetition is critical in order for children to learn new words, commands, or phrases. A good guideline is to repeat words in threes. For instance, if children are being instructed to wash their hands for snack time, say *lavar las manitas, lavar las manitas, lavar las manitas*, or "wash hands, wash hands, wash hands."
- Singing words and phrases daily to establish routine and familiarity with scheduling is also very important. For example, you can sing *vamos a recoger* or "clean up" whenever playtime is over.
- Music, dance, and body movement are especially important to convey ideas and allow freedom of expression in Spanish. Naming body parts, learning opposites, giving commands are especially easy to do through music. Dancing to "slow and fast" music, for example, allows children to learn the Spanish words *despacio y rápido*. This form of expression also gives

them the opportunity to speak the words without stressing about the pronunciation.

• Pair new and longtime students together to reinforce the learning. New students will be more receptive when new information is coming from a friend.

GUIDELINE 4

Go Outside the Classroom
• Take field trips to places where Spanish is spoken, such as Mexican restaurants or grocery stores. This will help children take chances speaking the language and give them the opportunity to build confidence, not to mention learning about the culture and real-life situations.

• Invite Spanish-speaking guests to visit the classroom and share a special talent, such as cooking.

Look for concerts and musical performances that showcase the Mexican culture. Folklórico and mariachi band performances are as educational as they are entertaining.

Through a Spanish immersion program setting, students are preparing for the opportunity to be challenged in a world where language diversity is valuable at many levels. Language immersion programs not only widen students' educational and economic potential, but also develop a deeper appreciation for different cultures and ethnicities. Language immersion is a promising method of education with benefits that will last a lifetime.

Source: Photos and text contributed by Iris Ochoa, Director, Bright Years Child Learning Center, League City, Texas.

who were stay-at-home moms to return to the labor pool. In a survey of five thousand employees at five companies, 57 percent of women and 33 percent of men with children younger than six years old report that they spend unproductive time at work because of child care concerns. Eighty percent of employers report that child care problems force many employees to lose work time.[23] To meet the needs of working parents, employers are increasingly called on to provide affordable, accessible, quality child care. According to the U.S. Chamber of Commerce, corporate-supported child care is one of the fastest growing employee benefits. But employer-sponsored child care is not new: The Stride Rite Corporation started the first on-site corporate child care program in Boston in 1971.[24]

On-site child care provides a number of advantages for parents:

• It is on-site. Parents can take their children to work with them.
• Parents can drop in on breaks for lunch to check on and care for their children.
• Mothers with infants can stop in to breast-feed.
• Parents can carpool with their children, saving time in the drop-off and pick-up process.
• Parents have the peace of mind knowing their children are close, safe, and well cared for.

Many corporations have child care management programs that operate their child care programs for them. For example, Bright Horizons is a provider of employer sponsored child care and partners with over 850 employers.[25] (See the Linking to Learning feature for more information about such child care programs.) Other employers provide different types of child care assistance. Some employers offer flexible work hours to make it easier for parents to make child care arrangements. Some employers allow their employees to take paid time off to care for mildly ill children. They see this as a positive return on the investment. Aetna Insurance Company estimates the savings realized from parental leave policies to be about $1 million per year. The company cut post-childbirth turnover by 50 percent by extending parental leave to six months, allowing a part-time return, and training supervisors to manage maternal leaves.[26]

Bristol-Myers Squibb is a leader in employee work-life programs and was named one of the 2012 *Working Mother* "100 Best Companies for Working Mothers" for its dedication to family-friendly benefits. Bristol-Myers Squibb offers on-site child development centers at five of its corporate campuses. Services include full- and part-time child care for children eight weeks to five years and full day kindergarten.[27] In addition, Bristol-Myers Squibb offers a comprehensive array of work-life programs and services to meet the needs of working families over the course of their career with the company, including the following:

Childcare discounts. Offers financial assistance at several national child care centers with locations near the work sites.

Resource and referral services. Counselors help with planning and referrals for parenting and child care, lactation, children's education, and elder care.

Lactation services. Subsidizes the purchase of a Medela breast pump and offers free consultation with a lactation specialist. Sites also make private space available to nursing mothers.

Prenatal program. Provides telephone support with medical practitioners during pregnancy. There's also a self-study program for employees who are expecting a child.[28]

MILITARY CHILD CARE

The Department of Defense (DoD) military child development system (CDS) provides daily services for the largest number of children of any employer in the United States. Military child care is provided in nine hundred centers and 5,500 Family Childcare Homes in more than three hundred geographic locations, both within and outside the continental United States. Ninety-eight percent of the DoD Child Care Centers are accredited, compared to 8 percent of the civilian child care centers.[29]

Military families face challenges that are not found in other work environments. Shifting work schedules that are often longer than the typical eight-hour day and the requirement to be ready to deploy anywhere in the world on a moment's notice require a child development system that is flexible in nature yet maintains high standards. Frequent family separations and the need to move, on average, every three years place military families in situations not often experienced in the civilian world. For this population, affordable, high-quality child care is paramount if they are to be ready to perform their missions and their jobs. It is also important to military personnel that child care services be consistent at installations throughout the military.

Four main components make up the DoD CDS: child development centers, family child care, school-age care, and resource and referral programs. Through these four areas, the DoD serves more than two hundred thousand children (ages six weeks to twelve years) daily. The system offers full-day, part-day, and hourly (i.e., drop-in) child care; part-day preschool programs; before- and after-school programs for school-age children; and extended-hour care, including nights and weekends.[30]

BEFORE- AND AFTER-SCHOOL CARE

In many respects, public schools are logical places for before-school and after-school care; they have the administrative organization, facilities, and staff to provide such care. In addition, many taxpayers and professionals have always believed that schools should not sit empty in the afternoons, evenings, holidays, and summers. Using resources already in place for child care makes good sense.

The before- and after-school child care programs of Broward County, Florida, provide students with the following:

- An inclusive child care program that is safe and nurturing in a comfortable environment
- A culturally enriching program that promotes the physical, intellectual, emotional, and social development of each child
- A program that meets the highest quality of child care standards

Before- and after-school care programs play an increasingly important role in school-based programs and in the lives of children and families. Although opportunities for play and exercise are important in these programs, more and more parents want them to provide help with homework, time to study, and enrichment activities such as music and the arts.

Currently, Broward County serves more than twenty thousand children in 180 before- and after-school child care programs. Programs at elementary schools and centers are either school district operated or operated by private providers.[31]

Nadine Rudek-Kelly leads a kindergarten before- and after-school program that offers a curriculum of a variety of activities including academics, arts, crafts, stories, and physical activities. The student-to-teacher ratio for this program is 10:1. In the before-school program, children engage in quiet activities and eat a light breakfast before the start of the school day. In the after-school program, the children do homework, participate in games, science projects, and outdoor play, and receive homework help.[32]

The Maricopa School District in Maricopa, Arizona, has a before- and after-school program that offers a loving, safe, fun, and educational learning environment. Their curriculum includes science, homework help, art, music, crafts, creative dramatic play, games, and group projects. During the summer months, children take field trips as well. The goal of their programs is to provide a nurturing, friendly, and safe environment that encourages children to build on their classroom experiences and expand their horizons.[33]

PROPRIETARY CHILD CARE

Some child care centers are run by corporations, businesses, and individual proprietors for the purpose of making a profit. Some for-profit centers provide before- and after-school programs for school-age children as well. Many of these programs emphasize their educational component and appeal to middle-class families who are willing to pay for the promised services. Knowledge Universe is the nation's largest private early childhood education provider of school-age education and care with 1,700 centers.[34] Its KinderCare Learning Centers operates more than 1,600 community-based centers across the country, serving more than 250,000 children and employing approximately 47,000.[35] Child care is a $38 billion service industry, with more and more entrepreneurs realizing they can make money in caring for the nation's children.

WHAT CONSTITUTES QUALITY CARE AND EDUCATION?

As child care grows and expands across the nation, it focuses our attention on a number of critical issues. One of these is how to provide and maintain high-quality care for each child. Although there is much debate about quality and what it involves, we can nonetheless identify the main characteristics of quality programs that provide care and education for children and families. Some critical components of high-quality care include the following:

- Low staff-to-child ratios and small groups of children (the fewer the children for each adult, the better it is for each child)
- Primary caregiver assignments for each small group of children
- Continuity of care (the same primary caregiver remains with a cohort of children for more than one year)
- Caregivers actively and regularly involve and communicate with families
- An emphasis on good nutrition and nutrition education for both children and parents
- Proper health maintenance and safety (e.g., making sure child care settings have safe and well maintained playgrounds)
- Cultural and linguistic continuity.[36] For example, a caregiver who shares a cultural background with a child is much more likely to naturally engage in practices which are in harmony with those of the home. The ability to place children directly under the care of a provider who shares their cultural heritage can help increase the capacity of a child care facility to provide appropriate care.[37]
- Teachers who are responsive to young children and interact in warm and caring ways
- Teachers who know how each child learns, grows, and develops, and who engage in developmentally appropriate practices

Each of these components is a necessary part of providing for high-quality education.

PROGRAM ACCREDITATION

Accreditation is a voluntary process by which programs assess and improve the quality of their center and family child care homes. Accreditation involves meeting higher standards than states and local licensing requirements. The accreditation process usually involves the administration, staff, and parents assessing a center's strengths and weaknesses based on criteria provided by an accrediting agency such as the following:

- National Association for the Education of Young Children
- National Accreditation Commission
- National Early Childhood Program Accreditation
- National Association for Family Child Care[38]

Areas frequently included in accreditation are relationships between staff and parents, curriculum, staff training, health and safety standards, and environment of the program.[39] NAEYC has established a national, voluntary accreditation system to help families identify high-quality programs. To achieve NAEYC accreditation, early childhood education programs volunteer to be measured against the NAEYC Early Childhood Program Standards. Today, nearly 6,745 NAEYC-accredited early childhood education programs serve families around the nation. Accreditation is administered through NAEYC's National Academy of Early Childhood programs. See the Linking to Learning feature at the end of the chapter. NAEYC program accreditation standards can be found on the NAEYC website and include relationships, curriculum, teaching, assessment, health, teachers, families, community relationships, physical environment, and leadership and management.

A center that is NAEYC accredited helps build a stronger team of teachers, administrators, and families working together to improve quality for children; has improved standards for the overall program; and receives publicity through NAEYC's website. NAEYC-accredited programs are committed to excellence and set forth high standards for quality.

Ultimately, the accreditation question is "does it matter?" The answer is yes! Research indicates that accredited centers provide children a higher quality care environment than do unaccredited centers.

HEALTHY CHILD CARE ENVIRONMENTS

At all age levels, a healthy environment supports children's physical and mental health. The environment should also be attractive and pleasant. The rooms, home, or center should be clean, well lit, well ventilated, cheerful, well maintained, and with separate areas for toileting (and for changing diapers), eating, and sleeping. Caregivers teach infants and toddlers healthy habits such as hand washing after toileting, before and after mealtime, and after other appropriate activities. According to the Centers for Disease Control and Prevention, frequent hand washing is one of the most important factors in maintaining your health and children's health and avoiding illness and preventing the spread of infection and disease.[40]

A healthy environment also provides a relaxed and happy eating environment. Areas should be disinfected properly before eating. Substantial research clearly indicates that a healthy diet and environment contribute to children's overall health and well-being.[41] Early childhood is a stage of life in which lifelong nutritional habits are developed and obesity is prevented. For infants and children, a major source of chemical pesticide exposure is through their food. Research shows that children's levels of chemical pesticide exposure drops quickly and significantly when they are switched from a normal diet to an organic one.[42] The Little Dreamers, Big Believers Daycare in Columbus, Ohio, uses ingredients that are 70 percent organic. Children eat meals with foods such as rigatoni with tomato sauce, garlic bread, and broccoli, all designed to provide healthy habits in accord with the MyPlate nutritional guide.[43]

A healthy environment also supports children's mental health. Caregivers support children's mental health when they provide responsive and loving care and create environments that have a balance of small and large open areas. Small areas provide the opportunity for infants and toddlers to be alone or in small groups. The open areas encourage active involvement with larger numbers of children. In addition, child care staff collaborate with and involve parents to help them know about and understand the importance of children's mental health and how they can help their children.

LEAD-FREE ENVIRONMENT.   In general, children less than six years old are more likely to be affected by lead than are adults because of increased contact with lead sources in the environment, such as lead-contaminated house dust and soil. Children also absorb lead more easily. Children's developing nervous systems are also more susceptible to the unfavorable health effects of lead, including developmental delay and behavioral problems.[44] The Centers for Disease Control and Prevention recommends taking these precautions in the classroom to keep children healthy and minimize any potential risk in the future:

1.   Wash children's hands frequently and always before they eat.
2.   Do not let children eat food or use pacifiers that dropped on the floor or outside.
3.   Remove all shoes when entering the center or use doormats.[45]

Cadmium is also a harmful lead product found in children's bracelets and charms sold in stores across the United States. Child care providers have to be ever vigilant in their role of providing lead-free environments.

NONTOXIC PESTICIDES. Exposure to pesticides at schools is associated with illnesses among school employees and students. Rates of illness from pesticide exposure at schools are higher in school staff than in children because staff members are more likely to handle pesticides. However, children may be particularly susceptible to pesticide toxicity because their organ systems have not reached developmental maturity. Exposure to pesticides can produce coughs, shortness of breath, nausea, vomiting, headaches, and eye irritation.[46]

In child care programs, keep all surfaces free of food and water, and reduce opportunities for pests to enter the building. Sanitary food habits, properly handling garbage, and sealing food in airtight containers help prevent problems with pests. Also, periodically vacuuming furniture and draperies can reduce dust mites and other pests. The Voice from the Field feature that follows, "The Eco-Environment in Early Childhood Settings," provides an excellent example of the many dimensions of a child care environment!

RESEARCH ABOUT CHILDCARE AND CHILDREN

Research reveals that high-quality early care and education have influences that last over a lifetime. A valuable source of research about child care comes from the Study of Early Child Care and Youth Development (SECCYD) by the National Institute of Child Health and Human Development (NICHD). This is a comprehensive longitudinal study initiated by NICHD designed to answer the many questions about the relationship between child care experiences and characteristics and children's developmental outcomes. The study collected features of child care and the experiences children have in different nonmaternal child care settings. Listed below are some of the study's findings on the use of child care and its effects on children and families. The study results make it clear that professionals must provide high-quality programs and must advocate for that high quality with the public and state legislators. Reflect on what surprises you most as you review the following study results.[47]

Hours in Child Care
- At their first entry into nonmaternal care, children average 29 hours of care per week.
- By twelve months, children in care average 33.9 hours a week of care.

Type of Care
- Forty-four percent of children receive child care in child care centers and 25 percent in child care homes; 12 percent are cared for by their father or their mother's partner; 10 percent are cared for at home by nannies or babysitters; and 9 percent are cared for by grandparents.

Maternal Attitudes and Child Care
- Mothers who believe their children benefit from their employment tend to place their infants in care earlier and for more hours in center-based child care.
- In contrast, mothers who believe maternal employment carries high risks for their children tend to put their infants in care for fewer hours and are especially likely to rely on the infant's father for child care.

Social, Emotional, Cognitive, and Health-Related Child Outcomes
- Poor-quality child care is related to an increased incidence of insecure infant-mother attachment (the child does not feel safe and will not be as willing to trust his or her parent) at fifteen months, but only when the mother is relatively low in sensitivity and responsiveness.

The Eco-Environment in Early Childhood Settings

Little Green Tree House is an eco-friendly preschool and child care center in the Chicago area. We promote a message of positive world consciousness and the importance of a healthy learning environment for children. Our professional teachers, coupled with an eco-friendly environment, facilitate the optimal growth and development of the whole child. We facilitate this growth by ensuring that our teachers are of the highest quality with suburb training and education on early childhood education and development. All of our teachers are also trained on the importance of a healthy learning environment by becoming familiar with our school's eco-friendly practices.

In the development stages and the building of both of our schools, we paid special attention to the materials that were used. From the low volatile organic compound (VOC) paint on all the walls, to the flooring and the lighting, special measures were taken to use recycled materials as well as to conserve energy. Little Green Tree House conserves a lot of energy by using light-emitting diodes (LEDs) as a major source of light in the school. LED light offers a long service life and high-energy efficiency. The classrooms are also equipped with large windows and skylights that provide an abundance of natural light.

All of our furniture is purchased through Community Playthings. Community Playthings, a company committed to environmental protection, uses only maple that has been certified by the Forest Stewardship Council (FSC) in the production of all of their products. We take special care to purchase toys that are polyvinyl chloride (PVC) and bisphenol A (BPA) free. We use Green Guard Certified mattresses, which emit low VOC, in the cribs, along with organic crib sheets for the babies and organic cotton sheets for the older children.

All food consumed by the children comes from an organic food catering company. This company purchases as much food as they can from local organic farms. All food is served to the children using stainless steel cups, plates, bowls, and serving utensils to avoid unnecessary waste.

One of our largest conservation efforts comes from the use of cloth diapers on all the children who are not potty trained. We strongly believe that keeping what would be an extremely excessive amount of disposable diapers out of landfills is a huge benefit to the environment. All of our cloth diapers are cleaned and treated with a small amount of bleach at an offsite location. This location specializes in the cleaning of cloth diapers.

The children do their part by helping the teachers plant and manage our organic rooftop gardens. On our roof, we have four organic gardens that are 4 feet wide by 6 feet long. The children help to water the gardens by using recycled rain from the school's rain barrel. Along with our rooftop gardens, the children also participate in adding to and learning about our school's compost bin. The teachers guide the children during the process of properly caring for the gardens and compost bin by including eco-friendly lesson plans into the curriculum. Some examples of eco-friendly lesson plans are learning about plants and animals, life cycles, how plants grow, and recycling. A lot of the eco-friendly content learned is basic knowledge because it has to be comprehended by such young children, but nonetheless such knowledge is extremely important. We believe that if the children start out at a young age in an eco-friendly environment, they will carry that philosophy with them into their older years, and it will be second nature for them to conserve in years to come.

Source: Contributed by Sarah Stiltner and Erin Lyon, Executive Directors of Little Green Tree House, Chicago, Illinois.

It is clear that high-quality child care has beneficial outcomes for children and families. You will be involved in advising parents about child care. This research data helps you be informed and knowledgeable. High-quality child care will continue to be important for children's well-being and provide greater social skills, increased academic success, higher self-esteem, and better nutrition and physical health.

The more that you can do to promote high-quality healthy programs, the better it will be for you, the children, and their families.

SAFE ENVIRONMENTS

Safe and healthy environments go together. In addition to what we have discussed, healthy environments also include keeping children safe emotionally. Caregivers provide safe environments through responsive relationships and by developing close and nurturing bonds with the children they care for. Responsive and close relationships enable infants and toddlers to experience trust and feel safe with you and in your program. More and more research tells us that healthy development depends on safe experiences during the first few years of life.[48]

Safe child care centers supervise children at all times.[49] Safe centers enforce strict security measures and install security cameras so that staff can monitor traffic. For example, Kiddie Academy buildings are equipped with secure entries and exits that require a pass or identification card for entry. Some buildings also use fingerprint verification and video monitoring. They also conduct background checks on all employees. The Learning Experience Academy of Early Education has an automatic electronic security system through which the staff can do the following:

- Check teacher-to-student ratios any time of the day
- Verify the location of a student
- Track each employee in the building
- Track critical medical information of a child or teacher
- View exact time in/time out of both staff and children
- Verify which authorized person dropped off, or picked up each child[50]

Keeping children safe physically contributes to their feeling safe and trusting emotionally.

Child care providers need to give children opportunities to learn social and academic skills through daily activities such as mealtime. What are some ways you could provide opportunities to ensure that children are learning important nutritional concepts and skills?

RESPECTFUL ENVIRONMENTS

A respectful environment is one in which caregivers deeply care about children and families. Caregivers create respectful environments by listening, observing, and being aware of children's verbal and nonverbal communications. Arranging the classroom in a way that maximizes social interaction promotes a safe, supportive, and engaging classroom climate. For example, if children are seated in a circle or horseshoe shape, this maximizes the eye contact you have with them and that they have with each other.[51] Closely looking at and observing children enables you to "read" children's behavior by asking yourself: "How will I respond to what the child is saying to me?"

A respectful environment also honors and supports children's unique individualities. Each child's unique individuality is a product of the interactions of such dimensions as temperament, gender, race, language, culture, and socioeconomic status.

CULTURALLY APPROPRIATE PRACTICE.   Respectful environments include culturally appropriate practices. Children who are Hispanic remain the largest minority group of underserved children, and the child care issues of access, affordability, and quality are of critical concern to their community. Fewer than half of Hispanic children birth to age three attend a center-based early education childhood program, compared to 66 percent of African American children and 59 percent of white children.[52] Because of limited access to high-quality programs, Hispanic children start kindergarten well behind their peers.[53]

Here are some things you can do to create a culturally respectful environment for your children.

- Greet families in a culturally sensitive manner. For example, some Hispanic families prefer the father to be greeted first, then the mother, and the children last.
- Provide inclusive artwork. For example, murals include children with different skin and hair colors.
- Use linguistically appropriate materials and provide books in English and Spanish.
- Adjust teacher-infant interaction style according to culture. Although most infants who are Hispanic are calmed with quick, repetitive, choppy phrases and back patting, infants who are Latino, for example, are calmed through soft, smooth talking, cradling, and gentle rocking.
- Apply limits to cultural accommodation when necessary. Discuss compromises with parents. For example, some cultures allow infants to eat items they could choke on such as hot dogs. In this case, explain the dangers of certain foods and ask parents to bring alternative snacks.
- Communicate with parents and other family members in your program. You must place a high priority on daily communication about children's progress. In addition, share with parents how your program and community agencies provide information in such critical areas as child development and nutrition.

Check Your Understanding: Respect

SUPPORTIVE ENVIRONMENTS

A supportive environment means that you will spend time with children, pleasantly interact with them, and encourage and help them. Supportive environments encourage and promote children's routine social interactions. A supportive environment accommodates children's individual differences and provides for active play. The Read, Play, and Learn program in Baltimore, Maryland, provides a supportive environment for their children. Children engage in games, songs, experiments, reading, dramatic play, and projects. In the Sensory Area, children explore and manipulate various textures and devices to support their psychological needs. Teachers use story themes to support children's needs. For example, *The Kissing Hand* storybook helps children adjust to leaving home for the first time. Family involvement components help children incorporate materials and favorite items from home into their day.[54] A supportive environment also offers a wide range of learning materials. This type of environment also promotes children's mental health and encourages child-centered activities.

Child care involves much more than merely providing physical care. All care givers should provide children with love and affection and should meet each child's full range of social, emotional, and physical needs.

Supportive programs should have written, developmentally based curricula for meeting children's needs. A program's curriculum should specify activities for children of all ages. Caregivers can use these activities to stimulate infants, provide for the growing independence of toddlers, and address the readiness and literacy skills of four- and five-year-olds. All programs include curricula and activities that meet the social, emotional, and cognitive needs of all children. Supportive programs use developmentally appropriate practices to implement the curriculum and achieve their program goals.

Watch this video to see how an early childhood classroom is set up to provide the many types of environments to meet each child's needs.

CHALLENGING ENVIRONMENTS

A challenging environment provides opportunities for infants and toddlers to be actively involved with other children, staff, and parents. These interactions are extremely important as children learn about their world and themselves. A child care program is not developmentally appropriate if it does not offer sufficient challenges to growing children. A challenging environment supports children's social interaction and lays the foundation for school readiness and other life outcomes. A challenging environment provides materials and activities that are matched to the needs, interests, and abilities of children and provide for many hands-on activities that support seeing, touching, feeling, and moving. Supportive and challenging environments complement each other.

Good care and education provides for children's needs and interests at each developmental stage. For example, infants need good physical care as well as continual love and affection and sensory stimulation. Toddlers need safe surroundings and opportunities to explore. They need caregivers who support and encourage active involvement. However, within these broad categories of development, individual children have unique styles of interacting and learning that you must also accommodate.

CAREGIVERS AND ENVIRONMENTS.   Caregivers are the key to all environments. They are the ones who passionately care about children and create the environments that are safe, healthy, supportive, respectful, and challenging. Every child wants and needs a teacher who is inspired and willing to do what it takes to create appropriate environments for them. This means that you will engage in ongoing professional development and gain the knowledge you need to grow as a professional in order to promote the educational environment all children need.

CAREGIVER-TO-CHILD RATIO

The ratio of adults to children is an important part of high-quality child care, and ratios also influence the environments used for children. The ratios should be sufficient to give children the individual care and attention they need. NAEYC guidelines for the ratio of caregivers to children are 1:4 for infants and toddlers and 1:6 to 1:10 for preschoolers, depending on group size.[55]

The American Academy of Pediatrics recommends the ratios and standards shown in Table 7.2. You should check the ratios for the state and city in which you live.

Research shows that when programs meet these recommended child-to-staff ratios and recommended levels of caregiver training and education, children have better outcomes.[56] Teachers have to provide attentive care for all children. When they have too many children, either individually or in a group, teachers cannot do this, and this contributes to low-quality child care. Low-quality care for all children—regardless of whether they were in child care centers or homes—is associated with poorer school readiness and language performance.[57]

TABLE 7.2 | Child Care Ratios and Group Size

Age	Maximum Child-to-Staff Ratio	Maximum Group Size
Birth–24 Months	3:1	6
25–30 months	4:1	8
31–35 months	5:1	10
3-year-olds	7:1	14
4–5-year-olds	8:1	16
6–8-year-olds	10:1	20

PROFESSIONAL STAFF DEVELOPMENT

Staff and professional development is another dimension of high-quality child care. All teachers should be involved in an ongoing program of training and development. The Child Development Associate (CDA) certification program is a good beginning for staff members to become competent and maintain necessary skills. Program administrators should also have a background and training in child development and early childhood education. Knowledge of child growth and development is essential for all child care professionals. They need to be developmentally aware and child oriented in all phases of delivering high-quality child care.

Providing staff training and development is an excellent idea, but it is only the first step. The next step after training and development is to implement what has been learned in the staff training. In this sense, staff development and training is a two-part process: learning and implementation. The California Child Care Program requires all child care providers to have 15 hours of preventative and health safety training. In this program, caregivers learn how to respond to breath-

Research clearly shows that care giver–child warmth is one of the most important dimensions of a high-quality child care program. What are some things that you will do in your program to help ensure that it conveys a feeling of warmth and familiarity for children?

ing and cardiac emergencies, first aid and injury prevention, and food preparation and sanitation practices that reduce the spread of infectious diseases. They then implement what they have learned at their child care center.[58] Other professional staff development training is available in technology, early childhood literacy, bullying prevention, discipline and classroom management, differentiation of instruction, response to intervention, safety, and nutrition.

SMART START: HELPING PROGRAMS BE SUCCESSFUL. Smart Start North Carolina is a nationally recognized initiative that helps ensure that all children enter school healthy and ready to succeed. Smart Start's vision is to have every child reach his or her potential and be prepared for success in a global community. Smart Start brings together all the people involved in a young child's life—families, teachers, doctors, caregivers, social workers, and many others—to ensure that children have all they need for healthy growth and development.

Smart Start connects families to physicians, as well as state insurance programs, to keep kids healthy. Smart Start programs help improve parenting skills and teach parents how to effectively read at home with their children. Smart Start connects families to high-quality child care and often helps families pay for this care. Smart Start also improves the quality of child care programs by providing support to improve facilities and staff skills.

Importance of Smart Start. Experiences during the earliest years literally shape the structure of the brain. Children's healthy growth is directly linked to early childhood experiences. Young children exposed to intense and prolonged stress associated with cyclical or generational poverty, military deployment, sudden parental unemployment, or other conditions require comprehensive intervention to ensure their healthy and productive development.[59] Smart Start is funded through state and private funds. By referring families and communities to the resources they need to support children's growth and development, Smart Start lays the foundation to nurture responsible, productive citizens who will make positive contributions to our society.[60]

ACCOMMODATING DIVERSE LEARNERS IN CHILD CARE AND OTHER EARLY CHILDHOOD PROGRAMS

Child care is a critical concern for families and for early childhood professionals. For parents, the quality and security of child care has implications for psychological well-being, management of work/family demands, and continuity of employment. For children, the quality of care has implications for their health, social and physical development, and their education and lifelong success.

CHILDREN OF DIVERSE CULTURES

Accommodating children of diversity is an on-going challenge for child care and other programs. Although the use of nonparental care has grown for all socioeconomic groups, the type, quality, and cost burden for parents remain highly stratified along demographic lines.[61] For example, children whose parents are Caucasian, highly educated, and affluent are more likely to be in center-based care arrangements. Children from Hispanic, poorly educated, immigrant, and less affluent families are more likely to be cared for by relatives.[62]

Too often, parents' child care choices are viewed as a single, isolated consumption choice. In reality, parents' child care choices are a part of a dynamic interplay between decisions about employment, child-rearing, and other family values. Therefore, choosing child care is as much a social transaction as it is an economic one.[63] In addition, when selecting child care, parents rate warmth of caregivers, utilization of a play-based curriculum, and educational level of caregivers as the most important factors. One challenge of child care is to provide these qualities in a way that responds to families' culture and language.[64]

One of the best ways to do this is by creating a family atmosphere. When you think about it, what intrinsic qualities do families have that you would want for your child while you were away at work? Familiarity? Warmth? Kindness?

Familiarity, or the easiness of interaction, is achieved by intimately getting to know your families. Intimacy can be hard to balance with professionalism. Achieve intimacy by asking questions about parents' interests; follow up on how their weekend activities went; and ask in a nonintrusive way about family life. Showing a genuine interest in and concern for parents as individuals goes a long way to create an easy, intimate relationship that leaves parents feeling comfortable and confident about leaving their children with you.

Caregiver **warmth** is more important to parents than the education of the caregiver or even the type of curriculum utilized by the program.[65] A warm environment is achieved through a few simple efforts on your part. Ask for pictures from home of the children with their families, pets, or favorite toys and place them around the room in frames or matted with construction paper. Display pictures of caregivers and children.

warmth Displaying or exhibiting kindness and genuine affection.

This contributes to a more family-like, warm atmosphere where caregivers and parents are both honored and the children remain the center of focus. Parents love to see children's artwork and other artifacts. Placing them around the room goes a long way toward creating warmth.

Warmth is also achieved by making the center and children's areas comfortable and inviting. Comfort and approachability should not be sacrificed in the effort to run a clean and efficient caregiving environment. But even in the most sterile of environments, warmth can be achieved by being genuine, kind, interested, and involved.

CHILDREN WITH SPECIAL NEEDS

Child care professionals must also accommodate children with special needs. Accommodations for children with special needs are primarily made in these ways: changes in the child care/classroom environment; changes in learning materials; and changes in instructional processes.

- Continuously change groups based on assessments and needs. These instructional arrangements include large groups, small groups, peer partners, one-to-one instruction, and/or independent activities.

- Accommodating changes in teaching strategies in response to children's needs influences children's abilities to participate and be successful. These changes in teaching strategies include simplifying directions, use of concrete materials/examples, sequencing learning tasks from easy to hard, repeated opportunities to practice skills, and direct physical assistance.

- Arranging the learning environment to meet children's needs is important for every early childhood setting. When rearranging the classroom environment, make sure that it meets the specific needs of children and that centers and materials are accessible for all children.

- Provide children with assistance and instruction. A child's need for assistance may range from individual instruction to individual supervision. Assistance can vary from day to day and can be provided by volunteers, aides, and peers.

- Providing children with alternative activities is a good way of accommodating to meet a child's needs.

ACTIVITIES FOR PROFESSIONAL DEVELOPMENT

ETHICAL DILEMMA

"THE BOY WHO ESCAPED CHILD CARE."

Rebeka Holly, lead teacher for a child care program, was shocked to receive a phone call from the police stating that Bobby Hernandes, one of her children, had "escaped" the child care center. Bobby wandered across a busy highway, strolled in and out of an auto shop, helped himself to gum and a soft drink at a convenience store, and walked into a nearby sports bar. The story of "the boy who escaped child care" went viral on the Internet and social media, with demands to shut the child care facility down. Rebeka is furious at Stacy Holcomb, the teacher in charge of Bobby, for not properly supervising her children.

Rebeka understands that a huge mistake was made, but she also knows her child care program has the potential to provide high-quality care. She hopes that this situation can be used to spur her center to become a high-quality program. Furthermore, the child care program is located in an area serving low-income parents. However, parents are pulling their children from the program. Television channels and local papers are calling for interviews, and now the state licensure board is threatening to "clean house."

What should Rebeka do? Should she recommend that the child care center fire Stacy? Should Rebeka resign her position to acknowledge her own mistakes? Should Rebeka speak to the local news media? Should she hire her own lawyer? Who ultimately is at fault in this situation, Rebeka or Stacy? What would you do if you were Rebeka? What would you do if you were in charge of the state licensing board?

ACTIVITIES TO APPLY WHAT YOU LEARNED

1. The world of child care is changing in many ways, including programs that are trying to meet the needs of all parents and the number of programs that are trying to be high quality. Conduct Internet research and find three examples of programs that meet the needs of diverse groups of parents as outlined in the vignettes of child care in America today that appear at the beginning of this chapter. Post your findings on your class discussion board.

2. There are many different types of child care all designed to meet the particular needs of individual parents and families. Based on your current views of child care, in what type of child care program would you be most inclined to enroll your child? Provide three reasons for your decision. On your class discussion board, ask several of your classmates to share their preferred child care choices.

3. Observe a child care program and ask permission to take notes of how providers provide healthy, safe, respectful, supportive, and challenging environments for children. Use PowerPoint to post your notes on your classroom discussion board and ask for opinions on your findings.

4. **KEY ASSESSMENT:** Suppose you were the director of a child care program and the parents of four-year-old Alex, who has mild Down syndrome, want to enroll him in your child care program. How would you respond to Alex's parents? What would you do to prepare yourself for including Alex? The staff? The children? Create a blog based on your experiences about how you can accommodate diverse learners in your child care program/classroom and post it to share with classmates. Use the rubric provided to guide your work.

LINKING TO LEARNING

The following agencies and programs, which can be located easily online, provide additional information about topics discussed in this chapter.

Child Care Aware

Child Care Aware helps families learn more about the elements of quality child care and how to locate programs in their communities.

Child Care Bureau

This agency includes information on the Child Care and Development Block Grant, links to other Administration on Children and Families sites, and other information within the Department of Health and Human Services, with links to other related child care sites.

Childcare.gov

This is a site for parents, child care programs, and early childhood educators. It brings all federal agency resources together in one place.

National Association for the Education of Young Children (NAEYC)

The NAEYC site provides information about the accreditation process for preschool and child care programs.

National Child Care Information Center

Sponsored by the Child Care Bureau, Administration for Children and Families, Department of Health and Human Services, this agency provides a central access point for information on child care and lists the licensure regulations for all fifty states regarding child care, center care, and other kinds of care.

National Resource Center for Health and Safety in Child Care and Early Education

Funded by the Maternal and Child Health Bureau of the Department of Health and Human Services, this group lists the child care licensure regulations for each state. It also has health and safety tips and full-text resources.

FEDERAL and STATE GOVERNMENTS

Supporting Children's Success

LEARNING OUTCOMES

1. Explain how federal programs influence early childhood education through legislative acts.
2. Describe and analyze how state standards are changing teaching and learning today.
3. Explain how you can accommodate diverse learners to benefit all children.

ONE of the remarkable political events of the last decade has been the use of early childhood education to achieve federal and state educational goals and to reform education. As a result, more federal and state dollars are being poured into early childhood programs, making this decade a very exciting and challenging time for all early childhood professionals and their programs. The U.S. Department of Education's fiscal year 2013 $69.8 billion budget advances President Obama's agenda to reform the nation's schools.[1] However, with increased federal and state funding come mandates, control, and restructuring. Federal and state laws, regulations, and dollars are changing what early childhood programs look like and how they function. Federally funded programs such as Head Start and Early Head Start are leading the way in changing how the early childhood profession cares for and educates young children.

FEDERAL PROGRAMS AND EARLY CHILDHOOD

Federal legislation has had a tremendous influence on the educational process and this will continue into the future. Currently, the Obama administration is committed to providing the support that our youngest children need to prepare to succeed in school and careers. The years before a child enters kindergarten are critical for children's futures, for the workforce, and for the role and place of the United States on the global stage. As a result, President Obama continually urges states to impose high standards across all publicly funded early learning settings, develop new programs to improve opportunities and outcomes, engage parents in their child's early learning and development, and improve the early education workforce.[2] As you read this chapter, you will learn how and why federal and state governments are changing the field of early childhood education.

THE ECONOMIC OPPORTUNITY ACT OF 1964

The **Economic Opportunity Act of 1964 (EOA)** was part of President Lyndon Johnson's war on poverty. It implemented several social programs to promote the health, education, and general welfare of people from low socioeconomic backgrounds and was designed to put people to work. The EOA provided for the beginning of Head Start in 1965. The EOA was later updated as the Head Start Act of 1981. The passage of the Economic Opportunity Act of 1964 marks the contemporary beginning of federal, political, and financial support for early childhood education.[3] **Head Start** is one of the longest-running programs to address systemic poverty in the United States. Its programs include **Early Head Start**, Head Start, Family and Community Partnerships, Migrant and Seasonal Head Start, and American Indian/Alaska Native Head Start.

ELEMENTARY AND SECONDARY EDUCATION ACT (ESEA)

In 1965, Congress passed the **Elementary and Secondary Education Act (ESEA)**, which serves to more fully fund primary and secondary education by providing funds to help educate children from low-income families. This portion of ESEA is known as **Title I**. Eligibility for Title I funds is based on children's eligibility for free or reduced-price school lunches, which is based on their family's income. Funds are used to provide additional academic support and learning opportunities so that children can

Economic Opportunity Act of 1964 (EOA) Implemented several social programs to promote the health, education, and general welfare of people from low socioeconomic backgrounds.

Head Start One of the longest running programs to address systemic poverty in the United States.

Early Head Start A federal program serving pregnant women, infants, toddlers, and their families.

Elementary and Secondary Education Act (ESEA) Federal legislation that funds mainly elementary and secondary education.

Title I Section of the Elementary and Secondary Education Act (ESEA) that provides monies to supplement the education of children from low-income families.

No Child Left Behind Act (NCLB) Federal law passed in 2001 that has significantly influenced early childhood education.

master challenging curricula and meet state standards in core academic subjects. For example, funds support extra instruction in reading and mathematics, as well as special preschool, after-school, and summer programs to extend and reinforce the regular school curriculum. More than 66,646 schools, two-thirds of all the public schools in the United States, use Title I funds, which amounts to 3.1 billion dollars, and serves more than 21 million children, half of whom are in grades K–5. Therefore, it is very likely that you will teach children served by Title I at a Title I school.[4]

NO CHILD LEFT BEHIND

In 2001 Congress reauthorized the Elementary and Secondary Education Act of 1965 as the **No Child Left Behind Act (NCLB)**. NCLB funds primary and secondary education and is designed to improve student achievement and school performance. The 2001 reauthorization of the NCLB radically and rapidly changed how the United States conducts its educational business. NCLB emphasizes state and district accountability, mandates state standards for what children should know and be able to do, includes a comprehensive program of testing in grades three to twelve, and encourages schools to use teaching methods that demonstrate their effectiveness in helping children learn.

NCLB targets six fundamental areas:

- The increased accountability of teachers and schools for children's school achievement.
- An emphasis on literacy and reading so that all children read on or above grade level by third grade.
- Insistence that schools and teachers use programs and curriculum that increase demonstrated achievement based on scientific research.
- Support for teacher professional staff development to enhance their abilities to teach all children so they achieve high standards.
- The use of educational technology in institutional programs.
- Parent involvement in schools and in decision-making procedures.
- More choices for parents and children to attend better public and charter schools.[5]

NCLB is a significant educational act that will continue to influence what and how you teach for many years to come. The act also influences pre-K education because there is a major emphasis on getting children ready for school. Many federally funded programs now use guidelines mandated in the No Child Left Behind Act to develop goals and objectives for their own programs.

At the time of this writing, Congress is in the process of filing different versions of bills to reauthorize NCLB. This reauthorization will probably occur after the 2016 presidential election, and it will likely include such initiatives as the following:

- The federal government's ongoing commitments to closing the achievement gap between cultural and socioeconomic groups. We have discussed how the persistent achievement gaps across age, culture, socioeconomic backgrounds, and gender keeps America's children from doing their best and being their best. The federal government is determined to prevent and eliminate these gaps.
- Encouraging the preparation and hiring of high-quality teachers, so that all children are taught by well-trained teachers. Currently, many children, especially those in urban schools, are taught by poorly qualified teachers.
- Providing for universal, high-quality infant, toddler, and pre-kindergarten early childhood programs for all children so they come to school ready to learn.
- Adequate funding for important children's and educational programs outside of NCLB, including child health and nutrition programs, Head Start, child care services, and programs to serve children with disabilities.

NCLB AND LITERACY EDUCATION

A far-ranging and significant influence of NCLB is that it has put literacy and reading first in early childhood programs by trying to ensure that every child in the United States can read at grade level by the end of third grade. This means that efforts to provide young children with the literacy skills they need begin in Early Head Start and Head Start programs. For example, the Department of Health and Human Services (which operates Head Start) provides programs with assistance regarding how they can prepare children to be ready to begin reading and writing when they enter school. Programs place particular emphasis on both child and family literacy so that children can develop the skills they need to become lifelong readers, and at the same time, parents can develop the skills they need to improve their own lives and help their children become proficient readers. Head Start invests considerable resources in early literacy, including providing resources for training and technical assistance to ensure that every Head Start classroom is promoting reading, vocabulary, and language skills.[6]

Currently, all early childhood programs, including Head Start, emphasize the development of children's early literacy skills by involving parents and grandparents. Literacy skills are seen as a key to success in school and life.

The federal legislative and financial influence on early childhood education—indeed, on all of education, from birth through higher education—is vast and significant. You can count on the fact that you, your colleagues, and the children you teach will continue to be under the direction of federal mandates and guidelines. Consequently, you must be aware of the influence of federal and state governments on you and your profession. Additionally, you must be willing to be politically involved in influencing legislation and its implementation in early childhood programs and classrooms.

HEAD START PROGRAMS

Head Start is a national program that promotes school readiness by enhancing the social and cognitive development of children through the provision of educational, health, nutritional, social, and other services to children and families. The Head Start program provides grants to local public and private nonprofit and for-profit agencies to provide comprehensive child development services to economically disadvantaged children and families, with a special focus on helping preschoolers develop the early reading and math skills they need to be successful in school.[7]

Head Start programs engage parents in their children's learning and help them in making progress toward their educational, literacy, and employment goals. Significant emphasis is placed on the involvement of parents in the administration of local Head Start programs.[8]

The Improving Head Start for School Readiness Act of 2007 reauthorized Head Start through 2012. Congress continues to fund Head Start until such time as it is reauthorized. This act helps more children arrive at kindergarten ready to succeed. The legislation increases teacher qualifications by requiring that 50 percent of Head Start teachers nationwide have a minimum of a baccalaureate degree (BA or BS) in early childhood education or a related field by 2013. Currently, 62 percent of Head Start teachers have the required degree.[9] It also requires Head Start programs to develop career ladders and annual professional development plans for full-time staff. In addition, it requires that all Head Start programs use research-based practices to support the growth of children's preliteracy and vocabulary skills.

Head Start has always been and remains a program for children of poverty. Although it currently reaches a significant number of poor children, increasing federal support for Head Start will likely increase the number of poor children served. However, we must keep in mind that the federal government is using Head Start to reform all of early childhood education. Federal officials believe that the changes they make in the Head Start curriculum—what and how teachers teach and how Head Start operates—serves as a model for other programs as well.

Head Start (for children three to five years of age) and Early Head Start (for children from birth to three years of age) are comprehensive child development programs that serve children, families, and pregnant women. These programs provide comprehensive health, nutritional, educational, and social services to help children achieve their full potential and succeed in school and life. Currently, the programs serve low-income children and families who are eligible for Head Start programs. This Head Start is called an entitlement program, because children and families who qualify are entitled to the services. However, only about 50 percent of eligible children and families receive these services because of the lack of funding to support full implementation. In addition, the numbers of children and families served by particular states and regions can be less than the national average.[10]

As public schools provide more kindergarten and preschool programs, Head Start now serves younger children, primarily three- and four-year-olds. Head Start is administered by the Administration for Children and Families (ACF) in the Department of Health and Human Services (HHS). Some educators and politicians think Head Start should be administered by the Department of Education. Others disagree. Currently, these two federal agencies collaborate to enhance and expand the Head Start programs to benefit all children from every aspect.

As of 2013, the Head Start program has an annual budget of more than $8 billion and serves some 1.2 million low-income children in approximately 49,200 Head Start classrooms. Of these nearly 1.2 million children, 2 percent are five years old and older; 48 percent are four-year-olds; 34 percent are three-year-olds; and 50 percent are three years old and under. Forty percent of the children are Hispanic and 29 percent are Black/African American. The average cost to educate a child in Head Start is $8,000 annually. Compare this cost to $8,703 per child, the price it costs to give a quality preschool education to every three- and four-year-old in the nation.[11] Head Start has a paid staff of 123,000 and 1.3 million volunteers.[12]

Head Start programs serve diverse geographic regions all across the United States. The El Paso, Texas, Head Start program serves 3,850 children and is the third-largest Head Start in the state of Texas. Head Start is an example of the federal government helping low-resource and underserved populations achieve their potential.[13]

HEAD START PERFORMANCE STANDARDS: EDUCATION AND CHILD DEVELOPMENT

Both Head Start and Early Head Start must comply with federal performance standards, designed to ensure that all children and families receive high-quality services.

Head Start Program Performance Standards
Federal guidelines for Head Start and Early Head Start, designed to ensure that all children and families receive high-quality services.

The **Head Start Program Performance Standards** play a central role in defining quality services for low-income children and their families. The Performance Standards are the mandatory regulations that programs must implement in order to operate a Head Start or Early Head Start program. These standards define the objectives, features, and services of a quality Head Start program; they specify the services that should be delivered to both young children and their families. These standards include the following:

(1) Child development and education approach for all children.

(1) In order to help children gain the skills and confidence necessary to be prepared to succeed in their present environment and with later

responsibilities in school and life, agencies' approach to child development and education must:

(i)   Be developmentally and linguistically appropriate;

(ii) Be inclusive of children with disabilities;

(iii) Provide an environment of acceptance that supports and respects gender, culture, language, ethnicity, and family composition;

(iv) Provide a balanced daily program of child-initiated and adult-directed activities, including individual and small group activities; and

(v)   Allow and enable children to independently use toilet facilities when it is developmentally appropriate and when efforts to encourage toilet training are supported by the parents.

(2) Parents and families must be:

(i)   Invited to become integrally involved in the development of the program's curriculum and approach to child development and education;

(ii) Provided opportunities to increase their child observation skills and to share assessments with staff that will help plan the learning experiences; and

(iii) Encouraged to participate in staff-parent conferences and home visits to discuss their child's development and education.

(3) Social and emotional development agencies must support social and emotional development by:

(i)   Encouraging development that enhances each child's strengths by:

   (A) Building trust;

   (B) Fostering independence;

   (C) Encouraging self-control by setting clear, consistent limits, and having realistic expectations;

   (D) Encouraging respect for the feelings and rights of others;

   (E) Supporting and respecting the home language, culture, and family composition of each child in ways that support the child's health and well-being; and

   (F) Planning for routines and transitions so that they occur in a timely, predictable, and unrushed manner according to each child's needs.

(4) Cognitive and Language Agencies must provide for the development of each child's cognitive and language skills by:

(i)   Supporting each child's learning, using various strategies, including experimentation, inquiry, observation, play, and exploration;

(ii) Ensuring opportunities for creative self-expression through activities such as art, music, movement, and dialogue;

(iii) Promoting interaction and language use among children and between children and adults; and

(iv) Supporting emerging literacy and numeracy development through materials and activities according to the developmental level of each child.

(5) Physical Development

(1)   In center-based settings, grantee and delegate agencies must promote each child's physical development by:

   (i) Providing sufficient time, indoor and outdoor space, equipment, materials, and adult guidance for active play and movement that support the development of gross motor skills;

(ii) Providing appropriate time, space, equipment, materials, and adult guidance for the development of fine motor skills according to each child's developmental level; and

(iii) Providing an appropriate environment and adult guidance for the participation of children with special needs.

(2) In home-based settings, grantee and delegate agencies must encourage parents to appreciate the importance of physical development, provide opportunities for children's outdoor and indoor active play, and guide children in the safe use of equipment and materials.

(6) Infants and Toddlers

(b) Child development and education approach for infants and toddlers.

(1) Agencies' program of services for infants and toddlers must encourage:

(i) The development of secure relationships in out-of-home care settings for infants and toddlers by having a limited number of consistent teachers over an extended period of time. Teachers must demonstrate an understanding of the child's family culture and, whenever possible, speak the child's language;

(ii) Trust and emotional security so that each child can explore the environment according to his or her developmental level; and

(iii) Opportunities for each child to explore a variety of sensory and motor experiences with support and stimulation from teachers and family members.

(2) Agencies must support the social and emotional development of infants and toddlers by promoting an environment that:

(i) Encourages the development of self-awareness, autonomy, and self-expression; and

(ii) Supports the emerging communication skills of infants and toddlers by providing daily opportunities for each child to interact with others and to express himself or herself freely.

(3) Agencies must promote the physical development of infants and toddlers by:

(i) Supporting the development of the physical skills of infants and toddlers including gross motor skills, such as grasping, pulling, pushing, crawling, walking, and climbing; and

(ii) Creating opportunities for fine motor development that encourage the control and coordination of small, specialized motions, using the eyes, mouth, hands, and feet.

(7) Preschoolers

(c) Child development and education approach for preschoolers.

(1) Agencies, in collaboration with the parents, must implement a curriculum that:

(i) Supports each child's individual pattern of development and learning;

(ii) Provides for the development of cognitive skills by encouraging each child to organize his or her experiences, to understand concepts, and to develop age appropriate literacy, numeracy, reasoning, problem solving and decision-making skills, which form a foundation for school readiness and later school success;

(iii) Integrates all educational aspects of the health, nutrition, and mental health services into program activities;

      (iv) Ensures that the program environment helps children develop emotional security and facility in social relationships;

      (v) Enhances each child's understanding of self as an individual and as a member of a group;

      (vi) Provides each child with opportunities for success to help develop feelings of competence, self-esteem, and positive attitudes toward learning; and

      (vii) Provides individual and small group experiences both indoors and outdoors.

    (2) Staff must use a variety of strategies to promote and support children's learning and developmental progress based on the observations and ongoing assessment of each child.[14]

HEAD START CHILD DEVELOPMENT AND EARLY LEARNING FRAMEWORK.
The Head Start Child Development and Early Learning Framework shown in Figure 8.1 specifies the domains of school readiness and identifies essential areas of learning and development that shape the Head Start curriculum. This child development and early learning framework is important for you for several reasons:

- It specifies learning outcomes that are essential to children's success in school and life.
- It ensures that all children in Head Start programs work toward the same learning outcomes.
- It impacts what children learn in all preschool programs, not just Head Start.

PROGRAM OPTIONS

Head Start and Early Head Start programs have the freedom to tailor their programs to meet the needs of the children, families, and communities they serve. To determine strengths and resources, every three years local programs conduct a community survey (the number of families and children living at or below the poverty level, projected benefits of Head Start in meeting the social needs of children and families in the community, health status of children and families in the community, etc.). Staff then designs their program options based on these data. Head Start programs may choose from one of these options:

1. The *center-based option* delivers services to children and families using the center as the base, or core. Center-based programs operate either full-day or half-day for thirty-two to thirty-four weeks a year, the minimum required by the Head Start Performance Standards, or they operate full-year programs. Center-based staff members make periodic visits to family homes.[15]

2. The *home-based option* uses the family home as the base for providing services. Home visitors work with the parents and children to improve parenting skills and to assist parents in using the home as the child's primary learning environment. Twice a month children and families come together for field trips and classroom experiences to emphasize peer group interaction.[16] The home-based option has these strengths:
   - Parent involvement is the keystone of the program.
   - Geographically isolated families have an invaluable opportunity to be part of a comprehensive child and family program.
   - An individualized family plan is based on both a child and a family assessment.
   - The family plan is facilitated by a home visitor, who is an adult educator with knowledge of and training in all Head Start components.
   - The program includes the entire family.

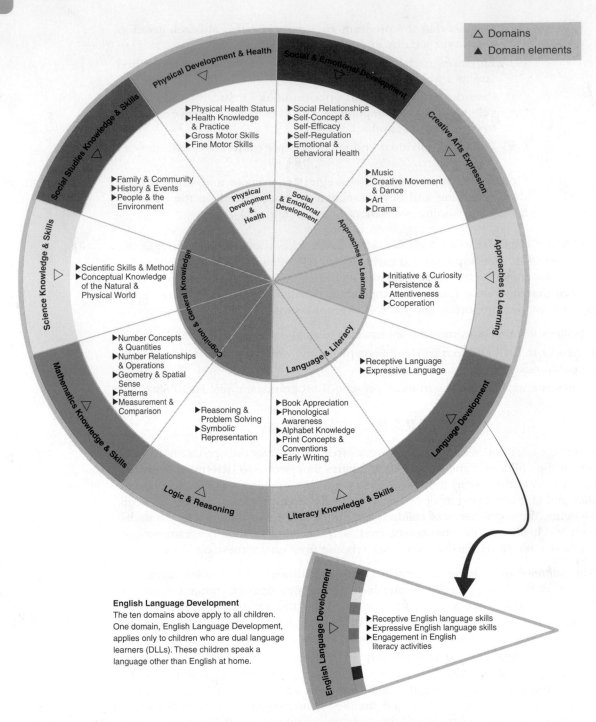

FIGURE 8.1 | Head Start Child Development and Early Learning Framework
The framework represents the foundation of the Head Start approach to school readiness. It aligns with and builds from the five essential domains of school readiness identified by the national education goals panel (see inner circle) and lays out essential areas of learning and development. The framework can be used to guide curriculum, implementation, and assessment to plan teaching and learning experiences that align to school readiness goals and track children's progress across developmental domains. The domains—and domain elements—apply to all three- to five-year-olds in Head Start and other early childhood programs, including dual language learners and children with disabilities.

Source: U.S. Department of Health and Human Services. Accessed from http://eclkc.ohs.acf.hhs.gov/hslc/tta-system/teaching/eecd/Assessment/Child%20Outcomes/HS_Revised_Child_Outcomes_Framework%28rev-Sept2011%29.pdf.

3. The *combination option* combines the center- and home-based options. The combination options must provide class sessions and home visits that result in an amount of contact time with children and families equivalent to the services provided through the center-based program option or home-based option.[17]

4. The *family child care option* includes programs created specifically to meet unique community and family needs. Many parents believe their children benefit from a homelike setting. Head Start agencies have found that family child care is a suitable arrangement when parents are working, in training, or need care for more than one child. The recognition of this setting as an option in Head Start is particularly timely given the changing circumstances that occur in many of today's families.

The Voice from the Field, "Higher Horizons Head Start," that follows provides a description of a combination program that implements a full-day center-based program for preschool children as well as home- and center-based services for infants, toddlers, and pregnant women.

Head Start prides itself on tailoring its programs to the children and families in the local community. In fact, this goal of meeting the needs of families and children at the local level is one of the program's strengths, and one that makes it very popular with parents.

> **Check Your Understanding:** Head Start

ELIGIBILITY FOR HEAD START SERVICES

To be eligible for Head Start services, children must meet age and family income criteria. Head Start enrolls children ages three to five years from low-income families. Income eligibility is determined by whether family incomes fall below the official federal poverty line, which is set annually by the U.S. Department of Health and Human Services. Poverty guidelines for 2013 are shown in Table 8.1.

Ninety percent of Head Start children have to meet the income eligibility criteria. The other 10 percent of enrollment can include children from families that exceed the low-income guidelines. The median income of the Head Start families is $22,714.

TABLE 8.1 | 2013 Poverty Guidelines for the 48 Contiguous States and the District of Columbia

Persons in Family/Household	Poverty Guideline ($)
For families/households with more than 8 persons, add $4,020 for each additional person.	
1	11,490
2	15,510
3	19,530
4	23,550
5	27,570
6	31,590
7	35,610
8	39,630

Higher Horizons Head Start

Higher Horizons operates full-day, full-year Head Start and Early Head Start programs for children from six weeks to five years of age in one of the most culturally diverse communities in the Washington, DC, metropolitan area. The Head Start programs offer full-day center-based services for children in two locations. Early Head Start offers home- and center-based services for infants, toddlers, and pregnant women. Children, families, and staff are representative of the diverse community; over forty-nine of the children speak languages other than English, including Spanish, Creole, Urdu, Somali, Cambodian, Punjabi, and Vietnamese.

PERFORMANCE STANDARDS

Higher Horizons is guided by Head Start Program Performance Standards. Major elements of the standards include child health and development, family/community engagement, early childhood development, and management systems and procedures. Higher Horizons involves parents and community representatives in all aspects of the program, including policy development, program design, and curriculum and management decisions.

THE HEAD START DAY

A routine day for Head Start children includes transportation pickup from an apartment complex on an agency-owned school bus. Other children are dropped off daily by parents or caregivers. Once children arrive, they are observed for general physical and mental health. Any unusual or observable concerns are reported to the health specialist for follow-up with the teacher and parent. Children are engaged in activities throughout the day, with an afternoon rest period. After the rest period, children begin preparing for departure by bus or receive a snack and participate in organized activities.

A typical daily schedule includes the following:

Arrival: Children are greeted in their home language; personal items (coats/hats) are placed in individual storage areas (cubbies). Teaching staff observe children for health inspections (colds/flu, signs of abuse/neglect, etc.).

Breakfast, Cleanup, Toothbrushing

Large Group Time: This is a time when there is group participation. Children and teaching staff make plans for the day; discuss the weather and news; children discuss happenings from home, etc. For example, teaching staff may read a book related to the plans they make and discuss the kites children brought in for "Kite Day." Throughout large group time, there are opportunities to build and expand vocabulary. For example, children use the local newspaper to find words that begin with *K* when discussing kites.

Gross Motor Activities—Outdoors/Gym: This is an opportunity for organized activities. Children have balls, hula hoops, obstacle course items, etc. Teaching staff arrange opportunities for children to choose activities to build teams, ensure that all children are actively engaged, and encourage physical activity. Children have access to the outdoor play areas with equipment to swing, climb, explore, and run.

Small Group Time—Individualization: Teaching staff work with children individually to develop skills in physical development (putting things together, solving puzzles, making projects with blocks, etc.). Teachers work with children in the art area to compare and match colored pieces of paper and children paint pictures using their imagination as creative thinkers. Children also have access to the dramatic play area and they arrange these items to set up a store. The computer area is available during small group time. Two computers in each classroom support children's development and learning in the areas of problem solving, fine motor control and eye-hand coordination, and other activities that help children make the bridge between the concrete and the abstract.

Large Group Time: Children review activities from the small group time; they share their activities with each other. Large group time also provides time for children to plan for the next day and discuss the outcomes of some of the activities they were involved in during small group time. Children may be introduced to music and movement during this time. Songs with lots of repetition, action songs, and songs with finger plays are also shared during large group time.

Lunch, Cleanup, Toothbrushing

Rest/Quiet Time

Snack, Parent Pick Up or

Music/Movement/Individualized Work Until Pickup: Individualized work may include a listening activity with a CD player or MP3 player. Children may select musical instruments to play, and small groups of children play in pairs, trios, or large group. Teaching staff ask children to pantomime movements of animals and insects (butterfly, elephant, etc.). Individualized work may focus on supporting a child in an area that he/she requires additional support such as vocabulary development, learning mathematical concepts in the block area, and artwork for creativity and self-expression.

MEALTIME

Meals are served family style (meaning that children eat together around a table) in each classroom. Children have the opportunity to help with food service, such as table setting and food distribution. Children help themselves to the food offered at breakfast, lunch, and snack. Adults in the classroom sit at each table, sharing the same food the children eat, and use this time to encourage the use of language to discuss both classroom and home activities. The menus are reflective of the diverse population served, which includes weekly vegetarian meals.

Meal adjustments are made for children with special dietary needs or food allergies. Vegan and vegetarian diets are recognized, and soy products are used for children with milk allergies. Special nutrition activities are regularly planned in each classroom. For example, each classroom is assigned a vegetable garden. Children plant vegetables (tomatoes, squash, pumpkins, melons, etc.) each spring and are responsible for watering, feeding, and tending to the growth of the vegetables. Once the vegetables are ready to harvest, they are brought to the classroom for cooking and eating. Children read stories about healthy food, and classrooms are responsible for monthly program-wide nutrition activities. Classrooms select a topic and are responsible for the activity. For example, children visit the local grocery store and select different varieties of apples (Gala, McIntosh, Fuji, Golden Delicious) to share with the classrooms and describe taste and textures.

THE CURRICULUM

Higher Horizons believes that the first five years of life are critical to a child's lifelong development. School readiness goals have been developed based on Head Start's definition of school readiness; these goals are aligned with the Virginia's Foundation Blocks for Early Learning and the Head Start Child Development and Early Learning Framework. Teachers plan daily activities using *The Creative Curriculum* approach to learning for children from infants through the preschool years. This resource-based curriculum helps staff plan and provide consistent and responsive care in an environment that starts children on the path to a lifetime of engaged learning. The curriculum for infants and toddlers helps staff build relationships with children by creating meaningful daily routines and experiences that respond to individual children's strengths and interests. For example, in the "cotton ball race," children learn to predict the effects of air movement on an object while considering the location of the air source. Children use straws to blow the cotton ball and see how far they can make it travel. They also blow a marble and a magnet to compare and contrast the amount of wind needed and what location they needed to be in to blow the objects to a certain predetermined point.

PARENT/FAMILY INVOLVEMENT

Parents play an active role in collaborating with classroom staff. Staff encourage parents to visit the classrooms and participate in two formal conferences and two home visits during the program year. The information gained during these staff–parent conferences enhances parents' knowledge and understanding of the developmental progress of the children in the program. During parent conferences, staff share that children are able to serve themselves and are independent and can help with simple tasks. Parents are often amazed at the types of items found in the home that can be used to support learning. For example, household items can be used for sorting, classification, and counting.

Higher Horizons Head Start continues to focus on developing and implementing quality programs that reflect current research and best practices and promoting the Head Start goal of school readiness for children.

Source: Text and photo contributed by Mary Ann Cornish, Executive Director, Higher Horizons Head Start and Early Head Start, Falls Church, Virginia.

Ten percent of a program's enrollment must include children with disabilities, and homeless children are also eligible for Head Start. Quite often, the actual enrollment in local programs for children with disabilities surpasses the minimum 10 percent requirement.

EARLY HEAD START

Early Head Start (EHS), launched in 1995, is designed to provide year-round comprehensive child and family development services for low-income pregnant women and families with infants and toddlers ages birth to three years. The purpose of the program is to enhance the physical, social, emotional, and intellectual development of children; support parents' efforts to fulfill their parental roles; and help families move toward self-sufficiency.[18] EHS is also a program for low-income families who meet federal poverty guidelines.

Head Start's entry into the field of infant and toddler care and education through EHS has achieved many accomplishments.[19]

- EHS provides services to the long-neglected age groups of infants and toddlers.
- EHS is a leader in the field of infant and toddler education.
- EHS programs produce statistically significant, positive impacts on standardized measures of children's cognitive, social-emotional, and language development, as well as lower levels of aggressive behavior.[20]

MIGRANT AND SEASONAL HEAD START PROGRAM

migrant family A family with school-aged children that moves from one geographic location to another to engage in agricultural work.

Migrant and Seasonal Head Start A federal program designed to provide educational and other services to children and families who earn income in agricultural work.

seasonal family A family with children who are engaged primarily in seasonal agricultural labor and who have not changed their residence to another geographic location in the preceding two-year period.

A **migrant family** is a family who moves from one geographic location to another within a two-year period for the purpose of engaging in agricultural work. Migrant Head Start provides services tailored to the unique needs of migrant families in some of the most rural areas in the United States. Services provided to migrant children and their families are identical to those of other Head Start programs, even as they address the unique needs of migrant children and families. **Migrant and Seasonal Head Start** programs emphasize serving infants and toddlers so that they do not have to accompany their parents to the fields or be left with young siblings.

A **seasonal family** is a family with children who are engaged primarily in seasonal agricultural labor and who have not changed their residence to another geographic location in the preceding two-year period. Migrant Head Start services offer positive, nurturing child development programs for children ages birth to school-entry age. Thirty-five percent of Migrant and Seasonal Head Start's enrollment is composed of infants and toddlers. Programs are center-based, full day, and structured to meet local needs.

For example, the focus of Fresno Migrant/Seasonal Head Start (FMSHS) is to promote the school readiness of low-income children by enhancing the social and cognitive development through the provision of health, education, nutrition, transportation, social, and other needed family services.

FMSHS encourages growth, independence, and self-sufficiency of the children and families through the many enrichment activities offered. Recruitment of children with disabilities is one of FMSHS's main priorities, and numerous children are eligible for program participation.[21]

AMERICAN INDIAN/ALASKA NATIVE HEAD START PROGRAMS

The American Indian/Alaska Native program of Head Start provides American Indian and Alaska Native children (birth to age five) and their families with comprehensive health, education, nutritional, social, and developmental services designed to promote school readiness.

The Migrant and Seasonal and American Indian/Alaska Native Head Start Program branches serve over 58,000 children nationwide. The Aleutian Pribilof Island Association Head Start program provides a half-day program that operates September through May and is designed to support children's physical, intellectual, and social growth. Currently, there are four center-based programs that collectively provide education, special needs, mental health, nutrition, and social services to a maximum of 72 children of preschool age (3–5 years) and their low-income families. Parents are encouraged to become involved in all aspects of the program and are provided with education, information, and referrals to assist them in reaching their goals.[22]

HEAD START RESEARCH

A question that everyone always asks is, "Do Head Start and Early Head Start programs work?" By *work*, people generally mean, "Do these programs deliver the services they are authorized and funded to deliver, and do these services make a difference in the lives of children and families?"

Over the last decade, the federal government has been aggressive in attempting to ensure that the programs it funds provide results. Consequently, we have seen a tremendous increase in federal monies allocated for research of federally funded programs and a corresponding increase in the number of research studies designed to measure the effectiveness of those programs.

The 2010 Head Start Impact Study reveals these results:

- *Program quality.* On average, Head Start children attend classrooms of good quality, and these classrooms are of higher quality than classrooms in other center-based programs.[23]

- *Head start access.* Access to Head Start has positive impacts on children's preschool experiences and school readiness:

   o For the four-year-old group, progress by the end of the Head Start year concentrates on language and literacy, including positive improvements in vocabulary, letter-word identification, spelling, pre-academic skills, color identification, letter naming, and parent-reported emergent literacy.

   o For the three-year-old group, benefits include improvements in vocabulary, letter-word identification, pre-academic skills, letter naming, elision (phonological processing or understanding letter and word sound), parent-reported emergent literacy, perceptual motor skills and prewriting, and applied problem solving (math).

   o Children attending Head Start show greater cognitive progress than do the control group children. Three-year-old children who had attended Head Start demonstrated modest gains in language, literacy, prewriting, and math skills. Four-year-old children demonstrated modest gains in language and literacy skills.[24]

- *Cognitive impacts.* By the end of first grade, only a single cognitive impact was found for each group. Children who attended Head Start as three- and four-year-old children do significantly better on vocabulary.[25]

- *Social-emotional impacts.* By the end of first grade, there was some evidence that children who attend Head Start as three-year-olds have closer and more positive relationships with their parents or significant primary adult than do children who have not. Of that same group, children with special needs showed improvements in the social-emotional domain by the end of first grade. Meanwhile, children who attended Head Start as three-year-olds showed less hyperactive and problem behavior by the end of Head Start; favorable social skills and positive approaches to learning at the end of the age four year; and less hyperactive behavior, increased social skills, and positive approaches to learning by the end of kindergarten.[26]

HEAD START PROGRAMS INCREASE IN PARENT INVOLVEMENT.   The results from research on parent involvement with their Head Start children is interesting and revealing.

- Head Start parents read more often and for longer periods of time at each sitting to their children compared to children and parents who are not in Head Start.
- Even after children are no longer attending Head Start, parents appear to "invest" more in their children. This is particularly true for fathers who are not living in the homes of their children. They spent more days visiting their children when their children were enrolled in Head Start as well as after they were no longer enrolled.
- Head Start programs that raised children's cognitive test score also tended to raise parents' involvement with their children.[27]

IMPLICATIONS FOR TEACHING.   Here are some specific things you can do:

- Encourage your students' parents to volunteer in your program and classroom. As you involve parents in your program, suggest ways for them to be more involved in their children's lives at home. As parents are more involved with their children, childrens' achievement increases.
- Share children's achievements with parents. Thank and praise parents for their involvement and encouragement of their children's achievements. As a result, parents invest more time, effort, and energy in helping their children succeed.
- Help children to be more pleasant. Researchers speculate that one of the reasons Head Start parents spend more time with (invested in) their children is because their children are more pleasant to be with. Consider how you can make your children more pleasant to be with. Some strategies are teach children behavioral control, teach manners, and get children involved in community service activities. Remember, every parent wants a child who is pleasant to be around. As children do better, their parents tend to like them more!

HEAD START FADE-OUT EFFECT

Even though the overall results of the Head Start Impact Study are generally positive, the big issue is the "fade-out" effect of Head Start benefits to children at the end of first grade. The fade-out effect refers to the fact that for some early childhood programs, the benefits children receive in a particular program tend to decrease or "fade out" over time, generally after a year or two. So, positive outcomes for children, such as enhanced vocabulary, increased reading and math readiness, and increased school readiness skills, tend to fade out as children progress through kindergarten and first grade. Many early childhood professionals believe that the causes of the fade-out include a lack of continuity of program services from preschool to kindergarten to first grade; a lack of high-quality teachers who have high achievement standards for all children in kindergarten and first grade; and poor-quality schools. We will hear much about the pros and cons of long-term benefits of Head Start in the years to come.

EARLY HEAD START RESEARCH FINDINGS.   Findings from a number of research studies conclude that Early Head Start makes a positive difference for children and families in terms of school success, family self-sufficiency, and parental support of child development. There are significant benefits for Early Head Start families:[28]

- EHS provides children with better vocabulary and improved cognitive and social-emotional development.

- EHS programs produce significant and positive impacts on the entire family system, establishing greater warmth and supportiveness between parent and child, more parent–child play, more stimulating home environments, more daily reading and increased support for language and learning, less spanking by mothers and fathers, more employment hours, and more hours spent in education and job training.
- EHS families who enroll during pregnancy have a greater likelihood of breastfeeding as compared to those not enrolled in EHS. There are positive impacts on children's cognitive and social-emotional development at 36 months of age.

CONCERNS WITH FEDERAL EARLY CHILDHOOD EDUCATION PROGRAMS.

As with all programs, Head Start has some associated issues of concern. Some of the issues are inherent in what we have discussed so far, and some are making Head Start a center of national attention.

Accountability. Part of the federal government's ongoing effort to improve Head Start involves making it more accountable for expenditures, children's achievement, and overall program performance. It is likely that Head Start administrators and other personnel will be challenged to enhance performance in all three of these

Children pull for their team at the tug-of-war station during the annual Head Start Field Day at Banita Creek Park in Nacogdoches, Texas.

areas. As you might expect, accountability does not come easily for some programs and agencies. As we have discussed, part of the changing educational climate is that the public wants to be assured that programs, especially those serving young children, achieve the goals for which they are funded.

Federal Control and Influence. One concern about federal legislation, regulations, and funding is that they represent an increasing encroachment of the federal government into state and local educational programs. Historically, the U.S. educational system is based on the idea that states and local communities should develop and implement educational programs and curricula, not the federal government. Opponents of federal control fear that America's highly valued local control is endangered and may even become extinct. Federal funding of any kind brings with it federal control in the form of regulations and guidelines.

REFORM AND RENEWAL OF HEAD START PROGRAMS.

Beginning in 2011, all of the nation's 1,600 Head Start and Early Head Start programs had to meet new performance criteria in order to have their grants renewed. Each Head Start program must develop school readiness goals, including the expectations of children's status across the domains of language and literacy, cognition and general knowledge, approaches to learning, physical well-being, motor development, and social and emotional development that will improve their readiness for kindergarten.[29] Each Head Start's program's classroom quality is measured by the Classroom Assessment Scoring System (CLASS). This is an observational assessment that focuses on teacher-child classroom interactions.[30]

Head Start programs that do not measure up to the standards as measured by CLASS will not have their grants renewed. This is a historic event in the fifty-year history of the Head Start program. This marked the first time that Head Start programs have had to prove that they prepare their children for kindergarten in order to keep and/or have their grants renewed.

Reflect and Apply: Benefits

HEAD START'S INFLUENCE.   Head Start is a big business and serious business. It has a complex operating structure, standards, and regulations. It also has a vast federal bureaucracy of personnel, regional offices, and training centers. Head Start is entrenched in the early childhood field and exerts a powerful influence on how the field functions and operates. In addition, Head Start is supported by the National Head Start Association (NHSA), a powerful, nonprofit lobbying and advocacy agency that serves to protect Head Start and promote its best interests. It wields tremendous power in the halls of Congress.

National Curriculum. The possibility of a national curriculum is closely associated with federal control and Head Start's influence. Head Start began as, and is based on, local option initiatives; in other words, local Head Start programs have been responsible for developing programs for the people and children that they represent and serve. Currently, however, an ongoing process of erosion is eating away at the autonomy of local programs to deliver local options within the programs. The ongoing push toward common national standards currently underway will have some influence on the goals and curriculum of Head Start and all of early childhood education, especially K–3.

Improving Teacher Quality. Teacher quality and qualifications are always a predominant issue when Head Start comes up for federal reauthorization every five years. The issue revolves around what percentage of Head Start teachers should have bachelor and associate degrees. Achieving the goal of high-quality personnel challenges administrators of all Head Start programs. Nonetheless, high-quality teachers and other staff are the heart and soul of any educational program, and each child deserves the best teacher possible. The federal government decreed that by September 30, 2013, one-half of Head Start teachers should have a bachelor's degree. Currently, over 62 percent of Head Start teachers have a bachelor's degree.[31]

Regardless of the issues associated with Head Start, one thing is certain: Head Start will continue to be an influential program affecting all early childhood programs.

NATIONAL NUTRITION PROGRAMS

The Family and Nutrition Service programs of the U.S. Department of Agriculture (USDA) provide national support for feeding America's children. Programs like Head Start strive to look at the whole child by not only offering academic progress but also by supporting healthy lifestyles. The nutrition component of Head Start focuses on promoting good nutrition and eating habits in children and families.

NATIONAL SCHOOL LUNCH PROGRAM.   The National School Lunch Program is a $9 billion annual federal nutrition program that provides breakfast, lunch, and snacks free or at a reduced rate for many of the nation's children. This program annually serves 31.2 million students in 101,000 schools.[32]

In the Abilene (Texas) Independent School District (ISD), for instance, about 60 percent of students qualify for the free or reduced-price meals annually.[33] Abilene ISD took advantage of the National School Lunch Program and the opportunities to provide a wider variety of fresh fruits and vegetables, including healthier dessert options such as low-fat pudding, fruit parfaits, and fruit cobblers.

Children from families with incomes below the federal poverty level are eligible for free meals. The USDA's threshold at which children are eligible for free meals and milk and reduced-price meals are obtained by multiplying 2013 federal income poverty guidelines by $1.30 and $1.85, which are $29,965 and $42,643, respectively.[34]

In addition to providing funding for school lunches, the USDA also sets rules and standards for school lunches. For example, beginning in the 2014–2015 school year, all snacks and vending machine foods must contain fruits, vegetables, dairy products, protein foods, or whole grain–rich foods that include at least a quarter cup of fruits or vegetables.

TITLE I EARLY CHILDHOOD PROGRAMS

Title I of NCLB provides financial assistance through state educational agencies to local educational agencies and schools with high numbers or percentages of poor children to help ensure that all children meet challenging state academic content and student academic achievement standards.[35] In 2013, the federal government spent almost $13 billion on Title I services.[36] You may hear a teacher say "I teach at a Title I school." This means that schools have a high percentage of poor children.

Title I focuses on several different objectives, all supporting the goal of giving children a high-quality education:

- Ensuring that high-quality academic assessments, accountability systems, teacher preparation and training, curriculum, and instructional materials are aligned with challenging state academic standards so that students, teachers, parents, and administrators can measure progress against common expectations for student academic achievement

- Meeting the educational needs of low-achieving children in the nation's highest-poverty schools, limited-English-proficient children, children from migrant families, children with disabilities, Native American children, neglected or delinquent children, and young children in need of reading assistance

- Closing the achievement gap between high- and low-performing children, especially the achievement gaps between minority and nonminority students

- Providing children with an enriched and accelerated educational program, including the use of school-wide programs or additional services that increase the amount and quality of instructional time

- Elevating the quality of instruction by providing staff in participating schools with substantial opportunities for professional development

- Affording parents substantial and meaningful opportunities to participate in the education of their children

Here is one example of a Title I Early Preschool which is representative of how Title I works. Columbia, Missouri, Public Schools offer developmentally appropriate preschool education services to children with developmental needs. Services are provided at no cost to eligible children. The preschool program serves over 650 children, with twenty-six classrooms located in elementary schools throughout the district. This program is designed to prepare children for successful school entry. Active family involvement is required to help children achieve this success. An early childhood teacher and instructional assistant plan age-appropriate learning experiences to promote development in literacy, communication, decision-making, and problem-solving. Teachers follow the HighScope teaching curriculum and a variety of other teaching resources to meet the developmental needs of each child.[37]

Federal initiatives like the National School Lunch and Breakfast Programs allow students under the poverty line to have healthy snacks and lunches daily.

All Head Start programs endeavor to build collaborative relationships with local agencies and programs. These collaborative approaches are designed to better serve children and families and to maximize the use of resources.

DEPARTMENT OF DEFENSE CHILD CARE

Military child care is an important part of military families' support network. Just as nonmilitary families depend and rely on quality child care for the successful growth and development of their children, so do military families. The Department of Defense (DoD) has recognized the need to help provide military families with quality and affordable child care and currently oversees nearly eight hundred Child Development Centers (CDCs) on military installations worldwide. Offering a safe child care environment and meeting professional standards for early childhood education, military child care accommodates the special needs of military families by extending hours to meet the work and deployment needs and schedules of their installation's population.[38]

The National Association of Child Care Resource and Referral Agencies (NACCRRA) is one organization that helps military families find quality child care programs individualized for each family. NACCRRA refers different military child care programs based on whether the parent is active or inactive, location of military installation, and even which war the parent is currently deployed in! For example, Operation Military Child Care (OMCC) serves military children ages birth to 12 years with families serving in one of six deployments.[39]

These programs offer assistance to military personnel and their families to ensure that their children are getting a quality education while they are off facing many challenges for our country.

SURE START.   A Department of Defense Education Activity (DoDEA) program for children at overseas installations, **Sure Start** is based on the Head Start model. The Sure Start program assists qualified preschool-aged children by providing education, health, and social services based on income and need guidelines.[40] Sure Start's comprehensive model, although appropriate for all preschool children, targets preschoolers who are at risk for school failure because of economic circumstance or other health and/or family factors.[41]

Sure Start A Department of Defense Education Activity (DoDEA) program based on the Head Start program model for command-sponsored children at overseas installations.

standards Statements of what students should know and be able to do.

Military families need and rely on quality child care as a part of their support network to ensure their children are getting a quality education while in the care of others.

FEDERAL AND STATE LEARNING STANDARDS

Have you asked yourself, "What should I teach?" How do you answer this question? Perhaps you reply that you will teach your children reading, writing, and mathematics. But let's look at your answer for a minute. What reading skills will you teach? Will you teach phonics? Word meaning? Vocabulary development? In what order will you teach these skills? To what achievement level will you teach them? These questions are not easily answered; and not all teachers answer them the same way.

Standards, statements of what students should know and be able to do, help answer questions about what to teach children and what they should learn. As a result, local, state, and, increasingly, national standards influence every facet of the practice of early childhood education, including how teachers teach and how children learn. Standards help you and other teachers better answer the "What should students learn? "and "What should I teach?"

FOUNDATIONS OF THE STANDARDS MOVEMENT

The standards movement is a little over thirty years old—not long in the timeline of major events in the history of education, but tremendously influential in its impact on education today. Three federal initiatives have played a very large role in the development and implementation of the current standards movement:

- ***A Nation at Risk: The Imperative for Educational Reform, National Commission on Excellence in Education (1983).*** The U.S. Department of Education created the National Commission on Excellence in Education to provide a report about the quality of education in the United States. The commission recommended, among other things, curriculum reform, more rigorous and measurable standards, and higher expectations for the nation's students.[42]

- ***Goals 2000: Educate America Act (2000).*** This act was designed to ensure that all students reached high levels of achievement. Goals 2000 established eight national education goals. Goal three specified that by the year 2000, all students will leave grades 4, 8, and 12 having demonstrated competency over challenging subject matter including English, mathematics, science, foreign languages, civics and government, economics, the arts, history, and geography, and every school in America will ensure that all students learn to use their minds well, so they may be prepared for responsible citizenship, further learning, and productive employment in our nation's modern economy.[43] Goal four of this act stated that by the year 2000, U.S. students would be first in the world in science and mathematics achievements.

- ***No Child Left Behind Act (2001).*** The former Elementary and Secondary Education Act of 1965, rechristened The No Child Left Behind Act (NCLB), is currently the main federal law affecting education from kindergarten through high school. NCLB mandates goals for improving education in elementary, middle, and high schools by setting high expectations for students, teachers, and administrators of each state, with the goal of greater educational achievement for all students.[44]

COMMON CORE STATE STANDARDS (CCSS)

All 50 states have state standards for what their students should know and do. If you are not familiar with your state standards, now would be a good time for you to learn about them. They will influence your teaching. However, educators, politicians, and the public realize that what students learn depends on where they live. State standards are not uniform across states. What students learn in California is not necessarily what children learn in New York. The public's desire for uniformity among state standards laid the foundation for CCSS.

Additional reasons for the development and implementation of the CCSS include the following:

- The Great Recession of 2008–2012 further documented the need for a well-trained work force. Leaders of businesses and industry have complained that they cannot find the highly skilled and educated workers they need to compete nationally and internationally. Business leaders look to the public schools for well-educated workers. They want the schools to beef-up their standards and teaching and provide highly educated students for the workforce of today and tomorrow.

- The United States has consistently ranked behind other nations in test scores of reading and mathematics.[45] Politicians believe the lack of U.S. student achievement is a threat to national security and is eroding U.S. global economic and political influence.

All of the above set the stage for the development of National Common Core Standards.

IMPLEMENTING COMMON CORE STANDARDS. The National Governors Association (NGA) and the Chief Council of State School Officers (CCSSO) launched the Common Core State Standards initiative, a state-led effort to construct national academic standards that would prepare students for success in higher education and future careers. In 2014 and 2015, two assessment agencies will begin administering tests, replacing old state exams, to review whether teachers and students are meeting the goals of the CCSS.

WHAT ARE COMMON CORE STATE STANDARDS?

Common Core State Standards (CCSS) National benchmarks in math and English created to have uniformity no matter where students attend public schools.

The **Common Core State Standards** are national benchmarks in math and English created to have uniformity no matter where students attend public schools. They are part of a state-led effort to give all students the skills and knowledge they need to succeed. The federal government was not involved in the development of the standards. Individual states choose whether or not to participate in and adopt these standards. Currently, the Common Core State Standards are based on best practices in national and international education and represent what American students need to know and do to be successful in college and careers (see Figures 8.2 and 8.3). Thus, you will hear teachers talk about getting their students "career and college" ready. This career and college readiness begins in kindergarten.

That's the perspective teacher Christie Neise has about the new curriculum, as well. "We've been doing this already," says the kindergarten teacher at Northmore Elementary in West Palm Beach, Florida, during training on the new standards. "The focus will just have to be a little sharper."[46]

CLOSING THE ACHIEVEMENT GAP WITH STANDARDS

There is a lot of discussion today about the education achievement gap. The achievement gap is the difference between what certain groups of children know and are able to do as opposed to what other social and ethnic groups of children know and are able to do. The achievement gap is wide between white children and black and Latino children. Consider this example:

> The 26-point reading achievement gap between white and Hispanic fourth-graders in 2007 was not significantly different from the 25-point gap in 2009. The reading achievement gap between black and white fourth-grade students in 2009 (26 points) was not measurably different from the gap in 2007.[47]

CCSS are often cited as one way that teachers and schools can help all children learn what they need to know, and as a result close the achievement gap. Certainly CCSS do play a role in helping close achievement gaps; however, standards by themselves cannot close these gaps. A number of other things are required, including the following:

- Programs for young children at an early age that will help them gain the knowledge, skills, and behaviors necessary for them to enter school and be successful.
- A highly effective teacher who is well prepared to teach all children regardless of diversity and socioeconomic background and who can help all children achieve at least one grade level at the end of the school year.[48]
- Parent education programs designed to help parents gain the knowledge and skills that will aid them in helping their children get ready to learn before they come to school. Parents are the most important part of a child's education and are essential to a child's well-being and school achievement.[49]

IMPLICATIONS FOR TEACHING.   Here are some things you can do to make sure that you help all young children learn and, as a result, eliminate achievement gaps:

- ***Be familiar with the Common Core State Standards and your state standards.*** These standards are important because they outline what each and every child should know and be able to do, not just *some* children.

	Key Ideas and Details	Craft and Structure	Integration of Knowledge and Ideas	Range of Reading and Level of Text Complexity
Kindergarten	• With prompting and support, ask and answer questions about key details in a text. • With prompting and support, retell familiar stories, including key details. • With prompting and support, identify characters, settings, and major events in a story	• Ask and answer questions about unknown words in a text. • Recognize common types of texts (e.g., storybooks, poems). • With prompting and support, name the author and illustrator of a story and define the role of each in telling the story.	• With prompting and support, describe the relationship between illustrations and the story in which they appear (e.g., what moment in a story an illustration depicts). • With prompting and support, compare and contrast the adventures and experiences of characters in familiar stories.	• Actively engage in group reading activities with purpose and understanding.
Grade 2	• Ask and answer such questions as *who, what, where, when, why,* and *how* to demonstrate understanding of key details in a text. • Recount stories, including fables and folktales from diverse cultures, and determine their central message, lesson, or moral. • Describe how characters in a story respond to major events and challenges.	• Describe how words and phrases (e.g., regular beats, alliteration, rhymes, repeated lines) supply rhythm and meaning in a story, poem, or song. • Describe the overall structure of a story, including describing how the beginning introduces the story and the ending concludes the action. • Acknowledge differences in the points of view of characters, including by speaking in a different voice for each character when reading dialogue aloud.	• Use information gained from the illustration and words in a print or digital text to demonstrate understanding of its characters, setting, or plot. • Compare and contrast two or more versions of the same story (e.g., Cinderella stories) by different authors or from different cultures.	• By the end of the year, read and comprehend literature, including stories and poetry, in the grades 2–3 text complexity band proficiently, with scaffolding as needed at the high end of the range.

FIGURE 8.2 | Common Core Standards for English Language Arts, Reading and Literature in Kindergarten and Second Grade

Source: © Copyright 2010. National Governors Association Center for Best Practices and Council of Chief State School Officers. All rights reserved.

- ***Develop your lesson plans and teaching activities so that they incorporate the CCSS.*** CCSS focus on the essential knowledge, skills, and behaviors that all children need to know.
- ***Focus on what your children will be tested on at the end of the year.*** You and other teachers should not "teach to the test"; however, you need to be aware of what your children will be tested on.

	Operations and Algebraic Thinking	Number and Operations in Base Ten	Measurement and Data	Geometry	Mathematical Practices*
Grade 1	• Represent and solve problems involving addition and subtraction. • Understand properties of multiplication and the relationship between addition and subtraction. • Add and subtract within 100. • Work with addition and subtraction equations.	• Use place value understanding and properties to add and subtract. • Understand place value. • Extend the counting sequence.	• Measure lengths indirectly and by iterating length units. • Tell and write time. • Represent and interpret data.	• Reason with shapes and their attributes.	• Make sense of problems and persevere in solving them. • Reason abstractly and quantitatively. • Construct viable arguments and critique the reasoning of others. • Model with mathematics. • Use appropriate tools strategically. • Attend to precision. • Look for and make use of structure. • Look for and express regularity in repeated reasoning.
Grade 3	• Represent and solve problems involving multiplication and division. • Understand properties of multiplication and the relationship between multiplication and division. • Multiply and divide within 100. • Solve problems involving the four operations, and identify and explain patterns in arithmetic.	• Use place value understanding and properties of operations to perform multi-digit arithmetic.	• Solve problems involving measurement and estimation of intervals of time, liquid volumes, and masses of objects. • Geometric Measurement: understand concepts of area and relate area to multiplication and to addition. • Geometric Measure: recognize perimeter as an attribute of plane figures and distinguish between linear and area measures.	• Reason with shapes and their attributes.	

FIGURE 8.3 | Common Core Standards for Mathematics Grades 1 and 3

- *Differentiate your instruction so that you can provide for the diverse learning needs of all your students.* One instructional approach does not fit all, and in today's educational environment increasing numbers of teachers differentiate their instruction to help ensure that all students learn. Some ways to differentiate instruction are as follows:
  o Group children for instructional purposes based on the skills they know and need to learn.
  o Provide children with different levels of instructional materials.
  o Provide individual instruction to children who need help, such as struggling readers.
  o Use peer teaching. Children learn from each other and they love to help others.
  o Use reading buddies. Reading buddies don't have to be at the same reading level. What is important is that children are reading away from the teacher and are having opportunities to read. Remember what Vygotsky said about "competent others" providing assistance in the zone of proximal development.
- *Make the best use of your classroom time for instructional purposes.* When children are meaningfully engaged in learning activities, there is a better chance for them to learn what they need to know and do. Remember, you have a limited amount of time with children, so strive to make the best use of it. At the same time, your teaching should be developmentally appropriate and children should be involved in activities they find interesting and worthwhile. Keep in mind that children need opportunities to play and interact with each other.
- *Integrate technology into your teaching and learning.* Children enjoy technology, and are very comfortable using it. Furthermore, technology adds interest to their learning, and at the same time, it helps children achieve what the standards require.
- *Work with families and parents to help them understand what you are teaching their children and why.* Seek family members' cooperation so they can help support and encourage in the home what you are teaching in the classroom. Sending simple lessons home, such as a packet of learning activities that children and family members can do together, helps involve parents in the teaching–learning process and impresses on them and their children the importance of school achievement.

One first grade teacher sends home each night a book bag containing books for children to read with their parents. Also included in the book bag is an evaluation sheet for the parents and students to fill out regarding the time they spent reading together and what parents believe are areas in which their children might need help.

Closing the achievement gap between cultures, races, and socioeconomic groups is an ongoing process, but it is one to which you must dedicate yourself. After all, helping all children succeed is why we teach and is what we dedicate our lives to.

STANDARDS ARE CHANGING TEACHING AND LEARNING

As indicators of what children should know and be able to do, standards are changing the ways teachers teach, how and what students learn, and the ways schools operate. Let's review some of the ways standards are shaping teaching and learning.

INTENTIONAL TEACHING. Standards have transformed (some would say reformed) teaching from an input model to an output model. As a result, teachers are no longer able to say, "I taught Salvador how to compare and contrast two versions of

intentional teaching
The process of teaching children the skills they need for success based on specific goals and standards.

alignment The arrangement of standards, curriculum, and tests so that they complement one another.

curriculum alignment The process of making sure that the content of the curriculum matches what the standards say students should know and be able to do.

data-driven instruction
A type of teaching in which analysis of assessment data is used to make decisions about how to best meet the instructional needs of each child.

the same story." Now the question is, "Is Salvador able to compare and contrast two versions of the same story?" **Intentional teaching** is the process of teaching children the skills they need for success based on specific goals and standards. Intentional teachers create environments, consider the curriculum and tailor it to children as individuals, plan learning experiences, and interact with children and families with purposefulness and thoughtfulness.[50] Intentional teachers, intentionally and with purpose, plan lessons, teach, and assess in order to ensure that their students are learning the CCSS and achieving at high levels.

CURRICULUM ALIGNMENT.   Increasing student achievement is at the center of the standards movement. Teachers view standards, tests, and teaching alignment as a viable and practical way to help ensure student achievement. **Alignment** is the arrangement of standards, curriculum, and tests so that they complement one another. In other words, the curriculum should be based on what the standards say students should know and be able to do; tests measure what the standards indicate. **Curriculum alignment** is the process of making sure that what is taught—the content of the curriculum—matches what the standards say students should know and be able to do.

DATA-DRIVEN INSTRUCTION.   Standards have brought about a shift in focus from covering subject matter to meeting the needs of each student. There is only one way to determine whether or not the needs of the students are being met: through an ongoing analysis of data collected from assessing children. In **data-driven instruction** the analysis of assessment data is used to make decisions about how to best meet the instructional needs of each child. To use data-driven instruction, start by analyzing existing data on each student from their cumulative record files to get a general profile of each student. Then align objectives to assessments by planning collaboratively with your grade-level colleagues to determine when you will be teaching district and state standards and how you will assess each standard. Next, gather data by using formal assessments, informal assessments, and technology. Use the data to guide your next steps in the instructional process. Which students are ready to move on? Which students need remediation? Which students need enrichment? Just remember that making data-based decisions to guide instruction is an ongoing process. You should be constantly assessing, analyzing, and adjusting throughout the school year.[51,52]

THE CONTRIBUTIONS OF STANDARDS.   We can conclude our discussion of standards by asking ourselves: Why is this important to us? The standards movement has done a number of things for the early childhood profession as well as for teachers and young children. Standards have helped the profession sharpen its focus regarding what young children should know and be able to do. As a result, many early childhood professionals have come to the conclusion that young children are much more capable than they realized or gave them credit for.

Check Your Understanding: Standards

As early childhood professionals have rediscovered the children they teach, they are in the process of rediscovering themselves. Teachers are engaged in more professional development than ever before, and much of this professional development involves learning how to teach with standards. In this sense, standards have reenergized the teaching profession.

COMMON CORE STANDARDS AND PROFESSIONAL DEVELOPMENT GO HAND IN HAND.   Common Core Standards don't implement themselves. Teachers spend a great deal of time in work sessions, planning sessions, and learning about the standards and how to implement them. You will be involved in **horizontal planning**, in which you collaboratively plan with your grade-level colleagues. You will also engage in **vertical planning** with teachers in grades below and above you. For example, as a second grade teacher you will plan with K, 1, 3, and 4 teachers to make sure that learning is seamless across grades.

One thing that you can count on as you teach with the new Common Core State Standards is that you will be very involved in meetings with your same-grade colleagues and colleagues from across your school and district about how to best implement the standards. The Voice from the Field, "Five Essential Steps for Implementing the Common Core State Standards," will help you understand, from a professional perspective, what is involved in implementing the CCSS in your grade level and school.

This video provides you a partial rationale for a standards-based curriculum. As you watch it, listen closely to what the teacher says about standards and how standards and what children know and are able to do, drives instruction.

horizontal planning
Collaboratively planning with your grade-level colleagues.

vertical planning
Collaboratively planning with teachers in grades below and above that which you teach.

Reflect and Apply: Implementation

ACCOMMODATING DIVERSE LEARNERS

Now that you have read about various Head Start programs, let's further explore the services available for children with disabilities in these programs. Head Start is critical for children with or at risk of developing disabilities because the program emphasizes addressing children's various abilities, learning styles, and conditions. Often, Head Start is the first place a child's disability or developmental delay is identified. This identification can lead to early intervention, which has tremendous benefits for young children and their families. Early intervention can lead to remediation or amelioration of disabilities and reduced special education costs and costs borne by families. Specially trained personnel work collaboratively with community agencies to provide services to children with disabilities.

Head Start has specific guidelines that specify that services provided to children with disabilities must be appropriate and inclusive. Here are some examples you can use in your early childhood classroom to benefit *all* children:

1. Although providing lists of children's therapy schedules is useful for teachers, do not post them; you do not want to publicly identify individual children with disabilities.

2. Encourage independence by providing opportunities for children to try new things. One good approach to get children to try new things is to break down goals into small steps. This is called "chunking" and is very effective.

3. Include *all* students in field trips. Carefully plan your trips to allow each child to benefit from the experience.

4. Just as your classroom has books showing children from many different cultural groups, also include books with pictures that show children with disabilities.

5. Promote acceptance of children with disabilities in all you do and say to your children, parents/families, and the community. Positive attitudes about children and inclusive classrooms begin with you!

Five Essential Steps for Implementing the Common Core State Standards

With the introduction and adoption of the Common Core State Standards by forty-six states, new challenges arise about how to implement them in a manner that acknowledges the hard work of teachers and school administrators across schools on all grade levels. It can be daunting when considering the many initiatives that have come and gone across school districts. The journey will take considerable effort and time on the part of all members of the school community—students, teachers, administrators, and families. It is one of the biggest shifts in the education of K–12 students in the last thirty years.

The CCSS are designed to prepare all students for college and careers. In the primary grades, the content and skills in English language arts and mathematics necessary to ensure student success are in great focus. The CCSS levels the playing field for all students and school districts. We are looking at the same document that delineates outcomes for students at each grade level. However, the road to achieving those standards is left to the discretion of school districts and, in some cases, individual schools.

Based on our own experiences implementing the CCSS, here are five recommendations that will support you in your teaching with standards.

STEP 1

Familiarize Yourself with the Common Core Standards.

The school administration must provide the time and space for teachers to read, interpret, and discuss the CCSS document in its entirety. Teachers must have an opportunity to speak with their colleagues, raise questions, and find applications to the current work in their classrooms. Teachers should become familiar with the standards of their grade and that of grades above and below them in order to be more effective teachers. To implement the content effectively, they must be aware of what the students are expected to know and do at the end of the grade.

STEP 2

Set Realistic Goals for the School.

The school's leadership must decide, in consultation with teachers and school district officials, the one or two areas for deep focus during the school year. All areas of the CCSS cannot be addressed at once, and it will only serve to overwhelm school leaders, teachers, and students. It is best to choose a focus based on areas in need of improvement in your school and/or district.

STEP 3

Communicate Expectations and Goals with Students and Parents.

Schools must conduct information sessions for parents and guardians. They, too, need to have some level of understanding. Their children are greatly impacted by the implementation of the CCSS. For students and parents to be active participants in their education, we need to communicate what is expected and required of students.

STEP 4

Collaborate with Other Teachers and Administrators.

By its design, the CCSS encourage teachers to plan and implement units, which are not included in all curriculums. Collaboration between teachers to create the necessary units will result in the most effective instruction for our students. It will also encourage consistency across grade levels to ensure all students are receiving the same content and skills.

STEP 5

Create and Administer Meaningful Assessments.

The CCSS creates a continuum of learning throughout the grades; not all skills are taught to mastery. Our assessments should reflect the goals set by the standards. Teachers should analyze assessments and discuss adjustments to reach these goals. This is where formative assessment is our friend. When teachers collaborate on the assessment tools and assess the work produced by students, they see the effect of their teaching. When all teachers are looking at the same assessment results, deeper conversations will happen and collaborative decisions made.

As educators, we often feel the pressure of implementing new and different ideas and strategies that state and federal education departments set. The frequent changes in expectations can be frustrating, discouraging, and time consuming. However, the CCSS creates a national level of academic achievement for all students. When all teachers and administrators have meaningful conversations about the implementation of the CCSS, change will happen where it matters most, in the classroom.

Source: Contributed by Annabell Martinez, Principal, and Elizabeth Bradstreet, Kindergarten Teacher, PS 124, Brooklyn, New York.

All Head Start programs endeavor to build collaborative relationships with local agencies and programs. These collaborative approaches are designed to better serve children and families and to maximize the use of resources.

INCLUSION AND COLLABORATION

The Head Start program of Upper Des Moines Opportunity, Inc., operates twenty-five fully inclusive preschool classrooms. We have three classrooms specific to toddlers, ages eighteen to thirty-six months. We also have twenty-two classrooms set up for children ages three to five. Our programs are designated for all children, regardless of race or disability. We use *The Creative Curriculum* as a part of our ongoing instruction and observation of children in the classroom. We also use the *Ages and Stages Questionnaire* for developmental and social-emotional screening for children from birth to five years. In addition, we use Positive Behavior Supports for guiding children's behavior.

Our Head Start programs take pride in the strength of our partnerships with local school districts and other local education agencies. Because of the strength of these relationships, we are able to collaborate in program design and offer natural or least-restriction environments to all children.

In Early Head Start, our staff is trained in case management of children with special needs. They take the lead position in coordination of services to our children and their families. These services are provided in the home, in the classroom, or in a child care setting. Support service staff trained in specific areas of early childhood development help in our toddler rooms. We use the Child Study model to continually update staff on individual progress, concerns, and needs of our children. We employ many interpreters of different languages because we serve a very diverse population.

Our Head Start classrooms for children aged three to five years offer many opportunities for inclusion. In some centers, we dually enroll children, allowing them the opportunity to spend half a day in Head Start and the other half in an early childhood special education (ECSE) classroom. We also have classrooms in which Head Start teachers and ECSE teachers work side by side, allowing for full-day programming for all children in the least restrictive settings. We operate Head Start classrooms in which the lead teacher has a degree in early childhood special education and associate(s) have backgrounds in early childhood, or the lead teacher has a background in early childhood and associate(s) are qualified to work with children having special needs. Support service staff help in all of our classrooms for three- to five-year-olds, and they, too, use the Child Study team approach to communicate the progress, needs, and concerns of all children.[53]

ACTIVITIES FOR PROFESSIONAL DEVELOPMENT

ETHICAL DILEMMA

"THIS EDUCATIONAL FASHION STATEMENT IS WRONG!"

Metropolitan school district is in the process of implementing the Common Core State Standards (CCSS). However, not all of the early childhood faculty see eye to eye on the CCSS. Some of the more vociferous in the school district argue that the standards will actually lower the bar for students, counteracting the Metropolitan ISD's reputation of being one of the more elite school districts in the state. Third grade teacher Kathy Fair has jumped on the "dumbing down" bandwagon. Kathy believes that the CCSS are the "educational fashion of the moment" and that they won't

last long. "I don't see why we have to teach to the lowest common denominator. This common core thing is too common!" On the other hand, first grade teacher Samantha Smith is a strong supporter of the CCSS and believes they will be beneficial for her children and the district. She is irked that Kathy is so vocally opposed to the standards. She thinks her point of view needs to be heard too.

What should Samantha do? Let Kathy continue making her wild assertions? Should Samantha risk an open confrontation with Kathy at the next faculty meeting scheduled for next week? Or, should Samantha pull Kathy aside and try to reason with her? Should Samantha post her support for the CCSS on Facebook? What should Samantha do? What would you do?

ACTIVITIES TO APPLY WHAT YOU LEARNED

1. Why do the benefits of Head Start seem to fade out in grade one? Participate in an online discussion that addresses this question. Be sure to consider such things as the way children are taught in kindergarten through first grade. What are some things you would do to help ensure that the fade-out effect does not happen? Post your suggestions to your class discussion board.

2. **KEY ASSESSMENT:** Second grade teacher Erica Rodriguez keeps asking herself the question: "Are the standards meeting their intended purpose of helping ensure that each and every child will achieve and learn?" Erica is a determined and dedicated teacher. She wants data to answer her question. She thinks that by reviewing teacher blogs and researching the beliefs of teachers of the year, she will get the information she needs. For example, she read the comments of Pam Williams, Georgia Teacher of the Year, who said, "I have seen much growth in English language

arts and reading informational text across disciplines." Erica needs your help finding additional information to support the argument that standards are meeting their intended purpose. Review teacher blogs and statements of teachers of the year. Post the highlights of your research on your class discussion board. Conclude your post with a one hundred-word statement about standards helping children achieve. Use this rubric to guide your work.

3. Head Start programs are often the "front line" in the identification of children with disabilities.

   a. Visit two Head Start programs and identify how they screen for and identify children with disabilities. Pay particular attention to how staff engage and interact with parents of children who have or may have a disability.

   b. Access the website of the Head Start programs and review their guidelines for including children with disabilities in their program.

   c. Create a PowerPoint of your findings and post it to your class discussion board.

LINKING TO LEARNING

The following agencies and programs, which can be located easily online, provide additional information about topics discussed in this chapter.

Early Head Start National Resource Center

The EHS NRC is a storehouse of early childhood expertise that promotes the building of new knowledge and the sharing of information.

Fatherhood Initiative

An overview of this initiative presents facts, statistics, and reports of the Department of Health and Human Services' involvement and activities with the Fatherhood Initiative.

National Head Start Association (NHSA)

The NHSA is a nonprofit organization dedicated to meeting and addressing the concerns of the Head Start community.

National Migrant and Seasonal Head Start Association

This nonprofit organization seeks to advocate for resources, create partnerships, and affect public policy for migrant and seasonal children and their families.

Common Core State Standards

The Common Core State Standards provide a consistent, clear understanding of what students are expected to learn, so teachers and parents know what they need to do to help them.

Office of Head Start

United States Department of Health and Human Services official website for Head Start contains information on legislation and regulations, program services, and current information and research concerning Head Start.

University of Colorado-Denver: Centers for American Indian and Alaska Native Health-Head Start Research Center

The goals of the American Indian and Alaska Native Head Start Research Center (AIANHSRC) are to operationalize and implement a research and training agenda for American Indian/Alaska Native (AI/AN) Head Start and Early Head Start Programs.

U.S. Department of Agriculture Food and Nutrition Service

This service provides information about the USDA's role in providing healthy and nutritious meals for children.

CHAPTER

9

INFANTS and TODDLERS

Foundation Years for Learning

LEARNING OUTCOMES

1. Describe what infants and toddlers are like.
2. Explain how research is influencing the care and education of infants and toddlers.
3. Describe how theories of development explain infant and toddler motor development.
4. Describe how theories of development explain infant and toddler cognitive development.
5. Describe how theories of development explain infant and toddler language development.
6. Explain why there is a renewed emphasis on infant and toddler psychosocial, emotional, and mental health.
7. List the ways you can provide quality programs and environments for infants and toddlers.
8. Describe how you can accommodate diverse infants and toddlers.

INTEREST in infant and toddler care and education is at an all-time high and will likely continue at this level well into the future. The growing demand for quality infant and toddler programs stems primarily from political and cultural trends. For example, Stephanie and Brent Hill, a young couple in Houston, just had their first baby, Addie, three months ago. Stephanie says, "With the economy the way it is, I just have to work to help keep the family afloat. I need to know she's *really* being cared for." It is also fueled by parents who want their children to have an early start and get off on the right foot so they can be successful in life and work. Raoul Hernandez, dad to two-year-old Daniel, is looking for a program that can help Daniel get a good start. "He's so smart—he's like a sponge. I want to be sure he gets as much as he can right now so that he'll be ready for school in a few years." The popularity of early care and education is also attributable to a changing view of the very young and the discovery that infants are remarkably competent individuals. Let's examine the ways that infants' and toddlers' development and early experiences shape their lives.

WHAT ARE INFANTS AND TODDLERS LIKE?

Think for a minute about your experiences with infants. What characteristics stand out most in your mind? Review the developmental profiles of Sara, Dakota, and Avanti in Portraits of Infants and Toddlers. The following discussion will help you understand children's development across four domains—social-emotional, cognitive, motor, and adaptive (i.e., daily living). After you read this text, reflect on and answer the questions that accompany the portraits.

Have you ever tried to carry on an extended conversation with an infant? They are full of coos, giggles, smiles, and sparkling eyes! Or have you ever tried to keep up with a toddler? A typical response is, "They are into everything!" The infant and toddler years between birth and age two are full of developmental milestones and significant events. **Infancy**, life's first year, includes the first breath, the first smile, first thoughts, first words, and first steps. During **toddlerhood**—from twelve to twenty-four months—two of the most outstanding developmental milestones are walking and rapid language development. Mobility and language are the cornerstones of autonomy that enable toddlers to become independent. How you, other early childhood professionals, and parents respond to infants' first accomplishments and toddlers' quests for autonomy determines how they grow and master life events.

UNDERSTANDING CHILD DEVELOPMENT

Understanding the major development processes that characterize the formative years of infants and toddlers helps you fully grasp your roles as educator and nurturer. Here are some important considerations:

- Recognize that infants and toddlers are not the miniature adults pictured in many baby product advertisements; children need many years to develop fully and become independent. This period of dependency and your responses to it are critical for children's development.
- Keep in mind that "normal" growth and development milestones are based on averages, and the average is simply the middle ground of development. Know the milestones of different stages of development to assess children's progress or lack of it.

PORTRAITS OF INFANTS AND TODDLERS

SARA

General Description 9 months old, Caucasian female; lives with her mother and grandmother; expresses her feelings easily and openly; loves to eat

Social-Emotional	Cognitive/Language	Motor	Adaptive (Daily Living)
• Begin to demonstrate separation and stranger anxiety. Sara cries when her mother leaves the room or when a stranger peeks into her stroller. • Develop trust in primary caregivers if they are responsive. Sara's mother is responsive to her cues and cries. • Use social referencing and strong attachments to primary caregivers to feel secure. Sara scans her teacher's face to see if a noisy toy is safe. • Express a variety of emotions such as anger, sadness, grief, and happiness. Sara frowns when her father says goodbye, and gives him a joyous smile when he returns. • Infants can begin to self-regulate, but need adults to help them when they are tired or distressed. When Sara is tired she sucks her thumb. Grandma then picks her up and rocks her.	• Object permanence skills increase. By 8 months of age, begins to look for observed objects that are placed or moved out of sight. When mom put the toy behind her back, Sara crawled around her to retrieve the toy. • Repeat actions that have an effect. Sara pulled the tail of the toy dinosaur to hear a song. • Can begin to learn sign language at approximately 8 months and learn to say the words in their language or use sign language for their primary caregivers. Sara exclaimed "Mama" when her mother entered the room.	• Sit, at first wobbly, then well, freeing hands to manipulate objects. By 8 months of age, Sara sits and hardly ever topples over. • Learn to move in a variety of ways. Sara crept on her tummy at 7 months, crawled on hands and knees by 8 months, and pulls to stand on sturdy objects (such as a coffee table) by 10 months. • First use raking grasp (using all fingers), then scissors grasp (using thumb and fingers), and then pincer grasp (using thumb and first finger) to pick up objects. Nine-month-old Sara uses a pincer grasp to pick up a Cheerio. • Bring hands together in midline around 8 months of age. Sara bangs two objects together.	• Begin to eat solid food when fed by adult. Sara opens her mouth as her mother approaches with a spoon full of soft cereal. She "tells" her mom that she doesn't want any more by turning her head, putting her lips together, or arching back. • Begin to pick up food such as Cheerios with fingers. At 9 months, Sara seems to delight in picking up Cheerios one by one.

DAKOTA

General Description 15 months old, Native American male; lives with his father; attends child care 8 hours a day; is cautious around strangers; loves to be close to family members

Social-Emotional	Cognitive/Language	Motor	Adaptive (Daily Living)
• Securely attached children explore away from primary caregivers, but often return for comfort and attention. Dakota plays with books, and then he brings one to his teacher.	• Often imitate adults and peers to accomplish goals. Dakota tries to get up on the couch after his dad sits down.	• Many children walk—Dakota toddles across the room. Each day he adjusts his walking to different surfaces. Dakota slows down as he walks in the mud.	• Use a spoon, sometimes awkwardly, as wrist strength grows. Dakota scooped up his yogurt with his spoon and licked off the yogurt.

236

Social-Emotional	Cognitive/Language	Motor	Adaptive (Daily Living)
• Continue to experience separation and stranger anxiety. Dakota appears cautious when a stranger enters the room or when mom leaves. • Begin to demonstrate autonomy. Dakota protests when his teacher tries to put a bib on him. • Use strategies to calm himself (self-regulation). Dakota reaches for his dad or his bunny when he is tired. • Communicate with and imitates peers. Dakota communicates with peers by smiling, vocalizing, frowning, retreating, giving objects, and taking objects. • Friendships and prosocial behaviors develop as early as 1 year of age—Dakota, who likes to be with his friend Olivia, is upset when she doesn't come to school.	• Pretend with objects aimed at them. Dakota pretends to drink from a toy cup. • Say approximately 10 words and/or use sign language, but still communicate primarily with body cues and gestures. Dakota and his teacher Margo enjoy a moment as he points at the butterfly. She says, "beautiful butterfly," and he tries to repeat it. Margo knows how important it is to talk to children. • Understand many more words/phrases than they can say. Dakota toddles to his shoes when his father says, "Get your shoes" without pointing.	• Enjoy crawling and walking up steps—placing one foot up and then placing the other foot on that step. Dakota went up and down his grandparent's steps, walking up and then crawling backward down the steps. • Turn cardboard pages of books alone or when read to by an adult. Dakota enjoys sitting in the book area at his school and turning the pages of a book by himself. • Enjoy putting objects into containers and dumping them as they explore the concept of space. Dakota puts large dominoes in a slot in the lid of a plastic container and later vigorously dumps them out.	• Use pincer grasp (thumb and first finger together) well to pick up small objects and hold a cup with a lid on it. Dakota picks up his sippy cup with both hands and brings it up to his mouth. • Remove own hat and socks (if loose fitting). Dakota takes his socks off continually throughout the day.

AVANTI

General Description 22 months old, African American male; lives with his mother and father; attends a family child care program; has a friend at his child care and education center; is persistent at solving problems

Social-Emotional	Cognitive/Language	Motor	Adaptive (Daily Living)
• Continue to demonstrate strong attachments to primary caregivers. Seek these adults for enjoyment and security. Avanti likes to sit on his teacher's lap as she reads him a story. • Self-regulation may be challenging at times. Avanti cries and falls to the floor when frustrated. At other times he rubs his blanket on his face to calm down or go to sleep. • Use prosocial behaviors. Avanti shows concern for peers when they are hurt or distressed. He handed Sara her blanket when she cried. • Peers take turns during play. Avanti and Sandi laugh as they take turns chasing each other.	• Experiment with sequential strategies to accomplish goals. Avanti tries many strategies to get the toy out of the box. • Direct pretend action to toys. Avanti moves the toy car across the floor and makes car noises. • Imitate actions, even after a delay in time. Avanti watches a peer kiss a doll and then does the action when he gets home. • Say words by 18 months to inform, reject, request, refuse, and demand—at 22 months use two words together. Avanti states "eat banana" emphatically to his teacher. Later he says "no banana" to refuse a bite of banana.	• Run with increased co-ordination. Avanti seems to run energetically everywhere he goes, but still falls at times. • Walk up steps, putting both feet on each step. Avanti's parents stayed close as he practiced going up stairs. • Increased fine motor skills allow children to manipulate more objects in increasingly complex ways. Avanti pressed on the spot on the bear's foot to hear it sing a song and then turned it upside down to hear it sing another song.	• Become increasingly independent, wanting to do things all by themselves. Avanti likes to unzip the zipper on Mom's sweater while she is wearing it. • Use a spoon to feed self, but still spill at times. Avanti uses a spoon for 5 minutes and then eats with his hands. • Put feet into their shoes (or big people's shoes). Avanti put his feet into his dad's shoes and joyfully clomped around the living room.

(Continued)

Social-Emotional	Cognitive/Language	Motor	Adaptive (Daily Living)
• Peers interact with words, gestures, imitation, and glee. Avanti and Tamera laugh excitedly as they poke their fingers into their playdough. • Avanti may be aggressive at times. Teachers and parents teach him words to say, show him how to be gentle, and work together with his parents.	• Follow two-step directions. Avanti's mother told him to get the ball and take it in the kitchen.	• Use an overhand or fist grasp with utensils and crayons. Avanti held his chalk tightly, with his whole hand over the chalk.	

Developmentally Appropriate Questions:

- Self-regulation and self-soothing play important roles in children's development. What are two important roles that self-soothing plays? What are two behaviors that children use to soothe and comfort themselves?
- What reasons can you give for why Dakota expresses separation and stranger anxiety?

- Is Avanti's language development "normal" for a child of 22 months? Avanti uses two-word phrases to express himself. What are these two-word phrases called?
- How is Sara's mother supporting her need for developing trust and attachment? What are some things that you can do to support infants in their quest for trust?

Sources: Contributed by Donna S. Wittmer, former professor of early childhood education at the University of Colorado–Denver. Donna is the author of *Focusing on Peers: The Importance of Relationships in the Early Years* (ZERO TO THREE, 2008) and is co-author, with Sandra Petersen, of *Endless Opportunities for Infant and Toddler Curriculum* (Pearson, 2013) and *Infant and Toddler Development and Responsive Program Planning: A Relationship-Based Approach* (Pearson, 2014).

infancy The first year of life.

toddlerhood Children twelve to twenty-four months.

- Know each child as an individual and what is normal for each child.
- Remember to care for and reach the whole child—the physical, social, emotional, intellectual, and linguistic.
- Take into account gender and socioeconomic, cultural, and family background, including nutritional and health history, to determine what is normal for individual children. Consider that when children are provided with good nutrition, health care, and a warm, loving environment, development tends toward what is normal for each child.

CULTURE AND CHILD DEVELOPMENT

culture A group's way of life, including basic values, beliefs, religion, language, clothing, food, and practices.

Many factors influence how children grow and develop; for example, reflect on the influence of parents, siblings, home, and schools. But what about culture? **Culture** is a group's way of life, including basic values, beliefs, religion, language, clothing, food, and various practices. Child rearing, for instance, is influenced by the culture of a particular group. Think for a minute about how the following routines, which are culturally based, affect children's developmental outcomes:[1] For example, Hispanic infants younger than 1 year of age were more likely to have been breast-fed and those who were four to five months of age were more likely to be eating pureed baby foods on a daily basis. Research also shows that six- to eleven-month-old Hispanic children are more likely than non-Hispanic children to eat fresh fruits, fruit-flavored drinks, baby cookies, and foods such as soups, rice, and beans that are common in many Hispanic cultures.[2]

BOTTLE OR BREAST-FEEDING. Whether children are held during a feeding, whether they are allowed or encouraged to hold the bottle, what feeding position is used, how frequently they are fed, and whether a bottle is used to induce sleep all depend on a culture's perspective. For example, the United States is predominantly a bottle-feeding culture. Breast-feeding is usually done in private because breasts are seen as sexual in nature. But in many eastern countries, breasts are seen as functional, so there is no shame in being uncovered or feeding children in public. In still other cultures, where religions prohibit the showing of women's bodies, there is a taboo of breast-feeding in front of men, though not necessarily other women. Similarly, different cultures have different views on promoting babies' independence, which affects breast-feeding practices. In western cultures such as those in western Europe and the United States, babies are often fed at specific intervals to encourage the baby to be self-soothing and independent, whereas in many eastern cultures, such as those in some African countries, children are seen as being naturally dependent and in need of care and so are fed on cue in short intervals all day and night. In addition, in the West, where many women work outside the home, and in the United States, where workplaces are not required to provide child care, breast-feeding is not an option for many women. Conversely, in many other cultures, it is an accepted practice for nursing mothers to aid one another in feeding their children.

FEEDING SOLID FOODS.   Culture dictates when and which foods are introduced; whether mess and waste are permitted; how much child choice and independence are allowed or encouraged; what utensils are used; and where and when feeding occurs. For example, women in the United States commonly express discomfort about children nursing after they have teeth. The American Academy of Pediatricians recommends that babies be breast-fed a minimum of one year, and the World Health Organization recommends a minimum of two years, but in many cultures, weaning can continue for several years.[3,4] When and how people encourage eating solid foods also differs by cultures. I'm sure you have seen a toddler covered with gooey food from head to toe and waving an unused fork or spoon. In the United States, this behavior might be seen as encouraging the child's independence and sense of self. However, in other areas of the world, especially in places where food may be scarce, such an exhibition might be considered wasteful.

TOILETING.   One's culture also determines such child-rearing practices as the age toileting begins, whether the goal is independent use of the toilet or reduction in number of diapers needed, how much adult involvement or time is required, how toileting accidents are handled, and whether diapers, training pants, or disposable pants are used. The American Academy of Pediatrics (AAP) states that before children are twelve months of age, they have no control over bladder or bowel movements. In the United States, many children start to show signs of being ready to start toilet training between eighteen and twenty-four months of age. The AAP cautions that some children may not be ready until thirty months or older.[5] In the United States, it is generally accepted that boys are harder to toilet train than girls and that they shouldn't be toilet trained until they are older. However, in many other cultures, such as China, both girl and boy infants are often toilet trained by seven or eight months old. In other cultures, using diapers is uncommon or even unheard of, whereas other cultures may view diapers as unsanitary. In the United States, recommended toilet-training methods range between rigid and child-centered, whereas in other countries, toilet training is a more traditional part of culture.

NAPPING.   How often, how long, and where a child naps; and how much adult assistance and participation are required for a child to fall and stay asleep, also depend on culture. Culture influences sleeping and waking times, including whether sleep is consolidated into a single continuous period and thus is associated with a single specific "bedtime." Whether sleep is confined to nighttime or to private spaces or may occur acceptably in daytime or in public spaces, and whether a child sleeps alone or in groups, varies by culture. In the United States, independence in almost every aspect of life is emphasized and valued, so it is common for babies to sleep alone, often in their own rooms. But other cultures, such as those throughout Asia, South America, and Africa, are more collectivist; they value interaction and aiding one another. As a result, in those cultures, it is uncommon for infants to sleep alone and may even be considered unkind because it causes the children to be unnecessarily lonely. In the United States, it is generally accepted that babies need lots of sleep, but the emphasis is on having babies sleep at regular intervals. Other cultures often promote communal sleeping among all age groups at different times of the day.

USE OF COMFORT ITEMS.   Whether a child is allowed or encouraged to use a pacifier or thumb, blanket, stuffed animal, or other object to provide comfort, and if so, when, where, and how often the child is allowed to use it, are all culturally connected. Again, the United States emphasizes independence, and as a result, it is generally frowned upon for children to be "dependent" on comfort items past a certain age. Usually parents see the age of two or three as the cutoff mark, but parents of children even one year old sometimes want their babies to quit pacifiers "cold turkey." Children often face a great deal of pressure from parents, dentists, pediatricians, and teachers to quit their thumb-sucking and "blankies," but pressure can cause a sense of shame or a reversion to even more reliance on items. Most current practices encourage parents to allow their children to simply "grow out of it." In other countries where poverty is an issue, comfort items may not be available to children at all.

DISCIPLINE.   The tone used when a child is disciplined or reprimanded for actions that are not approved of by adults varies; whether or not physical punishment is used varies; and margin for error and how that is tolerated varies from culture to culture. In the United States, the debate still rages about the acceptability of spanking. There are demographics of parents who are more likely to use spanking as discipline. For example, studies find that most parents who spank in the United States tend to have little education, are young parents, are single parents, and may have significant levels of depression and stress.[6] Spanking is also most commonly used among parents who were spanked themselves and who tend to think, "I was spanked, and I turned out fine." This group of parents is more likely to live in the South and to self-identify as conservative Christians.[7] When asked why they used spanking, this demographic of parents reply that they believe spanking is effective and that the child is to blame for the punished behavior; in other words, they believe that the child "deserved" to be spanked.[8] Interestingly, research shows that African American children are spanked significantly more often than children from Caucasian and Mexican-American families. African American children are also verbally reprimanded more often than their peers at ages two and three years.[9] As you can see, there are many factors, including socioeconomic status, marital status, religion, region, and race, that are factors in discipline decision making. However, these studies on spanking have found that children who were spanked as one-year-olds tend to behave more aggressively at ages two and three and do not perform as well as other children on a test measuring thinking skills at age three.[10] Some cultures condone only family members punishing or disciplining children, whereas others who live in more collectivist societies tend to take a more, "it takes a village to raise a child" approach, which allows non-family members to take part in discipline practices.

You need to consider the cultural practices of your families and form close partnerships with family members. It is very likely that you will experience cultural practices that are different from your own, but it is important that you try to understand them and respect them if they are safe, healthy, and developmentally appropriate for the child.

RESEARCH AND INFANT/ TODDLER EDUCATION

For the past decade, brain and child development research have received a lot of attention. Brain research has focused especially on the first three years of life. As we discuss these early years, let's review some interesting facts about infant and toddler brain development and consider the implications they have for you as a professional.

First, review Figure 9.1, which shows the regions of the brain and their functional processes. The brain is a fascinating and complex organ. Anatomically, the young brain is like the adult brain, except smaller. Whereas the average adult brain weighs approximately 3 pounds, at birth the infant's brain weighs ¾ pound; at six months, 1½ pounds; and at two years, 2¾ pounds. So, you can see that during the first two years of life the brain undergoes tremendous physical growth. The brain finishes developing physically at age ten, when it reaches its full adult size.

NEURAL SHEARING

At birth the brain has 100 billion neurons, or nerve cells—all the brain cells it will ever have! As parents and other caregivers play with, respond to, interact with, and talk to young children, brain connections develop and learning takes place. As those connections are repeatedly used, they become permanent. In contrast, brain connections that are not used or are used only a little may wither away. This withering away, or elimination, is known as **neural shearing**, or **pruning**. Consequently, children whose parents seldom talk or read to them may have difficulty with language skills later in life. This process helps explain why children who are not reared in language-rich environments may be at risk for academic failure.

neural shearing (pruning)
The selective elimination of synapses.

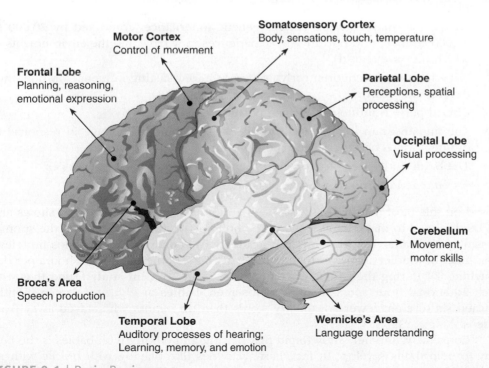

Somatosensory Cortex
Body, sensations, touch, temperature

Motor Cortex
Control of movement

Frontal Lobe
Planning, reasoning, emotional expression

Parietal Lobe
Perceptions, spatial processing

Occipital Lobe
Visual processing

Cerebellum
Movement, motor skills

Broca's Area
Speech production

Temporal Lobe
Auditory processes of hearing; Learning, memory, and emotion

Wernicke's Area
Language understanding

FIGURE 9.1 | Brain Regions
Brain research has made educators aware of the importance of providing young children with stimulating activities early in life.

SYNAPTOGENESIS

synaptogenesis The rapid development of neural connections.

By the time of birth, those billions of neurons will have formed more than 50 trillion connections, or synapses, through a process called **synaptogenesis**, the proliferation of neural connections. This process continues to occur until the age of ten. During just the first month, the brain forms more than 1,000 trillion more synaptic connections between neurons. These connections and neural pathways are essential for brain development, and it is children's experiences that help form these neural connections. Thus infants whose parents or other caregivers talk to them are more likely to develop larger vocabularies; using different words and speaking to infants in complex sentences increase the infants' knowledge of words and their later ability to speak in complex sentences.[11]

AGE-APPROPRIATE EXPERIENCES

sensitive periods Periods of developmental time during which certain things are learned more easily than at earlier or later times.

However, children need not just any experiences but rather the right experiences at the right times. There are developmental windows of opportunity, or **sensitive periods**, during which it is easier to learn something than it is at another time. For example, the critical period for language development is the first year of life. It is during this time that the auditory pathways for language learning are formed. Beginning at birth, an infant can distinguish the sounds of all the languages of the world. But at about six months, through the process of neural shearing, infants lose the ability to distinguish the sounds of languages they have not heard. By twelve months, their auditory maps are pretty well in place.[12] It is literally a case of use it or lose it.

We can draw several conclusions about the brain:

- Babies are born to learn. They are remarkable learning instruments; their brains make them so.
- Children's brain development and their ability to learn throughout life rely on the interplay between nature (genetic inheritance, controlled by 20,000 to 25,000 genes)[13] and nurture (the experiences they have and the environments in which they are reared).
- What happens to children early in life has a long-lasting influence on how they develop and learn.
- Critical periods influence learning positively and negatively.
- The human brain is quite "plastic"; it has the ability to change in response to different kinds of experiences and environments.
- The brain undergoes physiological changes in response to experiences.
- An enriched environment influences brain development.

Based on this information, there has been a rapid evolution of television shows and DVDs designed to make babies smarter by building on the plasticity and the sponginess of their brains. But the American Academy of Pediatrics recommends no television time for toddlers younger than two. On average, babies spend 1.2 hours per day watching TV during their first two years of life, and a recent study found that with each additional hour spent in front of a screen, babies at eight to sixteen months learned six to eight fewer vocabulary words than do infants who stayed away from videos.[14]

Conversely, another study found that playing and talking with babies is the best way to help them develop. In fact, basic activities like playing with blocks with an eighteen-month-old can improve his or her language skills six months later. To make the most of the amazing abilities of all children, the best thing to do is interact with them, not turn on the television.[15]

NATURE AND NURTURE

So, which of these factors—nature (genetics) or nurture (environment)—plays a larger role? On the one hand, many traits are fully determined by heredity. For example, your eye color is a product of your heredity. Physical height is also largely influenced by heredity—as much as 90 percent. Certainly height can be influenced by nutrition, growth hormones, and other environmental interventions; but by and large, an individual's height is genetically determined. And other traits, such as temperament and shyness, are highly heritable. Thus, we can say that many differences in individuals are due to heredity rather than to environmental factors.

On the other hand, nurture—the environment in which individuals grow and develop—plays an important role in what individuals are and how they behave. For example, the years from birth to age eight are extremely important environmentally, especially for nutrition, stimulation of the brain, affectionate relationships with parents, and opportunities to learn. Think for a moment about other kinds of environmental influence—such as family, school, and friends—that affect development. This would be a good time to review Bronfenbrenner's ecological theory and how interacting environmental influences affect children's development. For children with disabilities who may have limited capability for interacting with their environment, think about the potential impact on their development. For children who are from diverse cultural, linguistic, or socioeconomic backgrounds, think about the potential impact their environments have on their development.

A generation ago, we believed that nature and nurture were competing entities and that one of these was dominant over the other. Today we understand that they are not competing entities; both are necessary for normal development, and it is the interaction between the two that makes children the individuals they are (see Figure 9.2).

MOTOR DEVELOPMENT

What would life be like if you couldn't walk, run, or participate in your favorite activities? Motor skills play an important part in all of life. Even more so for infants and toddlers, motor development is essential because it contributes to their intellectual and skill development. Figure 9.3 lists infant and toddler motor milestones.

BASIC PRINCIPLES OF MOTOR DEVELOPMENT

Human motor development is governed by certain basic principles:

- Motor development is sequential.
- Maturation of the motor system proceeds from gross (large) to fine (small) behaviors. For example, as part of her learning to reach, Maria sweeps toward an object with her whole arm. Over the course of a month, however, as a result of development and experiences, Maria's gross reaching gives way to specific reaching, and she grasps for particular objects.
- Motor development occurs from *cephalo* to *caudal*—from head to foot (tail). This process is known as **cephalocaudal development**. At birth Maria's head is the most developed part of her body; thereafter, she holds her head erect before she sits, and she sits before she walks.
- Motor development proceeds from the *proximal* (i.e., midline, or central part of the body) to the *distal* (i.e., extremities), known as **proximodistal development**. Thus Maria is able to control her arm movements before she can control her finger movements.

cephalocaudal development The principle that development proceeds from the head to the toes.

proximodistal development The principle that development proceeds from the center of the body outward.

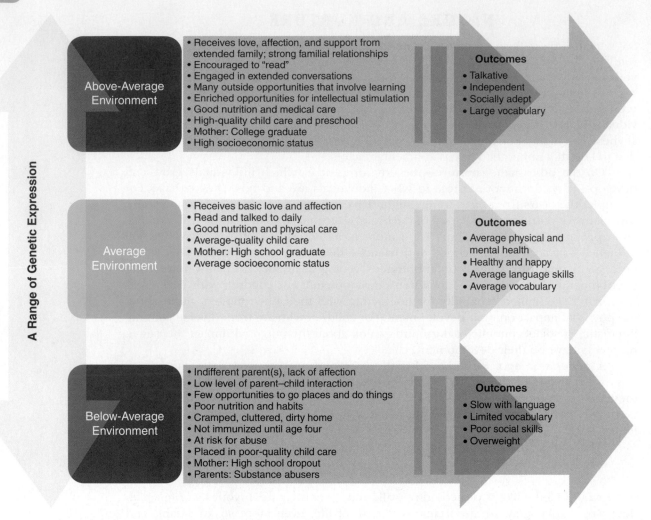

FIGURE 9.2 | The Interplay of Nature and Nurture

TOILET TRAINING

Motor development plays a major role in social and behavioral expectations. For example, toilet training (also called *toilet learning* or *toilet mastery*) is a milestone of the toddler period that often causes a great deal of anxiety for parents, professionals, and toddlers. Many parents want to accomplish toilet training as quickly and efficiently as possible, but frustrations arise when they start too early and expect too much of their children. Because toilet training is largely a matter of physical readiness and cultural acceptance, most child-rearing experts recommend waiting until children are two years old before beginning the training process.

The principle behind toilet training is that parents and teachers can help children develop control over an involuntary response. When an infant's bladder or bowel is full, the urethral or sphincter muscles open; the goal of toilet training is to teach children to control this involuntary reflex and use the toilet when appropriate. Training involves maturational development, timing, patience, modeling, preparing the environment, establishing a routine, and developing a partnership between the child and parents/teachers. Another necessary partnership is that between parents and the professionals who are assisting in toilet training, especially when parents do not know

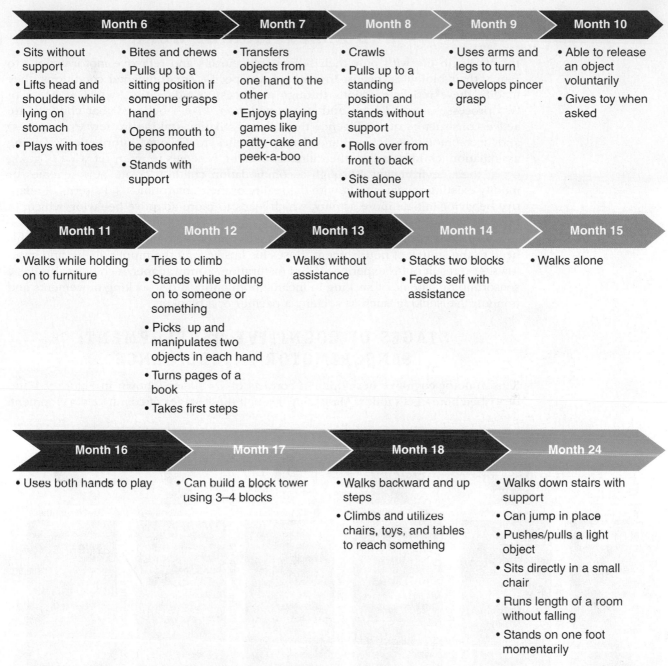

FIGURE 9.3 | Infant and Toddler Motor Milestones

what to do, are hesitant about approaching toilet training, or want to start the training too soon. The key for toilet training is to follow the lead of the child.

INTELLECTUAL DEVELOPMENT

Reflect on children's cognitive development and remember that a child's first developed schemata, or schemes, are sensorimotor. According to Piaget, infants do not have "thoughts of the mind," or private behaviors. Rather, they come to know their world by acting on it through their senses and motor actions. Piaget said that infants construct (as opposed to absorb) their schemes using reflexive sensorimotor actions.

ASSIMILATION, ACCOMMODATION, AND ADAPTATION AT WORK

Infants begin life with only their billions of neurons and reflexive motor actions to satisfy their biological needs. In response to specific environmental conditions, they modify these reflexive actions through a process of adaptation, which consists of two processes, *assimilation* and *accommodation*. Piaget believed that children are active constructors of intelligence through assimilation (taking in new experiences) and accommodation (changing existing schemes to fit new information). During assimilation, children adjust their already-existing schemes to interpret what is going on in their environment. Through accommodation children create new schemes or modify existing schemes to fit with the reality of their environments. Patterns of adaptive behavior initiate more activity, which leads to more adaptive behavior, which, in turn, yields more schemes.

Consider sucking, for example, an innate sensorimotor scheme. Kenny turns his head to the source of nourishment, closes his lips around the nipple, sucks, and swallows. As a result of his experiences and maturation, Kenny adapts or changes this basic sensorimotor scheme of sucking to include both anticipatory sucking movements and nonnutritive sucking, such as sucking a pacifier or a blanket.

STAGES OF COGNITIVE DEVELOPMENT: SENSORIMOTOR INTELLIGENCE

Sensorimotor cognitive development consists of six stages (shown in Figure 9.4 and described here). Let's follow Madeleine through these stages of cognitive development.

Birth–1 month	1–4 months	4–8 months	8–12 months	12–18 months	18–24 months
Stage I. Reflexive Action • Innate reflexive action—sucking, grasping, crying, rooting, swallowing • Experiences enabling reflexes to become more efficient (i.e., amount of sucking needed for nutrition) • Little or no tolerance for frustration or delayed gratification • Beginning to modify reflections to accommodate the environment	**Stage II. Primary Circular Reactions** • Behaviors focused on own body • Acquired adaptations • Reflexive actions gradually being replaced by voluntary actions (i.e., repeatedly putting hand in mouth) • Circular reactions resulting in modifications of existing schemes	**Stage III. Secondary Circular Reactions** • Increased awareness of and response to people and objects in the environment • Ability to initiate activities • Fascination with effects of actions • Beginning of object permanence	**Stage IV. Coordination of Secondary Schemes** • Knowledge of cause-and-effect relationship • Increased deliberation and puposefulness in responding to people and objects • First clear signs of developing object permanence • Actively searching for hidden objects • Combines new behavior to achieve goals • Behaves in particular ways to achieve results • Likes push–pull toys	**Stage V. Experimentation/Tertiary Circular Reactions** • Active experimentation through trial and error, leading to new outcomes • Much time spent experimenting with objects to see what happens • Insatiable curiosity • Differentiates self from objects • Realizes that "out of sight" is not "out of reach" or "out of existence" • Initial understanding of space, time, and causality	**Stage VI. Representation Intelligence** • Development of cause-and-effect relationships • Beginning of representational intelligence; child mentally representing objects • Engages in symbolic, imitative behavior • Beginning of sense of time • Egocentric in thought and behavior

FIGURE 9.4 | Stages of Sensorimotor Cognitive Development

STAGE 1: REFLEXIVE ACTION (BIRTH TO ONE MONTH). During this stage Madeleine sucks and grasps everything; she is literally ruled by reflexive actions. Because reflexive responses are undifferentiated, Madeleine responds the same way to everything. But sensorimotor schemes help her learn new ways of interacting with the world, and new ways of interacting promote her cognitive development.

Grasping is a primary infant sensorimotor scheme. At birth the grasping reflex consists of closing the fingers around an object placed in the hand. Through experiences and maturation, this basic reflexive grasping action becomes coordinated with looking, opening the hand, retracting the fingers, and grasping, thus developing from a pure reflexive action to an intentional grasping action. As Madeleine matures in response to experiences, her grasping scheme is combined with the delightful activity of grasping and releasing everything she can get her hands on.

STAGE 2: PRIMARY CIRCULAR REACTIONS (ONE TO FOUR MONTHS). The milestone of this stage is the modification of the reflexive actions of stage 1. Sensorimotor behaviors not previously present in Madeleine's repertoire of behaviors begin to appear: habitual thumb sucking (indicating hand–mouth coordination), tracking moving objects with the eyes, and moving the head toward sounds (indicating the beginning of recognition of causality). Thus Madeleine starts to direct her own behavior rather than being totally dependent on reflexive actions.

Primary circular reactions also begin during stage 2. In the first few months of life, Madeleine's behaviors—that is, her basic reflexive responses—involve her own body. Piaget called this stage primary. And Madeleine repeats the same behaviors over and over again—for example, constantly putting her hand and thumb to her mouth. Consequently, these actions are called circular reactions. By the end of this stage—at four months—Madeleine will have "practiced" her primary circular reactions hundreds of times, laying the cognitive and behavioral groundwork for the more coordinated and intentional actions of stage 3.

primary circular reactions Repetitive actions that are centered on the infant's own body.

STAGE 3: SECONDARY CIRCULAR REACTIONS (FOUR TO EIGHT MONTHS). **Secondary circular reactions** begin during this stage. This process is characterized by repetitive actions intended to get the same response from an object or person; for example, Madeleine repeatedly shakes a rattle to repeat the sound. Repetitiveness is characteristic of all circular reactions. *Secondary* here means that the reaction is elicited from a source other than the infant. Madeleine interacts with people and objects to make interesting sights, sounds, and events happen and last. Given an object, Madeleine uses all available schemes, such as mouthing, hitting, and banging; if one of these schemes produces an interesting result, she continues to use that scheme to elicit the same response. Imitation becomes increasingly intentional as a means of prolonging interest.

secondary circular reactions Repetitive actions focused on the qualities of objects, such as their shapes, sizes, colors, and noises.

Piaget also referred to this stage of cognitive development as "making interesting things last." Madeleine manipulates objects, demonstrating coordination between vision and tactile senses. She also reproduces events for the purpose of sustaining and repeating acts. The intellectual milestone of this stage is the beginning of **object permanence**. When infants in stages 1 and 2 cannot see an object, it does not exist for them—out of sight, out of mind! During stage 3, however, awareness grows that things that are out of sight continue to exist. Parents and infant/toddler caregivers spend a lot of time playing with their children. One of the fascinating games they play is "find the hidden object." Playing this game is a good way to determine whether or not children have developed the cognitive scheme of object permanence and also gives insight into how children "think."

object permanence The concept that people and objects have an independent existence beyond the child's perception of them.

STAGE 4: COORDINATION OF SECONDARY SCHEMES (EIGHT TO TWELVE MONTHS). During this stage, "coordination of secondary schemes," Madeleine uses means to attain ends. For instance, she moves objects out of the way (means) to get another object (end). She also begins to search for hidden objects, although not always in the places they were hidden, indicating a growing understanding of object permanence.

STAGE 5: EXPERIMENTATION/TERTIARY CIRCULAR REACTIONS (TWELVE TO EIGHTEEN MONTHS).

tertiary circular reactions Modifications that infants make in their behavior to explore the effects of those modifications.

This stage, the climax of the sensorimotor period, marks the beginning of truly intelligent behavior. Stage 5 is the *stage of experimentation*. Madeleine's experiments with objects to solve problems are characteristic of intelligence that involves **tertiary circular reactions**; she repeats actions and modifies behaviors over and over to see what will happen. This repetition helps develop understanding of cause-and-effect relationships and leads to the discovery of new relationships through exploration and experimentation.

Physically, stage 5 is also the beginning of the toddler stage, with the commencement of walking. Toddlers' physical mobility, combined with their growing ability and desire to experiment with objects, makes for fascinating and often frustrating child rearing. Madeleine is an avid explorer, determined to touch, taste, and feel all she can. Although the term *terrible twos* was once used to describe this stage, professionals now recognize there is nothing terrible about toddlers exploring their environment to develop their intelligence. What is important is that teachers, parents, and others prepare environments for exploration. As Madeleine's mom describes it, "I keep putting things up higher and higher because her arms seem to be getting longer and longer!" Novelty is interesting for its own sake, and Madeleine experiments in many different ways with a given object. For example, she may use any available item—a wood hammer, a block, a rhythm band instrument—to pound the pegs in a pound-a-peg toy.

symbolic representation The ability to use mental images to stand for something else.

symbolic play The ability of a young child to have an object stand for something else.

STAGE 6: REPRESENTATIONAL INTELLIGENCE (EIGHTEEN MONTHS TO TWO YEARS).

This is the stage of transition from sensorimotor to symbolic thought. **Symbolic representation** occurs when Madeleine can visualize events internally and maintain mental images of objects not present. Representational thought enables Madeleine to solve problems in a sensorimotor way through experimentation and trial and error and predict cause-and-effect relationships more accurately. She also develops the ability to remember, which allows her to try out actions she sees others do. During this stage Madeleine can "think" using mental images and memories, which enable her to engage in pretend activities. Madeleine's representational thought does not necessarily match the real world and its representations, which accounts for her ability to have other objects stand for almost anything: A wooden block is a car; a rag doll is a baby. This type of play, known as **symbolic play**, becomes more elaborate and complex in the preoperational period.

In summary, we need to keep in mind several important concepts regarding infant and toddler development:

Exploration and experimentation are essential to toddler development and well-being. You can support these developmental processes by creating challenging environments in which toddlers can explore with a wide variety of materials.

- Chronological ages associated with Piaget's stages of cognitive development are approximate; children can do things earlier (and later) than Piaget thought. Focus on children's cognitive behavior, which gives a clearer understanding of their level of development and can guide developmentally appropriate education and caregiving.

- Infants and toddlers do not "think" as adults do; they know their world by acting on it and thus need many opportunities for active involvement.

- Infants and toddlers actively construct their own intelligence. Children's activity with people and objects stimulates them cognitively and leads to the development of mental schemata (schemes).

- At birth infants do not have knowledge of the external world. They cannot differentiate between themselves and the external world. For all practical purposes, they are the world.

- The concept of causality, or cause and effect, does not exist at birth. Infants' and toddlers' concepts of causality begin to evolve only through acting on the environment.

- As infants and toddlers move from one stage of intellectual development to another, later stages evolve from, rather than replace, earlier ones. Schemes developed in stage 1 are incorporated and improved on by the schemes constructed in stage 2, and so forth.

Check Your Understanding: Piaget

LANGUAGE DEVELOPMENT

Language development begins at birth. Indeed, some developmentalists argue that it begins *before* birth. The first cry, the first coo, the first "da-da" and "ma-ma," the first words—all are auditory proof that children are participating in the process of language development. Language helps define us as human and represents one of our most remarkable intellectual accomplishments. But how does the infant go from the first cry to the first word a year later? How does the toddler progress from saying one word to saying several hundred words a year later? Although everyone agrees that children do learn language, not everyone agrees about how. How *does* language development begin? What forces and processes prompt children to participate in one of the uniquely human endeavors?

If you said that parents are forces that encourage children to participate in language development you are absolutely right. We cannot overestimate the role parents play in the language development of their children. Ask yourself these questions:

- What techniques does the parent use to encourage and support the child's literacy development?

- What are some developmentally appropriate ways the parent engages the child?

THEORIES OF LANGUAGE ACQUISITION

Just as we use theories to help us explain children's intellectual (Piaget) and social-emotional development (Erikson), so too must we use theories to help explain children's language development. The following are the major ways we explain language development.

HEREDITY FACTORS.   Heredity plays a role in language development in a number of ways. For one, humans have the respiratory and laryngeal systems that make rapid and efficient vocal communications possible. For another, the human brain makes language possible. The left hemisphere is the center for speech and phonetic analysis; it is the brain's main language center. But the right hemisphere also plays a role in our understanding of speech intonations, which enables us to distinguish between declarative, imperative, and interrogative sentences. Without these processing systems, language as we know it would be impossible.

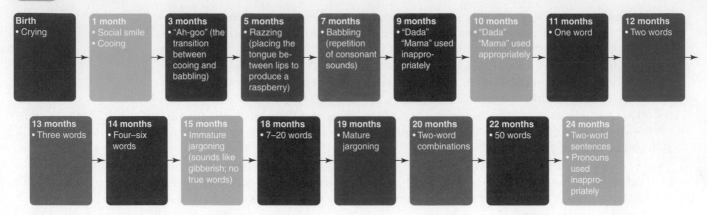

FIGURE 9.5 | Milestones of Language Development in Infants and Toddlers

Children's language development is linear and progressive—each stage builds upon the next. It is important for you to provide rich language opportunities for infants and toddlers so that each child may progress to each level and gain the language competency she needs in order to fulfill her full promise of capabilities.

Some theorists believe that humans are innately endowed with the ability to produce language. For example, Eric Lenneberg studied innate language acquisition in considerable detail in many different kinds of children, including the deaf. According to Lenneberg, "all the evidence suggests that the capacities for speech production and related aspects of language acquisition develop according to built-in biological schedules."[16] These built-in schedules are similar to sensitive periods.

The idea of the sensitive period of language development also had a particular fascination for Montessori, who believed there were two such sensitive periods. The first begins at birth and lasts for about three years. During this time children unconsciously absorb language from the environment. The second period begins at age three and lasts until about age eight. During this time children are active participants in their language development and learn how to use their power of communication. Milestones of language development are illustrated in Figure 9.5.

ENVIRONMENTAL FACTORS.   Although the ability to acquire language has a biological basis, the content of the language—syntax, grammar, and vocabulary—is acquired from the environment, which includes parents and others as models of language. Development depends on talk between children and adults and between children and children. Optimal language development ultimately depends on interactions with the best possible language models. Thus the biological process may be the same for all children, but the content of their language will differ according to environmental factors. Children in language-impoverished homes will not learn language as well as children reared in linguistically rich environments.

SEQUENCE OF LANGUAGE DEVELOPMENT

Regardless of the theory of language development you choose to adopt as your own, the fact remains that children develop language in predictable sequences, and they don't wait for us to tell them what theory to follow in their language development! They are very pragmatic and develop language regardless of our beliefs.

BABY SIGNING.   Think of the number of ways you use signs, that is, gestures to communicate a need or emotion. You blow a kiss to convey affection or hold your thumb and little finger to the side of your head to signal that you're talking on your cell phone. I'm sure you can think of many other examples. Now apply this same principle to young children who have needs and wants and emotional feelings long before they learn to talk. As a result, there is a growing movement in support of teaching children to use signs and gestures to communicate desires or signify objects and conditions before they learn language. This is called **baby signing**.

Beginning at about five months, babies can learn signals that stand for something else (e.g., a tap on the mouth for food, squeezing the hand for milk). However, there is no universal agreement about whether to teach babies a common set of signs or to use ones that parents and children themselves make up.

Regardless of the signs used, Linda Acredolo and Susan Goodwyn, popularizers of baby signing, identify these benefits:

- Reduces child and parent frustration
- Strengthens the parent–child bond
- Makes learning to talk easier
- Stimulates intellectual development
- Enhances self-esteem
- Provides a window into the child's world[17]

As an infant/toddler caregiver, you must respond to and interact with infants and toddlers in responsive ways that support their mental, physical, language, and social development.

Children are remarkable communicators without words. When they have attentive parents and caregivers, they become skilled communicators, using gestures, facial expressions, sound intonations, pointing, and reaching to make their desires known and get what they want. Pointing at an object and saying, "Uh-uh-uh" is the same as saying, "I want that rattle" or "Help me get the rattle." Responsive caregivers can respond by saying, "Do you want the rattle? I'll get it for you. Here it is!" Responsiveness is one attribute of attentive caregivers; it is the ability to read children's signs and signals, anticipating their desires even though no words are spoken.

baby signing Teaching babies to use signs or gestures to communicate a need or emotion.

HOLOPHRASIC SPEECH.   The ability to communicate progresses from sign language and sounds to the use of single words. Toddlers become skilled at using single words to name objects, to let others know what they want, and to express emotions. One word, in essence, does the work of a whole sentence. These single-word sentences are **holophrases**.

The first words of children are just that, first words. Children talk about people—dada, papa, mama, mummie, and baby (referring to themselves); animals—dog, cat, kitty; vehicles—car, truck, boat, train; toys—ball, block, book, doll; food—juice, milk, cookie, bread, drink; body parts—eye, nose, mouth, ear; clothing and household articles—hat, shoe, spoon, clock; greeting terms—hi, bye, night-night; and a few actions—up, no more, off.

The one-word sentences children use are primarily *referential* (used to label objects, such as "doll") or *expressive* (communicating personal desires or levels of social interaction, such as "bye-bye" and "kiss"). The extent to which children use these two functions of language depends in large measure on caregivers and parents. For example, children's early language use reflects their family's verbal style. Thus how parents speak to their children influences how their children speak.[18]

holophrases The single words children use to refer to what they see, hear, and feel (e.g., *up, doll*).

Motherese or Parentese. Research studies verify that caregivers talk to infants and toddlers differently from the way adults talk to each other. This distinctive way of adapting everyday speech to young children is called **motherese** or **parentese**.[19] Parentese has several characteristics:

- The sentences are short, averaging just over four words per sentence with babies. As children become older, the length of sentences mothers use also becomes longer. Mothers' conversations with their young children are short and sweet.

motherese (parentese) The way parents and others speak to young children in a slow, exaggerated way that includes short sentences and repetition of words and phrases.

- The sentences are highly intelligible. When talking to their young children, mothers tend not to slur or mumble their words, perhaps because mothers speak more slowly to their children than they do to adults in normal conversation.
- The sentences are unswervingly well formed—that is, they are grammatical sentences.
- The sentences are mainly imperatives and questions, such as "Give Mommy the ball," and "Do you want more juice?" Since mothers can't exchange a great deal of information with their young children, their utterances direct their children's actions.
- Mothers use sentences in which words like *here, that*, and *there* are used to stand for objects or people: "Here's your bottle," "That's your baby doll," "There's your doggie."
- Mothers expand or provide an adult version of their children's communication. When a child points at a baby doll on a chair, the mother may respond by saying, "Yes, the baby doll is on the chair."
- Mothers' sentences involve repetitions: "The ball, bring Mommy the ball. Yes, go get the ball—the ball—go get the ball."

telegraphic speech Two-word sentences that express actions and relationships (e.g., "Milk gone").

SYMBOLIC REPRESENTATION. Two significant developmental events occur at about the age of two. First, the development of symbolic representation occurs when something—a mental image, a word—is used to stand for something else not present. Words become signifiers of things—ball, block, blanket. Parents and teachers help children by using the names of things directly ("This is a ball") or indirectly ("Tell me what this is"). They can also use physical labels (*chair*) and use the names of things in conversations with children ("This is a shoe; let's put your shoe on").

The use of words as mental symbols enables children to participate in two processes that are characteristic of the early years: symbolic play and the beginning use of words and sentences to express meanings and make references.

VOCABULARY DEVELOPMENT. The development of a fifty-word vocabulary and the use of two-word sentences is the second significant achievement that occurs at about age two. This vocabulary development and the ability to combine words mark the beginning of *rapid language development*. Vocabulary development plays a very powerful and significant role in school achievement and life success. Research repeatedly demonstrates that children who come to school with a large vocabulary achieve more than their peers who do not have an expanded vocabulary.[20] Adults are the major source of children's vocabularies.

The process of language development begins at birth—perhaps even before. What are some things parents, teachers, and caregivers can do to promote a child's language development?

TELEGRAPHIC SPEECH. You have undoubtedly heard a toddler say something like "Go out" in response to a suggestion such as "Let's go outside." Perhaps you've said, "Is your juice all gone?" and the toddler responded, "All gone." These two-word sentences are called **telegraphic speech**. They are the same kind of sentences you use when you text message; the sentences are primarily made up of nouns and verbs, generally without prepositions, articles, conjunctions, and auxiliary verbs.

GRAMMATICAL MORPHEMES. There is more to learning language than learning words; there is also the matter of learning grammar. Grammar is the way we change the meanings of sentences and place events and actions in time: past, present, and future tense. Grammatical morphemes are the principal means of changing the meanings of sentences. A *morpheme* is the smallest unit of meaning in a language. It can be a word, such as *no*, or an element of a word, such as *-ed*. A morpheme that can stand alone, such as *child*, is a *free morpheme*. A morpheme that cannot stand alone is a bound morpheme. *Kicked* consists of the free morpheme *kick* and the bound morpheme *-ed*. Morphological rules govern tenses, plurals, and possessives.

The order in which children learn grammatical morphemes is well documented; the pattern of mastery is orderly and consistent. The first morpheme to be mastered is the present progressive ("I drinking"), followed by prepositions (*in* and *on*), plural (*dolls*), past irregular ("toy fell"), possessive ("Sally's doll"), uncontractible verb ("it is"), articles (*a, the*), past regular (*stopped*), third-person regular ("he runs"), uncontractible auxiliary ("I am going"), contractible verb (*that's*), and contractible auxiliary ("I'm going").[21]

NEGATIVES.   If you took a vote on a toddler's favorite word, "No!" would win hands down. When children begin to use negatives, they simply add *no* to the beginning of a word or sentence ("no milk"). As their *no* sentences become longer, they still put *no* first ("*no* put coat on"). Later, they place negatives appropriately between subject and verb ("I no want juice").

When children move beyond the use of the one-word expression "no," negation progresses through a series of meanings. The first meaning conveys nonexistence, such as "no juice" and "no hat," meaning that the juice is all gone and the hat isn't present. The next level of negation is the rejection of something. "No go out" is the rejection of the offer to go outside. Next, the use of *no* progresses to the denial of something the child believes to be untrue. If offered a carrot stick under the pretense that it is candy, the child will reply, "No candy."[22]

By the end of the preschool years, children have mastered most language patterns. Because the basis for language development develops in these early years, no amount of later remedial training can completely make up for development that should have occurred during this sensitive period of language learning.

IMPLICATIONS FOR TEACHING

A high priority for early childhood professionals is to provide programs that support and facilitate children's language development. You must recognize that when children come from culturally or linguistically diverse backgrounds, certain patterns may emerge as they acquire a second language, or if they are simultaneously learning two languages, or if they are being reared in a home where no adults speak fluent English; these patterns may mimic speech or language disorders or delays. Another priority is to provide a child–staff ratio that supports language development. For example, in a recent study of the effects of a reduced child–staff ratio on children's development, researchers found that in programs with ratios of 1:4 for infants and 1:6 for toddlers, language proficiency improved dramatically when compared to programs with higher ratios.[23] Below are some guidelines that will help you promote children's language development. For children with disabilities that impact their speech or language acquisition, it is just as important to implement the guidelines to promote their language development.

Treat children as partners in the communication process.

- Many infant behaviors—smiling, cooing, and vocalizing—serve to initiate conversation and professionals should be responsive.

Initiate conversations with infants and toddlers.

- Conversations are the building blocks of language development. Attentive and caring adults are infants' and toddlers' best stimulators of cognitive and language development.

Talk to infants in a soothing, pleasant voice, with frequent eye contact.

- Simplify verbalization—not by using baby talk—but by speaking in an easily understandable way. For example, instead of saying, "we are going to take a walk around the block, so you must put your coat on," you could say, "let's get coats on."

Use children's names when interacting with them.

- Using children's names personalizes the conversation and builds self-identity.

Use a variety of means to stimulate and promote language development.

- Include reading, stories, singing songs, and listening to music.

Encourage children to converse and share information.

- Provide children with opportunities to talk and interact with adults, other children, and more developed peers.

Help children learn to converse in various settings.

- Take children to different places so they can use their language with a variety of people.

Have children use language in different ways.

- Children need to know how to use language to ask questions, explain their feelings and emotions, tell what they have done, and describe things.

Give children experiences in the language of directions and commands.

- It is important for children to learn that language can be used as a means to an end—a way of attaining a desired goal.

Converse with children about what they are doing and how they are doing it.

- Children learn language through feedback.

Talk to children in the full range of adult language.

- Include past and present tense.

Help children learn the names of people and things.

- Learning names is an important part of vocabulary development. Label things as you interact with children.

Provide many experiences so that children have lots of things to talk about.

- The more experiences children have, the more they can talk about. Help expand speaking skills by helping them describe experiences.

Reflect and Apply: Language Development

PSYCHOSOCIAL AND EMOTIONAL DEVELOPMENT

The first of Erikson's psychosocial stages, *basic trust vs. basic mistrust,* begins at birth and lasts about one-and-a-half to two years. Trust for young children means they learn to rely on the sameness and continuity of their caregivers' responses to them. They can count on having their diapers changed; being fed when they are hungry, and that they will be embraced with love and affection. Basic trust develops when children are reared, cared for, and educated in an environment of love, warmth, and support.

SOCIAL BEHAVIORS

Social relationships begin at birth and are evident in the daily interactions between infants, parents, and teachers. Infants are social beings with a repertoire of behaviors they use to initiate and facilitate social interactions. Because *social behaviors* are used by everyone to begin and maintain a relationship with others, healthy social development is essential for young children. Regardless of their temperament, all infants are capable of and benefit from social interactions.

CRYING.   Crying is a primary social behavior in infancy. It attracts parents or caregivers and promotes a social interaction of some type and duration, depending on the skill and awareness of the caregiver. Crying has a survival value; it alerts caregivers to the presence and needs of the infant. However, merely meeting the basic needs of infants in a perfunctory manner is not sufficient to form a firm base for social development. Parents and caregivers must react to infants with enthusiasm, attentiveness, and concern for them as unique persons.

IMITATION.   Imitation is another social behavior of infants. They have the ability to mimic the facial expressions and gestures of adults. When a mother sticks out her tongue at a baby, after a few repetitions, the baby will also stick out its tongue. This imitative behavior is satisfying to the infant, and the mother is pleased by this interactive game. Since the imitative behavior is pleasant for both persons, they continue to interact for the sake of interaction, which in turn promotes more social interaction. Social relations develop from social interactions, but we must always remember that both occur in a social context, or culture.

Infants and toddlers are on a developmental trajectory. Social behaviors like imitation are positive indications of proper development. However, not all children develop the same way, and some may need early intervention to help them on their developmental journey.

ATTACHMENT AND RELATIONSHIPS

Bonding and attachment play major roles in the development of social and emotional relationships. **Bonding** is the process by which parents or teachers become emotionally attached, or bonded, to infants. It is the development of a close, personal, affective relationship. It is a one-way process, which some maintain occurs in the first hours or days after birth. **Attachment**, on the other hand, is the enduring emotional tie between the infant and the parents and other primary caregivers; it is a two-way relationship and often endures over a lifetime.

Attachment behaviors serve the purpose of getting and maintaining proximity; they form the basis for the enduring relationship of attachment. Parent and teacher attachment behaviors include kissing, caressing, holding, touching, embracing, making eye contact, and looking at the face. Infant attachment behaviors include laughing, crying, sucking, making eye contact, babbling, and general body movements. Later, when the infant is developmentally able, attachment behaviors include following, clinging, and calling.

bonding A parent's initial emotional tie to an infant.

attachment An emotional tie between a parent/caregiver and an infant that endures over time.

ADULT SPEECH.   Adult speech has a special fascination for infants. Interestingly enough, given the choice of listening to music or listening to the human voice, infants prefer the human voice! This preference plays a role in attachment by making the baby more responsive. Infants attend to language patterns they will later imitate in their process of language development; they move their bodies in rhythmic ways in response to the human voice. Babies' body movements and caregiver speech synchronize to each other: Adult speech triggers behavioral responses in the infant, which in turn stimulate responses in the adult, resulting in a "waltz" of attention and attachment. Today, the focus in studying infant social development is on the caregiver-to-infant relationship, not on the individuals as separate entities.[24]

MULTIPLE ATTACHMENTS.   Increased use of child care programs inevitably raises questions about infant attachment. Parents are concerned that their children will not attach to them. Worse yet, they fear that their baby will develop an attachment with the caregiver rather than with them. However, children can attach to more than one person, and there can be more than one attachment at a time. Infants attach to parents, or to the primary caregiver, as well as to others—child care providers, siblings, and parents, resulting in a hierarchy of attachments in which the latter attachments are not of equal value. Infants show a preference for the primary caregiver, usually the mother.

Parents should not only engage in attachment behaviors with their infants, but they should also select child care programs that employ caregivers who understand the importance of the caregiver's role and function in attachment. High-quality child care programs help mothers maintain their primary attachments to their infants in many ways. The staff keeps parents well informed about infants' accomplishments, but parents are allowed to "discover" and participate in infants' developmental milestones. A teacher, for example, might tell a mother that today her son showed signs of wanting to take his first step by himself. The teacher thereby allows the mother to be the first person to experience the joy of this accomplishment. The mother might then report to the center that her son took his first step at home the night before.

THE QUALITY OF ATTACHMENT.   The quality of infant–parent attachment varies according to the relationship that exists between them. A primary method of assessing the quality of parent–child attachment is the Strange Situation, an observational measure developed by Mary Ainsworth (1913–1999) to assess whether infants are securely attached to their caregivers. The testing episodes consist of observing and recording children's reactions to several events: a novel situation, separation from their mothers, reunion with their mothers, and reactions to a stranger. Based on their reactions and behaviors in these situations, children are described as being securely or insecurely attached, as detailed in Figure 9.6.

Secure Attachment
- Secure infants use family members as a secure base from which to explore their environments and play with toys.
- When separated from a parent, they may or may not cry, but when the family member returns, these infants actively seek the member and engage in positive interaction.
- About 65 percent of infants are securely attached.

Avoidant Attachment
- Avoidant infants are unresponsive/avoidant to family members and are not distressed when family members leave the room.
- Avoidant infants generally do not establish contact with a returning family member and may even avoid him or her.
- About 20 percent of infants demonstrate avoidant attachment.

Resistant Attachment
- Resistant infants seek closeness to family members and may even cling to them, frequently failing to explore.
- When family members leave, these infants are distressed and on the parent's return may demonstrate clinginess, or they may show resistive behavior and anger, including hitting and pushing. These infants are not easily comforted by a parent.
- About 10 to 15 percent of infants demonstrate resistant attachment.

Disorganized Attachment
- Disorganized infants demonstrate disorganized behavior.
- They look away from parents and approach them with little or no emotion.
- About 5 percent of children demonstrate disorganized attachment.

FIGURE 9.6 | Individual Differences in Attachment

The importance of knowing and recognizing different classifications of attachment is that you can inform parents and help them engage in the specific behaviors that will promote the growth of secure attachments.

FATHERS AND ATTACHMENT. Fathers—and their roles in families—are a prominent part of early childhood education today. Many fathers have played important roles in child rearing and have engaged in shared and participatory parenting. Currently, there is an increased emphasis on ways to encourage fathers to become even more involved in their families and in child rearing.

Fathers who feed, diaper, bathe, and engage in other caregiving activities demonstrate increased attachment behaviors, such as holding, talking, and looking.[25] Early childhood educators can encourage fathers to participate in all facets of caregiving and can conduct training programs that will help fathers gain the skills and confidence needed to assume their rightful places as coparents in rearing responsible children.

TEMPERAMENT AND PERSONALITY DEVELOPMENT

Children are born with individual behavioral characteristics, which, when considered as a collective whole, constitute **temperament**. This temperament, or essentially what children are like, helps determine the development of their personalities. Personalities develop as a result of the interplay between these particular characteristics and the environment.

temperament A child's general style of behavior.

There are nine characteristics of temperament: level and extent of motor activity; rhythm and regularity of functions such as eating, sleeping, regulation, and wakefulness; degree of acceptance or rejection of a new person or experience; adaptability to changes in the environment; sensitivity to stimuli; intensity or energy level of responses; general mood (e.g., pleasant or cranky, friendly or unfriendly); distractibility from an activity; and attention span and persistence in an activity. Based on these nine temperament characteristics clustered together, there are three classifications of children: the *easy child*, the *slow-to-warm-up child*, and the *difficult child* (see Figure 9.7).[26]

I cannot overemphasize, particularly in child care programs, the importance of developing a match between children's temperament and the caregiver's child-rearing style. As the parenting process extends beyond the natural parents to include all those who care for and provide services to infants, it is reasonable to expect that all who are a part of this parenting cluster will accommodate their behavior to take infants' basic temperaments into account.

INFANT AND TODDLER MENTAL HEALTH

The early childhood profession has always emphasized the importance of providing for children's social and emotional development. One of the benefits of recent research into the importance of early learning is the rediscovery that emotions and mental health play a powerful role in influencing development, especially cognitive development and learning. Infant/toddler mental health is synonymous with healthy social and emotional development. The terms are used interchangeably. **Infant/toddler mental health** involves the developing capacity of the child to experience, regulate (manage), and express emotions, and to form close and secure interpersonal relationships.[27] Think of your own emotions and the ways they influence your daily well-being and approaches to learning. If you are mad or angry right now, your attention is focused elsewhere, and these words don't carry the importance they would if you were happy, focused, and attentive. Now think about many of the stressful and traumatic events that affect children each day and the negative impacts these have on their lives.

infant/toddler mental health The overall health and well-being of young children in the context of family, school, and community relationships.

Easy Children

- Few problems in care and training
- Positive mood
- Regular body functions
- Low to moderate intensity of reaction
- Adaptability and positive approach to new situations

Slow-To-Warm-Up Children

- Low activity level
- Slow to adapt
- Withdraw from new stimuli
- Negative mood
- Low intensity of response

Difficult Children

- Irregular body functions
- Tense reactions
- Withdraw from new stimuli
- Slow to adapt to change
- Negative mood

FIGURE 9.7 | Children's Temperaments
Reflect on each of these three temperaments, and provide examples of how each could affect the outcome of children's development.

There is growing attention focused on ensuring that all young children are reared and educated in environments that will ensure their optimum mental health and well-being and their growth and development to their fullest potential. Figure 9.8 illustrates some risk factors and potential causes of poor mental health in children; the associated outcomes; and some remedies available to early childhood professionals, community services providers, mental health experts, and others.

GROWTH OF THE INFANT MENTAL HEALTH MOVEMENT.   Ever since the 2012 shooting rampage at Sandy Hook Elementary in Newtown, Connecticut, in which twenty kindergarten children and six adults were killed, the mental health movement has gained steam.

There are several reasons for the growth of the early childhood mental health movement:

- A growing realization that we must provide for the whole child—the physical, social, emotional, mental, and spiritual.
- The understanding that brain research supports the importance of relationships to the growth and development of young children.
- The understanding that high-quality early environments and nurturing relationships are essential for children's optimal development.
- Renewed interest in how children are affected by multiple risk factors in their lives, including societal and media violence, maternal depression, abusive home environments, the absence of fathers from the home, parent and teacher stress, and the lack of **continuity of care** (the ongoing nurturing relationship between children and their caregiver) in families and early childhood programs.

continuity of care
The ongoing nurturing relationship between a child and his or her caregiver.

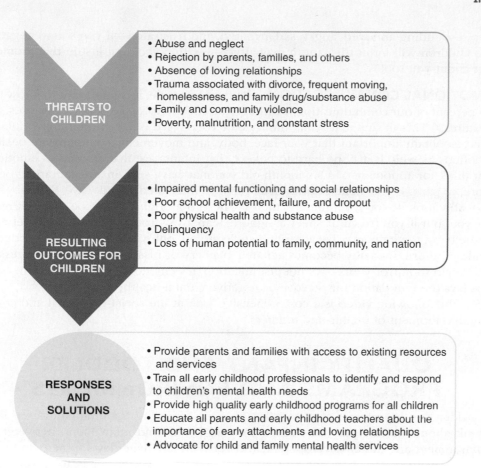

• Abuse and neglect
• Rejection by parents, families, and others
• Absence of loving relationships
• Trauma associated with divorce, frequent moving, homelessness, and family drug/substance abuse
• Family and community violence
• Poverty, malnutrition, and constant stress

THREATS TO CHILDREN

• Impaired mental functioning and social relationships
• Poor school achievement, failure, and dropout
• Poor physical health and substance abuse
• Delinquency
• Loss of human potential to family, community, and nation

RESULTING OUTCOMES FOR CHILDREN

• Provide parents and families with access to existing resources and services
• Train all early childhood professionals to identify and respond to children's mental health needs
• Provide high quality early childhood programs for all children
• Educate all parents and early childhood teachers about the importance of early attachments and loving relationships
• Advocate for child and family mental health services

RESPONSES AND SOLUTIONS

FIGURE 9.8 | Threats to Children's Mental Health, Resulting Outcomes, and Solutions

IMPLICATIONS FOR TEACHING. Some approaches to promoting continuity of care include the following:

- Screening teachers prior to hiring to determine their beliefs about the importance of relationships and the best ways to provide for them.
- Having infants and toddlers and their caregivers choose each other to arrive at a "best fit."
- Having caregivers stay with the same children for at least a year.
- Providing help and support to grandparents who become the primary caregivers of infants and toddlers.

EMOTIONAL SENSITIVITY. Research finds that the brains of infants as young as seven months old demonstrate sensitivity to the human voice and to emotions (angry or happy) communicated through the voice that is remarkably similar to that observed in adult brains.

This means that infants pick up emotional "vibes" around them; even if they don't understand the what or why of the emotions—they still *feel* them. This can affect the development of the child's attachments, relationships, language development, self-regulation, and temperament positively and negatively. Therefore it is important for you to be mindful of the tone of voice you use with and around infants and toddlers, indeed all children. Speak to infants and toddlers kindly, happily, positively, enthusiastically, gently, soothingly, and excitedly, depending on the situation.

Avoid sounding annoyed, angry, sad, irritated, and frustrated—if you sound negative, the children will intuit this, and it may affect how they feel, not just in that moment, but about you too!

EMOTIONAL COMMUNICATION.　At the same time, it is important to know that 55 percent of our communication is through our facial expressions, body postures, and gestures.[28] This means that while the tone of your voice is very important to infants, it is also vitally important that your face, body, and movements communicate positive emotions as well. It may be hard to believe that infants are that attuned to emotions, but think for a moment of a six-month-old you may have seen in a restaurant, grocery store, or park. If you smile brightly, lean forward interestedly, and wave, the baby will probably look at you for a minute, then break into a bright smile, coo, or even reach for you. But if you frown or sneer at, ignore, lean away from, or lower your eyebrows at the baby, the baby may try a hesitant smile at you, but when that doesn't produce a smile in return, the baby becomes agitated, may cry or fuss, and her facial expression will begin to mirror yours—it's not just imitation, it's emotional communication! All of this lays the foundation for positive or negative mental health.

The following video is a comprehensive look at the social-emotional and cognitive development of infants and toddlers.

QUALITY INFANT AND TODDLER PROGRAMS AND ENVIRONMENTS

Consider the importance of a holistic approach to caring for infants and toddlers. Think about the interplay between emotional health and attachment, between the environment and motor development, and between language development and emotional sensitivity. My goal for you after reading this discussion is to never again think "He's just a baby—he doesn't understand (need, want, or feel). . . ." As a result, it should be clear how important quality infant and toddler programs are for all children.

DEVELOPMENTALLY APPROPRIATE PROGRAMS

All early childhood professionals who provide care for infants and toddlers—indeed, for all children—must understand and recognize the process of developmental appropriateness, which provides a solid foundation for any program. The NAEYC states that early childhood professionals must understand the importance of providing programs for infants and toddlers that are different and unique from programs for older children. Developmentally appropriate programs for infants and toddlers are distinctly different from all other types of programs—they are not a scaled-down version of a good program for preschool children. These program differences are determined by the unique characteristics and needs of children during infant and toddler years.

Consider the following:

- Changes take place far more rapidly in the first two years than during any other period in life.
- During infancy, as at every other age, all areas of development—cognitive, social, emotional, and physical—are intertwined.
- Infants especially are totally dependent on adults to meet their needs.
- Very young children are especially vulnerable to adversity, violence, and abuse because they are less able to cope actively with discomfort and stress.[29]

Infants and toddlers learn through their own experiences, trial and error, repetition, imitation, and identification. Adults guide and encourage this learning by ensuring that the infant-toddler environment is safe and emotionally supportive. An appropriate program for children younger than three invites play, active exploration, and movement. It provides a broad array of stimulating experiences within a reliable framework of routines and protection from excessive stress. Relationships with caregivers and other people are emphasized as an essential contribution to the quality of children's experiences.[30]

Providing different programs of activities for infants and toddlers involves helping parents and other professionals recognize that infants, as a group, are different from toddlers and need programs, curricula, and facilities specifically designed for them. They need developmentally appropriate curricula.

It is also important to match caregivers with children of different ages. Not everyone is emotionally or professionally suited to provide care for infants and toddlers. Both groups need adults who can respond to their particular needs and developmental characteristics. Infants need especially nurturing professionals; toddlers, in contrast, need adults who can tolerate and allow for their emerging autonomy and independence.

CURRICULA FOR INFANTS AND TODDLERS

Curricula for infants and toddlers consist of all the activities and experiences they are involved in while under the direction of professionals: feeding, washing, diapering/toileting, playing, learning, and having stimulating interactions, outings, being involved with others, having conversations, and participating in stimulating cognitive and language experiences. Caregivers must plan the curriculum so that all activities are developmentally appropriate. However, not everyone agrees that planning for infants and toddlers should be such a linear process. Some think that planning should be more circular—that is, based on responses to child and teacher interactions. I believe planning is a combination of linear, circular, and relational processes. The Lesson Plan feature "How to Plan a Curriculum for Infants and Toddlers" is a Competency Builder that shows you how to plan a curriculum that promotes relationships and responds to children's needs and interests.

PREPARING ENVIRONMENTS TO SUPPORT INFANT AND TODDLER DEVELOPMENT

Research studies repeatedly show that children who are reared, cared for, and taught in environments that are enriched are healthier, happier, and more achievement oriented than are children who are not raised in such environments.[31] Environments for infants and toddlers should be inviting, comfortable, healthy, safe, supportive, challenging, and respectful. You must plan in order to create environments with these features.

Looking at and observing environments will help you think about what you can include in your environments for infants and toddlers. Also, as you plan, think about how you can make the environment as homelike as possible. Infants and toddlers like and need environments that are cozy, warm, and safe places to be. You can customize your children's homelike environment with curtains, family pictures on the walls, a couch, and so forth. Make sure that your home away from home includes objects from children's cultures.

PROVIDE FOR HEALTH AND SAFETY. Many programs use security cameras, observation windows, electronic access systems, and computer tracking of child and teacher attendance as part of their security program. Safe environments are essential

LESSON PLANS

How to Plan a Curriculum for Infants and Toddlers: Day to Day the Relationship Way

Talitha (nine months old) leans against her teacher while laughing and giving her a quick hug.
Marcus (thirteen months old) figures out how to make music with a small drum.
Kareem (eighteen months old) climbs into a teacher's lap with a book in his hand.
Tanya (twenty-four months old) splashes water with her peers in a small water table.

All of these fortunate infants and toddlers have something in common. They attend programs in which teachers know how to plan a curriculum that is responsive and promotes relationships.

WHAT IS AN INFANT AND TODDLER CURRICULUM?

A curriculum for infants and toddlers includes everything that they experience (from their perspective) from the moment they enter the program until they leave to go home. Every experience makes an impression on how children view themselves, others, and the world. Caring teachers plan a curriculum that is (a) relationship based and (b) responsive to infants' and toddlers' needs, interests, and developmental levels as well their families' goals for their children.

WHY ARE RELATIONSHIPS IMPORTANT IN CURRICULUM?

A relationship is a bond of caring between two people that develops over time. In a relationship-based program, teachers support all the relationships that are key to children's development—parent–child, teacher–child, teacher–family, and child–child relationships. Children need these sustaining, caring relationships to provide them a sense of self-worth, trust in the positive intentions of others, and motivation to explore and learn. To thrive, they need protection, affection, and opportunities to learn.

HOW CAN YOU PLAN AND IMPLEMENT A RESPONSIVE CURRICULUM?

In a responsive curriculum, teachers interact with children and plan day to day the relationship way. Teachers make daily and weekly changes in the environment and in their interactions in response to each child's needs, interests, goals, and exploration of concepts. How do you do this? First, you *respect*, then you *reflect*, and then you *relate*.

STEP 1

Respect

- *Respect infants and toddlers as competent, and honor their individual differences.* Recognize that infants and toddlers are active learners and thinkers who are using many different strategies to figure out how things work. In an emotionally supportive environment, they become problem solvers, make good choices, and care about others. Respect that children are unique human beings with different styles (e.g., some eat fast and others slowly), different interests, and one-of-a-kind personalities. Each child is valued as a child, not just for what adults want the child to become.

- *Respect that children will be motivated to learn if you provide a responsive environment.* It should engage them and appeal to a variety of ages, cultures, and individual needs. Provide opportunities for children to choose from such things as blocks, creative materials, sensory experiences, manipulatives, books, dramatic play, and active play opportunities.

- *Respect that play is the way that infants and toddlers learn.* When infants and toddlers aren't sleeping or eating, they should be playing with toys, people, and objects. As they make choices, infants and toddlers focus on their important goals for learning and nurturing—opening and closing a door on a toy, filling a hole on the playground, playing with a friend, turning a page in a book, putting objects in containers, or climbing on a teacher's lap for a hug. As they play, they explore concepts such as how objects fit into various spaces, cause and effect, object permanence, how to comfort another child, or what they can do with different sizes of paper (e.g., crumple, stack, make into a ball, color on it, cover up toys). Children will pursue their goals in an emotionally supportive and physically interesting environment. For example, a child who feels secure might work for long periods of time on figuring out how to stack blocks. Anything that infants and toddlers decide to do in an interesting and relationship-based program supports their learning in all domains of development—emotional, social, cognitive, language, and motor. Nurturing and responsive adults stay close by, support children's play, and meet their emotional needs by using all of the strategies described in the next sections.

STEP 2

Reflect

- *Reflect with families to learn about each child's unique interests, explorations, and culture.* If you are open and interested, families will share with you new words that their children are saying, their children's latest physical accomplishments and blossoming interests, how they celebrate holidays, or what they want for their children.
- *Reflect through observing children.* Each day observe children to know them well. Each teacher in the room should choose a few children to focus on each week and then take pictures or write notes to capture children's needs, interests, goals, and strategies. Use an observation and planning guide to capture your observations. Also, a developmental checklist allows you to capture the sequence and quality of a child's development over time and then use the information for responsive planning.
- *Reflect on your observations at least weekly with other teachers and often with families.*
  - What is the child trying to do, and how is the child trying to do it?
  - What is the child learning? (Not "what am I teaching?") What concepts (e.g., space, time, social interactions, expressing emotions, ways to open containers) is the child exploring?
  - What is the child telling you he or she needs? (More positive attention, more affection, new strategies to use when another child takes a toy, more room to learn to walk?)
  - What is new in the child's development? For example, is he or she learning to climb or jump, comfort peers, use two words together, or ask questions?

STEP 3

Relate

- *Relate to children by providing the basics—moment-to-moment responsive adult interactions.* Infants and toddlers need to feel that you really care about them.
  - Comfort distressed children.
  - Respond to children's cues and signals—for example, a frown that indicates discomfort, a cry that indicates distress, a plop in the lap with a book that means "Please read to me," sounds that indicate concentration and enjoyment, and words that communicate.
  - Talk responsively with children, abundantly describe your own and the children's actions, provide reasons and explanations, and engage in cooing, babbling, and word conversations.
  - Sing, read, play with children, and respond in nurturing ways to children's need for sleep, food, and comfort.
  - Guide children to learn how to be prosocial by noticing when they are kind, modeling helpfulness, and demonstrating how to care for others.
  - Be open and receptive to what each child is learning in the moment, and follow each child's lead during play.
  - Encourage the children to experiment and problem solve.
  - When a child becomes frustrated, scaffold learning and motivation by helping just enough to support the child's learning *how* to do the task.
  - Remember that sometimes you facilitate children's concentration and peer play by sitting near and observing with engaged interest.
- *Relate during routines.* Consider routines such as diapering/toilet learning, feeding/group eating, and nurturing to sleep as central parts of the curriculum for infants and toddlers. Use these times to support children's emotional

(Continued)

development and other learning. Talk to children to help them learn language, show affection to help them build a sense of self-worth, and respond to their cues of hunger and tiredness to help them learn to trust themselves and others.

- *Relate by using the observations and reflections to make changes.* Make such changes day-to-day and week-to-week in your interactions, the environment, opportunities, and routines.
  - Plan new ways to support healthy relationships between teachers, children, peers, and families. For example, to help a child who has started to bite peers, plan for a teacher to stay near to help the child learn new behaviors to get needs met.
  - Even though much of the environment and materials stay the same for the children's sense of security and stability, choose a few new songs to sing, books, toys, changes in the environment, and new opportunities (e.g., art and sensory materials, puzzles, manipulatives, large-motor equipment) based on the children's interests and learning. Continue reading favorite books and singing familiar songs while introducing a few new ones each week.

Source: Contributed by Donna S. Wittmer and Sandra H. Petersen, authors of *Infant and Toddler Development and Responsive Program Planning: A Relationship-Based Approach,* 3rd ed. (Upper Saddle River, NJ: Pearson, 2014). Donna was a professor of early childhood education at the University of Colorado-Denver. Sandy works for Zero to Three with the National Infant Toddler Child Care Initiative and Early Head Start and is also an instructor for WestEd Laboratories with the Program for Infant and Toddler Caregivers (PITC).

for infants, toddlers, teachers, and families. Here are some guidelines you can use to provide safe environments for infants and toddlers—and for all children:

- Areas used for diapering and toileting are separate from areas used for cooking, eating, and children's activities.
- Mattresses used for infants are firm; avoid soft bedding, such as comforters, pillows, fluffy blankets, or stuffed toys.
- All infant and toddler toys are made of nontoxic materials and sanitized regularly, and they are safe, durable, and in good condition.
- All electrical outlets accessible to children are covered and maintained to prevent shock.
- All required policies and plans of action for health emergencies requiring rapid response (such as choking or asthma attacks) are posted.
- Locations and telephone numbers of emergency response systems, and posted and up-to-date family contact information and consent for emergency care, are readily available.
- Playground equipment and surfaces are maintained to avoid injury to children.
- Teachers, staff, volunteers, and children wash their hands with soap and running water after diapering and toilet use, before and after food-related preparation or activity, after hands have become contaminated with blood or other body fluids, after handling pets or other animals, before and after giving medications, before and after bandaging a wound, and after assisting a child with toilet use.
- Staff and volunteers wear nonporous gloves when in contact with blood or other visibly bloody body fluids.
- Spilled body fluids are immediately cleaned up and disinfected according to professionally established guidelines. Tools and equipment used to clean spills are promptly disinfected, and blood-contaminated materials are disposed of in a plastic bag with a secure tie.[32]

Observe and Analyze

autonomy An Erikson concept that says as toddlers mature physically and mentally, they want to do things by themselves with no outside help.

SUPPORT DEVELOPMENTAL NEEDS. Supportive environments enable infants to develop basic trust and toddlers to develop **autonomy**. Autonomy occurs as toddlers mature physically and mentally and want to do things by themselves with no outside help. Infant care should be loving and responsive to their needs. The trusting infant depends on others to meet his or her needs. Toddlers want to do things for themselves and be independent. Support infant/toddler developmental needs in these ways:

- Respond immediately to an infant's expressions of need or discomfort; soothe and comfort the child. Meet infants' and toddlers' needs in warm, sensitive ways.

- Provide for their choices while taking into account their temperament, emotions, and individuality.

- Express love and be affectionate to your children. Toddlers may need extra or continual confirmation that they are loved and that trusted adults are there for them. Tell them, "I love you!"

- Give infants and toddlers your undivided attention—respond to their actions. Be alert to the baby's cues that he or she is ready to interact or play, or that he or she needs a break from activity.

- Create a stable, nurturing environment that is consistent. Make an extra effort to maintain schedules that are in synch with the baby's rhythms.

- Provide appropriate stimulation and freedom for a child to explore and master new experiences.

- Encourage families to have their infants and toddlers receive regular health checkups because illness and hospitalization often threaten a toddler's developing autonomy.

- Talk and read to children constantly. Engage them in conversations, comment on what they are doing using rich language and feeling words, and explain their surroundings to them.

- Encourage mastery of self-help skills and socialization, but support children's reliance on security objects such as a pacifier, blanket, or favorite stuffed animal and other successful self-coping strategies as they are needed.

- Validate all expressions of emotions and teach appropriate behaviors in high-emotion situations.[33]

- Treat each child as special and important.

PROVIDE CHALLENGING ENVIRONMENTS.   Challenging environments enable infants and toddlers to explore and interact with a wide variety of materials. It is important for you to provide all children with developmentally appropriate challenges. Challenging curriculum enables children to go from their present levels of development and learning to higher levels. Providing an enriched environment is a powerful way to promote infants' and toddlers' overall development. Here are some things you can do to provide challenging environments for infants and toddlers:

- Include a wide variety of multisensory, visual, auditory, and tactile materials and activities to support all areas of development—physical, social, emotional, and linguistic.
  - Hold, play with, and be responsive to infants and toddlers—you are the best toy a child has.
  - Provide mirrors for infants and toddlers to look at themselves and others. Talk with the children about how they look. Encourage them to laugh and smile at themselves, you, and others.
  - Provide visually interesting things for children to look at—mobiles, pictures, murals, and so on.
  - Provide toys and objects that children can manipulate—feel, suck, and grasp.
  - Provide objects and containers that children can use to put in or dump out.

- Provide responsive toys that make sounds, pop up, and so on, as children manipulate or act on them.
- Include materials for large and small muscles for reaching, grasping, kicking, pulling up, holding on, walking, and so forth.
- Enable children to be actively involved. An essential component of a challenging but appropriate environment is that it encourages active involvement. Active involvement is at the heart of constructivist approaches to early childhood education. So, providing opportunities for infants and toddlers to be active supports their learning and provides them with feelings of accomplishment and achievement. You should do the following:
  - Take infants and toddlers on walks so they can observe nature and people.
  - Provide safe floor space indoors and grassy areas outdoors so children can explore and move freely.
  - Allow infants and toddlers to crawl, pull up, walk, move freely, and safely explore.
  - Provide activities based on children's interests and abilities—a key to responsive and relational caregiving.
  - Provide low open shelves that allow children to see and select their own materials.
- The environment should promote language all of the time. Provide for a full range of language and literacy development.
  - Read, read, and read to infants and toddlers. Read aloud with enthusiasm, which shows children how much you love to read.
  - Read from all kinds of books—stories, poems, and so on.
  - Provide books (washable, cloth, etc.) for children to "read," handle, manipulate, and mouth.
  - Sing for and with children. Play a wide variety of music. Sing while changing diapers and other teacher–child activities.
  - Talk, talk, talk.
- Use technology and apps as developmentally appropriate. Now would be a good time to review the Voice from the Field, "Older Toddlers in the World of Apps," on page 268.

PROMOTE RESPECTFUL SOCIAL DEVELOPMENT AND INTERACTIONS.

Social interactions involve how children interact and get along with other children, their teachers, and others; they also include how teachers relate to and get along with the children they care for and other children. Here are some things you can do to promote respectful social development and interactions:

- Play games and engage in activities that include small groups of children.
- Play with toys that involve more than one child. For example, use a wagon and let one child pull another.
- Allow and encourage infants and toddlers to make choices. You can do this by asking them questions that encourage choice making. For example, "Can I help you dry your hands? Or can you do it by yourself?" or "You get to decide." Encourage autonomy with statements such as "That is something you can do."
- Give infants and toddlers the time they need and want to engage in an activity. Some infants and toddlers complete activities quickly; others need more time.
- Provide opportunities for infants and toddlers to engage in activities with others.
- Provide for friendship-making opportunities:
  - Provide for parallel play. Parallel play is when two children sit next to each other while they play, but may not necessarily interact. Donna Wittmer, author of

Focusing on Peers: The Importance of Relationships in the Early Years, says "Kids move from parallel play to parallel aware play. They'll look over at their buddy, smile, and even imitate him by stacking blocks the same way." This is a sign toddlers are becoming more social and are building skills that lead to friendships.

- Group children with familiar faces so that they can form recognition and comfort with their peers.
- Schedule play opportunities at a time of day that is not right before nap time, eating times, or go-home time—all times of the day that infants and toddlers are likely to be more fussy or irritable. Help situations stay meltdown free by enabling children to put their best foot forward.
- Model collaborative play such as helping one toddler roll a ball to another toddler. Provide lots of encouragement and positive feedback to encourage sharing and kindness.
- Be observant and on guard for the need to step in to prevent mishaps or meltdowns, but don't intervene too soon. Let children grow in independence as they are able.
- Label emotions to develop mutual empathy. For example, if Jack takes Emily's truck away, say quietly to Jack, "Look, Emily's crying. She feels sad that you took her truck. She'll feel happy if you give it back." If you need to, you can help Jack give the truck back by guiding his hands, then help him ask for a turn (be sure that he gets a turn soon to encourage him to share in the future!).

Reflect and Apply: Relational Caregiving

ACCOMMODATING DIVERSE LEARNERS

Meet Gabby, a two-month-old Caucasian infant. She is new to your care, and you are beginning to build a relationship with her. Like all babies, Gabby must begin to learn how to self-regulate. **Self-regulation** is a child's ability to gain control of bodily functions, manage emotions, maintain focus and attention, and integrate cognitive, physical, and social-emotional abilities. The growth of self-regulation is a developmental milestone across early childhood that begins in infancy that influences all aspects of behavior.[34] Babies must learn to increasingly self-regulate and control their emotions over time. Responsive caregivers act as helpers, external regulators, who help babies learn to gain self-control. Therefore, when you care for Gabby, you act as an extension of, or as a support for, her internal ability to regulate.

Several factors influence a baby's ability to move from external to internal self-regulation. Temperament is one factor. Temperament traits like mood, irritability, and adaptability affect a baby's capacity for emotional regulation. **Goodness of fit**—how well a teacher recognizes and responds or adapts to a child's temperament—also affects the learning of self-regulation. You develop a goodness of fit by working with babies' temperaments, not against them. You can work to lessen or soften some of the difficult features of temperament, and you can emphasize the strengths of temperament, but you can't change an infant's temperament! This means that you make changes in your own style of relating and change the environment to work with the baby's temperament.[35]

Granted, it is taxing to care for a baby who fusses nonstop or who sleeps for only an hour here and there, or a toddler who bites or who constantly throws tantrums. Negative behaviors give

self-regulation A child's ability to gain control of bodily functions; manage emotions, maintain focus and attention; and integrate cognitive, physical, and social-emotional abilities.

goodness of fit How well a teacher recognizes and responds or adapts to a child's temperament—also affects the learning of self-regulation.

VOICE FROM THE FIELD

Older Toddlers in the World of Apps

Many of today's older toddlers around the world are learning basic language and cognitive skills with apps for smartphones and tablets. Toddlers are truly children of the technological generation. Many toddlers are more skillful in manipulating apps than are their parents and caregivers! The following are some applications that help toddlers and their parents learn in the technological age. A number of caveats are in order, however:

• Not all children are fortunate enough to live in families with the means to provide their toddlers access to appropriate technology. You can make tablets accessible to older toddlers in your programs.

• As in all things, with all children, you must balance their involvement with apps (especially children age two years and under) and their need for interaction with other environmental stimuli, such as *you* and an enriched environment. Also review the American Academy of Pediatrics position statement on media use by children younger than two years and a joint position statement issued by the National Association for the Education of Young Children and the Fred Rogers Center for Early Learning and Children's Media *Technology and Interactive Media as Tools in Early Childhood Programs Serving Children From Birth Through Age 8.*

"I Hear Ewe"

Whenever your children tap on an animal or vehicle icon, the game announces what animal or vehicle it is and plays a recording of how it really sounds!

A great way to introduce toddlers to animals and vehicles!

"Letters A to Z"

Animated flashcards designed to help children learn the letters of the alphabet in a fun and engaging way!

Each flashcard contains characters and creatures that come to life in illustrated scenes accompanied by sound effects to describe the letters!

"Drawing Pad"

Drawing Pad is a mobile art studio designed exclusively for the iPad! The beautiful user interface puts the fun into creating art.

An entertaining and kid-friendly app that enables children to choose different colors, tools, and includes stamps.

Source: Used with permission from Darren Murtha Apps.

you cues and clues that the infant or toddler is having difficulty with self-regulation. You help Gabby learn self-regulation when you provide her with manageable challenges that are part of everyday life, like waiting to be fed or self-soothing into sleep. When you offer manageable challenges while providing external support, you help Gabby build self-regulation and personal responsibility.[36]

Here are some strategies you can use to help Gabby and other infants and toddlers develop self-regulation.

• ***Build a close relationship with Gabby:*** This helps her regulate her emotions and actions because she learns to trust you to fulfill her needs. She can rely on

268

you for consistent care and constant attention. As a result, Gabby gradually learns to quiet and control herself. To build close relationships do the following:[37]

- **Observe closely and respond:** Babies always give you cues to let you know when they are ready to play or when they are tired, hungry, or full. Be aware of and accepting of individual differences reflected in each baby's needs. For example, when Gabby is two months old, she cries loudly when she is hungry; if you respond promptly so that she does not become distressed, she will learn to trust you. Then, by the time she is four months old, she will be able to only whimper to cue you to her needs.[38]

- **Provide structure and predictability:** Babies need consistent caregivers who provide continuity of care. You strengthen your relationship with Gabby as she trusts the continuity of your relationship with her. For example, if you follow a regular sleep schedule each day, Gabby will feel safe because she learns what to expect.[39]

- **Show empathy and caring:** When caregivers identify children's needs and respond to them as significant, infants and toddlers feel good about themselves and are better able to handle their emotions. When Gabby reaches eight months of age and cries when her mother leaves in the morning, you can use a soft, soothing voice to empathize and reassure her, "It's so hard for you. I know you feel so sad." You can hold her and rub her back to offer empathy and strengthen your relationship with her.[40]

- **Define age-appropriate limits:** Help Gabby know what is expected. When she is a ten-month-old, you can tell her, "No biting. That hurts me." As Gabby grows, be consistent in expressing expectations and setting rules or consequences. The goal is to guide children and set limits so that they feel supported and valued, not judged and rejected. When Gabby grows into a curious toddler and wants to explore, you can verbalize and model limits. Tell her, "Wait for me, Gabby. We go out together," as you take her hand and help her open the door.[41]

- **Play!** When you play with babies and toddlers, you help them learn to find answers to problems and also help them develop the attention they need to attend to tasks.[42] Help Gabby develop self-regulation through play:

  - **Model language:** Early on, Gabby won't have many words, so you should describe what she is doing and what you and she are doing together. This responsive approach helps Gabby build understanding between her actions and words. Soon Gabby will be talking! She will also begin to use "self-talk" to help her control her own behavior. As her language and emotional development progresses, you can encourage Gabby to use her words to express her feelings and thoughts rather than immediately acting on her impulses.[43]

  - **Be a consultant:** As children begin to pretend, their play scripts are very straightforward and uncomplicated. When Gabby is younger, her pretend script may consist of using a brush to brush her own hair. When you take part in her play, you can help her grow her script by showing her how to brush the hair of a doll and your own hair. When you insert new roles or ideas into pretend situations and toys, Gabby learns to apply her behavior to the new scenario, which increases her self-regulation.[44]

Helping Gabby and other babies develop self-regulation helps them grow into a child ready for school and for life. As a result, Gabby will be able to understand what teachers and others ask of her in given situations, be able to monitor her own behavior to see if it matches, and maintain or change what she is doing based on her evaluation of the behavior.

ACTIVITIES FOR PROFESSIONAL DEVELOPMENT

ETHICAL DILEMMA

"POSTPARTUM MOM?"

Carlie is an infant and toddler caregiver at an early learning center. She has always enjoyed caring for Jacob, a happy-go-lucky two-year-old, and interacting with his mother, Amanda. Amanda just started bringing her new baby, Adam, to the early learning center, and Carlie has noticed that Amanda is often out of sorts, disheveled, short tempered, and that she often looks dejected, and her voice and affect are mostly flat. Amanda is so different from the way she was before she gave birth that Carlie is concerned. One day when

Amanda picked up Jacob and Adam, Carlie was shocked to see Amanda give Adam a shake when he wouldn't stop crying. Before she can say anything, the family is out the door. Carlie thinks Amanda might have postpartum depression, and she's concerned for Adam and Jacob.

What should Carlie do? Should she consult a supervisor or call Amanda's husband and share her concerns? Should Carlie alert Child Protective Services? Should Carlie talk to Amanda, or wait for more evidence that the children are in danger before she makes a decision? What do you think Carlie should do?

ACTIVITIES TO APPLY WHAT YOU LEARNED

1. Visit a parenting blog or website and peruse the posts. What are parents saying about their infants and toddlers? What are their questions, concerns, and delights? How does this give you a picture of what infants and toddlers are like? Post your findings on your online journal.

2. Conduct an Internet search of scientific magazines, teacher magazines, and newspapers for the latest brain research relating to infants and toddlers.

3. Observe a program that provides care for infants and toddlers. Is the curriculum developmentally appropriate? Explain what you liked most and least about the program. What suggestions would you make for improving the curriculum? Share your suggestions with your classmates on your class discussion board.

4. Which stage of sensorimotor cognitive development do you think is most important in an infant/toddler's development and why? Post your opinion in a Facebook note and tag your friends to start a friendly debate.

5. Select five books for infants and five for toddlers. Tell why you selected each and give examples for how you would use them in your infant/toddler program. Post your ten books on your class discussion board.

6. **KEY ASSESSMENT:** Caregiver–infant/toddler relationships are an important part of the care of these children. In fact, in the infant-toddler stages of development, the relationships that exist between children and caregivers/parents may be the most important contributor to healthy social-emotional and cognitive development. You have been invited to make a fifteen-minute presentation to the local association of the National Association for the Education of Young Children (NAEYC) on "How to Build Infant-Toddler-Caregiver Relationships." Identify five caregiver actions/behaviors that would promote relationships with infant and toddlers. For example, one relationship might be "responding appropriately to infants' cries and sounds." Another example might be "meet infants and toddlers needs in warm, sensitive ways. Use the rubric provided to guide your work.

7. Identify three ways curricula for infants and toddlers influence the environment and vice versa. Then research on the Internet the infant/toddler programs in your area. Pay attention to what their websites say about curricula, environments, and caregivers. Make a list of pros and cons of what you find.

8. How might a child's temperament affect how you care for him or her? Are there some behaviors that are difficult for you to empathize with or understand? Write a paragraph about how you will provide for goodness of fit between yourself and your charges when you come up against infants/toddlers with temperaments you find challenging. Post your paragraph on your class discussion board and ask for comments.

LINKING TO LEARNING

The following agencies and programs, which can be located easily online, provide additional information about topics discussed in this chapter.

Brain Development in Infants and Toddlers: Information for Parents and Caregivers

Provides an overview of resources available concerning the brain.

Early Brain Development: What Parents and Caregivers Need to Know

Presents facts about early brain development that parents and educators need to know.

Zero to Three

This organization's website concentrates exclusively on the miraculous first years of life, the critical period when a child undergoes the greatest human growth and development. The organization seeks to develop a solid intellectual, emotional, and social foundation for young children.

Technology and Young Children

Here you will find access to the joint position statement issued by the National Association for the Education of Young Children and the Fred Rogers Center for Early Learning and Children's Media, "Technology and Interactive Media as Tools in Early Childhood Programs Serving Children from Birth through Age 8."

THE PRESCHOOL YEARS

Readiness for School and Life

LEARNING OUTCOMES

1. List the reasons why preschools are so popular today.
2. Describe what preschool children are like and what they are able to do.
3. Explain why school readiness is important for the preschool years.
4. Explain the role of play in children's learning.
5. Explain what contributes to the new preschool curriculum.
6. Explain what the future holds for preschool children and education.

THE road to success in school and life begins long before kindergarten and first grade. This is why early childhood teachers, parents, and politicians view the preschool years as the cornerstone and foundation of success. The **preschool years** are playing a more important role in the educational process than they have at any other time in history, and they will continue to be the focus of public attention and financial support well into coming decades.

WHY ARE PRESCHOOLS SO POPULAR?

Preschools are programs for three- to five-year-old children before they enter kindergarten. Today, child care beginning at six weeks is commonplace for children of working parents, and many children are in a school of some kind as early as age two or three. More than 1.3 million children attend state funded pre-K, 1.1 million at age four. Reasons for the popularity of preschool programs are many and varied.

BROAD-BASED PUBLIC SUPPORT

All across the United States, the public and politicians are expressing their support for high-quality early childhood programs. Former Secretary of State Hillary Clinton has declared her dedication to early childhood education.[1] More than three hundred business leaders and organizations from forty-four states around the country signed an open letter to President Obama and members of Congress declaring support for early childhood programs.[2] In addition, many high-powered foundations are developing programs to support early childhood research and program development. These include the Pritzker Family Foundation's Early Childhood Accelerator Project and The Pew Charitable Trusts' home-visiting campaign.[3] It seems that preschool education's time has come, and more and more politicians and funding agencies are climbing on the bandwagon of support.

WORKING PARENTS

Working parents believe the public schools hold the solution to their child care needs so they advocate (rather strongly) for public schools to provide preschool programs. Some parents cannot afford quality child care; they believe preschools, furnished at the public's expense, are a reasonable, cost-efficient way to meet their child care needs. The alignment of the public schools with early childhood programs is becoming increasingly popular. Some think it makes sense to put the responsibility for educating and caring for all of the nation's children under the sponsorship of one agency—the public schools.

For their part, public school teachers and the unions that represent them are anxious to bring early childhood programs under the umbrella of the public schools. Public school teachers see their involvement as a step toward bringing higher-quality programs to more children. The unions see preschool teachers as another source for growing membership.[4]

HIGHLY EDUCATED WORKFORCE

A more highly educated workforce will increase economic growth.[5] Business leaders see early education as one way of developing highly skilled and more productive workers.[6] Many preschool programs include work-related skills and behavior in their curriculum. Many of the dispositions for learning, such as self-regulation and understanding, accepting, and following rules and routines, are essential workplace behaviors and are developed in preschool. Likewise, being literate begins in the early years, and literacy is an essential workforce skill. Research supports the importance of preschool early literacy learning as a basis for successful reading.[7] Learning to read is a high priority for our nation's schools. It makes sense to lay the foundation for reading as early as possible in the preschool years.

EQUAL OPPORTUNITY

Many believe that early public schooling, especially for children from low-income families, is necessary if the United States is to promote equal opportunity for all. They argue that low-income children begin school already far behind their more fortunate middle and upper class counterparts and that the best way to keep them from falling hopelessly behind is for them to begin school earlier. Extensive research shows that investing in our children is important and is not as expensive as some people believe.[8]

RESEARCH BASED AND COST EFFECTIVE

High-quality early education benefits children of all social and economic groups. It helps prepare young children to succeed in school and become better citizens; they earn more money, pay more taxes, and commit fewer crimes.[9] Consider what the research outlined below reveals about the cost benefits of spending taxpayer money in the early years.

Perry Preschool Project[10]

- For every dollar spent, $16 was saved in tax dollars.
- Sixty-six percent of the program group graduated from high school on time, compared to 45 percent of the control group.
- The control group suffered twice as many arrests as did the program group.

Chicago Child–Parent Center Program[11]

- For every dollar invested in the program, $7.10 was returned.
- Participants had a 51 percent reduction in child maltreatment.
- Participants had a 41 percent reduction in special education placement.

New Jersey Abbott Preschool Program[12]

- Increased receptive vocabulary scores by an additional four months, a particularly significant finding since this measure is strongly predictive of general cognitive abilities.
- Increased scores on measures of early math skills by 24 percent over the course of the year.
- Increased print awareness scores by 61 percent over the course of the year. Children who attended the program know more letters, more letter-sound associations, and are more familiar with words and book concepts at entry to kindergarten.

Los Angeles Universal Preschool[13]

- The percentage of children scoring near proficient on the social and emotional skills needed to do well in kindergarten increased 72 percent.
- English language learners (ELLs) who scored significantly lower than their non-English-learner peers closed the gap in skills such as demonstrating proficiency in using crayons, washing hands, controlling impulses, expressing needs, counting to ten, and recognizing letters of the alphabet, as well as shapes and colors.
- In general skills, such as writing their first names, recognizing rhyming words, and using books, ELLs' gains exceeded those made by non-English-learners.

EAGER TO LEARN

Three- and four-year-old children are ready, eager, and able to learn. Recognizing the strong connection between a child's early development and success later in life, more states are funding preschool programs for four- and even three-year-olds.[14] The National Research Council concluded in its study *Eager to Learn: Educating Our Preschoolers* that the last thirty years of child development research demonstrated that "two- to five-year-old children are more capable learners than had been imagined, and that their acquisition of linguistic, mathematical, and other skills relevant to school readiness is influenced (and can be improved) by their educational and developmental experiences during those years.[15]

EARLY INTERVENTION

For children with disabilities or delays, preschool programs also offer opportunities for early intervention. For example, Montgomery County Public Schools in Rockville, Maryland, implemented its Preschool Education Program (PEP) to address the needs of children ages three to five years with developmental delays or disabilities. All children in PEP have an individualized education program (IEP) with learning goals and objectives based on needs identified through assessment and testing. The goals and objectives guide teachers as they support children's improvement and progress. Most children have delays in more than one area and receive services for speech/language, occupational, and/or physical therapy.[16]

WHAT ARE PRESCHOOLERS LIKE?

Today's preschoolers are not like the children of previous decades. Many have already attended one, two, or three years of child care or school. They have watched hundreds of hours of television, and many are technologically sophisticated. Many have also experienced the trauma of family divorce or the psychological effects of abuse. Many have experienced the glitz and glamour of boutique birthday parties or hardships of living below the poverty level. Both collectively and individually, the experiential backgrounds of today's preschoolers are quite different from those of previous generations.

I have stressed the individuality of each child while at the same time understanding the commonalities of developmental processes for all children. Within this context of individuality and developmental commonalities, introduce yourself to two preschoolers in the "Portraits of Preschoolers" in the following feature. While reading this chapter, think about the characteristics and needs of these preschoolers and how you would teach them if they were in your classroom.

PHYSICAL AND MOTOR DEVELOPMENT

Understanding preschoolers' physical and motor development enables you to understand why active learning is so important. One noticeable difference between preschoolers and infants and toddlers is that preschoolers have lost most of their baby fat and have taken on a leaner, lankier look. This slimming down and increasing motor coordination enables them to participate with more confidence in the locomotor activities so necessary during this stage of growth and development. Both girls and boys continue to grow several inches per year throughout the preschool years. Table 10.1 shows the average height and weight for preschoolers.

Preschool children are learning to use and test their bodies. It is a time to learn what they can do individually and how they can do it. Locomotion plays a large role in motor and skill development; it includes activities of moving the body through

PORTRAITS OF PRESCHOOLERS

AIDROSS

General Description 3 years old, Middle Eastern male; friendly, talkative, cheerful; fascinated with trucks; has traveled to many countries; lives with father, mother, and younger brother; both parents are attending graduate school

Social-Emotional	Cognitive/Language	Motor	Adaptive (Daily Living)
• Beginning to encourage classmates to follow classroom rules • Becomes upset when asked to stop a preferred activity during transition times • Shows concern when classmates are sad/upset • Developing a preference for playing with 2 to 3 classmates	• Can count objects up to 10 with 1 to 1 correspondence • Tells a story using pictures • Can identify names of classmates in print • Enjoys answering questions during whole group time	• Writes name independently • Uses tweezers to pick up small objects • Uses scissors to cut out simple shapes • Kicks a ball to a friend • Can hop on one foot	• Uses toilet independently • Usually washes hands without prompting • Dresses self independently; can use Velcro fasteners but needs help with laces • Uses eating utensils appropriately • Follows classroom routines easily (takes out folder and puts his backpack away)

JAMILAH

General Description 4 years old, African American female; very bright and talkative with a great personality; makes friends easily; always happy; lives with mother, father, and 2 older siblings

Social-Emotional	Cognitive/Language	Motor	Adaptive (Daily Living)
• Engages in cooperative play on her own • Takes turns voluntarily • Enjoys helping others • Learns from her mistakes • Helps others make the right choices	• Rote counts to 35 and can use 1 to 1 correspondence up to 35 • Can answer "why" questions • Can pick out nonrhyming words out of a set of 3 • Can sort objects by attributes	• Creates movements to the beat of music • Can gallop, jump, skip, and hop on one foot • Uses writing tools correctly • Able to cut out shapes and objects such as butterflies and frogs	• Able to make appropriate decisions when it comes to safety • Able to dress herself • Can tie her shoes • Understands the order of daily routines

Developmentally Appropriate Questions:

- Aidross encourages his classmates to follow classroom rules. How would you develop a learning situation in which Aidross can be a team leader and help other children who don't follow the classroom rules?

- Transition times are often difficult for children and teachers because children can and do engage in inappropriate activities. What would you do to help Aidross, who doesn't like to stop an activity and transition, and others develop transition routines?

- Jamilah seems to have the ability to make "right" choices. How would you let Jamilah help her peers learn to make "right" choices?

Source: Contributed by Principal Felicia Sprayberry and teachers at the Popo and Lupe Gonzalez School for Young Children, Denton ISD, Denton, Texas.

TABLE 10.1 | Average Height and Weight of Preschoolers

Age	Males Height (inches)	Males Weight (pounds)	Females Height (inches)	Females Weight (pounds)
3 years	37.5	32.0	37.0	31.0
3.5 years	39.0	34.0	38.5	32.5
4 years	40.0	36.0	40.0	35.0
4.5 years	41.5	38.0	41.0	38.0
5 years	43.0	40.5	42.5	40.0

Source: National Center for Health Statistics in collaboration with the National Center for Chronic Disease Prevention and Health Promotion, www.cdc.gov/growthcharts.

space—walking, running, hopping, jumping, rolling, dancing, climbing, and leaping. Preschoolers use these activities to investigate and explore the relationships among themselves, space, and objects in space.

Preschoolers also like to participate in fine-motor activities such as drawing, coloring, painting, cutting, and pasting. They need programs that provide action and play, supported by proper nutrition and healthy habits of plentiful rest and good hygiene.

SOCIAL-EMOTIONAL DEVELOPMENT

A major responsibility of preschool teachers is to promote and support children's social-emotional development. Positive social-emotional development enables children to learn better and to succeed in all school and life activities. During the preschool years (ages three to five), children are in Erikson's psychosocial development stage of initiative versus guilt. During this stage, children are fully involved in locomotive activities and the enjoyment of doing things. They are very active and want to plan and be involved in activities. They want to move and be active.

IMPLICATIONS FOR TEACHING.   You can help support children's initiative in these ways:

- *Give children freedom to explore.* Lisa Frank, in her Bright Futures Pre-K classroom, has students try anything from yoga to sign language. Lisa always makes it an enjoyable experience. For example, she transformed her classroom into a magical ocean experience, complete with blue cling wrap and sea creature stickers on the window, an ocean sound CD during naptime, and an edible ocean made of blueberry Jell-O and Swedish fish.[17]

- *Provide projects and activities that enable children to discover and experiment.* Science means success for Wendy Butler-Boyensen's preschool children. She motivates her young students by exploring different scientific themes each month, from hiking through local wetlands to studying the solar system.[18]

- *Encourage and support children's attempts to plan, make things, and be involved.* Carla Lyles of Chicago, Illinois, listens, observes, and engages her students in conversations to determine their interests. For example, when her children expressed interest in building houses, she took them on a construction site field trip to explore the renovation of homes in their community. The class created a book filled with photos and captions from their excursion, and even enjoyed an onsite school visit by the backhoe driver they befriended on their trip.[19]

self-regulation The ability of preschool children to control their emotions and behaviors, to delay gratification, and to build positive social relations with each other.

executive function See *self-regulation*.

SELF-REGULATION.   During the preschool years, children are learning **self-regulation**, also referred to as **executive function**. Self-regulation is the ability to plan, initiate, and complete an activity; control emotions and behaviors; delay gratification; maintain attention; respond to feedback; and build positive social relations with others. Teaching self-regulation is a major teacher task during the preschool years.

Implications for Teaching. The following guidelines will enable you to teach self-regulation so preschool children can guide their own behavior:

- *Provide a variety of learning experiences.* Young children are very good at creating diversion when none is available. Often teachers think they cannot provide interesting learning experiences until children are "under control," when, in fact, the real problem is that children may be out of control because they have nothing interesting to do!

- *Arrange the environment to help children do their best.* Make sure activities are arranged so there is enough space for them and so they are protected from the traffic of other children.

- *Get to know each child.* Establish relationships with parents and support children's strengths as well as their needs. As you get to know each child, you can begin to tailor activities to each child's specific needs. Christine Lyall of Culver City Schools at the Office of Child Development tailors activities to her students' needs by being sensitive to their various learning styles. For example, she accommodates mathematical–logical intelligence by using hands-on materials and rhythmic patterning activities, which she makes herself. Christine attends to children's musical–rhythmic intelligence by composing her own songs about concepts the class is learning, and the children are captivated! She also addresses the often under-recognized bodily–kinesthetic intelligences of her students by incorporating dance and movement into learning strategies.[20]

- *Set clear guidelines for what is and is not appropriate behavior.* Guide behavior with rational explanations in a climate of mutual respect and caring.

- *Work with children to establish a few simple group rules.* Some appropriate rules are take care of other people; take care of yourself; and take care of the classroom. Teach and reinforce these rules continuously throughout the school year.

- *Use the child's home language as often as possible.* Make every effort to show children you support their culture and respect their language. For example, preschool teacher Trudy George uses children's home language through her "World Day" activity. Her students are taught greetings in different languages (e.g., "Hola," "Adiós") and read stories about children from different nations.

- *Coach children to verbally express their feelings.* Help children use either their home language or English, and model how to solve social problems with others using words. For many children, this will mean providing appropriate words and offering possible solutions and guidance when these problems arise.

- *Model self-control by using self-talk.* "Oh, I can't get this lid off the paint. I am feeling frustrated [take a deep breath]. Now I'll try again."

COGNITIVE DEVELOPMENT

operation A reversible mental action.

Preschoolers are in the preoperational stage of intellectual development. Characteristics of the preoperational stage are as follows: (1) children grow in their ability to use symbols, including language; (2) children are not capable of operational thinking (an **operation** is a reversible mental action), thus Piaget named this stage *preoperational*;

(3) children center on one thought or idea, often to the exclusion of other thoughts; (4) children are unable to conserve; and (5) children are egocentric.

Preoperational characteristics have particular implications for teachers.

IMPLICATIONS FOR TEACHING.   Here are some ways you can promote preschool children's cognitive development:

- *Provide concrete materials to help children see and experience concepts and processes.* Children learn from touching and experimenting with actual objects, as well as from pictures, stories, and media. When you read stories about fruit and nutrition, bring in a collection of apples for children to touch, feel, smell, taste, classify, manipulate, and explore. Collections also offer children an ideal way to learn the names of things, classify, count, and describe.

- *Use hands-on activities that give children opportunities for active involvement in their learning.* Encourage children to manipulate and interact with the world around them so they can construct concepts about relationships, attributes, and processes. Through exploration, preoperational children begin to collect and organize data about the objects they manipulate. For example, when children engage in water play with funnels and cups, they learn about concepts such as measurement, volume, sink/float, bubbles and the prism, evaporation, and saturation.

- *Give children many and varied experiences.* Diverse activities and play environments lend themselves to teaching different skills, concepts, and processes. Children should spend time daily in both indoor and outdoor activities. Give consideration to the types of activities that facilitate large and fine motor skills and social, emotional, and cognitive development. For example, outdoor play activities and games such as climbing, throwing and catching balls, and riding tricycles enhance large-motor development; fine-motor activities include using scissors, stringing beads, coloring, writing, and completing simple puzzles.

- *Scaffold appropriate tasks and behaviors.* Preoperational children learn to a great extent through modeling. For example, children should see you and other adults reading and writing daily. Provide opportunities for children to view brief demonstrations by peers or professionals on possible ways to use materials. For example, after children have spent time in free exploration with blocks and math manipulatives, you can show children patterning techniques and strategies they may want to experiment with in their own play.

- *Provide a literacy-rich environment to stimulate interest in and development of language and literacy.* Display class stories and dictations, children's writing, and charts of familiar songs and finger-plays. Have a variety of literature for students to read, including books, magazines, and newspapers. Make sure paper and writing utensils are abundant to motivate children in all kinds of writing. Daily literacy activities should include opportunities for shared, guided, and independent reading and writing; singing songs and finger-plays; and creative dramatics. In addition, read to children every day.

- *Allow children periods of uninterrupted time to engage in self-chosen projects.* Children benefit more from a few extended blocks of time that provide for in-depth involvement in meaningful projects than they do from frequent, brief periods of time.

Indoor and outdoor play contributes to children's cognitive development. Preschool teachers can help children learn many concepts as they participate with children in play—both indoors and outdoors. What are some concepts these children are learning through their involvement in play?

LANGUAGE DEVELOPMENT

Preschool children's language skills grow and develop rapidly. Vocabulary and sentence length increase as children continue to master syntax and grammar. During their third year or earlier, children add helping verbs and negatives to their vocabulary; for example, "No touch" or "I don't want milk." Sentences also become longer and more complex. During the fourth and fifth years, children use noun or subject clauses, conjunctions, and prepositions to complete their sentences. "No" is a common part of preschool children's language. This is a sign of children's desire for independence and autonomy. Preschoolers want to do things for themselves!

During the preschool years, children's language development is diverse and comprehensive and constitutes a truly impressive range of learning. Even more impressive is the fact that children learn intuitively, without a great deal of instruction, the rules of language that apply to the words and phrases they use. You can use many of the language practices recommended for infants and toddlers with preschoolers as well.

SCHOOL READINESS AND YOUNG CHILDREN

School readiness is a major topic of discussion regarding preschool and kindergarten programs. The early childhood profession is reexamining readiness, its many interpretations, and the various ways the concept is applied to educational practices.

school readiness
When children have the knowledge and abilities necessary for success in kindergarten.

For most parents, **school readiness** means that their children have the knowledge and abilities necessary for success in kindergarten. But what does readiness for kindergarten really include?

Readiness is no longer seen as consisting solely of a predetermined set of specific capabilities children must attain before entering kindergarten. Furthermore, the responsibility for children's early learning and development is no longer placed solely on the child or the parents but rather is seen as a shared responsibility among children, parents, families, early childhood professionals, communities, states, and the nation. Regardless of the child or family's diversity or background (culture, language, socioeconomic status, disability, etc.), readiness remains a shared responsibility.

For example, states are taking the initiative to ensure preschool children are ready for kindergarten. Texas School Ready! is a program that certifies preschool education classrooms that effectively prepare their students for kindergarten. Based on children's assessment scores as they enter kindergarten, the preschools they attended are—or are not—certified. This certification system is an incentive for all preschools to prepare their children for kindergarten.

SCHOOL READINESS

Some early childhood professionals and many parents believe that time cures all things, including a child's lack of school readiness. They think that as time passes and as children grow and develop physically and cognitively they become ready to achieve. This belief is manifested in school admissions policies advocating that children remain out of school for a year if they are found not ready by means of a school readiness test.

Assuming that passage of time brings about readiness is similar to the concept of unfolding, popularized by Froebel. Unfolding implies that development is inevitable and certain and that a child's optimum degree of development is determined by heredity and a biological clock. Froebel likened children to plants and parents and teachers to gardeners, whose task it is to nurture and care for children so that they can mature according to their genetic inheritance and maturational timetable. The concept of unfolding continues to be a powerful force in early childhood education; it is based on the belief that maturation is predictable, patterned, and orderly.

However, although much of child development does occur in predictable ways, it is not the same for all children. Some children may have delayed development and, for others, development may be advanced. In addition, teachers and parents cannot and should not simply wait for children to develop or acquire age-appropriate skills and behaviors. Creating rich and supportive environments helps ensure that all children will develop to their appropriate levels.

READINESS FOR LEARNING

As the United States moves closer to universal preschool with all three- to five-year-old children attending public-supported early childhood programs, readiness issues take on greater importance and significance. Preschool is the portal to kindergarten and the process of schooling through grade twelve and beyond. Preschool experiences and success set the trajectory for how well children achieve in kindergarten and beyond. This reality helps explain why early childhood educators are so interested in and concerned about preschool readiness skills and behaviors.

Unfortunately, America's children enter preschool programs at uneven levels of preparedness and readiness for learning what the public schools expect of them. Socioeconomic background, culture, language, and maternal education all contribute to children's readiness for learning. In fact, significant learning and educational and preparedness gaps exist at children's entry to preschool.[21] Many children enter preschool well prepared to learn what is necessary for entry into kindergarten as depicted in Figure 10.1. On the other hand, many children will struggle to learn essential readiness skills and behaviors and will continue to fall behind their more advantaged peers. To help level the playing field of preschool education and to ensure that all children learn essential knowledge, skills, and behaviors, all fifty states and the District of Columbia have identified early learning guidelines (ELGs) to direct teachers and programs. For example, the Florida Voluntary Prekindergarten (VPK) Education Standards cover these six domains:

- Physical development
- Approaches to learning
- Social and emotional development
- Language communication and emergent literacy
- Cognitive development and general knowledge
- Motor development[22]

You must be very familiar with your state's ELGs and use them as you plan and teach. Consider the readiness skills of language and social expression, which we discussed earlier, and independence, impulse control, interpersonal skills, experiential background, motor skills, academics, approaches to learning, and physical and mental health. All are important and necessary for a successful school experience. Even with individual states identifying important readiness skills, the level of preparedness varies dramatically from child to child, particularly children who are from diverse backgrounds. Some of this unevenness of preparedness may be based on the way the cultural background views the skill (as more or less important) or may be based on the (perhaps limited) capabilities of the child due to a disability or delay. Figure 10.1 shows important factors for kindergarten readiness. These are some of the things children should know and be able to do before they enter kindergarten.

INDEPENDENCE.   Independence means the ability to work alone on a task, take care of oneself, and initiate projects without always being told what to do. Independence also includes mastery of self-help skills, including, but not limited to, dressing skills, health skills (toileting, hand washing, using a tissue, and brushing teeth), and eating skills (using utensils and napkins, serving oneself, and cleaning up).

- Is encouraged to learn from and participate in a wide range of activities in the home and community
- Has gained confidence from past experiences to explore new ideas and environments
- Has the support and encouragement of family members to do things
- Is familiar with many kinds of books

- Is able to perform basic self-help/self-care tasks such as toileting, dressing, feeding, etc. See the portraits of children in this chapter
- Is willing to try new things
- Is encouraged to be self-reliant in approaching new learning tasks
- Has a desire to be and is learning to be independent
- Is responsible about taking care of materials and cleaning up

- Has the coordination necessary to participate in playground and other physical activities requiring running, jumping, climbing, etc.
- Is able to use and manipulate crayons, paintbrush, buttons, zippers, etc.
- Can hold a pencil/crayon and engages in "writing" and coloring activities

- Engages appropriately in conversations with peers and adults including teachers and other parents/caregivers
- Can express needs and wants in their primary language
- Has an interest in and eagerness for learning
- Engages in symbolic/imaginative play with self and peers

- Has enthusiasm for learning
- Identifies and names letters of the alphabet
- Is able to write first name
- Identifies numbers 1–5
- "Reads" and interacts with books and other print materials
- Counts five to ten objects correctly
- Recognizes primary shapes and colors
- Follows one to two step directions

- Plays and interacts collaboratively with peers
- Participates successfully in groups
- Gets along with and plays with peers and adults
- Is friendly and is able to make friends
- Shows empathy and caring for others

- Stays focused/pays attention during activities
- Controls impulses and self-regulates
- Can sit still and listen
- Is learning how to share
- Can take turns

- Is physically healthy and has received required check-ups, immunization, and medical evaluations
- Can identify own feelings, self-regulate, and calm self
- Is reasonably able to delay instant gratification
- Can accept comfort from adults

- Demonstrates enthusiasm for learning
- Shows initiative and curiosity
- Engages in self-initiated/directed activities
- Demonstrates engagement and perseverance
- Shows some planning and reflection

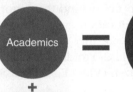

Experiential Background + Independence/Self-Care + Motor Skills + Language/Expression + Academics = Ready for Kindergarten + Interpersonal/Social Skills + Impulse Control + Physical and Emotional Health + Approaches to Learning

FIGURE 10.1 | Building Blocks of Kindergarten Readiness

IMPULSE CONTROL. **Impulse control**, or the ability to resist or moderate one's immediate reactions, urges, and desires, relates to self-regulation, which we discussed earlier. Controlling impulses includes working cooperatively with others, not hitting other children or interfering with their work, developing an attention span that permits involvement in learning activities for a reasonable length of time, and being able to stay seated for a while. Children who are not able to control their impulses are frequently labeled hyperactive or learning disabled.

impulse control See *self-regulation*.

ATTENTION SKILLS. Attention skills are a corollary of self-regulation. Paying attention to a task and the teacher are critical for school readiness. The ability to sustain attention for progressively longer periods of time is a predictor of achievement and school success.

INTERPERSONAL SKILLS. Interpersonal skills include getting along and working with peers, teachers, and other adults. Asked why they want their children to attend preschool, parents frequently respond, "to learn how to get along with others." One interpersonal skill children are encouraged to develop is "sharing with others." Every preschool program is an experience of participating in a community of learners in which children have the opportunity to interact with others to become successful in a group setting. Interpersonal skills include working cooperatively with others, learning and using basic manners, and most important, learning how to learn from and with others. Collaboration is a valuable skill and asset.

EXPERIENTIAL BACKGROUND. Experiential background is important to readiness because experiences are the building blocks of knowledge, the raw materials of cognitive development. Children must go places—the grocery store, the library, the zoo—and they must be involved in activities—creating things, painting, coloring, experimenting, and discovering. Children can build only on the background of information they bring to a new experience. Varied experiences are the context in which children learn new words, and the number and kinds of words children know are major predictors of later school success. Again, the unevenness of experiences before and during children's preschool enrollment is a major contributor to the school preparedness gap.

MENTAL/EMOTIONAL HEALTH. Given the events surrounding The Sandy Hook elementary school shooting on December 14, 2012, and other acts of violence, more professionals are focusing on how to promote positive mental health as a way of preventing aggression and violence. Certainly, children must have good nutritional and physical habits that enable them to participate fully in and profit from any program. At the same time, they must also have positive, nurturing environments and caring professionals to help them develop a self-image and mental health necessary for positive daily living.

It is no surprise then that early childhood professionals are taking into account children's emotional development as an important factor in school readiness. Research clearly shows that young children with aggressive and disruptive behaviors are much less likely to do well in school.[23]

Implications for Teaching. Here are several ways you can support children's mental/emotional health:

- Observe children, listen to them, and note typical and atypical behavior.
- Use modeling, role play, and group discussion to help children learn appropriate behavior.

- Devote class time to instructing children how to identify and label feelings, how to appropriately communicate with others about emotions, and how to resolve disputes with peers (e.g., using words instead of fists).

- Help parents gain the parenting skills they need to help their children. Surprisingly, increasing numbers of parents lack the parenting skills necessary for rearing children in the twenty-first century. Helping parents improves children's emotional and behavioral outcomes and enables families to provide sensitive, responsive care. In addition, good parenting techniques help curtail families' use of inconsistent and harsh discipline practices.

DIMENSIONS OF READINESS

Readiness for life and learning begins at birth and is affected and influenced by many factors.

IMPLICATIONS FOR TEACHING. Here are some things to keep in mind about the many dimensions of readiness:

- *Readiness is never ending.* Readiness is a continuum throughout life—the next life event is always just ahead, and the experiences children have today prepare them for the experiences of tomorrow.

- *All children are always ready for some kind of learning.* Children always need the experiences that promote learning and get them ready for the next step. The kind and quality of experiences children have—or don't have—influence their readiness for learning.

- *Schools and teachers are responsible for the education of each child.* Today, teachers don't play the blame game. They recognize that readiness is the responsibility of all. Schools should get ready for children and offer a curriculum and climate that allow for a full range of learning.

- *Readiness is individualized.* Three-, four-, and five-year-old children exhibit a range of abilities. Although all children are ready for learning, not all children are ready for learning the same thing at the same time, or in the same way.

- *Readiness is a function of culture.* You have to be sensitive to the fact that different cultures have different values regarding the purpose of school, the process of schooling, children's roles in the schooling process, and the roles of the family and culture in promoting readiness.

- *Readiness is a function of family income, maternal education, and parenting practices.*[24] Helping families get their children ready for school is as important as getting the children themselves ready for school.

- *Readiness involves the whole child.* Readiness includes physical well-being, positive social and emotional development, language development, cognitive development, and enthusiasm for learning.

approaches to learning
How children react to and engage in learning and activities associated with school.

APPROACHES TO LEARNING. Approaches to learning are the inclinations, dispositions, and learning styles necessary to interact effectively with the learning environment. Children will need to use approaches to learning if they are to be ready to move on to kindergarten.

Four-year-old Mario is working hard to complete a puzzle. The puzzle is harder than the ones Mario has previously worked on. Mario picks up a puzzle piece and looks at it and then scans the puzzle, trying to decide where it fits. Mario tries it one way. It doesn't fit. He turns the piece around and tries again. Yes! He is successful! Mario worked on the puzzle a long time. His teacher praises him, "Mario, you worked hard and you finished that puzzle."

Mario demonstrated that he has certain dispositions that will serve him well when he enters kindergarten. He's able to persist with a task, try something different when what he first tried did not work, and has the self-control necessary to pay attention. These dispositions are part of approaches to learning. Approaches to learning include the following:

1. *Curiosity/initiative.* The child chooses to engage and participate in a variety of new and challenging activities.
2. *Persistence.* The child is able to persist in and complete a variety of tasks and activities.
3. *Attention.* The child demonstrates increased attentiveness during teacher-directed activities.
4. *Self-direction.* The child is able to set goals, make choices, and manage time and effort with increased independence.
5. *Problem solving.* The child is able to solve problems in a number of ways, including finding more than one solution, exploration, and interactions with peers.
6. *Creativity.* The child is able to approach tasks with increased flexibility, imagination, and inventiveness.[25]

Check Your Understanding: Behavioral Skills

PLAY AND PRESCHOOL CHILDREN

Montessori thought of play as children's work and the home and preschool as workplaces where learning occurs through play. This comparison conveys the total absorption, dedication, energy, and focus children demonstrate through their play activities. They engage in play naturally and enjoy it; they do not select play activities because they intentionally set out to learn. They do not choose to put blocks in order from small to large because they want to learn how to seriate, nor do they build an incline because they want to learn the concept of *down* or the principles of gravity. However, the learning outcomes of such play are obvious.

Children's play is full of opportunities for learning, but there is no guarantee that children will learn through play all they need to know when they need to know it. Providing opportunities for children to choose among well-planned, varied learning activities enhances the probability that they will learn what they need to know through play.

PURPOSES OF PLAY

Children learn many things through play. Play activities are essential for their development across all developmental domains—the physical, social-emotional, cognitive, and linguistic. Play enables children to accomplish many things: Develop physical and social skills; develop literacy skills; practice language processes; enhance self-esteem; achieve knowledge, skills, and behaviors; learn concepts, prepare for adult life and roles (e.g., learn how to become independent, make decisions, and cooperate/collaborate with others); and master life situations.

Montessori said that play is children's work. The children in this picture are actively involved in building and constructing. Why is this type of activity an important part of the play process? What are some concepts these children are learning?

VALUE OF PLAY: LITERACY

Early childhood educators have long recognized the value of play for social, emotional, and physical development. Recently, however, play has achieved greater importance as a medium for literacy development. It is now recognized that literacy develops in meaningful, functional social settings rather than as a set of abstract skills taught in formal pencil-and-paper settings.

ENHANCING LITERACY. Literacy development involves a child's active engagement in cooperation and collaboration with peers; it builds on what the child already knows. Play provides this setting. During observation of children at play, especially in free-choice, cooperative play periods, you can note the functional uses of literacy that children incorporate into their play themes. When the environment is appropriately prepared with literacy materials in play areas, children engage in reading and writing activities in collaboration with other children.

To demonstrate how play in an appropriate setting can nurture literacy development, consider the following classroom setting in which the teacher has designed a veterinarian's office to go along with a class study on animals, focusing in particular on pets.

The dramatic play area is designed with a waiting room, including chairs; a table filled with magazines, books, and pamphlets about pet care; posters about pets; office hour notices; a No Smoking sign; and a sign advising visitors to check in with the nurse when arriving. On the nurse's desk are patient forms on clipboards, a telephone, an address and telephone book, appointment cards, and a calendar. The office contains patient folders, prescription pads, white coats, masks, gloves, a toy doctor's kit, and stuffed animals for patients.

SCAFFOLDING LITERACY ACTIVITIES. The teacher, Betty Meyers, guides students in using the various materials in the veterinarian's office during free-play time. For example, she reminds the children to read important information they find in the waiting area, to fill out forms about their pets' needs, to ask the nurse for appointment times, or to have the doctor write out appropriate treatments or prescriptions. In addition to giving support, Betty also models behaviors by participating in the play center with the children when she first introduces materials.

MATERIALS AND SETTINGS. When selecting settings to promote literacy in play, choose those that are familiar to children and relate them to themes. Suggestions for literacy materials and settings for the dramatic play areas include the following:

- A fast-food restaurant, ice cream store, or bakery includes menus, order pads, a cash register, specials for the day, recipes, and lists of flavors or products.

- A supermarket or local grocery store can include labeled shelves and sections, food containers, pricing labels, cash registers, telephones, shopping receipts, checkbooks, coupons, and promotional flyers.

- A post office to mail children's letters needs paper, envelopes, address books, pens, pencils, stamps, cash registers, and labeled mailboxes. A mail carrier hat and bag are important for children who deliver the mail, and they need to identify and read names and addresses.

- A gas station and car repair shop, designed in the block area, can have toy cars and trucks, receipts for sales, road maps for help with directions to different destinations, automotive tools and auto repair manuals for fixing cars and trucks, posters that advertise automobile equipment, and empty cans of different products typically found in service stations.[26]

KINDS OF PLAY

Children engage in many kinds of play: social, cognitive, informal, sociodramatic, outdoor, and rough-and-tumble.

SOCIAL PLAY.   Much of children's play occurs with or in the presence of other children. **Social play** occurs when children play with each other in groups. Mildred Parten, a children's play researcher, developed the most comprehensive description and classification of the types of social play, as follows.

- *Unoccupied play.* The child does not play with anything or anyone; the child merely stands or sits without doing anything observable.
- *Solitary play.* Although involved in play, the child plays alone, seemingly unaware of other children.
- *Onlooker play.* The child watches and observes the play of other children; the center of interest is others' play.
- *Parallel play.* The child plays alone, but in ways and with toys or other materials similar to the play of other children.
- *Associative play.* Children interact with each other, perhaps by asking questions or sharing materials, but do not play together.
- *Cooperative play.* Children actively play together, often as a result of the organization of the teacher.[27]

Social play supports many important functions. It provides the means for children to interact with others and learn many social skills. Play provides a context in which children learn how to compromise ("OK, I'll be the baby first, and you can be the mommy"), learn to be flexible, resolve conflicts, and continue the process of learning who they are. Children also learn what skills they have, such as those relating to leadership. In addition, social play provides a vehicle for practicing and developing literacy skills; children have others with whom to practice language and learn. And social play helps children learn impulse control; they realize they cannot always do whatever they want. Finally, social play negates isolation and helps children learn how to have the social interactions so vital to successful living.

COGNITIVE PLAY.   Froebel, Montessori, and Piaget all recognized the cognitive value of play. Froebel through his gifts and occupations and Montessori through her sensory materials saw children's active participation with concrete materials as a direct link to knowledge and development. Piaget's theory influences contemporary thinking about the cognitive basis for play; from a Piagetian perspective, play is literally cognitive development.

INFORMAL PLAY.   Proponents of learning through **informal play,** or **free play,** activities maintain that learning is best when it occurs spontaneously in an environment that contains people and materials with which children can interact. Learning materials may be grouped in centers—a kitchen center, a dress-up center, a block center, a music and art center, a water or sand area, and an outdoor climbing area—usually with items such as tricycles and wagons that are good for promoting large-muscle development.

The atmosphere of this kind of preschool setting tends to approximate a home setting, in which learning is informal, unstructured, and unpressured. Talk and interactions with adults are spontaneous. Play and learning episodes are generally determined by the interests of the children and, to some extent, teachers, based on what they think is best for children. The expected learning outcomes are socialization, emotional development, self-control, and acclimation to a school setting.

social play Play of children with others and in groups.

informal (free) play Play in which children participate in activities of interest to them.

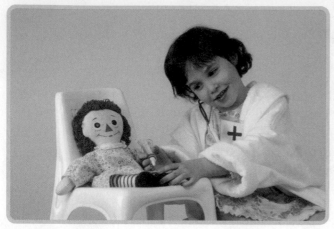

Dramatic play promotes children's understanding of concepts and processes. Here, play allows children to explore their feelings and ideas about medical practitioners and medical settings.

sociodramatic play Play involving realistic activities and events.

fantasy play Play involving unrealistic notions and superheroes.

In a quality program of free play, both indoors and outdoors, teachers are active participants. Sometimes they observe, sometimes they play with the children, sometimes they help the children, but they never intrude or impose. When well-managed, the free-play format enables children to learn many things as they interact with interesting activities, materials, and people in their environment.

SOCIODRAMATIC PLAY. Dramatic or *pretend play* allows children to participate vicariously in a wide range of activities associated with family living, society, and cultural heritage. Dramatic play is generally of two kinds: **Sociodramatic play** usually involves everyday realistic activities and events, whereas **fantasy play** typically involves fairy-tale and superhero play. Dramatic play centers often include areas such as housekeeping, dress-up, occupations, dolls, school, and other situations that follow children's interests. Skillful teachers think of many ways to expand children's interests and then replace old centers with new ones. For example, after a visit to the police station, a housekeeping center might be replaced with an occupations center.

In sociodramatic play, children have an opportunity to express themselves, assume different roles, and interact with their peers. Sociodramatic play centers thus act as a nonsexist and multicultural arena in which all children are equal.

OUTDOOR PLAY.   Children's outside play is just as important as their inside play. Children need to relieve stress and tension through play, and outdoor activities provide this opportunity. However, plan for what children will do and what equipment will be available; outdoor play is not an opportunity for children to run wild.

Children at the Grove School planted over twenty different types of vegetable and herb seeds in the planting beds. Rain barrel water and compost and worm bin fertilizer help children nurture a healthy harvest ready for sampling and donating! The outdoor play area also includes turf grass, shaded areas, a greenhouse, and an outdoor classroom sand pit with water.[28]

Outdoor environments and activities promote large- and small-muscle development and body coordination as well as language development, social interaction, and creativity for all children. Plan to make your playground a learning environment.

Many teachers also enjoy bringing the indoor learning environment outdoors, using easels, play dough, or dramatic play props to further enhance learning opportunities. In addition, taking a group of children outdoors for story or music time, sitting in the shade of a tree, brings a fresh perspective to daily group activities. As with indoor activities, provisions for outdoor play involve planning, supervising, and helping children be responsible for their behavior.

Adapting Outdoor Play for Children with Disabilities. Here are some ways you can adapt your outdoor space to accommodate children with disabilities.

- Position a child with physical challenges to achieve maximum range of motion, muscle control, and visual contact with materials and other children. A child might need to lie on his or her side or use a bolster to access materials and interact with other children during activities such as gardening and painting.
- Furnish specifically adapted play and recreation equipment when necessary. This might include modified swings, tricycles, and tables to accommodate independent participation in activities.

- Encourage the children to use their own means of getting around—whether a wheelchair, walker, or scooter—to participate in the activities and games of other children.
- For a child with limited use of hands and upper body, provide activities for the lower body and feet, such as foot painting, splashing in a wading pool, digging in the garden or sand, and kicking a ball.
- For a child with limited use of feet, legs, and lower body, provide activities such as painting, water table, sandbox, and gardening, which the child can do independently and successfully with the upper body. Always ensure correct positioning of the child's torso.
- Increase the width of balance beams and modify slippery surfaces to support better balance.
- Use softer balls (e.g., foam balls) or lightweight objects to facilitate throwing and catching when a child lacks strength or endurance.
- Use large balls (e.g., beach balls) and other large objects to make catching easier for a child who is unable to grasp smaller objects.[29]

ROUGH-AND-TUMBLE PLAY.   All children, to a greater or lesser degree, engage in rough-and-tumble play. One theory says that children play because they are biologically programmed to do so; that is, it is part of children's genetic heritage to engage in play activities. Indeed, there is a parallel between children's rough-and-tumble play and behaviors in the animal kingdom—for example, run-and-chase activities and pretend fighting. Rough-and-tumble play activities enable children to learn how to lead and follow, develop physical skills, interact with other children in different ways, and grow in their abilities to be part of a larger group.

TEACHERS' ROLES IN PROMOTING PLAY

You are the key to promoting meaningful play in early childhood programs. What you do and your attitudes toward play determine the quality of the preschool environment and play events. For example, the accompanying Voice from the Field, "Using Blocks to Help Preschoolers Build Mathematical Skills," demonstrates how you can use block play to help children meet preschool math standards.

As far as possible, implement the curriculum through play. Integrate specific learning activities with play to achieve specific learning outcomes. Play activities should match children's developmental needs and be free of gender and cultural stereotypes. Be clear about curriculum concepts and ideas you want children to learn through play.

Providing a safe and healthy environment is an important role that applies to the playground as well as to inside facilities. Outdoor areas should be safe for children to play in. Usually, states and cities have regulations requiring a playground to be fenced and have a source of drinking water, a minimum number of square feet of play area for each child, and equipment that is in good repair. Careful child supervision is a cornerstone of playground safety.

Play is an important part of children's lives and the early childhood curriculum. You and others need to honor, support, and provide many opportunities for children to play.

THE NEW PRESCHOOL: CURRICULUM, GUIDELINES, AND GOALS

Today's preschool is not the preschool of yesterday. Much has changed in how preschools operate and what is expected of children.

COMPETENCY BUILDER

Using Blocks to Help Preschoolers Build Mathematical Skills

Froebel, the father of kindergarten, introduced blocks to the early childhood curriculum with his creation of gifts. Froebel developed these materials to facilitate children's creativity and provide opportunities for them to construct geometric forms. Many preschool classrooms today have a block center or area dedicated to block play. These play areas include a variety of blocks that vary in size, shape, color, and texture. When children have time to explore and experiment with these resources, they have the opportunity to develop the foundation for mathematical concepts related to algebra, geometry, and measurement.

When including blocks in the early childhood mathematics classroom, consider the following ideas.

STEP 1 Use a Variety of Instructional Approaches

- Give children time to explore freely with blocks during center time as well as other times during the day. Providing opportunities for free play allows children to develop various intuitive geometric concepts and problem-solving skills while tapping into their innate mathematical interest about the world around them.
- Informally guide children's individual block play to help them connect prior learning experiences or deepen their understanding of a concept. Pose questions about the children's play to provoke mathematical conversations. For example, when a child sorts blocks into different groups, ask the child about these groupings with questions such as:
  - Why did you put these blocks together?
  - What other blocks could you put into this group?
  - What is the name of this group?
- Use blocks in small group or whole group instruction to introduce or review mathematical concepts such as counting or identifying various shapes.

STEP 2 Provide Children with Different Types of Blocks to Explore

Incorporate a variety of manipulatives—including different types of blocks—for young children to use in the preschool classroom. Providing these materials will allow children to explore mathematical concepts such as sorting, patterns, measurement, and geometry. The accompanying table lists some of the common types of blocks used in preschool classrooms and some of the mathematical concepts children develop when using these materials.

Type of Block	Mathematical Concepts	Examples
Building/architect blocks	Patterns, sorting, geometry, measurement, spatial relationships, counting	Children will build various structures with these materials. Consider playing an "I Spy" type of game where children find different shapes in their creations.
Pattern blocks	Patterns, sorting, geometry, measurement, spatial relationships, counting	Children can practice making patterns with these blocks or creating "new" shapes.
Snap cubes	Patterns, sorting, measurement, counting	Children can use blocks to determine the length/width of various objects in the room.

Type of Block	Mathematical Concepts	Examples
Color tiles	Patterns, sorting, measurement, counting	Children might use these blocks to measure objects in the classroom or to start thinking about how many color tiles might cover a certain object in the classroom (area).
Tangrams	Patterns, sorting, geometry, measurement, spatial relationships, counting	Provide children with opportunities to create "new" shapes with tangrams. Children can trace the perimeter of these designs and have friends try to create their new shapes.
Three-dimensional geometric models	Patterns, sorting, geometry, measurement, counting	These solids not only provide examples of various three-dimensional shapes, but also allow children different types of materials to sort.
Color cubes	Patterns, sorting, measurement, counting	Children can use these cubes to start understanding the concept of capacity. For instance, have children explore how many cubes different objects in the classroom can hold.
Attribute blocks	Patterns, sorting, geometry, measurement, counting	Children can practice sorting these blocks into various groups. Allow children to develop groups and labels instead of telling them to sort by color or by shape. Children will develop groupings that are more interesting with this flexibility.

(Continued)

STEP 3 — Ask Children a Variety of Questions

It is important to ask children thought-provoking questions that will allow them to explore a variety of mathematical concepts. Asking children questions about their block structures not only provides them with the opportunity to engage in mathematical conversations about their work, but also gives you the occasion to explore children's mathematical knowledge. For example, if a preschooler made a pattern using pattern blocks, you might ask the following questions:

- Tell me about your creation. What did you make? (Give the child an opportunity to use his or her words to describe the blocks.)
- What type of pattern did you make?
- If I wanted to add to your pattern, what blocks would I have to use?
- Is there a block that looks the same as the three green triangles?

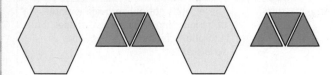

As you ask these questions, encourage children to use their own words to describe their work. Also, verify your understanding of the child's descriptions, as demonstrated below.

Ms. Jones: What type of pattern did you make?
Alicia: We used one yellow block and then three green blocks.
Ms. Jones: So you used one yellow hexagon and three green triangles, and then another yellow hexagon and three green triangles?
Mason and Alicia: Yes.

Providing children with opportunities to explore and construct with blocks helps lay the foundation for future mathematical success. These experiences not only allow children to deepen their understanding of algebra, geometry, and measurement, but they also offer children time to practice their problem-solving skills. In addition, children will engage in meaningful mathematical conversations with their peers and their teacher.

Source: Contributed by Elisabeth Johnston, assistant professor in the Department of Elementary and Early Childhood Education at Slippery Rock University, Slippery Rock, Pennsylvania. Her current research relates to how preschool teachers can support young children's mathematical development. Elisabeth taught second grade at a gifted and talented magnet school for six years in Texas, where she was responsible for teaching math to a diverse group of second graders.

ACCOMMODATING DIVERSE LEARNERS

typically developing The majority of developmental milestones at the time at which most young children achieve them without deficits in social or communication areas.

Meet Han Ling. Preschool is her first opportunity to go to school. Han Ling is **typically developing** (meaning that she reaches the majority of developmental milestones at the appropriate time and does not have deficits in social areas) and enjoys coloring, story time, and playing on the swing set outside. In preschool, Han Ling must learn the rules of a more structured environment, such as sitting for longer periods of time, and she must learn pre-math and language skills. With so much to teach her, it is easy to forget that Han Ling's first job as a preschool-aged child is play. Play is the true language of children. It is how they learn social norms, hone peer interactions, express their emotions, engage in their environment, and learn problem solving. However, play does not always erupt spontaneously.

IMPLICATIONS FOR TEACHING. Here are some tips to encourage Han Ling in play:

- Provide different play opportunities by arranging your room in centers. Block centers with blocks of varying weights and sizes, dramatic play centers with dress-up clothes, home centers with pretend food and cooking appliances, and manipulative centers with toys such as dolls, action figures, or cars are just a few examples of centers that elicit play.
- Change out your centers as you rotate your units. For example, if you are in a transportation unit, put toy boats, bicycles, cars, trucks, and trains in the manipulative center. Your students will begin to act out and internalize the information you've given them in their play.

292

- Start a rotation of three or four children grouped by their personalities, strengths, and weakness for each center. Don't put students in a center by themselves. Play is a wonderful opportunity to help Han Ling learn social skills and problem solving, which is much more difficult to do solo. It is natural and acceptable for centers and the children in them to occasionally blend into one another.
  - When children repeatedly combine, like the block center with the manipulative center or the home center and the dress-up center, go ahead and combine them. This may make your groups larger but also more vibrant and conducive to greater social skill building.
  - Move children into different groups. You may not find the perfect group for every child right away.
- Play! For most children, play comes naturally, but for some, especially if they are unfamiliar with the toys or the other children, have high anxiety, or if they are developmentally delayed, may not readily engage in play. You notice that Han Ling seems unsure and doesn't participate very much. To help Han Ling, do the following:
  - Choose similar or complementary toys. If Han Ling has a mommy doll, you pick up the daddy doll and the baby doll. Once you show interest, Han Ling will likely take the initiative and tell you what part to play or what to say. Let her lead you, and don't ask too many direct questions.
  - If Han Ling does not take the initiative in play, you can ask for directions in a roundabout way, saying, "Hmm, I'm not sure which one to be, the dad or the baby. . . ." She will likely take the lead and tell you what role to take.
  - To begin a play sequence, start with a scenario that Han Ling will be familiar with, like fixing breakfast or going to the grocery store. Once she is on familiar ground, Han Ling may become more directive and steer the pretending in other directions.
- Use play as an opportunity to observe your students. Through their play, they are communicating to you their strengths and weaknesses, their home lives, relationships, fears and insecurities, as well as greatest joys and interests. Use this information to become a better teacher for them.
- Remember that play is a way children "work things out," explore, and communicate.

So, if Han Ling uses language or acts out behavior that is overly aggressive or abusive, make a note of the situation, time, and date. Report it to the school counselor and your principal. Ask them whether you should notify the family or Child Protective Services. Play can be an adventure for both Han Ling and for you. If you accommodate play in your classroom, both you and your students will learn a lot and enjoy the school day.

Increasingly, the responsibility for setting the preschool curriculum is being taken over by state departments of education through **guidelines** (or **standards**), statements of what students should know and be able to do. Typically preschool standards are called guidelines because states do not require preschool attendance. Now would be a good time to access your state's preschool guidelines. Keep these in mind as you prepare preschool curricula and lesson plans. The feature "Planning and Teaching: Lesson Plans for Preschoolers," is a great example of how Shannon Keller uses her state's preschool guidelines to plan for her preschoolers.

guidelines (standards)
Preschool statements of what children should know and be able to do.

PRESCHOOL GOALS

As preschool programs have grown in number and popularity over the last decade, they have also changed in purpose. Traditional purposes of preschool are to socialize children, enhance their social-emotional development, and prepare them for kindergarten and first grade. A second purpose of preschools is to teach basic academic skills related to literacy, math, and science. In addition, preschools are now promoted as places to accomplish numerous goals including the following:

- *Support and develop children's innate capacity for learning.* Preschool programs seek to develop in children an interest in and love of learning as early in life as possible. Brain research clearly shows that birth to age five is a critical time for learning.[30]

- *Deliver a full range of health, social, economic, and academic services to children and families.* Indeed, family well-being is considered a justification for operating preschools; in fact, increasingly, preschool education is seen as a family affair.

- *Close achievement gaps.* Closing the *achievement gap* that exists between white and African American and Hispanic students is a high priority for the United States and the early childhood profession. In fact, the achievement gap may be a *preparation gap.* Many children enter kindergarten without the skills they need—from identifying colors to not being able to sit still. They have a hard time playing catch-up.[31]

- *Educate children for the global world of tomorrow.* The United States wants to continue to be a world leader. A well-educated workforce helps achieve this goal, and the preparation of a well-educated workforce begins in preschool.[32]

Given the popularity of and reasons for preschools, it is little wonder that the preschool years are playing a larger role in early childhood education and will continue to do so.

ACADEMICS.   As academics play a more central role in preschool curricula, some key areas of knowledge include these:

- Names, addresses, and phone numbers (including their own)
- Colors, sizes, shapes, and positions such as *under*, *over*, and *around*
- Numbers and prewriting skills, shape identification, letter recognition, sounds, and rhyming
- Simple sentence structure
- Simple addition and subtraction
- Ways to handle a book[33]

CHARACTER EDUCATION.   Many schools and school districts identify, with parents' help, the character traits they want all students to demonstrate. Children need multiple opportunities to learn about and demonstrate character traits such as positive mental attitude, persistence, respect for others, cooperation, honesty, trustworthiness, and sensitivity.

Kim Gorka develops community-mindedness in her young children at Children's Palace Preschool and Childcare. The children complete a different theme every week and, in December, the children volunteer. Everyone brings in a wrapped gift for "a friend we don't know," and the children give all the presents to New Horizons Shelter and Women's Center. The children just love this, and Gorka feels it's one of the best things they do. It is a good way to teach children the joys of not getting anything out of it except the feeling of being a good person.[34]

MUSIC AND THE ARTS.   Brain research supports the use of music and the arts to encourage learning in all areas. Preschoolers can learn about music and the arts in many ways:

- Varied materials (e.g., crayons, paint, clay, markers) to create original work
- Different colors, surface textures, and shapes to create form and meaning

LESSON PLANS

Lesson Planning in the Preschool

PLANNING AND TEACHING: LESSON PLANS FOR PRESCHOOLERS

Planning for teaching is a lot like planning for a trip: There are certain essential steps you should follow if you want children to learn new things and for them and you to have a good time!

- Identifying goals and objectives for teaching and learning is like identifying your destination (e.g., New York City).
- Selecting the methods you will use is like deciding how you are going to get to New York—by car, bus, train, or plane.
- Selecting the materials you will need is similar to selecting what you will need on your trip—clothing, suitcase, tickets, maps.
- Selecting specific activities is like selecting what you will do when you get to New York—walk in Central Park, visit Chinatown, or zip to the top of the Empire State Building.
- Evaluation and assessment come into play after you have taught your lesson, just as you would assess whether you had a good time on your trip.

    Here are four steps to follow:

STEP 1

Identify the Goals and Objectives of Your Lesson

You may find goals and objectives already selected for you in state or local standards.

    Your lesson will need to address all of the goals in an integrated way. Remember, however, that although state standards set goals, you have the creativity to teach your way using your professional knowledge, talents, and abilities.

STEP 2

Select the Materials You Will Need

Compile a list of materials that you will need to execute the activity. Are the materials safe and developmentally appropriate?

STEP 3

Select Activities and Adapt Them for Individual Needs

As you develop activities, keep in mind children's prior knowledge, their cultural backgrounds, and their individual and collective interests, and use them as a basis for your activities.

STEP 4

Assessment/Evaluation

Determine how you will assess what your children learned. Relate your assessment to the standards and your lesson plan objectives. Here is how Shannon Keller plans for her preschool children. Notice how Shannon achieves the four steps discussed above.

IT ALL "QUACKS" UP

(2- to 3-day lesson on addition)

IDENTIFY GOALS AND OBJECTIVES

2008 Texas Prekindergarten Guidelines V.A. 8: Child uses concrete models or makes verbal word problems for adding up to five objects

(Continued)

Focus

The teacher will model for students how to join objects together. The students will then practice joining (adding) objects together and create their own verbal word problem regarding addition by stating "2 ducks and 1 more duck makes 3 ducks."

SELECT THE MATERIALS YOU WILL NEED

Materials

- *Little Quack* by Lauren Thompson (published by Simon & Schuster)
- 5 rubber ducks
- 5 duck erasers (counters) for each pair of students
- 1 pond story mat (1/2 sheet of blue construction paper) for each pair of students

SELECT THE ACTIVITIES AND ADAPT THEM FOR INDIVIDUAL NEEDS

Vocabulary

join—to put objects together
adding—joining quantities

Activity

The teacher will share the story *Little Quack* with students. After reading the story, the teacher chooses five students to help her retell the story and to model how to join objects together using rubber ducks. The teacher groups students into pairs. The teacher will give each student pair a pond story mat and five duck counters. The teacher retells the story of *Little Quack* while students act the story out on the pond story mat. The teacher checks for understanding and knowledge using the questions below. Student pairs will be encouraged to create a story problem for joining. Allow student pairs to share their problems and continue with questioning.

ASSESSMENT/EVALUATION

Quality Questions

- *Knowledge:* What kind of animal is Little Quack?
- *Comprehension:* What happened to the ducks in the story?
- *Application:* Did Little Quack and his brothers and sisters jump in the pond at the same time? Can you show how the ducks got in the pond?
- *Analysis:* Why do you think the group of ducks in the pond grew bigger?
- *Synthesis:* What would have happened to the number of ducks in the pond if Little Quack didn't join his brothers and sisters?
- *Evaluation:* What did you like about this book and activity? Why?
- *Evaluation Option:* Informally assess student's knowledge of joining objects together (addition) by having students illustrate the problem they created on a piece of paper. Look to see if students were able to draw a picture of two groups of objects and a picture of both groups joined into one large group. This form of evaluation allows the teacher the opportunity to see which students understand the concept of joining objects.

Source: Contributed by Shannon Keller, former preschool and kindergarten teacher at Curtsinger Elementary, Frisco, Texas. Shannon now teaches third grade.

- Art as a form of self-expression
- Music activities, including varieties of simple songs and movement to various tempos
- Dramatic play with others

For example, Love A Lot Preschool in New York City offers music and piano classes for their students. Music and movement classes for preschools provide an outlet for creative energy in which the children learn to read music through individual and group lessons and sing songs and finger-plays.[35]

WELLNESS AND HEALTHY LIVING. When children are not healthy, they cannot achieve their best. Helping children learn healthy habits will help them do well in school. Healthy habits include the following:

- Good nutritional practices, including a balanced menu and essential nutrients
- Trying new foods
- Management of personal belongings such as keeping track of one's possessions
- Ability to dress oneself appropriately
- Personal hygiene, such as washing one's hands and wiping one's nose

For example, Nobel Learning Communities' preschools throughout the nation have implemented the "New Physical Education" early childhood program, which emphasizes physical activity, teaching good nutrition, reducing health risks, and introducing movement into the early stages of development. The "New PE" classes are more inclusive, active, and fun than traditional physical education programs, and they engage students through the use of energetic music, toys, and bright colors.[36]

We want children to be involved in child-initiated and active learning. These children wanted to make pudding after the teacher read *Geronimo Stilton's Cookbook*. What are some things children can learn by making and eating pudding?

LITERACY IN THE PRESCHOOL

Emergent literacy means children's communication skills are in an emerging state—in the process of developing.[37] Teachers and parents can support emergent literacy in preschool children not only by reading *to* them, but also by reading with them and encouraging their participation in the process of reading. One of the ways to support children's involvement is by supporting and encouraging their **modes of response**, the various ways they respond to learning, activities, and materials.

Elisabeth Epstein reads a book on seals to her children and then engages them in activities such as jumping like seals, pretend swimming, drawing pictures of seals, and comparing what seals eat to what other animals eat.

Emergent literacy also involves writing. Remember it was Montessori who said that writing comes before reading. For many children, writing becomes a pathway, a stepping stone, a scaffold for emerging into reading.

LANGUAGE. Language is the most important readiness skill. Children need language skills for success in both school and life. Important language skills include *receptive language*, such as listening to the teacher and following directions; *expressive language*, demonstrated in the ability to talk fluently and articulately with teachers

emergent literacy
Children's communication skills are in an emerging state; in the process of developing.

modes of response The various ways children respond to books and conversations.

and peers, to express oneself in the language of the school, and to communicate needs and ideas; and *symbolic language*, knowing the names of people, places, and things as well as words for concepts and adjectives and prepositions. Knowledge of the letters of the alphabet and vocabulary are two of the most important factors in being able to read.[38] These crucial readiness skills are especially critical for children from linguistically diverse backgrounds and for children with disabilities or delays in speech and/or language.

Conventional Literacy Skills. Conventional literacy skills refer to such skills as decoding (turning written words into spoken words), oral reading fluency, reading comprehension, writing, and spelling. The use of these skills is evident within all literacy practices, and they are readily recognizable as being necessary or useful components of literacy.[39]

Conventional reading and writing skills developed in the years from birth to age five years have a clear and consistently strong relationship with later conventional literacy skills. Six variables have medium to large predictive relationships with later measures of literacy development.[40] These are the following:

- **Alphabetic knowledge (AK)**: Knowledge of the names and sounds associated with printed letters.
- **Phonological awareness (PA)**: The ability to detect, manipulate, or analyze the auditory aspects of spoken language (including the ability to distinguish or segment words, syllables, or phonemes), independent of meaning.
- **Rapid automatic naming (RAN) of letters or digits**: The ability to rapidly name a sequence of random letters or digits.
- **Rapid automatic naming (RAN) of objects or colors**: The ability to rapidly name a sequence of repeating random sets of pictures of objects (e.g., "car," "tree," "house," "man") or colors.
- **Writing or writing name**: The ability to write letters in isolation on request or to write one's own name.
- **Phonological memory (PM)**: The ability to remember spoken information for a short period of time.[41]

An additional five early literacy skills are also important and show a moderate relation to later literacy success. These include the following:[42]

- Concepts about print: knowledge of print conventions (e.g., left-right, front-back) and concepts (book cover, author, text)
- Print knowledge: a combination of elements of AK, concepts about print, and early decoding
- Reading readiness: usually a combination of AK, concepts of print, vocabulary, memory, and PA
- Oral language: the ability to produce or comprehend spoken language, including vocabulary and grammar
- Visual processing: the ability to match or discriminate visually presented symbols

SUPPORTING ENGLISH LANGUAGE LEARNERS' LANGUAGE AND LITERACY SKILLS

Greater numbers of children of immigrants are entering preschools today. Here are some things you can do to support English Language Learners (ELLs) in five important literacy domains. As you review these activities, consider how you can apply them to your classroom teaching.

---

conventional literacy skills Skills such as decoding (turning written words into spoken words), oral reading fluency, reading comprehension, writing, and spelling.

alphabetic knowledge (AK) Knowledge of the names and sounds associated with printed letters.

phonological awareness (PA) The ability to detect, manipulate, or analyze the auditory aspects of spoken language (including the ability to distinguish or segment words, syllables, or phonemes), independent of meaning.

rapid automatic naming (RAN) of letters or digits The ability to rapidly name a sequence of random letters or digits.

rapid automatic naming (RAN) of objects or colors The ability to rapidly name a sequence of repeating random sets of pictures of objects (e.g., "car," "tree," "house," "man") or colors.

writing or writing name The ability to write letters in isolation on request or to write one's own name.

phonological memory (PM) The ability to remember spoken information for a short period of time.

Alphabetic knowledge: *Activities that target letter recognition.* Comparing alphabets or writing systems in other languages.

* Take an alphabet walk around the school, and look for letters in the environment.
* Place children in groups of four or five, and have them use their bodies to form letters.
* Divide the class in half, and give one half lowercase letter cards and the other half matching uppercase cards. Have the children find their matches.
* Teach Spanish-speaking students a song of the English alphabet.

Phonological awareness: *Activities that emphasize the sounds that make up words.* Presenting the sounds of other languages to make words.

* Word-to-word matching: Do *pen* and *pipe* begin with the same sound?
* Sound isolation: What is the first sound in *rose*?
* Odd word out: Which word starts with a different sound—*bag, nine, beach, bike*?

Book and print concepts: *Activities that show how books look and how they work.* Show how books have covers and front and back pages. Show that letters make up words.

* Leave multiple pieces of familiar text posted in the room at children's eye level, available for them to be read independently.
* Use magnetic letters, word tiles, and name cards to emphasize similarities and differences between words and letters.

book and print concepts Activities that show how books look and how they work.

Vocabulary knowledge: *Activities that emphasize words and their meaning.* Emphasizing that there are words in other languages that mean the same things as words in English.

* Give each student a card with one word on it, and have them form two circles, one inside the other. When the teacher calls out "inside" or "outside," the students in that circle show their cards to the students in front of or behind them, who must come up with the definitions. The circles then rotate to make new partners.[43]

vocabulary knowledge Activities that emphasize words and their meanings.

Discourse skills: *Activities that encourage telling stories, explaining how the world works, building a fantasy world using English.* Demonstrating that other languages have similar forms although they may seem a bit different.

* Discuss the storyline of short DVDs, and point out characters, scenes, and time changes; review the story periodically.
* Play guessing games like I Spy, and have students give specific clues about a hidden object or picture.[44]

discourse skills Activities that encourage telling stories and explaining how the world works.

Bilingual preschool teacher Monica Gil offers these best practices for use with ELLs.

BEST PRACTICE 1. Involve parents in their children's education as early and thoroughly as you can. At your first parent meeting, discuss opportunities for parental involvement!

Parents are the biggest influence for promoting learning and success in education. My colleagues and I find that students with the most aptitude come from homes where parents are actively engaged in their children's lives and who value education.

Educate parents to recognize that playtime can be used as learning time. Send weekly newsletters home outlining what students will study in class and suggest ways they can expand on them at home. Simple activities, such as counting the blocks she plays with or observing growing plants, will greatly enhance their child's capacity to learn.

BEST PRACTICE 2.   Set high expectations.

Most preschool students are naturally ready to learn and experience new ideas. Always consider children's undeveloped differences and attitudes. Truly believe in your students! You must absolutely know that each and every one can learn! Make modifications and differentiate each lesson you teach. When you expect the very best from your students, they can and will rise to the challenge.

BEST PRACTICE 3.   Incorporate collaborative learning.

Form small learning groups or pairs. First, learning groups enable you to create advanced critical thinking opportunities for the students in your classroom. After all, two (or more) thinking minds are better than one! Second, most students are eager and excited to talk and work with their classmates. Students achieve greater success with a challenging curriculum while also gaining the essential groundwork for working as part of a team. Collaborative problem solving becomes a gratifying and invigorating part of the day.

BEST PRACTICE 4.   Assess students often.

One of your duties is to determine each child's knowledge base from the moment they enter your classroom. To maximize learning potential, comprehensively assess students throughout the day, week, and year. Use data from these assessments to direct both whole group and individual instruction. Use your assessment information to intentionally plan and differentiate your instruction.

BEST PRACTICE 5.   Use visuals and movement.

Teaching young children requires a great amount of energy. Reading becomes a highly expressive skill. Make books of all genres (fiction and nonfiction) come to life. Visuals and movement also provide a basis for comprehension. Students can easily grasp and internalize the concepts using visual aids because they provide a clear and functional understanding in a meaningful way.

BEST PRACTICE 6.   Build word walls.

Use word walls. ELLs are learning two languages at once so it is important to provide them with a rich academic vocabulary. Having a large vocabulary in a native language helps students learn another language more easily.

Providing a print-rich environment through word walls and labeling helps students across a range of reading levels. Emergent readers benefit by understanding that print conveys a message. Advanced readers build their vocabulary by having the word resources in the classroom. Regularly replacing words on the wall naturally introduces and familiarizes students with hundreds of words. Reading, writing, and comprehension develop rapidly!

Check Your Understanding: Literacy Skills

THE DAILY SCHEDULE

What should a preschool day be like? Although a daily schedule depends on many things—your philosophy, the needs of children, parents' beliefs, and state and local standards—the following suggestions illustrate what you can do on a typical preschool day. Because an important preschool trend is toward full-day

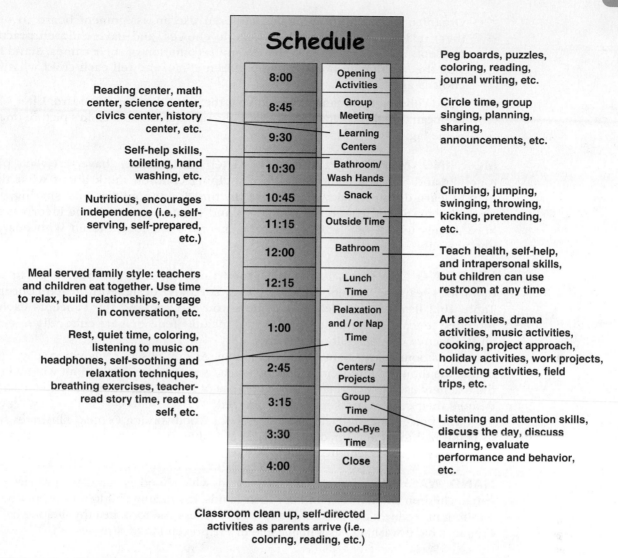

Reading center, math center, science center, civics center, history center, etc.

Self-help skills, toileting, hand washing, etc.

Nutritious, encourages independence (i.e., self-serving, self-prepared, etc.)

Meal served family style: teachers and children eat together. Use time to relax, build relationships, engage in conversation, etc.

Rest, quiet time, coloring, listening to music on headphones, self-soothing and relaxation techniques, breathing exercises, teacher-read story time, read to self, etc.

Peg boards, puzzles, coloring, reading, journal writing, etc.

Circle time, group singing, planning, sharing, announcements, etc.

Climbing, jumping, swinging, throwing, kicking, pretending, etc.

Teach health, self-help, and intrapersonal skills, but children can use restroom at any time

Art activities, drama activities, music activities, cooking, project approach, holiday activities, work projects, collecting activities, field trips, etc.

Listening and attention skills, discuss the day, discuss learning, evaluate performance and behavior, etc.

Schedule

8:00	Opening Activities
8:45	Group Meeting
9:30	Learning Centers
10:30	Bathroom/ Wash Hands
10:45	Snack
11:15	Outside Time
12:00	Bathroom
12:15	Lunch Time
1:00	Relaxation and / or Nap Time
2:45	Centers/ Projects
3:15	Group Time
3:30	Good-Bye Time
4:00	Close

Classroom clean up, self-directed activities as parents arrive (i.e., coloring, reading, etc.)

FIGURE 10.2 | Sample of a Daily Schedule

and full-year programs, this preschool schedule is for a whole-day program as shown in Figure 10.2.

OPENING ACTIVITIES. As children enter, greet each child individually. Daily personal greetings make children feel important, build a positive attitude toward school, and provide an opportunity for them to practice language skills. Greetings also give you a chance to check each child's health and emotional status. Greeting time is a nice opportunity to incorporate "greetings from around the world," which could reflect the diversity of children and families in the program.

Children usually do not arrive all at one time, so the first arrivals need something to do while others are arriving:

- Offer free selection of activities or let children self-select from a limited range of quiet activities (such as puzzles, journals to write in, or markers to color with).

- Organize arrival time by having children use an assignment board to help them make choices. Limit the available choices, and have children practice concepts such as colors and shapes and recognition of their names. Stand beside the assignment board when children come, and tell each child what the choices are.
- Hand children their name tags and help them put them on the board. Later, children can find their own tags and put them up. Include each child's picture on the name tag.

MORNING MEETING/PLANNING. After all children have arrived, plan together and talk about the day ahead, helping children think about what they plan to learn during the day. This is also the time for announcements, sharing, and group songs. Songs from other languages and cultures can easily be incorporated here. Songs using sign language can be incorporated for children with hearing impairments.

LEARNING CENTERS. After the group time, children are free to go to one of various learning centers, which are organized and designed to teach concepts. Table 10.2 lists types of learning centers you can use and the concepts each is intended to teach. Learning centers should include items that are culturally relevant and reflective of a diversity of cultures.

Classroom space is always at a premium. As you observe this video, pay attention to the thoughtful ways in which the teachers use space. Think about what criteria the teachers used to determine their "good use of space." Determine how the teachers defined their centers and kept them organized.

The Voice from the Field, "The Preschool Woodworking Center," illustrates how to make real tools and building materials available. Be sure to provide goggles and other precautions for children's safety.

HAND WASHING. Before any activity in which food is handled, prepared, or eaten, children should wash and dry their hands. Instructing children in proper hand-washing procedures can prevent the spread of illness and form healthy lifelong habits. Frequent hand washing has a major role in the prevention of diseases.

SNACKS. Provide a nutritionally sound and culturally relevant snack that the children can serve (and often prepare) themselves. You will need to find out whether any children have food allergies, such as to peanuts, which can cause serious health risks. More programs at all levels emphasize healthy and organic snacks. For example, Crawmer's Critterz Preschool believes nutrition provided without additives, chemicals, and coloring benefits children as they grow and strive to be the best they can be! Meals that are made from whole foods, not premade or frozen, provide their students with extra nutrition that students with packed meals just miss out on. Crawmer's Critterz prides themselves on cooking tasty meals from scratch that their kids love.[45]

OUTDOOR ACTIVITY/PLAY/WALKING. Help children practice climbing, jumping, swinging, throwing, and using body control. Incorporate walking trips and other events into outdoor play. Outdoor play is becoming a much more important part of the preschool curriculum and program.

BATHROOM/TOILETING. Bathroom/toileting times offer opportunities to teach health, self-help, and intrapersonal skills. Children should also be allowed to use the bathroom whenever necessary.

TABLE 10.2 | Types of Classroom Learning Centers

Theme-Based Centers	Concepts
Use theme centers as an extension of classroom themes: • Space • Dinosaurs • The Ocean • All About Me • My Family Generally a classroom theme lasts for 1–2 weeks and occasionally longer. Children can use theme centers for varying amounts of time from 15 to 30 minutes and during their free time.	• Use language skills, participate in sociodramatic play, verbalization. • Identify role(s) as a family member. • Cooperate with others in joint activities. • Learn how to cooperate and practice good habits of daily living, such as sharing, taking turns, and following rules.

Subject Centers	Concepts
• *Literacy/Language:* Be sure to change books frequently. Add ten new books every two to three weeks. The goal is to have preschoolers familiar with one hundred books. Also include books from all genres, for example, picture books, fiction, science, and so on.	• Verbalization, listening, directions, how to use books, colors, size, shapes, names, print and book knowledge, vocabulary development, print awareness.
• *Writing:* Provide various and plentiful materials for writing: paper, blank books, folded paper, envelopes, markers, pencils, and so forth. Every center should have materials for writing.	• Learn word knowledge, alphabet, words have meaning, words make sentences, and so forth. • Learn that writing has many useful purposes; written words convey meaning.

• *Math:* Provide plastic number tiles, math cards, pegboards.
  • Provide many concrete materials to promote hands-on experiences.
  • Provide picture books about math and read stories involving math.
	• Understand meanings of whole numbers.
	• Recognize the number of objects in small groups without counting and by counting.
	• Understand that number words refer to quantity.
	• Use one-to-one correspondence to solve problems by matching sets and comparing number amounts and in counting objects to ten and beyond.
	• Understand that the last word stated in counting tells "how many"; children count to determine number amounts and compare quantities (using language such as "more than" and "less than").
	• Order sets by the number of objects in them.
	• Develop spatial reasoning by working from two perspectives on space as shapes of objects are examined and relative positions are inspected.
	• Find shapes in the environment and describe them.
	• Build pictures and designs by combining two- and three-dimensional shapes.
	• Solve such problems as deciding which piece will fit into a space in a puzzle.
	• Discuss the relative positions of objects with vocabulary such as "above," "below," and "next to."
	• Identify objects as "the same" or "different," and then "more" or "less," on the basis of attributes that can be measured.
	• Identify measurable attributes such as length and weight, and solve problems by making direct comparisons of objects on the basis of those attributes.

(Continued)

TABLE 10.2 | Types of Classroom Learning Centers *(continued)*

Content-Based Centers	Concepts
• *Science:* Provide books on science, materials for observing, discovering relationships, and for learning about nature, plants, animals, and the environment.	• Develop skills in observation, size, shape, color, whole/part, figure/ground, spatial relations, classifying, graphing, problem-solving skills. • Learn how to observe, make comparisons, classify, and problem-solve. • Investigate and explore.
• *Life Science:* Provide various plants and animals, terrariums, and habitats.	• Understand plant and animal care and habitats.

• *Art/Music/Creative Expression:* Provide materials for painting, coloring, drawing, cutting, pasting.
  • Engage children in activities involving singing and movement.
  • Provide puppets and puppet theater to encourage dramatic and creative expression.
	• Listen to a wide range of musical styles.
	• Learn color relationships and combinations.
	• Engage in creative expression, aesthetic appreciation, satisfaction.
	• Create representations of home and places in the community.
	• Participate in group singing, finger-plays, and rhythm.

Activity Centers	Concepts
• *Construction/Blocks:* Provide a variety of different kinds of blocks. (See the Voice From the Field feature on p. 290.)	• Describe size, shape, length, seriation, spatial relationships. • Develop problem-solving skills.
• *Woodworking:* Use real tools and building materials. Be sure to provide for children's safety (goggles and so forth). (See the Voice From the Field feature on p. 305.)	• Following directions, learning how to use real tools, planning, discovering whole/part relationships, process of construction.

• *Dramatic Play:* Various materials for home activities.
  • Provide many props such as clothing, costumes, hats, shoes, etc.
  • Provide child-size stove, table, chairs, refrigerator, sink, etc.
  • Provide outfits and props from many occupations—health, safety, etc.
	• Learn language skills, sociodramatic play, functions, processes, social skills.
	• Engage in pretend and imaginary play.
	• Learn roles and responsibilities of community workers.

• Water/sand play	• Measuring weighing (what floats, capacity, etc.). • Learn social skills and responsibility (e.g., cleanup).

Technology Centers	Concepts
• *Computer/Technology:* Computers, printer, scanner, fax machine, digital camera, video camera. A computer center can have one or more work stations or can have one or more laptops or handheld devices.	• Socialization, keyboarding, how technology can solve problems. • Learning basic technology skills. • Writing (using e-mail, word processing). • Use technology to learn basic math and language skills. • Use technology to play games.

The Preschool Woodworking Center

The woodworking center is one of my favorite learning centers in preschool and kindergarten. The woodworking center is a favorite of children too. A woodworking cen-

ter provides many learning opportunities for children and is certainly worth the time and effort involved in setting it up, properly supervising it, and ensuring the safety of the children who use it.

BENEFITS OF WOODWORKING FOR CHILDREN

Judy Dalrymple, preschool teacher at St. Paul Christian Learning Center, touts these benefits of a woodworking center:

- Encourages children's creativity
- Gives children the opportunity to develop small motor skills
- Introduces children to tools they may not have used before, such as saws, screwdrivers, sandpaper, hammers, etc.
- Develops eye–hand coordination

Other woodworking center benefits include the following:

- Supports science, technology, engineering and math (STEM) skills, including making, following, and reading plans; building projects; testing ideas; and classification, seriation, measuring, etc.
- Teaches vocabulary development including learning and using all of the correct terms for woodworking tools and materials. Teach the names of tools and materials in English, Spanish, and other languages, as appropriate, for the children in your classroom (e.g., hammer–*el martillo*).

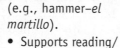

- Supports reading/literacy skills, including the reading and use of nonfiction literature like *The Kids' Building Workshop* by Craig and Barbara Robertson
- Involves children in active, hands-on and minds-on learning

- Develops independence and self confidence

GUIDELINES FOR USING THE WOODWORKING CENTER

Follow these guidelines when implementing and offering a woodworking center.

Practice safety first! Safety first in the woodworking center involves these things:

- Orientate the children to the center and the rules for using the center.
- Demonstrate the proper use of tools.

- Provide safety glasses. All children must wear safety glasses when using the center.
- Provide adult supervision. This means you supervise the woodworking center or others you have trained supervise. Grandparents are excellent candidates for helping you set up and manage a woodworking center. Ask for parent/grandparent/community volunteers from people who have a background and interest in woodworking. Judy recommends two adults and two children in a woodworking center at one time.

WOODWORK OPERATING PROCEDURES

- Provide real tools for children to use. The tools can be either child size or adult size.
- A woodworking center is noisy. Set your woodworking area up either in an out of the way area or outside. Some programs "containerize" their woodworking center, storing it inside and moving it outside when appropriate.
- Judy recommends a child-size work bench. Ask your adult volunteer to build one!
- Follow the two-adult, two-child format.
- Let children plan and design the projects they will build.

- Use children's woodworking experience as a gateway for them to write about and electronically document their experiences.

LUNCH. Lunch should be a relaxing time, and the meal should be served family style, with professionals and children eating together. Children should set their own tables and decorate them with place mats and flowers they can make in the art center or as a special project. Children should be involved in cleaning up after meals and snacks. On the other hand, in many programs, preschool children go to the school cafeteria for their lunch. Children at the Albany California Children's Center receive a hot family-style lunch, such as spaghetti or teriyaki chicken, made fresh daily from their in-house kitchen.[46] Try to make this a relaxing experience also.

RELAXATION. After lunch, children should have a chance to relax, perhaps to the accompaniment of teacher-read stories, CDs, and music. This is an ideal time to teach children breathing exercises and relaxation techniques.

REST TIME. Give children who want or need to rest an opportunity to do so. Provide quiet activities for children who do not need to or cannot sleep on a particular day. Don't force children to sleep or lie on a cot or blanket if they cannot sleep or have outgrown their need for an afternoon nap.

CENTERS OR SPECIAL PROJECTS. Engage children in center activities or projects. Projects can also be conducted in the morning, when some may be more appropriate, such as cooking something for a snack or lunch. Projects can include holiday activities, collecting things, art activities, and field trips.

GROUP TIME. End the day with a group meeting to review the day's activities. Such a meeting develops listening and attention skills, promotes oral communication, stresses that learning is important, and helps children evaluate their performance and behavior.

Observe and Analyze

HELPING PRESCHOOLERS MAKE SUCCESSFUL TRANSITIONS

transition A passage from one learning setting, grade, or program to another.

A **transition** is a passage from one learning setting, grade, program, or experience to another. Young children face many such transitions in their lives. The transition from preschool to kindergarten can influence positively or negatively children's attitudes toward school and learning. You can help ensure that the transition is a happy and rewarding experience. Children with special needs who are making a transition from a special program to a mainstreamed classroom need extra attention and support.

Increasingly large amounts of public funds are now dedicated to educating young children with the intent of boosting their chances for success in elementary school and beyond. Preschool learning environments are quite different from traditional elementary school classroom settings, and it is imperative children establish competencies critical to their school success and achievement.[47]

Preschool and kindergarten staff can collaborate and work out a transitional plan. Continuity between programs is important for social, emotional, and educational reasons. Children should see their new setting as an exciting place where they will be happy and successful. You can suggest that kindergarten teachers make booklets about their programs, including photographs of the kindergarten children, letters from them, and pictures of kindergarten activities. You can then place these booklets in your reading center, where your preschool children can read about the programs they will attend. Below you will read how teachers help transition their preschoolers into kindergarten.

It is also important to prepare children and their parents as much as possible for what to expect in the new setting:

- Educate and prepare children ahead of time for any new situation. Children can practice certain routines as they will do them when they enter their new school or grade. For example, Amy Christensen helps transition four-year-old preschoolers into kindergarten as the "Begindergarten" teacher at Gertie Belle Rodgers Elementary in Mitchell, South Dakota. She teaches a half-day morning transition class in the elementary school, which allows four-year-olds to become acquainted with the school and experiment and explore as they meet new friends. Amy writes a weekly newsletter for parents that gives details of the week and recaps children's accomplishments. For example, students read about Yao Ming, the Chinese professional basketball player, and his talent in basketball. They brainstormed about what their special talents are. The children were very creative and drew a page for a class book to be displayed at their end-of-the-year program.[48]

- Alert parents to new and different standards, dress, behavior, and parent–teacher interactions. Preschool professionals, in cooperation with kindergarten teachers, should share curriculum materials with parents so they can be familiar with what their children will learn.

- Let parents know ahead of time what their children will need in the new program (e.g., lunch box, change of clothing).

- Provide parents of children with special needs and bilingual parents with additional help and support during the transition.

- Offer parents and children an opportunity to visit the new program. Children will better understand its physical, curricular, and affective climates if they visit in advance. Teachers can incorporate methods they observed into their own program that will help children adjust to the new settings. For example, students attending Kokomo (Indiana) Center Schools are "gearing up" for kindergarten. At the annual "Ready, Set, GO!!! Kindergarten Round-Up," future kindergartners and their parents receive registration information, are introduced to available resources, and "race" to activities that are a great preview of the kindergarten year.[49]

- Exchange class visits between preschool and kindergarten programs. Class visits are an excellent way to have preschool children learn about the classrooms they will attend as kindergartners. Having kindergarten children visit the preschool and tell preschoolers about kindergarten provides a sense of security and anticipation.

- Hold a "kindergarten day" for preschoolers in which they attend kindergarten for a day. This program can include such things as riding the bus, having lunch, and participating in kindergarten activities.

The nature, extent, creativity, and effectiveness of transitional experiences for children, parents, and staff will be limited only by the commitment of all involved. If professionals are interested in providing good preschools, kindergartens, and primary schools, we will include transitional experiences in the curricula of all pre-school programs.

Reflect and Apply: Preschool Curriculum

THE FUTURE OF PRESCHOOL

The further growth of public preschools for three- and four-year-old children is inevitable. Growth to the point that all children are included will take decades, but it will happen. Most likely, the public schools will increasingly focus more on programs for four-year-old children and then, over time, include three-year-olds. A logical outgrowth of this long-term trend will be for the public schools to provide services for even younger children and their families.

One thing is certain: Preschool, as it was known a decade ago, is not the same today; and ten years from now it will again be different. Your challenge is to develop your professional skills so that you can assume a leadership role in the development of quality universal preschool programs.

UNIVERSAL PRESCHOOL

When you think of the idea of universal preschool, what comes to mind? Universal preschool means different things to different people. For some it means free and required for *all*; for others it means free and accessible for *all*; for some it means voluntary and free for some children; and for others it means accessible for some with pay. For purposes of our discussion, universal means free and accessible for *all*.

Thanks to President Obama's call for universal preschool, it is fast becoming a program whose time has come, and it now has a chance of becoming a permanent part of the American public school system. While not all children have free access to public school, I predict they will in the next ten years—unless there is another Great Recession. Preschool should be the beginning of public schooling. Research is clear that universal preschool benefits *all* children. Of course, it will take many more years before every four-year-old in every state has the opportunity for a free public preschool education.

RIGOROUS ACADEMIC STANDARDS

Increasingly preschool is seen as the place where children get ready for kindergarten and as a means for closing achievement gaps. We can consider this as a new era in early childhood education. The introduction of rigorous academic standards into the preschool is a result, in part, of the adoption of the Common Core State Standards (CCSS) by states and school districts. The introduction of curriculum and instructional strategies that focus on the Common Core State Standards are an effort by educators to make sure that when preschoolers enter kindergarten, they are ahead of the curve rather than behind it. You can think of the preschool curriculum as readiness for the Common Core State Standards!

The emphasis on more rigorous preschool curricula can also be attributed to President Obama's call for high-quality universal preschool for all four-year-old children. As a result, there is more attention focused on what makes a preschool program high quality. One hallmark of a high-quality program is how well children achieve.

HIGH-QUALITY TEACHERS

The call for high-quality preschool programs is accompanied by a call for high-quality teachers. However just as there is a heated debate about what constitutes high-quality preschools, the same is true for agreeing on what is involved in the preparation and certification of high-quality preschool teachers.

INCREASED USE OF TECHNOLOGY

Increasingly, preschool teachers are embracing iPads, laptops, and apps, such as "Handwriting without Tears," to support their teaching and children's learning. More preschools are entering school used to and comfortable with technology. As the academic focus turns more to literacy and math, more preschool programs will use technology and apps to teach essential skills in these areas.

Additionally, we know that preschool children have a natural and intense curiosity. Technology devices and apps are one way to engage children's curiosity and at the same time promote an interest in science and technology.

PRE-K–3 CONTINUUM

As a result of President's Obama's call for universal preschool, there is a renewed emphasis on making preschool the beginning of the educational experience. Except when attached to the public schools, preschools are often viewed as separate from mainstream education. Linking preschool education to full-day kindergartens and grades one to three provides a seamless path for learning. Done in the right way, this Pre-K–3 initiative can close achievement gaps and improve the quality of education for all children.

INCREASED FUNDING FOR HIGH-QUALITY PRESCHOOL PROGRAMS

One of the ongoing issues of federal, state, and local governments is whether they will or will not invest funds for early childhood programs. When there is not enough money to fund all priorities, which is always the case, different constituencies compete for funding, and questions of priority abound. Do we fund juvenile justice programs, jails, senior health care, or preschools? Numerous research studies such as those at the beginning of our discussion show that investing in high-quality preschool programs has short- and long-term educational and monetary benefits. You can use these data as you advocate for investing in high-quality preschool programs for young children.

ACTIVITIES FOR PROFESSIONAL DEVELOPMENT

ETHICAL DILEMMA

"I THINK WE SHOULD DO SOMETHING!"

Kindergarten teacher Maria Aguilar teaches in a small East Coast state that has not offered a public preschool program. Maria, a strong advocate for early education, was ecstatic when she heard that her state finally was going to provide support for pre-kindergarten education. However, in the days following the initial announcement, Maria was very disappointed to learn that the state was planning to fund only five pilot pre-kindergarten classrooms, and they would serve only about seventy-five four-year-old children. Maria was so upset by the news, she scheduled a meeting with Stephanie Andrade, her elementary principal. "Stephanie, how can the state legislature be so short-sighted? We know the advantages of high-quality preschool programs for young children! Why can't our state do its part and provide proper funding! I'm tired of all of these excuses about no money because of hard times and the recession! I think we should do something! Why don't we contact our state representatives and put some pressure on them to provide more funding?" Stephanie was not pleased with Maria's suggestions. "Now Maria, we have to take a step at a time. We should be happy with the funding we get. Let's not do anything to embarrass ourselves or the politicians who are providing the funding!"

What should Maria do? Should she visit her state representatives and share her opinions with them? Should she take Stephanie's advice and keep quiet? Should she take a more proactive approach and contact the local teachers' union and get them involved? Or, should Maria take another course of action? What should Maria do? What would you do?

ACTIVITIES TO APPLY WHAT YOU LEARNED

1. Create a short survey for the parents and staff of a local preschool. Ask them why preschool programs are important to them and what they think are the benefits to children and families. Post your survey results with your comments on your early childhood education discussion board and ask for feedback on the results of your survey.

2. Choose a domain of development: physical, cognitive, social-emotional, or language. Create a list of activities in your preschool environment that stimulate growth and maturity in that domain. Share this information with your classmates on your class discussion board.

3. **KEY ASSESSMENT:** You have been invited to speak to the local NAEYC affiliate on the topic "School Readiness: What Teachers and Parents Can Do." Develop your presentation outline using these questions: What is readiness? Why is children's readiness for school important? What should be the critical features of a preschool that is "getting children ready for school"? What are five key skills and behaviors a child should have on entering kindergarten? Post your outline on your Facebook page or share with your class using PowerPoint. Use the **rubric** provided to guide your work.

4. Go online and research the outdoor play facilities of preschool programs. Also, look at the outdoor play designs of commercial playground companies. List five things that you find new and interesting. Share this information with your classmates.

5. Based on material presented in this text, develop a set of ten guidelines for ensuring that preschool programs are developmentally appropriate. Visit a local preschool. Look at the environment, curriculum, and teaching practices. Is there anything exceptional? Anything that can be improved? Write a two hundred-word reflection about developmentally appropriate practice in the preschool. Share this with your classmates and ask for comments.

6. After reviewing all the information in this chapter, create a three- to five-minute video podcast addressing the statement, "In ten years, the future of preschool will be _____." Discuss what changes you think will take place in preschools. Also state what you would like to be doing professionally in the early childhood field in the next decade.

LINKING TO LEARNING

The following agencies and programs, which can be located easily online, provide additional information about topics discussed in this chapter.

International Association for the Child's Right to Play

The membership of this interdisciplinary organization affiliated with the International Play Association (founded in Denmark in 1961) is open to all professionals working for or with children. Their website includes a position statement on the need for recess in elementary schools and resources on playground games and activities.

Pre-K Now

Here you will find a website dedicated to the advancement of high-quality, voluntary pre-kindergarten for all preschool-age children. It is a public education and advocacy campaign that features up-to-date information on the reform of education for young children.

Preschool Teacher

This website is dedicated to pre-K teachers and serves as a place to share classroom ideas.

KINDERGARTEN EDUCATION

Learning All You Need to Know

LEARNING OUTCOMES

1. Explain what kindergarten is like today.
2. Describe high-quality environments for kindergarten children.
3. List the physical, social-emotional, and cognitive characteristics of kindergartners.
4. Explain what the kindergarten curriculum is like.
5. List the ways in which you can accommodate diverse kindergarten learners.

AS we begin our discussion of kindergarten children, programs, and environments, perhaps you are thinking back to your kindergarten or pre–first-grade school experiences. I am sure you have many pleasant memories that include your teachers and classmates, as well as what you learned and how you learned it. It is good that you have these fond memories, but we can't use just memories to build our understanding of what today's high-quality kindergartens are and should be like because kindergarteners of today are nothing like they were a decade ago.

THE KINDERGARTEN TODAY

Kindergarten today is in an ongoing transitional process from a program that previously focused primarily on social and emotional development to one that emphasizes academics, especially early literacy, math and science, and activities that prepare children to think and problem-solve. These changes represent a transformation of great magnitude and will continue to have a lasting impact on the kindergarten curriculum and the education of young children.

THE CHANGING KINDERGARTEN

The kindergarten classroom of today is very different from the kindergarten of yesterday, and it requires a different kind of teacher. Elizabeth Plotkin, a Kindergarten Teacher of the Year, says that her goal as a teacher is to provide opportunities for children to make positive memories in the school environment; build a foundation of finding joy in learning; and to claim each day as a chance to be the change in a child's life. Elizabeth believes that making connections between children's lives and the curriculum creates engaged learners.[1] Kindergarten Teacher of the Year Abby Lowe says one of the most rewarding things about being a teacher is watching her students grow. She wants her students to always feel smart and have a love for school.[2]

High-quality kindergarten teachers adjust in response to changes in what society demands of kindergarten education. Here are some of the ways kindergarten is evolving and the reasons why:

- ***Longer school days and the transition from half-day to full-day programs.*** National Education Association (NEA) President Dennis Van Roekel believes that full-day kindergarten provides our youngest students more time to explore, learn, and grow in an engaging and supportive environment.[3] Today, four million children are enrolled in kindergarten in the United States.[4] For their part, parents feel that their children benefit by being in a classroom environment and away from home for longer periods during the day. For example, Amy Hartley, a kindergarten parent, believes that attending full-day kindergarten benefited her two oldest children and sees similar results in her kindergartner. Amy says her children learned social skills and how to get along with others. Amy also believes that, because there are so many requirements in kindergarten, it's nice that her children can spend the morning on academics and the afternoon on some of the other activities.[5]

The following are reasons for longer school days and full-day kindergarten programs:

Provides better transition from kindergarten to first grade
- Helps children adapt to the demands of longer school days in the primary grades.
- Provides more time for children to participate in activities and projects.

Supports children's academic and social development

- Enables children with developmental delays and those at risk for school problems to have more time to complete projects and more time for socialization with peers and teachers.
- Gives teachers more time to plan curriculum, incorporate a greater number of activities into the school year, and offer more in-depth coverage of each standard.

Provides greater achievement in literacy, math, social skills, and science

- Emphasizes academics, especially reading, math, and science.
- Specifies, according to state and district standards, what children should know and be able to do.
- Helps kindergartners be better prepared for the primary grades.

Provides a framework for the accountability movement with emphasis on achievement

- Holds teachers and schools accountable for children's achievement.
- Helps children avoid school grade failures.
- Increases teachers' use of tests and assessments to plan instruction and promote achievement.
- Increases possibilities of preventing achievement gaps.

Works toward the almost universal goal of having all children reading by entry into first grade and on grade level by grade three

- Recognizes that literacy and reading are pathways to success in school and life and that learning to read is a basic right for all children.

If you want to gain a good picture of what is expected of kindergarten children today, now would be a good time to review the kindergarten standards for your state. Be sure to review their depth and breadth across all of the content areas.

Today, kindergarten is a universal part of schooling, enrolling children from different cultures and socio-economic backgrounds and, subsequently, different life experiences. What are some things you can do to ensure that kindergarten experiences meet the unique needs of each child?

THE ESCALATED CURRICULUM. After reviewing your state's kindergarten standards, you are probably thinking something like this: "Wow, a lot of what they're doing in kindergarten I did in first grade!"

A number of reasons account for the escalated kindergarten curriculum. First, since 1990, there has been a decided emphasis on academics in U.S. education, including early childhood education. This academic emphasis is due in part to national issues of better-trained workers and international economic competitiveness for your state. Second, many parents believe an academic approach to learning is the best way for their children to succeed in school and the world of work. Third, the standards, testing, and high-quality education reform movement encourages greater emphasis on academics. Fourth, the federal government sees kindergarten and the primary grades as important to the national goal of being a world leader. The federal government also believes that learning twenty-first century work skills begins in kindergarten and before.

These higher expectations for kindergarten children are not necessarily bad. A changing society means changing educational practices. Also, we know that children today are more capable than we previously thought. However, achieving higher expectations for children in developmentally appropriate ways is one of the major challenges facing you and the early childhood professional today.

WHO ATTENDS KINDERGARTEN?

Froebel's kindergarten was for children three to seven years of age. In the United States, kindergarten is for five- and six-year-old children before they enter first grade. The age at which children enter kindergarten differs from state to state and district to district. Some parents and early childhood educators support an older rather than a younger kindergarten entrance age because they think older children are more ready for kindergarten and will learn better. Consequently, it is not uncommon to have children in kindergarten who are seven years old by the end of the year. In the past, children had to be five years of age prior to December 31 for kindergarten admission; today the trend is toward an older admission age. For example, Maryland children must be five years old by September 1 rather than by the previous date of December 31.[6] Current legislative practices indicate that states and school districts will continue to push back the kindergarten entrance age so that kindergarten children will continue to be "older." However, young children really need to be in some kind of educational program. If children are going to be older as they enter kindergarten, then we need preschools for four- and five-year-old children.

REDSHIRTING.   You may have heard of the practice of **redshirting** college football players—that is, holding a player out a year for him to grow and mature. The theory is that the extra year will produce a better football player. The same practice applies to kindergarten children, with about 6 percent of children entering kindergarten being academically redshirted—held out of school for a year.[7] Parents and administrators who practice redshirting think that the extra year gives children an opportunity to mature intellectually, socially, and physically. Redshirting might have some benefit for children who are immature and whose birthdates fall close to the cut-off for school entrance. Some affluent parents redshirt their sons in particular because they want them to be the oldest members of the kindergarten class. They reason that their children will be class leaders, will get more attention from the teachers, and will have another year under their belts, all the better to handle the increasing demands of the kindergarten curriculum.

redshirting The practice of postponing the entrance into kindergarten of age-eligible children to allow extra time for social-emotional, intellectual, and physical growth.

RESEARCH AND REDSHIRTING.   An analysis of research data regarding children's achievement in reading and math found that redshirted children have slightly higher reading knowledge and skills at the end of first grade than do children who started kindergarten on time. In mathematics, however, redshirted children's scores were somewhat behind those of children who had started kindergarten on time. Research also suggests that children who are older than their peers score higher on achievement tests and are less likely to repeat a grade or to be diagnosed with learning disabilities than are younger students in the same class.[8]

Rather than the constant juggling of entrance ages, what is needed are early childhood programs designed to serve the needs of all children, regardless of the ages at which they enter school. At the heart of this issue is disagreement about whether developmental maturation or school experiences are the more potent factor in children's achievement. Research studies comparing age and school effects suggest that academic achievement is closely tied with age,[9] and that achievement gaps begin long before kindergarten as the following Voice from the Field feature, "The Kindergarten Achievement Gap Begins Before Kindergarten," points out. Also, for children who are not ready for kindergarten or who find kindergarten too challenging, there are other kinds of programs.

KINDERGARTEN PROGRAMS

Given the changing kindergarten curriculum, the almost universal nature of kindergarten, and the prevalence of a variety of abilities and disabilities, it is not surprising that some children are not ready for many of the kindergarten demands placed

The Kindergarten Achievement Gap Begins Before Kindergarten

In the opening pages of the third edition of NAEYC's *Developmentally Appropriate Practice in Early Childhood Programs Serving Children from Birth Through Age 8*, the authors discuss the early childhood achievement gap as one of the critical issues faced by children and early childhood professionals. Here is what they say:

> All families, educators, and the larger society hope that all children will achieve in school and go on to lead satisfying and productive lives. But that optimistic future is not equally likely for all of the nation's schoolchildren. Most disturbing, low-income and African American and Hispanic students lag specifically behind their peers on standardized comparisons of academic achievement throughout the school years, and they experience more difficulties while in the school setting.

The achievement gap between students of various races, cultures, and socioeconomic backgrounds is a serious issue, which all of us as early childhood educators must address. Many children come to school already behind their more advantaged counterparts because they are not prepared to meet the demands of contemporary schooling. The extent and seriousness of the achievement gap is further illustrated in the results of a survey of Michigan kindergarten teachers:

- Thirty-two percent of kindergarten teachers were not satisfied with the abilities of their kindergarten students when they started school, with an additional 50 percent being only somewhat satisfied.

- According to the teachers, only 65 percent of children entered kindergarten classrooms ready to learn the curriculum.
- Eighty-six percent of teachers report that students who are behind academically at kindergarten entrance impact a teacher's ability to effectively provide instruction to the rest of the class.

Awareness of the extent of the problem is only one part of our efforts to reduce and eliminate achievement gaps. Taking effective action is the other part of the solution. Here are two things that we can do as early childhood professionals:

- Advocate that *all* children, particularly English language learners and children from low-income backgrounds, have the opportunity to participate in high-quality preschool programs. There is growing consensus that providing universal preschool for all children will help them socially and academically as they continue through the elementary grades.
- Advocate for "ready schools and ready communities" so that the schools children attend and the communities they live in are united in their efforts to provide the health, nutrition, and educational experiences all children need in order to be successful in school and life.

In addition, there are many specific things that preschool and kindergarten teachers can do to help children catch up with their more advantaged peers. Intentional teaching of essential academic skills will go a long way toward helping eliminate the kindergarten achievement gap.

* C. Copple and S. Bredekamp, eds., *Developmentally Appropriate Practice in Early Childhood Programs: Serving Children from Birth Through Age 8,* 3rd. ed., (Washington, DC: NAEYC, 2009), 8.

† R. Snyder, "Education Reform," 2011: accessed on January 9, 2013, at http://www.ecic4kids.org.

---

on them. As a result, teachers and schools have developed alternative kindergarten programs.

developmental kindergarten (DK)
A kindergarten designed to provide children with additional time for maturation and physical, social, emotional, and intellectual development.

DEVELOPMENTAL KINDERGARTEN. The **developmental kindergarten (DK)** is a prekindergarten for kindergarten-aged children who are developmentally or behaviorally delayed; it is viewed as one means of helping them succeed in school. School districts have specific criteria for placing children in developmental kindergartens:

- Kindergarten-eligible children are given a kindergarten screening test to identify those who have special learning or behavioral needs. Many states require that all children take a screening test prior to kindergarten enrollment.
- Parents and preschool teachers who believe that children are not ready for kindergarten consult with the school district and/or their local school about the placement of individual children.

For example, the Troy, Michigan, School District has a DK program that provides meaningful and challenging experiences that build on children's prior knowledge.

Their integrated program of teacher-directed and child-initiated learning allows children many opportunities to manipulate materials, explore and discover ideas, interact with others, and develop at their own unique rate. This program fosters the development of a positive self-image and enhances children's growth toward their individual potential.[10]

TRANSITIONAL KINDERGARTEN.   A **transitional kindergarten (TK)** is designed to give children the time they need to achieve what is required for entry into first grade. These children are really getting two years of kindergarten to achieve what others would normally achieve in one. A transition class is different from a nongraded program in that the transition class consists of children of the same age, whereas the nongraded classroom has children of different ages.

The concept of transition classes implies, and practice should involve, linear progression that promotes ongoing achievement and success. Children are placed in a transition kindergarten so that they can continue to progress at their own pace. The curriculum, materials, and teaching practices should be appropriate for each child's developmental age or level.

Proponents of transitional programs identify these benefits:

- Promotes success, whereas retention is a regressive practice that promotes failure
- Provides for children's developmental abilities
- Enables children to be with other children of the same developmental age
- Provides an appropriate learning environment
- Puts children's needs ahead of the desire to place them in a particular grade
- Provides additional time for children to integrate learning—often referred to as the **gift of time**

Students at Honor Roll Elementary School who attend TK classes engage in a well-integrated, nurturing environment that focuses on socialization and active learning. Teachers work with children so they are able to complete their work independently, read and write, and discover their five senses. Academic skills are further developed through phonics-based reading, hands-on math activities, spelling, and simple grammar. Music, art, and physical play are also important parts in the TK curriculum.[11]

Children are born to learn. Learning is not something children get ready for but is a continuous process. What factors do you think are critical for children's readiness to learn?

transition kindergarten (TK) A kindergarten designed to serve children who may be old enough to go to first grade but are not quite ready to handle all of its expectations.

gift of time The practice of giving children more time in a program or at home to develop physically, emotionally, socially, and cognitively as preparation for kindergarten.

Check Your Understanding: Redshirting

FULL-DAY/HALF-DAY PROGRAMS.   All across the United States, school districts, families, and children face dilemmas and decisions about conducting and participating in full-day or half-day kindergarten programs. Currently, about 70 percent of kindergarten children are enrolled in some type of full-day kindergarten program—either public or private. At the present time, ten states and the District of Columbia require school districts to provide publically funded kindergarten programs. Thirty-four states require school districts to provide half-day kindergarten and six states do not require kindergarten.[12]

In my own state of Texas, kindergarten is not mandatory; however, once school districts provide kindergarten programs either whole or half day, they must continue to offer them. The benefits for children attending full-day kindergarten programs are numerous and beneficial.[13]

- Higher long-term achievement
- Higher achievement for disadvantaged and low-income children and for those receiving Title I services
- Higher reading scores in early grades
- Fewer grade retentions
- Higher test scores
- More time spent in individualized instruction

mixed-age grouping
Students in two or three grade levels combined in one classroom with one teacher.

MIXED-AGE/MULTIAGE GROUPING. Mixed-age grouping provides another approach to meeting the individual and collective needs of children. In a multiage group, there is a diversity of abilities, at least a two-year span in children's ages, and the same teacher. Multiage groups do the following:

- Provide materials and activities for a wider range of children's abilities.
- Create a feeling of community and belonging; most mixed-age groups have a feeling of family because children spend at least two years in the group.
- Support children's social development by providing a broader range of children to associate with. Older children act as teachers, tutors, and mentors, and younger children are able to model the academic and social skills of their older class members.
- Provide for a continuous progression of learning.

Today more teachers and schools are using multiage grouping to support kindergarten learning. Principal Dawn Gonzales says that by grouping students by ability rather than age, teachers are better able to respond to the student's needs. In addition, research shows that multiage classrooms can be beneficial to academic achievement. Collaboration and friendships are gained across all age groups, creating a unique community. Older students have an opportunity to become role models and to reinforce their own understanding through teaching. Younger students get to preview concepts they'll study later.[14]

looping A single-graded class of children staying with the same teacher for two or more years.

LOOPING. Looping occurs when a teacher spends two or more years with the same group of same-age children. In other words, a teacher involved in looping begins teaching a group of kindergartners and then teaches the same group as first graders and perhaps as second graders. Another teacher might do the same with second, third, and fourth graders. Kindergarten teacher Carla Rodriguez lists these advantages of looping:

- Teachers, students, and parents develop a deep relationship because of the longer amount of time together.
- Teachers understand the children's family dynamics and the expectations of the parents.
- Teachers develop a deeper understanding of children's learning styles.
- The second year, the students are already familiar with classroom procedures and expectations. Furthermore, the teacher already knows the needs of the students and can jump right in.

RETENTION. Along with the benefits of kindergarten education come other issues as well. One of these is retention. Children who are retained, instead of participating in kindergarten graduation ceremonies with their classmates, are destined to spend another year in kindergarten. Many of these children are retained, or failed, because teachers judge them to be immature or because they fail to measure up to the district's or teachers' standards for promotion to first grade.

Across our country, more children are being retained in kindergarten. These children are failing kindergarten because they are presumably not ready for the demands of first grade. Yet the early years of schooling are crucial in determining the child's long-term attitudes toward self, teachers, and learning. Children who emerge from the early years feeling good about themselves, respecting teachers, and enjoying learning will regard education as exciting and as a positive challenge. On the other hand, children who leave the early years of schooling feeling badly about themselves, with a low regard for teachers, and turned off to learning may find recess the best part of the school day.[15]

Do children do better the second time around? Despite our intuitive feelings that children who are retained will do better, research evidence is unequivocally contrary to that notion: Children *do not* do better the second time around. In fact, studies show that children do worse and that retention causes children to drop out.[16]

Reflect and Apply: Programs

ENVIRONMENTS FOR KINDERGARTNERS

NAEYC Standard 1 at the beginning of this chapter identifies one of your professional roles as being able to create environments that are healthy, respectful, supportive, and challenging for each child and to create a setting for positive learning experiences.

THE HEALTHY ENVIRONMENT

A healthy setting is important for all children. A safe, clean, well-maintained classroom with a positive atmosphere and social climate increases student and staff self-esteem and student achievement.[17] A healthy environment includes having children practice healthy habits. In Arlington, Virginia, schools have installed hand-sanitizer dispensers in all classrooms and have large supplies of gel available. When children come in from recess or go to lunch without time for a restroom break, they get a squirt of the gel. Principal Karen Hodges has her children sing the ABC song while they wash their hands, because washing hands for the time it takes to sing the song is long enough to kill the germs.[18]

A healthy environment also includes a relaxed and happy eating environment. Areas should be disinfected properly before eating. Substantial research clearly indicates that a healthy diet and environment contribute to children's overall health and well-being.[19]

HEALTHY FOODS. Since 2004, the federal government has required that every school district participating in the national school lunch and breakfast program develop a wellness plan to help children eat healthier foods.[20] Schools now include more fruits, vegetables, and whole grains on lunch trays. Connecticut schools prohibit the sale of soda and other sugary drinks, and deep fryers are disappearing from school cafeterias nationwide. Many schools already banned junk food in vending machines, and even classroom birthday parties are under attack. Alternative healthy foods that children can bring for birthdays are sealed yogurts, bagels, and fruits.[21] At Louisa May Alcott Elementary School in Chicago, children eat home-cooked breakfast and lunch made mainly from locally farmed products. Lunches include meals such as baked penne with Italian chicken sausage, ratatouille, and rosemary-roasted potatoes.[22]

celiac disease An immune reaction to eating gluten, a protein found in wheat, barley, and rye.

gluten sensitivity A spectrum of disorders, including celiac disease and wheat allergy, in which gluten has an adverse effect on the body (also called *gluten intolerance*).

504 plan A provision under the Americans with Disabilities act that specifies a child with a disability cannot be excluded from participating in federally funded free programs.

GLUTEN FREE.   Increasing numbers of children have been diagnosed with **celiac disease** and **gluten sensitivity** or (gluten intolerance). Celiac disease is an immune reaction to eating gluten, a protein found in wheat, barley, and rye. Eating gluten triggers an immune response. Over time, this reaction prevents absorption of some nutrients. This is known as malabsorption.[23] Some children with celiac disease and gluten sensitivity bring their lunches from home. Increasing numbers however participate in their schools gluten-free lunch menu. Under the Americans with Disabilities Act (ADA), a child with a specific disability, which can include celiac disease and gluten sensitivity, is eligible to participate in the free and reduced-price school lunch program. This is known as a **504 plan**. A 504 plan is a provision under the Americans with Disabilities Act that specifies a child with a disability cannot be excluded from participating in federally funded free programs. This includes school free and reduced-price lunch programs. Here is a sample of a gluten-free menu from the Chesterfield Public County School District in Chesterfield, Virginia.[24]

Monday

Burger on gluten-free bun

Entrée salad: Cheese

Side Choices

Steamed broccoli

Tossed salad

Baby carrots

Assorted fruit/juice/milk

Friday

Chicken filet on gluten-free bun

Entrée salad: Chicken fajita

Side Choices

Mixed vegetables

Tossed salad

Fresh veggies, with dip

Assorted fruit/juice/milk

ORGANIC FOODS.   Growing and eating organic foods is part of the greening of America and its schools. Creating lesson plans about organic foods, the benefits of organic food, and organic agriculture enables children to be familiar with organic products. If there's an organic farm near the school, a field trip is a good way to really teach children about organic farming. You can also talk about the environmental impact of choosing organic products and ways children can talk to their parents (or even to the school cafeteria staff) about using more organic products. If there is space, starting a classroom organic garden is a wonderful way for children to take home lessons about organic foods. Students can research organic gardening methods on the Internet or in books; start a classroom compost pile; and take care of their plants using organic methods. Casa dei Bambini Montessori School in Santa Maria, California has an organic snack menu:[25]

Beverages

Organic carrot juice, water, organic rice milk

Monday

Organic whole grain crackers with organic hummus

Organic persimmons and apples

Tuesday

Organic vegan blueberry muffins

Dried apricots and cranberries

Wednesday

Organic granola bars with sunflower butter and flax

Various fruit

Thursday

Soy and regular organic yogurt

Organic whole grain crackers

Various fruit

Friday

Quesadillas with organic cheese and blue corn tortillas

Organic vegetables and vegan ranch dips

THE RESPECTFUL ENVIRONMENT

A **respectful environment** is one in which teachers show respect for children, colleagues, and families, and in schools, children are respectful of adults and peers. This psychologically friendly environment contributes to a respectful environment and includes the attitudes, feelings, and values of the school and community.

In a respectful classroom, teachers treat children courteously, talk with them about in- and out-of-school activities and events, and show a genuine concern for them as individuals with specific needs. Unfortunately, not all children get the respect they need and want at home or at school. Some children, especially children with behavior and attention problems, can be subjected to verbal abuse by teachers and children. This is one reason why your respectful classroom means so much to each child.

respectful environments Environments that show respect for each individual child and for their culture, home language, individual abilities or disabilities, family context, and community.

THE SUPPORTIVE ENVIRONMENT

A **supportive environment** creates a climate in which children can do their best work. Teachers have high expectations, and students are expected to succeed.[26] The supportive environment consists of the immediate physical surroundings, social relationships, and cultural settings in which children function and interact. To help create a supportive social environment, *all* children of all cultures, genders, socioeconomic levels, and backgrounds are valued and included in all activities.

supportive environments Environments in which teachers believe each child can learn and help children understand and make meaning of their experiences.

IMPLICATIONS FOR TEACHING.   Here are some things you can do to create a supportive environment:

- *Meet children's safety needs.* Children feel safe and secure socially and emotionally when they have teachers who care about and help them.
- *Have a balance between teacher-initiated and child-initiated activities.* Children should be able choose to do things that they consider challenging and also things they do very well.
- *Provide a classroom arrangement and materials for active learning.* In a supportive environment, children are listening to stories, telling stories, dictating stories, looking at and reading books independently, singing, relating events that happened outside school, and talking, talking, talking. Children are also using computers interactively with appropriate games and tasks, solving puzzles,

counting napkins to put on the table to match the number of children, and measuring heights and weights. In other words, the teachers, the classroom arrangement, and the materials support children's active learning.

- *Emphasize social and emotional development as well as academic achievement.* Generally, age is the only criterion that determines whether a child may enroll in kindergarten. This means that some children come to kindergarten emotionally immature and more than a little self-centered. However, in any group of five-year-olds, there are children who function more like four-year-olds and others who are like six-year-olds. And, overall development isn't the only type of difference that exists. Some children are sociable, whereas others do not get along well with their peers.

A curriculum that helps children feel good about themselves also helps them become aware that other children also have needs and rights. In a good kindergarten environment, children learn to wait, to share, to take turns, and to help others as they also gain confidence in their own abilities and self-worth.[27]

Watch the following **video**. Think about the questions that teachers need to ask themselves to promote active learning. Focus on some of the key instructional strategies the teacher used to ensure that her children would be involved actively in the classroom activity of discovery.

THE CHALLENGING ENVIRONMENT

A challenging learning environment provides curricula that are neither too easy nor too hard. Teachers adjust learning levels to children's abilities while also making it possible for children to meet Common Core State Standards (CCSS) and state and local expectations. Challenging environments match children's abilities and achievement levels so that they are successful. A challenging kindergarten classroom is responsive to children's cultures and socioeconomic backgrounds. In challenging environments, teachers are attentive to individual students and provide them with one-on-one attention and instruction as appropriate.

In challenging environments, teachers assess children's learning on a daily basis to inform instructional decisions and provide necessary assistance. Challenging learning environments that encourage the active involvement of students can sometimes be difficult for teachers to create and manage.

IMPLICATIONS FOR TEACHING.   Here is how you can create a challenging environment for your students:

- Be knowledgeable about children's academic, social, and cultural backgrounds.
- Meet each child at his or her developmental level, foster that stage, and scaffold him or her to the next level.
- Use diverse and appropriate teaching approaches to provide meaningful learning opportunities for each child.
- Differentiate instruction and activities.
- Engage children in projects and small group activities, while also enabling children to do their best work.
- Integrate technology into your teaching to focus on academics and cognitive learning and to engage children. The Voice from the Field feature, "Interactive Whiteboards in the Classroom," provides you with six best practices.
- Design learning activities that help children think and problem-solve at their own level.
- Intentionally teach children to achieve the Common Core State Standards.

VOICE FROM THE FIELD

Interactive Whiteboards in the Kindergarten Classroom

Today's young children are "digital natives." They are immersed in a world of technology that brings them information and media on demand. As a result, when they begin their school-based experience, they require that same high level of engaging information from their learning environment. Integration of a variety of technology tools is necessary for a high-quality education. One of those tools, the interactive whiteboard, is an essential resource in today's early childhood classrooms.

SIX BEST PRACTICES FOR USING INTERACTIVE WHITEBOARDS IN KINDERGARTEN

Best Practice 1 Where? Mount whiteboards at a level where children can easily reach and interact with them. This can be at floor level or a low wall so that students can best view the board while in whole group instruction.

Best Practice 2 Who? The real power of whiteboards and other technology lies in engaging students' interactive learning. For example, instructional activities that require students to move objects to retell a story, match patterns, and roll interactive dice in a math lesson are all ways to engage students in meaningful learning.

Best Practice 3 What? The interactive whiteboard is a powerful tool to support learning in both literacy and math content for young children. Devote time to good basic training using the intuitive software that comes with the interactive whiteboard. The whiteboard program comes with many interactive tools and premade templates that can make designing an activity a breeze for you. Invest time up front to learn the features of the software to save valuable time and increase the quality of the instructional activities.

Best Practice 4 With? Collaborate with colleagues! Sharing digital files via e-mail or intranet enables you and other teachers to work together. Teams of teachers can divide tasks by subject areas or Common Core Standards and share work with others. Online networks such as Smart Exchange provide lessons you can customize for your individual classroom.

Best Practice 5 When? Using whiteboard technology to extend and differentiate learning is great, but whiteboards do not take the place of good teaching. Young children benefit most from their time engaged in hands-on learning with real objects and through instruction time with you and their classmates.

Best Practice 6 How? Use the interactive whiteboard to assist in accommodations for students with all types of special needs. Use an iPad and remote desktop apps such as SplashTop to accommodate students who may not be able to access the whiteboard in a typical way. For example, a student with limited movement can move shapes on the whiteboard from the back of the room using supplemental devices. Children can write using a keyboard.

Using the most current technology such as interactive whiteboards in early childhood classrooms provides students with the twenty-first-century tools they need to be twenty-first-century learners.

Source: Contributed by Pamela Beard, M.Ed., elementary teacher at Forest Ridge Elementary, College Station, Texas.

THE PHYSICAL ENVIRONMENT

Environments that support learning are essential if we want *all* kindergarten children to be successful.

CLASSROOM ARRANGEMENT AND ORGANIZATION. An effective environment classroom is organized to promote student interaction and learning. Desks, tables, and workstations are clustered together; work areas have a variety of learning materials to encourage group projects, experiments, and creative activities.

A high-quality kindergarten classroom is one in which children feel at home. You should collaborate with your children to personalize your classroom. Using plants, rugs, beanbag chairs, and pillows can make the classroom homelike and cozy. Prominently displayed artifacts give children a sense of pride and ownership.

Here are some things you can do to provide a high-quality physical environment for kindergarten:

- Provide many materials that support children learning to read and write, such as paper, pencils, crayons, and all kinds of books.
- Provide access to and use of technology. Children are adept with technology, and it provides for interaction and learning.
- Organize children into groups of different sizes and ability levels. This provides for social interaction and cooperative learning and encourages children to help others (scaffolding).
- Use a variety of different instructional approaches, such as small groups, large groups, seat work, center time, free activity choice time, individual one-on-one work with children, and free play time.
- Adapt your classroom arrangement so it meets the learning and social needs of your children. For example, set aside time for children to work in groups, assign group projects, and assign projects that include different cultures.
- Arrange your classroom so that it supports district common core and state learning standards. For example, to meet reading content standards, make books easily accessible to students and provide free reading time. Also, make sure the classroom has a comfortable area for group and individual reading times.
- Make supplies and learning materials readily accessible to children. Store materials on open, labeled shelves (using pictures and words).

Environments that are healthy, respectful, supportive, and challenging create the kindergarten stage on which children and teacher collaborate for success.

WHAT ARE KINDERGARTEN CHILDREN LIKE?

Kindergartners have similar developmental, physical, and behavioral characteristics that characterize them as kindergartners—children ages five to six years. Yet, at the same time, they have characteristics that make them unique individuals. To sample this uniqueness, review the two portraits of kindergarten children and respond to the accompanying developmentally appropriate questions.

PHYSICAL DEVELOPMENT

Kindergarten children have a lot of energy, and they want to use it in physical activities such as running, climbing, and jumping. Their desire to be involved in physical activity makes kindergarten an ideal time to involve children in projects of building—for example, making **learning centers** resemble a store, post office, or veterinary office.

learning centers Areas of the classroom set up to promote student-centered, hands-on, active learning, organized around student interests, themes, and academic subjects.

From ages five to seven years, children's average weight and height approximate each other. For example, at six years, boys, on average, weigh 46 pounds and are 45 inches tall; girls, on average, weigh about 44 pounds and are 45 inches tall. At age seven, both boys and girls weigh, on average, 50 pounds and are about 48 inches tall (see Table 11.1).

SOCIAL-EMOTIONAL DEVELOPMENT

Kindergarten children are in Erikson's industry versus inferiority stage of social-emotional development. During this stage, children are continuing to learn to regulate their emotions and social interactions.

PORTRAITS OF KINDERGARTNERS

DION

General Description 5-year-old African American male; very energetic and excitable; attended preschool; no siblings in the single-parent home

Social-Emotional	Cognitive	Motor	Adaptive (Daily Living)
• Can take turns and share, but doesn't always want to • Plays contentedly and independently without constant supervision • Has a good sense of humor, and enjoys sharing jokes and laughter with adults • Is often embarrassed by his own mistakes, wants to fit in and learn the rules; seeks approval of adults	• Can concentrate on a single task for 15 minutes or more at a time • Is interested in cause and effect; wants to know more about how and why things in his world work and happen • Asks more analytical questions and weighs the choices available to him • Is project minded; likes to plan buildings, act out scenarios, and create drawings related to his play	• Throws ball overhead; catches bounced balls • Displays high energy levels; he finds inactivity difficult, seeks active games, and enjoys climbing, sliding, swinging, and dancing • Is interested in performing tricks like standing on his head, performing dance steps, and enjoys practicing complex body coordination skills like swimming and riding bicycles • Can walk down stairs, alternating feet without using a handrail	• Manages mealtime tools and skills independently (carries lunch tray, opens milk carton, uses fork, spoon, and napkin) • Dresses himself independently and generally chooses appropriate clothing; sometimes needs help with zippers or buttons, experiments with tying shoes • Is able to say his name, address, age, and birthday • Organizes and maintains his own possessions at school (backpack, jacket, water bottle, cubby)

ALANA

General Description 6-year-old Hispanic female; shy and quiet; lives in a bilingual home; has an older, younger, and twin sister

Social-Emotional	Cognitive	Motor	Adaptive (Daily Living)
• Is interested in procedures, rules and rituals • Is increasingly aware that others sometimes have feelings different from her own • Will play in a mixed-gender group, but prefers to play with girls • Often chooses friends based on shared activities and immediate environment rather than shared interests	• Knows the difference between left and right • Understands the difference between even and odd numbers; can complete simple addition and subtraction problems • Is interested and eager to expand her vocabulary—about 3,000 new words this year • Draws people with details, often including eyelashes, eyebrows, hair and clothing accessories	• Uses simple combinations of movements such as running and kicking a ball or jumping and twisting • Can move in time with music or a beat, varying movement with fast and slow beats • Has fairly good control of pencils, crayons, and scissors; can cut on a straight or curved line • Skillfully uses a computer mouse and many keyboard controls	• Folds and puts away some of her own clean laundry • Brushes her own hair; needs help with ponytails and braids • Prepares her own PB&J sandwiches • Is learning to use proper etiquette to answer the telephone

Developmentally Appropriate Questions:

- Consider the fact that Dion is a young kindergartner. Does his profile reveal causes for concerns?
- Dion finds "inactivity difficult." What implication does this have for how you teach him?
- Dion comes from a single-parent home. Will this influence how you teach him? How you relate to his mother and family?

- Why do you think Alana prefers to play with girls? Is this a problem?
- Do you think Alana's development is "normal" for kindergarten? Is there anything in her profile that you would consider a red flag? What are two things you would do to teach to Alana's strengths?

Source: Contributed by Barb Tingle, kindergarten teacher at Sahuarita Primary School, Tuscon, Arizona, 2009 Freeport-McMoRan Sahuarita District Teacher of the Year, 2008 Wal-Mart Regional Teacher of the Year, and 2010 AZ Educational Foundation Ambassador for Excellence; and Deborah Palmer, Director of Shepherd's Fold Preschool, NACCP Director of the Year.

TABLE 11.1 | Average Height and Weight of Kindergartners

Age	Boys Height (inches)	Boys Weight (pounds)	Girls Height (inches)	Girls Weight (pounds)
5 years	43	40.5	42.25	40
6 years	45.25	45.5	45.25	44
7 years	48	50	47.75	50
8 years	50.5	56	50.25	56

Note: Remember that averages are just that, averages. Children have individual differences. Ongoing growth and development tend to accentuate these differences.
Source: Adapted from 2000 CDC Growth Charts: United States, National Center for Health Statistics; accessed on January 22, 2014, at http://www.cdc.gov/growthcharts.

IMPLICATIONS FOR TEACHING. The stage of industry versus inferiority is a critical one for young children. It is during this time that they look to and depend on parents and teachers for recognition of and support for successful accomplishment. In addition, they need guidance and models for appropriate social behavior. While the roots for appropriate behavior begin in the toddler and preschool years, the blooming of caring, kindness, and appropriate behaviors occurs in kindergarten.

Here are some things you can do to promote kindergartners' positive social-emotional development:

- Provide opportunities for children to be mentally involved in problem solving and social activities with peers. For example, iPad apps, such as animal games that encourage children to collaborate with each other on matching animal sounds to pictures, are good ways to promote learning and interaction.
- Give children opportunities to be classroom leaders in projects and activities. Teacher Alice Hays gives every child in her class a job, from cleaning up to organizing learning centers to being classroom manager. She rotates these jobs on a weekly basis so that all children have a chance to be leaders. Learning and using leadership skills is an essential part of children becoming college and career ready.
- Teach and model how to make and keep friends. For example, you can have children work in many different kinds of groups to promote friendships. Group work also demonstrates the importance of working together to achieve a common goal.
- Model positive social and emotional responses. Read stories and discuss feelings such as anger, happiness, guilt, and pride. For example, when you understand that a child's challenging behavior is caused by problems at home, you can show greater concern and empathy and are better able to help children learn appropriate behaviors.
- State your expectations for appropriate behavior and discuss them with your children. For example, Glenwood Elementary School in Chapel Hill, North Carolina, sets clear expectations for student behavior in the classroom and in shared areas such as the gym, cafeteria, and playground. They have a positive school climate that encourages children to meet and exceed expectations and to excel academically and socially. The school places signs in different locations that explain how students are expected to behave. Each teacher has a system for rewarding students as they meet classroom expectations. Teachers also explain to their children what each expectation means and what it looks like when performed correctly.[28]
- Give children responsibility. Most kindergarten children are very confident and eager to be involved, and they want to and can accept a great deal of responsibility.

They like going places and doing things, such as working on projects, experimenting, and working with others. Socially, kindergarten children are both solitary and independent workers and, at the same time, desire to work cooperatively with others. They want to be industrious and successful.

- Kindergarten children's combination of a can-do attitude and their cooperation and responsibility make them a delight to teach and work with. Kindergarten Teacher of the Year Barb Tingle "enjoys working with her kids." Her classroom culture is based on growth and success. Barb strives to become an expert in both her children's strengths and weaknesses, and from there she designs a classroom that fosters success for all students. She believes that everyone is a teacher, and everyone is a student.[29]

COGNITIVE AND LANGUAGE DEVELOPMENT

Kindergarten children are in a period of rapid intellectual and language growth. They have a tremendous capacity to learn words and like the challenge of doing so. This helps explain their love of big words and their ability to say and use them. This is nowhere more apparent than in their fondness for dinosaurs and words such as *brontosaurus*. Kindergarten children like and need to be involved in many language activities.

Additionally, kindergartners like to talk. You should encourage their desire to be verbal by providing many opportunities to engage in various language activities such as singing, telling stories, drama, reciting poetry, and using tongue twisters. You can also read to children so they discover the joys of hearing stories, learning about words, and using their imaginations.

THE KINDERGARTEN CURRICULUM

The kindergarten curriculum includes activities that support children emotionally, socially, and academically in literacy and reading, mathematics, science, social studies, and the arts. As you think about how to implement curriculum and instructional activities keep in mind your kindergartener's developmental capabilities and their desire to play as they learn.

LITERACY, READING, AND KINDERGARTEN CHILDREN

Literacy education is always a topic discussed in virtually all educational circles, and early childhood professionals spend a lot of time preparing for how to promote it. Literacy achievement is one of the main objectives of kindergarten and primary school classrooms. *Literacy* means the ability to read, write, speak, and listen, with an emphasis on reading and writing well, within the context of a child's cultural and social setting.

Literacy education is a high priority for several reasons:

First, too many children and adults cannot read. More than 90 million in the United States lack the literacy skills for a fully productive life.[30]

Second, conventional reading and writing skills developed in the years from birth to age five years have a clear and consistently strong relationship with later conventional literacy skills.[31]

Third, businesses and industry are concerned about how unprepared the nation's workforce is to meet the demands of the workplace. Critics of the educational establishment maintain that many high school graduates do not have the basic literacy skills required for today's high-tech jobs. Therefore, teachers and schools, especially in kindergarten and the primary grades, feel the pressure to teach all to read at or above grade level so they will have the skills they will need for productive work and create a stronger foundation for school and life success.

literacy education
Teaching that focuses on reading, writing, speaking, and listening.

Fourth, the federal and state governments, especially through the Common Core State Standards, are at the forefront of making sure all children learn to read well and that they read on level by third grade. Not surprisingly, then, the goals for kindergarten learning are higher than they were in the past. The literacy terms in Figure 11.1 will prove helpful in our discussion of literacy.

EMERGENT LITERACY. Emergent literacy is used to explain and describe the process of how children interact with books and with writing, even though they cannot read in a conventional sense.[32] This process begins at birth and continues throughout preschool, kindergarten, and the primary grades. Children's emergent literacy activities include reading from pictures, writing while scribbling, dictating stories to teachers, and using **invented spelling**, children's attempts to use their best judgments about spelling.

invented spelling
Children's attempts to use their best judgments about spelling.

Emergent literacy emphasizes using environmental and social contexts to support and extend children's reading and writing. Children want to make sense of what they read and write. The meaningful part of reading and writing occurs when children talk to each other, write letters, and read good literature or have it read to them. All of this occurs within a print-rich environment, one in which children see others read, make lists, and use language and the written word to achieve goals.

Alphabet knowledge The knowledge that letters have names and shapes and letters can represent sounds in language.
Example: Children recognize and name the letters of the alphabet.

Alphabetic principle Awareness that each speech sound or phoneme in a language has its own distinctive graphic representation and an understanding that letters go together in patterns to represent sounds.
Example: Letters and letter patterns represent sounds of the language. Introduce just letters that are used a lot such as M, A, T, S, P, and H. Teach consonants first for sound–letter relationships.

Comprehension In reading, the basic understanding of the words and the content or meaning contained within printed material.
Example: Keisha is able to retell the story. Mario is able to tell who the main character is.

Decoding Identifying words through context and phonics.
Example: James can figure out how to read a word he does not know by using his knowledge of letters and sounds. Also, he uses context clues (information from pictures and the sentence before and the sentence after a word) to decode it. He looked at the picture with a "pile" of wood to figure out *pile,* a word he did not know.

Orthographic awareness The ability to analyze visually the appearance and structure of words.
Example: Ben knows the word *man* and uses that knowledge to read the word *fan.*

Phoneme The smallest unit of speech that makes a difference to meaning.
Example: The word *pig* has three phonemes, /p/ /i/ /g/.

Phonemic awareness The ability to notice, think about, and work with the individual sounds in spoken words.
Example: Alex can identify the words in a set that begin with the same sound: *boy, big, bike.*

Phonics The learning of alphabetic principles of language and knowledge of letter–sound relationships.
Example: Children learn to associate letters with the phonemes (basic speech sounds) to help break the alphabetic code.

Phonological awareness The ability to manipulate language at the levels of syllables, rhymes, and individual speech sounds.
Example: Maria can distinguish words that rhyme from those that don't rhyme. Whitney can match words that sound alike. Caroline can segment words into sounds. Angie can blend sounds into words.

Print awareness The recognition of conventions and characteristics of a written language.
Example: Alex pretends to read a bedtime story to his teddy bear. Also, he recognizes the Kentucky Fried Chicken sign on his way to school.

FIGURE 11.1 | Reading/Literacy Instructional Terminology

Reading to and with children is an excellent way to scaffold their learning and to invite them into processes and activities that support their literacy development. In emergent literacy, becoming literate is viewed as a natural process; reading and writing are processes that children participate in naturally, long before they come to school. No doubt you have participated with or know of toddlers and preschoolers who are literate in many ways. They "read" all kinds of signs (Taco Bell) and labels (Campbell's Soup) and "write" with and on anything and everything.

ENGLISH LANGUAGE LEARNERS. With the increasing demands for accountability and high academic achievement for all students, educational policy makers and the schools focus their attention on young children (ages three to eight years) from non-English-speaking backgrounds. Children who speak a language other than English in the home and are not fully fluent in English are considered **English language learners (ELLs)**. All children can benefit cognitively, linguistically, and culturally from learning more than one language. Research suggests that young ELL children are quite capable of learning subject matter in two languages. The rate of growth of ELLs in America's school systems over the past decade is dramatic. The number of school-age children who speak a language other than English at home rose from 4.7 to 11.2 million. States with the most ELLs include Texas, California, Nevada, Arizona, and New Mexico. Unfortunately, only 1 percent of early childhood teachers are certified to teach ELL students. As a group, ELL students struggle to become fluent in English, lag well behind in terms of academic achievement, and have dropout rates almost twice those of native English speakers.[33] This is why today, beginning in kindergarten and before, educators place a premium on helping ELLs learn English and become successful in school.

APPROACHES TO LITERACY AND READING FOR YOUNG CHILDREN. Literacy and reading are certainly worthy national and educational goals, not only for young children, but also for everyone. However, how best to promote literacy has always been, and continues to be, a debated topic. Here are some approaches to reading instruction that are incorporated into basic reading programs today.

Whole Word. One of the most popular methods used for literacy and reading development is the *sight word approach* (also called *whole word* or *look-say*), in which children learn whole words (e.g., *cat, bat, sat*) and develop a sight vocabulary that enables them to begin reading and writing. Visual–spatial learners in particular do well with a whole-word approach.

Implications for Teaching. Here are some things you can do to teach children to read with a whole-word approach:

- Label things in their classrooms (e.g., door, bookcase, desk) as a means of teaching sight vocabulary.
- Create a **word wall**. Word walls are a collection of words displayed on a wall or other display place in the classroom designed to promote literacy learning. Words for the word wall come from stories, sight vocabulary lists, and children's writing.
- Create an **interactive word wall.** Interactive word walls enhance vocabulary learning as children interactively engage in activities structured around words on the

Reading plays an important role in the kindergarten curriculum. Provide your children many opportunities to read different kinds of books, including nonfiction literature such as science, math, and alphabet books, fairy tales, biographies, cookbooks, and newspaper and magazine articles.

English language learners (ELLs) Children who speak a language other than English in the home and who are not fully fluent in English.

word wall Designed to promote literacy learning, collection of words displayed on a wall or another display place in the classroom.

interactive word wall A collection of frequently used words in the classroom that children use to make sentences or use in other classroom literacy activities.

word wall. In addition, children can take the words off the wall and use them to help with their spelling. Kindergarten teacher Mandy Richmond plays twenty questions with her children. She picks a word from the interactive word wall, and the children ask twenty questions to help discover the secret word![34]

- Use picture dictionaries and other dictionaries. Children love to look up words, and this supports their research skills.
- Have children match words to pictures and objects. This is one approach used in Montessori programs.
- Have children make their own books and keep journals. They can use whole words to write stories, poems, and such. Each child can have his or her own word box/file to keep words for reading and writing. Each time a child learns/uses a new word, he or she can put that word in the file.
- Use technology to support children's word learning and writing, for example iPad apps such as, Sight Word Bingo, Word Wall HD, and The Electric Company.

A good source of sight words is the Dolch Sight Words, a list of 220 words children need for reading fluency. Many of the 220 words, such as *the*, *what*, and *please*, cannot be sounded out and must be learned by sight.[35]

whole-language approach
Philosophy of literacy development that advocates the use of all dimensions of language, reading, writing, listening, and speaking, to help children become motivated to read and write.

Phonics. Another popular approach to literacy and reading is *phonics instruction,* which stresses letter–sound correspondence. By learning these connections, children are able to combine sounds into words (*C-A-T*). The proponents of phonics instruction argue that letter–sound correspondence enables children to make automatic connections between words and sounds and, as a result, to sound out words and read them on their own.[36]

Language Experience. Another method of literacy and reading development, the *language experience approach,* follows the philosophy and suggestions inherent in progressive education philosophy. This approach is child centered and maintains that literacy education should be meaningful to children, growing out of experiences that are interesting to them. Using children's own experiences for instructional purposes is a key element in such child-centered approaches. Many teachers transcribe children's dictated experience stories and use them as a basis for writing and for reading instruction.

The emergent literacy and reading models view reading and written language acquisition as a continuum of development. Think of children as being on a continuous journey toward full literacy development.

Whole Language. The **whole-language approach** to literacy development advocates using all aspects of language—reading, writing, listening, and speaking—as the basis for developing literacy. Children learn about reading and writing by speaking and listening; they learn to read by writing, and they learn to write by reading. Other characteristics of the whole-language approach are as follows:

- Spending time on the processes of reading and writing is an important part of learning to read. Consequently, from the moment they enter the learning setting, children are involved in literacy activities, that is, being read to; "reading" books, pamphlets, and magazines; scribbling; "writing" notes; and so forth.

- The whole-word approach is an important part of the whole-language approach.
- Reading, writing, speaking, and listening are taught as an integrated whole, rather than in isolation.
- Writing begins early; children are writing from the time they enter the program.
- Whole language is literature based. Children learn words by reading them and having teachers read to and with them. Also, children's written materials are used as reading materials.

Balanced Approach. As with most things, a balanced approach is generally the best, and many early childhood advocates encourage literacy approaches that provide a balance across all of the methods for teaching children literacy and reading in a print-rich environment. A **print-rich environment** includes labeling; bulletin boards with children's journals, stories, and such; word walls; a wide variety of books and magazines across all genres; the use of technology to support literacy development and reading; literacy stations (centers); a classroom library; and materials for writing.

> **print-rich environment** An environment that enables children to interact with many forms of print.

Other features of a balanced approach include the following:

- Intentional instruction in the skills necessary for learning to read: phonics, word recognition, and so forth
- Reading workshops, which is a teaching strategy that gives students the opportunity to choose books to read and to discuss them with another student in small groups
- Writing workshops, which is a teaching strategy that makes writing an integrated part of the curriculum by giving students the opportunity to draft, write, and edit their stories and composition
- Shared reading (see below)
- Guided reading, which is a teacher-directed approach that helps all children learn essential reading skills

A primary goal of kindergarten education is for children to learn how to read. Thus, teachers must instruct, support, and guide them in learning what is necessary to be successful in school and life.

SHARED READING. Teachers have used shared reading for decades as a means to engage children, support the reading process, and develop fluent readers. For many teachers, shared reading is part of their professional DNA, and you will want to make it part of your professional DNA as well! Conducting shared reading sessions is a natural part of the learning to read and beginning to read instructional process. It is a pathway for children to learn to read fluently and well. **Shared reading**, as the name implies, is a collaborative, interactive reading process between teacher and children in which they read and share a book. Teachers model the reading process for children by reading books aloud and inviting them to join in. Shared reading is an essential part of, and a complement to, a balanced approach to reading. Children love to read, and shared reading builds on children's natural interest in and desire to read books and be involved with the teacher and other children. Shared reading is the Vygotskian theory of social learning at work! Shared reading works exceptionally well with English language learners (ELLs) because it helps make written language understandable and interesting. A shared reading episode of a particular book generally occurs over a period of three to five days. It is not an instructional process that

> **shared reading** A collaborative, interactive reading process between teacher and children in which they read and share a book.

you want to hurry through. It is designed to be fun, interactive, and instructive. Consequently, shared reading involves multiple readings of a book. The shared reading routine usually involves the use of a "big" book and multiple smaller copies of the same book.

Here are steps to follow in the shared reading process:

Step 1:   *Select a book to read.* This can be a collaborative process between you and the children and the more books you read, the more choices the children will have. Children have their favorite books, so it is important to read their favorites (over and over again!) and to introduce new books. Generally, books used in shared reading are fiction, but the Common Core State Standards (CCSS) call for reading across all genres—fiction, non-fiction, reference, and informational. One of my favorite big books to read with children is *If You Give a Pig a Pancake* by Laura Numeroff.

Step 2:   *Introduce the book.* This step involves showing and discussing the cover; reading the title, author name, and illustrator name, and calling children's attention to other book features; and asking the children to predict what they think the book will be about. You can record these predictions on a big paper chart and go over them later.

Step 3:   *Read the book to the children.* As you read, point to the words, emphasize the right to left flow of the sentences, and let children help you read as appropriate. At the end of the story, engage children in a discussion. A good platform for discussion involves the 5 "W" questions: Who? What? When? Where? Why?

Step 4:   *Read the book again.* Involve the children by having them retell the story.

Step 5:   *Extend and enrich the story.* For example, have the children share with a reading buddy what part of the story was their favorite, have the children "rewrite" the story, and have the children illustrate the story. Shared reading is not a difficult activity for you and the children to engage in. Many very fine teachers have recorded their shared reading sessions on YouTube and Teacher Tube. I encourage you to access these and learn from them!

USE THE 5E MODEL TO PLAN LESSONS.   Part of your role as a kindergarten teacher is to write lesson plans, either individually or as a team member. Some school districts have prepared lesson plans that you will be required to use. Other districts may ask you to prepare lesson plans a week or two in advance. Whatever the case may be, a good lesson plan helps you be an effective teacher.

The 5E Model is a valuable approach to lesson planning. There are regional and even district differences in curriculum, but the use of 5E Model lessons is effective for any classroom, anywhere, for several reasons. First, this lesson plan approach is research based and enhances both teacher and student performance. Second, the 5E Model encourages and supports active learning and is constructivist in its approach and design. Third, the lessons are designed to develop knowledge while at the same time forming collaborative relationships between children and between children and teachers. Fourth, these lessons lend themselves easily to differentiation among various types of learners, allowing students to progress through varying levels of Bloom's taxonomy of inquiry. Finally, they are layered (structured to build on prior knowledge) to ensure that all learners are successful.

The 5E Model emphasizes these five Es:

- Engage
- Explore

- Explain
- Extend
- Evaluate

The 5E model lesson plan on pages 334–335 is an excellent example of the 5E approach.

WRITING WORKSHOP. Writing workshops help children gain skills and confidence they need to be good writers. Kindergarten teacher Lauren Gonzales uses writing workshops in her class. Lauren starts with "Kid Writing," a process using inventive spelling, in which children write their words any way they want, regardless of spelling. Lauren then moves on to phonetic spelling. She then teaches children what she calls "Star Writing," in which the children learn how to do the following:

- Write and spell sight words correctly
- Use spaces
- Use capital letters when needed
- Use correct punctuation

When Lauren thinks her children are ready she then uses the Six-Trait Writing Method.[37] (See the 5E Model lesson plan.) The six traits include the following:

- *Ideas:* Have children include ideas (people I know, things I do, things I have, places I go). More ideas lead to better writing.
- *Organization:* Have children look at the structure of their writing (beginning, middle, and end).
- *Voice:* Encourage children to find their writer's voice and write to their audience (a note to mom would be in a more informal voice than a story the child writes about her dog to read to the class).
- *Word choice:* Have children use word walls and encourage them to think about their word choice.
- *Sentence fluency:* Teach children to check for smooth writing and varied sentence structure (are my sentences easy to understand?).
- *Conventions:* Have children check their work for mechanics of writing (punctuation, capitalization, grammar, paragraphing, etc.).[38]

READER'S WORKSHOP. Duval County Florida schools conduct reader's workshops by immersing children in rich literature and mini-lessons that teach that reading is fun and exciting. In their workshops they use books with great stories and identifiable characters, settings, sequenced events, problems, and solutions. Haley Alverado's reading workshop classes look at four important components:

- *Connecting:* Haley begins the lesson by connecting yesterday's lesson with today's lesson. The previous day's lesson focused on *Goldilocks and the Three Bears*, and today's lesson focuses on a nonfiction book. The class then begins by drawing a chart comparing all the nonfiction features to the fictional story, *Goldilocks and the Three Bears*.
- *Teaching:* In the teaching component, Haley teaches children some of the features that are in the nonfiction text versus their previous readings. She lists things such as the following:
  - Has real pictures
  - Teaches things that we did not know before
  - Has captions and fun facts

LESSON PLANS

A Literacy 5E Lesson

Lesson Title: Pumpkin Venn Diagram

Time Frame for Lesson: Two days in October
Day 1—Read story and complete Venn diagram
Day 2—Journal-writing activity

Standards: Texas Essential Knowledge and Skills (TEKS):

(English Language Arts—Reading/Comprehension of Literary Text/Theme and Genre)

- K.6A Identify elements of a story including setting, character, and key events.
- K.8A Retell a main event from a story read aloud.
- K.8B Describe characters in a story and the reasons for their actions.
- K.10B Retell important facts in a text, heard or read. (Writing/Writing Process)
- K.13A Plan a first draft by generating ideas for writing through class discussion (with adult assistance).
- K.13E Share writing with others (with adult assistance).
- K.14A Dictate or write sentences to tell a story and put the sentences in chronological sequence.

Materials: Copy of the book, *The Biggest Pumpkin Ever* by Steven Kroll and illustrated by Jeni Bassett; a large piece of butcher paper; markers; student journals or writing paper; pencils; and crayons.

Targeted Vocabulary: Venn diagram, fertilizer/fertilized, manure, enormous, and admire.

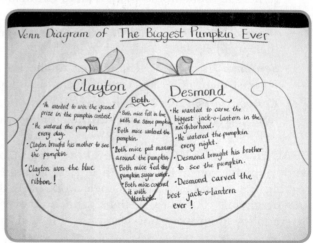

Lesson Procedure

Step 1—Engage: Introduce children in the text. Read *The Biggest Pumpkin Ever* by Steven Kroll.

Step 2—Explore: Have children raise their hands to do an open retell of the story. (An open retell is an opportunity for students to take turns telling the events of the story.)* Have them try to sequence the events of the story as each student raises his/her hand to volunteer a response. Ask, "What happened first? What did Desmond do to care for the pumpkin? What happened next?"

Step 3—Explain: The learner will compare and contrast the two main characters in the story, Desmond and Clayton, using a Venn diagram. Explain that today we are going to make a Venn diagram and that a Venn diagram is an illustration of how two things are alike and how they are different. Practice making a Venn diagram on the whiteboard together as a class, comparing two other things such as apples and oranges, dogs and cats, and so on.

Step 4—Extend: Using the butcher paper, draw two large intersecting circles, and draw features on them to resemble two large pumpkins. At the top of one pumpkin, write *Clayton*. At the top of the other pumpkin write *Desmond*.

Questions to ask:

- What did each mouse do to take care of the pumpkin?
- What did Clayton and Desmond want to do with their pumpkins?
- Where did each mouse live?
- Who else helped to care for the pumpkin?
- What happened to the pumpkin at the end of the story?

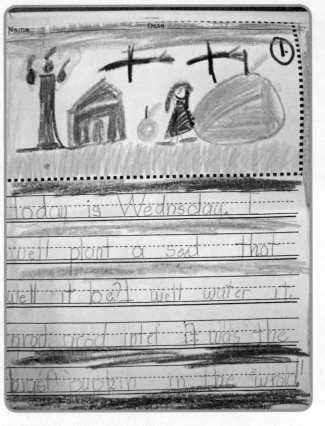

As children begin to answer these questions and discuss similarities and differences, the teacher writes sentences to fill in the Venn diagram based on their comments. If there is something specific to Clayton, write it on the pumpkin on the left. If it is specific to Desmond, then write it on the pumpkin on the right. If there is something that they both have in common, write it in the space where both pumpkins intersect. Once the Venn diagram is complete, encourage students to discuss among themselves what they can observe from the Venn diagram.

Step 5—Evaluate: Once students have completed the Venn diagram, have them do a writing activity about pumpkins. They may discuss in a small group or with a partner how to grow a pumpkin. They will then write a story "How to Grow a Pumpkin." This may be done on writing paper or in writing journals. This is an excellent time for differentiation of strategies to be used.[†] In evaluating the stories, a teacher may do so through informal observation by having the students read their entries to him or her. Or a more formal evaluation may be performed by using a rubric. The rubric should include rating the writer as "emerging," "developing," or "proficient" in the areas of ideas, organization, voice, word choice, sentence fluency, and conventions (this is commonly referred to as the Six-Trait Writing Method). This lesson also lends itself well to extension through science and social studies.[‡] The student writing sample meets the expectations defined in the rubric. The student performed the task with little to no help from the teacher.

[*]One way to ensure that every student has an opportunity to share is to write students' names on craft sticks. Teacher takes turns drawing a stick out of a cup and calling on that student to speak. This is a fair and unbiased technique.

[†]Suggestions for differentiating among various levels of learners: The high-level-ability learner may independently write in his/her journal with no help from the teacher. The average learner may need help sounding out words. The lower-level learner may need to dictate sentences to the teacher and then copy them over.

[‡]In an authentic kindergarten classroom, you could also do different 5E lessons focusing on science and/or math. In science, students could carve a pumpkin, plant the seeds, and observe them as they grow. In math, they could weigh a pumpkin, measure it, count the seeds, and so forth.

Source: Contributed by Lynne B. Rhodes, team leader and kindergarten teacher, Curtsinger Elementary School, Frisco, Texas. Photos by Jenny Clemens and Lynne R. Rhodes.

- ***Active involvement:*** In this part of the workshop, Haley has groups discuss things that they noticed in the nonfiction book. She adds additional features the children noticed.
- ***Linking:*** To link the lesson to independent reading, Haley gives each child a sticky note to place on any page that they find any of the nonfiction text features listed.[39]

MATH IN THE KINDERGARTEN

In today's kindergarten classroom, math, along with reading, plays a very prominent role. If you were to glimpse a kindergarten classroom, you might see groups and individual children engaged in such activities as graphing data from their observations and experiments; writing in their math journals; counting, sorting, and comparing concrete objects and keeping records of their work; making decisions about how to earn and spend money; working on computer math games and lessons; reading books about math; and engaged in math center activities. Kindergartners are active learners and like to learn with concrete materials in hands-on, "minds-on" active learning.

State standards primarily determine the subject matter content or "what gets taught" in the kindergarten. Take the kindergarten mathematics content standards for California, for example. They specify that students should understand small numbers, quantities, and simple shapes in their everyday environment and be able to count, compare, describe and sort objects, and develop a sense of properties and patterns. The standards describe the level at which students do these tasks so it is clear, for example, that a kindergartner should be able to "Compare two or more sets of objects (up to ten objects in each group) and identify which set is equal to, more than, or less than the other."[40]

How teachers teach math content to kindergartners is quite often left up to them, although in some school districts, teachers have to use and follow school district lesson plans. The primary reason more districts are using "scripted" lesson plans is because they want to ensure that all children are learning what the standards call for.

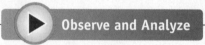

SCIENCE IN THE KINDERGARTEN

Science plays an increasingly important role in the kindergarten curriculum. If our children are to develop a love of science and the ability to think and express themselves scientifically, they need to learn about scientific concepts, methods, and attitudes while they are young. This gives them a foundation for future work in the sciences, math, language, and the arts. One of the most effective ways for young children to learn about science is through first-hand authentic objects and real specimens.

WHY IS TEACHING SCIENCE IN KINDERGARTEN IMPORTANT?   Science is assuming a more important role in kindergarten for these reasons:

- Science is an ideal vehicle for developing children's questioning minds about the natural world.
- Implementing the Science Standards can help our students take their place in a scientifically literate society.
- When children explore science, they acquire oral and written language for scientific expression and learn to read in new contexts.
- Science teaches children to appreciate the diversity of life and its interconnectedness.
- When children learn about nature, they respect and care for our planet and its natural resources.
- Learning scientific methods teaches children to view themselves as scientists.
- Exciting lessons in science can foster a lifelong love for the subject.[41]

SOCIAL STUDIES IN THE KINDERGARTEN

In kindergarten, the social sciences most often included are history, geography, economics, and civics.[42] For each of these disciplines you will want to include knowledge, concepts, and themes. Your teaching of the social studies should be content based and child centered, and you will want to make sure you consult your state's content standards for social studies.

Historically, social studies in the kindergarten focused on the **expanding horizons approach** (or *expanding environments approach*) for sequencing and selecting content. In this approach, children are at the center of the expanding horizons and at each grade level are immersed in a widening environment.

Today's teaching of the social studies is also designed to provide children with content knowledge and skills from the four social sciences. You will want to make sure you provide children with authentic content and activities that help them learn knowledge, apply knowledge, and engage in critical thinking.

IDEAS FOR TEACHING SOCIAL STUDIES.   The following are some ideas you can use to help you teach the social studies content standards of your state and school district:

- *Geography.* Emily Thompson teaches her kindergarten class about different cultures by placing a ribbon on a world map with the United States on one end and the other end on the country they are studying. Emily discusses with her students the different modes of transportation that are available for travel to the country. Children place pictures on the map above that country pertaining to the culture there. Emily then instructs the children to draw a picture, write a story, or create a poem to put on the map as well.

- *Economics.* Latonya Carter teaches her children about assembly lines through the use of creative arts. She draws a picture of a stick figure person using a different color crayon for each line drawn. After displaying the drawing on the wall, she then separates her class into small groups and gives each group member a different color crayon and one piece of paper per group. The piece of paper is passed down the line of students, and each student draws one line with their crayon matching Latonya's drawing. The class then discusses the importance of assembly lines, why each member must do his or her part, and the different products made on assembly lines.

- *Civics.* Brandon Phillips has his kindergarten children make a U.S. flag collage using large paper, magazines, crayons, scissors, and glue. He then discusses with the class that the flag is a national symbol, explains what the stars and stripes stand for, and discusses the role national symbols play in society. Children then tell Brandon where they've seen the American flag flown, and he makes a list of these places on chart paper. After the discussion, students individually draw pictures of other flags they have seen.

- *History.* Madelyn Hubbard teaches her kindergarten children about ancient cultures through photographs and online reproductions of wall paintings from ancient civilizations that illustrate life as it was lived in ancient times. She then asks the students to give her ideas about which animals lived at that time, which animals the people hunted, and what games the people played. Madelyn then has her students illustrate a picture of a day in their lives. The pictures include scenes such as driving to school, reading in class, recess, lunch, and playing with pets or siblings at home. After their drawings are complete, Madelyn hangs the students' pictures next to the pictures of the ancient civilization. The class then holds a discussion about the similarities and differences in the ancient civilizations and their own.

ARTS IN THE KINDERGARTEN

Teaching the arts in kindergarten consists of knowledge, skills, and concepts from these four areas: music, art, dance, and theater. Unfortunately the arts in the curriculum are not as highly valued as they should be. You can, however, teach the arts

expanding horizons approach Also called the *expanding environments approach*, an approach to teaching social studies in which the student is at the center of the expanding horizons and initial units, and at each grade level is exposed to an ever-widening environment.

"across the curriculum" by integrating them with reading, math, and science. All integration of the arts depends on these factors: time, opportunity, and materials.

TIME. Finding time to teach the arts is often a problem because of the emphasis on reading/literacy and math in the primary grades. Solve the problem by integrating the arts into your already scheduled time for teaching reading/literacy, math, science, and social studies. The following are ideas for integrating the arts into each of these areas:

Reading/Literacy. Students can act out the stories of their favorite book, thereby engaging in drama; students can illustrate a story that they or the class have written.

Math. Students can use art materials to make charts and graphs and to design and make different kinds of shapes. Students can also develop rules to describe the relationship of one shape to another: for example, "You can put two right triangles together to make a rectangle."

Science. Children can use their artistic skills to draw and paint various examples of the life cycle of butterflies or write and produce a public service announcement on the importance of personal health in the kindergarten classroom.

Social Studies. Students can learn about and sing many of the songs popular in their state's history; students can learn the folk dances of various cultural groups in their state.

OPPORTUNITY. The opportunities to teach the arts during the school year are endless. Consider the events that children are already experiencing in their everyday lives in their community. Was there a fire nearby? Is there a construction project? Did a storm pass through town? Did the zoo expand? Capitalize on such opportunities by weaving artistic elements such as puppetry, stories, drawing, or model building into the content areas. For example, in discussing the collapse of a bridge as the result of a flood, one teacher read the story *The Three Billy Goats Gruff*, and children made paper masks to depict the goats and built a bridge out of blocks and other found materials. Students clamored for a starring role as the troll. Every thematic unit provides opportunities for all of the arts, and children should be encouraged to explore ways to express ideas from the thematic units in an artistic way.

MATERIALS. Materials are just as important as time and opportunity. Materials include all of the materials related to the visual arts, paints, crayons, markers, brushes, and so on, as well as materials necessary for music and dance. For example, you can provide materials such as DVDs of folk dances, popular songs, and sing-along tunes. To encourage theater expression, children need props: clothes, hats, puppets, and plenty of materials such as cardboard boxes, glue, and tape for making their own stage settings and backgrounds. Keep in mind that the *process* of exploring the creative arts is more important than the finished *product*. Children are learning to enjoy learning when teachers respect the *process* of learning. You can create an arts center in which you have materials—paper, chalk, paintbrushes, pencils, and so on, with which children can represent the results of their scientific experiments, graph their math data, and illustrate their creative stories, poetry, and personal journals.

DEVELOPMENTALLY APPROPRIATE PRACTICE

Throughout this book I emphasize that in all things early childhood professionals do for and with children their efforts should be *developmentally appropriate*. Developmentally appropriate practice involves teaching and learning that is in accordance with children's physical, cognitive, social, linguistic, cultural, and gender development. Professionals help children learn and develop in ways that are compatible with children's ages and who they are as individuals, that is, respecting their background of experiences and culture.

Talking about developmentally appropriate practice is one thing; actually doing it is another. Here are some things you can do to make your kindergarten program developmentally appropriate and help children learn:

- Make learning meaningful to children by relating it to what they already know. For example, last week Blanca Davis and her children planted seeds and watched them sprout and grow. They talked about what plants need in order to grow and why some of their plants died. Yesterday, when the class pet, Fishey, died, Blanca took the opportunity to extend their discussion about living things and death. She selected two special books, *Goodbye Mousie* and *Jasper's Day,* to read to the children.

- Individualize your curriculum as much as possible to account for the needs of all children of all diversities of abilities and backgrounds. All children do not learn the same way, nor are they interested in learning the same things as everyone else all the time.

- Make learning physically and mentally active. Children should be actively involved in learning activities—building, making, experimenting, investigating, and working collaboratively with their peers.

- Involve children in *hands-on* activities with concrete objects and manipulatives. Emphasize real-life activities as opposed to workbook and worksheet activities.

Remember, developmentally appropriate practice begins with you.

ACCOMMODATING DIVERSE LEARNERS

Now that you have read about changes and issues in kindergartens today, let's focus our attention on the transition to kindergarten for children with disabilities. Most parents of typically developing children feel positive about their child's transition to kindergarten, but they nonetheless remain anxious about this major entry point into the world of school. Parents of children with disabilities share these worries and also have practical questions related to how, where, when, and who will provide their children's services. For the many parents who have worked hard to establish support systems in their preschools, the thought of starting all over again from scratch can seem daunting. The Individuals with Disabilities Education Act (IDEA) clearly articulates the importance of transitions for children with disabilities from early intervention programs to early childhood special education and inclusive kindergarten classrooms.

You can help facilitate all children's transitions to kindergarten by making a conscious effort to think about the acronym SCHOOL:

S: Start early. Schools must carefully bridge the distance between a play-based curriculum and the increasing academic demands of kindergarten. It is not unreasonable to start the transition process a full year to year and a half before kindergarten begins. For example, in the fall of a child's last year of preschool, teachers at the child's current school should contact the kindergarten to schedule times to meet and visit each program.

C: Collaborative team approach. Planning and making decisions with a collaborative team should involve families, preschool teachers, kindergarten teachers, school administrators, and any related service providers that the child sees (e.g., occupational therapists, physical therapists). For example, the team may observe several schools and choose the one that best meets the needs of the child.

H: Honor active involvement of families. This involvement may include teaching parents about the school and kindergarten and addressing their questions and concerns about how specialized services will be provided for their children. For example, parents may want to meet with the therapists or visit the school with their child prior to the beginning of school.

O: Observe current and future schools. Observe at the preschool and have the teachers and families observe at the kindergarten prior to the start of the kindergarten year. This will allow you to identify the needs and strengths of the child and prepare for any modifications or accommodations. For example, you may observe that the classroom arrangement of the preschool is easily replicated and meets the needs of *all* children.

O: Outline goals and anticipated outcomes. Work as a team to develop the goals and outcomes in the child's individualized education program. This may not be necessary for every child, but *all* children need goals and outcomes to ensure an optimal kindergarten experience. For example, a common kindergarten goal is following rules, routines, and directions. This can then include modifications or adaptations for children who need them.

L: Listen and learn. The child's previous teachers, therapists, and parents have a wealth of child-specific, relevant information that includes strategies or adaptations that have previously been successful. Having a collaborative dialogue also allows you to share the services and supports available at your school. For example, a parent might tell you that a child uses modified scissors when cutting or enjoys social praise.

> **Check Your Understanding:** Programs

ACTIVITIES FOR PROFESSIONAL DEVELOPMENT

ETHICAL DILEMMA

"FULL-DAY KINDERGARTEN POSES A PROBLEM"

In your state, full-day kindergarten is supposed to be offered by every public school starting in the fall of 2015. Although it is a statewide mandate for all school districts in your state, it may or may not happen in your district. District officials are saying that because of the poor economy, they are unable to afford to add the teachers and classrooms necessary to make the change from the traditional half-day schedule to a full-day schedule.

Sarah Collins is a kindergarten teacher and a strong advocate for full-day kindergarten. When Sarah heard the news about the delay, she scheduled a meeting with Paul Gardner, the district superintendent, to discuss her concerns about the delay of full-day kindergarten. During their conversation the superintendent said, "A lot of research shows that full-day kindergarten is very beneficial to kids, but there are a lot of districts like us who will have to wait until we find the money to make this happen." Based on her discussion with the superintendent, Sarah is very doubtful that the district will take any action to ensure that full-day kindergarten happens in the fall.

What should Sarah do? Should she keep quiet and say nothing? Or should Sarah try to talk with the board of education and present her case? Should Sarah ask the president of the local teachers' union to call a special meeting so she can persuade them to take action? Or should Sarah choose another course of action? What should Sarah do? What would you do?

ACTIVITIES TO APPLY WHAT YOU LEARNED

1. What do you like most about the kindergarten of today? What do you like least? Write an essay about your kindergarten experiences and post it to your class discussion board.

2. **KEY ASSESSMENT:** Identify for each of the following kindergarten classroom environments, healthy, respectful, supportive, and challenging, three things you do to support/enhance these areas.

Healthy

1.

2.

3.

Respectful

1.

2.

3.

Supportive

1.

2.

3.

Challenging

1.

2.

3.

Ask your professor to let you use PowerPoint to share your findings with the class.

Search for kindergarten teachers' Web pages for ideas to see how they make changes to their classroom environments to support these four areas. Use the rubric provided to guide your work.

3. Go online and research ways you can promote physical, social-emotional, and cognitive development for kindergartners. Identify five of your most important findings and share them by posting links on your class discussion board.

4. Think about ways kindergarten teachers integrate technology to help children learn the curriculum. How can you integrate technology in your classroom to help children learn math, science, reading/literacy, and social studies? Demonstrate to your colleagues the kinds of technology you would use.

5. How can you make children's transitions from early childhood special education programs to kindergarten easier? Conduct an online interview on Skype with a special education teacher to get his or her advice. Share these suggestions with your peers in a blog, online, or in a discussion.

LINKING TO LEARNING

The following agencies and programs, which can be located easily online, provide additional information about topics discussed in this chapter.

Dolch Sight Words

This site is dedicated to providing various educational activities to teach reading, including teachers teaching their students and parents teaching their children.

Kindergarten Connection

You will find new hints, tips, and information each week on this site dedicated to providing valuable resources to primary teachers.

Indian Child

This website provides various resources for parents and teachers. It offers tongue twisters, short stories, optical illusions, and other educational supplements for children.

National Kindergarten Alliance

The result of a summit of leaders from various kindergarten associations, organizations, and interest groups that met in January 2000 is posted here. This is a national organization that serves kindergarten teachers throughout the United States.

Susan Elizabeth Blow and History of the Kindergarten

This website outlines Blow's contributions to the development of the kindergarten and provides many links to Froebel and interesting kindergarten topics.

CHAPTER 12

THE PRIMARY GRADES

Preparation for Lifelong Success

LEARNING OUTCOMES

1. Explain how teaching in grades one to three is changing.
2. Explain the physical, motor, social, emotional, cognitive, and moral development characteristics of children in grades one to three.
3. Examine environments that support learning in grades 1–3.
4. Explain the instructional processes and teaching practices used in the primary grades.
5. Identify and analyze the curriculum content areas of the primary grades.
6. Describe how you can modify your classroom to accommodate children's learning needs.

TEACHING IN GRADES ONE TO THREE

Reform continues to sweep across the educational landscape. Nowhere is this more evident than in grades one to three. Changes include how schools operate and are organized, how teachers teach, how children are evaluated, and how schools involve and relate to parents and the community. State governments are specifying curriculum and testing agendas. Accountability and collaboration are in; schooling, as usual, is out.

NAEYC STANDARDS

THE PRIMARY GRADES AND CONTEMPORARY SCHOOLING

Gay Barnes is a first grade teacher and Alabama Teacher of the Year. Gay prides herself on her commitment to helping struggling students. She holds on to the notion that her teaching style should reflect what kind of teacher she would want her child to have. Gay is in charge of knowing her students as individual learners, knowing what they need to learn and how to plan and teach lessons that will take them to the next level of their learning. Gay believes when a child who has been puzzling over a concept for days suddenly has a magical 'Ah Ha!' moment, for that child in that instant, the learning is all her own.[1,2]

Teacher of the Year Talandria Gosha believes that every student is capable of learning and that students learn in various ways and rates. As a teacher, she enjoys researching, creating, implementing strategies, and learning about new opportunities to meet her students' needs. Her goal is to build on children's existing knowledge while teaching them something new each day. As a second grade teacher, Talandria values the beauty of growth in each individual student's progress.[3]

Third grade teacher Darcy Grimes, 2012 Teacher of the Year looks forward to coming to school every day to build relationships with her class. She believes that it can take a lot of time to create a learner-centered classroom, but the time she spends is worth it when she sees the excitement for learning on her children's faces. Darcy believes that in order to be an outstanding teacher she has to show her enthusiasm for learning to her students through humor, song, dance, and games and that she must create relationships and personal connections with each child in her classroom. Darcy sets high standards for all of her students, no matter what their background and past experiences, so they can work at their highest potential. Most of all, however, Darcy wants all of her students to be life-long learners and global citizens who can compete in this growing technological society. Darcy has her students use Web 2.0 tools to work collaboratively with classrooms in five different states and abroad in four different countries. These technological opportunities allow Darcy's students who live in a very rural area to have experiences working with other students around the world.[4]

LEARNING CONTEXTS

As we begin our discussion of living and learning in grades one to three, it will be helpful to look at the nature of primary grades today. The following are some of the major contexts of teaching in grades one, two, and three.

DIVERSITY. Schools and classrooms are more diverse than ever before. The percentage of racial/ethnic minority students enrolled in the nation's public schools increased to 48 percent in 2013.[5] This increase in minority enrollment largely reflects the growth in the percentage of students who are Hispanic. Hispanic students represent 23 percent of public school enrollment. The distribution of minority students in public schools differs across regions of the country, with minority public school enrollment (55 percent) exceeding white enrollment (45 percent) in the West.[6]

The number of school-age children who speak a language other than English at home is five million, or 76 percent of the population of this age range.[7] This means you will be teaching children from different cultures and backgrounds, and you will have to take those differences into account in your planning and teaching. In addition to cultural and linguistic differences, diversity is also reflected in children's socioeconomic status and in their physical, cognitive, social, emotional, adaptive, and communication abilities.

TESTING.   Testing is, and will continue to be, a part of contemporary school culture and instructional practices. For example, in the months of April and May, from P.S. 124 in Brooklyn, New York, to Lead Mine Elementary in North Carolina, to Frisco ISD in Texas, teachers focus on year-end teaching and testing. You too will be involved in helping students learn appropriate grade-level content so they can pass local, state, and national tests. In addition, you will use test data as a basis for your planning and instruction.

CHANGING TEACHER ROLES.   As you've read, the role of the early childhood teacher is changing rapidly and changing dramatically. This is particularly true for teachers in grades one to three. For example, it is likely that you will be a member of a **grade-level and across-levels planning** teams that meet regularly to plan, learn, debate, discuss, decide, and develop lessons and learning activities. You will collaborate with your colleagues on all types of projects and learning activities. Today, school is a place in which a premium is placed on collaboration and being a team player.

grade-level and across-levels planning Planning occurs in grade-level teams and across grade levels, for example, K–1. This is also called horizontal planning (same grade level) and vertical planning (grades above and/or below).

ACADEMICS.   The contemporary curriculum in grades one to three is heavy on reading and the STEM subjects (science, technology, engineering, and math). There is also an emphasis on the arts, social studies, character education, and health and wellness through physical education. Many of these areas, however, are integrated with the basic curriculum. For example, to integrate academics with children's projects and activities, fifth grade teacher Patricia Doyle at Pine Grove Elementary in St. Petersburg, Florida, taught a Family Recipe classroom project. The project included third, fourth, and fifth grade students in an activity that also involved their extended family members. Doyle wanted the students to learn about their ancestors and their ethnicity by producing cookbooks made up of favorite family recipes. The project covered many skills in many subjects: social studies, writing, technology, reading, research, speaking and presentation, math, and science.[8]

TECHNOLOGY USE AND INTEGRATION.   Children are different today from those of a decade ago because of new and different kinds of technology. Today's generation is the "dot-com" or Net Generation. They have grown up surrounded by technology and are familiar and comfortable with it. Children's involvement with computer games enables them to think abstractly and to make rapid-fire decisions. About three fourths (77 percent) of homes in the United States have Internet access.[9] This connectivity enables children to have almost immediate access to vast amounts of information that enrich their lives and learning. Also, consider how the use of cell phones and text messaging change the way children communicate. Here is how two third graders texted with each other about a school project:

Student 1:   Hey dyw to wrk with me for da project?
Student 2:   Yea. Dat's cool. U can pick the topic. Idc.

Because today's children are immersed in technology from the beginning of life, you need to find many opportunities to integrate technology into their learning activities. Provide opportunities for children to access the Internet, use digital cameras to gather information and document learning, create and transport reports on the Internet, and engage in electronic creativity discussions and the sharing of ideas.

Just as not all of your children have access to the Internet, not all of your children have the same access to technology. Making sure children have access to technology is an important factor when designing a classroom environment and planning curricula that promotes learning and motivation. You have to provide opportunities for children who don't have or use technology at home opportunities to use technology in your classroom.

HEALTH AND WELLNESS.   Physical education at all levels is undergoing a renaissance. One reason for its rejuvenation, especially in the primary and elementary grades, is the concern about the national epidemic of childhood obesity and increases in childhood diabetes. Physical education classes and programs are viewed as a way of providing children with the knowledge and activities they need to get in shape and stay that way for the rest of their lives.

ONGOING POLITICAL AND EDUCATIONAL CHANGES.   What politicians and lawmakers believe is best for children and how to teach them changes with every state and national election. Changes in politics in turn change how we teach children and what we teach them. For the past decade, politicians have placed a major emphasis on standards and academic achievement. The No Child Left Behind Act of 2001 (NCLB) focuses on teaching and learning and on meeting state and Common Core State Standards, especially in reading and math. Today there is a great emphasis on getting all students college and career ready (CCR), and this process begins in grades one, two, and three.

As a result of what we have discussed, you must look at teaching in grades one to three differently from how you would approach preschool and kindergarten education. You will want to consider new and appropriate approaches for teaching in these three important grades.

As you observe this video, pay particular attention to what the narrator has to say about the "balancing act" that primary grade teachers today have to perform between children's developmental needs and the demands of schooling. Reflect on some of the issues the narrator raises about teaching in the primary grades today and how teacher's role is changing to accommodate the demands of contemporary schooling.

WHAT ARE CHILDREN IN GRADES ONE TO THREE LIKE?

This text stresses the uniqueness and individuality of children, who also share common characteristics. Those common characteristics guide our practice of teaching, but we must always account for individual needs. All children are unique.

How are children of today different from the children of yesterday?

- Children of today are smarter than children of previous generations. There are a number of reasons for this: better health and nutrition, better-educated parents, better schooling, and access to and involvement with technology, such as computers, electronic devices, electronic games, learning systems, and television.
- Many children bring to school a vast background of experiences that contribute to their knowledge and ability to learn. However, many children do *not* have a rich array of experiences, and an increasing number live in poverty. Today, 23 percent of children under age eighteen live in poverty and come to school unprepared.[10]

- More children are from diverse racial, cultural, and socioeconomic backgrounds. In many communities and schools, children from minority backgrounds make up the majority. Many children from diverse populations come to school with health, home, and learning challenges.

Now let's take a look on at three typically developing children who are in classrooms today. After you review and reflect on the Portraits of First, Second, and Third Graders, answer the developmentally appropriate questions that accompany the feature.

PHYSICAL DEVELOPMENT

Two words describe the physical growth of primary-age children: *slow* and *steady*. Children at this age do not make the rapid and obvious height and weight gains of infants, toddlers, and preschoolers. Instead, they experience continual growth, develop increasing control over their bodies, and explore the things they are able to do. Primary children are building on the development of their earlier years.

From ages seven to eight, children's average weight and height approximate each other, as shown in Table 12.1. The weight of boys and girls tends to be the same until after age nine, when girls begin to pull ahead of boys in both height and weight. However, wide variations appear in both individual rates of growth and development and in the sizes of children. These differences in physical appearance result from genetic and cultural factors, nutritional intake and habits, health care, and experiential background.

MOTOR DEVELOPMENT

Six-, seven-, and eight-year-old children are in Erikson's industry versus inferiority stage. Thus, not only are children intuitively driven to initiate activities, but they are also learning to be competent and productive individuals. The primary years are a time to use and test developing motor skills. Children at this age should be actively involved in activities that enable them to use their bodies to learn and develop feelings of accomplishment and competence. Children's growing confidence and physical skills are reflected in games involving running, chasing, and their enthusiasm in organized sports of all kinds. A nearly universal characteristic of children in this period is their almost constant physical activity.

TABLE 12.1 | Average Height and Weight for First- to Third-Grade Children

Conduct your own survey of the height and weight of primary-age children. Compare your findings with this table. What conclusions can you draw?

Age	Males		Females	
	Height (inches)	Weight (pounds)	Height (inches)	Weight (pounds)
6 years	45.25	45.50	42.25	44.00
7 years	48.00	50.00	47.75	50.00
8 years	50.50	56.00	50.25	56.00
9 years	52.25	62.00	52.50	64.00

Source: Adapted from National Center for Health Statistics in collaboration with the National Center for Chronic Disease Prevention and Health Promotion (2004), www.cdc.gov/growthcharts.

PORTRAITS OF FIRST, SECOND, AND THIRD GRADERS

JACOB (1ST GRADE)

General Description 7-year-old African American male; great sense of humor; laughs at himself; an only child; loves music, trains, drawing, and writing

Social-Emotional	Cognitive	Motor	Adaptive (Daily Living)
• Makes friends; keeping friendships is very important to him • Emotionally sensitive; seeks approval; easily hurt • Does not respond well to criticism • Interacts equally well with boys and girls, however, appears to prefer engaging with girls	• Reads on grade level with good comprehension • Writing is at grade level • Admits that he is challenged by mathematics, but grades are of average performance	• Performs average on gross and fine motor skills, but still is unable to tie shoelaces • Participates in group games • Participates in all school activities	• Responds well to praise • Comes to school with necessary materials • Obeys class and school rules • Has a specific sense of style (hats and vests)

JAMEE (2ND GRADE)

General Description 8-year-old Hispanic female; well-spoken and great sense of humor; interested in music and art; lives with both parents and younger sister (2 yr old); she is one of the tallest students in her class

Social-Emotional	Cognitive	Motor	Adaptive (Daily Living)
• Friendly and outgoing • Has many friends • Often mediates disputes during recess • Empathetic	• Reads on grade level with good comprehension • Initially had trouble writing for sustained periods of time • Some challenges with basic math concepts, but perseveres	• Strong fine motor skills • Participates in all physical education activities • Loves to swim and dance	• Responds well to praise • Is a responsible student; comes to school with necessary materials • Is well groomed • Attentive in class and an active participant

BLAKE (3RD GRADE)

General Description 9-year-old Caucasian male; loves Legos, *Star Wars*, and telling imaginative stories; youngest of two children

Social-Emotional	Cognitive	Motor	Adaptive (Daily Living)
• Has difficulty expressing his feelings and often acts out when anxious or upset • Wants to play with all his classmates but is unsure how to approach them • Would rather work independently in a secluded part of the classroom • Once he talks about what is bothering him with an adult, he is able to return to regular activities	• Can concentrate on a single task for 5 minutes and benefits 1-1 support to make sure he is on task and understands directions • Benefits from concepts being modeled and then guided practice before being able to work on an assignment independently • Can complete one by two digit multiplication problems but might need a visual of the process before beginning • Can tell vivid stories, but needs a scribe to write them down	• Has difficulty sitting in one place for lengthy periods of time; taps or swings feet frequently • Can grasp a pencil, but he has trouble forming print letters; benefits from extra time or scribe • Uses simple combinations of movements such as running or jumping • Skillfully uses a mouse and keyboard	• Needs organizational support to keep track of his learning materials • Has a great sense of humor and wants to make others happy • Is unaware that his behaviors might distract others and often needs a reminder of this • Benefits from a consistent schedule • With a nurturing classroom environment, he is participating more in class discussions and taking more risks, especially when explaining his thoughts and feelings to others

(Continued)

Developmentally Appropriate Questions:

- Based on this brief portrait, what kind of learning "problems" does Blake have? What can you do to help Blake from "acting out"? Extend the length of time he can concentrate on a topic? Sitting in one place for a length of time?

- Consider that Jamee has some "challenges" with basic math concepts. What can you do to help ensure that young girls like Jamee do not develop math anxiety and instead enjoy and do well in math?

- Two of the children—Jamee and Jacob—enjoy music. Give two examples of how you can incorporate music and the arts in your teaching to promote children's learning.

Differences between boys' and girls' motor skills during the primary years are minimal—their abilities are about equal. Teachers therefore should not use gender as a basis for determining involvement in activities. On the contrary, we should promote *all* children's involvement in age-appropriate activities.

MATURITY IN THE PRIMARY GRADES. Although we refer to early childhood education as the years from birth to age eight, the primary, grades one to three, represent, in many ways, a divide in early childhood development. The primary grades are a period in which children are undergoing dramatic developmental change. Primary age children, while still children in many ways, are entering faster into the "tween" years or preadolescence than in previous decades. In third grade you will notice more evidence of the early onset of puberty, especially in girls. Growing up fast can be attributed in part to **puberty**, the period of profound physical and emotional developmental changes in the transition from childhood to adolescence. Health professionals attribute the early onset of puberty to lack of sound nutritional habits, childhood obesity; diet, especially consumption of meat and dairy products that contain hormones, industrial chemicals; and family genetics.[11]

The physical changes that accompany puberty can be confusing and traumatic for young girls, especially when they do not understand what is happening. This is where you will have to work closely with parents to help them educate their children about their children's developmental changes, and at the same time, you will have to collaborate with parents to help them understand their children's health and development and the emotional repercussions associated with it. Of course, the amount and kind of developmental information you provide depends on your school's policy regarding developmental topics. Thus, make sure you are well informed about what you can and cannot say and teach.

During the primary years we see evidence of continuing refinement of fine motor skills in children's mastery of many tasks they previously could not do or could do only with difficulty. They are now able to dress themselves relatively easily and attend to most of their personal needs. They are also more proficient at school tasks that require fine motor skills such as writing, making artwork, and using computers and other technology. In addition, primary children want to and are able to engage in real-life activities; they want the real thing. This makes teaching them easier and more fun because many activities have real-life applications.

SOCIAL DEVELOPMENT

Children in grades one to three (ages six through nine) are in Erikson's industry versus inferiority stage of social-emotional development. They are in **middle childhood**, a time when they gain confidence and ego satisfaction from completing demanding tasks. Children want to act responsibly and are quite capable of achieving difficult tasks and accomplishments. Children take a lot of pride in doing well. All of this reflects the industry side of social-emotional development.

puberty The period of profound physical and emotional developmental changes in the transition from childhood to adolescence.

middle childhood Describes children in Erikson's industry versus inferiority stage of social-emotional development, ages six to nine years, during which time they gain confidence and ego satisfaction from completing demanding tasks.

Children during this stage are at varying levels of academic achievement. Those who are high in academic self-esteem credit their success to such **mastery-oriented attributions** as trying hard (industriousness), paying attention, determination, and stick-to-itiveness. If they have difficulty with a task, they believe that by trying harder they will succeed.[12]

At the same time, children in this stage compare their abilities and accomplishments with their peers. When they perceive they are not doing as well as they could or as well as their peers, they may lose confidence in their abilities and achievement. This is the inferiority side of this stage of social-emotional development. Some children develop **learned helplessness**, a condition in which children attribute their failures to a lack of ability.

IMPLICATIONS FOR TEACHING. You, the teacher, can be helpful and supportive of children, providing them with tasks they can accomplish and encouraging them to do their best.

Here are some things you can do to accomplish this goal:

- Provide activities children can reasonably accomplish so they can experience the satisfaction that comes from a job well done.
- Apply Gardner's theory of multiple intelligences to your teaching, which will encourage children to excel at things they are good at. All children develop skills and abilities in particular areas. Build a classroom environment that enables children to be competent in their particular intelligence and learning style.
- Be supportive and encouraging of children's efforts. For example, "Good Job Aaron! See what you can do when you really try!"

EMOTIONAL DEVELOPMENT

Think for a moment about how important emotions are in your life and how emotions influence what and how you learn. When you are happy, life goes well! When you are sad, it is harder to be enthusiastic about doing what you have to do. The children you teach are no different. Emotions are an important part of children's everyday lives.[13] One of your responsibilities is to help them develop positive emotions and express their emotions in healthy ways.

IMPLICATIONS FOR TEACHING. The following activities give you specific ideas for how to support the positive social-emotional development of children in the industry versus inferiority stage of development:

- *Use literature to discuss emotions.* Children in grades one to three like to talk about their emotions and the emotions of characters in literature.[14] They are able to make inferences about characters' emotional states and discuss how they are or are not appropriate to the story. They can then relate these emotional states to their own lives and to events at home and in the classroom. Some good books to use to discuss emotional states include these:
  - *How Are You Peeling? Foods with Moods* by Saxton Freymann and Joost Elffers offers brief text and photographs of carvings made from vegetables that introduce the world of emotions by presenting leading questions such as "Are you feeling angry?"
  - *Today I Feel Silly: And Other Moods That Make My Day* by Jamie Lee Curtis follows a little girl with curly red hair through thirteen different moods including silly, grumpy, mean, excited, and confused.
  - *When Sophie Gets Angry . . . Really, Really Angry* by Molly Bang conveys young Sophie's anger when her mother allows her younger sister to play with her stuffed gorilla, the eventual calm she feels after running outside and crying, and the calm and relaxed return home.

mastery-oriented attributions Attributions that include effort (industriousness), paying attention, determination, and perseverance.

learned helplessness A condition that can develop when children perceive that they are not doing as well as they could or as well as their peers, lose confidence in their abilities and achievement, and then attribute their failures to a lack of ability. These children are passive and have learned to feel they are helpless.

FIGURE 12.1 | Journal Entry

Today's students want to use technology and unique programs to write, express themselves and be creative. Programs such as Wordle, in which students develop word clouds, provide them with an alternative way of expressing their thoughts and feelings.

- *Encourage children to express their emotions.* Beginning and ending the day with class meeting discussions is a good way to help children express their thoughts and feelings. This provides children a safe and secure outlet to say how they felt about their day.

- *Write about feelings.* Give children opportunities to keep journals in which they write about home, family life, classroom events, and how they feel about them. One teacher has her children create "word clouds" that they share with her and with their classmates if they choose. Figure 12.1 illustrates how Cassie, Mario, and Emily collaborated and used Wordle to develop a word cloud in response to their reading of Jamie Lee Curtis's book, *Today I Feel Silly, And Other Moods That Make My Day.*

- *Provide opportunities for play.* Play is a powerful outlet for releasing energy and expressing emotional states. Through fantasy and superhero play, children can express feelings and try out their growing range of emotions.

- *Provide for cultural differences.* Be aware of how the various cultures represented by your children feel about emotional expression. Some cultures are very emotive; others are not. Work with parents to learn how their cultures express certain emotions such as joy and sadness and determine the culturally unacceptable ways to express emotions.

childhood depression
A disorder affecting as many as 1 in 33 children that can negatively impact feelings, thoughts, and behavior and can manifest itself with physical symptoms of illness.

MENTAL HEALTH IN MIDDLE CHILDHOOD.   Just as we are concerned about the mental health of infants, toddlers, and preschoolers, so too are we very concerned about the mental health of children in the middle years. We are particularly concerned about **childhood depression**. As many as 1 in 33 children have depression.[15] Childhood depression manifests itself in the following ways: persistent sadness; withdrawal from family, friends, and activities that they once enjoyed; increased irritability or agitation; changes in eating and sleeping habits (e.g., significant weight loss, insomnia, excessive sleep); may complain of feeling sick; refuse to go to school; cling to a parent or caregiver or worry excessively that a parent may die.[16]

Children's good mental health begins at home and continues in your classroom. Part of your role is to work with parents to promote their children's mental health and support children's good mental health in your classroom.

IMPLICATIONS FOR TEACHING. In your teaching and collaboration with parents, here are some things you can advise parents to do:

- *Encourage children to play.* Play time is as important to a child's development as food. Play helps a child be creative, develop problem-solving skills and self-control, and learn how to get along with others.

- *Enroll children in an after-school activity, especially if they are otherwise home alone after school.* This is a great way for children to stay productive, learn something new, gain self-esteem, and have something to look forward to during the week.

- *Provide a safe and secure home environment.* Fear can be very real for a child. Try to find out what is frightening him or her. Be loving, patient, and reassuring, not critical.

- *Give appropriate guidance and discipline when necessary.* Be firm, but kind, and realistic with your expectations. The goal is not to control the child, but rather to help him or her learn self-control.

- *Communicate.* Parents need to make time each day after work and school to listen to their children and talk with them about what is happening in their lives and to share emotions and feelings.[17]

In your teaching of young children, here are some things you can do:

- *Create a sense of classroom belonging.* Feeling connected and welcomed is essential to children's positive adjustment, self-identification, and sense of trust in others and themselves.

- *Promote resilience.* Adversity is a natural part of life and being resilient is important to overcoming challenges and good mental health. Connectedness, competency, helping others, and successfully facing difficult situations all foster resilience.

- *Develop competencies.* Children need to know that they can overcome challenges and accomplish goals through their actions. Achieving academic success and developing individual talents and interests helps children feel competent and more able to deal positively with stress.

- *Ensure a positive, safe classroom and school environment.* Feeling safe is critical to students' learning and mental health. Promote positive behaviors such as respect, responsibility, and kindness. Prevent negative behaviors such as bullying and harassment.

- *Teach and reinforce positive behaviors and decision making.* Provide consistent expectations and support. Teach social skills, problem solving, and conflict resolution, which are supporters of good mental health.

- *Encourage helping others.* Children need to know that they can make a difference. Pro-social behaviors build self-esteem, foster connectedness, reinforce personal responsibility, and present opportunities for positive recognition.

- *Encourage good physical health.* Good physical health supports good mental health.[18]

COGNITIVE DEVELOPMENT

Concrete operational thought is the cognitive milestone that enables children in the primary elementary grades to think and act as they do. Children in the *concrete operations stage*, from about age seven to about age twelve, begin to use mental images and symbols during the thinking process and can reverse operations. For example, operations include many mathematical activities involving addition and subtraction, greater than and less than, multiplication, division, and equalities. A child is able to reverse operations when she can understand that when, for example, she adds two to three to get five, she can reverse this operation by subtracting two from five to get three. This is why it is a good idea for you to use concrete materials (e.g., rods, beads, buttons, blocks) to help children physically see operations as an aid for mental representation.

Concrete operational children begin to develop the ability to understand that change involving physical appearances does not necessarily change quality or quantity. They also begin to reverse thought processes by going back over and "undoing" a mental action just accomplished. Other mental operations children are capable of during this stage include the following:

- *One-to-one correspondence.* One-to-one correspondence is the basis for counting and matching objects. The concrete operations child has mastered the ability, for example, to give an iPod from the technology cart to each member of her work group.
- *Classification of events and time according to their occurrence.* For example, a child in the concrete operations stage can classify events as occurring before or after lunch.
- *Classification involving multiple properties.* Multiple classifications occur when a child can classify objects on the basis of more than one property, such as color and size, shape and size, shape and color, and so forth.

- *Seriation.* This is the ordering of people, objects, or events. For example, Mandy developed a chart showing the heights of children in her class from shortest to tallest.
- *Class inclusion operations.* Class inclusion also involves classification. For example, if you showed five apples, five oranges, and five lemons to a child in the concrete operations stage and asked him if there were more apples or fruit, he would be able to respond "fruit."

The process of development from the preoperational stage to the concrete stage is gradual and continual and occurs over a period of time as a result of maturation and experiences. No simple sets of exercises will cause children to move up the developmental ladder. Rather, ongoing developmentally appropriate activities lead to conceptual understanding.

Today there is great emphasis on children's cognitive development and activities that promote reading, math, and science. What are some things you can do to help children be successful in these areas?

MORAL DEVELOPMENT

Moral development is the process of developing culturally acceptable attitudes and behaviors toward others and the environment based on what society endorses and supports through rules, laws, and cultural norms as right and wrong.

TABLE 12.2 | Moral Development in the Primary Years

Theorist	Moral Stage and Characteristics	Implications for Teachers
Jean Piaget	1. *Relations of Constraint: Grades 1–2.* Concepts of right and wrong are determined by judgments of adults. Therefore, morality is based on what adults say is right and wrong.	• Provide children with many opportunities to engage in decisions and make decisions about what is right and wrong.
	2. *Relations of Cooperation: Grades 3–6.* Children's exchange of viewpoints with others helps determine what is good/bad and right/wrong.	• Provide opportunities every day for children to make decisions and assume responsibilities. Responsibility comes from opportunities to be responsible.
Lawrence Kohlberg	1. *Preconventional Level: Ages 4–10.* Morality is a matter of good or bad based on a system of punishment and reward as administered by adults in authority positions.	• Provide many examples of moral behavior and decisions. Use children's literature to help you achieve this goal.
	• *Stage 1: Punishment and obedience.* Children operate within and respond to consequences of behavior.	• Use children's out-of-classroom experiences as a basis for discussion involving values and decision-making.
	• *Stage 2: Instrumental–relativist orientation.* Children's actions are motivated by satisfaction of needs ("You scratch my back, I'll scratch yours").	• Provide children many opportunities to interact with children of different ages and cultures.

Jean Piaget and Lawrence Kohlberg are the leading proponents of a developmental stage theory of children's moral development. Table 12.2 outlines their stages of moral development during ages six to ten. Implicit to children's moral development is the process of moving or developing from what is known as "other regulation" (by parents, teachers, etc.) to self-regulation. Review Table 12.2 now and consider how you can apply the implications of this information to your teaching.

CHARACTER EDUCATION. Moral development is closely aligned with character education, which is rapidly becoming a part of many early childhood classrooms across the United States. Whereas everyone believes that children have to learn how to count, growing numbers of individuals also believe that schools have to teach children *what* counts. As character education is becoming a higher priority, curricula designed to teach specific character traits are now commonplace. In fact, the early childhood curriculum now consists of the six Rs: *r*eading, *w*riting, *a*rithmetic, *r*easoning, *r*espect, and *r*esponsibility.

Herrington Elementary School provides another example of ways to promote healthy, happy children in a school environment. Herrington is a school that seeks to promote community and working together to prevent bullying and hate. Herrington, a pre-K to grade five urban public school located in Pontiac, Michigan, has an enrollment

Character education is rapidly becoming a part of many early childhood classrooms across the United States. What characteristics do you think are important to teach children so that they develop positive morals and character skills?

of over four hundred students. Community is very important at Herrington, and the community presence is strong in the neighborhood and in the school. Each morning, all students eat breakfast together and then participate with teachers, support staff, and custodians in *harambee*, a Swahili term for "gathering," which means a call to unity for collective work. Throughout the school day, students are given opportunities to reflect on the golden rule and the community's values and to learn conflict resolution skills. Leading the district in scores and attendance rates, Herrington works hard to be a leader in the community. Character education ties the school's efforts together and provides the basis for unity. Herrington's lesson is clear: Promoting community involvement, unity, character education, and conflict resolution promotes healthy children, families, schools, and test scores!

All character education programs seek to teach a set of traditional core values that will result in civic virtue and moral character, including honesty, kindness, respect, responsibility, tolerance for diversity, racial harmony, and good citizenship. Efforts to promote character qualities and values are evident in school and statewide efforts. For example, all school districts in the states of Alabama, Arkansas, California, Florida, Georgia, Indiana, Louisiana, Nebraska, Tennessee, Utah, and Virginia are required to implement a comprehensive character education program for all children. Some of the traits included are honesty, fairness, responsibility for others, kindness, cooperation, self-control, and self-respect.[19]

IMPLICATIONS FOR TEACHING. So that children can broaden their core values help them understand that their world is larger than them and their immediate neighborhood. You can do this through many activities:

- Read books that teach character traits, often referring to the list of traits adopted by your school system.
- Use the special kids sections of the *Times News* (Character Counts and the Kids Scoop pages) to understand the importance of good character skills.
- Use visitors and artifacts from other states and countries to help students compare the values of where they live with other areas so that they can appreciate the similarities and differences, eliminate prejudice, and accept cultural differences.
- Study the traditions of other cultures and have international tasting parties with food, games, folktales, or stories about the cultures.
- Write letters to soldiers for several holidays, including Veterans Day, to encourage traits of appreciation and thankfulness.
- Make encouragement cards and small gifts for the cafeteria and maintenance workers and staff.
- Write to other classes and school groups to express gratitude and thanks when they have performed for your school.

ENVIRONMENTS THAT SUPPORT LEARNING IN THE PRIMARY GRADES

Environments play a major role in children's learning and success and are also a major determinant of what and how well children learn. Classrooms not only support children's learning, but they also help ensure that all children learn to their full capacities. Use these features to help you provide the best learning environment possible for all children.

THE PHYSICAL ENVIRONMENT

The following conditions support learning in the primary classroom:

- Materials are in abundant supply for reading, writing, language development, and content area development (e.g., books about math, science, social studies, and the arts).
- Learning centers reflect content areas.
- Children are seated in chairs at tables or in clusters of desks for roughly three to six children.
- Literature of all genres supports content area learning centers, and materials provide for and emulate real work experiences.
- Materials and instruction provide for interdisciplinary, integrated approaches.
- Program, learning, and environment are coordinated so that materials support and align with outcomes and standards.
- Teacher instruction (teacher-directed instruction and intentional teaching) and active student involvement are balanced.
- Centers support literacy. All centers have materials that support reading and writing.
- Children's products are displayed and valued.
- Schedules are posted where children can read them.
- Technology supports and enriches basic skill and concept learning. Children use technology to make presentations, projects, and reports.

SOCIAL ENVIRONMENT

The following conditions support an enriching emotional and social environment:

- Families, other adults, and the community are connected to classroom learning.
- Children are valued and respected. The classroom is a community of learners.
- Children live and learn in peace and harmony.
- High expectations for all are an essential part of the classroom culture.
- Assessment is continuous and appropriate and is designed to support teaching and learning.
- Thinking is considered a basic skill and is integrated through all areas of the curriculum.

ENVIRONMENTS THAT SUPPORT PRO-SOCIAL AND CONFLICT RESOLUTION EDUCATION

All early childhood professionals, parents, and politicians believe that efforts to reduce incidents of violence and uncivil behavior begin in the early years. Consequently, they place emphasis on teaching children the fundamentals of peaceful living, kindness, helpfulness, and cooperation.

IMPLICATIONS FOR TEACHING.   Follow these suggestions to foster the development of pro-social skills in your classroom:

- ***Be a good role model for children.*** Demonstrate in your life and relationships with children and other adults the behaviors of cooperation and kindness that you want to encourage in children. Civil behavior begins with courtesy and manners. You can model these and help children do the same.

- *Provide positive feedback and reinforcement when children perform pro-social behaviors.* When you reward children for appropriate behavior, they tend to repeat the behavior. ("I like how you helped Jake. I'll bet that made him feel better.")

- *Provide opportunities for children to help and show kindness to others.* For example, cooperative programs between your children and eldercare homes and other community agencies are excellent opportunities to practice kind and helping behaviors.

- *Conduct conflict-free classroom routines and activities.* Provide opportunities for children to work together and practice skills for cooperative living. Design learning centers and activities for children to share and work cooperatively.

- *Provide practice in conflict resolution skills.* Classroom exercises here include taking turns, talking through problems, compromising, and working out problems.

- *Use examples from literature to make your point.* Read stories to children that exemplify pro-social behaviors and provide such literature for them to read.

- *Counsel and work with parents.* Encourage parents to limit or eliminate altogether their children's watching violence on television, attending R-rated movies, playing video games with violent content, and buying or renting CDs with objectionable content.

- *Catch children "doing good."* Help children feel good about themselves, build strong self-images, and be competent individuals. Notice when children behave pro-socially and tell them that you are pleased with their actions. Children who are happy, confident, and competent feel good about themselves and are more likely to behave positively toward others.

TEACHING AND LEARNING IN GRADES ONE TO THREE

In the last five years, the educational spotlight has cast its beam on the primary grades, where the academic rubber really hits the road. Grades one to three are more academically challenging and rigorous now than they have ever been. Here are some examples: Politicians and educational reformers use the third grade as the demarcation for standards of achievement and grade promotion or retention. The federal government talks about all children being able to read on grade level by grade three. Thus, even though all teachers pre-K through third grade are responsible for ensuring that all children achieve this goal, it is in the third grade that this goal is measured and decisions are made about whether children will be promoted or retained. One of your major challenges of teaching in grades one to three will be to ensure that all of your children learn and achieve so that they can be promoted with their peers.

DOES CLASS SIZE MAKE A DIFFERENCE?

Class size is one of the variables in U.S. education that the public, politicians, and teachers believe influences student learning outcomes. At least twenty-four states, including my state of Texas, have mandated class size limits in the public schools. In Texas, the maximum class size in grades K–4 is twenty-two students (22:1). However, as a result of the Great Recession, many states, including Texas, have honored school district requests for exceptions to the maximum class size. As a result, many teachers find themselves with two to three more students in their classes. In one study of class size, conducted in Tennessee, class size was reduced by seven students to an overall class size of twenty-two; as a result, there was an increase of student achievement equivalent to three additional months of schooling over a four-year period.[20] Similar studies have also found achievement benefits to reducing class size. However, other studies have found mixed achievement effects or no achievement effects at all as a result of class size reduction. Class size reduction seems to have its greatest benefits for low-achieving students in the early grades. It is likely that given the current economic climate in the United States, class size will creep up by one to three students per class over the next few years, and as teachers and school administrators know, once class size is increased, it is difficult to reduce because of funding and other resource issues.

IMPLICATIONS FOR TEACHING

- Research is clear that teachers matter and that children who have highly effective teachers achieve at higher levels than those who don't. You should do everything you can to be a highly effective teacher and to do the best you can to teach each child.
- Research is also clear that regardless of class size, if teachers don't make productive use of classroom time and student involvement, then class size reduction has no benefits.
- Make the best use of student's time to maximize learning. Engage students productively in learning activities throughout the entire school day.

When teachers have high expectations for their children, and when children believe that their teachers respect and value them, children achieve at higher levels than those who believe their teachers don't care about them.[21] Always remember that student–teacher relations matter.

COMMON CORE STATE STANDARDS

The curriculum content of grades one, two, and three is pretty much determined by the Common Core State Standards (CCSS) and state and local standards. Take a few minutes now and review the CCSS and the standards for grades one, two, or three in your state. The CCSS for first grade reading, second grade math, and third grade reading and writing are shown in Figure 12.2.

The Common Core State Standards (CCSS) also create a context in which preparing primary children for career and college places an emphasis on ensuring that all students achieve to high levels. You will be involved in the implementation of the CCSS and will be part of grade-level teams collaborating to apply them to instructional practice. This emphasis on achievement results in many educational pressures that affect children and you. These include the end of social promotion and making sure all children can read on level by the end of third grade.

STANDARDS.   In forty-five states, the curriculum of grades one through three is aligned with the CCSS. As a result, you will be teaching content designed to help students learn what the CCSS specify. In fact, many school districts provide their teachers with lesson plans that suggest activities and instructional strategies based on the CCSS. You won't always get to teach exactly what you want to teach, when you want to teach it, and how you want to teach it. However, good teachers always find ways to include in the curriculum what they believe is important and developmentally appropriate. As many teachers have learned and are learning, teaching with the CCSS does not have to be dull and boring; you can make learning interesting and relevant to all your students' lives.

TEACHER ROLES.   Standards have transformed (some would say reformed) teaching from an input model to an output model. As a result, teachers are no longer able to say, "I taught Josh the use of structural cues to decode words." Now the

First Grade Reading	Second Grade Math	Third Grade Reading	Third Grade Writng
• Ask and answer questions about key details in a text • Identify words and phrases in stories or poems that suggest feelings or appeal to the senses • Use illustrations and details to describe its characters, setting, or events • With prompting and support, read prose and poetry of appropriate complexity for grade 1	• Represent and solve problems involving addition and subtraction • Understand place value • Measure and estimate lengths in standard units • Reason with shapes and their attributes	• Ask and answer questions to demonstrate understanding of a text, referring to the text as basis for answers • Determine the meaning of general academic and domain-specific words and phrases in a relevant text • Use information gained from illustrations and the words in a text to demonstrate understanding of the text	• Write opinion pieces on topics or texts, supporting a point of view with reasons • Write informative/explanatory texts to examine a topic and convey ideas and information clearly • Write narratives to develop real or imagined experiences or events using effective technique, descriptive details, and clear event sequences • Write routinely over extended time frames and shorter time frames for a range of discipline-specific tasks, purposes, and audiences

FIGURE 12.2 | Common Core Standards: Grades 1–3

questions are, "Is Josh able to use and apply decoding skills?" and "Will Josh do well on decoding skills on the state test?" Good teachers have good ideas about what and how to teach, and they always will. However, the time and opportunity to act on those good ideas are reduced by increasing requirements to teach to the standards and teach so that students will master the standards.

alignment The arrangement of standards, curriculum, and tests so they are in agreement.

CURRICULUM ALIGNMENT. Increasing student achievement is at the center of the standards movement. Policy makers and educators view standards, tests, and teaching alignment as a viable and practical way to help ensure student achievement. **Alignment** is the arrangement of standards, curriculum, and tests so that they complement one another. In other words, the curriculum should be based on what the standards say students should know and be able to do; tests should measure what the standards indicate. **Curriculum alignment** is the process of making sure that what is taught—the content of the curriculum—matches what the standards say students should know and be able to do.

curriculum alignment The process of making sure that what is taught matches the standards.

DATA-DRIVEN INSTRUCTION OF THE OUTCOMES OF STANDARDS AND TESTING. Accountability initiatives, including No Child Left Behind, have brought about a shift in focus from covering subject matter to meeting the needs of each student. There is only one way to determine whether or not the needs of the students are being met: through an ongoing analysis of data collected from assessing children. In **data-driven instruction**, teaching decisions are based on the analysis of assessment data to make decisions about how to best meet the instructional needs of each child. To use data-driven instruction, start by analyzing existing data on each student from their cumulative record files to get a general profile of each student. Then align objectives to

data-driven instruction The analysis of assessment data to make decisions about how best to meet the instructional needs of each child.

assessments by planning collaboratively with your grade-level colleagues to determine when you will be teaching district and state standards and how you will assess each standard. Next, gather data by using formal assessments, informal assessments, and technology. After gathering data, use it to guide your next steps in the instructional process. Which students are ready to move on? Which students need remediation? Which students need enrichment? Just remember that making data-based decisions to guide instruction is an ongoing process. You should be constantly assessing, analyzing, and adjusting throughout the school year.[22]

RESPONSE TO INSTRUCTION/RESPONSE TO INTERVENTION (RTI).   Response to Instruction/Intervention (RTI) is a multi-tiered approach to the early identification and support of students with learning and behavior needs. It is the opposite of the "wait to fail approach." RTI seeks to prevent academic failure through early intervention, frequent assessment, and increasingly intense instructional interventions/processes for children who continue to have difficulty. These are the essential components of RTI.

- ***Early intervention is essential for enhancing the child's success.*** RTI is founded on the principle that too little, too late is an inadequate approach to education. Instead, early intervention is considered the best chance of promoting children's success academically, developmentally, socially, and emotionally. If a child's difficulty is caught early enough and treated with the appropriate level of intensity, RTI can be essential in enhancing success.

- ***Use of multiple tiers of interventions.*** RTI uses a three-tiered approach to providing instruction and intervention, as shown in Figure 12.3, "The Three Tiers of Continuous Intervention/Instruction." Children advance through the three tiers based on their level of responsiveness to instruction or intervention. The less responsive a child is to instruction/intervention, the more intense the intervention/instruction becomes, as shown in Figure 12.4. Tier I consists of generalized, evidence-based core curricula and instruction that is provided to children school- and classroom-wide. For most children (about 80 percent), Tier I is sufficient to promote learning. However, for 15 percent of students, the generalized curriculum does not meet all of their needs, so they advance to Tier II intervention or instruction.

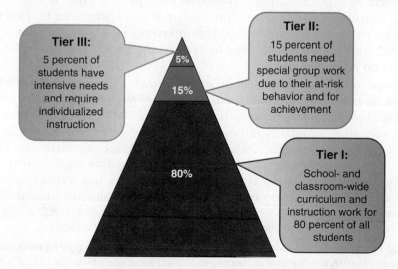

Tier III:
5 percent of students have intensive needs and require individualized instruction

Tier II:
15 percent of students need special group work due to their at-risk behavior and for achievement

5%

15%

80%

Tier I:
School- and classroom-wide curriculum and instruction work for 80 percent of all students

FIGURE 12.3 | The Three Tiers of Continuous Intervention/Instruction
Through RTI, teachers and schools provide ongoing assessments and instructional processes to assure that each child is successful.

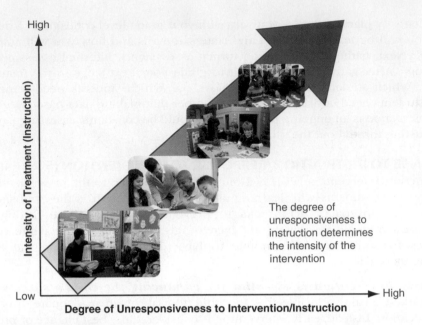

High

Intensity of Treatment (Instruction)

The degree of unresponsiveness to instruction determines the intensity of the intervention

Low   High

Degree of Unresponsiveness to Intervention/Instruction

FIGURE 12.4 | The RTI Model at Work
Through ongoing assessment, teachers match instructional practices to their students' learning needs, helping each child to achieve.

At Tier II, children receive a more intensified instruction because they show through ongoing assessment that they are not making adequate growth. In Tier II, children have increased opportunity to practice Tier I skills. When Tier II is insufficient, as it is for 5 percent of students, children move on to Tier III, where they can receive more individualized and focused intervention to meet Tier I benchmarks.

- *Problem-solving approach to determine most appropriate level of intervention for individual students.*[23] Teachers take a problem-solving approach to determining the tier in which a child belongs. If a child is unresponsive to Tier I instruction and intervention, then the child advances to Tier II, which provides more intense instruction and intervention. If Tier II is not adequately meeting students' needs, the teacher solves the problem by providing Tier III instruction and intervention.

- *Reliance on evidence-based practices and learning standards guide instruction and the use of intentional teaching methods that include embedded and explicit instruction at all tiers.*[24] RTI is meant to help children reach education standards through the use of evidence-based practices. Some evidenced-based practices include intentional teaching methods: embedded instruction and explicit instruction. **Embedded instruction** involves teaching skills and behaviors in the context of classroom routines and transitions. Under No Child Left Behind, teachers must use curriculum and instructional methods that are based on research to ensure children's academic success. RTI seeks to infuse each tier of intervention/instruction with evidence-based practices.

- *Use of monitoring to determine if students are making progress using multidimensional, authentic assessments that can identify the child's strengths and needs over time.*[25] Throughout the instruction, students are assessed for their learning and level of achievement. The data from these assessments are then used when determining which students need closer monitoring or intervention.

embedded instruction
Involves teaching skills and behaviors in the context of classroom routines and transitions.

Decisions regarding students' instructional needs are based on multiple assessment data taken over time. Authentic assessments, not just screening tools and standardized tests, should be used to make decisions regarding students' needs.

- *Holistic view of child development.*[26] RTI takes a holistic view of children as the approach to providing intervention/instruction. The holistic view of children takes into account social development, linguistic/literacy development, emotional development, cognitive development, physical and motor development, and other aspects such as character education, gender education, and culture, artistic, and socioeconomic context.

- *The critical contributions of parents and families to the success of the child.*[27] RTI recognizes that parents and families are critical to the overall success of the child. Without continuing support of families at home, RTI may have limited success in school. Families help reinforce and expand on what children learn at school, and teachers work to keep parents and families aware and informed of their children's successes, progress, and difficulties at each tier of instruction.

RTI and English Language Learners. As you can see from the many elements of RTI, it lends itself to success with a range of students, from children with disabilities to children struggling in an academic area to English language learners (ELLs). In fact, a recent study has found that RTI helps children who are ELLs make positive gains. In Chula Vista, California, the school district uses RTI to target children who are ELLs. They have seen a dramatic increase in test scores in reading and mathematics as a result. The district's superintendent, John Nelson, said RTI works because it changes teachers' thinking from an "I taught it and it's their fault if they got it or not" attitude to one of "I need to keep teaching it and support students approach."[28]

The RTI approach is also useful in helping make sure that children who don't know English aren't prematurely referred for special education evaluation, which raises the risk of mistaking a language barrier for a disability. Instead, RTI permits teachers to determine what kind of instruction a child needs on an individual level and to build on what the child can already do. This equals catching children before they fall.[29]

You will want to read and reflect on the *Frameworks for Response to Intervention in Early Childhood: Description and Implications,* a joint position statement of the Division for Early Childhood of the Council for Exceptional Children, the National Association for the Education of Young Children, and the National Head Start Association. The purpose of this joint statement is to define early childhood education's response to intervention and to promote a broader understanding and discussion of the topic.[30]

Reflect and Apply: RTI

DIFFERENTIATED INSTRUCTION IN THE PRIMARY GRADES

Differentiated instruction is an approach to teaching and learning for students of differing abilities in the same class, and all classrooms have differing abilities. The intent of differentiating instruction is to maximize each student's growth and individual success, meet each student where he or she is, and assist the child in the learning process.

There is no single set of strategies that constitutes differentiated instruction. Instead, the practice rests on principles that require you to continuously assess students and adjust instruction accordingly. If a teacher differentiates instruction, she frequently rotates students into small groups based on demonstrated knowledge, interest, and/or learning style preferences. The teacher then targets instruction

differentiated instruction An approach that enables teachers to plan strategically to meet the needs of every student in order to teach to the needs of each child and allow for diversity in the classroom.

to the needs of each group with the aim of moving all students toward high levels of achievement. A differentiated classroom is a dynamic environment in which students move in and out of learning groups based on achievement data, interests, and learning styles.

When you give directions in a differentiated classroom, start class with a small task, such as a review question or skill practice, and then meet with one small group at a time to provide specific directions for each group. Also write out directions for each group. Have the directions on the group's table or cluster at the beginning of the class or include the directions at a learning center or with a packet of learning materials that the students select. Then, use group lessons, activities, or graphic organizers to introduce concepts to the entire class before expecting small groups to work independently with a new concept or skill. Because of the integration of early childhood education and special education, instructional practices are blending, and those used by special educators are now routinely used in all primary grade programs.

intentional teaching
Developing plans, selecting instructional strategies, and teaching to promote learning.

INTENTIONAL TEACHING. **Intentional teaching** is the process of teaching children the skills they need for success. The intentional teacher:

- Has high expectations for each child and believes each child can and will learn
- Chooses the most appropriate instructional strategies to assure learning
- Plans using local, state, and Common Core State Standards
- Differentiates instruction to assure each child learns

Check Your Understanding: Instructional Strategies

CURRICULUM IN THE PRIMARY GRADES

In the primary grades, curriculum content areas take on greater emphasis. Children are not as concrete or literal, and the possibilities for new learning experiences and challenging activities are endless.

READING AND LANGUAGE ARTS IN THE PRIMARY GRADES

Just like preschool and kindergarten programs, today's primary grades emphasize literacy development, vocabulary, and reading. In fact, this emphasis is apparent in all the elementary grades, from pre-K to grade six. Parents and society want children who can speak, write, and read well.

LITERACY AND READING. I cannot overstate the importance of children's learning to read on grade level by the end of grade three. Unfortunately, millions of American children, many from low-income families, reach fourth grade without learning to read proficiently. Reading proficiently by the end of third grade is a crucial marker in a child's educational development.[31]

READ OR FAIL. More than thirteen states across the country have passed or are considering passing laws that mandate that children who do not read on grade level by grade three cannot be promoted to the fourth grade. They must repeat grade three. The research about grade retention is clear. It does not work.

What is needed are high-quality reading and literacy programs that begin in preschool (or before!), along with providing all children the instructional help and support they need to meet grade-level standards at each grade level. The economic cost of retaining children is substantial because of the need for additional teachers and classroom space to teach the retained students.

One of the best ways for children to develop language proficiency is for them to read, read, read. In the process, children develop a love of reading and reading becomes an important part of their daily lives.

Guided Reading. Guided reading is designed to help children develop and use strategies of independent reading. During guided reading, children read texts that are at their developmentally appropriate reading level and have a minimum of new things to learn. The children read in small groups (usually four to five or fewer) with their teacher.

Guided reading is beneficial for all students. For the more advanced readers, guided reading is a great way to introduce and practice skills that their peers may not be ready for. Guided reading offers struggling readers a safe setting for the extra support they need to master skills at a comfortable pace. When you teach guided reading in small groups, you can reinforce skills as many times as needed for the students to achieve mastery. The children are not pressured from the feeling that they are the only ones "not getting it."[32]

Guided reading is also very beneficial to teachers. Small group instruction allows teachers to pinpoint the strengths and weaknesses of individual students. It is an easy way for teachers to differentiate instruction, which makes it much easier to teach all students on their current level. Guided reading is also a great time to determine the reading level of the students or to group children with the same reading level; it gives a great deal of information about which reading strategies the students are using, as well as shows the progress each student has made.[33] Following are some guidelines for implementing guided reading:

- *Frequency:* You should teach guided reading every day. Guided reading sessions are short; fifteen minutes per group works well. Meeting with struggling readers daily is essential to their progress and success. Students reading on grade level should meet at least three times a week. Advanced readers need to meet at least once or twice a week as time permits.[34]

- *Content:* Because time is limited, guided reading activities are short and simple, yet they are quite effective owing to the individualized instruction. Guided reading gives students time to practice the skill with the support of the teacher. Afterward, students can apply the skills they learned as they play a learning game, use a book to go on a word hunt, or read leveled books (e.g., books targeted to a specific reading level). Provide constant support, take notes on student progress, and document the teaching strategies you use. These notes are very helpful because you can refer to them daily to plan future lessons or regroup the students based on their needs.[35]

- *Materials:* Use book bags and browsing boxes. Book bag books are leveled books that students read during self-selected reading (SSR), throughout the day, and at home. These book bags often hang on the back of students' chairs. The students choose the books for their book bags based on their individual interests from browsing boxes that are set up within reach of the students throughout the classroom. Browsing boxes are set up according to reading level to provide students with a wide array of reading choice and to also ensure that students are reading books that are just right for their reading level. You can also keep books used in guided reading in the book bags and let students take them home for practice. Here are some other suggested materials for guided reading:

- Dry erase boards/markers
- Magnetic letters
- Index cards
- Teacher-made skill practice games (Concentration, I Spy, etc.)
- Pencils/sticky notes
- Leveled books[36]

- *Grouping:* When you set up guided reading groups, give much thought and serious consideration to how to group the students based on ongoing assessment of their reading skills. Regroup students who have similar needs. As students master the skills practiced, they should then be regrouped. Students generally do not know what group they are in because the groups change constantly. It is easiest to call individual students to the reading table for instruction rather than naming each group because of the constant regrouping that should be happening and to protect the self-esteem of each student.[37]

- *Reading Levels:* When grouping for instruction, many teachers group according to each student's instructional reading level. There are three reading levels: independent, instructional, and frustration.
  - Children who are reading on the *independent level* can read the material independently. A child may be able to read the book independently, but may not be fluent. Independent books aim toward building fluency. A child's independent level is determined by the material she can read with no more than one word recognition error in each one hundred words.
  - A child's *instructional level* is determined from reading materials in which the child can read with no more than one word recognition error in twenty words. During guided reading, teachers provide reading materials at this level to effectively teach strategies to help students become better readers.
  - A child's *frustration level* is determined by the reading materials in which she makes many errors and struggles to read.

  A teacher's instruction should focus on the child's instructional level, not his or her frustration level. You can't teach a child from reading materials in which they are frustrated.

- *Management:* How can you manage guided reading and centers simultaneously? You must use good classroom management skills. Explicitly teach center expectations, activities, and routines, and have children practice them for several weeks before you begin guided reading. Monitor, praise good choices, and give consequences when needed for reinforcement. When you implement guided reading, children know well the central expectations and procedures. However, consistently reinforce procedures, rules, and expectations before, during, and after guided reading.[38]

Literacy Circles. Many teachers use literacy circles to support and enhance children's reading. **Literacy circles** are discussion groups in which children meet regularly to talk about books. Literacy circles are rarely the sole form of teaching reading but rather are a part of a balanced literacy program. As such, literacy circles are intended to act as a context in which children apply reading and writing skills. Groups are determined by book choice and are reader-response centered, meaning that discussion and conversation focus on what the readers thought and felt while reading the book. Literacy circles are structured so as to foster independence, responsibility, and reading

literacy circles Discussion groups in which children meet regularly to talk about books.

ownership. As such, literature circles are guided primarily by student insight and questions. As a result, literacy circles are flexible and fluid; they never look the same twice. To read how to implement literacy circles in your classrooms, read first grade teacher Candice Bookman's Voice from the Field on the following page.

IMPLICATIONS FOR TEACHING.   Here are five ways to help struggling readers:

1. Screen all students for potential reading problems and regularly monitor the progress of students who are at elevated risk for developing reading disabilities.
   - Accurately identify children at risk.
   - Use benchmarks or growth rates to identify children at varying risks for developing reading disabilities.

2. Provide differentiated reading instruction for all students based on assessments of current reading levels.
   - Provide differentiated instruction to students at varied reading levels for part of the day.
   - Differentiate instruction, including varying time, content, degree of support, and scaffolding, based on students' skills.

3. Provide intensive, systematic instruction on up to three fundamental reading skills in small groups to students who score below benchmark scores on universal screening.
   - Use curriculum that addresses the components of reading instruction (comprehension, fluency, phonemic awareness, phonics, and vocabulary) and relate to students' needs and developmental levels.
   - Implement this program three to five times a week for twenty to forty minutes.

4. Monitor the progress of Tier II students at least once a month. Determine whether students still require intervention. If so, design a Tier III intervention plan.
   - Monitor progress of Tier II students on a regular basis (at least eight times during the school year).
   - While providing Tier II instruction, monitor data to identify students who need additional instruction.

5. Provide intensive instruction on a daily basis that promotes the various components of reading to students who continue to show minimal progress after small group instruction.
   - Implement concentrated instruction that is focused on a small but targeted set of reading skills.
   - Adjust the overall speed of the lesson. Some students may require a slower pace in order to gain comprehension.
   - Plan and individualize Tier III instruction.
   - Ensure that Tier III students master a reading skill or strategy before moving on.

Children's Literature. One of the best ways to engage and encourage readers is through literature that appeals to them. For children, this means that literature needs to connect with them on their individual and developmental levels. The development of literature directed at children is at an all-time high, and there are various trends in children's literature that are aimed at creating a contemporary base of readers. Take,

VOICE FROM THE FIELD

COMPETENCY BUILDER

How to Use Literature Circles in the Elementary Grades

I can't imagine teaching without literature circles. There are just a few things that I think are important for any teacher willing to give literature circles a try.

STEP 1 — Have a Good, Strong Classroom Management System in Place

Students must know your expectations, and that if they don't make good choices for their behavior and use their time wisely, they will have an immediate consequence. I teach my expectations and we practice together for the first six weeks of school. Each day I ask the children to tell me what is important to remember about literature circles, and we discuss their responses as a class. We practice the entire routine, including where to get their literature tub (see below), what to do in their literature circles, and what to do when time is up. We practice each specific expectation I have for them. As the students go to literature circles, I actively monitor each group. I listen to their discussions, watch for off-task behavior, compliment good group work, give reminders or consequences when appropriate, and help with their activities when needed. I provide constant support until the students feel comfortable with the entire literature routine.

STEP 2 — Hold Students Accountable for Their Learning

This ensures that the time provided for literature circles is not wasted. Students know they will turn in their activities weekly and they will receive a grade. If the students do not work well together, it will be reflected in their grade. Students should have everything they need when they get to their literature circle so there is less of a chance for disruption such as wandering around the room or engaging in off-task behavior. I provide a tub for each group that holds their books, folders with the activities for the week, a dictionary, pencils, and so forth. If the children need anything different in a given week, for whatever reason, I provide it in the tub. Also, I let the students know in advance that things will be a little bit different that week.

STEP 3 — Give Each Group Member a Job

Each child has a responsibility for the week. Make sure that each member knows what the jobs are. I put a laminated list of jobs and descriptions in each group's folder. Since it is laminated, I write a student's name next to each job with an erasable marker, and then just erase it and rotate names weekly. In my class, the jobs during literature circles are as follows:

Material Manager: This child is responsible for picking up and putting away the tubs, passing out books and activities, and making sure they are put in the folders when completed. If there is anything missing from a tub for any reason, the material manager takes care of it.

Recorder: This child is responsible for writing down the ideas their group comes up with after the reading and group discussion. I often provide question stems to monitor comprehension. When I do not give them questions, the recorder is responsible for asking good thought-provoking questions and recording the responses of their group members. (This takes quite a bit of practice.) I expect the responses to be text dependent, so children must back up the question with a page number and proof from the text.

Word Wizard: This child is responsible for using the dictionary to look up and write the definition of any unfamiliar word encountered in their reading. Sometimes I make some suggestions of words that they may need to look up.

Illustrator: This child is responsible for drawing pictures of scenes from the book that go along with their learning. I may ask the children to find a part of the book they thought was funny, a turning point, a particular point of view, and so forth.

Graphic Organizer: This child is responsible for completing a graphic organizer to help the group comprehend what they are reading. These are sometimes story maps, Venn diagrams, T-charts, bubble maps, and such.

Teacher: I also have responsibilities during literature circles. While children work in their groups, I pull small groups of children for guided reading. I help them in areas of weakness, which may include phonics or comprehension skills. I have one group that I meet with daily to work on phonics skills. The other groups work on identifying the main idea, writing summaries, making inferences, understanding the author's purpose, and so forth.

366

4 Group Students in Different Ways

You can change groups when they are done with particular books and are ready to begin new ones. Comprehension skills and reading abilities will vary, but you can handle them in different ways. If you want skill levels to be close in each group, choose books with similar reading levels. One group may be reading chapter books, while another group is reading trade books on their level. The activities you give to each group will reflect what they are reading. If you want mixed-ability groups, partner children with different abilities.

5 Choose Books to Match Learning Goals

The books you provide to each group depend on the skill level of each group member. You can use literature circles for novel studies, and integrate content areas with nonfiction reading materials. When I have a mixed-ability group, I provide that group with different books on a particular topic written on different reading levels. Currently, I have a group reading about the solar system. I have provided them with six books, all on different reading levels. Each book contains different information, and my low-level reader has at least one book on his independent reading level.

THE VALUE OF LITERATURE CIRCLES

Literature circles are a great way to provide differentiated instruction to my class. They allow me to integrate reading with science and social studies as well as writing. When appropriate, I integrate English and grammar skills. Literature circles allow the class to learn practically every skill we learn in third grade in approximately forty-five minutes, while simultaneously giving me the flexibility to meet with students in small groups every day.

Source: Contributed by Candice M. Bookman, third grade teacher, Lawrence Elementary School, Mesquite Independent School District, Mesquite, Texas.

for example, the *Harry Potter* and the *Percy Jackson and the Olympians* series, which use different and new ways to tell a story; the plots are nonlinear, and they create or explain characters in new ways.[39] They use fantasy, magic, and mythology to appeal to and engage children, often creating lifelong readers. Underneath the contemporary trappings, they have themes that are classic and enduring. Themes such as a sense of belonging, a belief in hope for the future, the importance of relationships, and the importance of courage, will always appeal to children.[40] You can use classic and contemporary books in your teaching to engage and appeal to young readers. Some new books you might try are these:

- *Just Grace Walks the Dog* by Charise Mericle Harper. Third grader Grace is determined to have a pet, so she embarks on an adventure with her cardboard dog to prove to her parents that she is responsible and dependable enough to get a real dog.

- *Herbie Jones Sails Into Second Grade* by Suzy Kline. Herbie and his new friend Raymond start the first day of second grade with lots of fears and a teacher that takes them on adventures.

- *More Stories Huey Tells* by Ann Cameron. One of the five stories in this book is about Huey, a good problem solver, and when Huey and his older brother Julian get worried about their father's smoking, they find a way to work together to help him quit.

- *Lizzie Logan, Second Banana* by Eileen Spinelli. Lizzie's mom and her new dad are having a baby and Lizzie is worried her new dad will love the new brother more than her, so she signs up for a beauty contest and learns about families and love in the process.

- *PeeWee's Tale* by Johanna Hurwitz. The mother of nine-year-old Robbie doesn't like Robbie's guinea pig, PeeWee, so she has her husband set PeeWee loose in Central Park. PeeWee is lost in the wild environment until he makes a new friend who passes on a few survival strategies. PeeWee returns the favor by warning his friend about the city's plan to cut down the tree that she lives in.

Check Your Understanding: Strategies

MATH IN THE PRIMARY GRADES

Teachers are reemphasizing mathematics as an essential part of primary education. Just as reading is receiving a great deal of national attention, so too is mathematics. Some call this reemphasizing of mathematics the "new-new math," which emphasizes hands-on activities, problem solving, group work and teamwork, application and use of mathematical ideas and principles to real-life events, daily use of mathematics, and an understanding of and use of math understandings and competencies. The new math seeks to have students be creative users of math in life and workplace settings, but it also includes the ability to recall addition sums and multiplication products quickly. The ideas in following Voice from the Field will help you teach math.

CHILDREN FROM LOW-INCOME FAMILIES AND MATH.   Despite the efforts of standardizing math in the primary grades, children in general, and children who have low socioeconomic backgrounds in particular, continue to lag in performance.[41] All young children have the capability to learn and become proficient in math, but a lack of mathematical opportunities in early childhood settings and everyday experiences at home and in the community dampens this potential. There are two areas of math that are very important for children to learn early: numbers (including wholes, operations, and relations), and geometry (including spatial thinking and measuring).[42] Other math skills include classification, pattern skills, and problem solving.

It is important to realize that not every child acquires mathematical understanding at the same time, the same pace, or through the same modality. As a result, mathematics teaching needs to be across the spectrum of ability, just like teaching literacy. For example, embed math into everyday routines. When math becomes a part of everyday routines, as children explore their environment, they acquire basic math skills and concepts. Their school lives will involve the use of numerous math concepts on a daily basis. When you teach math to children early, across many environments and in a developmentally appropriate fashion, they acquire the skills they need to be successful!

PLANNING FOR MATH.   Helping children be successful includes planning for their learning. However, this means that you must be flexible and willing to try a variety of teaching techniques if you want your children to achieve meaningful mathematical learning. When you present mathematical concepts orally, visually, and kinesthetically, each child can move the information into long-term memory in a manner that works best for him or her. One way to appeal to different learning modalities is to integrate literature with mathematics. In order to meet the child's individual needs, you should incorporate tactile, auditory, and visual learning experiences. Using children's literature to help them make sense of math gives them a meaningful context for math concepts. It also helps math become relevant, familiar, and interesting. Just as importantly, it relates children's prior knowledge or experiences to math, motivates students to explore, and supports memorization. Another way to appeal to different learning modalities in math is to use manipulatives. When children can count beans, coins, and pattern blocks, they are able to understand concepts more readily, which boosts self-esteem and confidence in their math capabilities.

▶ **Observe and Analyze**

Bright Ideas for Teaching Math

Albert Einstein once said, "Do not worry about your problems with mathematics, I assure you mine are far greater." If it is true that one of the most intellectually gifted men in recent history had trouble with math, is it any wonder that our children sometimes suffer the same fate? Can it be that learning how to "do" math is such a difficult process that the vast majority of us will struggle and only a select few will go easily into the daunting world of equations, variables, and theorems? My answer to this question is a resounding NO! It is my belief and experience that young children take to math like they do to water. As long as they have guidance and aren't made afraid of the process before they begin it, they will do fine.

I've taught hundreds of students over the past nine years. During that time, the study of math has been an exploration of sorts. I've learned that numbers are like friends. Once you get to know them, they're lots of fun to be around. I do not claim to be an expert in the area of teaching math. I am simply one of many dedicated teachers who understand that in order to learn, children must be free to explore, ask questions, and make mistakes. From personal experience, I know there is no greater resource than my fellow teachers. Some of what I'm about to share I've learned from them. I hope these ideas for teaching math will help you and your students in some way.

- **Idea 1: Students must be comfortable with numbers in order to use them.** To be comfortable with numbers, children must recognize them, understand how they can be used, and have no fear of using them incorrectly. Most adults would agree that making mistakes and messing up occasionally is sometimes the best way to learn. Students will come to you with the idea they simply can't understand math. Your first job is to convince them they *can* and *will* be successful in math.
- **Idea 2: Give students real-world problems that have meaning for them.** Numbers are better understood when they represent physical things. Whether you're talking about fourteen ducks, thirty-two marbles, or even seven of your friends, numbers have meaning. Give students problems that show this representation. Ask them for a specific "unit" or item they're

counting. Their world is full of easy-to-use examples. Take advantage of this and help them relate to what they're learning.

- **Idea 3: Practice is important!** Young students must be strong in the operations of addition, subtraction, multiplication, and division. To gain strength they must practice whenever the opportunity presents itself. Use the classroom for organized practice. Quizzes, verbal answers to problems, and morning math are all ways to help students get in the necessary repetition. Small group or partner pairs are great for multiplication fact practice. I like to use the down time of waiting in line for student restroom breaks to go over division facts! However you get the practice in, make it efficient and effective.
- **Idea 4: Not all students learn the same way.** Today's teachers must employ different techniques to reach all of their students. My students use paper and pencil, flash cards, manipulatives, SmartBoard technology/Internet resources, rap songs, and even YouTube to help them navigate through their study of math. You will know what's best for your students. The important thing to remember is it won't be the same for all of them, and it's up to you to find what works.
- **Idea 5: Know what you want to accomplish with your students and let it guide your instruction.** Like many other teachers, I've been asked to realign my teaching to specifically address Common Core State Standards for math. In my opinion, these standards are an excellent way to bring cohesiveness to the different math concepts students are expected to master. Before you begin teaching, know exactly what your students need to accomplish. Fully understand the standard you're attempting to meet, and plan ahead, giving lots of thought to the activities that will help your students reach the goal. Assess formatively as often as necessary to make sure you're on the right road. Let what you learn *during* teaching guide what you do *while* you're teaching. Remember, learning is rarely a straight and narrow path. You and your students may have to go in several different directions to reach your goal. With input from your students, it's up to you to navigate the course.

I hope these ideas are helpful to you in your career. Always remember, you are a teacher. You change lives. You have the most important job in the world!

Source: Contributed by Nickie A. Blackburn, elementary teacher at Southside Elementary, Pike, Kentucky.

LESSON PLANS

5E Math Lesson Plan: Geometry

Lesson Title: Geometry: Getting Started

Time Frame for Lesson: 3 days

Day 1—Engage and explore
Day 2—Explain and extend
Day 3—Evaluate

Standards: Texas Essential Knowledge and Skills (TEKS)

- 3.8 Geometry and spatial reasoning. The student uses formal geometric vocabulary. The student is expected to identify, classify, and describe two-dimensional geometric figures by their attributes.

Graded assessment opportunity:

- 3.20 Writing/Expository and Procedural Texts. Students write expository texts to communicate ideas and information to specific audiences for specific purposes. Students are expected to: (i) create brief compositions that: (ii) include supporting sentences with simple facts, details, and explanations.

Materials: Chart paper, markers, toothpicks (in baggies labeled "sides"), mini-marshmallows (in baggies labeled "vertices"), student journals or writing paper, camera

Targeted Vocabulary: polygon, vertex, vertices, side

ENGAGE

Play "I Spy." On a large piece of chart paper, draw a picture of a simple house that is made out of basic 2D shapes. Ask your students, "Which shapes do you see?" As the students give you answers, highlight the shapes they are referencing and write the name of the shape out to the side.

Consider using a different color for each shape. This will help your lower-level and English language learners differentiate by color. Keep the chart paper posted throughout the entire geometry unit so that you can add vocabulary as needed and students can refer to it throughout.

EXPLORE

Mistakes are bound to happen in the explore portion of the lesson; this is part of learning. Let it happen! Take note of these misconceptions and address them during the explain portion.

Arrange your students into groups of 3–4. Make sure your lower-level learners are grouped with you. Challenge your groups to build the shapes mentioned in the Engage part of your lesson with the following materials:

- Show and distribute mini-marshmallow baggies and introduce them as "vertices."
- Show and distribute toothpick baggies and introduce them as "sides."

Say, "I will be listening for my mathematicians to use these vocabulary terms. Please refer to your materials as vertices and sides." By doing this, students will get used to the vocabulary terms associated with classifying 2D shapes. Give the students time to build.

You will want to actively monitor your students, encouraging the use of vocabulary. While you are working with your group, use quality questioning to guide your students to discover the attributes of basic geometry.

EXPLAIN

This is a very important part of the lesson. It is a time for students to reflect and for you to straighten out any misconceptions. More than likely, students will have built their circle using many sides and vertices, when in fact, a circle is unlike any other shape: it is made from one continuous curved line and is not considered a polygon. Also, if students built their rectangle using 6 vertices instead of 4, you'll need to address this and guide discussion on ways to change the length of the sides without compromising the number of needed vertices.

Have your students write the word "polygon" in their math journals. Ask, "What if I told you that all but one shape that you built today was a polygon? Which shape is unlike any other? (A circle.) "A circle is made up of one continuous curved line. It does not belong in the same category as the rest. What do the others have in common?" (They are made up of straight lines and vertices.) "Shapes that are made up of straight sides and vertices are called polygons." Define this word together in journals.

This is a great opportunity to introduce any and all vocabulary you need. To reach all levels of learning, show, build, hand-draw, and define each term. Examples include parallelogram, trapezoid, hexagon, pentagon, decagon, etc.

EXTEND

Take students outside with a mission to find as many 2D shapes as they can on the playground. Ask students to create a tally chart of each shape found and a hand-drawn picture. Come back together and allow the students to share their findings with a partner or group.

Your lower level-students may need a list of specific shapes that you want them to locate. Have checklists ready to go for these students, with the shapes you want them to find already listed. English language learners would benefit from a picture posted next to the shape. Your higher-level students will be inclined to find the harder, more intricate shapes. Give them freedom to find as many as possible.

EVALUATE

Evaluations do not always need to be paper and pencil; sometimes you need to think outside of the box! In this case, you need to assess if the students can use formal geometric vocabulary to identify, classify, and describe 2D shape by their attributes. What better way to test this than by having the students become the shapes?

Choose a location with a lot of floor space. Call on groups of students to participate in making shapes lying on the floor with their bodies. Explain that their body is the "straight side," and in order to create a "vertex," two sides must touch. If you pull a group of three names, have them build a triangle. If you pull a group of five, ask if they can build a pentagon. Ask, "How many sides does your shape have? How many vertices?" Once your students gain speed with the activity, consider having two groups compete: "Who can build the most accurate hexagon with the fastest speed, while also working the quietest?" The possibilities of how to use this activity are endless. If you're in need of a graded assignment, ask your students to write a paragraph comparing polygons with a circle. Students will need to show their learning by stating facts about polygons.

Something to consider: Snap a picture of the students building each shape in your vocabulary list. Print the pictures and have the students label the vertices and list important information about that shape on the back. These can be used as review flashcards.

Source: Contributed by Celeste E. Hanvey, M.Ed., third grade teacher, Curtsinger Elementary School, Frisco, Texas. Photos by Celeste E. Hanvey and Kathy Stroud.

Science fair activities enable children to do independent scientific work while collaborating with teachers, family members, and peers. The science fair project also encourages children to think scientifically, act like a scientist, and explore solutions to complex problems.

inquiry learning
Involvement of children in activities and processes that lead to learning.

SCIENCE IN THE PRIMARY GRADES

With a national emphasis on testing children in math and science, some critics of public schools contend that teachers spend too little time teaching science. They argue that children should receive high-quality science teaching and learning opportunities. One way schools are responding is by increasing opportunities for children to participate in science fairs and other organized activities designed to promote science teaching and learning.

INQUIRY-BASED LEARNING. Today's science teaching is *inquiry based;* that is, it is all about helping children learn to solve problems. **Inquiry learning** is the involvement of children in activities and processes that lead to learning. The process of inquiry involves (1) posing questions, (2) observing, (3) reading and researching for a purpose, (4) proposing solutions and making predictions, and (5) gathering information and interpreting it.

AT THE SCIENCE FAIR. It is very common for children in the primary grades to participate in school based and local science fairs. Science fairs promote and support the STEM subjects in the primary grades and provide the children with opportunities to be involved in STEM activities involving scientific thinking, exploring STEM activities in depth, and engaging in hands-on/minds-on learning. Science fair activities are a good way for children to explore areas that are of interest to them and to put the scientific method into practice. Science fair entries are usually in the form of a display or have accompanying artifacts such as student's experimental journals and materials/apparatus used in their projects. Guidelines for science fair entries include the following:

- Well identified, stated, and understandable problem
- Hypothesis stating and testing
- Data collection
- Data analysis
- Evidence of scientific thinking
- Conclusions about the research

Part of your role is to encourage all students to engage in science projects. Business and industry are demanding that public schools educate more scientists, especially women. Beginning in kindergarten, we have to develop a positive climate for girls to engage in STEM activities and to begin to consider STEM fields as appropriate career paths. In fact, helping children think about and consider careers is part of developmentally appropriate practice.

Girls Need Science, Too. Girls are underrepresented in science-based careers, especially in engineering, physics, technology, and math. This trajectory of underrepresentation begins in early childhood. Most children, boys and girls alike, are equally interested in science. The problem is how girls are taught and involved in science. The following are some things you can do to encourage and involve girls in science.

- Make sure all children have equal access to science materials and are involved in science experiments and activities.

- Since girls often excel in writing, encourage them to record their research and data collection in a science journal and in electronic format.

- Encourage all students to collaborate online by using blogs, Facebook, Twitter, YouTube, etc., to record and share their learning and the results of their experiments.

ENGINEERING FOR ALL. With the Common Core State Standards there is an increasing emphasis on getting children career and college ready. This emphasis on career and college readiness includes and involves children in STEM activities early. In STEM activities there is an emphasis on involving all children in engineering processes and activities. The process of being involved in engineering is being able to understand and use the engineering design process to solve problems. Figure 12.5 is an illustration of the engineering design process from Engineering is Elementary that you can use with your children.

LEGO® robotic engineering kits are an excellent way to introduce children to concepts of engineering at an early age. In addition, you can provide many other opportunities for children to learn basic engineering concepts, such as gears, wheels, pulleys, levers, and axles.

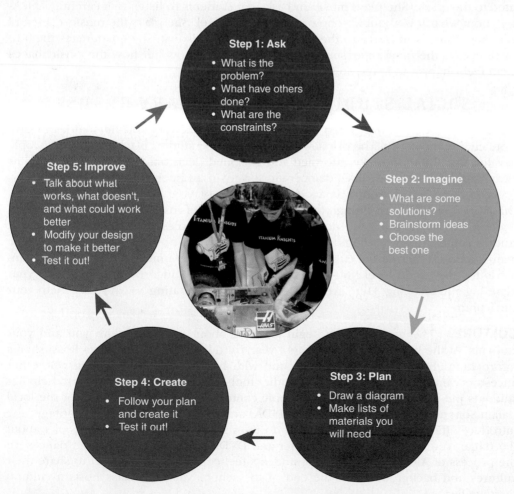

Step 1: Ask
- What is the problem?
- What have others done?
- What are the constraints?

Step 2: Imagine
- What are some solutions?
- Brainstorm ideas
- Choose the best one

Step 3: Plan
- Draw a diagram
- Make lists of materials you will need

Step 4: Create
- Follow your plan and create it
- Test it out!

Step 5: Improve
- Talk about what works, what doesn't, and what could work better
- Modify your design to make it better
- Test it out!

FIGURE 12.5 | Engineering is Elementary (EiE): Steps and Descriptions

ARTS IN THE PRIMARY GRADES

In the primary grades, the creative arts most often include music, theater, dance, and art. For each of these disciplines you will want to include knowledge, concepts, and themes. Your teaching of the arts should be content based and child centered, and you will want to make sure that you consult your state's content standards for the arts.

STEAM.   The arts are known to promote creativity, and many advocates of the arts today are encouraging the sciences to include arts with STEM to create STEAM. As a result, proponents of such a combination of STEM and the arts argue that this can enhance student learning and promote creative thinking and innovation.

This integration of the arts with STEM is not new to early childhood teachers. They routinely integrate all subjects including the arts, music, and dance across all content areas.

Today's teaching of the arts is designed to provide children with content knowledge and skills from the four disciplines listed in the preceding paragraph. Thus, in your teaching of the arts you will want to ensure that children are provided with authentic content and are engaged in activities that help them learn and apply knowledge of the arts. LaTonya Daniels encourages her students to appreciate and examine different styles of music as well as create dance presentations that are specifically related to the music. She plays music and asks her students to listen to it carefully, thinking about what it is about and how it makes them feel. She plays the music again and asks her students to move to the music. If the music is fast, she encourages them to move fast. At the same time, she asks her students to show her how the music makes them feel—happy, sad, and so forth.

SOCIAL STUDIES IN THE PRIMARY GRADES

Social studies are the integrated study of the social sciences and humanities to promote civic competence. The primary purpose of social studies is to help young people develop the ability to make informed and reasoned decisions for the public good as citizens of a culturally diverse, democratic society in an interdependent world.[43]

Teaching social studies is an important part of your responsibility as an early childhood teacher. Even though teachers devote a lot of instructional time to literacy/reading and math, you need not neglect the social studies. You can integrate social studies content with reading and math so that children are reading and engaged in math processes "across the curriculum." Be sure you are familiar with your state standards for the grade level you are teaching in order to incorporate them into your planning and teaching. Here are some ideas for incorporating social studies into your curriculum.

CULTURE.   The best place to begin teaching about culture is with you and your students. At the beginning of the school year, third grade teacher Alessia Rossi shares information about her Italian background with her students by showing where her ancestors came from. She uses social studies tools such as maps and globes to help her students put Italy in the world geographic context. She invites members of the local Italian Sons and Daughters of America (ISDA) to share Italian culture and heritage. She introduces Italian words and ties these to the reading lessons. She has books about the Italian culture in the reading center and DVDs with Italian songs and dances. In the process of Alessia's sharing, her students feel comfortable and start to share their cultures and backgrounds. At the end of the school year, the class hosts a cultural heritage festival.

TIME, CONTINUITY, AND CHANGE.   Just as culture is all around us, so we are surrounded by time, continuity, and change. Second grade teacher Kelie Shipley involved her students in a community history project in which her students research not only the history of their town, but also how the town is changing and why. In the course of the research, the children discovered that on one of the dedication plaques, the name of the person for whom their school is named was misspelled. They wrote letters to school and city officials, resulting in a new plaque. At the new dedication, relatives of the school's namesake came and talked about what school was like when they were in the second grade.

PEOPLE, PLACES, AND ENVIRONMENT. Your local museums, art institutes, and historical centers are wonderful resources for involving your students in learning about people, places, and the environment. For example, the Allen Memorial Art Museum in Oberlin, Ohio, collaborates with the Asian Art/Educational Outreach Funding Initiative of the Freeman Foundation and has developed Asian art educational programming for children and teachers. One of the lessons involves children ages five to eight in *gyotaku,* the Japanese art of fish painting, and *haiku,* a form of Japanese poetry.

INDIVIDUAL DEVELOPMENT AND IDENTITY. First grade teacher Ashley Gotkins incorporates the North Carolina Grade One Social Studies Standards into her teaching. They focus on neighborhoods and communities around the world. Ashley, whose grandmother was one-sixteenth Cherokee, uses her cultural heritage to teach about Native Americans and the Cherokee tribes. She builds her Native American lessons around these North Carolina Standards:[44]

- Describe the roles of individuals in the family.
- Identify various groups to which individuals and families belong.
- Compare and contrast similarities and differences among individuals and families.
- Explore the benefits of diversity in the United States.

INDIVIDUALS, GROUPS, AND INSTITUTIONS. On the first day of school, first grade teacher Tanika Ramsey holds a "morning meeting" in which all of the children introduce themselves. Then she talks about families, and what a family is. The children brainstorm about what things they can do to live peacefully in their classroom family. In the following days, Tanika expands the discussion to include what children can do to live harmoniously in the school. The children discuss school rules, interview administrators, staff, and other teachers and develop a "blueprint for school living." They share their blueprint with other kindergarten classes.

POWER, AUTHORITY, AND GOVERNANCE. Classroom living requires a lot of compromises and getting along with others. Second grade teacher Jacki Aochi believes she should share her "power" with children and can accomplish this goal by teaching her children how to resolve conflicts. In addition, Jacki conducts a morning meeting that consists of three parts. Each part takes about five minutes:

Having children map their community and compare it with maps of other communities around the world using Google Earth is an excellent way to involve students in understanding global similarities and differences.

- *Announcements:* Both she and the students make announcements related to classroom and school events and activities as well as life events such as birthdays, sporting events, and family activities.
- *Concerns:* The children discuss events inside and outside of the classroom and suggest resolutions for how they and others can turn the concern into a positive situation.

- *Being a Good Citizen:* Children have an opportunity to state what they are going to do during the day or week to be good citizens in the classroom, school, home, and community.

PRODUCTION, DISTRIBUTION, AND CONSUMPTION. Matt Blair teaches his third graders about the production, distribution, and consumption of consumer products by creating, selling, and distributing handmade cards. The children design and illustrate get well, birthday, and thank you cards and provide original verses and sentiments. They also package, sell, and distribute their cards. As part of the project, children visit design studios and printers and consult with marketing executives of local businesses. All proceeds from the sales of the cards go to a community charity selected by the children.

SCIENCE, TECHNOLOGY, AND SOCIETY. Second grade teacher Beverly Huang integrates her teaching of science, technology, and society with the teaching of the scientific method. (Review our discussion above.) She involves the children in a project in which they survey their homes and community to determine the ways in which computers influence how people live and work. The children post their own research questions, develop their surveys—both online and hard copy versions— analyze their data, draw conclusions, write their results in their science journals, and publish the results in their school newspaper.

GLOBAL CONNECTIONS. Melissa Gloria's students are third graders whose first language is primarily English, but they are learning Spanish as a second language. They are studying world cultures and use ePal Global Community (epals.com) to exchange letters, postcards, photographs, and journal entries via e-mail with their electronic pals in Ecuador. They collaborate by exchanging information about culture, history, and so on.

CIVIC IDEALS AND PRACTICES. First grade teacher Gretchen Reich uses the local community to teach civic pride. Her students engage in a project of learning about community agencies and how they help others. The students select agencies they would like to know more about, such as the Salvation Army, and invite agency members to their classroom to talk about what they do. As a result of their community civic involvement, the children decided to collect pennies to support the Salvation Army Red Kettle drive. In six weeks, the children raised $50. Also, once a month, the children bake cookies and take them to homes for senior citizens. Last month, in addition to baking cookies, the children also made cards and visited the Jewish Home for the Aged.

TEACHING THINKING

As we previously discussed, reasoning has been added as one of the six R's of early childhood programs. Educators believe that if students can think, they can meaningfully engage in subject matter curriculum and the rigors and demands of the workplace and life. As a result, many teachers are including the teaching of thinking in their daily lesson plans.

IMPLICATIONS FOR TEACHING. To promote thinking in your classroom follow these guidelines:

- Give children the freedom and security to be creative thinkers.
- Encourage children to search for other answers and alternative solutions rather than settling for one "right" answer. Ask open-ended questions ("Why do you think that?") rather than questions that require a yes or no response.

- Create classroom cultures in which children have the time, opportunity, and materials with which to be creative.
- Integrate thinking into the total curriculum so that children learn to think during the entire school day.

CONTEMPORARY TOPICS IN THE PRIMARY GRADES CURRICULUM

Curriculum changes are due in part to the influences of world events, politics, and new research and knowledge. Here are some recent additions to curriculum in the primary grades.

FISCAL EDUCATION. The financial recession (Great Recession) of 2008–2012 has had a great impact on the U.S. economy and education. As a result, the U.S. Department of Education is determined to educate children in fiscal matters, especially knowing how to manage money, how to save, and how to use mainstream banking services.

National Credit Union Administration (NCUA) Chairman Debbie Matz believes there is no better place for young people to learn these concepts than from their teachers at school, and no better partner to provide subject matter expertise for schools than financial institutions. Furthermore, in many underserved communities, studies show that parents learn about finances from their children, so youth financial education can benefit adults as well.[45]

Teacher Janice Belcuore integrates money concepts into her second grade class throughout the school year. Students alternate classroom jobs, such as door holder, line leader, and paper passer, at regular intervals. Some jobs earn more than others just like in the real world. Students get paid for their "jobs" twice a month, but they are required to pay rent—for their desks and chairs—save a certain amount each month, and keep a checkbook. A vital component of Janice's fiscal education is the checkbook because her students must enter their paycheck, deduct rent and debits, and save for expensive purchases—in other words, they must continuously use addition, subtraction, and carrying over in the real world. At the end of every month, children have the opportunity to "shop" with their money, and like the real world, they can go into debt, too! Missing homework assignments or inappropriate behavior costs Janice's students. In addition, each student completes a year-end fiscal report that includes comparing their spending and checks and balances with an adult family member. Janice's fiscal education is hands-on, real-world oriented, and meets state standards for math concepts. She hopes that these lessons will translate into lifelong learning about fiscal responsibility, which will impact how they behave in the global market.[46]

BULLYING EDUCATION. Bullying at all levels of education is a serious problem, but bullying in the primary grades has recently received a lot of national attention. Nine out of every ten elementary students are bullied by their peers.[47] Both the bullies and the bullied suffer higher levels of depression and other mental health problems throughout their lives than do those who are neither perpetrators nor victims.[48] And recently, news broadcasts across the country have shown us that victims are paying the ultimate price of bullying. In Baltimore, an eight-year-old third grader attempted to kill herself by jumping out a window.[49] In Chicago, a seven-year-old and a ten-year-old hanged themselves. In Texas, a nine-year-old boy hanged himself in the nurse's office.[50] This is a reality that must be faced by early childhood professionals. Suicide in response to bullying does not just occur in high school; it's happening in the first, second, and third grades too!

In response to the escalating awareness of bullying, schools are implementing anti-bully campaigns. Character education is also used to decrease bullying. Positive prevention programs focus on the power of words and how to use them positively rather than negatively. Such programs not only prevent bullying, they promote character, citizenship, and diversity. The positive approach focuses on solutions to bullying by instilling positive character traits through character education rather than by punishing negative behavior. This approach shows us that approaching bullying from a positive perspective, based on increasing positive traits in children rather than focusing on the negative and punishing behaviors, is a powerful way to address bullying. Schools using the positive approach rather than a punitive approach to bullying see amazing results. For example, national averages saw kindness, tolerance, and cooperation increase by 60 percent, name-calling decrease by 53 percent, bus discipline and distraction incidents decrease by 60 percent, and classroom distraction minutes decrease by 55 percent, extending available teaching time up to three weeks.[51]

TWENTY-FIRST CENTURY SKILLS. Our world is being transformed by technological advances, the "knowledge revolution," a global economy, and environmental changes.[52] Education has to keep up so that our children can be successful in the global community. To compete successfully for tomorrow's jobs, today's students need to learn to be future leaders who can think creatively, work collaboratively, use technology to solve problems effectively and peaceably, and take initiative. This means integrating the use of twenty-first century skills in every subject and at every grade to encourage students to learn the skills for the future, even as they learn the content.

Twenty-first century learning skills include the following:

- Information and communication skills such as media literacy, information literacy, and information and communication technology literacy.
- Thinking and problem-solving skills such as critical thinking and systems thinking, problem identification formulation and solution, creativity, and intellectual curiosity.
- Interpersonal and self-directional skills such as flexibility and adaptability, initiative and self-direction, social and cross-cultural skills, productivity and accountability, and leadership and responsibility.[53]

You will need to teach twenty-first century skills in a twenty-first century context. You can create the appropriate context by making content relevant to students' lives. You also create context by bringing the world into the classroom and taking the students out into the world. Also, be sure to incorporate twenty-first century content such as global awareness, financial, economic, and business literacy, civic literacy, and health literacy.[54]

WHY IS ENVIRONMENTAL EDUCATION IMPORTANT?

THE CHILD IN NATURE. Today, with the urbanization of the United States and with more people living in tighter urban spaces, many children are isolated from nature. This isolation from nature is also true for suburban children, who may spend their time in front of the television or glued to iPhones and iPads. Involving children in environmental education and involving them in activities relating to the outdoors and nature provides them opportunities to get in touch with the outdoors and be involved in meaningful ecological activities.

environmental education
Enables children to explore environmental issues, engage in problem solving, and find solutions for environmental issues.

Environmental education encourages children to think about their environment, their place in the environment, how they can be good stewards of their environment and how they can help others be good stewards of the environment. Environmental education is important for the following reasons:

- It enables children to act responsibly and be stewards of the environment.
- It increases student engagement in STEM: science, technology, engineering, and mathematics all lend themselves to the outdoors and to environmental/ecological issues.

- It connects classroom learning to the real world.
- It enables children to make decisions that influence the health and well-being of the environment today and tomorrow.

GREEN SCHOOLS AND GREEN CURRICULA.   All across the United States, schools are going green. Green schools are those in which the building creates a healthy environment conducive to learning while saving energy, resources, and money. Green schools and curricula are a response to eco-issues around the world and represent ways to save energy, conserve resources, infuse curricula with environmental education, build school gardens, and offer more healthy school lunches.

HORTICULTURAL THERAPY.   Horticultural therapy involves children in horticultural activities such as gardening and landscaping with the intent of improving children's cognitive, social, educational, and emotional development. Horticultural therapy is designed to improve the whole child, body, mind, and spirit. For example, at Cherry Ridge Elementary in Louisiana, children with autism planted a garden and raised lettuce, cabbage, radishes, pumpkins, and carrots. As a result of their gardening experiences, teachers report that the children have improved their grades and communication skills. Teachers also report that by taking care of and working in the garden, children are improving their concentration, self-esteem, and social skills.

Here are some things you could do to promote environmental education and involvement with your children:

- Involve your children in recycling activities.
- Read books that involve environment issues and that provide examples for children to be involved in environmental activities.
- Involve your children in outdoor activities relating to the common core and state standards. For example, many STEM activities lend themselves to children being involved in environmental issues such as alternative energy. For example, children can make pinwheels and use them as a basis for discussing the pros and cons of wind turbines and the generation of electricity.
- Create an outdoor educational environment in any land available to you on or adjacent to your school. Such mini-environments are a good way to involve the community and community agencies and to enable children to be more ecologically aware.

ACCOMMODATING DIVERSE LEARNERS

All early childhood teachers are inclusion classroom teachers at one time or another in their careers. Inclusion is defined as educating children with and without disabilities in the same classroom. The Division for Early Childhood (DEC) of the Council for Exceptional Children (CEC) and the National Association for the Education of Young Children (NAEYC) have identified inclusion as the preferred service delivery option for young children with special needs. However, there is no agreed-on model for developing and delivering these services. A classroom template for inclusion is not available, but it is essential that you believe that preparing all children to function in society is best achieved by creating environments for children whose diversity includes varying abilities, disabilities, and backgrounds.

The following are some ways you can create, implement, evaluate, and modify your classroom to create optimal learning conditions for all students:

- *Classroom schedule:* A consistent schedule helps students feel secure and adds to the predictability of the environment. A visual schedule reviewed orally every day benefits all children. In addition, some students will need their own individual schedules, particularly if their day includes therapists who assist them.

- *Routines:* Routines for different times of the day and scheduling a particular activity at the same time every day or on the same day every week is beneficial for students who need the stability of knowing what their day involves.
- *Transitions:* Develop transition strategies that support smooth transitions between activities. Use verbal cues (e.g., "five minutes before cleanup"), visual cues (e.g., picture schedules), auditory cues (e.g., timers), and praise after successful transitions.
- *Classroom curriculum:* An appropriate classroom curriculum includes activities that you can modify and adapt to meet the needs of each child.
- *Classroom management:* You must support and encourage appropriate behavior, prevent inappropriate behavior, and guide or redirect misbehavior when it does occur. In the inclusive classroom, you can achieve this goal by creating a positive management plan that addresses skill deficits. A **skill deficit** is the inability to perform a skill because the child does not possess that skill. For example, a child with a disability may have a social skill deficit associated with making friends and gaining popularity. Motivational deficits involve the unwillingness or lack of cooperation of children to perform a skill they possess, either entirely or at an appropriate level. For example, some children may be reluctant or hesitant to engage in an activity because of their disability. In contrast, some children may lack motivational self-control and be aggressive and intrusive in their behavior.
- *Rules:* State rules positively, limit their number, and make sure they are observable and measurable. Ensure that children's rules don't involve academic or homework issues that can unfairly impact students with disabilities or who are linguistically diverse.
- *Physical arrangement:* The four-desk cluster provides the most opportunities for students with disabilities to be included in the classroom. You can efficiently move from child to child, and at the same time the children support socialization, cooperation, and group work.
- *Grouping:* Grouping in the inclusive classroom is an excellent way to differentiate instruction to meet each child's needs. Appropriate assessment enables you to form appropriate groups.

skill deficit The term indicating that a child has not learned how to perform a particular skill or behavior.

ACTIVITIES FOR PROFESSIONAL DEVELOPMENT

ETHICAL DILEMMA

"CAUGHT IN THE MIDDLE"

Julia Le is a second grade teacher. One day she, her colleagues, and her students are stunned to learn that, Greg, a nine-year-old third grader, just committed suicide at school. The whole school community is shocked and grieving. Julia's students pepper her with tearful questions. "Why did he do it? How did he do it? Where will he go? But why?" Julia struggles to answer their questions. When Julia goes to her teaching mentor for advice on how best to help her students through this terrible time, her mentor empathizes but says, "It's not really your job to answer questions like that. That's what school counselors are for. If they keep asking you questions, just send them to the counselor." In addition, the principal tells Julia, "It's inappropriate for eight-year-olds to be talking about suicide." Julia just doesn't feel right about it. She did some research and found that the American Hospice Foundation (AHF) explains that the best policy is to tell children the truth and provide reassurance because fantasy is often more frightening than facts.[55] The AHF recommends that adults should give simple, honest, and age-appropriate explanations about loss or death.[56] Julia is caught between her school's "gag order" and her own sense of right and wrong.

What should Julia do? How should she answer her students' questions? How should Julia balance her own feelings and grieving with those of her students? What should Julia do? What would you do? Would you abide by the school's and your mentor's advice, or would you follow your feelings?

ACTIVITIES TO APPLY WHAT YOU LEARNED

1. Of all the ways that we identified in our discussion about how teaching and learning is changing in the primary grades, identify two that you think are most significant. Write a two-hundred word reflection on your selections and explain how they will influence your teaching. Ask for feedback on your class discussion board.

2. Skype with a local elementary school teacher and ask him/her about children's developmental changes he/she observes in the classroom. Which changes are the most obvious, and which are more subtle? Share your experience with your classmates.

3. Identify three reasons why classroom environments are so important to the teaching/learning process. Justify your reasons as though you were talking with a small group of parents of third graders. Reach out to your local parent-teacher association and ask if they would post your ideas on their website.

4. Observe classes in an elementary school in which the teachers use RTI. Ask the teachers to explain to explain to you RTI in action. What will you have to do to prepare yourself for teaching in the inclusive/RTI classroom? Ask your professor if you can make a fifteen-minute Power-Point presentation to your class about your experience.

5. **KEY ASSESSMENT:** One of the curriculum goals of many states is that all children should be able to read on grade level by grade three.

   a. Do you think this is an important goal?

   b. Why do you think this goal is set for grade three rather than another grade level, such as grades one or two?

   c. What are three things you and other teachers can do to help all children achieve the goal of reading on or above grade level by grade three?

   d. Create a Prezi presentation of your conclusions, post it on your class discussion board, and invite comments from other teachers. Use the **rubric** provided to guide your work.

6. How will you accommodate diverse learners in your inclusive classroom? Choose from the following differences that influence learning: ADHD, economic disadvantages, autism, or visual impairments. Give three examples of how you will accommodate the child.

LINKING TO LEARNING

The following agencies and programs, which can be located easily online, provide additional information about topics discussed in this chapter.

A to Z Teacher Stuff

This teacher-created site is designed to help teachers find online lesson plans and resources quickly and easily. It offers ideas on thematic units and lesson plans and contains a large collection of printable worksheets and pages.

CHARACTER COUNTS! National Homepage

This nonprofit, nonpartisan, nonsectarian coalition of schools, communities, and nonprofit organizations work to advance character education by teaching the six pillars of character.

Scholastic Teachers

The Scholastic Teachers website contains great resources for building student success, including lesson plans, activities, reproducibles, and thematic units. It also provides time-saving teacher tools, such as Standards Match, which lets you easily locate classroom resources aligned to your state standards.

TECHNOLOGY and YOUNG CHILDREN

Education for the Information Age

LEARNING OUTCOMES

1. Describe what the children of the Net generation are like.
2. Identify how technology is used with children with special needs.
3. Describe how you can integrate technology in your early childhood program.
4. Explain what parents and you can do to support children's use of technology.
5. List the ways you can use technology to accommodate diverse learners.

YOU need go no further than the daily newspaper (online, of course!) to see how technology is changing the face of education as we know it. Kindergarten teacher Kristi Meeuwse is a model of the technological twenty-first-century classroom teacher. She and her children use iPads in their daily lessons and activities. Kristi integrates iPads into her classroom and curriculum. Kristi and her children use KidBlog to blog with each other. Kristi says she has found even more ways to increase rigor, incorporate standards, personalize learning, and transform her classroom.[1] First grade teacher Carrie Jostmeyer says that the twenty-first century calls for us to change our paradigm of teaching and integrate technology in our classrooms. Technology has revitalized her approach to teaching.[2] Technological devices of all kinds are increasingly used in early childhood classrooms to enable collaboration, communication, and learning. Technology has changed, and will continue to change, the way children learn and the way you teach.

CHILDREN OF THE iGENERATION

Children today are technologically oriented. They are the last backpack generation and are confidently taking their place in the iGeneration. Children's growth, development, and learning are intimately tied to personal encounters with television, videos, electronic games, computers, iPads, and handheld technology in the home and schools. Many children, but not all, students have iPads, laptops, and handheld computers that they easily carry back and forth between home and school. American children spend more than seven hours a day with electronic devices.[3]

Today's young children do not remember a time in which they did not have the constant connectivity that technology brings. Here are some distinct characteristics that identify the iGeneration:

- Children today have the ability to multitask. They text and talk at the same time!
- Children have embraced technology as a tool for entertaining and learning.
- Children are very comfortable as the youngest members of the flip-screen generation.

Technology is an important part of the world of young children, and constant access to technology is here to stay. It has a great deal to offer, and there is much that young children can learn using technology in all domains—cognitive, social, emotional, and linguistic. Software is designed for children as young as six months; it is often referred to as *lapware* because children are held in their parents' laps to use it, and it is intended to be used by parents and children together.

You will find many software programs for the very young, such as Jumpstart Baby and Reader Rabbit Playtime for Baby, aimed specifically at children ages one to three. Jumpstart Baby leads children through eight activities, including wood-block puzzles and nursery rhyme sing-a-longs. Reader Rabbit Playtime for Baby allows young children to explore colors, shapes, songs, animals, letters, and numbers. There are also software programs for toddlers, such as Reader Rabbit Toddler, Reader Rabbit Playtime for Baby and Toddler, and Jumpstart Toddler.

TECHNOLOGY: A DEFINITION

Technology is the application of tools and information to support living and learning. With this definition, technology goes far beyond computers and games. Our definition

technology The application of tools and information used to support learning.

includes electronic and digital applications and devices. Such tools commonly found in early childhood programs include handheld computers, televisions, video cameras, iPhones, iPods, iPads, Kindles, digital cameras, and many types of assistive technology. As an early childhood teacher, you must plan to integrate the full range of technology devices in your classroom, learning centers, and activities.

TECHNOLOGICAL INTEGRATION IN EDUCATIONAL SETTINGS

Technology is changing and, in the process, changes the goals of education, what it means to be educated, and what literacy means. Literacy now has added dimensions: Students not only have to read, write, listen, and speak—skills fundamental to participation in a democratic society—but also have to use technology to be truly literate. In today's technological society, **technological literacy** means the ability to understand and apply and use technology in the home, school, and society. Technological literacy is becoming as important as the traditional components of literacy: reading, writing, speaking, and listening.

technological literacy The ability to understand and apply and use technology in the home, school, and society.

TECHNOLOGY STANDARDS. The International Society for Technology in Education (ISTE) has developed the National Educational Technology Standards (NETS) for students, the NETS•S, the standards for evaluating the skills and knowledge students need to learn effectively and live productively in an increasingly global and digital world.

NETS•S 1. Creativity and Innovation
Students demonstrate creative thinking, construct knowledge, and develop innovative products and processes using technology.

NETS•S 2. Communication and Collaboration
Students use digital media and environments to communicate and work collaboratively, including at a distance, to support individual learning and contribute to the learning of others.

NETS•S 3. Research and Information Fluency
Students apply digital tools to gather, evaluate, and use information.

NETS•S 4. Critical Thinking, Problem Solving, and Decision Making
Students use critical thinking skills to plan and conduct research, manage projects, solve problems, and make informed decisions using appropriate digital tools and resources.

NETS•S 5. Digital Citizenship
Students understand human, cultural, and societal issues related to technology and practice legal and ethical behavior.

NETS•S 6. Technology Operations and Concepts
Students demonstrate a sound understanding of technology concepts, systems, and operations.[4]

The emphasis in today's classroom is on technological integration, the infusion of technology in the learning setting to support children's learning and problem solving; to support and assist learning the curriculum content (Common Core State Standards), skills, and behaviors; and to enable and support purposeful learning. In other words, the use of technology is not an end in and of itself. Today's students must be able to use technology to analyze, explore, and learn.

DIGITAL LITERACY

Young children become immersed in digital media opportunities and develop **digital literacy**, the ability to use digital media for speaking, listening, reading, and writing purposes. Digital literacy includes not only traditional emergent literacy skills like reading and writing, but it also includes the psychomotor skills needed for keyboarding and texting and the problem-solving skills needed for navigating search engines; using iPhone apps and "flipping" on touch screen devices such as iPads; writing electronically; and sending and printing material such as messages, stories, and other electronic materials.

digital literacy The ability to use digital media for speaking, listening, reading, and writing purposes.

TECHNOLOGY AND SOCIAL COLLABORATION

As Vygotsky points out, and as this text emphasizes, social collaboration is important for young children's learning. Children seek out involvement and interaction with peers, siblings, parents, and you! Many digital games are designed for young children to support collaboration and social interactions, which as Vygotsky's theory suggests, leads to cognitive development. Technologies such as smartphones, blogs, instant messaging (IM), Instagram, Facebook, Twitter, Skype, YouTube, and iChat are ubiquitous. Likewise, collaboration and social interaction are abundant and commonplace in today's classrooms. All of these interactions allow young children to observe literacy skills at work within the social interaction of same age and older peers. These observations have a tremendous impact on young children's development and learning.[5] Collaborative technology use motivates children to be active and involved learners. One of your roles is to ensure that there is opportunity and time for peer collaboration with technology.

Observe how the teacher in this **video** uses an interactive whiteboard in her classroom for instruction. Pay particular attention to teacher–child interaction and reflect on advantages that accrue to both teachers and children by integrating technology in the instructional processes.

SUPPORTING CHILDREN'S TECHNOLOGY USE

In Cedar, Minnesota, School District No. 15, kindergarten teacher Sandy Benson says the children are better than the teachers with iPads. Kindergarten teacher Michelle Roy uses the free app chalkboard, which allows her children to practice sight spelling words, decode words, and write sentences. Michelle also uses member's apps and apps to reinforce phonics skills. All across the country, school districts report positive results from the integration of iPads with their Pre-K–3 classrooms. At Lakeville (Minnesota) school districts, teachers report increases in student engagement, increased student motivation, and gains in student learning.[6,7]

iPADS IN THE EARLY CHILDHOOD CLASSROOM

Earlier I mentioned Kristi Meeuwse as a model for technology use in the classroom and how she and her children use iPads in their daily lessons and activities. The following is a very illustrative description of what Kristi and her children do with iPads.

The use of iPads in the early childhood classroom has increased tremendously my students' abilities to engage in a variety of meaningful learning experiences across the curriculum. My kindergarten students use their iPads as a learning tool. However, technology without purpose does not yield desired results. Careful planning for the learning environment is a necessity. As students work together in small groups, they are engaging in cooperative learning. Cooperative learning creates an environment of active, involved, exploratory learning. It also develops social skills and higher-order thinking skills. Creating an environment where cooperative learning takes place throughout the day is important. It builds student confidence, knowing they can collaborate with others. Using iPads, students are constantly teaching each other how to do something. This sharing of information and exploration is seamless as we move from learning activity to learning activity throughout the day.

INTRODUCING iPADS. As I introduce my students to the iPads in the beginning of the year, I use small group instruction. Successful implementation depends on frontloading procedures, such as how to use and care for the iPad, modeling how we use iPads, and monitoring students' use of iPads. Once they are comfortable with procedures, I move to whole group instruction as well as allow students to use them independently on their own. Having appropriate expectations and a clear instructional goal will ensure positive results!

LITERACY IMMERSION WITH iPADS. iPads are an excellent way to enrich literacy instruction. When you immerse young children in literacy-rich classrooms, you develop the foundation of basic early literacy concepts, skills, and positive attitudes. This concept of literacy immersion centers on the idea that children need to learn in a literature-friendly environment. When we incorporate interdisciplinary connections to literacy, we increase student success. There are many appropriate apps available for young students. We use our iPads as eReaders to supplement our classroom leveled library. Students also engage in blogging activities, writing, and eBook creation on their iPads. For example, we use KidBlog, a free online blogging website that is secure for young children to blog with their classmates and with me. We use the Pages and eBook Magic App for writing and creating eBooks on the children's iPads. When students create their own eBook, I am able to sync it to all other iPads in the class, and all students then have a collection of books created by classmates.

Setting up the classroom for literacy immersion is deliberate and carefully planned. Children observe the teacher modeling reading and writing, they participate with the teacher in shared reading and writing and they participate in independent reading and writing activities all throughout the day. These activities are enhanced with iPads. Students may keep individual word lists on their iPads, and books that are on their individual reading levels (just right books). Having books that are "just right" at their fingertips enable students to read at any time they choose without having to get up and go search for one in the classroom. These books are available through Learning A-Z online as a purchase, or teachers may create their own with iBooks Author. Another helpful tool is keeping photographs of class anchor charts. Anchor charts are charts that are created with the class on a specific topic. It helps to "anchor" information in students' minds. This individualization of instruction makes the iPad a powerful tool for a large early childhood classroom. Students are able to work at their own pace.

NEW iPAD APPS. We use Safari to do research on the Internet. Proper student monitoring is necessary to check for appropriate content. This can be done by a teaching assistant walking around the room as well as checking the browser history on individual iPads. Working in small groups facilitates student monitoring. The camera on the iPad allows students to take photographs of objects in their environment to use in writing, math, science, and language arts activities. Students learn how to import images into their camera roll and then insert them in documents they create.

iPADS AND FIELD TRIPS.   Information technology is becoming more and more personal and portable. Learners are creating their own learning environments, integrating real time with virtual. Taking iPads on a field trip would allow students to capture what they are seeing, reflect on what they are learning, and create meaningful artifacts of the experience. The information collected on the trip could be put into an iMovie or Keynote to share with others and for assessment. For example, on a trip to the farm, students can take photographs of various animals and/or crops. Students will sort through their photos to evaluate which are most important to include in the iMovie. These photos could then be sequenced in order of events. Students can make comparisons between animals or crops. The evaluative process and synthesis of information develops higher-order thinking skills.

The use of iPads as a technology tool personalizes student learning and addresses learning styles. Daily instruction, modeling, guided practice, and the gradual release of responsibility for learning to the children is absolutely necessary for successful classroom integration of technology. With iPads in the classroom, the world is literally in children's hands![8]

IMPLICATIONS FOR TEACHING.   Young children's constant involvement with technology has a number of implications for you as an early childhood teacher:

- Build on the out-of-school technology experiences children bring to your classroom. Partner children who are more technologically adept with students who can benefit from one-on-one help. For example, you can partner children who can collaborate and help each other strengthen technological and reading, writing, and math skills.

- Provide enriched technology experiences for all students while ensuring that those students who lack technology competence receive appropriate assistance. For example, you can use an iPad to provide multiple methods of engagement, presentation, and expression. The iPad has multiple universal designs for learning features that enable children to receive technological assistance such as the screen reader for those visually impaired; mono audio feature for the hearing impaired; and zoom, closed captioning, and color configuration tools.[9]

- Involve parents in classroom programs of technology and enrichment. Parents can help you teach technology skills and can extend in-school technology learning at home.

Integrating technology into your teaching is a powerful way to enrich and extend learning. Be an enthusiastic supporter and user of technology and ensure that each child has high-quality technology experiences.

Observe and Analyze

The Voice from the Field, "How to Use Technology as a Scaffolding Tool in the Preschool Classroom," helps you introduce technology to young children as a means for acquiring literacy skills.

COMPETENCY BUILDER

How to Use Technology as a Scaffolding Tool in the Preschool Classroom

Technology can be an exciting tool to help children acquire early literacy skills. Using cameras, printers, scanners, and software provides endless possibilities for personalizing literacy activities.

STEP 1 Select the Equipment
You need several pieces of equipment to create literacy materials and activities.

Digital Camera

An inexpensive camera may work just as well as a special model designed for children. There are a number of features to consider:

- Resolution—the sharpness of the pictures expressed in pixels (the higher the resolution, the better the picture)
- Optical zoom—magnifies the images using a multifocal-length lens
- Image capacity—memory capability for images shot at high resolution
- Expansion slot for memory card
- LCD display for children to review pictures

Digital Video Camera

- Use to document events in the classroom.
- Use a tripod to ease use and avoid accidents.

Printer and Scanner

- A color printer is essential for book making and literacy material creation.
- Scanners can transfer children's writing samples and artwork into a digital format.

Digital Touchscreen Devices

- Digital devices, including the iPod touch, iPad and similar models, can be used by an adult in the classroom as a record-keeping tool. Some of these devices have built-in features, such as a calendar, address book, memo pad, clock, and calculator. Some models have Internet access, cameras, color screens, and audio capabilities, enabling them to record and show multimedia content.
  - This important documentation tool can record a child's progress.
- Children's work can be captured in photo or even video form.
- Software applications or appropriate apps are key for children's portfolio items.
- These devices can be used as tools for exploration and learning by young children. Children's apps need to be carefully evaluated for developmental appropriateness.

Learn to Use the Equipment

STEP 2 Most equipment is fairly user-friendly, requiring very little, if any, instruction to operate.

- Become familiar with all options and test them.
- Make sure equipment is easy for children to use.

The manufacturer may have tutorials that are downloadable from its website. Online training sites may also offer tips and training on using technology.

STEP 3 Choose the Software
Before you choose software or apps, decide on the literacy activity:

- For creating simple books or class slide shows, use a photo-management type of program—such as iPhoto, Kodak EasyShare, or Photo Kit Junior. Also presentation software, such as Keynote or Microsoft Power-Point, can be used for viewing the final product.
- For interactive books, authoring software is best—such as Classroom Suite, HyperStudio, or even Microsoft Word. Recently developed apps may also be appropriate and easy to use with digital devices.

STEP 4 Create Literacy Activities for the Children
When they create their own electronic books, children learn many print concepts, including reading text left to right and top to bottom, separating words with a space, and learning that words have meaning.

Electronic Book Templates

- Each child can create a book about himself or herself or can base it on a field trip, class project, or favorite book.
- Children can add their own pictures, voices, and text.
- Page-turning buttons in the bottom corners of each page allow children to navigate forward and backward through the book.

Child-Created Books

Children in preschool classes can learn to use digital cameras, download pictures to the computer, and use software to create books.

- Explain how to plug the camera into the computer and download the pictures.
- Show children how to use the photo management application.
- Teach children how to enter text and sounds into the program.
- Encourage children to work in small groups to benefit from cooperative play.

Document the Learning

- **Daily documentation.** Take digital photos in the classroom on an ongoing basis. Pictures of children's construction, artwork, or play activities can be shared immediately with them. The teacher may also want to share the images with the class as a review of the week's activities and projects.
- **Wall displays.** Displaying digital pictures in a hallway or on a classroom wall gives children documentation of events and an opportunity to review and revisit. Children's language skills are sparked as they review the pictures. They may also dictate a narrative about the pictures and events.
- **Portfolios.** Have digital photos, scanned photos, writing samples, and artwork in children's individual electronic portfolio files. At the end of the year, copy the images to a CD or DVD for families or create an electronic book or movie about each child. Families might also create their own books during a workshop at the end of the year. With simple instructions and a template, they can choose the images to place in children's books.

Technology is a scaffolding tool for literacy when educators and families know how to use equipment and apply it to young children's needs. Children gain print concepts and other early literacy skills, and the technology serves as a valuable documentation tool.

Source: Text contributed by Linda Robinson, Assistant Director, Center for Best Practices in Early Childhood, Western Illinois University, Macomb, Illinois. The center provides technology and assistive technology training, curricula, and online information to educators and families of young children.

DEVELOPMENTALLY APPROPRIATE TECHNOLOGY USE FOR YOUNG CHILDREN

Early childhood professionals value developmentally appropriate practice (DAP) in their work with young children. Thus it makes sense to use developmentally appropriate approaches when integrating technology in our teaching and learning. To help you in selecting and implementing technology with young children, the NAEYC and the Fred Rogers Center for Early Learning and Children's Media have published these guidelines for you to reflect on:

1. Select, use, integrate, and evaluate technology and interactive media tools in intentional and developmentally appropriate ways, giving careful attention to the appropriateness and the quality of the content, the child's experience, and the opportunities for co-engagement.

2. Provide a balance of activities in programs for young children, recognizing that technology and interactive media can be valuable tools when used intentionally with children to extend and support active, hands-on, creative, and authentic engagement with those around them and with their world.

3. Prohibit the passive use of television, videos, DVDs, and other noninteractive technologies and media in early childhood programs for children younger than two years, and discourage passive and noninteractive uses with children ages two through five years.

4. Limit any use of technology and interactive media in programs for children younger than two years to those that appropriately support responsive interactions between caregivers and children and that strengthen adult–child relationships.

5. Carefully consider the screen time recommendations from public health organizations for children from birth through age five years when determining appropriate limits on technology and media use in early childhood settings. Screen time estimates should include time spent in front of a screen at the early childhood program and, with input from parents and families, at home and elsewhere.

6. Provide leadership in ensuring equitable access to technology and interactive media experiences for the children in your care and for parents and families.[10]

TECHNOLOGY AND SPECIAL CHILDHOOD POPULATIONS

Technology has a profound effect on children with special needs, including very young children and students with disabilities. In today's rapidly developing technological world, technology is helping to bridge gaps between children's differences at rates many never dreamed possible.

The field of early childhood education is undergoing dramatic changes through its integration with the field of special education. As a result, early childhood professionals use assistive technology to help children and their families. According to Public Law 108-364, the Assistive Technology Act of 2004, **assistive technology** is "any item, device, or piece of equipment, or product system, whether acquired commercially off the shelf, modified, or customized, that is used to increase, maintain, or improve functional abilities of individuals with disabilities."[11]

assistive technology Any device used to promote the learning of children with disabilities.

Assistive technology covers a wide range of products and applications, from simple devices such as adaptive spoons and switch-adapted battery-operated toys to complex devices such as computerized environmental control systems. Increasingly, programs are using robots to interact with children with autism. This range in technology that is available to children with disabilities is generally described as being from low-tech to high-tech.

Assistive technology can work wonders for children with disabilities and really involve them in lessons and classroom activities.

USES OF ASSISTIVE TECHNOLOGY

Assistive technology is particularly important for students with disabilities who depend on it to help them communicate, learn, and be mobile. For example, for students with vision impairments, closed-circuit television can be used to enlarge print, a Braille printer can convert words to Braille, and audiotaped instructional materials help children so that they are able to hear. Closed-captioned television and FM amplification systems can assist students who are deaf or hard of hearing. Touch-screen computers, augmentative communication boards, and voice synthesizers can assist students with limited mobility or with disabilities that make communication difficult. Special education teacher in the Mount Vernon (Washington) school district, Cathy Maxwell, believes that exposure to technology during the first year of school is vital to a student's success in later academic years. Cathy also believes that through assistive technology, young children with disabilities can experience more success in communicating their needs and are able to make choices that provide the foundation for taking control of their educational future.[12]

Technology helps children with vision impairments see and children with physical disabilities read and write. It helps children who are developmentally delayed learn the skills they need to achieve at appropriate levels and enables other children with disabilities to substitute one ability for another and thus receive the special training they need. In addition, computer-assisted instruction provides software tools for teaching students at all ability levels, including programmed instruction for students with specific learning disabilities. Opportunities for using many forms of assistive technology are available to even very young children, from birth to age three. Some of these include powered mobility, myoelectric prostheses, and communication devices. Infants as young as three months interact with computers; eighteen-month-old children have drive-powered mobility devices and use myoelectric hands, and two-year-olds talk using speech synthesizers.

ASSISTIVE TECHNOLOGY AND LITERACY. Assistive technology can be included as an important tool in your work with children with special needs. One of your students with special needs may have trouble holding a pencil. Putting a pencil grip on the pencil makes it easier to hold. The pencil grip is an example of low-tech assistive technology.

An eReader, such as Barnes and Noble's Nook or Amazon's Kindle, may make a good tool for developing literacy in children with disabilities. Text size and font can be adjusted according to the child's needs, and unknown words can be pronounced and linked to a dictionary for a definition. Many eBooks for young children can be read to the child while the child follows along in the text. A child can input and save notes while reading a text the same way they can write on sticky notes to mark certain passages in a regular book. Thus eReaders may help a child with disabilities learn to read at higher independent levels with engaging texts.[13]

BENEFITS OF ASSISTIVE TECHNOLOGY

Technology permits children with special needs to use and enjoy knowledge, skills, and behaviors that might otherwise be inaccessible to them. In this way, technology empowers children with special needs; it enables them to exercise control over their lives and conditions of their learning. It enables them to do things previously thought impossible.

In addition, technology changes people's attitudes about children with disabilities. For example, some may view children with disabilities as unable to participate fully in regular classrooms; however, they may now recognize that instead of being segregated in separate programs, these children can be fully included in the regular classroom by using technology.

Figure 13.1 describes several examples of assistive technology for use with young children.

> **Check Your Understanding: Inclusive**

ACCOMMODATING FOR SOCIAL INTERACTION

For some children with disabilities, computers and other technology are the only means they have for communicating and socializing with peers and adults.

IMPLICATIONS FOR TEACHING. Here are some things you can do to help these children communicate and socialize:

- Have children work on projects together in pairs or small groups. Make sure the computer has several chairs around it to encourage children to work together.

BigKeys Keyboard.   BigKeys Keyboard is an assistive technology that has keys four times bigger than standard keyboard keys. It arranges letters in alphabetical order to assist young children and generates only one letter, regardless of how long a key is pressed. The BigKeys also accommodates children who cannot press down two or more keys simultaneously.

Big Red Switch.   Big Red Switch is a large, colorful switch to turn devices on and off. It is 5 inches in diameter with a surface that is easy to see and activate. It also has an audible click to help children make the cause-and-effect link.

QuickTalker12.   QuickTalker12 is an augmentative communication device that gives children a voice! It allows them to communicate by pressing on pictures.

Touch Windows 17.   Touch Windows 17 is a touch screen that attaches to the computer monitor and allows children to touch the screen directly rather than use a mouse. It can be used on a flat surface, such as a wheelchair tray, and is scratch resistant and resistant to breaking.

All-Turn-It Spinner.   An inclusion learning tool, All-Turn-It Spinner allows all children to participate in lessons on numbers, colors, shapes, matching, and sequencing. It is a spinner that is controlled by a switch for easy manipulating and has optional educational overlays, stickers, and books that can be purchased separately.

Talk Pad.   Talk Pad is a portable communication device that is designed to be used by children who need assistance with speech. It uses an electronic chip that records the voice and allows children with language limitations to be active participants in everyday activities.

FIGURE 13.1 | Examples of Assistive Technologies

Learning through technology is not inherently a solitary activity. You can find many ways to make it a cooperative and social learning experience.

- Provide children with opportunities to talk about their technology projects. Part of social development includes learning to talk confidently, explain, and share information with others.
- Encourage children to explore adult roles related to technology, such as newscaster, weather forecaster, and photographer. Invite adults from the community to share with children how they use technology in their careers. Invite a television crew to show children how they broadcast from community locations.
- Read stories about technology and encourage children to talk about technology in their lives and the lives of their families.

Reflect and Apply: Special Populations

INTEGRATING TECHNOLOGY IN EARLY CHILDHOOD PROGRAMS

Integrating technology into educational curriculum provides students with additional tools to enhance their learning. Technology in the classroom can help students become capable users, information-seekers, problem-solvers and decision-makers. School districts across the country are providing their students with technology devices. The Miami-Dade (FL) school district, the nation's fourth largest, plans to spend $63 million to purchase 150,000 laptops and tablets so all their 354,000 students will have access to them.[14]

SCIENCE, TECHNOLOGY, ENGINEERING, AND MATHEMATICS

STEM refers to the areas of science, technology, engineering, and mathematics. STEM initiatives started as a way to promote education in these related areas so that students would be prepared to study STEM fields in college and pursue STEM-related careers. Schools with a strong emphasis on STEM education often integrate science, technology, engineering, and mathematics into the entire curriculum.[15] According to the U.S. Bureau of Labor Statistics, professional information technology careers will increase well into the future.[16] Unfortunately, as jobs requiring a solid background in science, technology, engineering, and mathematics are growing, more students are choosing not to major in these areas. Scales Technology Academy (STA) in Tempe, Arizona, provides one-to-one laptops for all students from kindergarten through fifth grade and focuses on a high-technology curriculum.[17] STA is one of several schools that appeal to parents' preferences while integrating technology into the curriculum and providing a balance between core knowledge and twenty-first-century skills. Teachers empower students to be independent learners, critical thinkers, and problem-solvers. Teachers use interactive whiteboards, document cameras, and audio enhancements. The entire school campus features wireless Internet, promoting anytime, anywhere learning for all students.[18]

STEM The areas of science, technology, engineering, and mathematics.

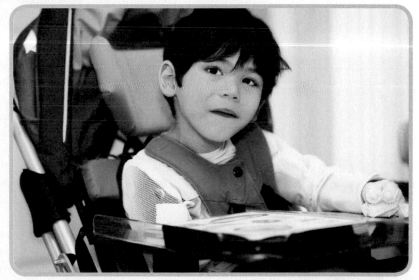

On a given school day, students benefiting from an education that integrates not only science and math, but also engineering and technology into the learning process may collaborate on an interactive whiteboard, use simulation programs to graph data from class projects, use handheld devices to collect and analyze data on local community environmental problems, and use technology to understand the basic physics of music. This helps to promote enthusiasm in the field of engineering and also to enhance the knowledge of our next generation of engineers and inventors. Students need an education with a solid foundation in STEM areas so that they are prepared to both work and live in the twenty-first century.

Assistive technology enables children with disabilities to participate in regular classrooms and to learn skills and behaviors not previously thought possible. What are some examples of assistive technologies that would enable this child and others with disabilities to learn?

INTEGRATING TECHNOLOGY IN YOUR PROGRAM

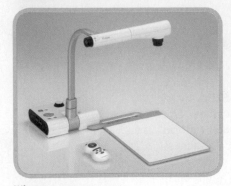

What are some ways you could use a document camera in your teaching?

ELMO Document Camera TT-02RX.
Courtesy of ELMO USA CORP.

Technology is such a fact of life in classrooms today that you will want to integrate technology into all of your instructional activities. Cathy Faris, instructional technology coach, and Karla Burkholder, director of instructional technology, at Northwest Independent School District near Fort Worth, Texas, provide these ideas for how you can integrate technology into your instruction:

- In pre-K, you can display children's books on a document camera and the students can circle characters or settings in the story. A document camera (also known as an image presenter, visual presenter, digital visualizer, or docucam) is a real-time image-capturing device that displays an object to a large audience. It magnifies and projects the images of actual, three-dimensional objects onto a big screen.

- In kindergarten, students use multimedia software to create a slide show that demonstrates their knowledge of phonemes. The students may choose pictures from a gallery to match the sound that the teacher assigns and then create a slide show either as a group or an individual project. Children save the slide show as a podcast to post to the teacher's website synced to an iPod.

- First grade students place their shared writing on a document camera, then use an interactive whiteboard or wireless chalkboard to highlight, circle, or make notes of important components in the writing sample.

- Second grade students use a digital video camera to record their participation in a science inquiry lesson. The children save the video to classroom computers for later review and study.

- Third grade students research a project on the Internet. They create a slide show to display their information. They also create a movie from the slide show pictures by saving photos and placing them into movie editing software. They save the movie as a podcast and place it on the teacher's website.

- In science, students use a document camera to focus in on insects, plants, rocks, minerals, and such. As the object becomes enlarged, the students can see its properties. This gives the students an opportunity to experience science in a way that they normally would not.

  - Scientific probes enable students to measure temperature, sound, and light. They graph the data, display it for discussion, and then print the reports.

  - Blogs allow students to share information, opinions, and experiences with other students via the Internet.

  - Student response systems (clickers), such as the CPS Pulse, enable teachers to capture real-time assessment data to gauge student comprehension, identify individual learning needs, and differentiate instruction.[19] This device is similar to polling the audience of a TV game show. In addition, teachers are able to document a student's progress over time.[20]

MP3 players and iPods enable children to participate in a wide range of activities and to learn basic knowledge and skills.

Of course not all children have the same access to technology, so making sure they have this access is an important factor when designing a classroom environment and planning curricula that promote learning. The following 5E lesson plan is an excellent guide for how to integrate technology in your teaching.

LESSON PLANS

Living and Nonliving Organisms 5-E

Grade Level: 1st Grade   **Subject Area:** Science

Lesson Title: It's Alive!!! Or Is It?

Texas Essential Knowledge and Skills: 1.9 Organisms and environments. The student knows that the living environment is composed of relationships between organisms and the life cycles that occur. The student is expected to:

(A) sort and classify living and nonliving things based upon whether or not they have basic needs and produce offspring

Technology Standards:

Creativity and innovation. The student uses creative thinking and innovative processes to construct knowledge and develop digital products. The student is expected to:

(B) create original products using a variety of resources

(C) explore virtual environments, simulations, models, and programming languages to enhance learning

Fundamental Questions:

How do you determine if something is classified as living or nonliving?

What is the difference between a living and nonliving thing?

What are the characteristics of a living thing?

What are the characteristics of a nonliving thing?

Why is it important for scientists to classify things in these categories?

Objectives:

We will identify the difference between living and nonliving organisms by predicting items that fall in each category.

We will analyze what characteristics make something living and not living by generating a list of "rules."

We will identify living and nonliving items by taking pictures of each and producing a digital poster.

We will justify why each item is classified as living or nonliving by creating a digital presentation that justifies the characteristics.

Materials:

Science journals, iPads, wireless Internet

Prior to the engage piece, provide inclusion students with a list of academic vocabulary that will be used as part of the lesson.

ENGAGE THE LEARNER

These activities mentally engage students with an event or question that capture students' interest and help them to make connections with what they know and what they can do.

Activity:

- In table groups, have students look at a virtual environment, such as a rainforest, using the SPHERE: 360 Degree Panorama Photography App by Spark Labs on iPads.

- In table groups, have the students discuss all of the things that they see in the panorama, whether it is living and nonliving, and how they determined it to be living or nonliving.

- Reconvene as a class and share with the students that scientists classify things for many purposes and this lesson focuses on classifying things as living and nonliving things.

- Pose the following questions: *Why do scientists need to classify items as living and nonliving? How can you tell if something is living or nonliving? What are some things that all living things have in common?* Generate a discussion about what makes something "alive."

Learners with special needs thrive in an environment that places emphasis on images.

If you do not have access to iPads, you can visit the web-based site at tourwrist.com and show the panorama on the projector.

This activity supports learners with special needs because working in groups gives them the opportunity to respond orally.

(Continued)

Post a screen shot of your anchor chart on your class website for students who were absent and for those who need additional time to review the activity.

- Use a whiteboard app such as Showme or Educreations to keep a running record and have students follow along in their science journal. (Resist the urge to correct misconceptions at this point.)

As inclusion students participate in this part of the lesson, it is vital that they be given continuous feedback. This serves as assurance that they are on track to the correct objective.

- After discussing the qualities of a living thing, go to each group and have them share the living things that their group saw in the panorama. Use the chart to check off the characteristics that apply to the living things.

- Keep going until all of the misconceptions are crossed off, and you will have the beginnings of a list of what all living things have in common. Have students circle the remaining living things in their science journal.

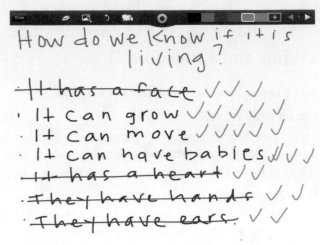

EXPLORE THE CONCEPT

Students encounter hands-on experiences in which they explore the concept further. They receive little explanation and few terms at this point, because they are to define the problem or phenomenon in their own words.

Activity: QR Code Scavenger Hunt

- Post QR codes around the room. Each QR code should be associated with a short video describing living or nonliving things that the students are familiar with in daily life. (Teachers can locate these videos on teacher-tube.com or schooltube.com.)
- Students will use the iPads to scan the QR code.
- In their journal, have students create a T-chart (living and nonliving) to record their discussions and predictions.

A QR code serves as a link between the virtual world and the physical world. A QR code can be created for free by using a web-based QR code creator such as qrcode.kaywa.com or qrstuff.com.

Students can utilize a free QR code reader that can be installed on the iPad via the App Store.

Inclusion students have a variety of ways they can "explain" the concept. Some thrive when expressing their understanding verbally, while others are more visual. It is crucial that you know your students and what helps solidify their learning.

EXPLAIN THE CONCEPT AND DEFINE THE TERMS

Only after students have explored the concept does the teacher provide the scientific explanation and terms for what they are studying.

Activity:

Review the results of the scavenger hunt. As a class, create an anchor chart to discuss the findings.

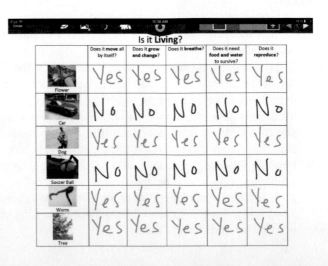

- Based on the chart, students should create a Thinking Map or other graphic organizer, such as a double-bubble, to compare and contrast the characteristic of living and nonliving things.

ELABORATE ON THE CONCEPT

This stage of the model helps students elaborate on their understanding of the concept. They are given opportunities to apply the concept in unique situations, or they are given related ideas to explore and explain using the information and experiences they have accumulated so far.

All students, especially inclusion students, tend to elaborate on parts of the lesson that you may not expect. As long as they have met the objective, take this opportunity to allow the student to make personal connections with the learning.

Activity: Expedition: Living and Nonliving

- Students will go outside and take pictures of some of the living/nonliving things using the iPads. Encourage them to take as many living and nonliving pictures as possible. Students will use the pictures to create a digital poster.

Allowing for a varied number of images supports learners at every level.

- Tell your students that today they have a "special" assignment. They are going to be living/nonliving scientific investigators.
- Let them know that they are going on a living and nonliving expedition. They will try and find as many living and nonliving things as they can.
- They will need their journal, pencil (hand lenses optional, goggles great for photo op), and group iPad. Before heading outside, have your students create a T-chart in their notebooks. Label the sections of T-chart living and nonliving.
- The target is for students to find at least five living things and five nonliving things to photograph and record on their charts.

Adjust this number based on individual needs.

EVALUATE STUDENTS' UNDERSTANDING OF THE CONCEPT

The final stage of the model is designed for the students to continue to elaborate on their understanding and to evaluate what they know now and what they have yet to figure out.

Activity:

Students will complete a digital presentation using whatever tools the class has access to. These may include:

iPad or iPods—30 Hands, Haiku Deck, Flip It!

Laptops or Tablets—Animoto, Haiku Deck Web Version, One True Media

This presentation should include objects they found on their living and nonliving expedition. It should answer the following questions:

Why do scientists classify things as living or non living?

What are do all living things have in common?

Show a few examples of living and non living things you found in your expedition. What makes them living/nonliving?

Source: Contributed by Cara Carter, Ashley Chapman, and Charles Cooper, Northwest ISD, Justin, Texas. (All images were obtained from www.morguefile.com and are copyright free.)

USING SMART BOARDS IN THE CLASSROOM

An interactive whiteboard such as the one marketed by Smart Technologies (the SMART Board) is one of the most valuable teaching and learning tools in the early childhood classroom. It can revolutionize the way you teach! The SMART Board projects a computer image onto a touch-sensitive whiteboard. You can write with digital ink using pen tools or with your finger! Teachers and students use their finger or hand as they would a mouse to drag and drop objects or click just as they would

The INTERWRITEMOBI enables teachers to interact with students, monitor student responses, and support student-centered learning.

using a mouse. Content displayed on the SMART Board becomes interactive so that students can move objects, click links, write on Web pages, and more. When young children interact with the whiteboard it engages them visually, kinesthetically, and aurally.

Here are some real classroom examples of SMART Board integration in the kindergarten, suggested by Pamela Beard, English as a Second Language specialist at Forest Ridge Elementary in College Station, Texas:

Math
- Students move images of red or green apples to construct a graph of their favorite kind of apple.
- Kindergarteners practice completing patterns using various clip art and the "infinite cloning" tool. This tool enables children to pull multiple copies of a single clip such as a red or blue bear, moving each one independently.
- Flash files include dice that roll when children click on them, a hundreds chart that they click to reveal patterns, a movable protractor, and more.

Writing
- Children do interactive writing, sharing digital ink pens to compose a journal entry.
- Teachers can change handwritten text into typed text for the children to read.

Reading
- Children highlight sight words using digital ink or move words into sentences using a poem for shared reading.
- Children sort words by long or short vowel sounds by physically moving them into a column chart.

Handwriting
- The whiteboard enables children to experiment with handwriting as they trace letters using larger gross motor strokes on a vertical surface.
- Children watch a quick animation of pen strokes needed to form a letter before they use the pen to practice on their own.

Science
- Movable models such as frog dissection or the water cycle make science interactive.
- Children record with an attached document camera, and the teacher can circle or use a spotlight tool to call attention to the results as they are replayed on the big screen.

Social Studies
- Teachers use the "Smart Capture" tool to digitally cut out pictures of historical characters to use as puppets for retelling the Thanksgiving story.[21]

Camcorders and flip cameras enable you to capture important learning events, document individual and small projects, and reinforce student skills. They also enable children to actively participate as researchers and authors.

With SMART Boards, you can have at your fingertips charts, journals, and models for instant display. Imagine your kindergarten class where students learn letters for the first time and are introduced to the letter "K," seeing various fonts of it on one slide; practicing it on a handwriting line; sorting pictures of things that start with that letter from things that don't; watching a five-minute videocast of *Sesame Street*'s clips of that letter; and finally putting it all in context by reading poetry focused on that specific letter. You can do it all by simply making a few clicks at the SMART Board![22]

USING TWITTER TO TEACH AND LEARN. Today, tweeting is one of the most used methods of communication there is! First grade teacher Jodi Conrad shares with you how **Twitter** is a learning experience for her children and her.

"My original intention for using Twitter in the classroom was to create an instant school and home learning connection. I wanted parents to have a conversation starter with their children the moment they walked out of school.

As I began using Twitter, I realized the benefits of using this social media tool were more far-reaching than I anticipated. I didn't expect the additional benefits such as enhancing our end-of-the-day classroom meeting by increasing community and student engagement, encouraging student reflection, and providing assessment data to guide future instruction. I found using Twitter supported the learning of writing skills. Students were learning how to summarize and how to write for an authentic purpose and specific audience. They learned about writing conventions in context, including grammar, spelling, keyboarding skills, and writing process skills. Additionally, our class has become connected with other classes in and out of our school district, and around the country. My students are learning essential twenty-first-century skills, including digital citizenship and how to use technology to collaborate and communicate with others in our global society.

Student response systems, also known as Classroom Performance Systems and "clickers" are an ideal way to get students actively involved in their learning.

Twitter An online social networking service and microblogging service that enables its users to send and read text-based messages.

Getting Started

1. Use Twitter. The best way to experience the potential of using Twitter in the classroom is to tweet. To be a consumer and contributor in the Twitter world go to Twitter.com and create your individual account. I use Twitter to support my own professional development. My professional Twitter account @JodiLeeConrad is used to tweet about what I am learning, to connect with other professionals and organizations, and to keep current on new research and teaching strategies.

2. Determine your purpose. Consider your audience and purpose. In my classroom, we end our day by gathering in front of the interactive whiteboard to reflect and discuss our learning. Students collaboratively create and send out a tweet to share our learning with parents and other followers. In addition to students tweeting about their learning, I use Twitter to communicate with parents about upcoming events, provide important reminders, and make parents aware of online learning resources.

3. Set up a Twitter account for your classroom. Create a Twitter account for your classroom at Twitter.com. You may want to use your class name. For example, MsConradAL1 is my classroom Twitter name. I used my name, school abbreviation (Abraham Lincoln), and 1 for first grade. Create a sense of ownership by getting students involved from the beginning and creating your Twitter name as a class.

4. Share your Twitter account with students. Explain to the class what Twitter is and how it will be used in the classroom. Twitter is a micro-blog. This means that you only have 140 characters to communicate your message. Twitter is a tool that is used to share ideas with others on the Internet. Let students know that parents will be invited to follow the class on Twitter.

5. Consider privacy settings and options. Twitter offers a variety of privacy settings. You will find many options in account settings. When selecting the settings to meet the needs of your classroom, consider your own comfort level with sharing information in this type of social media outlet and check with your district's technology department. They will be able to help you select the privacy settings that your district is comfortable with.

6. Share your Twitter name with parents and invite them to follow you. Explain to parents what Twitter is, your purpose for using it in the classroom, and the security measures you have in place to ensure the safety of the students. Share your Twitter name and invite parents to follow the class.[23]

BLOGGING IN THE CLASSROOM.   I'm sure that in your life, you are involved in many kinds of technology. I'll bet some of you are bloggers! You can use technology to your advantage in your classroom by creating your own blog and getting your children to blog. For those of you who don't blog, a **blog** is a Web publishing tool that allows you to self-publish commentary in a journal format, while adding artwork and links to other blogs or websites.

blog A Web publishing tool that allows you to self-publish commentary in a journal format, while adding artwork and links to other blogs or websites.

Why blog? Blogs are used to motivate children and give them authentic reasons to write. We have talked about authentic assessment and authentic environments. Authentic also applies to children applying what they learn to real-life activities and events and using the real world as a source of ideas.

Here is an excerpt from Kathy Cassidy's blog at the beginning of a new school year:

> Our first day of school was a busy one, but since the grade one students had been looking longingly at the iPads since they arrived in the classroom, we did take some time to get acquainted with these new tools. The grade two students were excellent teachers, passing on their knowledge to the younger students. We're looking forward to seeing how these captivating devices can help us to learn.[24]

TECHNOLOGY AND ASSESSMENT.   Increasingly, teachers are embracing technology as an efficient and helpful way to assess children's learning. Teacher Cheri Shirley walks you through how the assessment process can work.

Teachers can quickly and efficiently assess a child's literacy, phonological awareness, vocabulary, and math development using a netbook, notebook, Apple iPad, Apple iPod Touch, or laptop. Consider the following scenario:

It's September and Tracy Richard is ready to begin assessing her four-year-old pre-Kindergarten children. They have been in school for one month, and the children are comfortable in their new surroundings. Tracy is anxious to see what the children in her class know about letters, vocabulary, math, and phonological awareness. This beginning-of-the-year assessment will provide her with a benchmark and enable her to modify her instruction to better meet her children's needs. Tracy grabs her netbook, reminds her assistant that she will be in the conference room next door, and calls Cassie, the first child that she will assess.

Together, Tracy and Cassie walk to the conference room chattering about the "games" they will play on the "little computer." The room is set up so that there is a small table and two child-size chairs. Tracy sits next to Cassie and places the netbook where they both can see the screen and begins the letter assessment. One by one, letters appear on the netbook screen and Cassie quickly names them. Tracy easily scores each answer by discreetly tapping the arrows on the keyboard. Sixty seconds later and the letter knowledge assessment is complete! Tracy walks Cassie back to the classroom and repeats the process with the next child. After she has assessed each child's letter knowledge, she will systematically work through the remaining parts of the assessment. The entire assessment will take Tracy less than 20 minutes to complete with each child.

Tracy gets the netbook back out and connects it to the Internet in her classroom. She clicks on the "sync" icon on the desktop, and quickly her assessments synchronize with a secure server. In just a few seconds, she has a report on how well each of her children know the letters of the alphabet. She will have a class report as well as a report on each individual child. Tracy assesses which children have an emerging understanding of letters, and she will know exactly to which children she will need to provide additional assistance. Tracy now has the information she needs to plan her instruction in the weeks to come.

Mobile-to-Web technology allows teachers to quickly and accurately assess children at multiple checkpoints throughout the year. HTML-5 technology (the assessment process) is simplified by allowing the teacher to assess offline. Teachers can administer assessments outside the classroom in environments that are more conducive for assessment.

There are many benefits for early childhood teachers who assess children using one of the many, readily available mobile-to-Web assessment tools currently on the market. The benefits of technology-based assessment over traditional assessment methods include the following:

- More accurate assessment results
- Less time spent preparing materials for assessment
- Less time spent in administering the actual assessment, which results in more time devoted to teaching in the classroom
- More cost-effective
- More flexibility to choose the appropriate setting for the assessment
- Provides immediate feedback
- Results are easy to interpret and share with administrators and parents
- Results enable teachers to differentiate instruction with greater ease

Tracy Richard is part of a generation that has never been without technology. She understands and values its early childhood applications. The result is that she is able to deliver instruction to her children that will have a positive impact on student achievement.[25]

In your overall and day-to-day teaching, you will want to use best practices of technology instruction. In her Voice from the Field, technology support teacher Cathy Faris shares with you how to use some of the best practices for integrating technology with your teaching.

Reflect and Apply: PRO's

SUPERVISION OF CHILDREN'S INTERNET USE

Parents and teachers face a technological challenge in trying to separate the good from the bad on the Internet. One approach is to monitor constantly what their children access. However, for most parents, this is an impractical solution. Another approach is to use a filter, a computer program that denies access to sites parents specify as inappropriate. One such program, Net Nanny (see the Linking to Learning section at the end of the chapter) blocks access to chat rooms, stops instant messages, blocks violent games, and has the capability to filter Facebook usage.

USING TECHNOLOGY TO IMPLEMENT LEARNING THEORIES

The theories early childhood education (ECE) professionals use to guide their practice of developing pedagogy for children birth to age eight years lend themselves to implementation with technology. Teachers use technology to develop curriculum and instructional activities, and children use technology to learn knowledge and skills outlined in program, state, and national Common Core State Standards. Here are

Teaching Standards with Technology

Twenty-first-century learners must be able to collaborate, problem-solve, create, and be critical thinkers. Northwest Independent School District in Texas employs these best practices beginning in pre-Kindergarten:

Creativity. Students develop innovative products to demonstrate creative thinking using cross-platform technology applications such as Showme, Glogster, Animoto, Educreations. For the Spring 2012 science fair, students were given the option to use the tool of their choice for their presentations. The majority of students chose to create a digital application instead of the traditional science board. Many students used a virtual poster (Glogster), which allowed them to embed text, video, images, and research information all acquired using the iPad.

Collaboration. Collaboration combined with technology allows for limitless creative opportunities, for example, Skype, FaceTime, video conferencing, Dropbox file sharing, and social media such as Edmodo.

Edmodo is a social network that hosts protected classrooms in a virtual environment. Teachers set up virtual classrooms that provide opportunities for online learning. As a member of the virtual classroom, students view resources, take quizzes, engage in a forum or blog, upload assignments, and share opinions with an online poll.

The use of Skype also allows a class to communicate directly with a military pen pal in Iraq. This activity enabled students to gain an authentic perspective of a real-life soldier and have a working relationship with him. Students were able to work together to create a Veterans Day presentation using information, pictures, and videos directly from Iraq. For his birthday, they used Skype to hold a surprise party for him.

Problem Solving/Critical Thinking. Students use critical thinking skills to plan and conduct research, manage projects, solve problems, and make informed decisions using appropriate tools and resources. Research shows that there is a high demand for job applicants who are strong critical thinkers and problem solvers. Technology helps foster these skills by use of applications such as Creatagraph, CHARTGIZMO, Showme, and Blabberize.

Using Showme, a productivity app, students can annotate as well as use audio to explain a concept. An example is when students use the app to demonstrate steps taken to solve a math problem. The video can also be shared and used as a reference in Edmodo.

Differentiation. Planning for student differences, learning styles, and pacing in the classroom is a must for educators. The iPad addresses the different modalities of learning, such as tactile, kinesthetic, auditory, and visual, as do as apps such as Showme, Educreations, Toontastic, and StoryKit. Cara Carter, IT support teacher at Northwest ISD, says, "Meeting so many needs simultaneously is a challenge. Various apps engage the learners on all levels of Blooms Digital Taxonomy."

Assessment. Data gathered from assessment drive instruction are a vital component in today's classroom. Technology affords timely, specific, and authentic data. Assessment design can be both qualitative (Wallwisher, blogs, forums, Lino) or quantitative (PollEverywhere, Socrative, response systems).

Engagement/Own Their Learning. When children are given freedom in a nonthreatening environment to explore the digital world, they take charge of their own learning. We give choices and direction while students create products. "Children learn by being engaged, being challenged, and by discovering answers on their own. For example, Brigette Hinte, a teacher in Northwest ISD, says, "The iPads have opened up a new door in my classroom that provides these opportunities in endless ways!"

As educators, it is imperative that we meet the expectations of our digital natives. Students are on-demand learners and expect to be connected globally, immediately, and continuously, with immediate access to information and resources. Teacher Allison Connell says, "Students are begging me for more time to work on class work with technology instead of asking, 'when is recess?' That really excites me! Thank you, iPad!"

> "The students without financial access to technology tools at home often feel restricted. However, by using technology in the classroom, students obtain skills necessary to be successful in the outside world," — Cathy Faris, IT Support Teacher, NISD.

Now would be a good time for you to research each of the programs mentioned above and determine how you could use particular apps, software, and programs in your teaching.

Source: Contributed by Cathy Faris, Fort Worth, Texas.

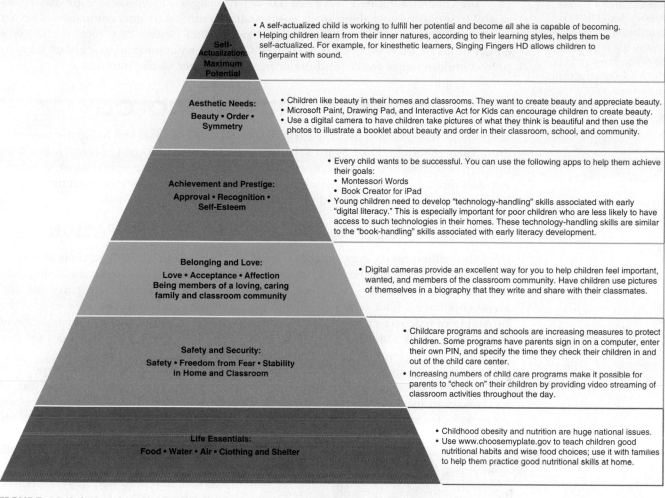

Self-Actualization: Maximum Potential
- A self-actualized child is working to fulfill her potential and become all she is capable of becoming.
- Helping children learn from their inner natures, according to their learning styles, helps them be self-actualized. For example, for kinesthetic learners, Singing Fingers HD allows children to fingerpaint with sound.

Aesthetic Needs: Beauty • Order • Symmetry
- Children like beauty in their homes and classrooms. They want to create beauty and appreciate beauty.
- Microsoft Paint, Drawing Pad, and Interactive Act for Kids can encourage children to create beauty.
- Use a digital camera to have children take pictures of what they think is beautiful and then use the photos to illustrate a booklet about beauty and order in their classroom, school, and community.

Achievement and Prestige: Approval • Recognition • Self-Esteem
- Every child wants to be successful. You can use the following apps to help them achieve their goals:
  - Montessori Words
  - Book Creator for iPad
- Young children need to develop "technology-handling" skills associated with early "digital literacy." This is especially important for poor children who are less likely to have access to such technologies in their homes. These technology-handling skills are similar to the "book-handling" skills associated with early literacy development.

Belonging and Love: Love • Acceptance • Affection Being members of a loving, caring family and classroom community
- Digital cameras provide an excellent way for you to help children feel important, wanted, and members of the classroom community. Have children use pictures of themselves in a biography that they write and share with their classmates.

Safety and Security: Safety • Freedom from Fear • Stability in Home and Classroom
- Childcare programs and schools are increasing measures to protect children. Some programs have parents sign in on a computer, enter their own PIN, and specify the time they check their children in and out of the child care center.
- Increasing numbers of child care programs make it possible for parents to "check on" their children by providing video streaming of classroom activities throughout the day.

Life Essentials: Food • Water • Air • Clothing and Shelter
- Childhood obesity and nutrition are huge national issues.
- Use www.choosemyplate.gov to teach children good nutritional habits and wise food choices; use it with families to help them practice good nutritional skills at home.

FIGURE 13.2 | Meeting Maslow's Hierarchy of Needs with Technology

some ways technology supports your implementation of Maslow's hierarchy of needs (see Figure 13.2).

At Stephens Elementary School in Madison, Wisconsin, students use computers and the Internet to support and extend learning within the classroom. All school computers are fully networked. Laser printers, "quick-take" and digital cameras, and scanners are available. All students receive keyboarding instruction in the third, fourth, and fifth grade classes. Each classroom has at least two computers, with additional computers housed in the school computer lab, accommodating weekly REACH (Reinforcement and Enrichment for All Children) classes. Students may use the Internet with parent permission and teacher supervision.[26]

A. M. Chaffee Elementary School in Oxford, Massachusetts, has similar policies. Teachers inform students that the use of the Internet is a privilege, not a right, and inappropriate use will result in the cancellation of the privilege and alternative assignments. Teachers, parents, and students sign agreements that they will use district technology appropriately. All district computers are equipped with filtering software, and students only access the Internet for school-related purposes. Students are taught Internet safety rules and copyright issues at the beginning of each year.[27]

The Children's Online Privacy Act (COPPA) Legislation designed to ensure the privacy rights of children and protect them from unscrupulous individuals and companies.

The Children's Online Privacy Act (COPPA) is designed to ensure the privacy rights of children and protect them from unscrupulous individuals and companies. The act requires Web operators to secure parental permission before they receive children's e-mail or home addresses.[28] It is likely that Congress will continue to legislate ways to protect children ages twelve and under from the danger of the Internet.

PARENTS AND TECHNOLOGY

Technology has changed the way early childhood professionals teach and the way children learn. It should come as no surprise that it has also changed parents' roles. With the help of technology, parents now have more resources for participating in, supervising, and directing their children's education. They also have more opportunities to be involved in school activities and monitor children's school programs.

TECHNOLOGY AND PARENT PARTICIPATION

Even though parenting may seem like a full-time proposition, many parents also have demanding work schedules, and many work two jobs to make ends meet. Juggling the demands of parenting and work causes anxiety and concern about parenting and about children's school achievement. Parents' questions and concerns often exceed the capability of teachers and school personnel to respond within the time constraints of the school day. In addition, many parents have difficulty getting to the school for parent conferences, programs, and assistance.

Technology, such as e-mail, and video-conferencing programs, such as Skype, offer new ways to exchange or gain information and to get help and assistance. Other uses of technology to increase parent involvement include school websites, teacher and classroom websites, and phone conferencing. Some teachers use their websites to regularly post pictures of students doing everyday activities in class. In Florida, the Polk County School District uses an online instructional system to help parents as well as students develop technological literacy. Parents can access student grades, discipline information, and a wealth of information about the district curriculum, as well as ideas for enrichment activities at home, through the district website. Many campuses in the district also offer classes to teach parents how to encourage Internet competence and safety.[29]

Another good way to involve parents and families is through a school/teacher/classroom website. Many teachers use a classroom website to share classroom correspondence, schedules, and many ideas for how to help children with homework and generally support their school success.

Using technology to document children's learning is an excellent way to have an ongoing record of children's achievement. It also provides an opportunity for children to make books about their progress and to electronically share with family, friends, and relatives.

Technology allows children to explore different worlds, access resources, and engage in learning activities on their own. How can you use computers and other technology to appropriately support children's learning?

Check Your Understanding: Parents

ACCOMMODATING DIVERSE LEARNERS

Now that you have read about technology and assistive technology in the early childhood classroom, let's review a common low-tech option often used in early childhood classrooms to help children acquire a way to communicate. **Picture Exchange Communication System (PECS)** is an augmentative/alternative communication system.[30] PECS is exactly what the name implies. Children using PECS learn to exchange a picture of a desired item to communicate. This is particularly useful for children with no verbal skills or limited verbal communication because the child learns to initiate interactions spontaneously and to make requests using pictures. These pictures can be photographs, line drawings, commercially prepared (i.e., Boardmaker), or teacher-made pictures. Your knowledge of PECS will enhance your ability as a teacher of *all* students within your classroom. Young children of all abilities can use pictures as an easy, inexpensive form of assistive technology. Let's meet a child using PECS and see how you can integrate communication goals of using PECs into your curriculum and classroom.

Eliana is a four-year-old girl with autism. She is nonverbal and spends the majority of her day in an inclusive classroom. Her teachers are using PECS to help her learn to communicate her needs, wants, and emotions. She is currently working on goal 4, and as her communication increases, her inappropriate behaviors are decreasing.

Picture Exchange Communication System (PECS) An augmentative/ alternative communication system that allows children to learn to exchange a picture of a desired item to communicate.

GOAL 1: THE PHYSICAL EXCHANGE

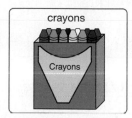

Using a highly preferred item, Eliana will pick up the picture, reach toward another person, and give the picture to the individual. This may be done during art time, when the picture of crayons is placed on the box of crayons and Eliana has to give the picture to the teacher.

GOAL 2: EXPANDING SPONTANEITY

Eliana will go to her communication board/book and pick up the picture and then go to a teacher and give him or her the picture. For example, at snack time, Eliana will pick a picture of a preferred snack and find an adult she can give the picture to.

GOAL 3: PICTURE DISCRIMINATION

Eliana will go to her communication board/book and pick out a picture from an array and then go to an individual and give him or her the picture. For example, during center time, Eliana will choose what center she wants to go to.

 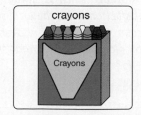 

GOAL 4: SENTENCE STRUCTURE

Now that Eliana can quickly and easily choose between pictures, the teacher creates pictures of multiword phrases (i.e., I want . . .) and Eliana can use them to combine a picture for "I want" with a picture of the preferred items.

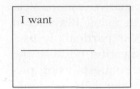

GOAL 5: RESPONSIVE AND SPONTANEOUS COMMENTING

Using pictures for "I see," "I hear," "I feel," and so on, Eliana will be taught to comment on her environment, express her likes and dislikes, and expand her communication.

As you can see, the pictures do not need to be elaborate or require the use of extensive art skills! Any teacher can use readily available pictures to assist all children in the class in communicating.

ACTIVITIES FOR PROFESSIONAL DEVELOPMENT

ETHICAL DILEMMA

"CALL ME A LUDDITE* IF YOU LIKE!"

Allondra Mendoza is not pleased at all with her son Brian's lack of involvement with technology in his second grade classroom. In fact, Allondra feels that Brian is not getting any experiences at all with technology. Brian complains about his teacher not having any technology in her classroom. Allondra has come to the conclusion that Brian's teacher, Janelle Merani is computer illiterate! "We try to give Brian many technological advantages at home. He has an iPad, iPhone, and a Kindle. We view our home as a technological oasis. However, when Brian goes to school, it's like the Sahara Desert!" Allondra has decided "she has had it" and asks for a parent teacher conference. During the conference, Janelle is very forth right and direct with Allondra. "You're right, Mrs. Mendoza! I don't like computers! Actually, I hate them! I think they're totally unnecessary, and I have no intention

of using technology in my classroom. Call me a Luddite if you like, but I've taught for over thirty years, and there's no need for me to change the way I teach now." Allondra can't believe her ears. She leaves the parent teacher conference thoroughly "ticked off" with Janelle's attitude and is determined to do something about it.

*One who opposes any technical or technological change.

What should Janelle do? Immediately get a meeting with the school principal and ask for Brian to be transferred to another classroom? Or, should Allondra go directly to the school board and demand Janelle's firing on the basis of incompetency? Or, should Allondra take her case to the local television station, which is always eager to publicize parents' dissatisfactions with the local school district? Or, should Allondra calm down, think it over, and be satisfied with Brian's technological desert? What should Allondra do? What would you do?

ACTIVITIES TO APPLY WHAT YOU LEARNED

1. **KEY ASSESSMENT:** Today's children are more technologically savvy than ever before, and many are ready and able to use technology in the classroom. Your challenge will be how to provide technology literacy—that is, the ability to understand, and use technology in the home, school, and society. Post a Prezi presentation to your class discussion board in which you provide three examples of how you will promote and increase children's technological literacy. As you prepare your Prezi, take into consideration these factors.

   a. The plans and ideas you have for how you will gain access to the technology that you want to use. For example, if you want to use iPads with your children but your district does not have any available, you may have to write a grant to your school's foundation or to a community agency to get the funds for the technology that you want. Many teachers today are in the "grant writing" business as a means of getting the technology they need to achieve their classroom goals.

   b. Be sure to consider *how* you will include *all* your children in becoming technologically literate. Reflect on what training and technological help you will need to achieve your goal of promoting technological literacy in your classroom. Use this **rubric** to guide your work.

2. Consult with a special education teacher about how he or she uses assistive technology and the kind of assistive technology used. You could also make arrangements to conduct your interview via Skype. Make a list of all of the different kinds of assistive technology the teacher uses and post this information to your classroom discussion board. This activity can be a good discussion starter for you and your classmates as a way of thinking and reflecting on the possibilities for assistive technology in your and their future classrooms.

3. By now you should understand that you will use technology as part of your instructional activities. Of all of the technological devices and methods for using technology, identify three technological devices (e.g., iPads) that you would want in your classroom and identify three technology-based activities (e.g., Twitter) that you would want to involve your children in. Post this information to your classroom discussion board and ask for feedback.

4. One of your roles as a teacher will be to provide parents with information about your technology use in your classroom and to advise them about how they can use technology in the home to help their children learn. Think of ways you can help parents stay informed about technology and ways you can involve them in their children's technological learning. Share your findings with your classmates in an online discussion.

5. Accommodating for children's learning means that you will make provisions for them to have access to the curriculum and learning materials in ways that they can learn within the disabilities they have. Think of five ways you can use technology to accommodate diverse learners. For example, how can you use technology to help English language learners? Write a two-hundred word message to your classmates about how you will accommodate diverse learners in your classroom and post it on your class discussion board.

LINKING TO LEARNING

The following agencies and programs, which can be located easily online, provide additional information about topics discussed in this chapter.

AbleNet

They have helped millions of children with a variety of disabilities discover the joy of playing with battery-operated and electronic toys. The Big Red Switch has allowed countless persons with disabilities to access the world around them at the slightest touch of a button.

Aurora Systems

They provide assistive technology for children with learning disabilities and dyslexia and support augmentative communication.

BigKeys

BigKeys offers keyboards for those who need larger keys in order to locate and operate the keys.

Net Nanny

This Internet filtering software delivers family-safe computing solutions for the home, library, education, government, and small/medium business markets.

Tack Tiles

Tack Tiles Braille System is a sophisticated teaching tool for all ages based on LEGO-type blocks. These Braille blocks provide a smoother, shorter, more interesting path to Braille literacy.

GUIDING CHILDREN

Helping Children Become Responsible

LEARNING OUTCOMES

1. Define behavior guidance.
2. Determine what it means to guide behavior in a community of learners.
3. Identify the social constructivist approach to guiding behavior.
4. Identify and apply ten steps to guide behavior.
5. Analyze the problems associated with physical punishment.
6. Determine how you can guide children with disabilities using reinforcement strategies.

WHAT IS GUIDING BEHAVIOR?

Guiding children's behavior is a process of helping them build positive behaviors through **behavior guidance**, a process by which children learn to control and direct their behavior and become independent and self-reliant. Behavior guidance is a process of helping children develop skills useful over a lifetime.

As you work with young children, one of your goals will be to help them become independent and able to regulate, or govern their own behavior. **Self-regulation** is the ability to plan, initiate, and complete an activity; control emotions and behaviors; delay gratification; maintain attention; respond to feedback; and build positive social relations with others.[1]

Another term we use when discussing children's behavior is **executive function (EF)**. EF refers to the ability of children to order their thoughts, process information in a coherent way, hold relevant details in short-term memory, and avoid distractions and focus on the task at hand.[2]

The ability of young children to control their emotional and cognitive impulses is a strong indicator of short- and long-term academic and life success. According to some research, self-regulation predicts academic achievement more reliably than do IQ tests.[3] In a national survey, 46 percent of kindergarten teachers said that at least half the kids in their classes had problems following directions.[4] In a Head Start study, teachers reported more than a quarter of their students exhibited self-control-related negative behaviors. It is estimated that more than five thousand children are expelled from pre-K programs annually because teachers feel unable to control them.[5] These are serious issues for children, schools, families, and society.

KEY TEACHER BEHAVIORS.   Three teacher behaviors are essential for promoting self-regulation in children:

1. Use of reasoning, verbal rationales, and explanations to guide behavior.
2. Gradually relinquishing control and encouraging children to be independent.
3. Creating a warm environment to support positive emotional growth.

These and other guidelines we discuss below will help you be confident and effective as a professional in guiding children's individual and group behaviors.

THE IMPORTANCE OF GUIDING CHILDREN'S BEHAVIOR

As an early childhood teacher, you will assume major responsibility for guiding children's behavior in up-close and personal ways. You will spend many hours with young children as a parent/family surrogate. As a result, you need to know and use a wide range of best practices for guiding children's behavior so they can become the responsible people that society, their parents, and you want them to be. There are a number of reasons why guiding children's behavior is important.

ACADEMICS.   Helping children learn to guide and be responsible for their own behavior is as important as helping them learn to read and write. Think for a moment about how many times you have said or have heard others say, "If only the children would behave, I could teach them something!" or "This student won't learn!" Appropriate behavior and achievement are interconnected; you can't have one without the other. Consequently, one of your primary roles as an early childhood teacher is to help children learn the knowledge, skills, and behaviors necessary to help them act responsibly.

NAEYC STANDARDS

behavior guidance The processes by which children are helped to identify appropriate behaviors and use them.

self-regulation (executive function) The ability to keep track of and control one's behavior.

executive function (EF) *See* **self-regulation**.

LIFELONG SUCCESS. Helping children learn to act responsibly and guide their behavior lays the foundation for lifelong responsible and productive living. As early childhood educators, we believe that the early years are the formative years. Thus, what we teach children about responsible living, how we guide them, and what skills we help them learn in the early years will last a lifetime.

PREVENTING DELINQUENCY PROBLEMS. The roots of delinquent and deviant behavior develop in the early years. From research we know what behaviors lead to future problems. For example, behavior characteristics of preschool children that are precursors of adolescent delinquent behavior problems and delinquency include disruptive behavior, overactive and intense behavior, irritability, noncompliance, and intensity in social interactions. All of these behaviors are preventable through diligent guiding and teaching in the early years. However, you can't and should not do all of the guiding in isolation. Involving parents and other family members in school-based programs and activities helps prevent many behavioral problems that are the basis for school failure. Collaborating with families early in their children's lives is an essential way to prevent problems before they begin.

CIVILITY. The public is increasingly concerned about the erosion of civility and what it perceives as a general breakdown of personal responsibility for bad behavior.[6] One reason the public funds public schools is to help keep society strong and healthy. Parents and the public look to you and the early childhood profession to help children learn to live cooperatively and civilly in a democratic society. Getting along with others and guiding one's behavior are culturally and socially essential and meaningful accomplishments. Society counts on you and your colleagues to educate responsible children for responsible democratic living.

Check Your Understanding: Process

GUIDING BEHAVIOR IN A COMMUNITY OF LEARNERS

Think for a moment of the early childhood classes you have taught, volunteered in or observed. In some of the classes, children were actively involved in meaningful activities based on local, state, and common core district and state standards. In other classrooms, the children and teachers seemed disorganized and aimless, with little real learning occurring. What makes the difference? There are three components of a well-run classroom: (1) the classroom is a community of learners, (2) the classroom is well-organized, and (3) there is a well-thought-out and implemented plan for guiding children's behavior and learning.

THE COMMUNITY OF LEARNERS

Lev Vygotsky said that all learning is social. Humans are social beings. Thus, it makes sense for you to create a social classroom environment that supports positive behaviors, and academic achievement.

Classrooms are and should be a community of learners in which children of all ages take shared responsibility for the physical, social, and learning environments. You, the teacher, must help children develop the behaviors for living and learning in the classroom.

A learning community is child-centered. All that you do in classrooms should focus on children's growth and development as persons and as learners. The practices you use and teach for guiding children's behavior are for their academic and behavioral benefit.

As a result of our guiding children's behavior—and helping them guide their own behavior—children can be successful, confident, responsible contributors to the learning community.

DEMOCRATIC LIVING.   In our efforts to help prepare all children to live effectively and productively in a democracy, we place increasing emphasis on providing them experiences that enable them to productively live and learn in democratic school and classroom communities. The idea of teaching democratic living through classrooms that are miniature democracies is not new. John Dewey was an advocate of this approach and championed democratic classrooms as a way of promoting democratic living.[7] However, running a democratic classroom is easier said than done. It requires a confident professional who believes it is worth the effort.

KEY FOUNDATIONAL PRACTICES.   **Learning communities** are grounded in key foundational practices, including morning meetings, respect for children, character education, and teaching civility.

learning communities
Communities grounded in key foundational practices, including morning meetings, respect for children, character education, and teaching civility.

Morning Meetings. You can promote cooperative living in which children help each other direct their behavior. Children are born seeking social interactions, and social relations are necessary for children's learning and development. Children's natural social groups and play groups are ideal and natural settings in which children assist each other in learning new behaviors and being responsible for their own behavior. The classroom as a whole is an important social group. Peers help each other learn. A good way to provide children time and opportunity to talk about behavior and classroom problems is through a morning class meeting.

Classroom meetings in which teachers and children talk serve many useful functions. They talk about expected behaviors from day to day ("When we are done playing with toys, what do we do with them?"); review with children what they did in a particular center or situation; and help them anticipate what they will do in future situations ("Tomorrow morning when we visit the Senior Citizen Center . . ."). In all these situations, children are cooperatively engaged in thinking about, talking about, and learning how to engage in appropriate behavior. They are learning to manage their own behavior!

You can also initiate, support, and foster a cooperative, collaborative learning community in the classroom in which children are involved in developing and setting guidelines and devising classroom and, by extension, individual norms of behavior. Teachers assist children but do not do things for them, and they ask questions that make children think about their behavior—how it influences the class, themselves, and others. This process of cooperative living occurs daily. Discussions grow out of existing problems, and guidance is based on the needs of children and the classroom. An excellent resource for learning about class meetings and how to conduct them is an NAEYC resource book, *Class Meetings: Young Children Solving Problems Together* by Emily Vance and Patricia Jimenez Weaver.

Respect for Children. Throughout this text I have repeatedly emphasized the necessity for honoring and respecting children as human beings. When children are respected and honored, they are much more likely to engage in behavior that is respectful and honorable.

Democratic learning environments require that students develop responsibility for their own behaviors and learning, that classrooms operate as communities, and that all children are respected and respectful of others. Reflect on Standard 1 of the NAEYC professional goals, promoting child development and learning, to create classroom and other environments that are respectful of children and families.

Character Education. Promoting character education continues to grow as a means of promoting fundamental behaviors that early childhood teachers and society believe are essential for living in a democratic society. For example, teachers and their students at Broad Street School in Bridgeton, New Jersey, learn just how far a simple act of kindness can go. The Caught Caring event is a program sponsored by the school's Character Education Committee, which aims to instill in students good citizenship. The committee gave certificates to twenty-nine students for promoting kindness and help that creates a positive atmosphere at the school. One student helped a classmate who was being bullied and had his glasses knocked off. Other students helped tie someone's shoes, opened a locker, shared their supplies, and invited a lonely student to eat lunch with them.[8]

civil behavior Acting in polite, courteous, and respectful ways.

TEACHING CIVILITY.   Civil behavior and ways to promote it are of growing interest at all levels of society. The specific teaching of **civil behavior**—how to treat others well and in turn be treated well—is seen as essential for living well in contemporary society. At a minimum, civil behavior includes manners, respect, and the ability to get along with people of all races, cultures, and socioeconomic backgrounds.

As you watch this **video** of Zeiller's classroom, pay attention to how the teachers speak about different verbal and nonverbal rules and cues used in the classroom and throughout the school. Think and reflect on how you can incorporate these classroom management practices in your classroom.

A SOCIAL CONSTRUCTIVIST APPROACH TO GUIDING CHILDREN

social constructivist approach Approaches to teaching that emphasize the social context of learning and behavior.

Both Piaget's and Vygotsky's theories support a social constructivist approach to learning and behavior. Teachers who embrace a **social constructivist approach** believe that children construct, or build, their behavior as a result of learning from past experiences and from making decisions that lead to responsible behavior. The teacher's primary role in the constructivist approach is to guide children in constructing their behavior and using it in socially appropriate and productive ways. This process begins in homes and classrooms.

You can use *scaffolding* and the *zone of proximal development* (ZPD) to guide children's behavior. Two other constructivist essentials, **adult–child discourse** and **private speech**, or *self-talk,* are also useful in guiding behavior.

adult–child discourse The talk between an adult and a child, which includes adult suggestions about behavior and problem solving.

The central belief that the development of a child's knowledge and behavior occurs in the context of social relations with adults and peers is foundational to Vygotskian and constructivist theory. This means that learning and development are socially mediated as children interact with more competent peers and adults. Consequently, as children gain the ability to master language and appropriate social relations, they are able to intentionally regulate their behavior. Below are ways you can guide children's behavior using scaffolding, the zone of proximal development, adult–child discourse, and private speech.

private speech Self-directed speech that children use to plan and guide their behavior.

GUIDING BEHAVIOR IN THE ZONE OF PROXIMAL DEVELOPMENT (ZPD)

The zone of proximal development (ZPD) is the cognitive and developmental space that is created when a child is in social interaction with a more competent person (MCP) or a more knowledgeable other (MKO). According to Vygotsky, the ZPD is the range of cognitive and behavioral abilities that a child can perform with assistance, but that she cannot accomplish independently. Teachers take children from the behavioral

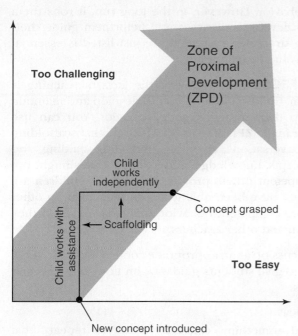

- Teachers
  - Give children guidelines for how to solve problems.
  - Hold class meetings to discuss how to handle classroom behavior problems.
  - Give children choices about how to handle particular situations.

- Peers
  - Meet at the classroom conference center to discuss how to share a book.
  - Make suggestions about how to help others control their anger.
  - Create a video to show others how to walk to the library and other places.

- Parents
  - Give support at home.
  - Provide routines and behavioral expectations.
  - Develop with child a checklist of good behaviors.

FIGURE 14.1 | The Zone of Proximal Development Applied to Guiding Behavior

and social skills they have in their ZPD and guide them to increasingly higher levels of responsible behavior and social interactions. Also, although we often think of guiding behavior as a one-on-one activity, this is not the case. Your role in guiding behavior includes large and small groups, as well as individual children. Figure 14.1 illustrates the ZPD and provides ideas for how to guide children's behavior within it. The ZPD is constantly moving and changing, depending on children's behavioral accomplishments and the assistance and scaffolding provided by others.

IMPLICATIONS FOR TEACHING.   Using our knowledge of Vygotsky's theories, we can develop some strategies to guide children's behavior. Here are some things you can do:

- Guide problem solving.

   "Tanya, what are some things you can do to help you remember to put the books away?"

   "Arturo, you and Juana want to use the easel at the same time. What are some ways you can both use it?"

- Ask questions that help children arrive at their own solutions.

   "Jesse, you can't use both toys at the same time. Which one do you want to use first?"

   "Carly, here is an idea that might help you get to the block corner. Ask Amy, 'Would you please move over a little so I can get to the blocks?'"

- Model appropriate skills.

   Practice social skills and manners (i.e., say please and thank you) with children.

   Listen attentively to children and encourage listening. For example, "Rodney has something he wants to tell us; let's listen to what he has to say."

In the short term, telling children what to do may seem like the easiest and most efficient way to manage classroom behavior. However, in the long run, it robs them of growth-producing opportunities to develop skills that will help them guide their behavior throughout their lives. Using strategies such as those just listed is essential and should become a routine part of your classroom life.

GUIDING BEHAVIOR WITH SCAFFOLDING.   One of the facts of teaching is that you are the leader in the classroom. Children look to you to develop and maintain appropriate expectations and to help them practice good behavior. You can use scaffolding to guide children's behavior in the ZPD (Figure 14.1). Recall that scaffolding involves informal methods such as conversations, questions, modeling, guiding, and supporting to help children learn concepts, knowledge, and skills that they might not learn by themselves. When more competent others provide help (you!), children are able to accomplish what they would not have been able to do on their own. In other words, children are capable of far more competent behavior and achievement if they receive guidance and support from you and other teachers.

Class Discussion.   You can use class discussion as an appropriate context for scaffolding. Here are some strategies you can use to give students guidance on how to guide their behavior during classroom discussions:

- Everyone listens to everyone's ideas.
- Children who don't understand something can ask others to repeat what they said.
- All children get a chance to participate; you may direct and facilitate the conversation to ensure that all children are involved.
- Encourage children to state their thoughts clearly.
- At the conclusion of the discussion, ask a child to summarize what was discussed.
- You and/or children write down the main points from the discussion. For example, at the beginning of the school year, in her first grade classroom, Rachael Flores observes what she believes are some early warning signs of bullying. Some children are engaging in rude behavior and there is mild shoving by some of the bigger boys. Rachael takes this opportunity to introduce the topic of bullying into the class morning meeting. Over several meetings, Rachael reads *The Band-Aid Chicken* by Becky Rangel Henton. As the children discuss bullying, they write down some ways they can deal with bullies:
  - Walk away.
  - Tell a teacher.
  - Ask a friend for help.
  - Tell the bully "Leave me alone!"
  - Walk with a friend.
  - Stand up for yourself.
  - Don't fight the bully. You might lose or get in trouble too.

Adult–Child Discourse. The scaffolding script that follows is illustrative of adult–child discourse. It is an example of a learning conversation, which invites student participation. This discourse centers on how student authors should act while they are sharing their stories:

Teacher: "Maybe we should now think about how to behave as the author during author's chair. What do authors do? Who can remember? Tina, would you like to start?"

Tina: "The author sits in the author's chair and speaks loud and clear."

Isabel: "The author should not fool around, like making faces or having outside conversations."

Shauna: "The author should not be shy and should be brave and confident."

The teacher continues to invite students to participate using this type of scaffolding. A list of responsibilities is created and used in subsequent lessons.[9]

You will want to conduct similar discourses with children as you help them develop their skills and behavior. Discourse can also involve talking about how children might solve problems, interact and cooperate with others, understand norms of social conduct, and act on values related to school and family living. You must initiate and guide this discourse and help children learn the new skills that will assist them in developing self-regulation.

Private Speech and Self-Guided Behavior. Jennifer, a four-year-old preschooler, is busily engrossed in putting a puzzle together. As she searches for a puzzle piece, she asks herself aloud, "Which piece comes next?" I'm sure you have heard children talk to themselves. More than likely, you have talked to yourself! Private speech, or self-talk, is commonplace among young children.

Private speech plays an important role in problem solving and self-regulation of behavior. Children use it to transfer problem-solving knowledge and responsibility from adults to themselves. When you use questions and conversations to guide children and to help them discover solutions, you help them use language as a problem-solving tool. In other words, you lead children to use speech to solve problems, and their language helps them guide their behavior. Now that we have looked at what guiding behavior is, why it is important for you to guide behavior, and the learning theories that can help you, let's dive into the ten steps for guiding behavior.

Check Your Understanding: Social Constructivist

TEN STEPS TO GUIDING BEHAVIOR

Thinking about and learning how to guide children's behavior within a constructivist framework enables you to apply the following ten standards as you teach young children. The goal of most parents and early childhood professionals is to have children behave in socially acceptable and appropriate ways that contribute to and promote life in a democratic society. You should view children's behavior as a process of learning by doing—with guidance. Children cannot learn to develop appropriate behavior and be responsible all by themselves; they must be guided and taught through precept and example. But just as no one learns to ride a bicycle by reading a book on the subject, children do not learn to guide themselves only by being told what to do. They need opportunities to develop, practice, and perfect their abilities to control and guide their own behavior. At the same time they need the guidance, help, support, and encouragement of you, parents, and early childhood professionals. Effective guidance of children's behavior consists of the following ten essential steps.

STEP ONE: ARRANGE AND MODIFY THE ENVIRONMENT

Environment plays a key role in children's ability to guide their behavior. For example, arrange your classroom so that children can independently get and return their own papers and materials, use learning centers, and have time to work on individual projects.

Parents and early childhood professionals have an obligation to help children learn appropriate behavior by guiding their actions and modeling correct behaviors. What role does setting rules play in guiding behavior?

In child care centers, early childhood classrooms, and family day care homes, teachers arrange the environment so it supports the purposes of the program and makes appropriate behavior possible. Room arrangement is crucial to guiding children's behavior; appropriate arrangements signal to children that they are expected to be responsible for their own behavior. And, it is much more pleasant to live and work in an attractive and aesthetically pleasing classroom or center. We all want a nice environment—children should have one, too.

Here are some guidelines to reflect on and help you arrange your classroom to assist children in guiding their own behavior:

- Have an open area in which you and your children can meet as a whole group for morning meetings, etc. Starting and ending the day with a class meeting allows children to discuss their behavior and plan for how they can do a better job.
- Make center areas well defined and accessible to all children. Make center boundaries low enough so that you and others can see over them for proper supervision and observation.
- Provide for all kinds of activities, both quiet and loud. Try to locate quiet areas together (e.g., reading area and puzzle area) and loud centers together (e.g., woodworking and blocks).
- Have appropriate and abundant materials for children's use, and locate them so that children can easily have access to them. Having to ask for materials promotes dependency and leads to behavior problems.
- Make materials easy to store and put away. A general rule of thumb is that there should be a place for everything, and everything should be in its place when not in use.
- Provide children with guidelines on how to use centers and materials. Time spent on teaching and reviewing guidelines and procedures is time well spent.

supportive classroom
Physical arrangement of the classroom so that it is conducive to the behaviors taught.

THE SUPPORTIVE CLASSROOM.   Arrange the physical setting into a **supportive classroom**, conducive to the behaviors you want to teach. If you want to encourage independent work, provide places and time for children to work alone. Disruptive behavior is often encouraged by classroom arrangements that force children to walk over or through other children to get to equipment or materials.

encouraging classroom
A classroom environment that rewards student accomplishment and independence.

THE ENCOURAGING CLASSROOM.   Your classroom should be a place where children can do their best work and be on their best behavior. It should be a rewarding place. The following are components of an **encouraging classroom**. Provide the following:

- Display of children's work
- Freedom of movement (within guidelines)
- Independent work
- A variety of workstations and materials based on children's interests

positive classroom
A classroom environment that promotes appropriate behavior and success.

THE POSITIVE CLASSROOM.   Your classroom should also be a place where children can receive positive energy and love. The following are characteristics of a **positive classroom**:

- Emphasize community and a culture of caring.
- Set high, yet clear and achievable expectations.
- Display consistent behavior.
- Develop open communication among all children and adults.

- Be an efficacious teacher, one who believes children can and will learn, and teach accordingly.
- Obtain sufficient materials to support learning activities.
- Establish and maintain routines.
- Plan for a daily balance between cooperation and independent learning.
- Observe children learning, reflect on how each learns best, and identify trouble areas.

TIME AND TRANSITIONS.   Time, generally more important to adults than to children, plays a major role in every program. The following guidelines relate to time and its use:

- *Do not waste children's time.* Children should be involved in interesting, meaningful activities from the moment they enter the center, classroom, or family child care home. Keep children productively engaged throughout the day.
- *Do not make children wait.* When children have to wait for materials or their turn, provide them with something else to do, such as listening to a story or playing in the block center. Problems can occur when children have to wait because they like to be busy and involved.
- *Allow transition time.* Transitions are times when children move from one activity to another. They should be as smooth as possible and as fun as possible. In one program, teachers sing "It's Cleanup Time!" as a transition from one activity to cleanup and then to another activity. Transition times offer a great opportunity to embed instruction. **Embedded instruction** is the process of engaging children in learning during daily activities, transitions, and routines. On Monday, kindergarten teacher Nancy Green has the children line up for lunch in alphabetical order; on Tuesday they line up according to the number on a craft stick they drew from a container; Wednesday by the color of their clothing; Thursday by the first letter of their last name; Friday by the vowel in their name (If you have an "O" in your name, etc.).
- *Provide time for rest, relaxation, and pleasure.* At Jefferson Elementary, the first and third graders practice yoga several times a week with their teachers. Max, a third grade student, says, "The thing I like about yoga is you can concentrate more, and you will get better grades." Sydney likes yoga "because it relaxes you and makes you smarter." Alejandro says, "I like the tree (pose) the best because I never give up. It makes me relax. Yoga is a good exercise for everyone in the classroom."[10]

embedded instruction
Is the process of engaging children in learning during daily activities, transitions, and routines.

STEP TWO: ESTABLISH APPROPRIATE EXPECTATIONS

Expectations set the boundaries for desired behavior. They are the guideposts children use in learning to direct their own behavior. When children know what adults expect, they can better achieve those expectations.

Setting appropriate expectations for children means you must first decide what behaviors are appropriate. Up to a point, the more we expect of children, the more and better they achieve. Generally, we expect too little of most children. However, having expectations for children is not enough. You have to help children know and understand what the expectations are and then help them meet these expectations. Some children need little help; others need demonstrations, explanations, encouragement, and support as they learn.

SET LIMITS.   Setting limits is closely associated with establishing expectations and relates to defining unacceptable behavior. For example, knocking over a block tower built by someone else and running in the classroom are generally considered unacceptable behaviors. Setting clear limits has three benefits. First, limits help you clarify in your own mind what you believe is acceptable and unacceptable behavior, based on your knowledge of child development, children, their families, and their culture. Second, clear limits help prevent inconsistency and help children act with confidence because they know which behaviors are acceptable. Third, limits provide children with security; children want and need limits. Remember, as children grow and mature, the limits change and are adjusted to developmental levels, programmatic considerations, and life situations.

DEVELOP CLASSROOM RULES.   Although I like to talk about and think in terms of expectations and limits, other early childhood professionals think and talk about classroom rules. The following are some guidelines about rules.

Plan classroom rules from the first day of class, and as the year goes on, involve children in establishing other classroom rules. In the beginning, children want and need to know what they can and cannot do. For example, rules might relate to transitioning from one learning center to another and following bathroom routines. Whatever rules you establish, they should be fair, reasonable, and appropriate to the children's age and maturity. And, you should keep rules to a minimum—the fewer the better!

Remind children of the rules and encourage them to always do their best to follow them. Later, review the rules, and have the children evaluate their behavior against the rules. Children are able to become responsible for their own behavior in a positive, accepting atmosphere where they know what the expectations are.

First grade teacher Katie Hopson and her children developed the following classroom expectations for her children to guide their behavior. In the morning meetings, Katie asked her children what they thought would be good rules to live by in their classroom. As a result, the children were a part of establishing the guideline for their behavior. Over the school year, if Katie and the children need to add new rules they will, based on the needs of the classroom.

1. Be kind and helpful.
2. Make good use of your time.
3. Always do your BEST work.
4. Follow directions.
5. Listen carefully.

Setting and establishing classroom rules is an important part of having a classroom that supports learning. As Katie did, involving students in the setting of classroom rules is a good idea.

Figure 14.2 provides you with additional ideas for classroom rules.

STEP THREE: MODEL APPROPRIATE BEHAVIOR

We have all heard the maxim "Telling is not teaching." Nevertheless, we tend to teach by giving instructions, and, of course, children do need instructions. Teachers soon realize, however, that actions speak louder than words.

Children see and remember how other people act. Quite often, after observing another person, a child tries out a new behavior. If this new action brings a reward of some kind, the child repeats it. Proponents of the modeling approach to learning believe that most behavior people exhibit is learned from the behavior of a model(s). They think children tend to model behavior that brings rewards from teachers, parents, and peers.

You can use the following techniques to help children learn through modeling:

- *Show.* For example, show children where the block corner is and how and where the blocks are stored.

Pre-Kindergarten	• Helping hands • Listening ears • Looking eyes • Quiet voices • Walking feet
Kindergarten	• Be kind to everyone • Raise your hand when you want to speak • Use inside voice • Walk inside the room • Listen to the teachers • Follow the school rules
First Grade	• Respect other people • Keep your hands and feet to yourself • Raise your hand for permission to speak in class • Walk quietly in the hallways • Move about quietly in the classroom
Second Grade	• Be a good listener • Be a good friend • Be polite • Be a hard worker • Be the best you can be
Third Grade	• Listen and follow directions • Raise your hand • Work quietly • Keep hands and feet to yourself • Walk silently in the halls • Be kind to others

FIGURE 14.2 | Examples of Classroom Rules, Pre-K–3

- ***Demonstrate.*** Perform a task while students watch. For example, demonstrate the proper way to put the blocks away and store them. An extension of this technique is to have children practice the demonstration while you supervise. Also have a child demonstrate to other children while you supervise.

- ***Model.*** Modeling occurs when you practice the behavior you expect of the children. For example, model and demonstrate social and group-living behaviors, using simple courtesies ("Please," "Thank you," "You're welcome") and practicing cooperation, sharing, and respect for others. You can call children's attention to desired behaviors when another child models it.

- ***Supervise.*** Supervision is a process of reviewing, maintaining standards, and following up. If children are not performing the desired behavior, you need to review the behavior. You must be consistent in your expectations: Children will learn that they do not have to put away their blocks if you allow them not to do it even once. Remember, you are responsible for setting up the environment that enables children's learning to take place. The Voice from the Field titled "How to Guide Children to Help Ensure Their Success" guides you through five steps to help children be responsible.

How to Guide Children to Help Ensure Their Success

Kenneth entered the kindergarten classroom on the first day of the school year, trailing several feet behind his mom, who appeared to be unaware of his presence. She called out a greeting to another mom, and the two of them had an extended discussion about events in the neighborhood. Kenneth glanced around the room and headed purposefully toward the housekeeping center, where he grabbed a baby doll, threw it out of the doll bed, and then ran to the block box and grabbed a large block in each hand. At this point I deflected his trail of destruction and redirected his progress. "Good morning, welcome to my class. My name is Ms. Cheryl. What's your name?" The whirlwind stopped briefly to mumble a response that I could not understand and glared at me in open hostility. "Let's go talk to Mom," I suggested, touching his shoulder and directing him toward his mom.

UNDERSTANDING BEHAVIOR

In our opening scenario, what important facts should we as educators recognize as signals that Kenneth has some behaviors that require adjustment to ensure his success in school?

- He seems unaware of the expected protocol for entering a classroom.
- His mother's apparent lack of interest in her child's behavior could be an indicator that Kenneth does not expect the adults around him to be involved with his activities.
- He may have been in an atmosphere that requires very little from him when it comes to following rules and, as indicated by his hostility, may see adult intervention as only restrictive rather than supportive and nurturing.
- Kenneth may even have an undiagnosed speech problem that prohibits adults and other children from understanding his needs. If adults in his world have failed to observe and interact with him, he is also probably lacking in basic language skills and vocabulary, which would limit his understanding.
- He appears to deal with his world in a very physical manner.

BEHAVIORS NECESSARY FOR SUCCESS IN SCHOOL

Behavior 1: Recognition of authority. Kenneth was not even aware that an adult was in charge of the classroom.

Behavior 2: Trust in adults. The process of building trust is lengthy, but Kenneth needs to learn to see adults as nurturing and supportive.

Behavior 3: Use of verbal skills rather than physical reactions. If Kenneth is lacking in language, his teacher can help provide language experiences: defining words, explaining everything in detail, showing and describing pictures, reading books aloud, helping with activities, and talk, talk, talking.

STEP 1 Plan
Plan what activities you will offer your children. What part of the day will you use for centers? How can you show your students the best ways to use materials? Where will your children keep their belongings?

STEP 2 Be Explicit
Be sure that all of your children fully understand the classroom expectations. For example, I give my children opportunities to practice how we are to walk in the hallways, play on the playground, eat in the cafeteria, and move about the classroom. Many behaviors that inhibit success in school occur because students are not made aware of appropriate and inappropriate school procedures.

STEP 3 Model Behavior
Model appropriate behaviors and use sociodramatic play to give children an opportunity to "act out" inappropriate behaviors. Lead a class discussion on appropriate versus inappropriate behaviors and allow children to discuss how they feel. Teach children how to handle these issues through conflict resolution methods. Remember, it takes numerous rounds of modeling and role playing to make an impact on behavior that has been ingrained for five years at home and is still the norm when students return home.

STEP 4 Develop Classroom Rules
Our classroom rules are as follows:
1. We listen to each other.
2. We use our hands for helping, not hurting.
3. We use caring language.
4. We care about each other's feelings.
5. We are responsible for what we say and do.

STEP 5 Reinforce

Helping children learn to guide their own behavior takes consistent reteaching and reinforcement. Encourage students to deal with their conflicts appropriately by providing an area for students to talk away from the group. For example, when two students are having a problem with a toy, in a calm voice intervene by asking the students, "Would you two like to go to the discussion area and talk about your feelings?" Spend time daily stating expectations so students get the practice they need to internalize appropriate behaviors.

Source: Contributed by Cheryl Doyle, National Board Certified preschool teacher, Miami, Florida.

IGNORING BEHAVIOR. Do not encourage children's misbehavior. Frequently, teachers see too much and ignore too little. Ignoring inappropriate behavior is probably one of the most overlooked strategies for managing an effective learning setting and guiding children's behavior. Some teachers feel guilty when they use this strategy; they believe that ignoring undesirable behaviors is not good teaching. Certainly, ignoring must be combined with positive guidance and teaching, but if you focus on building responsible behavior, there will be less need to solve behavior problems.

For example, if Charlie jumps up during circle time and grabs a book from the book rack to get attention, you don't want to reinforce his inappropriate behavior by giving him that attention. Instead, you might ignore his behavior while at the same time praising other children for sitting quietly and listening to you read the story. After several days of this strategy, Charlie will probably stay in the circle, at which point you can praise and encourage him for sitting and listening to the story as the other children are. Ignoring *can* work!

TEACHING PEACEFUL LIVING. Teaching peaceful living and how to get along with classmates is an important dimension of every classroom. Teaching peace, cooperative learning, and conflict resolution are important parts of helping children guide their behavior. The Voice from the Field , "Teaching Peace and Conflict Resolution in the Classroom," provides you with many practical ideas and activities for promoting peaceful living in your classroom.

Reflect and Apply: Peace

STEP FOUR: GUIDE THE WHOLE CHILD

Children are not one- or two-dimensional persons. Children are a unified whole. Review and reflect on Figure 14.3 (p. 424), which shows the various dimensions involved in guiding children in and across all domains. There is much discussion today about teaching the whole child—physically, socially, emotionally, cognitively, linguistically, and spiritually. The same applies to guiding behavior of the whole child. This renewed interest in the whole child reflects the profession's ongoing dedication to developmentally appropriate practice. The Association for Supervision and Curriculum Development (ASCD) leads a national effort to include the whole child in all instructional programs and practices. (See the Linking to Learning section at the end of this chapter.) As you work with your children, reflect on how you can promote their positive development in all dimensions.

DIFFERENTIATE GUIDANCE. Just as we differentiate instruction for each child, we also want to differentiate guidance for each child. This means that the one-size-fits-all

VOICE FROM THE FIELD

Teaching Peace and Conflict Resolution in the Classroom

Classrooms are communities of learners. Teachers and children need to live in peace and harmony. You can achieve this goal by teaching about peace, engaging children in peace-making activities, reading books about peace, and teaching specific skills for conflict resolution. In addition, teaching peace begins in the home and classroom, but expands to the school, the community, the nation, and the world. Teaching about other cultures of the world is included in a curriculum that encourages peaceful classrooms and relationships.

Here are some specific classroom conflict resolution strategies you can use to teach children peace:

- **Provide opportunities for children to help and show kindness to others.** Cooperative programs between primary classes and senior centers are excellent opportunities to practice kind and helping behaviors. Children can bake cookies and take them to the senior centers where they read to and with the senior citizens. The possibilities here are endless for showing acts of kindness and sharing.
- **Conduct classroom routines and activities so they are as free of conflict as possible.** Provide opportunities for children to work together and practice skills of cooperative living. Design learning centers and activities so children are able to share and work cooperatively. Children are great teachers, and they can help others learn. Also, children learn leadership roles by helping others. Children helping others can cross over grade levels—third graders can help kindergartners, and so on.
- **When real conflicts occur, provide practice in conflict resolution.** These skills include talking through problems, compromising, and apologizing. But a word of caution regarding apologies: Too often an apology is a perfunctory response on the part of teachers and children. Rather than just offering the often-empty words "I'm sorry," it is far more meaningful to help one child understand how another is feeling. To encourage empathic behavior, you can provide examples of conflict resolution:

"Vanessa, please don't knock over Lucila's building, because she worked hard to build it"; "Brandon, what's another way that you can tell Monica she's sitting in your chair—instead of hitting her, which hurts?" A meeting table in the classroom is a great way to provide opportunities for children and you to sit down and talk things out. Be sure that the "talking out" results in a resolution for how to do things better, for improved attitudes, and for new behaviors.

- **Read stories to children that exemplify prosocial behaviors.** Some good books for promoting peace and understanding are:
  - *Peace Begins with You* by Katharine Scholes. Expresses the different definitions and dimensions of peace, culminating with the responsibility of each individual to make the choice to be a peacemaker (ages four to eight).
  - *Somewhere Today: A Book of Peace* by Shelley Moore Thomas. Makes the concept of nonviolence a personal thing by describing recent events like violence in schools and communities and shows how we all can become a part of promoting peace (ages four to eight).
  - *Planting Trees in Kenya: The Story of Wangari Maathai* by Claire A. Nivola. Tells the story of environmentalist Wangari Maathai, the first woman from Africa to win a Nobel Peace Prize, for her direct response to the devastated natural resources

The classroom environment is one of the most important factors that enable children to develop and use appropriate behavior. The classroom should belong to children, and their ownership and pride in it makes it more likely they will act responsibly.

and poverty caused by the deforestation of her homeland (ages five to eight).

- *I Have a Dream* by Kathleen A. Wilson. Gives children the opportunity to experience Martin Luther King Jr.'s speech through the eyes of fifteen African American artists. Each artist depicts a portion of the story of the civil rights movement (ages four to eight).

- *The Colors of Us* by Karen Katz. Lena discovers that she and her friends and neighbors are all beautiful shades of brown. "I am the color of cinnamon. Mom says she could eat me up," says Lena. Then she sees everyone else in terms of delicious foods. Different ethnicities celebrate the color of their skin and the different shades of brown (ages four to eight).

- **Encourage children to do something else.** Teach children that one strategy for reducing conflict is to walk away and get involved in another activity. Children can learn that they do not always have to play with a toy someone else is playing with. They can get involved in another activity with a different toy; they can do something else now and play with the toy later. Chances are, however, that by getting involved in another activity, they will forget about the toy they were ready to fight for.

- **Have children take turns.** Taking turns is a good way for children to learn that they cannot always be first, have their own way, or do a prized activity. Taking turns brings equality and fairness to interpersonal relations. Also, devise ways to involve all children. For example, put every child's name on a craft stick, and you can pull a name to see who goes next.

- **Teach children to share.** Sharing is good behavior to promote in any setting. Children have to be taught how to share and how to behave when others do not share. You can help children to select another toy rather than hitting or grabbing. But keep in mind that during the early years, children are egocentric, and acts of sharing are likely to be motivated by expectations of a reward or approval, such as being thought of as a good boy or girl.

- **Have children ask for help.** Encourage children to ask others for help for solving problems. Many teachers have a rule that before children come to them for help, students should ask their peers for help. Teacher Lisa Bailey has this rule: "One, two, three—ask three before me." When given opportunities, children are good at solving problems and helping other children. Helping promotes collaboration and encourages compromise and problem solving.

- **Involve parents as part of the peace and conflict resolution processes.** Counsel and work with parents to encourage them to limit or eliminate children's exposure to violence. Suggest that they regulate or eliminate watching violence on television, attending R-rated movies, playing video games with violent content, and buying CDs with objectionable lyrics. Also, share with your families your expectations for peaceful living in your classroom. Share with parents activities you use to help children peacefully resolve conflicts. In addition, you can ask parents for their help and ideas in helping their children learn and live in peace.

approach to guidance doesn't work. Assess each child's behavioral strengths and weaknesses and select appropriate guidance for each child. For example, Amanda is a very responsible child and works and learns best with little guidance and with appropriate suggestions for how she can complete certain assignments and activities. Raul on the other hand, is a boisterous, active boy who needs constant reminders of rules and how to interact with others. While you will have rules that apply to the entire class, and while you will have behavioral guidelines that apply to everybody, individual children need more or less explicit guidelines, and some may need more of your attention than others. Figure 14.3 illustrates the different components of teaching the whole child.

STEP FIVE: KNOW AND USE DEVELOPMENTALLY APPROPRIATE PRACTICE

Knowing child development is the cornerstone of developmentally appropriate practice. You cannot guide the whole child if you do not know and understand where children are developmentally. Children cannot behave well when you expect too much or too little of them based on their development or when parents expect them to behave in ways inappropriate for them as individuals. A key for guiding children's behavior

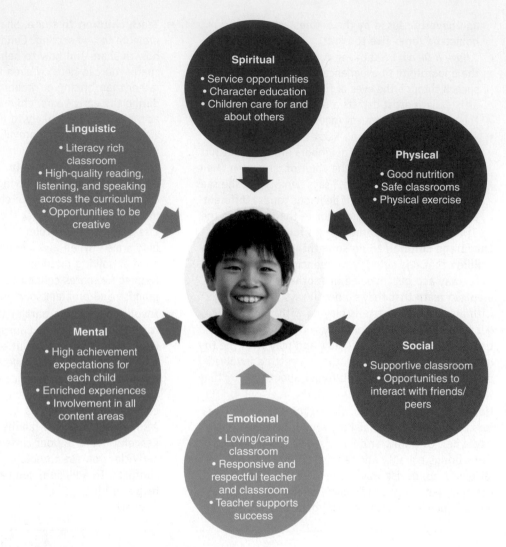

FIGURE 14.3 | Guiding the Whole Child

A key to guiding the behavior of the whole child is to guide his or her behavior across all development domains.

is to *really know what each child is like.* This is the real meaning of developmentally appropriate practice. You will want to study children's development and observe children's behavior to learn what is appropriate for all children and individual children based on their needs, gender, socioeconomic backgrounds, individual disposition, and culture.

STEP SIX: MEET CHILDREN'S NEEDS

Part of knowing children is knowing their needs. Can you really expect a child to sit quietly and pay attention if he is hungry? Can you expect appropriate social interactions from a child if she never learned to trust? Abraham Maslow believed that human growth and development is oriented toward **self-actualization**, the striving to realize one's potential. Maslow felt that humans are internally motivated by five basic needs that constitute a hierarchy of motivating behaviors, progressing from physical needs to self-fulfillment. Maslow's hierarchy moves through *physical needs, safety and*

self-actualization An inherent tendency to reach one's true potential.

security needs, *belonging* and *affection need*s, and *self-esteem needs*, culminating in self-actualization.

PHYSICAL NEEDS.   Children's abilities to guide their behavior depend in part on how well their physical needs are met. Children do their best in school, for example, when they are well nourished. Thus, parents should provide for their children's nutritional needs by giving them breakfast, and early childhood professionals should stress its benefits. For example, the brain needs protein and water to function well. Consequently, many teachers allow children to have water bottles at their desks and to have frequent nutritional snacks.

In addition, the quality of the environment is important. Children cannot be expected to behave appropriately if classrooms are dark and noisy and smell of stale air. And children need adequate rest to do and be their best. The ideal amount of rest is an individual matter, but preschoolers need between eleven and thirteen hours of sleep, whereas young school-age children need ten to eleven hours of sleep each night.[11] A tired child cannot meet many of the expectations of schooling.

SAFETY AND SECURITY NEEDS.   Children can't learn in fear. They should not have to fear their parents or teachers and should feel comfortable and secure at home and at school. Asking or forcing children to do school tasks for which they do not have the skills makes them feel insecure, and children who are afraid or insecure become tense. Consider also the dangers many urban children face—such as crime, drugs, or homelessness—or the emotional toll on children who constantly live in an atmosphere of domestic violence. Part of guiding children's behavior includes providing safe and secure communities, neighborhoods, homes, schools, and classrooms. Your classroom can provide children with the oasis of safety they need to feel comfortable and confident.

NEED FOR BELONGING AND AFFECTION.   Children need the sense of belonging that comes from being given jobs to do, having responsibilities, and helping make classroom decisions. Love and affection needs are satisfied when parents hold, hug, and kiss their children and tell them, "I love you." Teachers meet children's affectional needs when they smile, speak pleasantly, are kind and gentle, treat children with courtesy and respect, and genuinely value each child. An excellent way to show respect and affection for children and demonstrate their belonging is for you to personally greet them when they come into your classroom. A personal greeting helps children feel wanted and secure and promotes feelings of self-worth. In fact, all early childhood programs should begin with this daily validation of each child.

NEED FOR SELF-ESTEEM.   Children who view themselves as worthy, responsible, and competent act in accordance with these feelings. Children's views of themselves come primarily from parents, you, their classmates, and other adults. The foundations for self-esteem are success and achievement. Consequently, it is up to you to give all children opportunities for success.

SELF-ACTUALIZATION.   Children want to use their talents and abilities to do things on their own and be independent. You and parents can help young children become independent by helping them learn to dress themselves, go to the restroom by themselves, and take care of their environment. You can also help children set achievement and behavior goals ("Tell me what you are going to build with your blocks.") and encourage them to evaluate their behavior ("Let's talk about how you helped with cleanup after free play.").

These categories highlight children's basic needs that professionals and parents must consider when guiding children and helping them to develop responsibility for their behavior.

Inner control helps children work independently, which is an important social and behavioral skill necessary for ongoing school achievement.

locus of control The source of control over personal behavior, either internal or external.

social story A personalized, detailed, and simple script that breaks down behavior and provides rules and directions.

STEP SEVEN: HELP CHILDREN BUILD NEW BEHAVIORS

When guiding children, it is important for you to realize that it is not enough to model behaviors or state expectations. You cannot expect children to come up with appropriate behaviors on their own. You must be prepared to help children build new behaviors to replace malfunctioning or maladaptive behaviors that are getting in the way of their learning.

INTERNAL CONTROL (SELF CONTROL). Helping children build new behaviors means that you help them learn that they are primarily responsible for their own behavior and that the pleasures and rewards for appropriate behavior are internal, coming from within them, as opposed to always coming from outside (i.e., from the approval and praise of others). We refer to this concept as **locus of control**—the source or place of control. The preferred and recommended locus of control for young and old alike is internal. However, young children with disabilities often develop an *external* locus of control because the adults in their environment "overhelp" them with difficulties they experience as a result of their disability. Additionally, children without disabilities may also have difficulty with internal control. To avoid the development of an external locus of control in children with and without disabilities, foster an attitude of capability and independence:

DELAYING GRATIFICATION. We talk a lot about helping children develop self-control, but how can we do this? Well, as it turns out research can help us. Researchers inform us that preschoolers who learn to delay gratification are more likely to do well in school, avoid substance abuse, and generally do better in life than do children who can't delay their gratification.[12] Similar research reveals that delaying gratification and self-control are better predictors of a student's academic performance than an IQ test![13] So, what does this mean for you? How can you actively employ strategies to help children learn to delay gratification? Here are some examples:

- Develop a reasonable set of classroom rules and make sure that every child follows them.

- Develop classroom routines for what children are to do and how they are to behave, especially when they enter the school or classroom, during transitions from one learning center to another, and from classroom to lunch or recess. Helping children self-manage their behavior leads to self-control and delayed gratification.

- Provide children with classroom "cues and clues" for how to make decisions and be responsible. For example, provide children with social stories. A **social story** is a personalized, detailed, and simple script that breaks down behavior and provides rules and directions. Social stories can range from drawings featuring stick figures, to computer images, or even better, to digital photos featuring a specific child. Also a good way to give specific directions is with step-by-step photos to show how to engage in and complete certain tasks, such as hand washing, how to put away learning materials, etc.

- Provide appropriate "rewards" for children who focus on learning tasks for specific periods of time; who lead by example during routines such as standing in line or waiting their turn; and who complete a task from beginning to end.

- Embed management skills into classroom routines such as taking turns; being respectful and listening while others speak, and helping children learn that they can't always have what they want when they want it.

Helping children delay gratification and learn self-control may be one of the most valuable things you can do to help them be successful throughout their lifetimes.

TEACHER-CHILD RELATIONS IN GUIDING BEHAVIOR. Think for a minute about your social relations with others. How others treat you affects you emotionally, physically, and cognitively. The same is true for the children you teach. How you relate to them really matters and affects how well they achieve, as well as how well they do and behave. What are teacher behaviors that really matter in preventing children's behavior problems? Consider these:

- Responding to children in a timely fashion
- Anticipating student needs and emotions
- Giving frequent feedback
- Providing strong support for children's academic and social competence in the classroom setting

Researchers have found that the extent to which children can access the instructional and socialization resources of the classroom environment may be, in part, predicated on teacher–child interactions: The partnership between the quality of teacher–child relationships and later school performance is strong and persistent. The association is evident in academic and social spheres of school performance.[14]

In addition, teacher–child affection and warm relationship, can reduce aggressive behavior. Close teacher–child relationships may provide young children with resources (e.g., emotional security, guidance, and aid) that facilitate an 'approach' orientation—as opposed to an 'avoidant' or 'resistant' stance—toward the interpersonal and scholastic demands of the classroom and school.[15] The implication for you and other early childhood professionals is that you need to really care for your children and develop strong and affectionate relationships with them.[16]

STEP EIGHT: EMPOWER CHILDREN

Helping children build new behaviors creates a sense of responsibility and self-confidence. As children are given responsibility, they develop greater self-direction, which means that you can guide them at the next level in their ZPD. Without responsibilities children are bored and frustrated and become discipline problems—the very opposite of what we intend.

To reiterate, guiding behavior is not about compliance and control. And, it is not a matter of getting children to please adults with remarks such as, "Show me how perfect you can be," "Don't embarrass me in front of others," "I want to see nice groups," or "I'm waiting for quiet." Instead, it is important to instill in children a sense of independence and responsibility for their *own* behavior. For example, you might say, "Jasmine, you worked a long time cutting out the flower you drew. You kept working on it until you were finished. Would you like some tape to hang it up?"

You can do a number of things to empower children:

- *Give children responsibilities.* All children, from an early age, should have responsibilities—that is, tasks that are theirs to do and for which they are accountable. Being responsible for completing tasks—doing such things as putting toys and learning materials away—promotes a positive sense of self-worth and conveys to children that people in a community of learning have responsibilities for making the community work well.

- *Give children choices.* Life is full of choices—some require thought and deliberation, and others are automatic, based on previous behavior. But every time you make a decision, you are being responsible and exercising your right to decide. Children like to have choices, and choices help them become independent, confident, and self-disciplined. Making choices is a key to developing responsible behavior and inner control; it lays the foundation for decision making later. Here are some guidelines for giving children choices:

  - Give children choices only when there are valid choices to make. When it comes time to clean up the classroom, don't let children choose whether they want to participate. Instead, let them choose between collecting the scissors or the crayons.

  - Help children make choices. Instead of "What would you like to do today?" say, "Sarah, you have a choice between working in the woodworking center or the computer center. Which would you like to do?"

- *Help children succeed.* Children want to be successful, and you can help them in their efforts. For example, you can arrange the environment and make opportunities available for children to be able to do things. Successful accomplishments are a major ingredient of positive behavior.

STEP NINE: USE PRAISE AND ENCOURAGEMENT

When you have done a good job, you want to be told you have done a good job! Children are the same way. Children want to receive feedback in the form of praise and encouragement, and they want to feel good about their accomplishments.

With the blending of early childhood and special education, more teachers are incorporating praise in their repertoire of teaching strategies. Many special education practices are based on reinforcing appropriate behavior through praise and rewards. The Accommodating Diverse Learners section at the end of this chapter illustrates the use of different types of reinforcement to encourage children's efforts and promote their success. However, simply telling a child "Good!" or "Fantastic job!" doesn't really give her the feedback she needs in order to learn from her accomplishments and have ideas for how she can do even better. Using encouragement is a much better approach.

PROCESS PRAISE VERSUS PERSONAL PRAISE.   Praise is good for children, but it should be the right kind. Children need to be praised for what they do—their effort rather than who they are as a person. So, when Tony returns the blocks to the shelf you would say "Great job of putting the blocks away!" versus saying "Good job, Tony!" Research reveals that the kind of praise given to children influences their motivation later on. **Process praise** as opposed to personal praise provides the foundation for ongoing good behavior and achievement.[17]

process praise Praising children for what they do: "Eddy you did a very good job of teaching Amanda how to write her story on the iPad!" Process praise praises the child and what they accomplished.

ENCOURAGEMENT VERSUS PRAISE.   Think about when somebody says to you, "Good job!" You know what they are referring to but you don't know any of the specifics of the "good job." Perhaps you wanted more feedback on how you could do even better, or you wanted feedback about what part of your accomplishments were good and what part you might improve. The same is true for children. Encouragement provides children opportunities for improving and growing. When we encourage children, we provide them with greater levels of self-motivation and with suggestions for how they can develop new skills and behaviors.

Here are some other reasons why you should use encouragement:

- *Encouragement acknowledges the child's effort.* For example, kindergarten teacher Rebecca Winston does not generalize the work of her children by saying that it is "good" or "great." She points out David's accomplishment in creating purple when combining blue and red and Maya's curving brush strokes in her painting.

- ***Encouragement recognizes the child's success.*** Rebecca recognizes her children are unique and have individual accomplishments she needs to acknowledge. She says, "David, your painting is very colorful. You used lots of reds and blues. You actually made the color purple here. Do you see it?" "Maya, your bird is ready to fly! You used curved lines to make wings look real! You are very skilled at making curves and circles."

- ***Encouragement helps children self-evaluate their efforts.*** When teachers provide children with feedback about what they are doing, children learn to self-evaluate their efforts and successes without comparing their efforts with others. David can now try to see what other colors he can mix together to make new colors! Maya can try to create new drawing designs, such as zigzags or wavy lines!

STEP TEN: DEVELOP A PARTNERSHIP WITH PARENTS, FAMILIES, AND OTHERS

Involving parents and families is a wonderful way to gain invaluable insights about children's behavior. You and parents must be partners and work cooperatively in guiding children's behaviors.

KNOW YOUR CHILDREN.   An important rule in guiding behavior is to *know your children*. A good way to learn about the children you care for and teach is through home visits. If you do not have an opportunity to visit the home, a parent conference, e-mails, and phone calls are other ways you can collaborate to get the information you and they need. Either way, gather information concerning the child's health history and interests; the child's attitude toward schooling; the parents' educational expectations for the child; the school support available in the home (e.g., books, places to study); home conditions that would support or hinder school achievement (such as where the child sleeps); parents' attitudes toward schooling and discipline; parents' support of the child (e.g., encouragement to do well); parents' interests and abilities; and parents' desire to become involved in the school.

UNDERSTAND HOW PARENTS INFLUENCE CHILDREN'S BEHAVIOR. Research confirms that good parenting enhances academic achievement, whereas poor parenting often leads to poor academic achievement.[18] Unfortunately, the Great Recession of 2008–2012 had a tremendous impact on the nation's economy and the socioeconomic status (SES) of many families and children. Census Bureau data indicate that 46.2 million Americans—the highest number in the last fifty-two years—are now living in poverty.[19] What effect does the Great Recession have upon children's classroom and home behaviors? The answer is "a lot." Parents and other family members in low SES households interact and discipline their children differently than do parents and family members in higher SES groups.[20]

- The stresses of living in poverty, poor housing conditions, and parent unemployment inject more stress into the lives of all family members, especially children. Stressed parents have more intense emotional reaction to their children's' behavior than do parents who are not always stressed, and as a result, they use harsher discipline.[21]

- Highly stressed parents assume that their children intentionally misbehave. It is as though stressed parents are looking for ways that their children misbehave and get upset when they do. This leads to more frequent bouts of discipline.[22]

- Low socioeconomic parents believe in and use more harsh methods of discipline than do their higher socioeconomic counterparts.[23] This may be because of their lower levels of education, or it may be because of the ways they themselves were parented.[24] In either case, harsh discipline tends to lead to more negative outcomes for children.

Given the discipline practices of parents of low SES, you can do the following:

- Be especially sensitive to and observant of the behavior of children from low SES in your classroom, monitoring for signs abuse and neglect.
- Collaborate with your administrators and colleagues to develop parent-education programs for all parents to help them understand and to use appropriate methods of discipline.
- Child discipline and guidance is often a function of culture and race. You will want to educate yourself on the discipline practices of different ethnic groups. For example, some ethnic groups believe in and practice harsher methods of discipline than do parents from other ethnic groups.

INVOLVE PARENTS.   A visit or conference also offers an opportunity for you to share ideas with parents. For example, express your desire for children to do well in school; encourage parents to take part in school and classroom programs; suggest ways parents can help children learn; describe some of the school programs; give information about school events, projects, and meetings; and explain your belief about discipline. Many teachers also include this information on their class or school websites.

DEVELOP YOUR PHILOSOPHY.   A good way to clarify your beliefs is to develop a philosophy about what you believe concerning child rearing, guidance, and children. Now would be a good time to list three or four of your main ideas for guiding children's behavior. Knowing what behaviors you want to support in children also helps you determine what is developmentally appropriate for your children. In addition, knowing what you believe makes it easier for you to share with parents, help them guide their children's behavior at home, and counsel them about discipline.

PHYSICAL PUNISHMENT AND CHILDREN'S DEVELOPMENT

Is it possible to guide children's behavior without physical punishment? More and more, early childhood professionals agree that it is. Whether parents and professionals should spank or paddle as a means of guiding behavior is an age-old controversy. Some parents spank their children, following a "No!" with a slap on the hand or a spank on the bottom; some base their use of physical punishment on their religious beliefs. However, spanking is now mostly considered an inappropriate form of guidance. Thirty-one states have legislatively prohibited corporal punishment in schools.[25] However, this means in nineteen states corporal punishment is still allowed. The American Academy of Pediatrics strongly opposes striking a child for any reason. If a spanking is spontaneous, parents should later explain calmly why they did it, the specific behavior that provoked it, and how angry they felt. They also might apologize to their child for their loss of control.[26]

PROBLEMS WITH SPANKING.   There are several problems with spanking and other forms of physical punishment. First, physical punishment is generally ineffective in building behavior in children; it does not show children what to do or provide them with models for how to behave. Second, adults who use physical punishment are modeling physical aggression, saying, in effect, that it is permissible to use aggression in interpersonal relationships. Children who are spanked are thus more likely to use aggression with their peers.[27] Third, spanking and physical punishment increases the risk of physical injury to the child. Because spanking can be an emotionally charged situation, the spanker can become too aggressive, overdo the punishment, and hit the child in vulnerable places. Fourth, parents, caregivers, and teachers are children's sources of security. Physical punishment erodes the sense of security that children must have to function confidently in their daily lives.

In the long run, parents, you, and other early childhood professionals determine children's behavior. Thus, in guiding the behavior of children entrusted to their care, professionals and others must select procedures that are appropriate to their own philosophies and to children's particular needs. The best advice regarding physical punishment is to avoid it and use nonviolent means for guiding children's behavior. Helping children develop an internal system of control benefits them more than a system that relies on external control and authoritarianism. Developing self-regulation in children should be a primary goal of all professionals.

Observe and Analyze

ACCOMMODATING DIVERSE LEARNERS

Many young children exhibit problem behaviors in early childhood, and for most children these behaviors are transient or respond well to developmentally appropriate management techniques. In this text you have learned about some of these techniques. Unfortunately, some students do not respond to guidance strategies and require additional assistance. Positive reinforcement can be used for *all* children and *increases* the occurrence of appropriate behavior. Positive reinforcement is different from rewards. You can give rewards to children when they engage in desirable behavior, but if the reward does not lead to an increase in positive behavior, it is not actually a positive reinforcer. Here are some different types of positive reinforcement that you can use in your classroom.

TANGIBLE REINFORCEMENT

Tangible reinforcers are material objects a child wants, such as stickers, stamps, or certificates. A child's positive behavior is reinforced by access to these items that may not be related to the specific behavior. For example, a child who sits appropriately during circle time may be given a sticker.

ACTIVITY-BASED REINFORCEMENT

Activity-based reinforcement is access to fun or preferred activities that can reinforce a child's behavior. For example, allowing a child to have free time in the puzzle center if he finishes seat work is an activity-based reinforcement.

TOKEN REINFORCEMENT

Token reinforcement gives children points or tokens for appropriate behavior. These rewards have little value in themselves but can be exchanged for something the child wants. For example, giving children tickets that they can exchange for free time or trips to the "treasure chest" is a common token reinforcement system.

SOCIAL REINFORCEMENT

Social reinforcement is given out by teachers who express praise and approval for appropriate behavior. They may be verbal, "good job!" written with a smiley face, or expressions such as a smile, a pat on the back, or a wink.

NATURAL REINFORCEMENT

Natural reinforcement results directly from the child's behavior. For example, a child is struggling to open her juice. The child says "help," and an adult helps the child. The opening (of and getting the juice) is reinforcing. This successful interaction increases the likelihood that the child will *ask* for help in the future, rather than requesting assistance in a more inappropriate manner.

The goal is for children to behave appropriately with natural or social reinforcement. Meeting the needs of *all* children requires knowledge of different types of reinforcement to tailor your interventions to the individual needs of each child.

ACTIVITIES FOR PROFESSIONAL DEVELOPMENT

ETHICAL DILEMMA

"YOU CAN'T SPANK MY CHILD!"

Becky Belcher is outraged. Her eight-year-old daughter, Abigail, just came home and said that her teacher had used a meter stick to paddle her and three of her classmates in front of the other students. Abigail said, "I was scared! It really hurt! I felt like I was going to throw up!" Becky Belcher can hardly contain herself. "I don't want my child subjected to that kind of abuse. The school didn't call and tell me that they were going to spank Abigail. I signed a form that said that I didn't want Abigail spanked at school! If there's spanking to be done, it's my job not the school's job! If the school district thinks I'm going to put up with them assaulting my Abigail they got another thought coming! They broke the law!"

What should Becky Belcher do? Should she keep Abigail at home until the teacher is punished? Should she go directly to the police and file assault charges against the teacher? Should she take her case to the superintendent and school board? What should Becky Belcher do? What would you do?

ACTIVITIES TO APPLY WHAT YOU LEARNED

1. You were invited to speak to the parents' group of the local elementary school. Your topic is "What Is Guiding Behavior and Why Is It Important?" In preparation, create a Prezi so that you can share your plan with your classmates. Ask them for feedback and suggestions to improve your speech.

2. **KEY ASSESSMENT:** Think about the behaviors that are essential for living and learning in a community of learners in the grade level you want to teach. Go to YouTube and TeacherTube and find examples that other teachers use to develop a community of learners. As a result, develop a PowerPoint presentation based on what you will share with your class, which outlines five essential teacher behaviors/activities you think are absolutely necessary for developing and maintaining a community of learners. Use the rubric provided to guide your work.

3. Blog about how you can use the social constructivist approach to guide children. Include the importance of scaffolding, the zone of proximal development, adult child discourse, and private speech. Also, explain how you will incorporate these topics in your teaching and classroom.

4. Here you learned ten steps for guiding children's behavior. Although they are all important, rank-order the ten based on their importance to you. Your first choice will be 1, your second, 2, and so on. Share this list with your peers and compare the major differences in rank orders. How do you explain the reasons for your differences of opinions?

5. Interview two teachers and two parents about their views of physical punishment. The key point to focus on is the reasons and rationale for why they do or do not use physical punishment. What implications do the interviews have for your role as a teacher of young children?

6. Refer back and reflect on the chapter discussion about ways you can reward children for their behavior. How will you use tangible, activity-based, token, social, and natural reinforcement in your classroom? Go online and research behavior modification techniques. Which do you find most effective? Start a chat room discussion and discuss your results with your peers.

LINKING TO LEARNING

The following agencies and programs, which can be located easily online, provide additional information about topics discussed in this chapter.

Association for Supervision and Curriculum Development
This professional educational leadership organization is dedicated to advancing best practices and policies for teachers and students.

Center for Effective Discipline
This nonprofit organization provides educational information to the public on the effects of corporal punishment and on alternatives to its use.

University of Arkansas Division of Agriculture: Guiding Children Successfully
This site provides information, organized into different programs, on how to successfully guide children.

Virginia Cooperative Extension
Virginia Cooperative Extension provides several common-sense strategies for effectively guiding the behavior of young children so they can make positive choices, learn problem-solving skills, and learn respect and responsibility.

CHAPTER

15

MULTICULTURALISM

Living and Learning in a Diverse Society

LEARNING OUTCOMES

1. Identify reasons why America is multicultural.
2. Explain how you can infuse multicultural content into curriculum, programs, and activities.
3. Describe how you can teach English language learners.
4. Determine how you can meet the needs of diverse learners in your classroom.

AMERICA THE MULTICULTURAL

Read any U.S. Census Bureau population projection that you care to, and one thing is certain: The population of the United States is changing and will continue to be more and more diverse. In fact, by 2060, 1 in 3 residents will be Hispanic. Fifteen percent of the population will be black and 10 percent will be Asian. In addition, the United States will become even more of a nation of blended races, with 21 percent of the population of mixed ancestry.[1] For example, today marriages are more mixed than ever. Fifteen percent of all marriages are between spouses of different races or ethnicities.[2]

THE CULTURES OF OUR CHILDREN

In schools all across the United States, a very diverse population of immigrant children from other countries such as Mexico, El Salvador, Venezuela, Vietnam, Sierra Leone, and Pakistan are in our nation's schools. They are learning the content of schooling, and they are learning to speak English. Today, there are 4.7 million English language learners (ELLs) in our nation's schools.[3] Eighty-nine percent of children at Edison Elementary School in Long Beach, California, are ELLs.

MINORITY CHILDREN—THE EMERGING MAJORITY. Presently, minorities make up over half of the children born in the United States. The "tipping point" came in July 2011, when more minority babies were born than Caucasian children.[4] This trend will continue. In addition, California, Hawaii, New Mexico, and Texas, are minority majority states. For example, in Texas, 50.2 percent of the children are Hispanic.[5]

When we think of minority children and families, we might tend to think of African Americans and Hispanics. Yet minority children of all cultures attend our nation's schools. For example, Minnesota is the home to the largest number of Somali immigrants in the United States.[6] The United States is also home to 546,000 Haitian immigrants, with the majority residing in South Florida.[7]

The demographics of our nation's children and their families have tremendous implications for your professional practice. More students will require special education, bilingual education, and other special services.

The great diversity of young children in American schools creates interesting challenges for you and all early childhood educators. Issues of culture and diversity will continue to shape curriculum and instructional practices. Not only do children speak languages other than English, they also behave differently based on cultural customs and values, and they come from varied socioeconomic backgrounds and with different life experiences. In part, how you respond to the diverse makeup and needs of your children determines how well they fulfill their responsibilities as citizens in the years to come. The strategies and solutions for achieving this goal are not always easy, but they require our utmost attention and dedication. You and other early childhood professionals must prepare *all* children to live happily and productively in our society.

DEVELOPING YOUR CULTURAL COMPETENCE

As U.S. classrooms become more diverse, it is important for you to develop the cultural competence you need to effectively teach your students. **Cultural competence** is the ability to interact effectively with children, families, and colleagues of different

cultural competence
The ability and confidence to interact effectively with children, families, and colleagues of different cultures.

cultures, as well as an awareness of cultural differences and cultural values.[8] You practice cultural competence by treating everyone with respect, learning about other cultures, and incorporating cultural dimensions into all aspects of your teaching. In addition, you become culturally competent by creating strong home–school relationships: keeping in touch with parents and families, learning about and understanding their hopes and goals for their children, and involving them in your classroom and school. You need to learn the cultural backgrounds of your students. As classrooms become more diverse, you will want to incorporate children's cultures into your instructional activities.

"RULES OF ENGAGEMENT" FOR BEING A CULTURALLY RESPONSIVE TEACHER

Here are some "rules of engagement" for being a culturally responsive teacher.

- *Relationships matter.* There is a saying in early childhood education that "all education involves relationships." So, it is important for you to develop positive, respectful, and caring relationships with your children. Relationships really are at the heart of teaching and learning. By being interested in children and their cultures, you send a message that each child is worthy regardless of the child's cultural and racial background.

- *Safe environments are essential.* Children feel safe in their environments when they are cared for, respected and valued by you and their peers. Greeting each child at the door each morning with a smile and words of encouragement conveys to them that they are safe in your classroom and they can safely go about the day. A warm, inviting classroom is a place for children of all cultures to feel comfortable, wanted, and supported.

- *Engage all children in learning local and state standards.* Engage children in their learning so that they are successful. When children achieve and are successful, you value their achievements and accomplishments. This enables children to develop an attitude of worth and success.

- *Integrate children's cultures in the classroom.*
  - Pictures of children and their families posted around your classroom invite children to talk about themselves and their family. It also encourages them to share information about their families and their cultures. When children are comfortable talking about who they are, this is a sign that they and their culture are valued.

- *Accommodate children's learning styles.* Assess and determine how each child learns best, for example, through words and pictures, through concrete materials, by listening, by reading, etc. Integrate in your learning activities those that enable children to learn how they learn best. When children know that you accept and honor their learning styles, this is another "signal" to them that you value them and their culture.

- *Connect lessons and activities to children's everyday lives.*
  - Have children write and talk about themselves
  - Use children's artwork to decorate the classroom

- *Connect with and involve parents.*
  - Get to know parents and families and what they want for their children
  - Respect and honor parents' hopes for their children
  - Provide support through home visits and training sessions

MULTICULTURAL AWARENESS

Culturally competent teachers promote and teach multicultural awareness in their classrooms. **Multicultural awareness** is the process of developing in all children an appreciation and understanding of other people's cultures, socioeconomic status, and gender, including their own.[9]

Bringing multicultural awareness to your classroom does not mean teaching about certain cultures to the exclusion of others. Rather, multicultural awareness activities focus on diverse cultures while making children aware of the content, nature, and richness of their own. Learning about other cultures while also learning about their own culture enables children to integrate commonalities and appreciate differences without inferring inferiority or superiority of one culture over another.

The diversity of today's society is clearly evident in many classrooms. Teachers must teach lessons that are multicultural to help enrich children's learning experiences.

Promoting multicultural awareness in an early childhood program has implications far beyond the program itself. Cultural influences affect work habits, interpersonal relations, and children's general outlook on life. You must take these multicultural influences into consideration when designing curriculum and instructional processes for young and impressionable students.

Reflect and Apply: P.S. 188

TEACHING AND MULTICULTURAL INFUSION

One way to positively change the lives of children and their families is to infuse multiculturalism into early childhood activities and practices. **Multicultural infusion** means that multicultural education permeates the entire curriculum. From a larger perspective, infusion strategies ensure that multiculturalism becomes an essential part of your classroom.

FOSTER CULTURAL AWARENESS

It is important to teach children about other cultures, including their own. A lack of understanding about cultural differences leads to intolerance, suspicion, and even violence. Researchers believe that children are aware of racial differences by the time they are in preschool. They also believe that by age twelve, most children have developed an image of most racial and ethnic groups in the United States.[10] Fostering cultural awareness early is a good way to equip them with the knowledge they need before they develop racial stereotypes. As we say in early childhood, it is more effective to prevent than to remediate!

ASSESS YOUR ATTITUDES TOWARD CHILDREN.   In your teaching of young children, it is important that you assess your attitudes toward children and their families to ensure you are multiculturally sensitive and aware. Answer these questions:

- Do you believe that *all* children can and will learn?
- Are you willing to spend the time and effort necessary to help each child learn?

multicultural awareness
Developing in all children an appreciation and understanding of other people's cultures, socioeconomic status, and gender, including their own.

multicultural infusion
Making multiculturalism an explicit part of curriculum and programs.

- Are you willing to teach children individually according to their cultural and individual learning styles?
- Do you have high expectations for *all* children regardless of their race, socioeconomic status, or gender?
- Are you willing to work with the parents and families of your children to learn more about their culture, educational values, and lifestyle preferences?

As you reflect on these questions, you may find some areas in which you need more information and help from colleagues and mentors. What is important is that you are willing to enhance your cultural competence, learn, change, and become the teacher all children need and deserve.

DEVELOP CLASSROOM AWARENESS.   Be constantly aware that you are the key to a multicultural classroom. Therefore, integrate different cultures and populations across the school year and throughout the curriculum. It is not enough to only celebrate African American culture in February and Hispanic culture in September; to study women's contributions for Women's History Month in March or be attentive to disabilities in Disabilities Awareness Month in October. In addition, integrate the contributions and impacts of all cultures, genders, and abilities throughout the curriculum as a part of your everyday teaching and approach to interacting.

DEVELOP YOUR AWARENESS.   The following guidelines will help you gain multicultural competence and develop your own awareness as well as the awareness of your students:

- *Recognize that all children are unique.* They all have special talents, abilities, and styles of learning and relating to others. Provide opportunities for children to be different and to use their abilities. For example, kindergarten teacher Alma Brooks teaches a lesson that allows children to see the physical differences in one another. In this lesson she has the children paint pictures of themselves and write down what makes their physical characteristics and talents or special abilities different from those of others. At the end of the lesson, they all gather around and talk about their personal unique characteristics to emphasize that each person is different yet special.[11]
- *Get to know, appreciate, and respect the cultural backgrounds of all your children.* Visit families and community neighborhoods to learn more about cultures, religions, and ways of life. For example, kindergarten teacher Ally Smith knows that in D'hjira's culture people rarely wear shoes all the time, so she allows him to take off his shoes and socks during naptime.[12]
- *Infuse your children's cultures into your lesson planning and teaching.* Use all subject areas—math, science, language arts, literacy, music, art, and social studies—to relate culture to your children. For example, third grade teacher William Rodriguez teaches a Spanish language lesson by introducing a *balero*. A balero is a traditional Mexican toy that resembles a cup and ball. While children play with the balero, William introduces Spanish words, and numbers. As the children continue to play the game, they are surrounded with the Spanish language while also having fun learning a Spanish game.[13]
- *Use children's interests and experiences to form a basis for planning lessons and developing activities.* This approach helps students feel good about their backgrounds, cultures, families, and experiences. Also, when children relate what they are doing in the classroom to the rest of their daily lives, their learning is more meaningful. For example, third grade teacher Carol Read noticed that her children are fascinated and interested in insects, so she decided to do a lesson on silkworms. In this lesson she discusses what the silkworm eats, allows students

to observe silkworms, and brings the lesson to a close by allowing children to draw and label the body parts of a silkworm. She also uses this opportunity to discuss and teach the Chinese culture.[14]

- ***Use authentic situations to provide for cultural learning and under-standing.*** For example, a field trip to a culturally diverse neighborhood of your city or town provides children an opportunity to understand firsthand many of the details about how people conduct their daily lives. Such an experience provides wonderful opportunities for involving children in writing, cooking, reading, and dramatic play activities. What about setting up a market in the classroom? Second grade Teacher of the Year Jamee Miller generates new ways to expose her children to life beyond their neighborhoods through online exploration and digital field trips. Recently, her class experienced St. Augustine, Florida. Jamee spent weekends taking pictures and compiling them to create a virtual world for her children to experience. Such activities allow her children to prepare to live and work in diverse communities without going outside the classroom![15]

- ***Use authentic assessment activities to fully assess children's learning and growth.*** You will want to assess students within a cultural framework—this is a part of your implementing the whole child approach and is essential to developmentally appropriate practice. Portfolios are ideal means for children to learn and grow in a culturally sensitive, unbiased environment by allowing them to self-evaluate their work and progress while honoring and respecting their culture. For example, Madison, Connecticut, third grade teacher Sandra Brand allows her students to do student-led conferences using self portfolios to review their progress and assignments through the school year with their parents. If students have missing or incomplete assignments, then they explain why the work is incomplete or missing during the conference and their plans to plan to keep from failing to complete other assignments.[16]

- ***Be a role model by accepting, appreciating, and respecting other languages and cultures.*** It is important to communicate and demonstrate that uniqueness and diversity are positive. For example, third grader A'ishah wears a hijab or head scarf (concealing hair, ears, and neck) to school. Her classmates understand and respect her Muslim culture and practices. Second grader Rajiv eats foods that look and smell different from most of the other children in the classroom. During lunch, the children in class learn about the different foods he eats instead of thinking he is "weird" or different.[17]

- ***Be knowledgeable about, proud of, and secure in your own culture.*** Children will ask about you, and you should share your background with them. For example, kindergarten teacher Danasha Johnson shares her culture and experiences throughout the school year. She uses lessons and activities that discuss and explain the African American culture. Danasha discusses famous African American activists and those that have paved the way for equality for all races. Most important of all, she shares herself with her children. She invites other teachers to share their cultures with her class and uses this information to inform her lessons. In doing so, she models for her students that you can be both aware and proud of your own culture and still be accepting and sensitive to other cultures.

- ***Collaborate with your school administrators and colleagues to promote cultural awareness.*** Remember, it takes a school for multicultural infusion to

Early childhood educators must consider the diverse characteristics of students—including gender, ethnicity, race, and socioeconomic factors—when planning learning opportunities for their classes. What are some ways diversity can enrich the curriculum?

really be effective. For example, at Alain Locke Elementary School in Philadelphia, Pennsylvania, faculty and staff value each student as a unique individual, rich in diversity of culture and experiences. All staff members are actively involved in celebrating diversity through language, culture, and the arts.[18]

SELECT APPROPRIATE INSTRUCTIONAL MATERIALS.   In addition to assessing your own attitudes and infusing personal sensitivity into the multicultural classroom, you also need to carefully consider and select appropriate instructional materials to support multicultural infusion.

Multicultural Literature. Choose literature that emphasizes people's habits, customs, and general living and working behaviors. This approach stresses similarities and differences regarding how children and families live their *whole* lives and avoids merely noting differences or teaching only about habits and customs. Multicultural literature today is more representative of various cultural groups and provides authentic language experiences for young children. It is written by authors from particular cultures and contains true-to-life stories and culturally authentic writing styles. The following are some examples of the rich selection of multicultural literature available and authentic literature themes represented in cultures around the world.

- *Forgotten or Unknown Princesses* by Philippe Lechermeier and Rebecca Dautremer: A story of unique princesses that all have their own positive and negative attributes.
- *The Best Mariachi in the World* by J. D. Smith: A tale about finding one's own talent.
- *Teo in the Snow* by Violeta Denou: A story about Teo and his friends who go on a winter excursion in the mountain and do not always make safe choices in the pursuit of having fun.
- *Leon and Bob* by Simon James: A story about a boy whose father is away in the army and his imaginary friend who is his confidant and playmate.
- *Oh No!* by Rotraut Susanne Berner: A story about a hen who complains about everything, her friend who has a solution to every complaint, and their discovery that things are not always black and white.
- *Hush!* by Minfong Ho: A Thai lullaby about a mother who begs a mosquito, water buffalo, and other animals to let her baby sleep.
- *Nine-in-One Grr! Grr!* by Blia Xiong: A folktale from the Hmong people of Laos that answers questions in a beautiful, clever fashion.

Multicultural Science, Technology, Engineering, Math, and Arts (STEMA). It should come as no surprise that, given today's emphasis on science, technology, engineering, math, and arts (STEMA), there are many excellent books that integrate multiculturalism and STEMA (also sometimes known as STEAM). Consider the following books in your teaching:

- *Boy + Bot* by Ame Dyckman: A boy and a robot meet in the woods and play together, having a great time even through their differences.
- *How Many Seeds in a Pumpkin?* by Margaret McNamara: A wonderful read-aloud companion for math or science and a fun way to reinforce counting skills!
- *Math-terpieces* by Greg Tang: A challenging children's book with an innovative approach that targets four basic problem-solving rules.

- *Newton and Me* by Lynne Mayer: A great children's science book about a young boy who plays with his dog and discovers the laws of force and motion.
- *A Full Moon Rising* by Marilyn Singer: Poetic and informational book about the full moon and how it is appreciated throughout the world through celebrations and traditions.
- *Amelia to Zora* by Cynthia Chin-Lee: A book alphabetically listing stories, detailed collages, and illustrations from various events in the lives of twenty-six amazing women.
- *Riparia's River* by Michael J. Caduto: A lively story about non-point pollution that is action filled and informational.
- *Kunu's Basket* by Lee Decora Francis: Teaches children about patience through the experience of a young boy who makes baskets.

Thematic Teaching. Early childhood teachers often use thematic units to strengthen children's understanding of themselves, their culture, and the cultures of others. Thematic units are lessons based on groups of topics that are designed around activities and cover several areas of the curriculum. Thematic choices from a variety of cultures help children identify cultural similarities and encourage understanding and tolerance. Consider the following suggestions of themes:

- *Getting to know myself, getting to know others.* Kindergarten teacher Maci Daniels uses a toilet tissue activity to familiarize her children with one another. In this activity, Maci passes a roll of toilet tissue and tells students to take as many sheets as they like, without explanation as to what they will do with it. Once everyone has chosen their toilet tissue squares, Maci explains that the number of squares represents the number of things that the children must tell about themselves. This allows everyone to introduce themselves and get to know fun facts about their peers.[19]
- *What is special about you and me?* Second grade teacher Nicky Gunther has her children interview each other, taking note of the one special characteristic, interest, or hobby each student wants to be recognized for. She allows the children to read one another's lists after they have interviewed each other. Nicky then instructs the children to place their papers face down. At the end of the lesson Nicky calls out the special characteristics of each student to see if the children can guess each others' talents and special abilities.[20]
- *Growing up in the city.* Second grade teacher Candice Mason has a lesson in which her children illustrate on a square piece of paper what their city or neighborhood looks like. In their drawings, children draw the buildings that surround them, and houses, trees, or anything significant about their city. Once each child finishes drawing his or her city, Candice and the children combine the square pieces and make a mural.[21]
- *Growing up in my country.* Third grade teacher Timothy Reynolds gives his students one 8 × 11-inch piece of paper to illustrate their country of origin. On this page they include a picture and a short description of their country's beliefs and traditions. He also asks that they include flags and symbols that reflect their country. After they are all done, Timothy compiles each page and makes a class scrapbook for everyone to review.[22] For children born in the United States, Timothy explains that even though they are born here, they each have their own experiences, cultures, and traditions in this country. He asks them to write about their families' and communities' traditions, symbols, and beliefs and assures his students that it is OK if each of their papers look different, even though they are from the same country.

- *Tell me about Africa (South America, China, etc.).* Third grade teacher Kathy Lynn has her children learn firsthand about other cultures by setting them up with pen pals in different countries. Children in her classroom write to third graders in Uganda about their traditions, cultural etiquette, foods, etc.[23] Second grade teacher Donald Marcel uses the online pen pal service ePal to collaborate with art students in the Caribbean. His students post their artwork on the ePal portal and also get the opportunity to view Caribbean artwork as well.[24] You will want to review your school's policy on using services such as ePal.

TEACH YOUR LOCAL, STATE, AND COMMON CORE STATE STANDARDS (CCSS).

State standards and the Common Core State Standards (CCSS) cover all subjects and content areas. While your particular state may not specifically have a set of standards relating to multicultural awareness and infusion, more than likely the content standards do. For example, in the California English Language Arts Standards, first graders identify how language uses reflect region and cultures. They also have to compare and contrast different versions of the same stories that reflect different cultures.[25] In the Florida Social Studies Content Standards, second graders must compare the cultures of Native American tribes from various geographic regions of the United States.[26] Thus, your state standards will provide you many opportunities to infuse culture into all you teach.

Multicultural Accomplishments. Add to your classroom activities, as appropriate, the accomplishments of people from different cultural groups, women of all cultures, and individuals with disabilities. The following criteria are most important when picking materials for use in a multicultural curriculum for early childhood programs:

- Represent people of all cultures fairly and accurately.
- Represent people of diverse ethnic groups and people with exceptionalities.
- Be sure that historic information is accurate and nondiscriminatory.
- Be sure that materials do not include stereotypical roles or language.
- Ensure gender equity—that is, boys and girls must be represented equally and in nonstereotypical roles.

AVOID SEXISM AND GENDER-ROLE STEREOTYPING.

Current interest in multiculturalism in general and nondiscrimination in particular raises concern about sexism and gender-role stereotyping. **Sexism** is the attitudes, beliefs, and behaviors which result in the assumption that one sex is superior to another. In addition, the term also refers to the policies, practices, and activities that may prescribe traditional sex roles for boys and girls.

sexism Prejudice or discrimination based on sex.

Title IX of the Education Amendments Act of 1972, as amended by Public Law 93–568, prohibits such discrimination in the schools: "No person in the United States shall, on the basis of sex, be excluded from participation in, be denied the benefits of, or be subjected to discrimination under any education program or activity receiving federal financial assistance."[27] For example, the Mason Elementary School in Duluth, Georgia, encourages and supports girls and boys to participate in sports, choir, band, and extracurricular clubs. Their sports club is open to children who would like to play basketball, football, Frisbee, or soccer. Their coaches' goal is to make the most positive contribution possible to the physical, emotional, and social well-being of students. In the choir and band, children learn and perform a wide variety of musical styles to gain a better understanding of the elements of choral music. They also have a broadcast club, Junior Beta Club (academic honor society), academic achievement club, and health club.[28]

You and other early childhood professionals need to be concerned about the roots of sexism and **sexual harassment** and realize that these practices have their beginnings in children's early years in homes, centers, and preschools. You must constantly examine personal and programmatic practices, evaluate materials, and work with parents to eliminate sexism and ensure that no child is shortchanged in any way.

sexual harassment
Unwelcome sexual behavior and talk.

IMPLICATIONS FOR TEACHING. You can provide children with an open framework in which they can develop their gender roles. The following are some suggestions for avoiding gender stereotypes:

- *Provide opportunities for all children to experience the activities, materials, toys, and emotions traditionally associated with both sexes.* Give boys as well as girls opportunities to experience tenderness, affection, and the warmth of close parent–child and teacher–pupil relationships. Conversely, girls as well as boys should be able to behave energetically, get dirty, and participate in what are typically considered male activities, such as woodworking and block building.

- *Become conscious of words that promote sexism.* In a lesson on community helpers, taught in most preschool and kindergarten programs at one time or another, many words carry a sexist connotation. *Fireman, policeman,* and *mailman,* for example, are all masculine terms; nonsexist terms are *firefighter, police officer,* and *mail carrier.* Examine all your curricular materials and teaching practices to determine how you can make them free of sexist language.

- *Determine what physical arrangements in the classroom promote or encourage gender-role stereotyping.* Are boys encouraged to use the block area more than girls? Are girls encouraged to use the quiet areas more than boys? Do children hang their coats separately—a place for boys and a place for girls? All children should have equal access to all learning areas of the classroom; no area should be reserved exclusively for one sex. In addition, examine any activity or practice that promotes segregation of children by gender or culture. Cooperative learning activities and group work provide ways to ensure that children of both sexes work together.

As you collaborate with parents, be sure to discuss appropriate attire for all children that makes it possible for them to engage in a wide variety of indoor and outdoor activities. Your goal is to make sure that both genders are clothed so that they can participate freely in all activities.

- *Examine your behavior to see whether you are encouraging gender stereotypes.* Do you tell girls they cannot empty wastebaskets, but they can water the plants? Do you tell boys they should not play with dolls? Do you say that boys aren't supposed to cry? Do you reward only the girls who are always passive, well behaved, and well mannered? Follow these guidelines in your teaching:
  - Give all children a chance to respond to questions. Research consistently shows that teachers do not wait long enough after they ask a question for

most children, especially girls, to respond. Therefore, quick responders—usually boys—answer most of the questions. By waiting longer, you will be able to encourage more girls to answer.[29]

- Help all children become independent and do things for themselves. Discourage behaviors and attitudes that promote helplessness and dependency.
- Use portfolios, teacher observations, and other authentic means of assessing children's progress to provide bias-free assessment. Involving children in the evaluation of their own efforts is also a good way of promoting children's positive images of themselves.
- Encourage children to dress in ways that lead to full participation in all activities. Children should be encouraged to dress so they will be able to participate in a range of both indoor and outdoor activities. This is an area in which you may be able to help parents by discussing how dressing children appropriately can contribute to more effective participation. However, you have to work within what different cultures believe and practice about personal attire.

IMPLEMENT AN ANTIBIAS CURRICULUM AND ACTIVITIES.   The goal of an *antibias curriculum* is to help children learn to be accepting of others, regardless of race, ethnicity, gender, sexual orientation, socioeconomic status, or disability. Children participating in an antibias curriculum become comfortable with diversity and learn to stand up for themselves and others in the face of injustice. Additionally, in such a supportive, open-minded environment, children learn to construct a knowledgeable, confident self-identity.

Young children are constantly learning about differences and need a sensitive teacher to help them form positive, unbiased perceptions about differences among people. As children color pictures of themselves, for example, you may hear a comment such as, "Your skin is white and my skin is brown." You may be tempted, in the name of equality, to respond, "It doesn't matter what color we are—we are all people." Although this remark does not sound harmful, it fails to help children develop positive feelings about themselves. A more appropriate response might be, "Amanda, your skin is a beautiful dark brown, which is just right for you; Christina, your skin is a beautiful light tan, which is just right for you." A response such as this positively acknowledges each child's different skin color, which is an important step in developing a positive self-concept.

Check Your Understanding: Ability

Through the sensitive guidance of caring teachers, children learn to speak up for themselves and others. By living and learning in an accepting environment, children find that they have the ability to change intolerable situations and can have a positive impact on the future. This is part of what empowerment is about, and it begins in the home and in early childhood programs. An antibias curriculum should start in early childhood and continue throughout the school years. The book *Anti-Bias Education for Young Children and Ourselves* by Louise Derman-Sparks and Julie Olsen Edwards will help you learn more about anti-bias education.

tolerance The ability of children (and adults!) to recognize, accept, and respect the rights and beliefs of others.

TEACH TOLERANCE.   **Tolerance** is the ability of children (and adults!) to recognize, accept, and respect the rights and beliefs of others. Teaching tolerance is essential in every classroom in the United States today.

USE CONFLICT-RESOLUTION STRATEGIES AND PROMOTE PEACEFUL LIVING

We all live in a world of conflict. Television and other media bombard us with images of violence, crime, and international and personal conflict. Unfortunately, many children live in homes where conflict and disharmony are a way of life rather than an exception. Increasingly, early childhood professionals are challenged to help children resolve conflicts in peaceful ways. *Conflict-resolution strategies* help children learn how to solve problems, disagree in appropriate ways, negotiate, and live in harmony with others.

Your goal is to have children reach mutually agreeable solutions to problems without the use of power (e.g., fighting, hitting, pushing, or verbal taunts or threats). The following no-lose method of conflict resolution helps you achieve your goal:

1. Identify and define the conflict in a nonaccusatory way. ("Vinnie and Rachael, you have a problem—you both want the green paint.")

2. Encourage children to help in solving behavior problems. ("Let's think of how to solve this problem.")

3. Brainstorm solutions with children; accept a variety of solutions, and avoid evaluating them. ("Yes, you could both use the same paint cup. . . . You could take turns.")

4. Discuss with children each solution, and discuss the pros and the cons. ("Vinnie, that's a good idea—putting paint in the two paper cups so that both you and Rachael can use the green paint at the same time, thank you.")

5. Put the plan into action. ("See whether the two of you can get the green paint into the paper cups without help.")

6. Follow up to evaluate how well the solution worked. (After a few minutes, "Looks like your idea of how to solve your green paint problem really worked!")[30]

The following Voice from the Field, "How to Create Classroom Environments That Support Peaceful Living and Learning," will help you develop learning environments that support children's learning.

WELCOME PARENT AND COMMUNITY INVOLVEMENT

As we have noted earlier, as an early childhood teacher, you will work with children and families of diverse cultural backgrounds. You will need to learn about their cultural backgrounds so that you can respond appropriately to their needs. Let's take a look at the culture of some families who are of Hispanic descent and its implications for parent and family involvement.

Within the Hispanic culture, particularly families from Latin American countries, there is belief in the authority of the school and teachers. In many of these Latin American countries, it is considered rude for a parent to intrude in the life of the school. Parents believe it is the school's job to educate and the parent's job to nurture and that the two jobs do not mix. A child who is well educated is one who has learned moral and ethical behavior.

Hispanics tend to have strong family ties, believe in family loyalty, and have a collective orientation that supports community life; they have been found to be field dependent (i.e., learning best in group and highly organized environments) and sensitive to nonverbal indicators of feeling.[31] These traits are represented by an emphasis on warm, personalized styles of interaction, a relaxed sense of time, and a need for

How to Create Classroom Environments That Support Peaceful Living and Learning

Peaceful living begins with peaceful homes, peaceful classrooms, and peaceful communities. Today's children are surrounded by violence, aggression, and uncivil behavior. Many children live in violent homes, are victims of abuse, and are constantly bombarded with violence on television and other media. We have previously discussed the signs and symptoms of abuse and what you can do about it. We know that it is much more difficult to remediate than it is to prevent. Consequently, creating peaceful classrooms that promote peaceful and respectful living and learning will go a long way to keep children from developing aggressive behaviors that lead to violence and wasted lives.

STRATEGY 1

Create a Classroom Environment That Supports Peaceful Living

To create a classroom environment that supports peaceful living, include these dimensions:

- Create an environment that is warm, welcoming, and productive; supports a home-like atmosphere; that is attractive and one in which children feel comfortable and welcomed. Such an atmosphere has a calming influence on children and supports peaceful living.
- Use a "peace table," a place you and the children can sit to talk things over and talk about behavior and share thoughts and feelings about themselves and others. A peace table gives children a chance to develop classroom strategies for how to give and receive respect and do their best work.
- A peaceful environment is a well-organized environment. Arrange your learning environment so that children can help each other and work collaboratively. Create your environment so children have free access to a wide range of learning materials that support their learning. When children know where things belong and when they are able to help care for and maintain the classroom, they develop a sense of ownership and feel a responsibility for living with others in the classroom.
- Support children's independent learning and industriousness. Children like to be active and busy and, when

they are, there are fewer problems and more positive involvement and behavior.

- Be at your classroom door every morning. Greet each child with a smile, a handshake, and words of welcome and encouragement.
- Reduce clutter. Environments for young children should be as organized as possible and lack clutter. Cluttered and chaotic environments create a sense of anxiety and promote aggression. Closely examine your classroom to make sure that it is well-organized, uncluttered, and is an inviting and pleasant place to live and learn for you and your children.

Picture yourself in this classroom. You are discussing peaceful living with your students. What are some behaviors you would suggest to your students for living peacefully in their classroom?

STRATEGY 2

Collaborate with Parents

- Make parents your partners in peace. Invite parents into your classroom so they can see how you promote peaceful living and learning.
- Give parents tips and ideas for how they can create peaceful environments at home.
- Ask parents for their ideas for how to make your classroom a place of peace and learning.

STRATEGY 3

Teach and Practice Peaceful Dispositions

Dispositions are frequent and voluntary habits of thinking and doing. They are "habits of the mind." Childhood dispositions that support peaceful living include the following:

- Cooperation
- Friendliness
- Respectfulness
- Kindness
- Thoughtful behavior
- Helpfulness
- Empathy

There are many opportunities to conduct activities related to peaceful living. Here children are sharing ideas for how to live peacefully with all children regardless of socioeconomic background and culture. What are some activities you could incorporate in your classroom for peaceful living with children from all cultures?

STRATEGY 4 Integrate Peace into Your Curriculum

- Teach responsible and peaceful living. Give children many opportunities to be responsible and show that they are capable of responsible living by helping others and by being in charge of their own learning.
- In your morning meeting, talk about the dispositions that support peaceful living.
- Have children talk and write about qualities of life in a peaceful classroom. Talk about current events that relate to violence and what children think are solutions to violence.
- Create a chart of behaviors that support peaceful learning. Review the chart in class meetings. Send the chart home to parents. Discuss topics such as, "How do you want to be treated?"
- Read books about peaceful living. Constantly be on the lookout for books about peaceful living. For example, the Jane Addams Peace Association (Jane Addams won the Nobel Peace Prize in 1931, and was the first woman to do so) annually gives awards to children's books that promote peace and peaceful living. The 2010 Children's Book Award winner, *Nasreen's Secret School: A True Story from Afghanistan,* is a wonderful book about the importance of education.* When selecting books of any kind to include in your classroom, library, and learning centers, make sure the topics are appropriate for your children and their individual cultures and that they represent a wide array of topics.
- Have children role-play peaceful living and act out and demonstrate appropriate classroom behaviors that support peaceful attitudes and behaviors.

STRATEGY 5 Model Peaceful Living

Model the dispositions you want children to learn. Remember that children are always watching you and your behaviors. Children learn very quickly how you react to certain situations. Therefore, you must practice dispositions of cooperation, friendliness, and respectfulness. If you want children to work cooperatively with each other, then they should see you working cooperatively with them, your colleagues, and with their parents.

*Jane Addams Peace Organization, "About the Children's Books," accessed on August 26, 2013, from www.janeaddamspeace.org.

an informal atmosphere for communication. Given these preferences, a culture clash may result when Hispanic students and parents are confronted with the typical task-oriented style of most American teachers.

Although an understanding of the general cultural characteristics of Hispanics is helpful, it is important not to overgeneralize. Each family and child is unique, and care should be taken not to assume values and beliefs just because a family speaks Spanish and is from Latin America. It is important that teachers take time to discover the particular values, beliefs, and practices of families in the classroom.

You, the child's teacher, are the person in your school that Hispanic families will most likely trust the most. Consequently, you play an important role in the empowerment of children and parents. You can serve as a contact point, parent colleague, and a confidant.[32]

Use the following guidelines to involve Hispanic parents:

- *Use a personal touch.* It is crucial to use face-to-face communication in the Hispanic parents' primary language when first making contact. It may even take several personal meetings before the parents gain sufficient trust to participate actively. Home visits are a particularly good way to begin to develop rapport.

- *Provide bilingual support.* All communication with Hispanic parents, written and oral, must be provided in Spanish and English. In addition, many programs report that having bicultural and bilingual staff helps promote trust.[33]

- *Use nonjudgmental communication.* To gain the trust and confidence of Hispanic parents, avoid making them feel that they are to blame for something or are doing something wrong. Support parents for their strengths.

- *Address real concerns.* To keep Hispanic parents actively engaged, make plans that respond to a real need or concern. Communicate clearly what parents will get out of each meeting and how the meeting will help them in their role as parents.

- *Participate in staff development focused on Hispanic culture.* Understand the key features of Hispanic culture and its impact on students' behavior and learning styles. Everyone has the obligation to learn as much about children, their culture, and their backgrounds as possible.

- *Facilitate community connections.* As I have said, early childhood is a family affair and many Hispanic families may benefit from family literacy programs, vocational training, ESL programs, improved medical and dental services, and other community-based social services. Your school or early childhood program can serve as a resource and referral agency to support the overall strength and stability of the families.

Keep in mind that although the above suggestions specifically support Hispanic parent and family involvement, you can apply similar processes to involve parents of all cultures.

TEACHING ENGLISH LANGUAGE LEARNERS

ESL kindergarten teacher Monica Schnnee's passion is language in all its forms and from every land. Learning a language is learning about the world. Students in her class learn by listening, talking, reading, singing, writing, participating in experiences inside and outside the classroom. The most important part of their learning is "thinking." They think in English and in their home language to add to what they already know. Students write digital stories, record themselves reading poems, and share what they know with their friends and the world.[34]

Melanie Conger's, 2012 ELL Teacher of the Year and second grade teacher in Glendale, Arizona, teaching philosophy is based on "Yes, we can." Melanie thinks that all too often in ELL education the focus is on what students can't do. In a teaching world overwhelmed by negativity, her answer to anything her students are asked to do is "Yes, we can." Melanie believes ELL education, and teaching in general, needs more positivity.[35]

Most people assume that children who do not speak English when they enter school will learn English in the schools. Some people interpret this to mean that a child's native language (often referred to as the *home language*)—whether Spanish, French, Italian, Chinese, Tagalog, or any of the other languages, will naturally be suppressed. Title III—the English Language Acquisition, Language Enhancement, and Academic Achievement Act—of 2002 under NCLB neither prohibits nor promotes bilingual instruction.[36] Speaking of Chinese, more schools are teaching it as an important international language.

What are some school districts doing about this? Here is one example.

FALLBROOK UNION ELEMENTARY

The Fallbrook (California) Union Elementary School District's (FUESD's) student population comprises 33 percent English language learners and 58.4 percent students qualifying for the free or reduced-price lunches. Two schools are located on Camp Pendleton Marine Base, and many of our students come from active duty military families.

PANDA (PROMOTING AND NURTURING DYNAMIC ACADEMICS)

Prior to the advancement of this program, there were no foreign language programs offered at the elementary level in the school district. Parents consistently expressed great interest in the development of the PANDA Project, and we received more than seven hundred parent requests seeking placement in the program for their children.

MANDARIN CHINESE

Prior to offering the Mandarin learning opportunity, the district actively sought to educate parents and community members regarding the benefits to students in learning Mandarin Chinese. Mandarin is a tonal, character-based language, which is very different from English (an alphabetic Latin-based language). Mandarin Chinese is a tonal language with words created using just twenty-three beginning sounds (called initials), and thirty-two ended sounds (called finals). Initial and ending sounds are combined to create words, but in addition to initials and finals, Mandarin incorporates five different tones that vary the meaning of the words when spoken aloud.

Mandarin Chinese is a challenging second language to learn, and students need many opportunities to hear and speak the new language to reap the full benefits. In order for children to get those enriched opportunities, classroom instructional strategies reflect best practices and offer students a variety of learning supports such as visuals, manipulatives, cooperative learning, the integration of technology, and total physical response (TPR). TPR is a means of pairing auditory teaching practices (like discussions or talking) with other sensory input (such as physical movement) to reinforce the learning. With TPR, students respond physically to the words of the teacher. The activity may be a simple game such as Simon Says, or creating hand gestures to accompany different tones and words. All of these methods encourage a high level of student engagement and motivation to learn. For example, teacher Grace Cox employs a variety of teaching strategies, including TPR, modeling, and materials and artifacts to help students comprehend and retain lesson vocabulary. She uses a modified version of "There Was an Old Lady Who Swallowed a Fly" taught entirely in Mandarin Chinese using the best practices described above. Her students were engaged, motivated, and highly successful!

Professional development for teachers and administration has been critical as we established our program. Additionally, our district established a collaborative partnership with the Confucius Institute of San Diego State University to link our program directly with important resources, such as experts in Chinese culture, language, and instruction, as well as "sister schools" in China. The establishment of sister schools provides students with real-life opportunities to engage with Chinese-speaking peers and authentically implement acquired Mandarin language skills.

BENEFITS OF PANDA

Mandarin elicits right-brain activity, as opposed to English, which elicits more left-brain activity. Therefore, learning Mandarin in addition to English encourages more brain activity in both hemispheres, which improves global thinking and relating. For struggling students, Mandarin can be an instructional pathway to increase motivation and provide opportunities to develop mental flexibility. Furthermore, PANDA provides students with challenging and rigorous programs that will prepare them with critical skills needed to be professionally competitive in the twenty-first century. In addition, the U.S. Department of Education identifies Mandarin as a U.S. government priority language and supports programs like ours that provide students with early opportunities to develop Mandarin language skills that will later support the attainment of advanced Mandarin fluency. FUESD also believes the rigor of learning Mandarin provides gifted and talented students the opportunity to participate in a challenging and engaging program that will supply important language skills they can carry with them into their future endeavors at both the college and professional levels.[37]

ELLs: THE CHALLENGE OF EDUCATING ALL

The United States is experiencing a rapid increase in immigration, and by 2015 the Census Bureau estimates that immigrant children will account for 30 percent of the school-age population.[38] If you are working in Arizona, California, Nevada, Texas, New York, or New Jersey—the states that currently have the greatest immigrant representation—you will certainly teach students from immigrant families.[39] Some of the difficulties immigrant families face are as follows:

- One in every five children in immigrant families have difficulty speaking English.[40]
- Twenty-seven percent of immigrant children live in linguistically isolated homes. This means that in their homes, they are the only ones under the age of fourteen who know English.[41]
- Twenty-six percent of immigrant children's parents do not have a high school diploma or equivalent. Thirteen percent of immigrant children's parents do not have the equivalent of a ninth grade education.[42] This means that immigrant children will not get as much help with language development and school or homework activities as native-born children, and children of immigrants may be less prepared than their counterparts to start kindergarten. Three- and four-year-old children in immigrant families are less likely to participate in nursery school or preschool programs than their peers.[43]
- Spanish is second only to English as the most spoken language in the United States.[44] Spanish speakers often face discrimination in public and private sectors for not knowing English.

SUPPORTING ENGLISH LANGUAGE LEARNERS

José is a bright and energetic second grader. He excels in math, enjoys playing soccer, and collects baseball cards. He struggles with English as his second language. He and his family immigrated only six months ago. José is one of seventeen million children of immigrant families in the United States.[45]

As José's teacher, you will provide him with the knowledge and experiences necessary for him to be successful in school and life in the United States. Here are some steps you can take to help José:

- Play to José's strengths and interests.
  - José is good at math, so appeal to his analytical nature by providing reading material that is factual and observable. Magazines for children—like *Kids Discover*, *Muse*, *Ladybug*, and *Highlights*—are rich in graphs, tables, and photos and provide information José will find interesting.
  - José is interested in soccer, so provide stories and books about soccer to enrich his English-speaking and reading skills.
  - Help José organize soccer games during recess. Encourage him to take a leadership role, like team captain, and to teach others how to play. A leadership role and helping others will increase his acceptance into the classroom and will allow him to make friendships more easily.
- Make sure José understands you. After giving directions to the entire class, ask José quietly if he understands the directions and if he needs you to repeat anything more slowly or in more detail.
- Make sure your body language conveys to José that you accept him as a person and learner. When José feels accepted and welcomed by you, he is more likely to come to you for help rather than not seeking help at all.
- Initiate a buddy system. Assign a classmate to José to run interference in language and cultural differences. This buddy will be a mentor to José when he needs it. A buddy system increases familiarity and encourages José's acceptance into your classroom.
- Accommodate cultural differences.
  - Be knowledgeable of José's culture. Do a little research. Familiarize yourself with cultural norms so that you can appropriately respond to José. For example, certain symbols in certain cultures may mean different things. While you may use it to signal acceptance or a job well done, José may take it as an insult.
- Incorporate Spanish (or another language) into your classroom because doing so helps lay the foundation for language learning. For example, when introducing new vocabulary words, you should ask José for a translation in Spanish. The role of translator will give José a position of worth and knowledge in the classroom and will enhance his self-esteem.
- Encourage José to speak English when appropriate, but allow him to communicate with others freely in either Spanish or English.
- Have a "Spanish Hour" once a week in which José reads a book in Spanish to the class. The class can translate the story into English. This process encourages cultural discussions, acceptance, sharing, and language skills.

Watch the video about culture and language and listen to what professor Hamayan and the teacher have to say about the interrelationship between learning a second language and a second culture. As you listen, reflect on the implications their thoughts have for teaching and learning in your classroom. Identify some things you can do to use language to help children learn the culture and to use culture to help children learn the language.

DUAL LANGUAGE PROGRAMS

The following programs use English and another language to teach ELLs. Review and reflect on these programs. Your school will use one of these programs or a variant to teach ELLs.

TWO-WAY IMMERSION OR TWO-WAY BILINGUAL

- The goal is to develop strong skills and proficiency in both L1 (native language) and L2 (English)
- It includes students with an English background and students from one other language background
- Instruction is in both languages, typically starting with smaller proportions of instruction in English, and gradually moving to half in each language
- Students typically stay in the program throughout elementary school

DUAL LANGUAGE

- When called "dual language immersion," the program is usually the same as two-way immersion or two-way bilingual.
- When called "dual language," it may refer to students from one language group developing full literacy skills in two languages—L1 and English

One-Way Immersion:

- Either native English speakers or native speakers of the second language make up all or most of the students enrolled, and instruction takes place in two languages.
- At least the half instructional time is in the second language; in early grades, it may take up as much as 90 percent.
- There must be a distinct separation of the two languages.

Two-Way Immersion:

- Native speakers of English and native speakers of Spanish learn both languages in the same classroom.
- At least one-third of the students must be native speakers of the second language.
- The goal is to produce fully bilingual, biliterate students by the end of elementary school.

LATE EXIT TRANSITIONAL, DEVELOPMENTAL BILINGUAL, OR MAINTENANCE EDUCATION

- The goal is to develop some skills and proficiency in L1 and strong skills and proficiency in L2 (English).
- Instruction at lower grades is in L1, gradually transitioning to English; students typically transition into mainstream classrooms with their English-speaking peers.
- Differences among the three programs focus on the degree of literacy students develop in the native language.

EARLY EXIT TRANSITIONAL

- The goal is to develop English skills as quickly as possible, without delaying learning of academic core content.
- Instruction begins in L1, but rapidly moves to English; students typically are transitioned into mainstream classrooms with their English-speaking peers as soon as possible.

HERITAGE LANGUAGE OR INDIGENOUS LANGUAGE PROGRAM

- The goal is literacy in two languages.
- Content is taught in both languages, with teachers fluent in both languages.
- There are differences between the two programs: Heritage language programs typically target students who are non-English-speakers or who have weak literacy

skills in L1, whereas indigenous language programs support endangered minority languages in which students may have weak receptive and no productive skills. Both programs often serve American Indian students.[46]

SUPPORTING ENGLISH LANGUAGE LEARNERS AND THEIR FAMILIES. There are a number of things you can do to be culturally and educationally responsive to ELLs and their families.

- *Know children.* The heart of developmentally appropriate practice is that we get to know individual children and their backgrounds and experiences. When you know, really know, children, you can personalize your instruction to them.

- *Know your families.* This is key! What is home life like for the child? What life circumstances are the families dealing with? This is valuable information for you to use to plan how to respond to the child each day.

- *Draw on children's background knowledge.* Find out about your children's experiences. You can do this by talking to them individually and by asking them to share their experience on certain topics during circle times or the Morning Meeting.

- *Make classroom learning materials concrete.* Use the following:
  - Pictures and word cards
  - Concrete materials, such as number rods, to help with math

- *Model, show, teach.*

- *Scaffold children learning.*
  - Pictures, graphic organizers, and word charts are excellent ways to scaffold children's learning. Graphic organizers are in the form of circle maps, tree maps, and flowcharts. Graphic organizers help ELL children learn.

- *Integrate technology into your lesson.* All children, including ELLs, can learn with and through interaction with apps and technology.

- *Promote social behaviors.*
  - Remember that learning is social, so promote students to student interactions.

- *Teach children vocabulary they need to know.* Such familiar words and terms are the starting point for learning English and culture.

- *Organize your classroom to support language learning.* Provide materials and opportunities for children to write and speak their language and English.
  - Provide picture books, ABC books, and fiction and nonfiction books in child's language.
  - Read, read, read to children and have them read along with you. Let children "read" to each other.

Reflect and Apply: ELLs

ACCOMMODATING DIVERSE LEARNERS

There is a risk that children who are English language learners can be disproportionately placed in special education programs and classes. This often occurs because of a child's race, ethnicity, gender, language proficiency, and/or family income. As a result, students may not receive services, or they may receive services that do not meet their needs because they are misclassified or inappropriately labeled. In that event, a child's placement in special education classes can actually become a form of discrimination. As a teacher of the next generation, you will want to ensure that each child receives the best education and the right kind of services and accommodation so that all children can be successful.

Meet Rolo and Anh. They are both English language learners. Both are bright, friendly, and respectful second graders. But in the classroom, they both are having difficulties learning. Rolo works hard, but he just can't seem to get the knack for reading. Anh's teacher has to frequently get her attention because she stares off into space. Both Rolo and Anh struggle to recall information they have already learned. As they fall farther and farther behind their English-speaking classmates, Rolo and Ahn get more frustrated and more downhearted.

It is often very difficult to determine if a child's issues are language-acquisition related or learning disability related because many indicators of learning disabilities are also indicators of the language learning process. For example, lack of attention, difficulty interpreting verbal messages, difficulty retrieving stored information, and difficulty sequencing and organizing information are hallmarks of learning disabilities and also of problems in language acquisition.[47, 48] For this reason, Rolo and Anh have very similar classroom behaviors and both have been referred for special education services. But do they both have learning disabilities? Are their classroom problems actually language learning issues?

To determine if special education services are the right accommodation for both Rolo and Ahn, remember the acronym STOP and carefully consider the following before you decide to refer Rolo and Anh, or any other ELL child, to special education or special language attention support:

Sustain a classroom climate that supports the wide range of individual and family differences described above. Providing a wide range of instructional activities, and individualizing attention and instruction may be exactly what each child needs to succeed.

Try reasonable accommodations and modifications within your classroom that can improve the academic, social, and emotional skills of students and make special education unnecessary. Response to intervention (RTI), a data-based process and a diagnostic tool, is a method of academic intervention designed to provide early, effective assistance to children who are having difficulty learning.

Organize a prereferral team within your school or use one in existence. This may be called the child study team, student intervention team, teacher support team, or student success team. Regardless of its name, the purpose of the team is to identify, implement, evaluate, and document strategies in the general classroom prior to referral to special education.

Proficiency in English should be evaluated and not just assumed. Students who have been identified as "limited English proficient" should be evaluated and take part in the prereferral process in their native language prior to referral to special education.

Check Your Understanding: STOP

ACTIVITIES FOR PROFESSIONAL DEVELOPMENT

ETHICAL DILEMMA

"SPEAK ENGLISH FIRST!"

Beth Janison is a new first grade teacher in River Bend School District. River Bend has had a large influx of minority students during the past few years. In fact, the minority students are almost the majority. Not everyone thinks that the rapid increase in the minority student population is beneficial to the school district or town. Some of Beth's colleagues think that the school district is bending over (too far) backward to meet minority students' needs. At Beth's first meeting with Harry Holister, her new mentor teacher, he remarked, "Respecting minorities and catering to them are two different things. I stress with my parents that this is America and speaking English comes first. If they or their kids can't speak English, they better learn!"

What should Beth do? Should she agree with Harry and adopt a policy of English first? Should Beth seek out the director of multiculturalism for her district and discuss Harry's comments with her? Or, should Beth contact the local LULAC (League of United Latin American Citizens) and ask for their support? Or, should Beth pursue another course of action? What should Beth do? What would you do?

ACTIVITIES TO APPLY WHAT YOU LEARNED

1. Think about ways that you can help your students be more culturally aware of the cultures in their classroom. Go online and find ways teachers of the year foster cultural awareness. Share what you learned by posting the link on Facebook.

2. **KEY ASSESSMENT:** Stories and literacy play an important role in transmitting to children information about themselves, their culture, and how to live in a multicultural society.

   a. Review the multicultural books suggested in this discussion. List three ways you can use them in your classroom. Post your suggestions on your class discussion board.

   b. Identify five children's books that you think would be useful in teaching multicultural awareness and state why you chose the books. Use Prezi or some other presentation format to post your suggestions online. Ask your colleagues for feedback.

   Use the **rubric** provided to guide your work.

3. Review and reflect on the types of programs for teaching ELLs discussed here. Create a chart with the similarities and differences of each program and your assessment of each. Post this chart on your class bulletin board for your peers to review. Ask for their comments.

4. How can you use the acronym STOP to help accommodate your diverse learners? What other methods can you think of that will ensure that young children from diverse backgrounds are not disproportionately placed in special education programs and classes? Post your results to your class discussion board and get feedback from your classmates.

LINKING TO LEARNING

The following agencies and programs, which can be located easily online, provide additional information about topics discussed in this chapter.

Colorín Colorado
This free Web-based service provides information, activities, and advice for educators and Spanish-speaking families of English language learners (ELLs).

National Association for Bilingual Education (NABE)
The NABE is the only national professional organization devoted to representing bilingual learners and bilingual education professionals.

National Association for Multicultural Education (NAME)
The association brings together individuals and groups with interests in multicultural education from all levels and disciples of education. It has six points of consensus regarding multicultural education that are central to NAME's philosophy and serve as NAME's goals.

National Clearinghouse for English Language Acquisition and Language Instruction Educational Programs
Funded by the U.S. Department of Education, this clearinghouse collects, analyzes, and disseminates information relating to the effective education of linguistically and culturally diverse learners in the United States.

CHILDREN with DIVERSE NEEDS

Appropriate Education for All

LEARNING OUTCOMES

1. Identify the key strategies for teaching children with diverse needs.

2. Describe how you can support gifted and talented students.

3. Explain how to identify children who are abused and neglected and determine what you can do to help them.

4. Explain how you can help children who are homeless receive a quality education.

5. Explain how you can use social stories to accommodate children's needs.

CHILDREN with special needs are in every program, school, and classroom in the United States. As an early childhood professional, you will teach students who have a variety of special needs. These children may come from all socioeconomic backgrounds, racial and ethnic groups, and have exceptional abilities and/or disabilities. In fact, some students may have more than one exceptionality; they may be **twice exceptional.** For example, students may be gifted and also have a **learning disability**, a condition which causes a child to have difficulty learning or using certain skills.

Students with special needs are often discriminated against because of their disability, socioeconomic background, language, ethnicity, or gender. You will be challenged to provide for *all* your students an education that is appropriate for their physical, intellectual, social, and emotional abilities and to help them achieve their best. To meet this challenge, you should learn as much as you can about the special needs of children and collaborate with other professionals to identify and develop teaching strategies, programs, and curricula for them. Most of all, you need to be a strong advocate for meeting each child's individual needs.

CHILDREN WITH DISABILITIES

Children with special needs and their families absolutely must have the education and services that will help these children achieve their potential. You will be a part of the process of seeing that they receive such services. Unfortunately, quite often children with disabilities are not provided appropriate services and fail to reach their full potential. About 10 to 12 percent of the nation's students have some type of disability.[1] Table 16.1 lists the number of persons from ages three to twenty-one with disabilities in the

TABLE 16.1 | Number of Children Served by IDEA

All Disabilities	**6,552,766**
Specific learning disabilities	2,431,317
Speech and language impairments	1,416,060
Intellectual disability	463,321
Emotional disturbance	407,617
Multiple disabilities	131,458
Hearing impairments	79,215
Orthopedic impairments	65,345
Other health impairments	689,183
Visual impairment	29,217
Autism	378,876
Deaf-blindness	2,283
Traumatic brain injury	25,391
Development delay	368,873

Note: Data include children and youth ages three to twenty-one.
Source: National Center for Education Statistics; Table A-9-1.
Number and percentage distribution of children and youth ages 3–21 served under the Individuals with Disabilities Education Act (IDEA), Part B, and number served as a percentage of total school enrollment, by disability type: selected school years, 1980–1981 through 2009–2010, 2013.

56% of children receiving early intervention transitioned to kindergarten "very easily" versus 4% whose transition was "very difficult"	59% of children in early intervention have trouble communicating their needs	8% of children receiving special education services have emotional disturbances	African American students are 2.83 times more likely to receive special education and related services for intellectual disabilities than all other racial/ethnic groups combined and 2.24 times more likely for emotional disturbance	Asian children (ages 6-21) account for 8.1% of students receiving special education services for autism and developmental delays, more than any other race/ethnicity	Hispanic preschoolers represent 20% of the general population but are less likely to be served under Part B of IDEA than children of all other racial/ethnic groups combined	46% of American Indian/Alaska Native children with disabilities drop out of high school, nearly double the dropout rate of Caucasians with disabilities	African American students (ages 6–21) represent only 14.8% of the general population but comprise 44.8% of students with specific learning disabilities

Questions

• Might Hispanics with disabilities be overrepresented or underrepresented in these data? Why might this occur?
• Why do you think African American students are overrepresented in the population of students with disabilities? What other statistic helps explain this?
• What is the primary developmental delay with children in early intervention?
• Why is early intervention important for success in school?

FIGURE 16.1 | Children with Disabilities: Facts, Figures, and Questions
Early intervention is mandated in IDEA, Part C, for infants and toddlers with disabilities who are under the age of three. Disabilities include diagnosed developmental delays and physical or mental conditions that have a high probability of resulting in developmental delay, as well as other at-risk conditions at the state's discretion.

Source: U.S. Department of Education, Office of Special Education and Rehabilitative Services, Office of Special Education Programs, 30*th Annual Report to Congress on the Implementation of the Individuals with Disabilities Education Act, 2008,* vol. 1, Washington, D.C., 2012.

twice exceptional Students with dual exceptionalities.

learning disability A condition which causes a child to have difficulty learning and using certain skills.

various categories. These data are one reason for the laws to help ensure that children have special education and related services and that schools and teachers have high expectations for these children.

As we will discuss, the federal government has passed many laws protecting and promoting the rights and needs of children with disabilities. One of the most important of these federal laws is the Individuals with Disabilities Education Improvement Act of 2004 (IDEA).

In addition, Figure 16.1 provides you with interesting and useful demographic information about children's disabilities and races and cultures.

As with many special areas, the field of special education has a unique vocabulary and terminology. The glossary in Figure 16.2 helps you understand these terms as you read this text and as you work with children and families. As the fields of early childhood and special education continue to integrate and blend, you must learn more about the field of early childhood special education and the terminology associated with it.

INDIVIDUALS WITH DISABILITIES EDUCATION ACT (IDEA)

Individuals with Disabilities Education Act (IDEA) A federal act providing a free and appropriate public education to youth between ages three and twenty-one with disabilities.

The **Individuals with Disabilities Education Act (IDEA)** does the following:

• ensures a free appropriate public education that emphasizes special education and related services designed to meet the unique needs of these children
• ensures that the rights of the children with disabilities and their parents or guardians are protected
• assists states and localities to provide for the education of all children with disabilities
• assesses and assures the effectiveness of efforts to educate children with disabilities.[2]

Children with disabilities:
- The expression that replaces former terms such as handicapped. To avoid labeling children, do not use the phrase *disabled children*.

Co-teaching:
- The process by which a regular classroom professional and a special educator or a person trained in exceptional student education team teach a group of regular and mainstreamed children in the same classroom.

Differentiated Instruction:
- An approach to teaching and learning for students of differing abilities in the same class. The intent of differentiating instruction is to maximize each student's growth and individual success; meet each student where he or she is; and assist the child in the learning process.

Disability:
- A physical or mental impairment that substantially limits one or more major life activities.

Early intervention:
- Providing services to children and families as early in the child's life as possible to prevent or help with a special need(s).

Embedded Instruction:
- Instruction that is included as an integral part of normal classroom routines, often using naturalistic teaching strategies.

Exceptional student education:
- Replaces the term *special education*; refers to the education of children with special needs.

Integration:
- A generic term that refers to educating children with disabilities along with typically developing children. Such education can occur in mainstream, reverse mainstream, and full-inclusion programs.

Least restrictive environment (LRE):
- The use of special classes, separate schooling, or other removal of children with disabilities from the regular educational environment only when the nature or severity of the disability is such that education in regular classes with the use of supplementary aids and services cannot be achieved satisfactorily.

Mainstreaming:
- The social and educational integration of children with special needs into the general instructional process, usually a regular classroom program.

Normalized setting:
- A place that is normal, or best, for the child.

Reverse mainstreaming:
- The process by which typically developing children are placed in programs for children with disabilities, who are in the majority.

FIGURE 16.2 | Terminology Related to Children with Special Needs

IDEA defines **children with disabilities** as children with intellectual disabilities, hearing impairments (including deafness), speech or language impairments, visual impairments (including blindness), serious emotional disturbance, orthopedic impairments, autism, developmental delays; traumatic brain injury, other health impairments, or specific learning disabilities, and who, by reason thereof, need special education and related services.[3]

IDEA applies to infants and toddlers (ages zero to three) and students (age three through twenty-one). Infants and toddlers have needs unlike those of older children.

children with disabilities
IDEA defines children with disabilities as those children with intellectual disabilities, hearing impairments (including deafness), speech or language impairments, visual impairments (including blindness), serious emotional disturbance, orthopedic impairments, autism, developmental delays, traumatic brain injury, other health impairments, or specific learning disabilities, and who, by reason thereof, need special education and related services.

IDEA consists of four parts, but the parts of most interest to you are Part B and Part C, which are age specific.

IDEA, PART B.   Part B of IDEA is the foundation upon which all special education and related services rests.[4] Part B benefits students who are ages three through twenty-one. Part B details the general purposes of IDEA. IDEA also defines important terms, state and local education agency eligibility for funding, evaluation, procedural safeguards designed to protect children and their families' rights, conflict resolution, enforcement and use of funds, and grants for preschool programs. Most important to you, however, Part B describes free and appropriate public education, the least restrictive environment, and the individual education programs.[5]

IDEA, PART C.   Part C is designed to provide **early intervention**, a process of providing services and opportunities for children and families to benefit any child under age three who needs services because of developmental delays. However, Part C gives states discretion whether to serve infants and toddlers in programs. Part C also gives each state the option of serving at-risk toddlers. These are children who would be at risk of experiencing a substantial developmental delay if they did not receive early intervention services.[6]

THE SEVEN PRINCIPLES OF IDEA.   IDEA has established seven basic principles to follow as you provide education and other services to children with special needs:

1. *Zero reject.* IDEA calls for educating all children and excluding none from an education—**zero reject**. Before IDEA many children were excluded from educational programs or were denied an education.

2. *Nondiscriminatory evaluation.* A fair assessment is required to determine whether a child has a disability and, if so, what the student's education should consist of. This is a **nondiscriminatory evaluation**.

3. *Multidisciplinary assessment.* In this team approach, a group of people use various methods of evaluation to ensure that a child's needs and program are not determined by one test or one person.

4. *Appropriate education.* IDEA provides a **free and appropriate public education (FAPE)** for all students between the ages of three and twenty-one. *Appropriate* means that children must receive an education suited to their age, maturity, condition of disability, past achievements, and parental expectations.

5. *Least restrictive placement/environment.* Students with disabilities must, to the maximum extent appropriate for each one, be educated with students who do not have disabilities. The **least restrictive environment (LRE)** is not necessarily the regular classroom.

6. *Procedural due process.* IDEA provides schools and parents with ways to resolve their differences by mediation or by having hearings before impartial hearing officers or judges.

7. *Parent and student participation.* IDEA specifies a process of shared decision making, whereby educators, parents, and students collaborate in deciding the student's educational plan.

REFERRAL, ASSESSMENT, AND PLACEMENT.   Under IDEA, educators must follow certain procedures in developing a special plan for each child. Referral of the student for exceptional student services can be made by anyone, including a teacher, parent, doctor, or other professional. The referral is usually followed by a comprehensive individual assessment to determine whether the child possesses a disability and is eligible for services. In order for testing to occur, parents or guardians must give their consent.

---

early intervention
A process of providing services and opportunities for children and families.

zero reject The Individuals with Disabilities Education Act calls for educating all children and excluding none from an education. Before IDEA many children were excluded from educational programs or were denied an education.

nondiscriminatory evaluation A fair evaluation is required to determine whether a student has a disability and, if so, what the student's education should consist of.

free and appropriate public education (FAPE) A free education suited to children's age, maturity, condition of disability, past achievements, and parental expectations.

least restrictive environment (LRE) Placement that meets the needs of students who are disabled in as regular a setting as possible.

If a child is eligible for exceptional student services, the **child study team**, the group of individuals who determine a child's eligibility for special education, meets to develop an **individualized education plan (IEP)** for the child. Essentially, the IEP is a contract or agreement that specifies the school's plan for providing the child with FAPE and services. The child study team includes a parent or parent representative; the student, when appropriate; a special education teacher; a regular education teacher; a representative of the school district; and a principal, assistant principal, or coordinator of exceptional student services. The IEP must be reviewed annually and revised as appropriate. The child study team is also sometimes referred to as the Assessment, Referral and Dismissal (ARD) Team, which is also responsible for dismissing students from exceptional student education services when they are able to function in the regular classroom without services.

English Language Learners and Referral, Assessment, and Placement. The question of referral, assessment, and placement has always been a tricky one when it comes to children who are English language learners (ELLs). Data show that there is an overrepresentation of minorities in special education. The ELL population is both overrepresented and underrepresented in special education. Children who are ELLs are frequently and inappropriately referred for special education services based on tests that actually measure their language acquisition rather than their learning abilities. Also, recall from Figure 16.1 that Hispanic children constitute 20 percent of the general population, but receive special education services less than do all other racial and ethnic groups combined.[7] Therefore, ELLs often have the problem of actually having a learning disability that goes undiagnosed and unaccommodated based on the belief that language is the issue. Additionally, children who are ELLs may in fact be referred to special education but still not receive appropriate or adequate services because of a lack of bilingual special education teachers.

Indicators of Learning Disabilities. Distinguishing between incomplete second-language acquisition and a learning disability is a difficult but vitally important task. Many indicators of learning disabilities are also indicators of the language learning process. For example, lack of attention, difficulty interpreting verbal messages, difficulty retrieving stored information, and difficulty sequencing and organizing information are hallmarks of both learning disabilities and language acquisition. As a result, many argue that the only way a language disability can reliably be distinguished from second-language acquisition is to do a complete assessment in both languages. If problems are apparent only in the second language, it is probably a language acquisition issue; if they are present in both languages, it is a learning disability. However, this approach assumes that ELLs have acquired a solid foundation of language skills in their native language. What about the students who don't have a learning disability but who were disadvantaged in their native language and now are expected to perform in a second language?[8] The implications are challenging because these children are at such a great risk for failure.

Children with learning disabilities and children who are learning English have different needs that necessitate different interventions and educational strategies. Learning disabilities occur outside of children's control, and they do not go away. Children who have learning disabilities can and need to be taught compensatory strategies to help them persevere, to be successful, and to be well-educated. Conversely, a lack of proficiency in English has a cause and can be addressed educationally. Children who are ELLs need large amounts of meaningful interaction with language, in interactive situations, with appropriate scaffolding.[9]

INDIVIDUALIZED EDUCATION PLANS (IEPs). Because IDEA requires **individualization of instruction**, schools must provide for all students' specific needs,

child study team The group of individuals who determine a child's eligibility for special education.

individualized education plan (IEP) A plan for meeting an exceptional learner's educational needs, specifying goals, objectives, services, and procedures for evaluating progress.

individualization of instruction Providing for students' specific needs, disabilities, and preferences.

disabilities, and preferences, as well as those of their parents. Individualization of instruction also means developing and implementing an individualized education plan (IEP) for each student. The IEP must specify what the school and teachers will do for the child, how and when it will be done, and by whom it will be done, and this information must be in writing.

Purposes and Functions of the IEP. IEPs have several purposes. They do the following:

- Protect children and parents by ensuring planning for and the delivering of services.
- Guarantee that children will have plans tailored to their individual strengths, weaknesses, and learning styles.
- Help professionals and other instructional and administrative personnel focus their teaching and resources on children's specific needs, promoting the best use of everyone's time, efforts, and talents.
- Help ensure that children with disabilities receive a range of services from other agencies if needed, and must specify how a child's total needs will be met.
- Clarify and refine decisions about what is best for children, where they should be placed, and how they should be taught and helped.
- Ensure that children will not be categorized or labeled without discussion of their unique needs.
- Require review on at least an annual basis, encouraging professionals to consider how and what children have learned, determine whether what was prescribed was effective, and prescribe new or modified strategies.

In developing the IEP, a person trained in diagnosing disabling conditions, such as a school psychologist, must be involved, as well as a classroom professional, the parent, and, when appropriate, the child. Because so many classrooms of today are inclusive, more than likely you will have children with disabilities in your classroom. This means you will participate in the development of an IEP for one or several of your children.

INDIVIDUALIZED FAMILY SERVICE PLANS. The process of helping children with disabilities ages zero to three begins with referral and assessment. Referrals of children's agencies can come from a variety of sources, including the families of children, child care providers, and county departments of health and pediatrics. Frequently, the point of entry into services for children and families is a county or city agency. For example, the Baltimore County Infants and Toddlers Program (BCITP) provides services for families of children first through thirty-six months who may have developmental disabilities, delays, or special health needs.[10] Referrals result in the development of an **individualized family service plan (IFSP)**, which is designed to help families reach the goals they have for themselves and their children. IDEA Part C provides funds for infants and toddlers to receive early intervention services through the IFSP, which includes the following:

- Multidisciplinary assessment developed by a multidisciplinary team and the parents.
- Planned services to meet developmental needs, including, as necessary, special education, speech and language assistance, occupational therapy, physical therapy, psychological services, parent and family training and counseling services, transition services, medical diagnostic services, and health services.
- Supporting information, including a statement of the child's present levels of development; a statement of the family's strengths and needs in regard to enhancing the child's development; a statement of major expected outcomes for

individualized family service plan (IFSP) A plan designed to help families reach their goals for themselves and their children, with varied support services.

the child and family; the criteria, procedures, and timelines for determining progress; the specific early intervention services necessary to meet the unique needs of the child and family; the projected dates for initiation of services; the name of the case manager; and transition procedures from the early intervention program into a preschool program.

An IFSP requires an integrated, team approach to intervention. A **transdisciplinary team model** is one method of integrating information and skills across professional disciplines. In this model, all team members (including the family) teach, learn, and work together to accomplish a mutually agreed-on set of intervention outcomes. With a transdisciplinary model, one or a few people are primary implementers of the program; other team members provide ongoing direct or indirect services. For example, an occupational therapist might observe a toddler during meals and then recommend to the parent how to physically assist the child.

transdisciplinary team model Professionals from various disciplines working together to integrate instructional strategies and therapy and to evaluate the effectiveness of their individual roles.

Benefits of Family-Centered Services. Family-centered services are an important component of early childhood programming, and they will become even more important. Programs that embrace and use family-centered services achieve some important improvements in child developmental and social adjustment outcomes, decrease parental stress as a result of accessing needed services for their children and themselves, and recognize the family's role as decision maker and partner in the early intervention process.

INCLUSIVE EDUCATION

You will teach in an inclusive classroom. Today's teacher is a teacher of all children regardless of ability or disability. The inclusive classroom is one outcome of the ongoing integration of the fields of early childhood education and early childhood special education. In addition to guiding your teaching and professional development with the NAEYC Standards for Professional Preparation, you should also be guided by the Professional Standards for Preparation of Special Education Teachers. They are outlined for you in Figure 16.3. Review and reflect on these standards and what you need to do to achieve them.

INCLUSION.   IDEA requires that schools meet the needs of students with disabilities as much as possible in the general education classroom. Teachers use a variety of adaptations to ensure that all students, regardless of abilities, have equal access to a quality education. **Adaptive education** is aimed at providing learning experiences that help each student achieve desired educational goals. Education is adaptive when schools and classroom teachers modify learning environments to respond effectively to student differences and to enhance an individual's ability to succeed in such environments. Gayle Solis Zavala, a National Special Education Teacher of the Year, is constantly finding ways to improve her students' receptive and expressive language through multisensory activities. To appeal to both children with physical and cognitive disabilities and their nondisabled peers, she draws on board games, gardens, digital cameras, and puppetry. Her students have performed in a local arts festival, which helps them embrace different cultures and languages. Gayle has also developed schoolwide projects to teach her students entrepreneurship, respect, and other important life skills; these projects have included a pickle sale and an indoor plant care service.[11] You can read more about Gayle in the Voice from the Field, "Kids with Special Needs Need Extra Special Touch."

adaptive education Modifications in any classroom, program, environment, or curriculum that help students achieve desired educational goals.

The Full Inclusion Debate. Inclusion supports the right of all students to participate in natural environments, which most often are regular classrooms. **Full inclusion** means

full inclusion An approach whereby students with disabilities receive all instruction and support services in a general classroom.

Standard 1

- *Foundations*:
  I understand the field as an evolving and changing discipline based on philosophies, evidence-based principles and theories, relevant laws and policies, diverse and historical points of view, and human issues that have historically influenced and continue to influence the field of special education and the education and treatment of individuals with exceptional needs in both school and society.

Standard 2

- *Development and Characteristics of Learners*:
  I know and demonstrate respect for students as unique human beings. I understand the similarities and differences in human development and the characteristics between and among individuals with and without exceptional learning needs.

Standard 3

- *Individual Learning Differences*:
  I understand the effects that an exceptional condition can have on an individual's learning in school and throughout life. I understand that the beliefs, traditions, and values across and within cultures can affect relationships among and between students, their families, and the school community.

Standard 4

- *Instructional Strategies*:
  I possess a repertoire of evidence-based instructional strategies to individualize instruction for individuals with exceptional learning needs.

Standard 5

- *Learning Environments and Social Interactions*:
  I actively create learning environments for individuals with exceptional learning needs that foster cultural understanding, safety and emotional well-being, positive social interactions, and active engagement of individuals with exceptional learning needs.

Standard 6

- *Language*:
  I understand typical and atypical language development and the ways in which exceptional conditions can interact with an individual's experience with and use of language.

Standard 7

- *Instructional Planning*:
  I develop long-range individualized instructional plans anchored in both general and special education curricula.

Standard 8

- *Assessment*:
  I use multiple types of assessment information for a variety of educational decisions.

Standard 9

- *Professional and Ethical Practice*:
  I am guided by the profession's ethical and professional practice standards.

Standard 10

- *Collaboration*:
  I routinely and effectively collaborate with families, other educators, related service providers, and personnel from community agencies in culturally responsive ways.

FIGURE 16.3 | Content Standards for Educators of Individuals with Exceptional Gifts and Talents

Source: What Every Special Educator Must Know (2009, 6th ed. Revised). Council for Exceptional Children (CEC).

that students with disabilities receive the services and support appropriate to their individual needs entirely in their natural environments, such as general classrooms, playgrounds, family care centers, and child care centers. **Partial inclusion** means that students receive part of their instruction in the general classroom and the other part in pull-out classrooms, or **resource rooms**, where they work individually or in small groups with special education teachers.

Full inclusion receives a lot of attention and is the subject of great national debate for several reasons:

- Court decisions and state and federal laws mandate, support, and encourage full inclusion; many of the decisions relate to basic civil rights. For example, in the 1992 case *Oberti v. Board of Education of the Borough of Clementon School District*, the judge ruled that Rafael, an eight-year-old child with Down syndrome, should not have to earn his way into an integrated classroom but had a right to be there from the beginning.

- Some teachers feel they do not have the training or support necessary to provide for the disabilities of children in full-inclusion classrooms. Increasingly, early childhood teachers are also earning special education certification so they can be well prepared for the inclusive classroom. Also, more schools are requiring dual certification—early childhood and special education—as a basis for employment.

- Some parents of children with disabilities are dissatisfied with separate programs, which they view as a form of segregation. They want their children to have the academic and social benefits of attending general education classrooms.

Early childhood educators are very much involved in making inclusion work. In order for inclusion to be a reality in your classroom, there are a number of things you can do to ensure your success.

- **Understand Students and Their Needs**
  - Learn the characteristics of students with special needs
  - Learn about legislation affecting students with special needs
  - Become comfortable with students with special needs
  - Learn about and use assistive and educational technologies
- **Develop Skill in Instructional Techniques**
  - Modify instruction for students with special needs
  - Use a variety of instructional styles and media and increase the range of learning behaviors
  - Individualize instruction and integrate the curriculum
  - Provide instruction for students of all ability levels
  - Modify assessment techniques for students with special needs
- **Manage the Classroom Environment**
  - Physically adapt the learning environment to accommodate students with special needs
  - Foster social acceptance of students with special needs
  - Provide inclusion in varied student groupings
  - Use peer tutoring
  - Guide and manage the behavior of all students
  - Motivate all students
- **Collaborate with Other Professionals and Parents**
  - Work closely with special educators and other specialists
  - Work with and involve parents
  - Participate in planning and implementing IEPs

partial inclusion An approach whereby students with disabilities receive some instruction in a general classroom and some in a specialized setting.

resource room A room where students work individually or in small groups with special education teachers.

Kids with Special Needs Need Extra Special Touch

STEP 1 — Provide a Warm Welcome

I want to emphasize the importance of the "warm welcome" each day. A handshake or friendly pat on the back is a personal gesture that lets the students know they are important and you are glad to see them.

STEP 2 — Support Independence

Call this first day of school Independence Day. Students with disabilities, just as students without disabilities, find themselves facing this day with many of the same feelings and anxieties. Students with disabilities, however, especially students with English as a second language, may have little or no way to communicate their needs or feelings. They may walk or dash away or squat down refusing to move in fear of what is waiting ahead. In the cafeteria, it's like entering another world altogether, where once again they will be asked to wait in a line, but this time there are choices to make, a cashier to greet, a table that stretches for miles to sit at, and food wrapped in plastic bags and cartons to figure out how to open.

The choices for breakfast, and later for lunch, are eventually communicated by the students in a way that begins to give them independence and a communicative voice (i.e., pointing, verbalizing part or all of a word, sign language, or a picture communication board). Cafeteria staff give students PIN numbers to use whenever they get breakfast or lunch. Students carry their numbers with them to key in on what looks like a debit card machine. Consult with the cafeteria staff ahead of time to gain their support and patience. This is a functional and practical opportunity to learn numbers and add another important independent skill. For students with cognitive and/or physical limitation, a communication board or simple one-message voice output device can be used to convey any needed communicative message.

STEP 3 — Scaffold

Use scaffolding as a teaching strategy when orienting and teaching students with disabilities. As students learn to sign, verbalize, and select what they want to say on their picture boards, the teacher or staff can model or provide assistance to help a student learn a more independent response. Continuing on with the cafeteria scenario, a teacher's first reaction may be to open up a student's juice carton or wipe a soiled mouth or clothing. But, if the students are to learn to take care of themselves, they need to repeatedly practice these self-help skills. The reward is evident as the students finally open their own cartons and wave their hands in the air with delight and look to their teacher for praise.

STEP 4 — Praise

Praise is one of your biggest teaching tools in managing behavior:

"I like the way Jesus is staying in line. Great job, Jesus!"

"I like the way Ashley is keeping her hands to herself (gesturing with folded arms or hands in pocket)."

The students are always watching to see what gets the attention of teachers and staff. It is always more beneficial to voice positive praise, especially with the most challenging students.

STEP 5 — Develop a Social Contract

Establish a written social contract (pictures can be added to cue understanding) between the students and the teaching staff. Even if students are nonverbal or have limited communication skills, you can model appropriate choices about positive social interaction, use picture prompts, or capture the targeted behavior when it happens to add to the social contract. Allowing students to participate in creating the social contract is another example of giving them independence and self-advocacy. Some social contract behaviors are the following:

- Listen quietly to one another.
- Use nice words with each other.
- Establish eye contact.
- Enjoy humor (have fun), but humor should not be hurtful (don't make fun of one another).

A social contract is also an important opportunity to emphasize to paraprofessionals, volunteers, and other classroom personnel how the climate of the classroom should be. Everyone signs the contract, and we review it at least once a day to maintain its importance.

Establishing independence; providing opportunities to communicate; and a safe, nurturing climate is a recipe for success with all children.

Source: Contributed by Gayle Solis Zavala, CEC Teacher of the Year.

A Continuum of Services. Not all children with disabilities can receive all of the services they need in the regular classroom. This is why school districts provide for a range of services for their students based on individual children's needs. These services include teachers and aides who provide assistance to the classroom teacher, special education resource rooms, and separate special education classrooms. The Council for Exceptional Children (CEC), a professional organization of special educators, believes that a continuum of services must be available for all students and that the concept of inclusion is a meaningful goal.[12]

A *continuum of services* implies a full and graduated range of services available for all individuals, from the most restrictive placements to the least. For students with disabilities, a continuum of services would identify institutional placement as the most restrictive and a general education classroom as the least restrictive.

There is considerable debate over whether such a continuum is an appropriate policy. Advocates of full inclusion say that the approach works against developing truly inclusive programs. Given the great amount of interest in inclusion, discussion regarding both its appropriateness and the best ways to implement it will likely continue for some time.

CONSULTATION AND COLLABORATION

As an early childhood professional, you will participate in **consultation**, seeking advice and information from colleagues. You will also engage in **collaboration**, working cooperatively with a range of special educators, other professionals, parents, and administrators to provide services to students with disabilities and students at risk. Some of those professionals include the following:

- Diagnosticians, who are trained to test and analyze students' strengths and weaknesses
- Special educators, who are trained to instruct students with special needs
- **Itinerant teachers**, who travel from school to school, providing assistance and teaching students
- **Resource teachers**, who provide assistance with materials, planning, and teaching
- Physical therapists, who treat physical disabilities through nonmedical means
- Occupational therapists, who direct activities that develop muscular control and self-help skills
- Speech and language pathologists, who assess, diagnose, treat, and help prevent speech, language, cognitive communication, voice, swallowing, fluency, and other related disorders

Consultation with experienced teachers, experts in the field of special education, and administrators enables you to see your options more clearly, gain important knowledge and insight, and consider teaching and learning strategies you might not have thought of on your own. With collaboration you will be able to implement those strategies and new approaches with the help and support of others.

consultation Seeking advice and information from colleagues.

collaboration Working jointly and cooperatively with other professionals, parents, and administrators.

itinerant teachers Professionals who travel from school to school, providing assistance and teaching students.

resource teachers Professionals who provide assistance with materials and planning for teachers of exceptional students.

WITH COLLEAGUES.   Consulting and collaborating with colleagues, especially special education teachers, is an excellent and even necessary means of understanding students' needs and the best ways to meet those needs. Collaborating with your colleagues is an essential component of successful teaching and learning in an inclusive classroom. As a classroom teacher, you will be expected to provide information and ideas about content knowledge, curriculum objectives, curriculum sequence, and content evaluation. Special education teachers are expected to contribute information about disabilities, learning and motivation strategies that work with students with disabilities, and ideas about how to adapt curriculum to meet students' special needs.

Itinerant Special Educators. Many school districts use the services of a special education itinerant teacher, who is a valuable resource to you, your students, and their parents. This traveling teacher provides information, assists you in making helpful modifications to the classroom environment, coaches you in some new instructional techniques, and in some cases works directly with the child(ren) for part of each week.

The itinerant teacher gives you and parents information about a child's disability, explains any jargon or medical terms that may be present in evaluation reports, and refers the parents to helpful resources, such as pertinent websites or parent support groups. In addition, the itinerant teacher talks with you about how the physical environment is working for a child with a disability. Is the room fully accessible, is the equipment appropriate, and does the child seem to find all areas of the room inviting? The itinerant teacher may also loan equipment to you and help you provide more visual support for the child, such as a picture schedule or markings on the floor to indicate where children sit and line up.

embedded instruction Instruction that is included as an integral part of normal classroom routines.

naturalistic teaching strategies Incorporating instruction into opportunities that occur naturally or routinely in the classroom.

School districts are required to provide specialized instruction to students with disabilities, but the itinerant teacher will look for opportunities for **embedded instruction** that can use **naturalistic teaching strategies**. In these cases, the instruction will blend right into normal classroom routines. For example, if the child has a social objective to greet classmates using their names, a natural opportunity might prompt this behavior with a greeting song during arrival time or opening-circle time and again when classmates enter an area where the child is working during free-choice time.

In a collaborative teaching experience with an itinerant special education teacher, you can learn a lot and share together the joy of watching young children with special needs succeed in their very own neighborhood schools.[13]

Autism occurs on a spectrum; each child exhibits it uniquely. There is no cure for autism, but early intervention can help tremendously with symptoms and increase the quality of life for the child and the child's whole family.

WITH PARENTS.   The development of an IEP requires that you work closely with parents in developing learning and evaluation goals for students with disabilities. Also, some parents may want to spend time in your classroom to help you meet the needs of their children. All parents have information about their children's needs, growth, and development that will be helpful to you as you plan and teach.

WITH PARAPROFESSIONALS.   You may have one or more full- or part-time paraprofessionals in your classroom, depending on the number of students with disabilities and the nature of their disabilities. Classroom assistants can help you to provide multimodal instruction and assess students' skills. For example, Megan Molina is a paraprofessional in Wendy Stark's blended classroom. When Wendy is busy handling Brian's meltdown or spending a few extra minutes on making observation assessments for Teneka, Megan keeps the other children on task and helps them complete their lesson. Other times, Megan takes Cho for a walk when she becomes overstimulated so that she can regroup while Wendy continues teaching the rest of the class. Megan and Wendy spend a lot of time planning and preparing for class together.

WITH ADMINISTRATORS.   Administrators can help you with the legal, political, and procedural matters of teaching students with special needs in your classroom. Administrators can also help by providing more planning time and opportunities for special education and general education teachers to plan together and by employing a "floating" substitute to aid teachers and increase release time for teacher planning. In addition, in supporting **coteaching** partnerships, the collaboration of a regular classroom teacher and a special education teacher in teaching lessons and activities, administrators can give you access to a network of other services, information, and resources.

coteaching The collaboration of a regular classroom teacher and a special education teacher in teaching lessons and activities.

Check Your Understanding: Terminology

As you read now about children with autism and attention-deficient hyperactivity disorders, reflect on how you will consult and collaborate with colleagues and families to meet their needs.

CHILDREN WITH AUTISM SPECTRUM DISORDERS (ASD)

Autism is a complex developmental disability that appears during the first three years of life. It is the result of a neurological disorder that affects the normal functioning of the brain, impacting development in the areas of social interaction and communication skills. Children with autism typically show difficulties in verbal and nonverbal communication, social interactions, joint attention (sharing one's experience or event by following eye gaze, gesturing, or leading), and leisure or play activities. Autism affects each child differently and to varying degrees. Autism is currently diagnosed five times more often in boys than in girls, although we do not know why.[14] Its prevalence is not affected by race, region, or socioeconomic status. Since autism was first diagnosed in the United States, the occurrence has climbed to 1 in 88 children and 1 in 54 boys. Autism diagnoses are increasing at the rate of 10 to 17 percent per year, and autism is the fastest growing serious developmental disability in the United States.[15] More children will be diagnosed with autism in the coming years than with AIDS, diabetes, and cancer combined.

autism A developmental disability that typically appears during the first three years of life and is the result of a neurological disorder that affects the normal functioning of the brain, impacting development in the areas of social interaction and communication skills.

CHARACTERISTICS OF CHILDREN WITH AUTISM.   Autism can be diagnosed as early as eighteen months of age—and the earlier children with autism receive intense and consistent intervention, the more likely they are to have positive experiences in the school, the home, and later, the occupational realms.[16] Signs of autism in infants and toddlers can include fixation on objects, lack of response to people, failing to respond to their names, avoiding eye contact, and engaging in repetitive movements such as rocking or arm flapping.[17] Children with autism typically demonstrate the following characteristics:

- Deficits in receptive and expressive communication skills
- Difficulties in verbal and nonverbal communication

- Repetitive or "stereotyped" behaviors[18]
- Difficulty initiating and sustaining symbolic play and social interactions[19]
- Difficulties in social interactions
- Limited interests
- Difficult ties with joint attention-showing expressions by following eye gaze, gesturing, or leading
- Trouble keeping up with conversations[20]

CAUSES OF AUTISM. The cause of autism remains unknown. New research indicates that induced labor increases the chance of autism.[21] Twin and family studies suggest an underlying genetic vulnerability to autism. Researchers have identified several genes associated with autism and have found anomalies in multiple areas of the brain of people who have autism. Other studies found that children with autism have atypical levels of serotonin or other neurotransmitters in their brains. This suggests that autism results from the interference in typical brain development caused by glitches in the genes that organize brain growth and guide how neurons communicate with one another as the fetus develops in utero.[22] Still other research suggests that in infancy and toddlerhood brain synapses are pruned in such a way as to "turn on or off" the autism gene, indicating that autism is a synaptic disorder.[23] Still other researchers have found that there may be environmental triggers for autism spectrum disorders,[24] but contrary to popular belief, there is no scientific evidence of any relationship between vaccines and autism.[25] It is likely that the cause of spectrum disorders is likely due to a combination of all of these factors. Regardless of the cause, autism is a prevalent presence in American society and will continue to be so.

AUTISM AND IMMUNIZATIONS/VACCINES. Despite popular opinion, research does not support the belief that autism is caused by immunizations or vaccines.[26] Some parents believe that preservatives used in immunizations and vaccines causes or triggers autism and ADHD. Although public health officials advise parents that immunizations and vaccines do not cause health problems, including autism and ADHD, a growing number of parents are opting out of required immunizations and vaccinations. Public health officials are concerned for the children who are not vaccinated or immunized and the health threat they create for themselves, their peers, and the public at large.

applied behavior analysis (ABA) ABA is based on the learning theory of behaviorism, which states that all behavior is motivated by a purpose and is learned through systematic reinforcement.

play therapy The developmentally appropriate practice and model to incorporate social experiences and enjoyable interactions to enhance a child's pretend skills, joint attention, communication skills, and appropriate behavior.

INTERVENTIONS. There are a number of effective interventions for autism. One is **applied behavior analysis (ABA)**, the theory that behavior rewarded is more likely to be repeated than behavior ignored. To reinforce behavior, ABA therapists initiate a sequence of stimuli, responses, and rewards. For example, an ABA therapist who is working on joint attention with Leland, a child with ASD, will ask Leland to "show me" the red block (stimulus). If Leland points to the red block (response), the ABA therapist gives him an M&M (reward) or another appropriate reward such as a sticker. If Leland does not respond or points to a different colored block, the therapist ignores the behavior and repeats the stimulus.

Play therapy is another effective intervention for children on the autism spectrum. Play therapy uses developmentally appropriate practices and models to incorporate social experiences and enjoyable interactions to enhance a child's pretend skills, joint attention, communication skills, and appropriate behavior. Play therapy can take place individually between a therapist and one child, in a group with other children, or along with the parents. Unlike ABA, play therapy is generally child led.[27] For example, a play therapist working with Kate, who has autism, would use different toys to engage her.

Over time, the play therapist would challenge Kate's behaviors and content of play by initiating different play scenarios. The play therapist reflects and comments on Kate's emotions and activities in order to elicit and reward language development, play skills, and relationship development so that Kate can feel understood and valued for who she is.

MUSIC, ART, AND OCCUPATIONAL THERAPY. Music, art, and occupational therapies are also highly effective interventions for children with autism.[28] Music therapists or art therapists use their respective expressive mediums (musical instruments, singing, painting, clay, etc.) to provide children who have spectrum delays with different means of experiencing relationships and self-expression and expanding various other skills. These therapies are unique in that they give children with spectrum delays an opportunity to develop skills that have social utility. As a result, children gain in peer interaction, and self-esteem, and improve their everyday functioning. Physical and occupational therapists use a more body-centered approach to reach children with developmental delays. By swinging, receiving deep compressions to their body, climbing, and jumping, children's bodies are challenged and made more comfortable, thereby eliciting more language, social reciprocity, and joint attention. These types of therapies can also be done individually, in groups, or with parents to maximize the effects of therapy. For example, an occupational therapist might put Benjamin in a hammock swing and push him in it to stimulate his vestibular needs while engaging him in developmentally appropriate conversation.

Other methods of effective intervention include a highly supportive teaching environment; predictability and routine; family involvement; and working with young children in small teacher-to-child ratios, often one-to-one in the early stages. Later in the chapter we will describe how teachers can accommodate a child with autism disorder through the creation of a *social story*. Also, the following Voice From the Field illustrates how hands-on-activities such as baking have great benefits for children with autism.

In the video about social skills, the teacher is working with a student with mild autism. The object of the teacher's intervention is to help the child learn social skills and be able to play and interact with other children. Pay particular attention to *what* the teacher says to the student with autism before she goes to play with the other children and *what* she reminds the student of during her interaction with her friends. Reflect on the importance of telling the student exactly what to do.

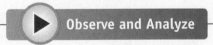
Observe and Analyze

CHILDREN WITH ATTENTION-DEFICIT HYPERACTIVITY DISORDER

Attention-deficit hyperactivity disorder (ADHD) is one of the most common neurobehavioral disorders involving the brain that affects emotions, behaviors, and learning.[29] Children with ADHD generally suffer with difficulties in three specific areas: *attention, impulse control, and hyperactivity*.[30] The causes of ADHD are unknown, but research strongly suggests that genetics plays a role. Studies of twins show that almost 80 percent of the influence of ADHD is due to genetic factors.[31] Other causes can be brain injury, environmental exposure to lead, alcohol and tobacco use during pregnancy, and premature birth and low birth weight. Despite popular opinion, research does not support the beliefs that ADHD is caused by eating too much candy and sodas, watching too much TV, parenting, or social and environmental factors

attention-deficit hyperactivity disorder (ADHD) Difficulty with attention and self-control, which leads to problems with learning, social functioning, and behavior that occur in more than one situation and have been present for a significant length of time.

Baking with Pre-Kindergarten Children with Autism

WHY BAKE WITH CHILDREN?

Children love to participate with hands-on activities. For example, baking with children of all ages and abilities has many benefits. They learn by exploring all five senses to gather information from the materials in front of them. Children will look, smell, hold, hear, and typically the big winner, *taste,* the items. You can use baking to incorporate many avenues of learning in one activity. Children with autism tend to be "picky" eaters; therefore, it is critical to open their world of trying new things and accepting unfamiliar textures and tastes. In addition, when peers observe peers or the teacher, this allows them to have a visual model of what to do and how to do it. Observing is a form of scaffolding. Baking with children with autism opens up the door to many avenues for teaching self-help skills, communication skills, fine motor skills, and social skills. Practicing all of these disciplines throughout the school day and in lessons provides more opportunities for each student to be independent and successful with his or her individualized educational programming (IEP).

TIPS BEFORE BAKING WITH CHILDREN

TIP 1 Be Organized!
Before starting a baking lesson (or any lesson) it is critical for you to be organized. Have all your supplies in advance—including any modifications or support systems students with autism need to be successful during any baking session.

TIP 2 Use Visual Prompts
Visual pictures of the baking rules and expectations enables students to remember what you want them to do. I use Boardmaker for every concept I teach my students. I display the picture prompts in color ink on one sheet of paper, then laminate them for durability and for re-use in other lessons. The first paper mat has pictures of the baking rules, another has the ingredients, and another is about turn taking. Essentially, the paper mats represent mini-social stories that are available in simple terms and with easy access during the baking session.

TIP 3 Use Your Materials to Teach the Standards
Once you have the supplies you need, keep some of them in a bin and others on the table out of reach for the students. Have plastic measuring cups and spoons for each student to use or play with. This opens a completely different "teachable moment." Before introducing the baking ingredients, ask the students to either label the color of the measuring cup or use a two- to three-word sentence depending on the child's communication level. Once they identify their color, you can put down the student's choice on color of measuring cups in the sequential size and discuss small, medium, or large cups. A student then can request the size of the cup she wants. Each student can take turns to pick the color and size of the measuring cup he or she wants. Now you just tapped into a pre-K math skill!

TIP 4 Collaborate and Practice with Your Team
Run through the steps and lesson first (pretending) before introducing it to the students. If possible, role-play with your team, which may include a therapist, paraprofessionals, volunteers, or parents. This helps you become comfortable with your role and how to keep the pace within the lesson. Children with autism cannot sit for a very long period of time. I allow each student to have a turn to stir the ingredients with a large wooden spoon. When it is their turn they are allowed to stand at the table. This offers them a change in position, to see what's in the large bowl by looking down at it.

TIP 5 Use Technology
Many children with autism spectrum enjoy videos. I play a video of children baking on the SMART Board. This helps convey what the word *baking* means, what happens when people bake, and what they can anticipate when I tell them the word *baking*.

TIP 6 Encourage New Behavior
Children with autism have a lot of sensory processing issues. I encourage these students to come out of their comfort zone to experience new things. For example, wearing a baker's hat or having an apron tied on their body. This is only for a brief period of time and may be only for their turn to stir the ingredients. This is determined on an individual-child basis.

TIP 7 — Do a Taste Test!

Children like to sample certain baking ingredients more than others. Of course the chocolate chips are a hit with my class, but not the flour or butter. So, if I bake three times a month, and this is my third baking lesson, I might change it up a bit. I create a graph of "LIKES" and "DO NOT LIKE," pairing them with visual icons of a happy face under the heading "likes" and an unhappy face under the label "do not like."

BAKING WITH THE CHILDREN

STEP 1 — Wash Hands!

The first step of baking is to wash hands before everyone begins. This allows you the opportunity to naturally teach "in the moment" that washing hands before touching food is very important.

STEP 2 — Praise!

Once all the students are seated around the table. Praise each person who is sitting nicely and has appropriate learning behaviors ready for baking.

STEP 3 — Review

Review the visual boards that you have on the table to discuss the baking rules, ingredients, and how to take turns. This shifts your energy to communicating to the students what they "can do" during this baking lesson. If you state to them "what you can do" and provide two choices, it will shift your lesson into a productive and successful learning opportunity. For example, have the children stir water in their measuring cups while they wait for their turn to stir the ingredients in the big bowl.

STEP 4 — Label

Labeling the baking materials and ingredients offers a fun way to incorporate language and communication skills. Students with autism can learn to say bowl, spoon, cup, butter, egg, and flour. For the nonverbal students, you can open the channels of learning by placing two choices in front of a student and ask the child to point to one. For example, "Timmy, point to the egg." "Good, you pointed to the egg. Egg starts with 'Ee,' and this is white. It is breakable and has liquid inside."

STEP 5 — Integrate Content Areas

As you put each ingredient into the big bowl for mixing, bring a little science into "the moment." Show the child this is a stick of butter and it is solid. Melt the butter in a clear bowl or measuring cup in the microwave and show them that the butter it is now a liquid.

STEP 6 — Take Turns

As for turn-taking, I use the visual mat and a simple song that repeats itself three times to allow each student the same amount of time to have the spotlight of stirring. This not only acts as a verbal timer, but also promotes communication.

Baking is teaching. Children with autism need to practice and have opportunities to experience "real life" activities to be successful and independent.

Source: Contributed by Laura Lee Reed, Ed.D., Golden Apple Teacher of the Year for Students with Autism, Lee County Florida School District.

---

such as poverty or family chaos. However, many things such as environment and poverty may make ADHD symptoms more prominent and contribute to the failure to resolve it. Still, the evidence is not strong enough to conclude that they are the main causes of ADHD.[32]

To be classified as having ADHD, by the age of twelve a child must display for at least six months at least six of the following characteristics to a degree that is maladaptive and inconsistent with developmental level. There are three types of ADHD: predominantly inattentive type, predominantly hyperactive-impulsive type, and combined type.

Children with ADHD show a persistent pattern of inattention and/or hyperactivity-impulsivity that interferes with functioning or development:

1. ***Inattention.*** Six or more symptoms of inattention for children up to age sixteen or five or more for adolescents seventeen and older and adults; symptoms of

inattention have been present for at least six months, and they are inappropriate for developmental level:

- Often fails to give close attention to details or makes careless mistakes in schoolwork, at work, or with other activities
- Often has trouble holding attention on tasks or play activities
- Often does not seem to listen when spoken to directly
- Often does not follow through on instructions and fails to finish schoolwork, chores, or duties in the workplace (e.g., loses focus, side-tracked)
- Often has trouble organizing tasks and activities
- Often avoids, dislikes, or is reluctant to do tasks that require mental effort over a long period of time (such as schoolwork or homework)
- Often loses things necessary for tasks and activities (e.g., school materials, pencils, books, tools, wallets, keys, paperwork, eyeglasses, mobile telephones)
- Is often easily distracted
- Is often forgetful in daily activities[33]

2. *Hyperactivity and Impulsivity.* Six or more symptoms of hyperactivity-impulsivity for children up to age sixteen, or five or more for adolescents seventeen and older and adults; symptoms of hyperactivity-impulsivity have been present for at least six months to an extent that is disruptive and inappropriate for the person's developmental level:

- Often fidgets with or taps hands or feet or squirms in seat
- Often leaves seat in situations when remaining seated is expected
- Often runs about or climbs in situations where it is not appropriate (adolescents or adults may be limited to feeling restless)
- Often unable to play or take part in leisure activities quietly
- Is often "on the go," acting as if "driven by a motor"
- Often talks excessively
- Often blurts out an answer before a question has been completed
- Often has trouble waiting his/her turn
- Often interrupts or intrudes on others (e.g., butts into conversations or games)[34]

There are additional conditions that children must meet:

- Several inattentive or hyperactive-impulsive symptoms were present before age twelve years.
- Several symptoms are present in two or more settings (e.g., at home, school or work; with friends or relatives; in other activities).
- There is clear evidence that the symptoms interfere with, or reduce the quality of, social, school, or work functioning.[35]

ADHD, COMBINED TYPE.   Children who have the combined type of ADHD exhibit both inattentive behaviors and hyperactive and impulsive behaviors. They may not show sufficient symptoms in either category to make a diagnosis of one type or another, but they do exhibit symptoms in both types to an extent that is enough to interfere with daily life and learning.[36]

ADHD AND GENDER.   ADHD is diagnosed about three times more often in boys (13.2 percent) than in girls (5.6 percent) and conservatively affects 8 percent of all students.[37] Boys are more likely to have the hyperactive component and thus are identified with ADHD more often and more quickly, whereas girls tend to show the symptoms of ADHD in different ways. However, both boys and girls can have any combination of symptoms. Some speculate that the typical hyperactive symptoms of boys disrupt the classroom more, and as a result, teachers are more likely to recommend testing and diagnosis.[38] Hallmark symptoms for boys tend to be impulsivity and inability to sit still or concentrate. Researchers speculate that because girls are socialized to please parents and teachers, they are more likely to compensate for their ADHD in behavior-appropriate ways. Symptoms for ADHD in girls are nonstop, uncontrollable talking; friendship difficulties; inordinate messiness; and difficulty paying attention,

All children, but particularly those with learning differences, learn best when they are involved with hands-on activities.

which may sometimes present as simply "not getting it." Some researchers have found that when these symptoms are identified, teachers tend to see them as evidence of a lack of the girl's academic abilities or intelligence rather than a symptom of a learning and behavior disorder, although it may well be that many girls who have ADHD are not diagnosed. As a result, girls may not get the help they need.

THE EFFECTS OF ADHD.   When ADHD is left untreated, children are more likely to experience lower educational achievement and are less likely to graduate from high school or college than their counterparts who have gotten help for their ADHD or those who don't have ADHD. They are also more inclined to have low self-esteem, antisocial thoughts, a pessimistic outlook on their future, and problems with their romantic relationships and jobs.[39] With the right combination of medication and intervention, children with ADHD have a better chance for a successful academic, personal, and career life. Interventions for ADHD include differentiated academic instruction, an approach to teaching and learning for students of differing abilities in the same class. The intent of differentiating instruction is to maximize each student's growth and individual success, meet each student where he or she is, and assist the child in the learning process.

TEACHING CHILDREN WITH ADHD.   You can apply these principles of effective teaching when you introduce, conduct, and conclude each lesson during the school day.[40]

Introducing Lessons. When you first introduce lessons, provide students with an advance organizer. Prepare students for the day's lesson by quickly summarizing the order of various activities. Explain, for example, that a review of the previous lesson will be followed by new information and that both group and independent work is expected. Next, review previous lessons on the topic. For example, remind children that yesterday's lesson focused on learning how to regroup in subtraction. Then review several problems before describing the current lesson. Be sure to set learning expectations. State what students are expected to learn during the lesson. For example, explain to students that a language arts lesson will involve reading a story about Paul Bunyan and identifying new vocabulary words in the story. Also, set behavioral expectations. Describe how students are expected to behave during the lesson. For example, tell children that they may talk quietly to their neighbors as they do their seat work or they may raise their hands to get your attention. Also, be sure to identify all materials that the children will need during the lesson, rather than leave them to figure that out on their own. For example, specify that children need their journals and pencils for journal writing or their crayons, scissors, and colored paper for an art project. Finally, remind students how to obtain help in mastering the lesson. For example, refer children to a particular page in the textbook for guidance on completing a worksheet. Many teachers have the "three students before me" (ask three peers for help before going to the teacher) rule.

Teaching Lessons. As you teach your lessons, be sure to support students' participation in the classroom. Provide students with ADHD with private, discreet cues to stay on task and an advance warning that they will be called on shortly. Avoid bringing attention to differences between students with ADHD and their classmates. At all times avoid the use of sarcasm and criticism. Integrate technology into your lessons. For example, use a document camera to demonstrate how to solve an addition problem requiring regrouping. The students can work on the problem at their desks while you manipulate counters on the projector screen. Be certain to continually check student performance. Question individual students to assess their mastery of the lesson. For example, you can ask students doing seat work (i.e., lessons completed by students at their desks) to demonstrate how they arrived at the answer to a problem, or you can ask individual students to state in their own words how the main character felt at the end of the story. As you perform ongoing student evaluation, identify students who need additional assistance. Watch for signs of a lack of comprehension, such as daydreaming or visual or verbal indications of frustration. Provide these children with extra explanations, or ask another student to serve as a peer tutor for the lesson. At the same time, describe how students can identify and correct their own mistakes. For example, remind students that they should check their calculations in math problems and reiterate how they can check their calculations. Also, remind them of particularly difficult spelling rules and ways to watch out for easy-to-make errors.

Help Students Focus. As lessons progress, help students continue to focus. Remind students to keep working and to focus on their assigned task. For example, you can provide follow-up directions or assign learning partners. These practices can be directed at individual children or at the entire class. Follow-up directions are effective and take different forms. For example, after giving directions to the class as a whole, provide additional *oral directions* for a child with ADHD. Ask whether the child understood the directions, and then repeat the directions together. Another way to provide follow-up direction is in writing. For example, write the page number for an assignment on the chalkboard, and remind the child to look at the board if he or she forgets the assignment.

Organizational Study Skills. Throughout your lessons, be sure to use cooperative learning strategies. Have students work together in small groups to maximize their own and each other's learning. Use strategies such as think-pair-share, in which you ask students to think about a topic, pair with a partner to discuss it, and share ideas with the group. Also, individualize instructional practices. For example, use partnered reading activities—pair the child with ADHD with another student who is a strong reader. Have the partners take turns reading orally and listening to each other. You can use scheduled storytelling sessions in which children retell a story that they have recently read. Keep a word bank or dictionary of new or hard-to-read sight-vocabulary words. Encourage computer games for reading comprehension. Schedule computer time for children to have drill and practice with sight-vocabulary words. Finally, make available to students a second set of books and other materials that they can use at home.

Time Management. Keep in mind that organization and study-skill strategies are particularly important for children with ADHD. They need to learn and use organization and study skills both throughout lessons and throughout their daily lives. The following list suggests different ways to help your students with ADHD develop and use organizational and study-skill strategies:

- *Assignment notebooks:* Provide the child with ADHD with an assignment notebook to help organize homework and seat work.
- *Color-coded folder:* Provide the child with color-coded folders to help organize assignments for different academic subjects (e.g., reading, mathematics, social science, and science).
- *Homework partner:* Assign the child a partner to help record homework and seat work in the assignment notebook and to help file worksheets and other papers in the proper folders.

Time management is an essential skill for children with ADHD because they tend to need extra help managing their time. Here are some tips to help students with ADHD learn to manage their time effectively:

- *Use a clock or wristwatch:* Teach the child with ADHD how to read and use a clock or wristwatch to manage time when completing assigned work.
- *Use a calendar:* Teach the child how to read and use a calendar to schedule assignments.
- *Practice sequencing activities:* Provide the child with supervised opportunities to break down an assignment into a sequence of short, interrelated activities.
- *Create a daily activity schedule:* Tape a schedule of planned daily activities on the child's desk.
- *Provide parents with time management strategies to use at home.*

BEHAVIORAL INTERVENTION. The purpose of behavioral intervention in the school setting is to assist students with ADHD in developing the behaviors that are most conducive to their own learning and that of classmates. Well-managed classrooms prevent many disciplinary problems and provide an environment that is most favorable for learning.

- *Define the appropriate behavior while giving encouragement:* Make encouragement specific for the positive behavior the student displays; that is, your comments should focus on what the student did right and should include exactly what part(s) of the student's behavior were desirable. Rather than praising a student for not disturbing the class, praise the student for quietly completing a math lesson on time.
- *Give praise immediately:* The sooner approval is given regarding appropriate behavior, the more likely the student is to repeat it.
- *Vary statements of praise:* The comments you use to praise appropriate behavior should vary; when students hear the same praise statement repeated over and over, it may lose its value.
- *Be consistent and sincere with praise:* Appropriate behavior should receive consistent praise. Consistency among teachers is important to avoid confusion on the part of students with ADHD. Similarly, students will notice insincere praise, which will make praise less effective.

CLASSROOM ACCOMMODATION. Children with ADHD often have difficulty adjusting to the structured environment of a classroom, determining what is important, and focusing on assigned work. Because they are easily distracted by other children or by nearby activities, many children with ADHD benefit from accommodations that reduce distractions in the classroom environment and help them stay on task.

- *Seat the child near you:* Assign the child with ADHD a seat near your desk or the front of the room. This seating assignment allows you to monitor and reinforce the child's on-task behavior.
- *Seat the child near a student role model:* This arrangement enables children to work cooperatively and to learn from their peers.
- *Provide low-distraction work areas:* As space permits, make available a quiet, distraction-free room or area for quiet study time and test taking. Students should be directed to this area privately and discreetly to avoid the appearance of punishment.

MEDICATION. Using medication to help children control their behavior is common. Some teachers and other education professionals object to medication for fear that some children are overmedicated. However, stimulant medications such as Adderall, Concerta, Focalin, and Ritalin can be a vital and effective component in helping children who have ADHD. Each medication affects children differently, and children may need to try different types and at different dosages before a right fit is found. Also, some stimulant drugs might not work for many children. In situations where stimulant drugs are not effective, nonstimulant drugs such as Strattera may be helpful. With the right combination of medication, behavioral interventions, and creative teaching, children with ADHD can be successful learners and students, which will set them up for success later in life.

INSTRUCTIONAL STRATEGIES FOR TEACHING CHILDREN WITH DISABILITIES

Sound teaching strategies work well for *all* students, including those with disabilities, but you must plan how to create inclusive teaching environments. There are many strategies that can help make your classroom a true learning environment.

universal design (UD)
A broad-spectrum solution that helps assure that environment, curriculum, and instructional strategies are accessible to all students.

UNIVERSAL DESIGN.   Universal design (UD) describes the adaptation of teaching strategies and technology to make the learning environment, the curriculum, and the instruction processes accessible to each young child—much in the same way that universal design in architecture incorporates curb cuts, automatic doors, ramps, and other accommodations for people with disabilities. Universal design ensures that learning is accessible to all students, and that success and achievement are feasible for students regardless of their differences. Universal design was established to integrate a greater number of students with disabilities into general education classroom settings. Universal design is based on two best practices: (1) Instruction is developmentally appropriate, and (2) teaching is based on a constructivist approach to learning. Developmentally appropriate practices and constructivist learning are based on the belief that children need multiple means of engagement, as well as practical experiences that support what they have learned.

For example, when teachers teach oral language and conversation skills, they use different modes of presenting the material and provide positive reinforcement. Teachers might record children's thoughts and ideas using written language, audio, or video to provide alternate ways for children to interact with the material. If the teacher is focusing on writing, she would embed writing into a variety of activities across the board, accept all students' attempts, and remain sensitive to the physical demands of writing that may be difficult for some students. She would also provide computers and other electronic devices to promote alternate routes to written expressive language.

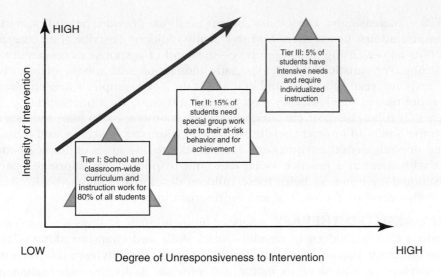

FIGURE 16.4 | The RTI Model

When it comes to universal design, flexibility is the key. For example, in a lesson on whole numbers and comparing number values, you would present numbers and value comparison using multiple media, such as oral directions, charts or diagrams, storybooks, blocks, or even cooking activities. The idea is to reach each child at the level he or she understands best. The teacher may introduce the concept of value comparison through graphs and group discussion one day, and then use a cooking experiment to demonstrate the concept practically ("Which is more: two cups of flour, or three cups of water?").

RESPONSE TO INTERVENTION/RESPONSE TO INSTRUCTION (RTI). As we know, **response to intervention/response to instruction (RTI)** (also referred to as response to intervention and instruction, or RTII), is a multitier instructional approach to the early identification and support of children with learning and behavior needs (Figure 16.4). RTI works by efficiently differentiating instruction for all students at their developmental levels. Children who are responsive to initial high-quality instruction (about 80 percent of the children) continue to be taught in the manner that is effective for them. Students who have difficulty, for whatever reason (about 15 percent), are engaged in increasingly smaller groups with increasingly need-oriented instruction, until they succeed. Some children (5 percent) may need individual and intense instruction, resulting in mastery of learning outcomes. RTI is successful because it incorporates increasingly intense instruction based on the individual needs of students.

response to intervention/ response to instruction (RTI) A multitiered approach to the early identification and support of students with learning and behavior needs.

HI-TECH OR LO-TECH? BOTH!

One of the challenges many teachers face is how to manage and guide children with disabilities. For example, some of the characteristics of children with autism and ADHD are that they have difficulty paying attention, staying focused, and developing social relationships. All these behavioral skills are necessary for learning in home and school and in getting along with others.

The use of robots and service animals are two alternatives that increasing numbers of teachers and families are turning to in order to help children stay on track, stay focused, and develop the skills they need to be successful in school (and life).

ROBOTS. Increasingly, robots are being used to provide helpful services for children and adults. Researchers find that many children describe their interactions with robots as reassuring and supportive—the kind of response necessary for living and learning. For autistic children, especially, interaction with robots enables them to attend, respond, read emotions, and communicate. For example, when children play with a robot named KASPAR, they tend to relax and enjoy their interaction.

Another robot, Keepon, encourages children to interact with him, and as a result, develop the ability to interact socially with their classmates, teachers, and others. The relaxing, nonjudgmental environment that robots provide gives children freedom to interact with them and practice social cues and responses. An informal, open, and conversational environment helps these children develop and master basic communication skills necessary for survival and for flourishing in the world.[41]

ANIMAL-ASSISTED THERAPY.   Service animals, such as dogs and cats, provide an opportunity for children to develop social skills and character skills relating to kindness and compassion; nurturance; loyalty and responsibility, especially responsible pet ownership; and to develop motor and physical skills through human–animal interactions. Service animals provide children the opportunity to be in a less restrictive environment, where they may interact and engage in learning opportunities with their peers. Children who need animal-assisted therapy often improve in their inability to trust others, learn appropriate touch, cooperate, problem-solve, concentrate, and express their emotions.[42] Learning these basic skills assists children in developing their ability to communicate effectively with their peers and adults, giving them the opportunity to learn and have a more productive and fulfilling role in their classrooms and homes.

For children with autism, service animals also provide comfort and security and another avenue for expressing emotions and interacting socially. For example, at Carson Elementary School, third grader, Jeremy, attends school with his service dog, Sam. Jeremy has muscular dystrophy, which makes it difficult for him to play with other children. As a result, he was becoming withdrawn and antisocial. However, teachers report that with Sam around, Jeremy is more outgoing, talkative, and social.

Service dogs need to be certified by agencies such as the National Service Animal Registry. Furthermore, not all schools and school districts allow animals in classrooms. Thus, you will want to check your school district's policy before you make any decisions about service animals in your classroom.

What does all of this mean for you? There is more than one way to assist children's learning. Certainly, you, the teacher, are the creator of environments and manager of the classroom. However, for children with particular disabilities, such as those with autism, robots and animal-assisted therapy may be one solution you have been looking for and that one or two of your children may need.

IMPLICATIONS FOR TEACHING.   The following ideas will also help you teach children with disabilities and create inclusive settings that enhance the education of *all* students:

- *Accentuate the positive:* One of the most effective strategies is to emphasize what children *can* do rather than what they *cannot* do. Children with disabilities have talents and abilities similar to those of other children.
- *Use appropriate assessment:* Include work samples, cumulative records, and appropriate assessment instruments. Parents and other professionals who have worked with individual children are sources of valuable information and can contribute to accurate and appropriate plans for them. Appropriate assessment includes using culturally sensitive tools and measures.

- *Use concrete examples and materials.*
- *Develop and use multisensory approaches to learning:* Use multisensory learning centers. Multisensory learning centers can assist in meeting diverse needs in an inclusive classroom; they can address various instructional levels with emphases on visual, auditory, and kinesthetic pathways to learning.
- *Model what children are to do:* Rather than just telling children what to do, have a child who has mastered a certain task or behavior model it for others. Also, ask each child to perform a designated skill or task with supervision. Give corrective feedback. Then let children practice or perform that behavior. Later, involve them in their own assessment of the behavior.
- *Make the learning environment a pleasant, rewarding place to be.*
- *Create a dependable classroom schedule:* All children develop a sense of security when daily plans follow a consistent pattern. Children with disabilities in particular benefit from dependable schedules because it provides routine and stability and a sense of control. However, allowing for flexibility is also important.
- *Encourage parents to volunteer at school and to read to their children at home.*
- *Identify appropriate tasks children can accomplish on their own:* Create opportunities for them to become more independent of you and others.
- *Use cooperative learning:* Cooperative learning enables all students to work together to achieve common goals. Cooperative learning has five components:
  - *Positive interdependence:* Group members establish mutual goals, divide the prerequisite tasks, share materials and resources, assume shared roles, and provide feedback to each other.
  - *Face-to-face interaction:* Group members encourage and facilitate each other's efforts to complete tasks through direct communication.
  - *Individual accountability personal responsibility:* Individual performance is assessed, and results are reported back to both the individual and the group, which holds members accountable for completing their fair share of responsibility.
  - *Interpersonal and small-group skills:* Students are responsible for getting to know and trust each other, communicating accurately and clearly, accepting and supporting each other, and resolving conflicts in a constructive manner.
  - *Group processing:* Group reflection includes describing which contributions of members are helpful or unhelpful in making decisions and which group actions should be continued or changed.
- *Develop a peer buddy system:* In a peer buddy system, classmates serve as friends, guides, or counselors to students who are experiencing problems. Variations are to pair an older student with a younger one who is experiencing a problem or to pair two students who are experiencing similar problems.[43]

DAILY REPORT CARDS HELP IMPROVE STUDENT BEHAVIOR. Most children are accustomed to receiving a six-week report card. However, we know that constant feedback about behavior and achievement provides students information they need to improve their behavior, and learn new skills and information. The What Works Clearinghouse (WWC), a U.S. Department of Education Agency, reviews educational research on a wide range of topics. The WWC reports that the use of daily report cards (DRCs) can improve the behavior of students with ADHD.[44] A DRC is aligned with behavioral and academic goals and with a student's individual educational plan (IEP). The teacher sends home the DRC that has information about the student's daily behavior and academic progress. Parents review and respond to the DRC and return it to the teacher.

So, what does research about the effectiveness of a daily report card have to do with you?

1. Many teachers provide parents ongoing information about their children's progress and behavior in the days and weeks between a six-week report card. Although this is a lot of work, it pays dividends in terms of building home–school relationships and student achievement.

2. Frequent reports to parents help ensure that teachers and parents/families are in agreement about children's behavioral and academic progress.

3. Sending home a DRC for children with disabilities who are in your classroom is a good idea and one you should consider. A weekly report card would work well for other students.

4. For some families, an electronic DRC or a weekly report would probably work better than a hard copy. An electronic DRC ensures that it gets home!

Consistent, ongoing, helpful feedback, including suggestions for improving behavioral and academic achievement is beneficial for every child and their families too.

TESTING STRATEGIES FOR CHILDREN WITH DISABILITIES. We've talked about the difficulty of using tests and assessments with children who have disabilities. We have known for a long time that too many children with disabilities are taking inappropriate state tests that produce results that don't reflect what the children really can do. States are responding by providing modified tests. For example, Pennsylvania is field-testing modified tests in math in all districts and is currently field-testing in reading and science in some districts. The modified assessment test is the same as the grade level standard test, but it has a simplified format that administrators and educators hope is accommodating enough that students' performance will more accurately reflect their capabilities and increase the number of children in special education scoring at a proficient level. The push for modified tests comes in part from some schools missing making Adequate Yearly Progress (AYP) as required by NCLB because too many exceptional children do not score at the proficient level. Teachers involved in the modified testing report that the process is much smoother than in previous years and that they believe the results can support the use of the modified tests.[45]

> **Check Your Understanding:** Strategies

CHILDREN WHO ARE GIFTED AND TALENTED

Children identified as gifted and talented receive services through the Jacob K. Javits Gifted and Talented Students Education Act of 2001. This act defines *gifted and talented children* as those who "give evidence of high performance capabilities in areas such as intellectual, creative, artistic, or leadership capacity or in specific academic fields, and who require services or activities not ordinarily provided by the school in order to fully develop such capabilities."[46] The definition distinguishes between *giftedness*, which is characterized by above-average intellectual ability, and *talented*, which refers to individuals who excel in such areas as drama, art, music, athletics, and leadership. Students can have these abilities separately or in combination; for example, a gifted student may also have a learning disability, and a student with an orthopedic disability may also be gifted.

CHARACTERISTICS OF GIFTED AND TALENTED CHILDEN. Most states have their own definitions of gifted and talented, so it is wise for you to check on the definition for your state. For example, in Illinois the definition of gifted and talented children includes children with outstanding talent who perform or show the potential for performing at remarkably high levels of accomplishment.[47] New York's definition includes pupils who show evidence of high performances capability and exceptional potential in areas such as general intellectual ability, special academic aptitude and outstanding ability in visual and performing arts. This definition includes those pupils who require educational programs or services beyond those normally provided by the regular school program in order to realize their full potential.[48] In Kentucky, gifted and talented students are identified as possessing demonstrated or potential ability to perform at exceptionally high levels in one or more of five areas: intellectual aptitude, specific academic aptitude, creative or divergent thinking, psychosocial skills, or in the visual or performing arts.[49]

PROVIDING FOR AND ACCOMMODATING GIFTED AND TALENTED CHILDREN

Regular classroom teachers often provide for gifted children through enrichment and acceleration. *Enrichment* allows children to pursue topics in greater depth and in ways different from that which the curriculum specifies. *Acceleration* permits children to progress academically at a quicker pace.

Classroom teachers can also use parents and resource people to tutor and work in special ways with these children and can provide opportunities for the children to assume leadership responsibilities. For example, children who are gifted and talented may be interested in tutoring other students who need extra practice or help. Tutoring can cut across grade and age levels. Students can also help explain directions and procedures to the class. In addition, teachers can encourage them to use their talents and abilities outside the classroom by becoming involved with other people and agencies.

Teachers can foster creativity through classroom activities that require divergent thinking and by using higher-order questions that encourage children to explain, apply, analyze, rearrange, and judge. Many schools have resource rooms for gifted and talented students, where children can spend a half day or more every week working with a professional who is interested and trained in working with them. Resource room pullout is the most popular of these methods.

In your work with children who are gifted, the more you can find out about them, the easier it will be for you to meet all of their exceptional needs. For example, one of the things that you will want to know is what motivates your children who are gifted and how you can take that intrinsic motivation and apply it to your teaching and children's learning. For many children, having the opportunity to use a block of time in any way they would like is a powerful motivating factor.

GIFTED AND TALENTED IDENTIFICATION. Children can receive the gifted and talented label through many avenues, but the most popular is generally through IQ testing, which is conducted at the request of teachers and families. Schools with a minority majority and low socioeconomic populations historically don't receive recommendations for IQ testing. Some schools are trying to fight this trend to ensure that all children have an equal opportunity to be seen as gifted and talented. The LA Unified School district now makes IQ testing for all second graders mandatory and has already seen a 9 percent increase in minority students identified as gifted and talented in just six months. One mother whose son is now recognized as gifted and talented says proudly, "Now he has something not everybody has, and it's going to follow him for the rest of his life. It could expand his life and open doors. It gives him the opportunity to be noticed."[50]

It is important to remember, however, that IQ testing is not the only way to measure giftedness or talent. IQ only measures certain qualities in a certain way. As a result, children who have learning disabilities or are English language learners (ELLs) but who may also be gifted and talented may not get the gifted and talented label, a label that can provide motivation, encouragement, and enriched education. As a teacher, you can take the initiative to recognize many types of intelligences. Recall Gardner's multiple intelligences and how they apply to individual children. You can play a huge part in securing the best education for all your students when you recognize their gifts!

HIGH-STAKES TESTS LEAVE MINORITY STUDENTS BEHIND

Today, students from preschool to high school are subjected to an almost endless array of tests. These tests are designed to measure everything from achievement, abilities, interests, and reading level to friendship preferences. When these tests are used to make critical decisions about students that have serious school and life consequences, they are called *high-stakes tests*. For example, standardized achievement tests are used to make decisions about whether Maria or Mario should be promoted to the next grade or whether Jennifer or Johnny has to attend summer school. But grade promotion and summer school attendance are not the only high-stakes decisions about young children that are based on tests.

Take the case of Amir Diego Howard, a bright third grader at Sierra Vista Elementary School. Amir's teacher thought he was a perfect candidate for the school district's gifted and talented (GT) program, so she referred him. Amir did well in the first two steps of the district's three-step process for admission into GT. First, Amir had his teacher's recommendation. Second, he scored at the 96th percentile on a national standardized achievement test. The third step was the problem. Amir failed to score an IQ of 133 on the Kaufman Brief Intelligence Test. "Sometimes they gave me these huge words that I don't even know," said Amir about the IQ test. "Like 'autobiography.' I don't know what that means. I'm only in the third grade." Unfortunately, across the country many language minority children like Amir fail to get into GT programs. Tests used to establish admission criteria discriminate against English language learners and minority students. Frequently, children who are English language learners don't have the language and the background experiences so they are not going to do well on standardized tests many use to identify gifted children.

The good news is that increasing numbers of school districts are doing something about the inequities of high-stakes testing and how criteria for GT and other programs discriminate against English language learners. For example, districts are broadening and/or changing their criteria by doing the following:

- Placing more emphasis on nonverbal criteria such as learning styles and creative behavior
- Eliminating passing scores on high-stakes tests as a condition of program admission
- Placing more emphasis on teacher recommendations
- Changing admission criteria to ensure that more minority and ELL students are in GT programs
- Using language-free tests that don't discriminate against English language learners and minority children

CHILDREN WHO ARE ABUSED AND NEGLECTED

Many of our views of childhood are highly romanticized. We tend to believe that parents always love their children and enjoy caring for them. We envision family settings full of joy, happiness, and harmony. Unfortunately for many children, their parents, and society, these assumptions are not always true. In fact, the extent of child abuse is far greater than we might imagine. In 2013, there were 3.3 million reports of child abuse involving nearly six million children.[51] Abuse knows no religious, ethnic, age, or economic boundaries. Children of all races and ethnicities can be victims of child abuse. In 2013, nearly one-half of all victims of child abuse and neglect were Caucasian, one-fifth were African American, and one-fifth were Hispanic. Thirty-two percent of the victims of child abuse and neglect are under the age of four. Children whose parents are unemployed are twice as likely to be victims of child abuse and two to three times more likely to suffer from neglect than are children whose parents are employed. To that effect, children from low socioeconomic families have more than three times the rate of child abuse and seven times the rate of neglect compared to other children. Additionally, children who live with a single parent who has a live-in partner are eight times more susceptible to abuse and neglect than children who live with their married biological parents.[52]

CHILDREN AS PROPERTY

Child abuse is not new; it has been documented throughout history. The attitude that children are property partly accounts for this record. Parents have believed, and some still do, that they own their children and can do with them as they please. The extent to which children are abused is difficult to ascertain, but it is probably much greater than most people realize. Valid statistics are difficult to come by because definitions of child abuse and neglect differ from state to state and reports are categorized differently. Because of the increasing concern over child abuse, social agencies, hospitals, child care centers, and schools are becoming more involved in identification, treatment, and prevention of this national problem.

Public Law 93–247, the Child Abuse Prevention and Treatment Act, defines *child abuse and neglect* as the

> physical or mental injury, sexual abuse, negligent treatment or maltreatment of a child under the age of eighteen by a person who is responsible for the child's welfare under circumstances which indicate that the child's health or welfare is harmed or threatened thereby as determined in accordance with regulations prescribed by the secretary.[53]

In addition, all states have some kind of legal or statutory definition of child abuse and mistreatment, and many define penalties for child abuse.

DEFINITION OF ABUSE

As you can see from the Child Abuse and Treatment Act, there are many kinds of child abuse. The general definition of abuse includes physical abuse, neglect, emotional abuse, and sexual abuse.[54] Consider:

- Children younger than one year had the highest rate of victimization of 21.2 per 1,000 children.
- More than 78 percent of reported child fatalities as a result of abuse and neglect were caused by one or more of the child victim's parents.[55]

PHYSICAL ABUSE.   Physical abuse includes, but is not limited to, hitting with an open hand, closed fist, or another object (such as a strap or switch); punching; shaking; throwing; kicking; burning; stabbing; drowning; electrocuting; tying up; or choking.[56]

CHILD NEGLECT.   Neglect is distressingly common; in fact, of all the types of abuse, neglect is probably the most common. Of the children who suffer from abuse, 75 percent (531,413 children) are specifically victims of neglect, meaning a parent or guardian failed to provide for the child's basic needs. Forms of neglect include medical neglect, educational neglect, physical neglect, and emotional abuse.[57]

EMOTIONAL ABUSE.   Just as debilitating as physical abuse and neglect is *emotional abuse*, which occurs when parents, teachers, and others strip children of their self-esteem. Adults take away children's self-esteem by continually criticizing, belittling, screaming and nagging, verbally berating, creating fear, and intentionally and severely limiting opportunities. Because emotional abuse is difficult to define legally and difficult to document, the unfortunate consequence for emotionally abused children is that they are often left in a debilitating environment.

SEXUAL ABUSE.   Finally, sexual abuse is one of the most inherently deplorable abuses of children. Sexual abuse is far more common than we like to acknowledge, and it likely occurs more frequently than we are able to ascertain. In fact, over 30 percent of victims never disclose the experience to anyone. Of the children who do disclose their abuse, either when confronted by an adult or when reporting themselves, 80 percent initially deny abuse or are tentative in disclosing, and of those who do admit their abuse, 75 percent tell someone accidentally or inadvertently. Sadly, more than 20 percent of the children who have admitted they suffered from sexual abuse eventually recant out of shame, guilt, or adult pressure, even though the abuse occurred.[58]

As a result, we can only conservatively estimate that sexual abuse wounds 135,000 children nationwide per year. This means that 1 in 4 girls are sexually abused and 1 in 6 boys are sexually abused. Additionally, 1 in 5 children are solicited sexually while on the Internet.[59] It is a crime that children are often doubted when they report their abuse; people commonly think that they "make it up," but children only falsely report sexual abuse .5 percent of the time.[60] If a child tells you she is being abused, believe her!

A misleading myth is that children are abused by strangers. It is overwhelmingly more likely that they are abused by family members or other people they know and trust, which contributes to the underreporting of sexual abuse. In fact, 30 to 40 percent of victims are abused by a family member, and at least 50 percent are abused by someone outside of their families whom they know and trust. In addition, approximately 40 percent of sexually abused children are also abused by older or larger children whom they know and who were likely victims of abuse themselves. As a result, we know that only 10 percent are abused by strangers. These statistics tell us that we cannot and must not assume that our students go home to safe homes: You must be aware and vigilant to the signs of abuse and take steps to protect the children you teach.[61]

Figure 16.5 will help you identify abuse and neglect. Remember that the presence of a single characteristic does not necessarily indicate abuse. You should observe a child's behavior and appearance over a period of time.

REPORTING CHILD ABUSE

As a teacher you are a mandatory reporter of child abuse. Other mandatory reporters include physicians, nurses, social workers, counselors, and psychologists. Each state has its own procedures and set of policies for reporting child abuse. It can be intimidating to report abuse, but just remember, 70 percent of child sex offenders have anywhere between one to nine victims and at least 20 percent have ten to forty victims; a

Physical Indicators

- Unexplained Bruises and Welts:
  - on face, lips, mouth
  - on torso, back, buttock, thighs
  - in various stages of healing
  - clustered, forming regular patterns
  - reflecting shape of article used to inflict (electric cord, belt buckle)
  - on several different surface areas
  - regularly appear after absence, weekend or vacation
- Unexplained Burns:
  - cigar, cigarette burns, especially on soles, palms, back or buttocks
  - immersion burns (sock-like, glove-like doughnut shaped on buttocks or genitalia)
  - patterns like electric burner, iron, etc.
  - rope burns on arms, legs, neck or torso
- Unexplained Fractures:
  - to skull, nose, facial structure
  - in various stages of healing
  - multiple or spiral fractures
- Unexplained Lacerations or Abrasion:
  - to mouth, lips, gums or eyes
  - to external genitalia

Physical Abuse

Behavioral Indicators

- Wary of adult contact
- Apprehensive when other children cry
- Behavior extremes:
  - Aggressiveness
  - Withdrawal
- Frightened of parents
- Reports injury by parents

Physical Indicators

- Difficulty walking or sitting
- Torn, stained or bloody underclothing
- Pain or itching in genital area
- Bruises or bleeding in external genitalia, vaginal or anal areas
- Venereal disease, especially in pre-teens
- Pregnancy

Behavioral Indicators

- Unwilling to change for gym or participate in PE
- Withdrawal, fantasy or infantile behavior
- Bizarre, sophisticated, or unusual sexual behavior or knowledge
- Poor peer relationships
- Delinquency or run away reports of sexual abuse by caretaker

Sexual Abuse

Physical Indicators

- Consistent hunger, poor hygiene, inappropriate dress
- Consistent lack of supervision, especially in dangerous activities or long periods
- Constant fatigue or listlessness
- Unattended physical problems or medical needs
- Abandonment

Behavioral Indicators

- Begging, stealing food
- Extended stays at school (early arrival and late departure)
- Consistently falling asleep in class
- Delinquency (e.g., thefts)
- State there is no caretaker

Physical Neglect

Physical Indicators

- Habit disorders (sucking, biting, rocking, etc.)
- Conduct disorders (antisocial, destructive, etc.)
- Neurotic traits (sleep disorders, speech disorders, inhibition of play)
- Psychoneurotic reactions (hysteria, obsession, compulsion, phobias, hypochondria)

Behavioral Indicators

- Behavior Extremes:
  - Compliant, passive
  - Aggressive, demanding
- Overly Adoptive Behavior:
  - Inappropriately adult
  - Developmental lags (physical, mental, emotional)
  - Attempted suicide

Emotional Maltreatment

FIGURE 16.5 | Indicators of Abuse

Source: The Parenting Education Resource Center, Prevent Child Abuse–New Jersey, http://www.PreventChildAbuseNJ.org.

serial child molester may have as many as four hundred victims in his or her lifetime.[62] So when you report abuse of any kind, but particularly sexual abuse, you are not only helping the one child you know about, but many, many others as well. Therefore, you need to be very familiar with your state and district policies about how to identify child abuse and how to report it.

The following guidelines should govern your response to a child with suspected abuse or neglect:

- *Remain calm:* A child may retract information or stop talking if he or she senses a strong reaction.
- *Believe the child:* Children rarely make up stories about abuse.
- *Listen without passing judgment:* Most children know their abusers and often have conflicted feelings.
- *Tell the child you are glad that he or she told someone.*
- *Assure the child that abuse is not his or her fault.*
- *Do what you can to make certain that the child is safe from further abuse.*
- *Do not investigate the case yourself:* Call the police or the child and family services agency.

How child abuse is reported varies from state to state. In Washington, DC, for example, if child abuse or neglect is suspected, you are to call the reporting hotline immediately at (202) 671-SAFE. To make a report, you would need to provide the following information:

- Name, age, sex, and address of the child who is the subject of the report, and names of any siblings and the parent, guardian, or caregiver
- Nature and extent of the abuse or neglect, as you know it (and any previous abuse or neglect)
- Any additional information that may help establish the cause and identity of persons responsible
- Your name, occupation, contact information, and a statement of any actions taken concerning the child

CHILDREN WHO ARE HOMELESS

While walking down a city street, you may have encountered homeless men and women, but have you seen a homeless child? Homeless children are the neglected, forgotten, often abandoned segment of the growing homeless population in the United States. The National Center on Family Homelessness estimates that there are as many as 1.62 million homeless children, living either with homeless families or on their own. This translates to 1 out of every 45 of your students being homeless. And sadly, children are the fastest-growing population among the homeless.[63]

CHILD OUTCOMES OF BEING HOMELESS

Homelessness has long-lasting and devastating effects upon children. They have at least twice as much traumatic stress, overall health problems, and emotional disturbances than do children who are not homeless. Many do not know where they will be sleeping at night, what they will get to eat the next day, or even if they will get to eat at all. Homeless children are more likely to suffer from nightmares, be teased by classmates, and have trouble staying awake during the day. As you can imagine, homelessness and its ramifications drastically affect not only children's personal and developmental well-being, but their school performance as well. Homeless children are less likely to graduate and thus are more likely to perpetuate the homeless cycle. School is difficult for children who are homeless. They exhibit such problem behaviors as short attention spans, weak impulse control, withdrawal, aggression, speech delays, and regressive behavior. They are at greater risk for health problems, and if they do enter school, they face many problems related to previous school experience (e.g., grade failure) and attendance (e.g., long trips to attend school). Grades and academic success suffer, and as a result, so does their self-esteem. Homelessness results in developmental delays and contributes to higher levels of adult homelessness.[64] Fortunately, more agencies are now responding to the unique needs of homeless children and their families.

Public Law 107–110, the McKinney-Vento Homeless Assistance Act of 2001, provides that "each State educational agency shall assure that each child of a homeless individual and each homeless youth has access to the same free, appropriate public education, including a public preschool education, as provided to other children and youth."[65]

COMBATING HOMELESSNESS

Some school districts have aggressively taken on this epidemic to combat homelessness. Here are some things that they have done:

- Nationwide, the McKinney-Vento Homeless Assistance Act requires school districts to establish "liaisons" between children who are homeless and their schools. In Richmond, California, an organization named Families in Transition (FIT) uses liaisons to identify and aid children who are homeless. FIT not only builds community ties, but also monitors homeless children's school attendance and grades.

- In Albuquerque, New Mexico, the school districts use liaisons to gain grant funding and to implement summer school programs, career programs, biweekly free tutoring, support groups, and free food programs for children who are homeless.[66] The mission statement of the Albuquerque Public Schools says that their project "shall provide the means, motivation, and encouragement needed for homeless students to reach their potentials as productive members of society in an educational environment that treats all students with dignity and respect."[67]

- In Minneapolis, Minnesota, the school districts (MPS) have taken steps to ensure that homeless students can stay enrolled in one school continuously by providing free transportation, whether by taxi, bus, or school bus, regardless of the pick-up or drop-off site. The schools train staff to recognize the signs of children who are between homes so that they can get them help. MPS also provides brand new backpacks and school supplies for homeless children, as well as allocating a certain amount of their funding to keep homeless children involved in extracurricular activities like sports, dance, music, and art.[68]

IMPLICATIONS FOR TEACHING   Regardless of where you teach and your district's policies, there are things you can do in your classroom and your community to aid children who are homeless:

- Challenge your own conception of homelessness. Regardless of your beliefs about adults who are homeless and accompanying stereotypes, children are not responsible for their families' poverty or home situations. Treat students and their families who are having economic difficulties respectfully and professionally, with empathy and an open mind.

- Know the signs of homelessness.

- Once you've identified children in your classroom who are homeless or are at risk to become so, you should do the following:

  - Stop teasing and bullying of children who are homeless.

  - Be careful of the language you use. If organizing outreach efforts in your classroom for homelessness, such as canned food drives and clothing drives, refer to circumstances in respectful and neutral ways.

- Don't single out children who are homeless.
- Encourage children who are homeless to participate in tasks that they enjoy and excel in to build their self-esteem.
- Make school feel safe, inviting, and consistent. To do so, maintain a routine, assure and reassure children when they are in doubt or afraid, and be available to listen to and encourage them. Provide them with a means to be expressive.
- Encourage children who are homeless to use the school counselor so that their emotional and developmental needs are met.
- In and out of the classroom setting, respect children and their families' privacy and wishes. Some parents and/or children do not want to be identified as homeless because of the stereotypes and stigmas attached. If a child does not wish to be identified as homeless, refrain from doing so to protect his or her privacy. Discuss with parents their wishes and how best to get them the help they need.
- Be an advocate. If one does not already exist in your school, work to establish a task force that incorporates social workers, school counselors, principals, teachers, parents, community members, and local businesses. Homelessness does not just affect one or two of us; when it affects our children, it affects us all. Follow Minneapolis's and Albuquerque's lead and encourage your task force to implement similar strategies. Be both creative and practical in order to build on these examples. Work with national and local groups to obtain funds and resources for your students who are homeless.

ACCOMMODATING DIVERSE LEARNERS

autism spectrum disorder A neurological developmental disorder characterized by a deficit in communication and social interactions, as well as by the presence of restricted and repetitive behaviors.

receptive language An individual whose skills appear to be typical but who has difficulty expressing himself or herself; interactions with peers are often contentious or stilted because of the difficulty of diverting from his or her own plans or adapting to peers' perspective.

social story A personalized, detailed, and simple script that breaks down behavior and provides rules and directions.

Meet Sean. He has just turned four years old and was diagnosed with **autism spectrum disorder**, a neurological developmental disorder characterized by a deficit in communication and social interactions as well as by the presence of restricted and repetitive behaviors. Sean is very attached to routine, and although his **receptive language** skills appear to be typical—he can understand spoken, written, or visual communication—he has difficulty expressing himself. In addition, Sean's social interactions with peers are often contentious or stilted because he has difficulty diverting from his own plans or adapting to his peers' perspective. How will you accommodate Sean in your classroom? One way you can help Sean acclimate to your classroom rules and routines is for you to write a **social story** for him. A social story is a personalized, detailed, and simple script that breaks down behavior and provides rules and directions. Social stories can range from drawings featuring stick figures, to computer images, or even better, to digital photos featuring Sean. To write a social story, follow these steps:

Step 1: Identify a behavior or activity you want Sean to comply with. You can use social stories to modify any kind of behavior, from toileting to peer interactions to transitions. However, each social story should focus on one thing at a time. For example, Sean is having difficulty transitioning from his mother's car to your classroom and the morning routine. Before writing the social story, observe Sean and talk with his parents to learn why the home-to-school transition is difficult for him. Is he concerned that his mother won't come back for him? Does Sean understand what will happen next? Are all transitions a source of worry for him? You will use this information to write Sean's social story.

Step 2: Write on the first page: "This is Sean." Use a picture of Sean. You can draw it and label it or use an actual photo. The photo should depict a part of Sean's life he will recognize. If he brings a Spider-Man action figure to school every day, have Spider-Man in the picture.

Step 3: Write on the second page: "On Monday morning, Sean gets into Mommy's car to come to school." Include a photo of Sean getting into his mother's car.

Always use the child's own language. Sean calls his mother "Mommy," so you use the word "Mommy." Keep in mind that different cultures use different words for parents. For example, Ali, whose parents are from Pakistan, calls his father "Abba." Contact Sean's parents and ask them questions about the words he uses. For Sean, using his language makes the story more real, more personal, and reinforces the importance of communication.

This is Sean.

On Monday morning, Sean gets into Mommy's car to come to school.

Step 4: Provide routines. Children with autism tend to like routines because they provide predictability. Sean's mother shares with you that if she takes a different route to school, Sean has a meltdown. As a result, driving to school can be a daily trauma.

Sometimes Mommy drives one way to school. If Mommy drives a new way to school, I will be safe. Mommy will keep Sean safe.

If I feel worried, I can say, 'I am safe and I am still going to school' or 'It's okay if Mommy goes a different way. I am still going to school.'

Step 5: On the third page, write: "Sometimes Mommy drives one way to school. If Mommy drives a new way to school, I will be safe. Mommy will keep Sean safe. If I feel worried, I can say, 'I am safe and I am still going to school' or 'It's OK if Mommy goes a different way. I am still going to school.'" Use a picture of Sean giving the "OK" or "thumbs-up" sign inside a car.

Step 6: Write on the fourth page: "When Sean gets to school, he can say, 'Bye Mommy, see you soon!'" Use a picture of Sean with a big smile on his face waving good-bye. Social stories are a behavior model and a linguistic script, so whenever you use them be sure to model the behavior you wish to reinforce.

If Sean is very attuned to time, instead of saying "See you soon," you can include the time his mother will return, saying "See you in three hours at 12 o'clock!" Use a picture of his mother next to a picture of a clock showing the correct time on the same page.

Step 7: Write on the fifth page: "Sean's job is to go to school. Sean can say, 'Hi, (teacher's name).'" Take a picture of yourself and insert it here.

Step 8: If Sean's next step in the routine is to hang up his backpack, give him instructions for hanging up his backpack. On the sixth page write: "Sean can hang his backpack on his hook. Now it is time to sit down." Use a picture of his hook with an arrow pointing to the next task of sitting down.

Step 9: If Sean does not know how to greet his classmates, it is important to provide him with the steps and the words to do so. On the seventh page write: "When I sit down, I can say 'Hi, Johnny!'" Use a picture of his classmates waving or giving high fives.

Step 10: Follow the same steps to make pages for Tuesday, Wednesday, Thursday, and Friday.

Social stories focus on the behavior you want Sean to use, not on negative behavior. Once you have written the social story, set aside time during the day to read it with Sean. Tell him that you made this very special book just for him. The first day, read it several times. You should read a social story as if it were a picture book with all the inflection and emotion you wish to model. Have Sean practice saying the words with you. Make a copy and send it home with Sean. Ask his parents to read it at home a few times but especially before bedtime and right before he leaves for school in the morning. On the drive over, have Sean's mother let him hold the book and read it to himself. The first few days you use the new story, read it with him as he gets out of the car. Eventually Sean will not need this added support.

Reflect and Apply: IEP

ACTIVITIES FOR PROFESSIONAL DEVELOPMENT

ETHICAL DILEMMA

BOY IN A DUFFEL BAG!

Shortly after six-year-old Chris left for school, his mother, Amy Baker, received a phone call from school asking her to come and pick up Chris because he was "jumping off the walls." Chris has autism and is in a special education class to help meet his needs. Amy rushed to the school and hurried down the hallway toward the classroom door. Outside the classroom, she heard Chris crying out "Mama, mama." Amy couldn't believe her ears! Her son's voice was coming from a duffel bag outside the classroom door. Amy frantically untied the duffel bag drawstrings and pulled Chris out. When Amy demanded an explanation from teachers and school administration, they downplayed the whole issue. They said they put Chris in a "therapy bag to calm him down." Amy became indignant, "Therapy bag or duffel bag, it's all the same to me! Why would anyone put Chris in a bag? If this school thinks they are getting away with this, they've got another thought coming!"

What should Amy do? Start a website petition asking for people to sign up to attend the next school board meeting? Or, should Amy contact the Council for Exceptional Children and see if they can help? Or, should Amy pull Chris from the public schools, place him in a private school, and forget the whole thing? Or, should Amy go to the local television stations and request air time to let her explain to the public what is really going on in their schools? What should Amy do? What would you do?

ACTIVITIES TO APPLY WHAT YOU LEARNED

1. **KEY ASSESSMENT:** Visit an inclusive classroom and observe a child with a special need during playtime. Develop an observational checklist to guide your observation. Note the materials available, the physical arrangement of the environment, and the number of other children involved. Try to determine whether the child is really engaged in the play activity. Hypothesize about why the child is or is not engaged. Make three recommendations for how you would ensure the full inclusion and engagement of this child in your classroom. Discuss your observations online in a PowerPoint, Prezi or other technological application with your colleagues. Use the rubric provided to guide your work.

2. Five-year-old Mackenzie is in your kindergarten class. Mackenzie is a high achiever, she loves to learn. She learns new things quickly and has an excellent memory. What are three ways that you can support Mackenzie's learning? Skype with a teacher and ask for advice and suggestions.

3. Get in touch with a local play therapist or child welfare agency and ask for information about how best to help a child in your classroom who has been sexually abused. Prepare a five-minute presentation on preventing sexual abuse for your class. Include your information in your presentation.

4. Conduct an Internet search to discover the state of homeless children in your area. Are you surprised by how many (or how few) there are? Why or why not? Collaborate with your classmates and develop a plan for how to raise awareness in your school district about homelessness. Post your plan on Facebook and ask for community help.

5. Create a social story to address an issue (other than transitioning) that children with autism typically have, using the steps and techniques described in this text. Compile the social stories of your classmates into a booklet and make copies so you all have a set of social stories for your future classrooms.

LINKING TO LEARNING

The following agencies and programs, which can be located easily online, provide additional information about topics discussed in this chapter.

Council for Exceptional Children

The council publishes extremely up-to-date news regarding education-related legislation; its website contains numerous links to other sites.

Council for Learning Disabilities

This is an international organization of and for professionals who represent diverse disciplines and who are committed to enhancing the education and life span development of individuals with learning disabilities. The council establishes standards of excellence and promotes innovative strategies for research and practice through interdisciplinary collegiality, collaboration, and advocacy.

National Association for the Education of Homeless Children and Youth (NAEHCY)

NAEHCY is a professional organization specifically dedicated to homeless education. It was established to ensure research-based strategies for effective approaches to the problems faced by homeless children, youth, and families. NAEHCY has created guidelines, goals, and objectives that outline strategies for dealing with government agencies and designing effective programs.

National Dissemination Center for Children with Disabilities

The dissemination and referral center provides information on disabilities and disability-related issues for families, educators, and other professionals.

Office of Special Education and Rehabilitation Services

This U.S. Department of Education office supports programs that assist in educating children with special needs, provides for the rehabilitation of youth and adults with disabilities, and supports research to improve the lives of individuals with disabilities.

Prevent Child Abuse America (PCA)

The PCA is a volunteer organization of concerned citizens that works with community, state, and national groups to expand and disseminate knowledge about child abuse prevention.

Teaching Children with Attention Deficit Hyperactivity Disorder

This organization's website provides many excellent ideas and specific strategies for teaching students with ADHD.

U.S. Department of Health & Human Services Administration for Children & Families

This governmental agency helps coordinate and develop programs and policies concerning child abuse and neglect.

CHAPTER

17

PARENTS, FAMILIES, and the COMMUNITY

Building Partnerships for Student Success

LEARNING OUTCOMES

1. Explain how the collaborative partnerships between families, schools, and communities are changing.
2. Explain how changes in parents and families influence teachers, schools, and you.
3. Identify the six types of parent involvement and explain how you can use each one.
4. Identify the community resources that are available to help you meet the needs of children and families.
5. Develop a plan to address absenteeism in your classroom and school.
6. Construct a plan to accommodate the needs of diverse learners in your classroom.

NAEYC STANDARDS

A positive and convincing relationship exists between family involvement and benefits for students, including improved academic achievement. This relationship holds across families of all economic, racial/ethnic, and educational backgrounds, as well as students of all ages. Students with involved parents, no matter their background, are more likely to earn higher grades and test scores, adapt well to school, attend regularly, have better social skills and behavior, and graduate and go on to higher education. Family involvement also has a protective effect; the more families can support their children's progress, the better their children do in school and the longer they stay in school.[1]

The public believes that nothing has a greater effect on students' level of achievement than parents. In fact, the public thinks that parents matter more than teachers![2] This makes parental involvement in children's education a huge priority for the nation's schools.

NEW VIEWS OF PARENT/ FAMILY PARTNERSHIPS

Schooling used to consist mostly of teaching children social and basic academic skills. But as society has changed, so has the content of schooling. Early childhood programs have assumed many parental functions and responsibilities, and now they also help parents and families with educational and social issues that affect them and their children in their daily lives.

PARENT EDUCATION–PARENT UNIVERSITIES

Parent–school cooperation, collaboration, and education are the new normal in many elementary schools across the country. One increasingly popular approach is for schools to conduct a **Parent University**, which provides parents knowledge and skills on a wide variety of topics. The Washoe County Nevada School District's Parent University offers sessions called Born to Learn, which help parents support their children's learning; Family Story Teller, designed to help parents read to their children; and Math and Parent Partnerships, in which teachers and parents work in teams to help parents understand new math.[3] At Hope-Centennial Elementary in Palm Beach County, Florida, the school operates a Parent University that helps parents inspire their children. Principal Julie Hopkins said she needs the involvement of her parents in their child's education and behavior to make the school a better place.[4]

Karen Marler, principal of Lacoochee (Florida) Elementary, helps parents take ownership of their children's education in order to increase student achievement. Teodora Romero wanted to help her children succeed in school, but she didn't know how. A Mexican immigrant who speaks almost exclusively Spanish, Romero felt overwhelmed by the assignments her third-grade son Luis and kindergarten daughter Berniece brought home. So, Principal Marler developed Parent University, which offers classes to help parents help their children and themselves. Classes include Help Children Read, Volunteering at School, and Parent Involvement.[5]

ACCOUNTABILITY AND REFORM

Current accountability and reform movements have convinced families that they should no longer be kept out of their children's schools. Families believe their children have a right to effective, high-quality teaching and care by high-quality

teachers.[6] Parents have become more militant in their demands for high-quality education. Schools and other agencies have responded by seeking ways to involve families in this quest for quality. Educators and families realize that mutual cooperation is in everyone's best interest.[7]

INVOLVEMENT CAUSES INVESTMENT

Research concerning parent involvement generally looks at the effects parent and family involvement has on child outcomes such as achievement, school attendance, and so forth. However, new research sheds light on the effects of parent involvement on parents themselves and how those effects in turn benefit children. Researchers investigated Head Start's parent involvement program and found that parent participation increases parents' involvement with their children. In other words, parent involvement encourages parents to "invest" themselves in their children. This investment takes the form of parents being more attentive to their children and being willing to spend more time with them in reading to them, doing math activities, and so forth.[8]

IMPLICATIONS FOR TEACHING

- Because parents are more likely to "invest" in their children when they are involved means that you should make every effort to involve *all* parents in your program.
- Begin early when involving parents—before the school year begins or at the very beginning of the school year. For example, first grade teacher, Carrie Jostmeyer, in Frisco (Texas) ISD calls every one of her students' parents and talks about the child's first day; tells parents how proud she is to be their child's teacher and invites the parents to come and visit and be involved in the child's classroom.
- Be a strong advocate for parents enrolling their children in preschool and other programs. This helps ensure that parents are involved and engaged early in the schooling process. As a result, they will invest in their children earlier.[9]

CHANGING FAMILIES: CHANGING INVOLVEMENT

The family of today is not the family of yesterday, nor will the family of today be the family of tomorrow. Family structures are changing in front of our eyes! Many children live with stepparents and have stepsiblings and half-siblings. Families are more diverse owing to divorce, separation, nonmarriages, international adoptions, and foster parenting. Families have single moms and dads and boyfriends and girlfriends who choose not to get married. Extended families include aunts, uncles, cousins, and others.

We know the importance of meeting the needs of *all* children in today's early childhood education and care settings. Here, we emphasize involving *all* families in school and community programs to help all children be successful. In the following sections, you will read about different family compositions and tips for involving all children and their families in school.

SINGLE-PARENT FAMILIES

The three main reasons for the changing American family are divorce, single parenthood, and changing laws and societal attitudes about marriage and families. In 2012, 41 percent of all births were to single women of all ages.[10] Depending on where you teach, as many as 50 percent of your children could be from single-parent families. Nationally, 26.3 percent of children in the United States live in single-parent families. More couples are choosing to bear children without getting married; there are

an estimated 13.7 million single parents in the United States who have custody of 21.8 million children. Most single parents with primary custody are women (82.6 percent).[11] About a quarter of single-parent family households live at or below poverty level.[12] This trend in childbearing and parenting will continue, and it has tremendous implications for you and how you involve single-parent families.

IMPLICATIONS FOR TEACHING

Tips for Involving Single Parents. With the above facts in mind, here are some things you can do to ensure that you involve single-parent families:

- *Accommodate family schedules by arranging conferences and events at times other than during the workday—perhaps early morning, noon, late afternoon, or early evening.* Some employers, sensitive to these needs, give release time to participate in school functions, but others do not. In addition, talk with your school administration about going to families, rather than having families always come to you and other teachers.

- *Remember, single parents have a limited amount of time to spend on involvement with their children's school and with their children at home.* When you talk with single-parent families, make sure that (1) the meeting starts on time, (2) you have a list of items to discuss, (3) you have sample materials available to illustrate all points, (4) you make specific suggestions relative to one-parent environments, and (5) the meeting ends on time. Because one-parent families are more likely to need child care assistance to attend meetings, plan for child care for every parent meeting or activity.

- *Suggest some ways single parents can make their time with their children meaningful.* As an early childhood teacher, you are expected to assist parents by providing them information to help their children in the best ways possible. For example, if a child has trouble following directions, show families how to use home situations to help in this area. Suggest that children can learn to follow directions by assigning responsibilities such as helping with errands, meal preparation, or housework.

- *Get to know families' lifestyles and living conditions.* From a professional standpoint, you want to be able to provide families with valid and reliable information based on their situations and circumstances. For instance, you can recommend that every child have a quiet place to study; but this may be an impossible demand for some households. Visit some of the homes in your community before you set meeting times; decide what family involvement activities to implement; and determine what you will ask of families during the year. All early childhood professionals need to keep in mind the condition of the home environment when they request that children bring certain items to school or carry out certain tasks at home. And, when asking for parents' help, be sensitive to their talents and time constraints.

- *Help develop support groups for single-parent families within your school, such as discussion groups and classes on parenting.* Be sure to consider the needs and abilities of single-parent families in your family involvement activities and programs. After all, single-parent families may represent the majority of families in your classroom.

- *Offer opportunities for single parents to volunteer time or services to the school.* For example, single mother Sarah Thomas is recognized as Bay City School District Volunteer of the Year. Sarah makes sure her two children witness her volunteering. Sarah believes volunteering is more than talking, it's doing for others—and that the more parents participate, the more everyone benefits.

FATHERS

More fathers are involved in parenting responsibilities today than ever before; in fact, more than one-fifth of preschool children are cared for by their fathers while their mothers work outside the home.[13] Fathers head 17.4 percent of single-parent families.[14] In addition, half of all U.S. children won't live with their fathers for part of their childhoods.[15] Nonetheless, many of these "nonresident" dads want to be and are involved with their children. The implication is clear: You and other early childhood professionals must make special efforts to involve all fathers in their programs.

More professionals now recognize that fathering and mothering are complementary processes. Many fathers are competent caregivers, directly supervising children, helping set the tone for family life, providing stability in a relationship, supporting a mother's parenting role and career goals, and representing a masculine role model for the children. And more fathers are turning to professional organizations such as the National Fatherhood Initiative (NFI), which offer online resources, tips, and a community for fathers to voice their concerns and seek help. The NFI also offers school-based programming and school-based organizations to build a foundation for father involvement. By encouraging father involvement, schools reap the benefits of safer, healthier communities, and a richer educational experience for children. When dads are involved, children get higher grades, have fewer behavioral problems, and are more likely to stay in school.[16]

There are many styles of fathering. Some fathers are at home while their spouses work; some are frequently absent because their work requires travel; some have primary custody of their children; some are single; some dominate home life and are controlling; some are passive and exert little influence in the home; some take little interest in their homes and families; some are surrogate parents; some are equal partners with their spouses in raising their children. There are as many kinds of fathering as there are fathers!

IMPLICATIONS FOR TEACHING

Ideas for Involving Fathers. Regardless of the roles fathers play, make special efforts to involve them. Here are some father-friendly ideas you can use to encourage their involvement:

- *Invite fathers to your class or program.* Make sure they are included in all your parent/family initiatives.
- *Make fathers feel welcome in your program.* For example, kindergarten students at Palm Pointe Elementary celebrated Father's Day with their dads by participating in "Donuts with Dad." Students presented their dads with arts and crafts to show appreciation for all fathers.
- *Send a simple survey home to fathers.* Ask them how they would like to be involved in their children's education. Keep in mind the six types of parent/family involvement shown in Figure 17.1, which we will discuss later.
- *Include books and other literature about dads in your classroom library.* Two good books are as follows:
  - *My Father Knows the Names of Things* by Jane Yolen. A child celebrates his father's expertise. Not only does dad know "a dozen . . . words for night," he knows about soaps, dinosaurs, bugs, and flowers.[17]
  - *My Father is Taller Than a Tree* by Joseph Bruiac. Thirteen unique father-and-son pairs who come from diverse backgrounds and live in different places. Even though the dads are not all the same, their relationships show us an

important truth: Even the simplest and most familiar activities become special when dads and kids do them together.[18]

- *Consider special programs.* For example, WATCH D.O.G.S. (Dads of Great Students) is the father involvement initiative of the National Center for Fathering that organizes fathers and father figures to provide positive male role models for the students and to enhance school security. Today, more than 2,811 active programs in forty-six states participate in the WATCH D.O.G.S. Program. At Green Valley (PA) Elementary[19] each day, a different student's father volunteers, arriving at 8:30 a.m. and staying until dismissal. Fathers walk the hallways, attend classes, play at recess, and help as needed. Fathers as role models are an important influence in the lives of many children today.

Check Your Understanding: Dads

MULTIGENERATIONAL FAMILIES

In January 2009, the nation and the world watched the new, *multigenerational* First Family move into the White House. President Barack Obama, the First Lady, Michelle Obama, their two daughters, and the First Grandmother, Marian Robinson, represent an emerging trend in today's families. **Multigenerational families** are those in which three or more generations share a common housing unit. Multigenerational households are making a significant comeback owing to the effects of the Great Recession on families and as demographic shifts change how families live.

multigenerational families Living arrangements in which three or more generations share a common housing unit.

GRANDPARENTS AS PARENTS.   More children than ever are living with their grandparents. Reasons for this increase include parental drug use, divorce, mental and physical illness, abandonment, teenage pregnancy, child abuse and neglect, incarceration, and death. One in 8 twenty-two- to twenty-nine-year-olds say that because of the Great Recession, they have boomeranged back to live with their parents after being on their own.[20] A record 49 million Americans, or 16.1 percent of the total U.S. population, live in a family household that contains at least two adult generations or a grandparent and at least one other generation.[21]

Many children today are *skipped-generation children*, meaning that neither of their parents is living with them and they are living with their grandparents or in some other living arrangement. About 1 in 14 U.S children live with a grandparent. In these **grandfamilies**, another term for children living with their grandparents, grandparents provide the primary care and education for their grandchildren. Grandparents in these skipped-generation households have all of the parenting responsibilities of parents, providing for their grandchildren's basic needs and care, as well as making sure that they do well in school. As a result, these grandparents need your support and educational assistance.

grandfamilies Children living with their grandparents.

Grandparents who open their homes to their grandchildren are often divided into two types of households—three-generational and skipped generation—reflecting different family situations, needs, and concerns.

Three-generation households include grandparents, adult children, and grandchildren. These households tend to form in response to financial difficulties, illness, divorce, adolescent childbearing, and in some instances, out of the grandparents' desire to help their children and grandchildren. A national survey of multigenerational household members (including those in three-generation households) cited unemployment and underemployment, health care costs, and home foreclosures among the top reasons for moving in together.[22]

Grandparents acting as parents for their grandchildren are a growing reality in the United States today. What are some things you can do to ensure that grandparents will have the educational assistance and support they need so that their grandchildren will be successful in school?

IDEAS FOR INVOLVING GRANDPARENTS. You must help grandparents learn to parent all over again, keeping in mind that they are rearing their grandchildren in a whole different generation from the one in which they reared their children. In addition, many grandparents are very unfamiliar with today's schools and what is involved.

IMPLICATIONS FOR TEACHING. Here are some things you can do to help grandparents help themselves and their grandchildren.

- Offer grandparents the same parent involvement opportunities you offer all parents. After all, they have many of the same needs as all parents who are trying to do their best by their children.

- Provide refresher parenting courses to help grandparents understand how children and schooling have changed since they reared their children.
- Link grandparents to support groups, such as Raising Our Children's Children (ROCC) and the American Association of Retired Persons (AARP) Grandparent Information Center.
- Offer grandparents opportunities to engage with children academically and socially. Many universities offer Grandparent University, where grandparents can relive memories of being at a university and their grandchildren can experience what college has to offer—dorm life, food, and classes. For example, children or grandchildren of Oklahoma State University (OSU) alumni are invited to OSU's Grandparent University summer program. Students choose from the fourteen majors available, including architecture, broadcasting, and horticulture, and also stay in dorms, attend classes in their major, and participate in campus activities.[23]

LINGUISTICALLY DIVERSE PARENTS AND FAMILIES

linguistically diverse parents Individuals whose English proficiency is minimal and who lack a comprehensive knowledge of the norms and social systems in the United States.

Linguistically diverse parents are individuals whose English proficiency is minimal and who may lack a deep knowledge of the norms and social systems in the United States. Linguistically diverse families often face language and cultural barriers that greatly hamper their ability to become actively involved in their children's education, although many have a great desire and willingness to participate.

Because the culture of linguistically diverse families often differs from that of the majority in a community, those who seek a truly collaborative involvement must take into account the cultural features that inhibit collaboration. Styles of child rearing and family organization, attitudes toward schooling, organizations around which families center their lives, life goals and values, political influences, and methods of communication within the cultural group all have implications for parent participation.

Linguistically diverse families often lack information about the U.S. educational system, including basic school philosophy, practices, and structure—which can result in misconceptions, fear, and a general reluctance to become involved. Furthermore, the U.S. educational system may be quite different from the ones these families are used to. In fact, they may have been taught to avoid active involvement in the educational process, preferring to leave all decisions concerning their children's education to professionals.

The U.S. ideal of a community-controlled and community-supported educational system must be explained to families from cultures in which this concept is not so highly valued. The traditional roles of children, teachers, and administrators in the United States also have to be explained. Many families need to learn to assume their roles and obligations associated with their children's schooling.

IMPLICATIONS FOR TEACHING

- Go where the families are—to their homes and neighborhoods. Churches and community centers are often comfortable places to interact with and inform parents.
- Communicate with linguistically diverse parents in their native language.
- Validate the cultures and languages of parents and children.
- Learn the cultures of your children and families.
- Talk to parents about their cultures. Ask them to help you incorporate their languages and customs in your classroom.
- Link parents with parents. Have parents who are involved in your school help new parents get comfortable and involved.

TEENAGE PARENTS

Teenage pregnancy is declining and is at its lowest rate in two decades. Nonetheless, teenage pregnancy rates are still cause for alarm. Consider these facts:

- 367,752 births occurred to mothers aged fifteen to nineteen years, a birthrate of 34.3 per 1,000 women in this age group.[24]
- As a group, Latino teenagers have the highest birthrate, with 56 births per 1,000.[25]
- Among the states, Mississippi has the highest birthrate of teens fifteen to nineteen years of age, with 68 births per 1,000. New Mexico is second, with 64 per 1,000, and Texas is third with 63 per 1,000. The national teen birthrate average is 42 per 1,000.[26]

From a public policy perspective this has the following implications:

- Pregnancy and birth are significant contributors to high school dropout rates among girls. Only about 50 percent of teen mothers receive a high school diploma.
- The children of teenage mothers are more likely to have lower school achievement, drop out of school, have more health problems, be incarcerated at some time during adolescence, give birth as a teenager, and face unemployment as a young adult.[27]

From an early childhood point of view, teenage pregnancies create greater demand for infant/toddler child care and for programs to help teenagers learn how to be good parents.

SUPPORTING AND HELPING TEENAGE PARENTS. At one time, most teenage parents were married, but today, most are not. Teenage parents come from culturally and linguistically diverse backgrounds. Despite society's advances over the last few decades, for teen moms, not much has changed. Two-thirds of teenage mothers live in poverty; less than 50 percent graduate high school; and only 2 percent of girls who are moms by the age of eighteen will graduate college by the age of thirty.[28] Furthermore, more teenage mothers are choosing to raise their children with assistance from their mothers and grandmothers. Regardless of their circumstances, teenage parents have the following needs:

- ***Support in their role as parents.*** Support can include information about child-rearing practices and child development and help in implementing the information in their interactions with their children. Teen Parents of Lubbock (Texas) enrolls young mothers age twelve to twenty-one years in weekly education meetings and monthly social activities or playdates with their mentor moms. The program enables teenagers to meet other young mothers like themselves and be in a support network that keeps them focused on school while raising their children.[29]

- *Support in their continuing development as adolescents and young adults.* Remember that younger teenage parents are really children themselves. They need assistance in meeting their own developmental needs, as well as those of their children. In spite of the reality television programs such as *Teen Mom* and *16 and Pregnant* that glamorize teen moms, they need a great deal of help and support.
- *Help with completing their education.* Some early childhood programs provide parenting courses as well as classes designed to help teenage parents complete requirements for a high school diploma. Remember that a critical influence on children's development and achievement is the mother's education level. For example, the Tupelo (Mississippi) School District offers the Link Centre, a high school advancement academy for teenage mothers so they can continue their education while receiving additional help, like parenting skills, not received in a traditional classroom.[30]

As early childhood programs enroll more children of teenage families, they must seek ways to creatively and sensitively involve these families.

- *Know what each parent in your program wants for his or her child.* Find out families' goals. What are their caregiving practices? What concerns do they have about their child? Encourage parents to talk about all of this, to ask questions, and to be honest with you about their goals for their children.
- *Build relationships.* Relationships enhance your chances for conflict management or resolution. Be patient. Building relationships takes time, but it enhances communications and understandings. You'll communicate better if you have a relationship, and you'll have a relationship if you learn to communicate!
- *Educate yourself and your parents.* Learn about the cultures and customs of your families. Help families and children learn the customs and practices of the United States and their local community.

LESBIAN, GAY, BISEXUAL, AND TRANSGENDER (LGBT) FAMILIES

More than likely, you will have in your classroom children from lesbian, gay, bisexual, and transgendered (LGBT) families. LGBT individuals and couples become parents in a variety of ways, including adoption, foster parenting, donor insemination, surrogacy, and previous heterosexual relationships.[31] Here are some important facts and figures you need to consider as you seek to involve and embrace all parents and families:

- Being raised in LGBT families does not impact normal childhood development. Studies show that the sexual orientation of a parent is irrelevant to the development of a child's mental health, social development, sexual orientation, and to the quality of the parent–child relationship.[32] Children raised in lesbian households are psychologically well-adjusted and have fewer behavioral problems than do their peers raised in heterosexual households. Children from lesbian families rate higher in social, academic, and total competence. They also show lower rates in social, rule-breaking, and aggressive problem behavior.[33]
- LGBT parents are more likely to be involved in their children's education, are more involved in school activities, and are more likely to report more consistent communication with school personnel than their heterosexual counterparts.[34]
- LGBT parents suffer from various types of exclusion from their school communities, such as being excluded or prevented from fully participating in school activities and events; being excluded by school policies and procedures; and

being ignored and feeling invisible. LGBT parents report mistreatment from other parents in the school community and from their children's peers at school.[35]

- Children may be stigmatized because of their parents' sexuality and be victims of teasing and bullying. Studies provide mixed results on whether children from LGBT families suffer from more teasing and bullying than do peers from heterosexual families. However, data show that about 45 percent of LGBT parents are either African American or Latino. This is important because it is possible that there is a greater degree of stigmatization of homosexuality in minority groups.[36]

- LGBT families are raising millions of children. Many of these children are adopted; children with same-sex parents are more likely to be foreign born.[37] These children may face not only prejudices about their country of origin, but also the prejudices against the sexual orientation of their families.

All parents deserve to be and should be involved in their children's education. What can you do to help LGBT families get involved in their children's education?

So what does this mean for you? Children in your classroom are your students regardless of their parents' sexual orientation and your own personal beliefs. They deserve the best you can give them. All parents deserve to be and should be involved. However, you may face some obstacles to successfully involving LGBT families from other parents, staff members, and community members. Perhaps your own prejudices may get in the way of your ability to provide all children with an equal and quality education.

IMPLICATIONS FOR TEACHING.   Here is what you can do:

- Treat each family member and child equally with dignity, respect, and honor. Under no circumstances should you participate in making disparaging, derogatory, or negative remarks to or about LGBT parents to other teachers, parents, students, or community members.

- Be aware of your own beliefs and how they may impact your teaching and treatment of others. Treat each family member and child equally, with dignity, respect, and honor.

- Collaborate with other staff members to arrange for a uniform response to teasing and bullying. Teachers and administrators should be a united front against discrimination and bullying to better support each child's education and sense of belonging.

- Create an environment of respect and safety. Studies show that LGBT parents whose children's schools have a comprehensive safe-school policy that protects students from bullying and harassment report the lowest level of mistreatment. A comprehensive curriculum based on diversity acceptance is also helpful. Work with your colleagues and school district administrators to support and use a comprehensive approach to exploring and welcoming diverse families.

- Invite and encourage LGBT families to attend school functions, volunteer, and participate in classroom activities as you do other families. Let them know you value and desire their input, presence, and participation. Make it clear that your classroom is a friendly, accepting, equalizing place by having classroom decorations reflect the diversity of all families, from bi-racial to LGBT to single parents.

- Include both parents in the parent-family relationship, not just the biological parent (if the child is not adopted). Encourage both parents' participation and input.

MILITARY FAMILIES

You may have heard the phrase, "When one member joins, the whole family serves," when it comes to service members and their families. This is certainly true today with the United States at war in several countries. Children are profoundly impacted by their families' involvement in military service. At the present time, there are 1.4 million servicemen and servicewomen away from home on active duty, so it is likely that you will have a child of a military family in your classroom.[38] Today's service families are unique in that they face a lifestyle that is often in upheaval and results in increased family separations owing to frequent deployment, recalls to active duty, and relocations. These are highly stressful and challenging times for service families. Here are some suggestions for how you can support children of military families.

IMPLICATIONS FOR TEACHING

- *Help children keep in contact with families.* Offer opportunities for children to write letters, e-mail, or talk to their parent on the phone. As a project for your students, you can honor your military parents by sending them a class package with a special gift, video, or letter. Many faith-based veterans groups and other community agencies will pay the postage for packages and letters for service personnel. For example, Cindy Bost of Youngsville, Pennsylvania, started Pennies for Postage to help families and organizations pay for postage to send care packages to service members overseas. Cindy started with bake sales and donation buckets in stores around town, but now some local organizations are on board.[39] You can also help kids keep a journal, scrapbook, or photo album of daily events to share with their mom or dad when that parent returns.

- *Get in touch with military families in your school and community.* You can help children in your class make contact with other children whose parents are on active military duty and give them a forum to talk about their thoughts and feelings.

- *Collaborate with the community to gain access to programs that support military families.* The Armed Services YMCA's Operation Hero is an onsite after-school program that focuses on character development and skill building in military children who have been identified by school personnel and parents as exhibiting low self-esteem or having difficulty adjusting both academically and socially in the school environment. Curriculum is designed to help children handle the challenges of military life, provide tools to help them succeed in school, and help develop a positive self-image while improving social and communication skills.[40]

  Such support groups offer many outlets for children and families to form new relationships, establish ties in a new place, and feel comfortable in a school. Frequently relocating is difficult for children. Imagine having to do that several times a year! So, if a military support group for families and children does not exist in your school or community, you can help organize one.

- *Understand and spot academic and behavior cues early.* Children may experience a decline in classroom performance while a parent is on active military duty; it may be hard for them to focus with so much to be worried about. Be understanding and supportive, and provide a listening ear to your children with deployed family members. Provide extra tutoring and other opportunities for children to learn and practice academics to help keep them on track.

- *Encourage parents to limit the amount of television children watch.* Young children should not watch war-related coverage without adult supervision. Children's fears and worries for their family members can lead to negative emotions, such as depression, anxiety, or aggression. Provide a nurturing relationship and classroom. Sadly, children do know about and are harmed by war and violence. You can produce an antidote for fear and violence by providing a positive and nurturing class and school environment.

PRISON/INCARCERATED FAMILIES

In the United States, 1 in every 34 adults (3.2 percent) are in jail or prison, probation, or on parole.[41] This means that at least 2.7 million minor children in the United States have a parent in prison.[42] Today, 1.1 million fathers and 120,000 mothers are behind bars.[43] Children with an incarcerated parent are two to three times more likely to engage in delinquent behavior.[44]

CHILDREN OF PROMISE.   The Children of Promise organization is a community-based, non-profit organization in Brooklyn, New York. It helps children cope with having a mother or father in prison. Children of Promise conducts after-school and summer programs and works with about two hundred children between the ages of six and sixteen, all of whom have at least one parent in prison.

The children write to their moms and dads every two weeks. They include photographs, report cards, and other items going on in their lives. Often the kids will ask each other: What did you tell your dad?[45]

GET ON THE BUS.   Faced with alarming statistics, community programs are taking an active role in preventing juvenile delinquency as well as giving children an opportunity to see their incarcerated parents. Get On The Bus, a Los Angeles-based nonprofit organization founded by Sister Suzanne Jabro, brings children and their guardians/caregivers from throughout the state of California to visit their mothers and fathers in prison every year around Mother's and Father's Day. Get On The Bus is a project of the Center of Restorative Justice. Maria Costanzo Palmer, program director, says that every child has a right to see, talk to, and touch their parents. On Mother's Day 2014, the program took busloads of children from every major city in California to three women's prisons, and on Father's Day it took busloads of children to seven men's prisons. Maria says that for many children, this is the only way that they get to visit their parents, many of whom are incarcerated over three hundred miles away. Kids on the bus learn that they are not alone and are not the only children with a parent in prison. Maria has this advice for you as a classroom teacher:[46]

- Be aware that in your classroom you may have children whose parents are in prison. Being aware of the fact that many children have incarcerated parents is the first step to helping them.
- Not all children of incarcerated parents know that their mother or father is in prison. Many families are careful of what they say about where the mother or father is, so approach each family carefully and get to know their needs. Ask them how you can help them.
- Let children know that they are loved by you and others. Remember, all children need affection and the security of knowing you care.[47]

LITTLE CHILDREN, BIG CHALLENGES: INCARCERATION.   In response to the growing numbers of incarcerated parents, Sesame Street has launched a bilingual program called Little Children, Big Challenges: Incarceration. The program is designed for children ages three to eight years who have incarcerated parents.[48]

IMPLICATIONS OF CHANGING FAMILY PATTERNS

Given the changes in families today, here are some things you can do to help parents:

- ***Provide support services for parents and their children.*** Support can range from being a listening ear to organizing support groups and seminars on single parenting. You can help families connect with other agencies and groups, such as Big Brothers and Big Sisters and Parents Without Partners. Through newsletters and flyers, e-mails, Web pages, and texting you can offer families specific advice on how to help children become independent and how to meet the demands of living in single-parent families, stepfamilies, and other family configurations.

- *Avoid criticism and being judgmental toward parents.* Examine your attitudes toward family patterns and remember there is no right family pattern in which all children should be reared. Be careful not to criticize parents for the jobs they are doing. Parents may not have enough time to spend with their children or know how to discipline them. Regardless of their circumstances, families need help, not criticism.

- *Offer educational experiences for parents and their children to participate in.* Offer experiences children might not otherwise have because of their family organization. For example, outdoor activities such as fishing trips and sports events can be interesting and enriching learning experiences for children who may not have such opportunities.

  Parents and students at Lura A. White Elementary School participated in a national program that promotes student reading outside of school and the involvement of parents in their children's reading. Awards were given to teachers and parents who made the program a success as well as students who read the most books. All participants and their families enjoyed a schoolwide barbeque.[49]

- *Be sensitive to the needs of the families in your classroom.* Avoid having children make presents for both parents when it is inappropriate to do so or awarding prizes for bringing both parents to meetings. Replace such terms as *broken home* with *single-parent family*. Be sensitive to the realities of children's home lives. For instance, when a teacher sent a field trip permission form home with children and told them to have their mothers or fathers sign it, one child said, "I don't have a father. If my mother can't sign it, can the man she sleeps with sign it?" Clarify with families how they would like specific situations handled; for example, ask whether you should send notices of school events, in what language, and to which (or both) parents.

- *Seek professional development training.* Request professional development training to help you work with families. Professional development programs can provide information about referral agencies, guidance techniques, and child abuse identification and prevention. You need to be alert to all kinds of child abuse, including mental, physical, and sexual abuse.

There are unlimited possibilities for a meaningful program of family involvement. Families can make a significant difference in their children's education, and with your assistance they can join teachers and schools in a productive partnership. The following Voice from the Field, "How to Create a Parent-Friendly School," shares effective strategies you can use to create a parent-friendly school.

As you think about how you will involve parents and families, reflect on the powerful influences families have in children's lives. It is in the context of the family unit that children learn about morality and character—essential developmental dimensions of their lives.

In the video about home/school communication, two teachers discuss how they communicate with and involve parents in their children's class work and learning. Pay particular attention to the methods the teachers use to communicate with and involve parents; reflect on how you can use their ideas in your teaching and your collaborative involvement with them.

VOICE FROM THE FIELD

COMPETENCY BUILDER

How to Create a Parent-Friendly School

Parent and community involvement makes the difference between schools being a place to go and a place to learn. "Our PTA brings the school community together and encourages student involvement in affective and academic areas," says Dr. Jesse D. Baker, principal of Stadium Drive Elementary School of the Arts in Lake Orion, Michigan. He cites events such as mother–son dances, daddy–daughter outings, family swim night at the local high school, and a parent-directed spirit week and fun run as examples of parent involvement. In addition, it is usual to have one or two parent volunteers in each classroom on most days. "When parents are welcomed and their decisions are respected, their involvement increases," says Baker.

Parent-friendly schools and programs do not just happen. They require hard work and dedication by everyone involved. Here are some ideas from Stadium Drive Elementary School that you can use to make your classroom and school more parent friendly

STRATEGY 1 — Show That You Care
Develop a compassionate culture toward students, families, and the community in general.

- Send flowers and letters and make telephone calls and visits to ill children or their families to show the extent of the staff's commitment to families.
- Welcome new families and encourage them to become involved.
- Encourage teachers to stand at their classroom doors each morning and greet youngsters as they enter.
- Organize a schoolwide effort to help a community member cope with a life-threatening condition. At Stadium Drive Elementary, students collect money. However, donations of food, offers of transportation, or care for children are other excellent ways to show you care.
- Collect canned goods for needy families at holiday times and throughout the year.
- Collect donations for victims of natural disasters.
- Conduct a coats-for-kids drive before cold weather sets in.
- Reward students' caring behaviors. Stadium Drive Elementary has a Pause to Recognize program that acknowledges caring and respectful behavior.

- Create a scholarship fund. Staff members at Stadium Drive each pay a dollar on Fridays for the privilege of wearing blue jeans, thus creating a scholarship fund for a graduating senior alumnus.

STRATEGY 2 — Communicate Frequently with Parents and the Community
Through multiple media, highlight the school's philosophy and activities that support that philosophy. "Communication is key to maintaining a nurturing culture between staff and families," says Jan Seeds, PTA president. Parents at Stadium Drive, named a parent-friendly school by *Parent Magazine,* stay connected with the school through regular communication.

- Make a calendar of school events available on public access cable and the school's website.
- Publish a weekly newsletter in paper and electronic form.
- Ask the PTA to produce a student directory of addresses and phone numbers.
- Call or e-mail parents to update them on classroom activities.

STRATEGY 3 — Solicit Feedback from Parents
Gather data from parents and the community regarding their needs and perceptions. Then use the data to set school goals. Gather written comments of parents regarding school climate. When requesting a teacher, one parent at Stadium Drive wrote, "My daughter was in her class last year. Through the different class volunteering I did, I was able to see how she managed her classroom and taught the children, and I was very impressed. Her attentiveness and compassion really helped bring out the best in children." Ask for opinions and suggestions.

STRATEGY 4 — Unite Parents and Staff in a Common Goal
Meeting the educational needs of all students should be everyone's top priority. Stadium Drive maintains a positive bond among all stakeholders and establishes school priorities as a result of formal and informal information gleaned from student, parent, and staff surveys.

- Provide funds for field trips and for visiting artists, musicians, dancers, and actors to come to your school to work with students. The PTA at Stadium Drive is responsible for this area.
- Extend the parent–teacher partnership whenever possible. At Stadium Drive's Curriculum Night, teachers explain grade-level curriculum and address specific

issues. Fall and spring conferences update parents on their children's progress.

5 Create Community Partnerships

Cooperative relationships can showcase school efforts and involve businesses in school activities. Partnerships beyond the Stadium Drive school walls exist with both businesses and civic organizations.

- Establish mutually beneficial relationships with local businesses. For example, students can make deposits at school to their bank savings account. Or a local art shop can frame—at no cost—student artwork going to state competition.
- Display student art and written work at local businesses and restaurants.
- Invite community artists, musicians, and journalists to judge student entries in competitions.
- Host senior citizens as special guests at school activities, recitals, concerts, and performances.
- Work with local charities. At Stadium Drive, staff and students work with the local Lions Club in an adopt-a-family program, with each classroom providing wrapped presents for a needy family during winter holidays.

6 Connect Parents and Students with the School

Programs and services that benefit and involve families can strengthen and unify the school community.

- Recruit parents at the beginning of the year, and then call them to volunteer for classroom help, special projects, and field trip chaperones, as well as in your school art room or media center. Stadium Drive uses this approach, and the growth in their volunteerism over the past six years has been significant—from 975 to nearly 5,000 volunteer hours.
- Tap into students from middle school and high school; they are often willing volunteers. At Stadium Drive, these older students volunteered more than six hundred hours last year.
- Thank all volunteers at the end of the year. For example, have a volunteer tea or picnic.

- Include nonacademic services for students and families, such as a school social worker, a county nurse, and special education ancillary staff.
- Offer counseling on child rearing, grief management, and conflict resolution.
- Recommend strategies for handling trauma, disruptive behavior, poor student choices, and psychological issues.
- Make referrals to outside agencies for child abuse, drug abuse, alcoholism, or domestic violence.
- Support students and parents with information and training on health issues.

7 Consider Family Needs

Make meeting times, child care arrangements, and other activities user friendly.

- Provide scholarships to aid students who would be otherwise unable to attend camp or field trips.
- Schedule PTA meetings, parent–teacher conferences, and personal contacts in the evening, before school, or immediately after school. Provide free child care.
- Encourage staff to meet at times convenient to parents.
- Provide before- and after-school child care and enrichment programs, such as cooking, dance, crafts, tumbling, magic, play-building, cartooning, art, and computer applications.
- Make school facilities available after hours to parents and the groups to which they belong for scouting, martial arts training, sports, home designing, or other community interests.
- Use the educational resources of the school and community to extend learning opportunities for families. For example, students at Stadium Drive design Web pages to exhibit classroom activities, and their concerts and musical productions are broadcast on local cable.
- Provide a parent section in the library for materials on child growth and parenting.

Source: Contributed by Dr. Jesse D. Baker, principal, Stadium Drive Elementary School, Lake Orion, Michigan.

parent/family involvement
The participation of parents and other family members in all areas of their children's education and development, based on the premise that parents are the primary influence in children's lives.

TYPES OF PARENT/FAMILY INVOLVEMENT

Parent/family involvement is a process of helping parents and family members use their abilities to benefit themselves, their children, and the early childhood program. Because families, children, and the program are all part of the process, all three parties should benefit from a well-planned program of involvement. Nonetheless, the focus in interactions between parent/family and the child is the family—and you must work with and through families if you want to be successful.

As you think about your role in parent and family involvement, reflect on the six types of parent involvement in Figure 17.1. These six types of parent/family involvement constitute a comprehensive approach to your work with parents. A worthy professional goal would be for you to *try* to have some of your parents involved in all six of these types of parental involvement throughout the program year. Your success as an involver of parents at all levels will depend in part on how well you collaborate with your colleagues, your parents, and your community.

TYPE 1: PERSONAL/INDIVIDUAL INVOLVEMENT AND EMPOWERMENT

- *Adult education classes.* Provide families with opportunities to learn about a range of topics such as child development, helping children learn to read, and basic math skills.
- *Training programs.* Give parents and other family members skills as classroom aides, club and activity sponsors, curriculum planners, and policy decision makers. When parents and other family members are viewed as experts, empowerment results.
- *Classroom and center activities.* Although not all families can be directly involved in classroom activities, encourage those who can. But remember

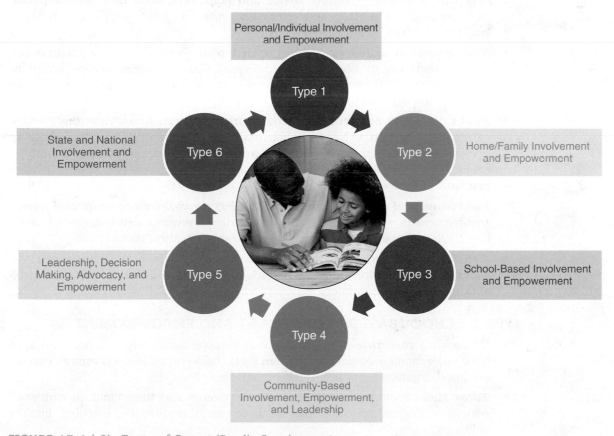

FIGURE 17.1 | Six Types of Parent/Family Involvement
There are basically six types of parent/family involvement as shown above. You should consider how you can involve some of your parents in all of the six types.

Source: G. S. Morrison (2014). *Fundamentals of Early Childhood Education,* 7th ed. Pearson; and G. S. Morrison (1978). *Parent Involvement in the Home, School, and Community.* Merrill.

that those who are involved must have guidance, direction, and training. Involving parents and others as paid aides can be an excellent way to provide both employment and training. Many programs, such as Head Start, actively support such a policy. Get as many parents involved in your classroom as you can.

- *Libraries and materials centers.* Families benefit from books and other articles relating to parenting. Some programs furnish resource areas with comfortable chairs to encourage families to use these materials. The Voice from the Field, "The Home Library: Transforming At-Risk Readers," gives you very specific ideas for how to give each child in your classroom a home library.

TYPE 2: HOME/FAMILY INVOLVEMENT AND EMPOWERMENT

- *Performances and plays.* These, especially ones in which children have a part, tend to bring families to school; however, the purpose of children's performances should not be solely to get families involved.

- *Telephone hotlines.* When staffed by families, they can help allay fears and provide information relating to child abuse, communicable diseases, and special events. Hotlines answered by a knowledgeable parent or family member, even if only during certain hours of the week, provide other parents and family members with a means of getting advice and help. Telephone networks or phone trees are also used to help children and parents with homework and to monitor latchkey children.

- *Newsletters/e-newsletters.* When planned with parents' help, newsletters are an excellent way to keep families informed about program events, activities, and curriculum information. Newsletters in parents' native languages help keep language-minority families informed.

- *Books and other materials for parents and children to use at home.* Provide material for parents to read to their children. For example, use book bags to encourage parental awareness of student learning. Also, sending out a monthly calendar of activities to be done at home is one good way to keep families involved in their children's learning.

- *Individualized education programs (IEPs) for children with special needs.* Involvement in writing an IEP is not only a legal requirement but also an excellent learning experience and an effective communication tool.

- *Websites for parents.* A website informs them about the activities of your classroom. Give suggestions for how parents can extend and enrich classroom projects and activities at home.

TYPE 3: SCHOOL BASED INVOLVEMENT AND EMPOWERMENT

- *Welcoming committees.* A good way to involve families in any program is to have other families contact them when their children first join a program. Parents are good organizers of these types of activities.

- *Tutor time.* Provide tutor time in which parents and their children can work with teachers on special topics such as math homework, teaching literacy skills, etc.

- *Participation in workshops.* These workshops introduce families to the school's policies, procedures, and programs. Most families want to know what is going on in the school and would do a better job of helping their children at home if they knew school policies and classroom procedures.

TYPE 4: COMMUNITY BASED INVOLVEMENT, EMPOWERMENT, AND LEADERSHIP

- *Family nights, cultural dinners, chili cook-offs, and potluck dinners.* Such events bring families and the community to the school in nonthreatening, social ways, such as the following:

  - At Country Heights Elementary School (Davies County, Kentucky) preschool teacher Connie Johnson invites a community librarian to come in and read books to her children. Connie also regularly sends home with her children information about public library activities and events. The public library staff visits over seventy-two preschool sites throughout the county.[50]

  - Hills Elementary (Iowa) has a large population of students who live in an impoverished part of town. The school started a community center that offers a monthly family night dinner program and provides opportunities for parents, teachers, and students to develop study and life skills.[51] And, speaking of community librarians and libraries, Justin Minkel, Arkansas Teacher of the Year, suggests in his Voice from the Field, that you work with parents and families to develop home libraries for children.

- *Parent support groups.* Parents need support in their roles. Support groups can provide parenting information, community agency information, and speakers.

- *Home visitations.* Home visitations are an excellent way to promote community/school/family involvement. For example, the Henderson County (Kentucky) schools conduct an annual home visitation blitz. The home visitation blitz sent out five hundred teachers and other school staff into the homes of three thousand students. Community members from attorneys to politicians to store owners and business executives provided and served a barbeque lunch for the home visitors. (See tips for conducting home visits in this text.)

TYPE 5: LEADERSHIP, DECISION-MAKING, ADVOCACY, AND EMPOWERMENT

- *Fairs and bazaars.* Involve families in many aspects of the decision-making process. Allow and encourage input in regard to fund-raising, planning, etc.

- *School parent councils.* Review the school's budget, recommend programs, sponsor events, solve problems, and raise funds for special school activities.[52]

- *School site councils.* Many decisions affecting the education of students are made in the schools. School-based decision-making is the responsibility of the school site council. For example school site councils hire teachers (in some cases), approve school rules, and decide if students will wear uniforms.[53]

- *Hiring and policy making.* Parents and community members can and should serve on committees that hire staff and set policy.

- *Curriculum development and review.* Parents' involvement in curriculum planning helps them learn about and understand what constitutes a quality program and what is involved in a developmentally appropriate curriculum. When families know about the curriculum, they are more supportive of it.

TYPE 6: STATE AND NATIONAL INVOLVEMENT/EMPOWERMENT.

Stand for Children is an independent organization that works with parents to engage them in advocacy for better public schools in Chicago and Illinois. Stand for Children held a series of telephone town halls in which they called seventy thousand people and asked them to listen in to a town hall meeting held by a panel of speakers. Parents were given the opportunity to join the real-time discussions and to ask questions. Town hall meetings included discussions about longer school days, how to build better public schools, and how to promote safety and reduce violence in schools and communities.[54]

The National Civic League (NCL) partners with local communities nationwide to increase by 50 percent the number of low-income children reading on grade level in third grade in at least a dozen states during the next ten years. In 2011, the city of Baltimore won the All-America City Award, presented by the NCL, for creating a grade-level reading campaign to achieve three goals by 2020:

1. Average daily attendance of 97 percent for students in grades K–3.
2. More than 80 percent of students reading at grade level by the end of third grade.
3. More than 80 percent of all children fully prepared for kindergarten.[55]

The Kentucky Department of Education sends out an issue of *ParentInfo,* an e-mail newsletter, with timely tips on how parents can help children succeed in school. Topics include college and career readiness, testing, school-based decision-making councils, bullying, technology, and more.[56]

Parents and students at Lura A. White Elementary School participated in the annual Books and Beyond, a national program that promotes student reading outside of school and the involvement of parents in their children's reading. Awards are given to teachers and parents who make the program a success and also to students who read the most books. All participants and their families enjoy a schoolwide barbeque. Kindergarten students read 6,720 books; first graders read 7,895 books; second graders read 5,635 books; and third graders read 8,116 books.[57]

Many early childhood teachers conduct home visits to help parents learn how to support their children's learning at home. What useful information can parents provide you about children's learning, experience, growth, and development?

Check Your Understanding: Target

HOME VISITATION

All across the United States, growing numbers of school districts are encouraging and supporting teachers to visit children's homes and ask parents for help in educating their children. Two home visits per year are required in the Head Start program, and home visits are becoming more commonplace in many school districts.[58] Teachers who do home visiting are trained prior to going on the visits. Although not every state or district pays extra for home visits, more schools are building them into the school calendar, with a certain number of days being set aside for home visiting. Some districts and programs provide released time for visitation by hiring substitute teachers to enable classroom teachers to make home visits.

A home visiting program demonstrates that teachers, principal, and school staff are willing to go more than halfway to involve all parents in their children's education. Home visits help teachers demonstrate their interest in students' families and understand their students better by seeing them in their home environment.

These visits should not replace parent–teacher conferences or be used to discuss children's progress. When done early, before any school problems can arise, they avoid putting parents on the defensive and signal that teachers are eager to work with all parents. Teachers who have made home visits say they build stronger relationships with parents and

VOICE FROM THE FIELD

COMPETENCY BUILDER

The Home Library: Transforming At-Risk Readers

Melinda started second grade with everything against her. She lives in poverty, her mom is illiterate in both English and Spanish, and she was severely abused at the age of six. At the beginning of the year, she owned only one book.

Despite these barriers, Melinda made extraordinary academic progress. She moved from a kindergarten level to a fourth grade level in the two years she was in my class. Her demeanor changed, too; she began smiling and laughing more often, and she became a confident scholar.

One reason for her success is simple—instead of one book at home, Melinda now has a home library of forty books.

THE 1,000 BOOKS PROJECT

Each of the twenty-five children in my class received forty books over the course of second and third grade, for a total of one thousand new books in their homes. I purchased the books through a combination of my own funds, donations from individuals and local organizations, and bonus points from Scholastic book orders. The kids received three types of books each month: copies of several class read-alouds, books their guided reading group had just read, and individual choices selected from Scholastic's website. The total cost for each student's home library was less than $50 each year.

I watched child after child become a different kind of writer, thinker, and human being because of her or his growth as a reader.

Steps for Building a Home Library and Family Literacy

STEP 1 **Create a Home Library Project**
Start small—before launching The 1,000 Books Project, I did a pilot version where my eight lowest readers each received ten books. Funding for the project can come from school or district funds, local businesses, or minigrants from organizations that support literacy. Whatever the size of the project, these three elements are essential:

- Have each child create a physical space at home for their books.
- Let the students choose most of the titles.
- Make sure the books aren't too hard or too easy for the student.

STEP 2 **Find a Time When Parents Can Come into Your Classroom to Read with Their Children**
My students' parents are invited to visit the classroom every Tuesday at 2:30 p.m. to read with their children. Sometimes the parent reads a book to the child; other times the child reads to the parent. I make sure I have books in the class library that are written in Spanish or other families' home languages for those parents who aren't as comfortable reading in English. Parents usually read to their own child first, then they read with other students whose parents weren't able to come that day, building a class community where families begin to know one another.

STEP 3 **Make Sure Your Books Reflect Your Students' Lives and Interests**
Because most of my students speak Spanish as a first language, three book baskets in my classroom library are filled with books in Spanish (nonfiction, fantasy, and realistic fiction). I make sure the books reflect the kids' interests as well as their family's cultural heritage. Be sure to include nonfiction, too—most students love nonfiction texts related to their interests. As an added bonus, photographs are better than drawings when it comes to helping children build vocabulary.

STEP 4 **Create "Talk Time" for Both Children and Their Families**
Kids need time to share their connections, questions, and opinions about each book they read. We do about fifty "think-pair-shares" a day where students turn to their conversation partner for that week and talk one-on-one about a question I pose. Inviting parents as "guest speakers" is a great way to enrich the context of a book. I invited a student's mom to speak about her experience moving to the United States from Mexico. She spoke in Spanish, with her daughter translating, and the students immediately noticed that this parent's reasons for leaving Mexico were the same as the motivations of European immigrants in the books we had been reading.

STEP 5 **Teach Parents, Too**
Students who make the most reading growth in my class are those who read almost every night at home. Many parents have already made reading a nightly activity, but some parents need guidance on how to help their children become readers. Each year I ask parents to set aside about twenty minutes a night for their child to read, and I provide them with a list of questions in both Spanish and English that they can ask their child after reading, such as, "What was your favorite part?" or "What questions did you have while you were reading?"

Source: Contributed by Justin Minkel, second and third grade teacher at Jones Elementary in Northwest Arkansas. He is the 2007 Arkansas Teacher of the Year, a 2006 Milken Educator, and a 2011 National Board Certified Teacher.

their children and improve attendance and achievement. Although many home visits do occur in the home, they do not always have to. Sometimes parents are more comfortable meeting teachers away from the home in places such as community centers, churches, or the local YMCA or YWCA. These visits are still considered home visits.

Here are some guidelines for how you can be successful in your program of home visitation.

PREPARE FOR THE VISIT.   Planning for home visitations are as important as conducting the visitation. It makes sense to have goals, objectives, and guidelines for these visitations as a means for successfully planning for them. Buder Elementary School in St. Louis, Missouri, has these goals for their home visitations:

- *Improve* academic achievement and test scores
- *Increase* student attendance
- *Increase* parental involvement
- *Increase* homework completion
- *Improve* behavior, decrease discipline referrals, and improve attitudes about school[59]
- *Schedule the visits:*
  - Make sure you give parents plenty of notice—a week or more.
  - Some schools have scheduled home visits in the afternoon right after school. Others have found that early evening is more convenient for parents. Some schedule visits right before a new school year begins. A mix of times may be needed to reach all families.
  - Work with community groups (e.g., Boys and Girls Clubs, housing complexes, 4-H, YMCAs, and community centers) to schedule visits in neutral but convenient spaces.
- *Make parents feel comfortable:*
  - Send a letter home to parents explaining the desire to have teachers make informal visits to all students' homes. Include a form that parents can mail back to accept or decline the visit.
  - State clearly that the intent of your thirty-minute visit is to introduce yourself to family members and not to discuss the child's progress.
  - Suggest that families think about special things their children would want to share with you, the teacher.
- *Reduce parents' worries.* One school included a note to parents that said "No preparation is required. In fact, our homes need to be vacuumed and all of us are on diets!" This touch of humor and casualness helps set a friendly and informal tone.
- *Make a phone call to parents who have not responded to explain the plan for home visits and reassure parents that it is to get acquainted and not to evaluate students.*
- *Enlist community groups, religious organizations, and businesses to help publicize the home visits.*[60]
- *At the visit, do the following:*
  - Get to know the parents and family. What is their attitude toward school and education?
  - Be sure to involve parents and children in a "hopes and dreams" conversation. What do parents want for themselves and their children? What do they want for their children? Ask children what their hopes and dreams are. Ask both parents and children how they think you can help their children accomplish their dreams and succeed in school.
  - Tell parents and children what your expectations are for them.

FAMILY CONFERENCES

Significant parent involvement occurs through well-planned and well-conducted conferences between families and early childhood professionals, informally referred to as **parent–teacher conferences** or **family–teacher conferences**. Such conferences are often the first contact many families have with a school and are critical both from a public relations point of view and as a vehicle for helping families and professionals accomplish their goals. The following guidelines will help you prepare for and conduct successful conferences:

- *Plan ahead.* Be sure of the reason for the conference. What do you want to accomplish? List the points you want to cover and think about what you are going to say.

- *Get to know the parents.* This is not wasted time; the more effectively you establish rapport with a parent, the more you will accomplish in the long run.

- *Avoid an authoritative atmosphere.* Do not sit behind your desk while the parent sits in a child's chair. Treat parents and others like the adults they are.

- *Communicate at the parent's level.* Use words, phrases, and explanations that parents understand and are familiar with. Avoid jargon or complicated explanations, and speak in your natural, conversational style.

- *Accentuate the positive.* Make every effort to show and tell parents what the child is doing well. When you deal with problems, put them in the proper perspective: Identify what the child is able to do, what the goals and purposes of the learning program are, what specific skills or concepts you are trying to get the child to learn, and what problems the child is having in achieving. Most important, explain what you plan to do to help the child achieve and what specific role the parents can play in meeting achievement goals.

- *Give families a chance to talk.* You will not learn much about them if you do all the talking, so encourage families to talk.

- *Learn to listen.* An active listener holds eye contact, uses body language such as head nodding and hand gestures, does not interrupt, avoids arguing, paraphrases as a way of clarifying ideas, and keeps the conversation on track.

- *Follow up.* Ask the parent for a definite time for the next conference as you are concluding the current one. Another conference is the best method of solidifying gains and extending support, but other acceptable means of follow-up are telephone calls, written reports, notes sent with children, emails, Twitter, and brief visits to the home. Even though these types of contacts may appear casual, they should be planned and conducted as seriously as any regular parent–professional conference. No matter which approach you choose, family–teacher conferences have many benefits:

  - Families see that you genuinely care about their children.
  - Family members can clarify problems, issues, advice, and directions.
  - Parents, family members, and children are encouraged to continue to do their best.
  - Conferences offer opportunities to extend classroom learning to the home.
  - In conferences you can extend programs initiated to help families or formulate new plans.

- *Develop an action plan.* Never leave the parent with a sense of frustration, unsure of what you will be doing or what they are to do. Every communication with families should end on a positive note so that everyone knows what is to be done and how.

parent–teacher conferences or **family–teacher conferences** Meetings between parents and early childhood professionals to inform the parents of the child's progress and allow them to actively participate in the educational process.

CHILDREN AND CONFERENCES. A frequently asked question is, "Should children be present at parent–teacher conferences?" The answer is, "Yes, of course, if it is appropriate for them to be present." In most instances, it is appropriate and offers a number of benefits:

- Children have much to contribute. They can talk about their progress and behavior, offer suggestions for improvement and enrichment, and discuss their interests.
- The locus of control is centered in the child. Children learn that they have a voice and that others think their opinions are important.
- Children's self-esteem is enhanced because they are viewed as an important part of the conference and because a major purpose of the conference is to help them and their families.
- Children become more involved in their classroom and education. Students take pride not only in their own accomplishments and their ability to share them, but also in the opportunity to help each other prepare for their conferences. A team spirit—a sense of community—can emerge and benefit everyone involved.[61]
- Children learn that education is a cooperative process between home and school.

As you reflect on the ways you can communicate with children and their families, also think about ways you can involve them in your classroom.

USING TECHNOLOGY TO INVOLVE PARENTS

The Internet provides an excellent way for you to reach out to parents and keep them informed and involved. For example, teachers use the Internet to post calendars, newsletters, discussion topics, assignments, assessment tools, spelling lists, and tips. Here are some ways you can electronically connect with families:

- ***E-mail.*** E-mail is fast, convenient, and for many families is the preferred mode of communication. E-mail increases communication between families and teachers and between faculty and outside personnel involved in working with individual students.
- ***Teacher website.*** Most school districts have a website that provides general information about the district and individual schools. Web pages are excellent ways to give parents and community members general information and let them virtually experience school and classroom events and accomplishments. For example, through the Internet, you can access many teachers' websites. Now would be a good time for you to do this.

  First grade teacher Marci McGowan uses her classroom website as an interactive tool to connect with families outside the classroom. She displays photos of student work and projects, access to other colleague teachers' websites for resources and information, and educational books and activities students can work on during the summer break. Most importantly, Marci's teaching philosophy is located on her website to guide and direct her teaching of young children. She also writes a letter to the children at the beginning of the year introducing herself, explaining what supplies to bring, and when and where to meet her on the first day of school.[62]
- ***Twitter.*** Twitter, a social-networking website delivering short (140 characters or less), text-based posts, is useful on many levels. Teachers can use Twitter to send out homework so that parents are automatically updated. Parents can follow teachers and see what their children are up to from any computer (from work, home, coffee shops) at any time of the day. Twitter can also bring students into contact with their community on a local and global level. Students in two Maine elementary schools have been exchanging messages through Twitter. Teachers

say the exercise was initiated to help students develop their writing skills by composing messages that must be 140 characters or less.[63]

- *Video chat.* Teachers can use free video chat providers such as Skype or Gmail to hold convenient conferences with parents. The use of Skype helped a family in Peculiar, Missouri, who had a parent who works overseas. Trey Coble participated in his son's parent–teacher conference via Skype.[64]

- *Teacher–parent blog.* Teachers can use a blog to connect with students and their families. Blogs can feature lesson summaries, concept introduction and exploration, and classroom notes, reminders, and news. Parents can leave comments, be more informed, and communicate with other parents in the class.

    Parents really appreciate the inclusion that the blogs provide. The fascination and engagement with technology that children have is something that helps motivate parents to be involved. One parent explains that her child is genuinely excited to come home and show her what's going on at school. Her child reads his own words and listens to his own voice on the Internet and finds this fascinating. She believes this knowledge helps him to better utilize Internet resources, and increases his understanding and awareness of the technologies.

You can involve your students in building a great classroom–parent relationship. The more student-led the online activities are, the more engaged and interested parents will be. First grade teacher Carrie Jostmeyer recommends these ideas:

- *Animoto videos.* Students create online presentations instead of slideshows using photos, graphics, music, and videos about what they are learning.

- *Student and classroom blogs.* Parents have access to what the students are learning about and discussing.

- *Flip camera videos.* Students can record themselves reading a book aloud and send it to their parents wherever they are. What an awesome e-mail to open up in the middle of the work day!

- *Weekly news report.* Students take the lead as anchors, news reporters, and camera crew, writing out what they learned in different content areas throughout the week and recording a news broadcast. You can burn copies of the broadcast for students to take home to watch with their parents.[65]

    Here are some guidelines to follow when you communicate with families electronically:

- Check with your school or program technology coordinator for guidelines and policies for Web page development and communicating electronically with parents.

- Remember that not all parents are connected to the Internet. There is still a "digital divide" in the United States; low-income parents and minorities are less likely to have Internet access. Consider how to provide families without Internet access the same information you provide to families who have Internet service. Here are some things you can do:
  - Use the cellphone to stay in touch with parents
  - Work with local libraries and make arrangements for parents to have Internet access
  - Research to see if any of your community partners can help you arrange for adopting a family to provide them Internet services

- Observe all the rules of politeness and courtesy that you would in a face-to-face conversation.

- Observe all the rules of courteous Internet conversations. For example, don't use all capital letters (this is similar to SHOUTING).
- Remember that just like handwritten notes, electronic mail can be saved. In addition, electronic notes are much more easily transferred.
- Be straightforward and concise in your electronic conversations.
- Establish ground rules ahead of time about what you will and will not discuss electronically.

There are unlimited possibilities for you to conduct a meaningful program of involvement for all parents and families. Families can make a significant difference in their children's education, and with your assistance they can join teachers and schools in a productive partnership.

As you think about how you will involve parents and families, reflect on the powerful influences families have in children's lives. It is in the context of the family unit that children learn about morality and character—essential developmental dimensions of their lives.

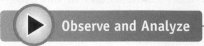

Observe and Analyze

COMMUNITY INVOLVEMENT

Early childhood professionals realize that neither they alone nor the limited resources of their programs are sufficient to meet the needs of many children and families. Consequently, professionals are seeking ways to link families to community services and resources. For example, if a child needs clothing, a professional who is aware of community resources might contact the local Salvation Army for assistance.

Using the community in your teaching is a wonderful way to help children and families come into contact with others and to tap into valuable social and educational services. Reflect on what people and organizations in your community you would use to help teach children the importance and value of the community in which they live.

COMMUNITY RESOURCES

The community offers a vital and rich array of resources to help you meet the needs of parents and children. Following are suggested actions you can take to use your community in your teaching:

- *Know your students and their needs.* Through observations, conferences with parents, and discussions with students, you can identify barriers to children's learning and discover what kind of help to seek.
- *Know your community.* Walk or drive around the community. Ask a parent to give you a tour to help familiarize you with agencies and individuals. Read the local newspaper, and attend community events and activities.
- *Ask for help and support from parents and the community.* Keep in mind that many parents will not be involved unless you personally ask them. The only encouragement many individuals and local businesses need is your invitation.
- *Develop a directory of community agencies.* Consult the business pages of local phone books, contact local chambers of commerce, and ask parents what agencies are helpful to them.
- *Compile a list of people who are willing to come to your classroom to speak to or work with your students.* You can start by asking parents to volunteer and to give suggestions and recommendations of others.

- ***Get involved with community-based agencies.*** For example, the Oakland Parents Literacy Project provides essential services to children and families. It is an extension of the region's social services network and provides free dinners for parents and children. Participation has grown dramatically, often hosting as many as five hundred people.[66] Each Wednesday night, the program holds reading events at three school locations. Parents and their children are invited for a two-hour session that includes dinner: Domino's Pizza provides cut-rate prices to the group and donates fruits and vegetables. There is reading by a guest and a free show—a clown, juggler, puppeteer, or magician to make the night complete. Every child who attends is given a book to take home. The goal of the program is to visit every Oakland elementary school during the school year.[67]

BENEFITS OF WORKING WITH COMMUNITY AGENCIES

As a teacher, you will experience numerous benefits when you collaborate with community agencies that work with parents and families.

- Teachers are often the first people to notice families in need of support. Connecting with community agencies allows you to refer families for support when family difficulties are too big for you to handle alone. For example, teachers notice when children in class have significant changes in behavior, look lifeless in class, and talk about stressful things at home as part of classroom sharing. Those may be signs of family stress that require professional intervention.

- Agencies provide an array of services that can help support families. Children whose parents receive support have less stress at home and are more able to learn in school. This makes your job easier and allows you to be more effective. For example, supportive relationships can help parents become more confident in raising children as parents learn concrete parenting skills, like teaching their children bedtime routines. Children who go to bed around the same time every night are more rested and are better able to learn in school.

- Community agency members can help you work with families to strengthen communication connections between home and school. Parent mentors help parents communicate with school personnel by listening to parent concerns, discussing and reframing problems, and helping set up a conversation with the teacher to discuss problems.

- Agency members are often aware of tangible resources to help families in need. For example, they can help connect you with a source for a free new coat for a child who does not have one or help connect families with counseling services to cope with stressful financial situations at home.

DEVELOPING TEACHER–COMMUNITY AGENCY CONNECTIONS

There are a variety ways you can connect to community agencies:

Step 1. Find out what the procedure is in your school for referring families to community agencies. Some community agencies may work directly with the school psychologist or counselor. Bring concerns about families to the appropriate school personnel who will then make the referral.

Step 2. Contact the agency over the phone or in person. Establish a positive working relationship with a specific person at the agency that you can easily make referrals to and at the same time someone you can trust to meet your family's needs. Agency staff change frequently and you want to make sure that the parents you refer for support actually find help. If possible have parents sign a release so you can talk about your concerns with the agency.

Step 3.   Make good referrals. If you are referring a parent to a voluntary program make sure the parent is aware of the program and wants the support it offers.

Step 4.   Keep in touch with the agency by checking in and providing feedback, especially if you notice positive changes in the child, parent, and family. Agencies like to receive feedback to know how their program is working.

PARENTS, CHILDREN, AND SCHOOL ABSENTEEISM

We talk about children in the classrooms as though they were just a natural part of the process of education. We take it for granted that children will be in our classroom every day for us to teach! But what if there were no children? For many children, this is exactly the problem: They are not in school! And as you are probably thinking right now, if children are not in the classroom they are not learning. This is exactly right!

chronic school absence
When children miss 10 percent of the school days in a school year.

While **chronic school absence** (missing 10 percent of the school year) is not a problem everywhere, it can reach surprisingly high levels even in the early grades. Nationwide, nearly 10 percent of kindergartners and first graders are chronically absent. In some communities, chronic early absence can affect 25 percent of all children in kindergarten through third grade across the entire district. Within particular schools in the same district, chronic early absence can range from less than 1 percent to more than 50 percent.[68] Here is what research on children's absenteeism concludes.

Chronic Absence Adversely Impacts Student Performance.   The negative impact of chronic absence is especially true for children living in poverty. All children, regardless of socioeconomic background, do worse academically in first grade if they are chronically absent in kindergarten. Chronic absence in kindergarten especially affects reading performance for Hispanic first graders. Among poor children, chronic absence in kindergarten predicts the lowest levels of educational achievement at the end of the fifth grade.[69]

So, you are probably thinking that one solution to chronic absenteeism is to get children in school. This is exactly right! Achieving the goal of reducing chronic absenteeism and having children in school requires collaboration between teachers, schools, families, and communities. You can implement some strategies universally, such as engaging all families from all backgrounds in education, but depending on the seriousness of the child's absenteeism and the factors contributing to his or her school absence, you may need to implement a more targeted approach to encourage school participation. Such targeted assistance ranges from offering incentives to attend school, such as field trips, to contacting truancy officers. Here are strategies that you can use in your efforts to reduce and eliminate absenteeism:

IMPLICATIONS FOR TEACHING

- Make every effort to involve or engage with all parents. Don't let any of your parents fall through the cracks. When parents feel that you value them and their children and want them to get involved, they are more likely to be involved and send their children to school.

- Stress with children and families the importance of school attendance. Talk about the importance of school attendance at your morning meetings. Send notes and newsletters with parents about providing them with reasons why it is important for their children to attend school.

- When children are absent, contact parents and inquire why children are not in school and ask what you can do to help.
- Offer classroom incentives for good attendance. Incentives can include certificates, awards, class field trips, etc.

Reflect and Apply: Home Visits

PARENTS' RIGHTS AND ACCOMMODATION OF DIVERSE LEARNERS

Now that you have read about the different ways to involve parents and bolster home–school collaboration, let's discuss some requirements for working with parents when their child has a disability. The Individuals with Disabilities Education Act of 2004 (IDEA) supports the belief that the education of children with disabilities is made more effective by strengthening the role of parents in the special education process. IDEA requires that parents participate in each step of the special education process and ensures this by giving parents the following protections:

- ***The right to give informed written consent and the right to confidentiality.*** Parents must give written permission before their child is evaluated, before services begin or are changed, and before information about their child is shared with anyone else.

- ***The right to receive written prior notice.*** Parents must receive written notice before any evaluations or assessments can take place and before each meeting to review the individualized family service plan (IFSP) or individualized education program (IEP).

- ***The right to a coordinated IFSP or IEP.*** A written plan is developed by a team of professionals and the parents to develop goals for the child and services that will best help reach those goals. This plan also describes when, where, and how services will be delivered.

- ***The right to receive services in natural environments and in the least restrictive environment.*** Services are focused on the family's and child's daily routines and are designed to be carried out within regular activities. The IFSP/IEP team must provide written justification if services are provided anywhere other than the natural environment or least restrictive environment.

- ***The right to review records.*** Parents may inspect, review, and receive a copy of their child's records.

- ***The right to a process to resolve disputes.*** Parents who feel their child's rights have been violated may file a written complaint or request mediation or a due process hearing.

Ensuring that children's needs are met and rights are upheld requires a system of communication that is consistent and mutually agreed on. Children's success at home and school is strengthened when this communication is reciprocal and positive. Parents and teachers have knowledge that, when shared, can benefit *all* children. Sharing back and forth between teachers and families is optimal because each has information the other may not have. The more information families and teachers have, the more they can collaborate to help children. Figure 17.2 shares information that families and teachers can use to effectively collaborate with each other to benefit all children.

Families share information on the child:

- History and development (milestones, medical information, and medication)
- Strengths and weaknesses at home
- Family dynamics that may affect learning and behavior
- Familial expectations
- Academic successes and deficits

Teachers share information on:

- Typical child development and developmental milestones
- The child's strengths and weaknesses at school
- School dynamics that may affect learning and behavior
- Resources available to assist families
- Scope and sequence of curriculum and possible modifications and adaptations

FIGURE 17.2 | Information Families and Teachers Use to Benefit Children

ACTIVITIES FOR PROFESSIONAL DEVELOPMENT

ETHICAL DILEMMA

"GETTING PARENTS TO EXERCISE THEIR RIGHTS IS THE HIGHEST FORM OF PARENT INVOLVEMENT"

Matt Hancock teaches second grade at Bridge City Elementary, a Title I school where 99 percent of the children are eligible for free or reduced lunches. Over the years, Matt has grown increasingly restive with his school's lack of efforts to increase student achievement and turn around its reputation as a "failing" school. The state legislature recently passed a "parent trigger law," giving parents the right to intervene in a struggling school and, among other things, give them the option to replace the principal, which Matt

thinks ought to happen. As Matt explains it, "There has to be shared responsibility between schools and parents for high student achievement. My kids are trapped in a failing school, and I want to make a difference. Getting the parents to exercise their legal rights is the highest form of parent involvement." On the other side of the issue, the district teachers' union is against the implementation of any parent trigger law provision. In fact, the president of the union has warned Matt, "Don't get involved!"

What should Matt do? Try to work with the union to get some much-needed improvements in his school? Or, should Matt take another course of action? Matt thinks he has no choice but to "take the issue public and get the local press involved." What would you advise Matt to do?

ACTIVITIES TO APPLY WHAT YOU LEARNED

1. Search the Internet for how current educational accountability and school reform movements are changing and shaping parents' attitudes about their involvement in and their relationship with the schools. Why are parents demanding more involvement in their children's schools? Conduct an online poll with your classmates regarding

their opinions pro or con for how involved they think parents and families should or should not be involved in their local schools. Use PowerPoint to share your poll results with your classmates.

2. Choose a demographic from the "Changing Families: Changing Involvement" section that interests you or you feel you need to learn more about in order to meet the needs of the children in your classroom. Create a PowerPoint presentation documenting research and general

information of this particular demographic and its implications for your classroom. Then create a list of ideas or events that you will use to encourage involvement of this family type in your classroom. Post your ideas to a teacher blog such as TeacherLingo and ask for comments.

3. **KEY ASSESSMENT:** Choose one type of parent/family involvement from the six types of parent/family involvement and develop a plan for parent/family involvement in a grade you plan to teach. Use the outline below.

   a. Identify the overall and specific objectives for your plan.

   b. Based on the type of involvement you choose, develop specific activities for involving families and providing services to them.

   c. Explain how you will involve different family types in your event (fathers, single parents, LGBT parents, military families, etc.).

   d. Explain how you will use community resources in your plan.

   Post your plan on your classroom discussion board and ask for comments from classmates. Use the rubric provided to guide your work.

4. Evaluate social services in your area and identify the particular services they offer to children and families. Compile a binder of resources that are easily accessible to children and families. Put the binder in your professional portfolio for future use.

5. A child in your kindergarten classroom has missed three consecutive days of school. You have decided to call a conference with the child's family to figure out what is going on. What questions would you ask about the child's frequent absences? What would you suggest to ensure the child misses no more days of school? What school or community resources would you involve to ensure the child has success in school? Post your information on your classroom discussion board.

6. Parents of children with disabilities have legal right regarding their involvement in the assessment and education of their children. Contact the special education services of two school districts in your area. Ask them to share with you the procedures they have put in place to assure that all parents' rights are respected and implemented. Ask your teacher if you can make a brief five-minute presentation to your class about what you learned.

LINKING TO LEARNING

The following agencies and programs, which can be located easily online, provide additional information about topics discussed in this chapter.

AARP
The AARP provides support and many interesting articles and links for grandparents who are rearing their grandchildren.

AVANCE
AVANCE is one of the oldest, largest, and most distinguished parenting and early childhood education programs in the country, providing innovative education and family support services to predominantly Hispanic families in low-income, at-risk communities.

Early Childhood Educators' and Family Web Corner
Early Childhood Educators' and Family Web Corner provides links to teacher pages, family pages, articles, and staff development resources.

Edvantia
Edvantia offers ways to keep abreast of what's happening with school–community partnerships to address the pressing needs of children and their families.

Family Education Network
This network is committed to strengthening and empowering families by providing communities with the counseling, education, resources, information, and training needed to promote a positive and nurturing environment in which to raise children.

National Coalition for Parent Involvement in Education
The coalition is dedicated to developing family–school partnerships throughout America; involving parents and families in their children's lives; and fostering relationships among home, school, and community, all of which can enhance the education of our nation's young people.

National Fatherhood Initiative
No other issue is as pervasive and destructive as father absence. Father absence is strongly linked to poverty, teen pregnancy, juvenile delinquency, abuse, suicide, and a host of other issues. This initiative is dedicated to giving our nation's children a brighter future by educating and engaging fathers.

National Parent Teacher Association (PTA)
The PTA calls for schools to promote partnerships that will increase parent involvement and participation in the social, emotional, and academic growth of children; it has voluntary National Standards for Parent/Family Involvement Programs.

National Network of Partnership Schools (NNPS)
NNPS invites schools, districts, states, and organizations to join together and use research-based approaches to organize and sustain excellent programs of family and community involvement that will increase student success in school.

APPENDIX

Time Line: The History of Early Childhood Education

1524 Martin Luther argued for public support of education for all children in his *Letter to the Mayors and Aldermen of All the Cities of Germany in Behalf of Christian Schools.*

1628 John Amos Comenius' *The Great Didactic* proclaimed the value of education for all children according to the laws of nature.

1762 Jean-Jacques Rousseau wrote *Émile,* explaining that education should take into account the child's natural growth and interests.

1780 Robert Raikes initiated the Sunday School movement in England to teach Bible study and religion to children.

1801 Johann Pestalozzi wrote *How Gertrude Teaches Her Children,* emphasizing home education and learning by discovery.

1816 Robert Owen set up a nursery school in Great Britain at the New Lanark Cotton Mills, believing that early education could counteract bad influences of the home.

1817 In Hartford, Connecticut, Thomas Gallaudet founded the first residential school for the deaf.

1824 The American Sunday School Union formed with the purpose of initiating Sunday Schools around the United States.

1836 William McGuffey published the *Eclectic Reader* for elementary school children. His writing had a strong impact on moral and literary attitudes in the nineteenth century.

1837 Friedrich Froebel established the first kindergarten in Blankenburgh, Germany. Frobel is known as the father of the kindergarten.

1837 Horace Mann began his job as secretary of the Massachusetts State Board of Education. Mann is often called the father of the common schools because of the role he played in helping set up the elementary school system in the United States.

1837 In France Edouard Seguin, influenced by Jean Itard, started the first school for the feebleminded.

1856 Mrs. Margarethe Schurz established the first kindergarten in the United States in Watertown, Wisconsin; the school was founded for children of German immigrants, and the program was conducted in German.

1860 Elizabeth Peabody opened a private kindergarten in Boston, Massachusetts, for English-speaking children.

1869 The first special education class for the deaf founded in Boston.

1871 The first public kindergarten opened in North America in Ontario, Canada.

1873 Susan Blow opened the first public school kindergarten in the United States in St. Louis, Missouri, as a cooperative effort with superintendent of schools William Harris.

1876 A model kindergarten was part of the Philadelphia Centennial Exposition.

1880 The first teacher-training program for teachers of kindergarten opened in Oshkosh Normal School, Philadelphia.

1884 The American Association of Elementary, Kindergarten, and Nursery School Educators founded to serve in a consulting capacity for other educators.

1892 The International Kindergarten Union (IKU) established.

1896 John Dewey started the Laboratory School at the University of Chicago, basing his program on child-centered learning with an emphasis on life experiences.

1905 Sigmund Freud wrote *Three Essays of the Theory of Sexuality,* emphasizing the value of a healthy emotional environment during childhood.

1907 In Rome, Maria Montessori started her first preschool, called Children's House; she based her now-famous teaching method on the theory that children learn best by themselves in a properly prepared environment.

1909 Theodore Roosevelt convened the first White House Conference on Children.

1911 Arnold Gesell, well known for his research on the importance of the preschool years, began his child development study at Yale University.

1911 Margaret and Rachel McMillan founded an open-air nursery school in Great Britain in which the class met outdoors; emphasis was on healthy living.

1912 Arnold and Beatrice Gesell wrote *The Normal Child and Primary Education*.

1915 In New York City Eva McLin started the first U.S. Montessori nursery school.

1915 The Child Education Foundation of New York City founded a nursery school using Montessori's principles.

1918 The first public nursery schools in Great Britain started.

1919 Harriet Johnson started the Nursery School of the Bureau of Educational Experiments, later to become the Bank Street College of Education.

1921 Patty Smith Hill started a progressive laboratory nursery school at Columbia Teachers College.

1921 A. S. Neill founded Summerhill, an experimental school based on the ideas of Rousseau and Dewey.

1922 With Edna Noble White as its first director, the Merrill-Palmer Institute Nursery School opened in Detroit, with the purpose of preparing women in proper child care. The Institute was known as the Merrill-Palmer School of Motherhood and Home Training.

1922 Abigail Eliot, influenced by the open-air school in Great Britain and basing her program on personal hygiene and proper behavior, started the Ruggles Street Nursery School in Boston.

1924 *Childhood Education,* the first professional journal in early childhood education, was published by the International Kindergarten Union (IKU).

1926 Patty Smith Hill at Columbia Teachers College founded the National Committee on Nursery Schools; now called the National Association for the Education of Young Children, it provides guidance and consultant services for educators.

1926 Founding of the National Association of Nursery Education (NANE).

1930 The International Kindergarten Union (IKU) changed its name to the Association for Childhood Education.

1933 The Works Projects Administration (WPA) provided money to start nursery schools so that unemployed teachers would have jobs.

1935 The first toy-lending library founded by Toy Loan in Los Angeles.

1940 The Lanham Act provided funds for child care during World War II, mainly for day care centers for children whose mothers worked in the war effort.

1943 Kaiser Child Care Centers opened in Portland, Oregon, to provide twenty-four-hour child care for children of mothers working in war-related industries.

1944 The National Association of Nursery Education published *Young Children*.

1946 Dr. Benjamin Spock wrote the *Common Sense Book of Baby and Child Care*.

1950 Erik Erickson published his writings on the eight ages or stages of personality growth and development and identified tasks for each stage of development; the information, known as Personality in the Making, formed the basis for the 1950 White House Conference on Children and Youth.

1952 Jean Piaget's *The Origins of Intelligence in Children* first published in English.

1955 Rudolf Flesch's *Why Johnny Can't Read* criticized the schools for their methodology in teaching reading and other basic skills.

1957 The Soviet Union launched *Sputnik,* sparking renewed interest in other educational systems and marking the beginning of the rediscovery of early childhood education.

1958 Congress passed The National Defense Education Act to provide federal funds for improving education in the sciences, mathematics, and foreign languages.

1960 Katharine Whiteside Taylor founded the American Council of Parent Cooperatives for those interested in exchanging ideas about preschool education; it later became the Parent Cooperative Preschools International.

1960 The Day Care and Child Development Council of America created to publicize the need for quality services for children.

1964 At its Miami Beach conference, the National Association of Nursery Education became the National Association for the Education of Young Children (NAEYC).

1964 Congress passed The Economic Opportunity Act of 1964, marking the beginning of the War on Poverty and the foundation for Head Start.

1965 Congress passed The Elementary and Secondary Education Act to provide federal money for programs for educationally deprived children.

1965 The Head Start program began with federal money allocated for preschool education; the early programs were known as child development centers.

1966 The Bureau of Education for the Handicapped established.

1967 The Follow Through program was initiated to extend Head Start into the primary grades.

1968 B. F. Skinner wrote *The Technology of Teaching,* which outlined a programmed approach to learning.

1968 The federal government established the Handicapped Children's Early Education Program to fund model preschool programs for children with disabilities.

1970 The White House Conference on Children and Youth.

1971 The Stride Rite Corporation in Boston was the first to start a corporate-supported child care program.

1972 The National Home Start Program began for the purpose of involving parents in their children's education.

1975 Congress passed Public Law–142, the Education for All Handicapped Children Act, mandating a free and appropriate education for all children with disabilities and extending many rights to the parents of such children.

1979 The International Year of the Child sponsored by The United Nations and designated by executive order.

1980 The first American *lekotek* (toy-lending library) opened its doors in Evanston, Illinois.

1980 The White House Conference on Families.

1981 Congress passed The Head Start Act of 1981 to extend Head Start and provide for effective delivery of comprehensive services to economically disadvantaged children and their families.

1981 Secretary of Education Terrell Bell announced the establishment of the National Commission on Excellence in Education.

1982 The Mississippi legislature established mandatory statewide public kindergartens.

1983 An Arkansas commission chaired by Hillary Clinton called for mandatory kindergarten and lower pupil–teacher ratios in the early grades.

1984 The HighScope Educational Foundation released a study that documented the value of high-quality preschool programs for poor children, a study cited repeatedly in later years by those favoring expansion of Head Start and other early-years programs.

1985 Head Start celebrated its twentieth anniversary with a joint resolution of the Senate and House "reaffirming congressional support."

1986 The U.S. Secretary of Education proclaimed this the Year of the Elementary School, saying, "Let's do all we can this year to remind this nation that the time our children spend in elementary school is crucial to everything they will do for the rest of their lives."

1986 Public Law 99–457 (the Education of the Handicapped Act Amendments) established a national policy on early intervention that recognizes its benefits, provides assistance to states to build systems of service delivery, and recognizes the unique roles of families in the development of their children with disabilities.

1987 Congress created the National Commission to Prevent Infant Mortality.

1988 Vermont announced plans to assess student performance on the basis of work portfolios as well as test scores.

1989 United Nations Convention adopted the Rights of the Child.

1990 The United Nations Convention on the Rights of the Child went into effect, following its signing by twenty nations.

1990 Head Start celebrated its twenty-fifth anniversary.

1991 Education Alternatives, Inc., a for-profit firm, opened South Pointe Elementary School in Miami, Florida, the first public school in the nation to be run by a private company.

1991 The Carnegie Foundation issued "Ready to Learn," a plan to ensure children's readiness for school.

1994 The United Nations declared 1994 the Year of the Indigenous Child.

1995 Head Start reauthorization established a new program, Early Head Start, for low-income pregnant women and families with infants and toddlers.

1999 As part of the effort to strengthen educational opportunities for America's six million students with disabilities, the Department of Education issued final regulations for implementing the Individuals with Disabilities Education Act (IDEA) of 1997.

1999 Florida became the first state in the nation to pass a statewide school voucher plan; the law gives children in academically failing public schools a chance to attend private, secular, or religious schools with public money.

2000 Head Start celebrated its thirty-fifth anniversary.

2002 President George W. Bush signed Public Law 107–110, the No Child Left Behind Act of 2001. NCLB contains four basic provisions: stronger accountability for results, increased flexibility and local control, expanded options for parents, and an emphasis on teaching methods that have been proven to work.

2003 The United Nations launched the Literacy Decade (2003–2012) in order to reduce world illiteracy rates. The theme is Literacy as Freedom.

2007 Congress passed the Improving Head Start for School Readiness Act of 2007, which reauthorized the Head Start program through 2012.

2009 President Barack Obama signed the American Reinvestment and Recovery Act of 2009, which provided more than $90 billion for education, nearly half of which went to local school districts to prevent layoffs and for school modernization and repair.

2010 Head Start Celebrated forty-five years of success.

2012 The U.S. Census Bureau released poverty data that revealed that child poverty remained at record high levels. More than one in five children in America, 16.1 million, live in poverty.

2013 In his State of the Union address, President Barack Obama called on Congress to expand access to high-quality preschool to every child in America. This initiated a renewed interest in the preschool movement.

ENDNOTES

CHAPTER 1

1. L. J. Schweinhart, J. Montie, Z. Xiang, W. S. Barnett, C. R. Belfield, and M. Nores, *Lifetime Effects: The High/Scope Perry Preschool Study Through Age 40* (Ypsilanti, MI: High/Scope Press, 2005).

2. University of North Carolina at Chapel Hill, "Benefits of High Quality Child Care Persist 30 Years Later," January 19, 2012; accessed on September 17, 2012, at http://uncnews.unc.edu/content/view/5032/107/; Promising Practices Network, March 2013; accessed on March 23, 2013, at www.promisingpractices.net/programs.asp.

3. W. S. Barnett, M. E. Carolan, J. Fitzgerald, and J. H. Squires, *The State of Preschool 2011: State Preschool Yearbook* (New Brunswick, NJ: National Institute for Early Education Research, 2011); accessed on September 17, 2012, at http://nieer.org/sites/nieer/files/2011yearbook.pdf.

4. Council of Chief State School Officers, "CA Teacher Named 2012 National Teacher of the Year," April 23, 2012; accessed on March 23, 2013, at www.ccsso.org/News_and_Events/Press_Releases/CA_Teacher_Named_2012_National_Teacher_of_the_Year.html.

5. National Association for the Education of Young Children, *2010 NAEYC Standards for Initial and Advanced Early Childhood Professional Preparation Programs*, April 2012; accessed on September 17, 2012, at www.naeyc.org/ncate/files/ncate/file/faculty/Standards/NAEYC%20Initial%20and%20Advanced%20Standards%203_2012.pdf.

6. Tina Repetti-Renzullo, "Teacher of the Year, Philosophy of Teaching," Teacher 2 Teacher; accessed on March 30, 2013, at http://teacher2teacher.lacoe.edu/teacher-of-the-year-philosophy-of-teaching.aspx.

7. Forum on Child and Family Statistics, *America's Children: Key National Indicators of Well-Being,* 2011; accessed on May 26, 2012, at www.childstats.gov/americaschildren/eco1.asp.

8. Evelyn Pringle, "Schools Failing Children With Disabilities," 2006; accessed on May 26, 2012, at www.lawyersandsettlements.com/articles/civil-human-rights/school_disability-00121.html.

9. Indiana Department of Education, "Melanie Park," September 27, 2011; accessed on September 18, 2012, at www.doc.in.gov/improvement/educator-effectiveness/melanie-park.

10. P. Anderson, "2011 Elementary Teacher of the Year," Hawaii Association for Health, Physical Education, and Recreation, and Dance, August 14, 2011; accessed on September 18, 2012, at http://hahperd.org/?p=189.

11. A. Borys and L. Chiarello, *Promoting Disability Awareness and Acceptance in Childhood;* accessed on September 18, 2012, at http://wiki.uiowa.edu/download/attachments/34245691/RHAB-Disability_Awareness_Manual.pdf.

12. Austin EcoSchool, "EcoSchool Principles," 2012; accessed on September 17, 2012, at http://austin-ecoschool.org/principle/.

13. J. Klein, "Childcare Centers Going Green: A Guide to Parents," *Gaiam Life*, 2011; accessed on September 17, 2012, at http://life.gaiam.com/article/childcare-centers-going-green-guide-parents.

14. Texas Association of School Administrators, "Teacher of the Year," 2012; accessed on September 19, 2012, at www.tasanet.org/?q=node/413.

15. A. M. Bush, "Boy's 'Second Voice' Helps Him Communicate," *Fosters.com*, January 1, 2010; accessed on September 19, 2012, at www.fosters.com/apps/pbcs.dll/article?AID=/20100101/GJLIFESTYLES/912299977/-1/CITLIFESTYLES10&template=citAParticle.

16. The Associated Press, "Program Pairs Autistic Students with Peer Tutors," *Education Week*, December 3, 2009; accessed on December 17, 2009, at www.edweek.org/ew/articles/2009/12/03/316933idtutoringprogram_ap.html?r=1234616367.

17. S. Sandall, M. L. Hemmeter, B. J. Smith, and M. E. McLean, *DEC Recommended Practices* (Longmont, CO: Sopris West, 2005), 113–118.

18. R. Allen, "The ABC's of Kindergarten," 2012–2013; accessed on September 19, 2012, at http://mrsallan.woodriver.k12.ne.us/miscstuff/12-13/ABC'sOfKindergarten.pdf.

19. M. Marquez, "My Philosophy of Teaching," Plano ISD; accessed on September 19, 2012, at www.pisd.edu/about.us/awards.ratings/maria.marquez.shtml.

20. National Association for the Education of Young Children, *NAEYC Initial Licensure Standards*, "Initial Licensure Programs" (Washington, DC: NAEYC, 2001), 15.

21. AllThingsPLC, "Research, Educational Tools, and Blog for Building a Professional Learning Community"; accessed on September 19, 2012, at www.allthingsplc.info/evidence/pinewoodelementaryschool/index.php.

22. National Association for the Education of Young Children, *NAEYC Standards for Early Childhood Professional Preparation Programs* (Washington, DC: NAEYC, 2009), 16.

23. Michelle Shearer, "Making a Difference–Shaping the Future," 2011, accessed on May 26, 2012, at www.ccsso.org/Documents/NTOY/Applications/2011NTOYfinMDapp.pdf.

24. *Daily Herald*, "Teachers Awarded Grants for Innovative Teaching," October 3, 2008; accessed on January 5, 2010, at www.dailyherald.com/story/?id=239576.

25. Indian Prairie School District, Robert E. Clow Elementary School, *Second Grade—Social Studies*; accessed on September 19, 2012, at http://clow.ipsd.org/academics_2_soc.html.

26. National Council for Accreditation of Teacher Education, *NCATE Unit Standards* (Washington, DC: NCATE, 2007).

27. M. Ackley, "Okemos Elementary School Teacher Named Michigan Teacher of the Year," May 14, 2009; accessed on January 8, 2010, at http://michigan.michigan.gov/mde/0,1607,7-140—214772—,00.html.

28. Ibid., 24.

29. Ibid., 24–25.

30. Northfield Public Schools, "Professional Learning Communities," 2012; accessed on September 19, 2012, at http://nfld.k12.mn.us/longfellow/curriculum/plcs/.

31. L. Killough, "Connecticut's 2010 Teacher of the Year Featured in the Advisor," Read. React. Respond. Blog CEA, December 3, 2009; accessed on January 8, 2010, at http://blogcea.org/2009/12/03/2010-teacher-of-the-year.

32. C. Copple and S. Bredekamp, *Developmentally Appropriate Practice in Early Childhood Programs,* 3rd ed. (Washington, DC: National Association for the Education of Young Children, 2009).

33. Universities.com, "Associate Degree in Early Childhood Education at Arkansas State University"; accessed on September 19, 2012, at www.universities.com/edu/Associate_degree_in_Early_Childhood_Education_at_Arkansas_State_University_Heber_Springs_AR.html.

34. Council of Chief State School Officers, "CCSSO Announces Finalists for 2012 Teacher of the Year," January 19, 2012; accessed on September 19, 2012, at http://www.ccsso.org/News_and_Events/Press_Releases/CCSSO_Announces_Finalists_for_2012_National_Teacher_of_the_Year.html.

35. The Partnership for 21st Century Skills, 2011; accessed on September 19, 2012, at www.p21.org/index.php.

36. E. Ezureick, "Teacher of the Year Bios," blog, May 1, 2009; accessed on May 28, 2012, at http://ezureick.wordpress.com/2009/05/01/teacher-of-the-year-bios/.

37. B. Tabor, "Outstanding Achievement," *Denton Record-Chronicle,* November 14, 2011; accessed on September 18, 2012, at www.dentonrc.com/local-news/education/in-the-schools-headlines/20111114-outstanding-achievement.ece.

38. Third Grade Teachers, A Free Online Community for Third Grade Teachers and Support Staff, blog, http://third-grade-teachers.ning.com/.

39. DEC/NAEYC, *Early Childhood Inclusion: A Joint Position Statement of the Division for Early Childhood (DEC) and the National Association for the Education of Young Children (NAEYC)* (Chapel Hill, NC: The University of North Carolina, FPG Child Development Institute, 2009).

40. Ibid.

CHAPTER 2

1. *Education News,* "Poor Schools and Poor Kids?", January 5, 2010; accessed on April 13, 2013, at www.educationnews.org/commentaries/20787.html.

2. U.S. Department of Health and Human Services, 2013 Poverty Levels Guidelines; accessed on June 14, 2013, at http://aspe.hhs.gov/poverty/13poverty.cfm.

3. M. Edelman, "Leaving the Littlest Ones Behind," 2010; accessed on May 28, 2012, at http://news.change.org/stories/leaving-the-littlest-ones-behind.

4. Education.com, Achievement Gap, accessed on November 8, 2011, at http://www.education.com/definition/achievement-gap/.

5. McKinsey and Company, *The Economic Impact of the Achievement Gap in America's Schools,* April 2009; accessed on May 28, 2012, at http://mckinseyonsociety.com/the-economic-impact-of-the-achievement-gap-in-americas-schools/.

6. Ibid.

7. Ibid.

8. N. Fouad, G. Hackett, S. Haag, et al. "Barriers and Supports for Continuing in Mathematics and Science: Gender and Educational Level Differences," updated 2010; accessed on May 28, 2012, at http://www.sciencedirect.com/science/article/pii/S0001879110001168.

9. Ibid.

10. Children's Defense Fund, Addressing the Achievement Gap Symposium, July 25, 2012; accessed on June 14, 2013, at http://www.childrensdefense.org/policy-priorities/early-childhood-education-care/ets.html.

11. S. Lewis, *A Call for Change: The Social and Educational Factor Contributing to the Outcomes of Black Males in Urban Schools* (Washington, DC: Council of the Great City Schools, 2010), accessed on May 28, 2012, at http://graphics8.nytimes.com/packages/pdf/opinion/A-Call-For-Change.pdf.

12. Center for Educator Compensation Reform, General Compensation Question, "Does Evidence Suggest That Some Teachers Are Significantly More Effective Than Others at Improving Student Achievement?"; accessed on May 28, 2012, at http://cecr.ed.gov/guides/researchSyntheses/Research%20Synthesis_Q%20A1.pdf.

13. D. Johnson and A. Rudolph, "Beyond Social Promotion and Retention-Five Strategies to Help Students Succeed," 2001; accessed on May 28, 2012, at http://www.ncrel.org/sdrs/areas/issues/students/atrisk/at800.htm.

14. NEA Today, "How Do We Increase Teacher Quality in Low-Income Schools?", May 24, 2011; accessed on June 14, 2013, at http://neatoday.org/2011/05/24/how-do-we-increase-teacher-quality-at-low-income-schools/.

15. U.S Department of Defense, Education Activity, "2011 Teacher of the Year," November 3, 2010; accessed on June 14, 2013, at http://www.dodea.edu/newsroom/pressreleases/11032010.cfm.

16. U. Bronfenbrenner, *The Ecology of Human Development: Experiments by Nature and Design* (Cambridge, MA: Harvard University Press, 1979).

17. Center for Health and Health Care in Schools, "School Based Health," 2011; accessed on April 13, 2013, at http://www.healthinschools.org/about-us.aspx.

18. Population Reference Bureau, "More Mothers of Young Children in U.S Workforce" November 7, 2011; accessed on June 14, 2013, at http://www.prb.org/Publications/Articles/2012/us-working-mothers-with-children.aspx.

19. M. Brick, TinyEYE Therapy Services, "Overview"; accessed on April 13, 2013, at www.scribd.com/doc/11476769/TinyEYE-Collaborating-With-Families-for-Preschool.

20. National Center for Family Literacy, "Toyota: Committed to Moving Families Forward"; accessed on April 13, 2013, at www.famlit.org/toyota.

21. *Science Daily,* "Number of Stay-at-Home Dads Increasing," July 17, 2007; accessed on August 27, 2009, at www.sciencedaily.com/upi/index.php?feed=TopNews&article=UPI-1-20070617-12130500-bc-us-fathers.xml.

22. Centers for Disease Control and Prevention, "Unmarried Childbearing," January 18, 2013; accessed on June 14, 2013 at http://www.cdc.gov/nchs/fastats/unmarry.htm.

23. Centers for Disease Control and Prevention, "Marriage and Divorce," February 19, 2013; accessed on April 13, 2013, at http://www.cdc.gov/nchs/nvss/marriage_divorce_tables.htm.

24. "School Family Community Partnership Ideas," n.d.; accessed on April 13, 2013, at www.naperville203.org/parents-students/ProgramIdeasPS.asp.

25. Center for the Improvement of Child Caring, "Parenting Skill-Building Programs," n.d.; accessed on September 19, 2012, at www.ciccparenting.org/cicc_sbp_11.asp.

26. Joseph A. Lopez, "The Cost of Publicly Financed Dental Care in Relation to Community Water Fluoridation in Texas,"

Texas Medical Center Dissertations (via ProQuest), paper no. AAI1480447, January 1, 2010; accessed on August 5, 2013, at http://digitalcommons.library.tmc.edu/dissertations/AAI1480447.

27. Ibid.

28. American Lung Association, "Asthma and Children Fact Sheet," November 2011; accessed August 15, 2013, http://www.lungusa.org/lung-disease/asthma/resources/facts-and-figures/asthma-children-fact-sheet.html.

29. Oregon Public Health Division, "Childhood Lead Poisoning: Going, But Not Gone," *CD Summary* 62, no. 13 (June 18, 2013); accessed on August 24, 2013, at https://public.health.oregon.gov/DiseasesConditions/CommunicableDisease/CD-SummaryNewsletter/Documents/2013/ohd6213.pdf.

30. National Institute for Environmental Health, "Lead Poisoning," 2010; accessed on May 28, 2012, at http://kids.niehs.nih.gov/explore/pollute/lead.htm.

31. Centers for Disease Control and Prevention, "Children and Diabetes," 2012 update; accessed on May 29, 2012, at http://www.cdc.gov/diabetes/projects/cda2.htm.

32. American Diabetes Association, "Diabetes Basics, Definitions"; accessed on May 29, 2012, at http://www.diabetes.org/diabetes-basics/type-1/.

33. Children with Diabetes, "What You Should Know," 2005; accessed on May 29, 2012, at http://www.childrenwithdiabetes.com/cgi-bin/cwdprintpage.pl?url=http://www.childrenwithdiabetes.com/d_0n_d00.htm.

34. American Heart Association, "Overweight in Children," 2012 update; accessed on May 28, 2012, at http://www.heart.org/HEARTORG/GettingHealthy/WeightManagement/Obesity/Overweight-in-Children_UCM_304054_Article.jsp#.

35. J. Harrington, "Identifying the 'Tipping Point' Age for Overweight Pediatric Patients," *Science Daily,* February 11, 2010; accessed on May 28, 2012, at http://www.sciencedaily.com/releases/2010/02/100211121832.htm.

36. American Academy of Children and Adolescent, "Obesity in Children And Teens," 2011, accessed on May 28, 2012, at http://www.aacap.org/cs/root/facts_for_families/obesity_in_children_and_teens.

37. R. Nauert, "Misperception of Weight Ups Teen Depression Risk," *Psych Central* (2009); accessed on May 28, 2012, at http://psychcentral.com/news/2010/06/29/misperception-of-weight-ups-teen-depression-risk/15189.html.

38. New Mexico AppleSeed, "Full Stomachs = Full Minds: A Guide to 'Breakfast After the Bell,'" 2011; accessed on May 28, 2012, at http://nmappleseed.org/www.nmappleseed.org/Publications_files/Final%20breakfast%205%3A9.pdf.

39. L. Brown, W. Beardslee, and D. Prothrow-Smith, *Impact of School Breakfast on Children's Health and Learning: An Analysis of the Scientific Research,* November 17, 2008; accessed on May 28, 2012, at http://bestpractices.nokidhungry.org/download/file/fid/263.

40. University of Michigan Health Systems, "Obesity and Overweight," 2011; accessed on May 28, 2012, at http://www.med.umich.edu/yourchild/topics/obesity.htm.

41. V. Strauss , "School Junk Food Ban Works, Study Finds," *The Washington Post,* May 30, 2010; accessed on May 28, 2012, at http://voices.washingtonpost.com/answer-sheet/health-1/school-junk-food-ban-works---.html.

42. Robert Wood Johnson Foundation, "Arkansas Schools, Parents Adjusting Well to State Efforts to Curb Obesity," June 17, 2008;

accessed on May 28, 2012, at http://www.rwjf.org/newsroom/product.jsp?id=31911.

43. Nutrition Services Department, RUSD Center for Food and Justice, "Riverside Unified School District Farmers' Market Salad Bar Program," September 2010; accessed on May 28, 2012, at https://saladbars2schools.org/pdf/Riverside-SBP.pdf.

44. T. Shanks, Y. Kim, V. Loke, and M. Destin, *Assets and Child Well-Being in Developed Countries, Children and Youth Services Review* (St. Louis, MO: Center for Social Development, 2010), accessed on May 28, 2012, at http://csd.wustl.edu/Publications/Documents/WP09-66.pdf.

45. Centers for Disease Control and Prevention, "Violence Prevention," May 18, 2012; accessed on May 28, 2012, at http://www.cdc.gov/ViolencePrevention/.

46. Ibid.

47. Ibid.

48. California State University, Television and Health, "Television Statistics," 2010; accessed on May 28, 2012, from http://www.csun.edu/science/health/docs/tv&health.html.

49. Ibid.

50. National Institute on Media and the Family, "Children and Media Violence," November 2006; accessed on May 28, 2012, from http://www.mediafamily.org/facts/facts_vlent.shtml.

51. Eyes on Bullying, Education Development Center Inc., "Child Care," 2010; accessed on May 28, 2012, at http://www.eyesonbullying.org/childcare.html.

52. WebMD, Health and Parenting, "Bullying—What Children Should Do If They Are Bullied," December 23, 2010; accessed on May 28, 2012, at http://www.webmd.com/parenting/tc/bullying-what-children-should-do-if-they-are-bullied.

53. *Science Daily,* "More Than 25% of Teenagers Have Suffered Cyber Bullying in the Past Year," December 15, 2010; accessed on May 28, 2012, at http://www.sciencedaily.com/releases/2010/12/101214085734.htm.

54. National Center for Mental Health Promotion and Youth Violence Prevention, "Preventing Cyber Bullying in the School and the Community," 2009; accessed on May 28, 2012, at http://www.promoteprevent.org/Publications/center-briefs/Cyberbullying%20Prevention%20Brief.pdf.

55. United States Census Bureau, "Hispanic Heritage Month 2011: Sept. 15–Oct. 15," August 26, 2011; accessed on April 13, 2013, at http://www.census.gov/newsroom/releases/archives/facts_for_features_special_editions/cb11-ff18.html.

56. S. Dewan, "Southern Schools Mark Two Majorities," *New York Times,* January 6, 2010; accessed on April 13, 2013, at www.nytimes.com/2010/01/07/us/07south.html.

57. K. A. Magnuson, H. R. Sexton, P. E. Davis-Kean, and A. C. Huston, "Increases in Maternal Education and Young Children Language Skills," *Merrill-Palmer Quarterly*; accessed on September 20, 2012, at http://findarticles.com/p/articles/mi_qa3749/is_200907/ai_n32127514/.

58. State Council on Alcohol and Other Drug Abuse, "Cultural Competency Definition," August 22, 2008; accessed on August 10, 2013, at www.scaoda.state.wi.us/docs/main/CulturalCompetencyDefinition.pdf.

59. Council for Exceptional Children, Cultural and Linguistic Diversity; accessed on September 20, 2012, at www.cec.sped.org/AM/Template.cfm?Section=Cultural_and_Linguistic_Diversity&Template=/TaggedPage/TaggedPageDisplay.cfm&TPLID=36&ContentID=5541.

60. Green Building Council, "Green Building Research"; accessed on September 18, 2012, from http://www.usgbc.org/Docs/Archive/General/Docs3402.pdf.

61. The Garden Club of America, "Elizabeth Abernathy Hull Fund for Early Environmental Education," 2012; accessed on April 13, 2013, at http://www2.gcamerica.org/gca-awards-Hull-Award.cfm.

62. George Morrison, "How the Rise of China Will Change Everything," *Jola Montessori* 81 (2008); accessed on April 13, 2013, at http://jola-montessori.com/article/george-morrison-12/.

63. The White House, "Changing the Equation in STEM Education"; accessed on April 13, 2013, at http://www.whitehouse.gov/blog/2010/09/16/changing-equation-stem-education.

CHAPTER 3

1. Teacher Lingo, Lingo Message Boards, *Assessment*; accessed April 13, 2013, from http://teacherlingo.com/forums/post/210359.aspx.

2. M. Sommerville, *Kindergarten's 3 R's: Respect, Resources and Rants,* April 12, 2008; accessed April 13, 2013, from http://kidney-garden.blogspot.com/.

3. Ibid.

4. Texas Education Agency, Texas Essential Knowledge and Skills for English Language Arts and Reading: Subchapter A: Elementary, 2008; accessed April 13, 2013, from http://ritter.tea.state.tx.us/rules/tac/chapter110/ch110a.pdf.

5. M. Rose, "Make Room for Rubrics," accessed April 13, 2013, at http://teacher.scholastic.com/professional/assessment/room-forubrics.htm.

6. J. M. Hintze and W. J. Matthews, "The Generalizability of Systematic Direct Observations Across Time and Setting: A Preliminary Investigation of the Psychometrics of Behavioral Observation," *School Psychology Review 33,* no. 2 (2004): 258–270.

7. NMSA, C. Garrison, and M. Ehringhaus, *Formative and Summative Assessments in the Classroom*; accessed April 13, 2013, from http://www.scribd.com/doc/28317120/Formative-and-Summative-Assessment.

8. Ibid.

9. CO ST §22-1-116, http://mb2.ecs.org/reports/Report.aspx?id=31.

10. CO ST §22-7-504, http://mb2.ecs.org/reports/Report.aspx?id=31.

11. J. O'Brian, "How Screening Assessment Practices Support Quality Disabilities Services in Head Start," *Head Start Bulletin* 70 (April 2001): 20–24.

12. P. Hartigan, "Pressure-Cooker Kindergarten," *The Boston Globe,* August 30, 2009; accessed April 13, 2013, from www.boston.com/community/moms/articles/2009/08/30/pressure_cooker_kindergarten/?page=1.

13. S. J. Bagnato, J. T. Neisworth, and K. Pretti-Frontczak, *LINKing Authentic Assessment and Early Childhood Intervention: Best Measures for Best Practices,* 4th ed. (Baltimore, MD: Paul Brookes, 2009).

14. Testimony of Ben Allen, Ph.D., Research and Evaluation Director, National Head Start Association, Before the National Research Council Committee on Developmental Outcomes and Assessments for Young Children. July 6, 2007; accessed April 13, 2013, from http://policy.gmu.edu/currents/volume8/issue01/NHSABenAllenTestimony.pdf.

15. National Education Association, *NEA Policy Brief: English Language Learners Face Unique Challenges,* 2008; accessed August 10, 2009, from www.nea.org/assets/docs/mf_PB05_ELL.pdf.

16. Ibid.

17. Ibid.

18. Ibid.

19. Ibid.

20. WIDA Consortium, *WIDA Focus on Language and Culture: Variables Affecting Individual Academic Achievement*; accessed April 13, 2013, from www.wida.us/resources/focus/Bulletin1.pdf.

21. Ibid.

22. Ibid.

23. *The Seattle Times,* "Seattle Special-Ed Teachers Suspended for Refusal to Give Test," March 6, 2009; accessed April 13, 2013, from http://seattletimes.nwsource.com/html/education/2008819875_suspension06m.html.

CHAPTER 4

1. B. Beatty, "Past, Present and Future," *The American Prospect, Online Edition* (November 2004); accessed August 16, 2012, at www.prospect.org/cs/articles?article=past_present_and_future.

2. S. Broughman, S. Tourkin, and N. Swaim, "Private School Universe Survey: Survey Documentation for the School Year 2009–10," National Center for Education Statistics, July 2012; accessed April 30, 2013, from http://nces.ed.gov/pubs2012/2012323.pdf.

3. J. A. Comenius, *The Great Didactic of John Amos Comenius,* ed. and trans. M. W. Keating (New York: Russell & Russell, 1967), 58.

4. J. Rousseau, *Émile; Or, Education,* trans. B. Foxley (New York: Dutton, Everyman's Library, 1933), 5.

5. A. W. Boyd, "Redshirting: Holding Back to Get Ahead," The Daily Record.com. July, 2012, accessed on April 30, 2013, at http://www.dailyrecord.com/article/20120719/NJNEWS/307190060/Redshirting-Holding-back-get-ahead-?odyssey=nav|head.

6. Roger DeGuimps, *Pestalozzi: His Life and Work* (New York: Appleton, 1890), 196.

7. A. Hassan, *Chapter 1: Shipyard Day Care Centers of World War II: The Kaiser Experiment*; accessed on April 30, 2013, from http://wwiishipyarddaycare.tripod.com/intro.htm.

8. K. Wellhousen and J. Kieff, *A Constructivist Approach to Block Play in Early Childhood* (New York: Delmar, 2002).

9. R. D. Archambault, ed., *John Dewey on Education—Selected Writings* (New York: Random House, 1964), 430.

10. M. Montessori, *The Discovery of the Child,* trans. M. J. Costelloe (Notre Dame, IN: Fides, 1967), 22.

11. American Montessori Society, "The Glass Classroom," 2013; accessed on April 30, 2013, at http://www.amshq.org/Montessori%20Education/History%20of%20Montessori%20Education/the_glass_classroom.aspx.

12. Forest Schools; accessed on August 13, 2012, from www.forestschools.com/history-of-forest-schools.php.

13. Partnership for the 21st Century Skills, "Framework for 21st Century Learning," March 2011; accessed on April 30, 2013, at http://www.p21.org/storage/documents/1.__p21_framework_2-pager.pdf.

14. eSchool News, *Support grows for common standards,* May 5, 2009; accessed on April 30, 2013, from www.eschoolnews.com/2009/05/05/support-grows-for-common-standards/.

15. S. Malburg, "Understanding the Basics of Title I Funds." Bright Hub Education, October 2012; accessed on April 30,

2013, at http://www.brighthubeducation.com/teaching-methods-tips/11105-basics-of-title-1-funds/.

16. Texas Department of Agriculture, "Income Eligibility Guidelines," 2012; accessed on April 30, 2013, at http://www.squaremeals.org/Publications/IncomeEligibilityGuidelines.aspx#CACFP.

17. US Department of Education, "Improving Basic Programs Operated by Local Educational Agencies (Title I, Part A)," 2011; accessed on April 30, 2013, from www2.ed.gov/programs/titleiparta/index.html.

18. M. Rich, "No Child Law Whittled Down by White House," *New York Times*, July 6, 2012; accessed on April 30, 2013, at http://www.nytimes.com/2012/07/06/education/no-child-left-behind-whittled-down-under-obama.html?pagewanted=all.

19. US Department of Education Archives, *A Nation At Risk: The Imperative for Educational Reform*, April 1983; accessed on April 30, 2013 at http://datacenter.spps.org/uploads/SOTW_A_Nation_at_Risk_1983.pdf

20. C. Copple and S. Bredekamp, eds., *Developmentally Appropriate Practice in Early Childhood Programs: Serving Children from Birth Through Age 8*, 3rd ed. (Washington, DC: National Association for the Education of Young Children, 2009), xii.

21. S. Mintz, *Huck's Raft: A History of American Childhood* (Cambridge, MA: Belknap Press, 2004), 7–13.

22. D. Elkind, *The Hurried Child: Growing Up Too Fast Too Soon* (Reading, MA: Addison-Wesley, 1981).

23. Mintz, *Huck's Raft*, 7–13.

24. J. Locke, *An Essay Concerning Human Understanding* (New York: Dover, 1999), 92–93.

25. *Troxel v. Granville* (99-138) 530 U.S. 57 (2000) 137 Wash. 2d 1, 969 P.2d 21, affirmed; accessed on August 24, 2013, at www.law.cornell.edu/supct/html/99-138.ZS.html.

26. N. Smith, "Why New Grads are Homeward Bound," *Business News Daily*, May 22, 2012; accessed on April 30, 2013, from http://www.businessnewsdaily.com/2568-college-graduates-returning-home.html.

27. California Department of Education, American Indian Early Childhood Education Program; 2012, accessed on April 30, 2013, at www.cde.ca.gov/sp/ai/ec/.

28. L. A. Maxwell, "American Indian Preschoolers Focus of Parent Outreach Effort," *Education Week*, July 24, 2012; accessed on April 30, 2013, at http://blogs.edweek.org/edweek/early_years/2012/07/families_with_american_indian_preschoolers_focus_of_parent_outreach.html?qs=American+indian+preschoolers.

29. FindLaw, U.S. Supreme Court, *Plessy v. Ferguson* (1896), 163 U.S. 537 (1896) 163 U.S. 537; accessed on April 30, 2013, from http://caselaw.lp.findlaw.com/cgi-bin/getcase.pl?court=us&vol=163&invol=537.

30. FindLaw, U.S. Supreme Court, *Brown v. Board of Education* (1954) 347 U.S. 483 (1954) 347 U.S. 483; accessed on April 30, 2013, from http://caselaw.lp.findlaw.com/scripts/getcase.pl?court=US&vol=347&invol=483.

31. Education Week, "Achievement Gap," updated July 7, 2011; accessed on April 30, 2013, from http://www.edweek.org/ew/issues/achievement-gap/.

32. G. Orfield, "Reviving the Goal of an Integrated Society: A 21st Century Challenge," The Civil Rights Project, UCLA, May 2010; accessed on April 30, 2013, from www.projectcensored.org/top-stories/articles/2-us-schools-are-more-segregated-today-than-in-the-1950s-source/.

33. E. Richmond, "Schools More Segregated Today than in the Late 1960s," *The Atlantic*, June 11, 2012; accessed on April 30, 2013, at http://www.theatlantic.com/national/archive/2012/06/schools-are-more-segregated-today-than-during-the-late-1960s/258348/.

34. National Center for Education Statistics, "Findings in Brief: Reading and Mathematics 2011, National Assessment of Educational Progress at Grades 4 and 8," 2011; accessed on April 30, 2013, at http://nces.ed.gov/nationsreportcard/pdf/main2011/2012459.pdf.

35. McKinsey and Co., *The Economic Impact of the Achievement Gap in America's Schools: Summary of Findings*, June 2009; accessed on April 30, 2013, from www.mckinsey.com/App_Media/Images/Page_Images/Offices/SocialSector/PDF/achievement_gap_report.pdf.

36. FindLaw, *Title IX and Education*; accessed on April 30, 2013, from http://library.findlaw.com/1996/Jan/11/126069.html.

37. Ibid.

38. Education Week, *Stereotype of Mathematical Inferiority Still Plagues Girls*, August 22, 2008; accessed on April 30, 2013, from www.edweek.org/ew/articles/2008/08/27/01girls_ep.h28.html?qs=gender+differences+in+education.

39. J. Rehmeyer, "Gender Equality Closes Math Gap," *ScienceNews*, June 5, 2008; accessed on April 30, 2013, from www.sciencenews.org/view/generic/id/32949/title/Math_Trek__Gender_equality_closes_math_gap.

40. Ibid.

41. National Center for Learning Disabilities, *What Is FAPE and What Can It Mean to My Child?*, 2013; accessed on April 30, 2013, from www.ncld.org/at-school/your-childs-rights/laws-protecting-students/what-is-fape-and-what-can-it-mean-to-my-child.

42. Ibid.

43. Ibid.

44. Ibid.

45. US Department of Labor, "Current Disability Employment Statistics," July 2012; accessed on April 30, 2013, at http://www.dol.gov/odep/.

46. Ibid.

47. L. J. Schweinhart, J. Montie, Z. Xiang, W. S. Barnett, C. R. Belfield, and M. Nores, *Lifetime Effects: The High/Scope Perry Preschool Study Through Age 40* (monographs of the High/Scope Educational Research Foundation, 14) (Ypsilanti, MI: High/Scope Press, 2004), 3.

48. ASCD, The Whole Child Initiative; accessed on April 30, 2013, from http://www.wholechildeducation.org.

CHAPTER 5

1. M. A. Spencer Pulaski, *Understanding Piaget* (New York: Harper & Row, 1980), 9.

2. Ibid.

3. G. A. Davis and J. D. Keller, *Exploring Science and Mathematics in a Child's World* (Columbus, OH: Pearson, 2009), 12.

4. National Association for the Education of Young Children, *Developmentally Appropriate Practice in Early Childhood Programs: Serving Children from Birth Through Age 8*, 3rd ed., C. Copple and S. Bredekamp, eds. (Washington, DC: NAEYC, 2009), 11.

5. Ibid., 12.

6. Ibid.

7. Catherine M. Kearn, EdD, early childhood professional and adjunct professor, Carroll University, Waukesha, Wisconsin; Elena Bodrova, senior researcher at Mid-Continent Research for Education and Learning, Denver Colorado; and Deborah Leong, professor of psychology and director of the Center for Improving Early Learning.

8. G. Boeree, "Erik Erikson"; accessed on July 24, 2012, from http://webspace.ship.edu/cgboer/erikson.html.

9. V. Drake, "Micronutrients and Cognitive Function," *Oregon State University, Linus Pauling Institute Newsletter*, Summer 2011; accessed on July 24, 2012, at http://lpi.oregonstate.edu/ss11/cognitive.html.

10. M. Wood, "B Vitamins and the Aging Brain Examined," *US Department of Agriculture*; accessed on July 24, 2012, at http://www.ars.usda.gov/is/pr/2010/100817.htm.

11. Ibid.

12. M. Hegarty, "Supporting School Success: Fueled to Succeed," Scholastic Parents Site; accessed on July 24, 2012, at http://content.scholastic.com/browse/article.jsp?id=1297.

13. Centers for Disease Control and Prevention, "NCHS Data Brief: Prevalence of Obesity in the United States, 2009–2010," 2011; accessed on July 24, 2012, at http://www.cdc.gov/nchs/data/databriefs/db82.htm#of.

14. USDA, Household Food Security in the United States in 2010, September 2011; accessed on July 24, 2012, at http://www.ers.usda.gov/publications/err-economic-research-report/err125.aspx.

15. US Department of Agriculture, USDA School Meals: Healthy Meals, Healthy Schools, Healthy Kids, updated February 16, 2012; accessed on August 20, 2012, at http://www.fns.usda.gov/cga/factsheets/school_meals.htm.

16. NAEYC, *Principles of Child Development and Learning That Inform Developmentally Appropriate Practice*; accessed on July 24, 2012, at www.naeyc.org/about/positions/dap3.asp.

17. B. K. Hamre and R. C. Pianta, "Early Teacher-Child Relationships and the Trajectory of Children's School Outcomes Through Eighth Grade," *Child Development* 72 (2001): 625–638.

18. G. W. Ladd and K. B. Burgess, "Do Relational Risks and Protective Factors Moderate the Linkages Between Childhood Aggression and Early Psychological and School Adjustment?" *Child Development* 72 (2001): 1579–1601.

19. Ibid.

20. B. Hart, and T. Risley, *Meaningful Differences in the Everyday Experience of Young American Children*; accessed on December 10, 2012, at http://www.lenababy.com/Study.aspx.

21. C. Stump, "Repeating a grade: The Pros and Cons," *GreatSchools*, 2011; accessed on August 16, 2012, at http://www.greatschools.org/special-education/health/659-repeating-a-grade.gs?page=2.

CHAPTER 6

1. National Association for the Education of Young Children, *Accreditation Matters*; accessed on January 2, 2013, at www.naeyc.org/academy/AccreditationMattersWhyEarn.asp.

2. National Association for the Education of Young Children, *Summary of NAEYC-Accredited Programs for Young Children*; accessed on January 2, 2013, at http://oldweb.naeyc.org/academy/summary/center_summary.asp.

3. T. Williams, "Livingston Parish Schools Experiencing Explosion of Pre-K Students," *WAFB 9News* WAFB, 2012; accessed on January 2, 2013, at http://www.wafb.com/global/story.asp?s=7171942.

4. PEW, "Business Case for Early Childhood Investments," June 14, 2011; accessed on January 2, 2013, at www.readynation.org.

5. Ibid.

6. B. Obama, "Organizing for America: Education"; accessed January 2, 2013, at www.barackobama.com/issues/education/.

7. PEW, "Business Case for Early Childhood Investments," June 14, 2011; accessed on January 2, 2013, at www.readynation.org.

8. PEW, "Long-Term Economic Benefits of Investing in Early Childhood Programs," June 14, 2011; accessed on January 2, 2013, at http://www.readynation.org/docs/researchproject_dickens_bartik_200802_brief.pdf.

9. M. Montessori, *The Secret of Childhood,* trans. M. J. Costello (Notre Dame, IN: Fides, 1966), 20.

10. Ibid., 46.

11. M. Montessori, *The Absorbent Mind,* trans. Claude A. Claremont (New York: Holt, Rinehart and Winston, 1967), 25.

12. Montessori, *Dr. Montessori's Own Handbook,* 131. Published March 26, 2009.

13. A. S. Epstein and M. Hohmann, *The HighScope Preschool Curriculum* (Ypsilanti, MI: HighScope Press, 2012).

14. HighScope, "The HighScope Difference," 2012; accessed on September 4, 2012, at http://www.highscope.org/Content.asp?ContentId=410.

15. Reprinted by permission of HighScope Educational Research Foundation, 600 N. River St., Ypsilanti, MI 48198-2898.

16. Ibid.

17. HighScope Educational Research Foundation, 2002. *Child Observation Record (COR) for Infants and Toddlers* (Ypsilanti, MI: HighScope Press, 2002); HighScope Educational Research Foundation 2003, *Preschool Child Observation Record (COR)*, 2nd ed. (Ypsilanti, MI: HighScope Press, 2003); HighScope Educational Research Foundation & Red-e Set Grow, 2013, *OnlineCOR* [computerized assessment system]; accessed on January 3, 2013, at http://www.onlinecor.net/.

18. Ibid.

19. HighScope, "Educational Programs: Early Childhood," 2012; accessed on July 26, 2012, at www.highscope.org/Content.asp?ContentId=63.

20. This section is adapted from L. Gandini, "Foundations of the Reggio Emilia Approach," in J. Hendrick, ed., *First Steps Toward Teaching the Reggio Way* (Upper Saddle River, NJ: Merrill/Prentice Hall, 1997), 14–25.

21. Reprinted by permission from L. Malaguzzi, "No Way. The Hundred Is There," trans. L. Gandini, in *The Hundred Languages of Children: The Reggio Emilia Approach*, eds. C. Edwards, L. Gandini, and S. Forman (Greenwich, CT: Ablex), 3.

22. The College School: Early Childhood Atelier, "The Atelier"; accessed on January 2, 2013, at www.thecollegeschool.org/page.cfm?p=66.

23. R. K. Edmiaston and L. M. Fitzgerald, "How Reggio Emilia Encourages Inclusion," *Educational Leadership* 58, no. 1 (2000): 66. Update contributed by Valerie Dolezal, principal of Grant

Early Childhood Center, in Cedar Rapids, IA, on January 14, 2010; accessed on January 2, 2013, at http://grant.cr.k12.ia.us/.

24. H. Helm and L. Katz, *Young Investigators: The Project Approach in the Early Years* (New York: Teachers College Press, 2001).

25. McKinsey and Co., *The Economic Impact of the Achievement Gap in America's Schools: Summary of Findings*; accessed on January 2, 2013, from http://mckinseyonsociety.com/the-economic-impact-of-the-achievement-gap-in-americas-schools/.

26. Ibid.

27. Ibid.

CHAPTER 7

1. V. Wright, M. Chau, and Y. Artani, "Who Are America's Poor Children?", National Center for Children in Poverty, January 2010; accessed on January 3, 2013, at www.nccp.org/publications/pdf/text_912.pdf.

2. Ibid.

3. Bureau of Labor Statistics, U.S. Department of Labor, "Employment Characteristics of Families Summary," April 26, 2012; accessed on January 2, 2013, at http://www.bls.gov/news.release/famee.nr0.htm.

4. Baby Center, "How Much You'll Spend," 2011; accessed on March 29, 2013, at www.babycenter.com/0_how-much-youll-spend-on-childcare_1199776.bc; National Association of Child Care Resource & Referral Agencies, "Price of Child Care," 2011; accessed on January 2, 2013, at http://www.naccrra.org/sites/default/files/default_site_pages/2011/childcareinamericafacts_2011_final.pdf.

5. National Association of Child Care Resource and Referral Agencies, "The Child Care Workforce"; accessed on November 24, 2009, at www.naccrra.org/policy/background_issues/cc_workforce.php.

6. P. J. Sainz, "Latino Children Are Behind in Preschool Enrollment," June 20, 2008; accessed on November 25, 2009, at www.preschoolcalifornia.org/media-center/latino-children-are-behind-in-preschool-enrollment.html.

7. National Association of Child Care Resource & Referral Agencies, "Unequal Opportunities for Preschoolers," February 2009; accessed on March 29, 2013 at http://issuu.com/naccrra/docs/unequal-opportunities.

8. National Association of Child Care Resource & Referral Agencies, "Child Care in America Fact Sheet," Introduction, 2012; accessed on March 29, 2013, at http://www.naccrra.org/public-policy/resources/child-care-state-fact-sheets-0.

9. L. Lippman, S. Vandivere, J. Keith, and A. Atienza, Child Trends Research Brief, Child Care Used by Low-Income Families; Variations Across States, June 2008; accessed on January 3, 2013, at http://www.childtrends.org/Files/Child_Trends-2008_07_02_RB_ChildCareLowIncome.pdf.

10. National Association of Child Care Resource & Referral Agencies, Child Care in America Fact Sheet, 2012; accessed on January 3, 2013, at http://www.naccrra.org/public-policy/resources/child-care-state-fact-sheets-0.

11. S. Shellenbarger, "When Granny Is Your Nanny," *Wall Street Journal*, June 24, 2009; accessed on January 3, 2013, at http://online.wsj.com/article/SB10001424052970204621904574245973124738260.html.

12. E. Brandon, "When Your Nanny Is Granny," April 17, 2009; accessed on January 3, 2013, at http://images.usnews.com/money/personal-finance/retirement/articles/2009/08/17/when-your-nanny-is-granny.html.

13. ARP, "GrandFacts, State Fact Sheets for Grandparents and Other Relatives Raising Children," October 2012; accessed on January 3, 2013, at http://www.aarp.org/content/dam/aarp/relationships/friends-family/grandfacts/grandfacts-texas.pdf.

14. AARP, "GrandFacts, State Fact Sheets for Grandparents and Other Relatives Raising Children," October 2010; accessed on January 3, 2013, at http://www.aarp.org/content/dam/aarp/relationships/friends-family/grandfacts/grandfacts-california.pdf.

15. C. Thompson, "Grandparents Raising Grandchildren," Baby Zone, June 1, 2009; accessed on January 3, 2013, at www.babyzone.com/mom_dad/love_friendship/grandparents-and-extended/article/raising-grandchildren.

16. National Association of Child Care Resource & Referral Agencies, Child Care in America Fact Sheet; accessed on January 3, 2013, at http://www.naccrra.org/public-policy/resources/child-care-state-fact-sheets-0.

17. Florida Family Child Care Home Association, "What Is Family Child Care?", 2013; accessed on January, 3, 2013, at www.familychildcare.org/index.php?page=parents. FFCCHA is a non-profit state association. Used with permission.

18. Sarah Hutcheon Child Development, "Helping Youth Avoid Risky Behavior: Family-Based Program," 2009; accessed on March 29, 2013, at www.medicalnewstoday.com/articles/150150.php; Florida Family Child Care Association, "What Is Family Child Care?" (n.d.); accessed January 3, 2013, at www.familychildcare.org/index.php?page=parents.

19. ONEGeneration, "About Us," 2013; accessed on March 29, 2013, at http://onegeneration.org/about-us/.

20. Ibid.

21. National Child Care Information and Technical Assistance Center, Statistical Information on Child Care in the United States, March 2008; nccic.acf.hhs.gov/poptopics/statistics.pdf.

22. Kidco, "About Us," accessed on March 29, 2013, at http://www.kidco-childcare.org/AboutUs.html.

23. Virginia Kids Count, "Business on Board with Childcare," 2012; accessed on March 29, 2013, at http://www.wvkidscountfund.org/who-we-are.

24. Lee McIntyre, "Childcare on Board," Federal Reserve Bank of Boston, 2000; accessed on March 29, 2013, at www.bos.frb.org/economic/nerr/rr2000/q3/daycare.htm.

25. Bright Horizons, "About Us," 2013; accessed on March 29, 2013, at http://solutionsatwork.brighthorizons.com/About-Us.aspx.

26. Ibid.

27. Bristol-Myers Squibb, "Bristol-Myers Squibb Named a 2012 Working Mother 100 Best Company," 2012; accessed on March 29, 2013, at http://www.bms.com/news/features/2012/Pages/WorkingMother100BestCompany.aspx.

28. Bristol-Myers Squibb, "Bristol-Myers Squibb Named a 2012 Working Mother 100 Best Company," 2012; accessed on March 29, 2013, at http://www.bms.com/careers/benefits/pages/familydependentcare.aspx.

29. Child Care Exchange, "Exchange," March/April 2011; accessed on March 29, 2013, at http://www.childcareexchange.com/catalog/product/the-proud-story-of-military-child-care/5019826/.

30. Ibid.

31. Broward County Public Schools, "Before & After School Care," 2012; accessed on March 29, 2013, at www.broward.k12.fl.us/k12programs/bascc.

32. "Kindergarten Wraparound Program," (n.d.); accessed on March 29, 2013, at www.town.raynham.ma.us/Public_Documents/RaynhamMA_Recreation/Childcare%20Program%20Description.

33. Maricopa School District, "Copa Kids Care" (2001–2013); accessed on March 29, 2013, at www.maricopausd.org/filestore/CopaKidsParentHandbook0910.pdf.

34. Child Care Exchange, "The Exchange Top 50, North America's Largest For Profit Child Care Organizations," January/February 2009, p. 23; www.childcareexchange.com/library/5018521.pdf.

35. Child Care Exchange, "Reflecting on the Past 25 Years of For Profit Child Care," Exchange, January/February 2012; accessed on March 29, 2013, at http://www.childcareexchange.com/catalog/product/reflecting-on-the-past-25-years-of-for-profit-child-care/5020317/.

36. J. P. Bianchi, Colorado's Children Campaign, "Quality Child Care: An Investment in Families, an Investment in Colorado's Economy," March 2009; accessed on March 29, 2013, at http://www.eric.ed.gov/PDFS/ED539114.pdf.

37. "The Critical Importance of Cultural and Linguistic Continuity for Infants and Toddlers"; accessed on March 29, 2013, accessed at http://condor.admin.ccny.cuny.edu/~mmcenter/tk/gwilgus/linguisticdevelopment.htm.

38. Child Care Aware, "Accreditation," 2013; accessed on March 29, 2013, at http://childcareaware.org/parents-and-guardians/parent-information/accreditation.

39. Ibid.

40. Centers for Disease Control and Prevention, March 29, 2013; accessed at www.cdc.gov/features.handwashing.

41. M. Story, K. Kaphingst, R. Robinson-O'Brien, and K. Glanz, "Creating Healthy Food and Eating Environments: Policy and Environmental Approaches," Annual Review Public Health, November 21, 2007; accessed on March 29, 2013, at http://publhealth.annualreviews.org.

42. All for Natural Health, "Organic Food Benefits Children Too" (2007–2012); accessed on March 29, 2013, at www.all4naturalhealth.com/organic-food-benefits.html.

43. Little Dreamers, Big Believers, "Organic Food Day Care," June 2, 2008; accessed on March 29, 2013, at http://www.littledreamersbigbelievers.com/#!Programs/cee5.

44. Centers for Disease Control and Prevention, "Potential Exposure to Lead in Artificial Turf: Public Health Issues, Actions, and Recommendations," January 17, 2013; accessed on March 29, 2013, at www2a.cdc.gov/HAN/ArchiveSys/ViewMsgV.asp?AlertNum=00275.

45. Ibid.

46. Centers for Disease Control and Prevention, "Reducing Pesticide Exposure at Schools," 2007; accessed on March 29, 2013, at www.cdc.gov/niosh/docs/2007-150/.

47. E. K. Shriver, National Institute of Child Health and Human Development, "Study of Early Child Care and Youth Development," November 2012; accessed on March 29, 2013, at http://www.nichd.nih.gov/research/supported/Pages/seccyd.aspx.

48. National Resource Center for Health and Safety in Child Care, University of Colorado Health Sciences Center at Fitzsimons, "A Parent's Guide to Choosing a Safe and Healthy Child Care"; accessed on March 29, 2013, at http://nrckids.org/RESOURCES/ParentsGuide.pdf.

49. Ibid.

50. Learning Experience Academy of Early Education, "About Us," 2013; accessed on March 29, 2013, at http://whippany.tlechildcare.com/aboutus-preschool-kindergarten-daycare-childcare.php.

51. School of Graduate Studies & Continuing Education, "Creating a Safe and Engaging Classroom Climate," 2009; accessed on March 29, 2013, at www.uww.edu/learn/diversity/safeclassroom.php.

52. National Council of La Raza, "Early Care and Education Policy"; accessed on March 29, 2013, at www.nclr.org/content/policy/detail/55516/.

53. Ibid.

54. Read, Play and Learn, "Supportive Environment" (n.d.); accessed on March 29, 2013, at www.readplaylearn.com/philosophy/environment.htm.

55. Texas Association for the Education of Young Children, "Comments/Recommendations Texas Day Care Minimum Standards Revisions," October 2009; accessed on March 29, 2013, at www.texasaeyc.org/docs/Texas%20Minimum%20Standards%20Revisions%20Comments%20TAEYC%20October%202009.doc.

56. NICHD Early Child Care Research Network, "Child Outcomes When Child Care Center Classes Meet Recommended Standards for Quality," American Journal of Public Health 88, no. 7 (1998): 1072–1077.

57. K. McCartney, E. Dearing, B. A. Taylor, and K. L. Bub, "Quality Child Care Supports the Achievement of Low-Income Children: Direct and Indirect Pathways Through Caregiving and the Home Environment," 2007; accessed on March 29, 2013, at http://www.sciencedirect.com/science/article/pii/S0193397307000652.

58. California Child Care Health Program (n.d.); accessed on March 29, 2013, at http://www.ucsfchildcarehealth.org/.

59. Stephanie Fanjul, Smart Start Communications & Development Director, The North Carolina Partnership for Children, Inc. (personal communication, February 24, 2010).

60. Ibid.

61. Ibid.

62. Ibid.

63. Ibid.

64. A. K. Rose, "Parental Decision Making About Child Care," Journal of Family Issues 29, no. 9 (2008): 1161–1184; accessed on March 29, 2013, at http://jfi.sagepub.com/cgi/content/refs/29/9/1161.

65. Ibid.

CHAPTER 8

1. U.S. Department of Education, "Funding Highlights"; accessed on June 20, 2013, at http://www.whitehouse.gov/sites/default/files/omb/budget/fy2013/assets/education.pdf.

2. The White House, "Education"; accessed on June 20, 2013, at www.whitehouse.gov/issues/education.

3. U.S. House of Representatives, Committee of Ways and Means, "Headstart"; accessed on June 20, 2013, at http://waysandmeans.house.gov/media/pdf/110/head.pdf.

4. New America Foundation, "Federal Education Budget Project"; accessed on July 12, 2013, at http://febp.newamerica.net/background-analysis/no-child-left-behind-act-title-i-distribution-formulas.

5. Almanac Policy Issues, "Executive Summary: The No Child Left Behind Act of 2001"; accessed on July 8, 2013, at http://www.policyalmanac.org/education/archive/no_child_left_behind.shtml.

6. U.S. Department of Health and Human Services, "Head Start Fact Sheet: 2012,"; accessed on July 5, 2013, at http://eclkc.ohs.acf.hhs.gov/hslc/mr/factsheets/2012-hs-program-fact-sheet.html.

7. U.S. Department of Health and Human Services, Administration for Children and Families, "About the Office of Head Start"; accessed on June 25, 2013, at http://www.acf.hhs.gov/programs/ohs.

8. Ibid.

9. New America Foundation, Federal Education Budget Project, Background & Analysis, "Head Start," 2013; accessed on July 18, 2013, at http://febp.newamerica.net/background-analysis/head-start.

10. The Pew Charitable Trusts, Pre-K Now, "Head Start and Pre-K Collaboration," 2011; accessed on July 31, 2012, at www.preknow.org/policy/headstart.cfm.

11. U.S. Department of Health and Human Services, "Head Start Fact Sheet: 2012,"; accessed on July 5, 2013, at http://eclkc.ohs.acf.hhs.gov/hslc/mr/factsheets/2012-hs-program-factsheet.html

12. The Pew Charitable Trusts, "Cost of Providing Quality Preschool Education to America's 3- and 4-Year Olds"; accessed on July 12, 2013, at http://www.pewtrusts.org/news_room_detail.aspx?id=19562.

13. Region 19 Head Start, "Enrollment and Eligibility"; accessed on July 8, 2013, at http://www.esc19hs.net/Enrollment%20Information.htm.

14. Head Start, "Education and Early Childhood"; accessed on July 8, 2013, at http://eclkc.ohs.acf.hhs.gov/hslc/standards/Head%20Start%20Requirements/1304/1304.21%20Education%20and%20early%20childhood%20development.htm.

15. U.S. Department of Health and Human Services, "45 CFR Part 1306-Head Start Staffing Requirements and Program Options," Administration for Children and Families; accessed on July 7, 2013, at http://eclkc.ohs.acf.hhs.gov/hslc/standards/Policy%20Clarifications%20and%20FAQs/j_pc.htm.

16. Ibid.

17. Ibid.

18. Early Childhood Learning and Knowledge Center, "Quality Early Head Start Services: A Summary of Research-Based Practice that Support Children's Families and Expectant Parents," 2009; accessed on July 8, 2013, at http://eclkc.ohs.acf.hhs.gov/hslc/tta-system/ehsnrc/Early%20Head%20Start/design-planning/ehs-101/ehs%20quality%20final%203-02%20%282%29.pdf.

19. Ibid.

20. Ibid.

21. Community Action Partnership of Madera County, Helping People, Changing Lives Community Action, "Fresno Migrant and Seasonal Head Start"; accessed on July 8, 2013, at https://www.maderacap.org/TextPages/fresno_migrant_and_seasonal_head_start.aspx.

22. Ibid.

23. M. Puma, S. Bell, R. Cook, and C. Heid, *Head Start Impact Study: Final Report*, (Washington, DC: U.S. Department of Health and Human Services, 2010), xxiii–xxvi; accessed on June 29, 2013, at http://www.acf.hhs.gov/programs/opre/resource/head-start-impact-study-final-report-executive-summary.

24. Ibid.

25. Ibid.

26. Ibid.

27. A. Gelber and A. Isen, "Children's Schooling and Parents' Investment in Children: Evidence from the Head Start Impact Study," NBER Working Paper No. 17704, National Bureau of Economic Research, December 2011; accessed on July 12, 2013, at http://www.nber.org/papers/w17704.pdf?new_window=1.

28. M. Puma, S. Bell, R. Cook, and C. Heid, *Head Start Impact Study*, January 2010.

29. Early Childhood Learning & Knowledge Center, "Policies and Procedures for Designation Renewal of Head Start and Early Head Start Grantees," updated December 1, 2011; accessed on May 30, 2012, at http://eclkc.ohs.acf.hhs.gov/hslc/standards/Head%20Start%20Requirements/1307.

30. Teachstone, "What Is the CLASS™ Tool?," 2012; accessed on May 30, 2012, at http://www.teachstone.org/about-the-class/.

31. New America Foundation, *Head Start Exceeds Requirement That Half of Teachers Earn BA in Early Childhood*, 2013; accessed on July 12, 2013, at http://earlyed.newamerica.net/blogposts/2013/head_start_exceeds_requirement_that_half_of_teachers_earn_ba_in_early_childhood-83778.

32. National School Lunch Program, FAQ, 2011; accessed on June 29, 2013, at www.fns.usda.gov/cnd/lunch/aboutlunch/NSLPFactSheet.pdf.

33. V. Watson, "AISD Sends Sweets Packing," *Reporter News*, April 22, 2010; accessed on July 31, 2012, at www.reporternews.com/news/2010/apr/22/aisd-sends-sweets-packing/?print=1.

34. U.S. Department of Agriculture Food and Nutrition Service, "SY 2012-2013 Income Eligibility Requirements for National School Lunch Program"; accessed on July 8, 2013, at http://www.fns.usda.gov/cnd/governance/notices/iegs/iegs.htm.

35. U.S. Department of Education, Title I, Part A Program (updated 2011); accessed on June 29, 2013, at www2.ed.gov/programs/titleiparta/index.html.

36. New America Foundation, Federal Education Budget Project, Background & Analysis, "No Child Left Behind Act–Title I Distribution Formulas"; accessed on July 12, 2013, at http://febp.newamerica.net/background-analysis/no-child-left-behind-act-title-i-distribution-formulas.

37. Columbia Public Schools, "CPS Title I Preschool Program: Welcome to Title I Preschool," 2012; accessed on June 29, 2013, at http://www.columbia.k12.mo.us/depts/title.php.

38. U.S. Department of Defense, "Military Homefront-Overview," updated 2012; accessed on July 31, 2012, at www.militaryhomefront.dod.mil/portal/page/mhf/MHF/MHF_HOME_1?id=20.40.500.94.0.0.0.0.0.

39. National Association of Child Care Resource and Referral Agencies, "What Program Is Right for Your Family?"; accessed on July 31, 2012, at www.naccrra.org/MilitaryPrograms/army/fee-assistance-programs/.

40. Department of Defense Education Activity, "Early Childhood Education: Welcome to Sure Start"; accessed on July 31, 2012, at www.dodea.edu/curriculum/eChildhood.cfm?cId=ss.

41. Ibid.

42. A. G. de Leon, "After 20 Years of Educational Reform, Progress, but Plenty of Unfinished Business," *Carnegie Results* 1, no. 3 (2003); accessed on May 29, 2012, at http://www.carnegie.org/results/03/index.html.

43. "Goals 2000: Educate America Act," January 1, 1994; accessed on December 2, 2013, at http://www2.ed.gov/legislation/GOALS2000/TheAct/index.html.

44. Ibid.

45. Paul E. Peterson, Ludger Woessmann, Eric A. Hanushek, and Carlos X. Lastra-Anadón, "Globally Challenged: Are Students Ready to Compete?," August 2011; accessed on June 4, 2012, at http://www.hks.harvard.edu/pepg/PDF/Papers/PEPG11-03_GloballyChallenged.pdf.

46. A. Ross, "New Rules Make Kindergarten Count for More," *The Palm Beach Post*, August 20, 2011; accessed on May 29, 2012, from http://www.palmbeachpost.com/news/schools/new-rules-make-kindergarten-count-for-more-1765416.html.

47. National Center for Education Statistics, "Achievement Gaps: How Hispanic and Whites Students in Public Schools Perform in Mathematics and Reading on the National Assessment of Educational Progress," National Assessment of Educational Progress, June 2011; accessed on May 29, 2012, from http://nces.ed.gov/nationsreportcard/pubs/studies/2011459.asp.

48. U.S. Department of Education, "Great Teachers and Great Leaders," updated May 2011; accessed on May 29, 2012, at http://www2.ed.gov/policy/elsec/leg/blueprint/publication_pg5.html.

49. Head Start, "Parent and Family Services"; accessed on May 29, 2012, at http://heartlandheadstart.org/page4.html.

50. C. Copple and S. Bredekamp, *Developmentally Appropriate Practice in Early Childhood Programs; Serving Children from Birth to Age 8,* 3rd ed. (Washington, DC: NAEYC, 2009).

51. Gary W. Baird, Principal, Lead Mine Elementary School, Raleigh, North Carolina. January 2010.

52. Mary Jo Madvig, Early Childhood Program Director, Upper Des Moines Opportunity, Inc., Des Moines, Iowa. January 2010.

CHAPTER 9

1. J. Klinkner, *Cultural Sensitivity When Caring for Infants and Toddlers.* Wisconsin Child Care Improvement Project, Inc.; accessed on December 28, 2006, at www.wccip.org/tips/Infant_Toddler/Cultural_Sensitive_Info.html.

2. J. Mennela, P. Ziegler, R. Briefel, and T. Novak, "American Dietetic Association. Feeding Infants and Toddlers Study: The Types of Foods Fed to Hispanic Infants and Toddlers," Suppl. 1, 106 (2006). Pubmed.gov article. Found on http://www.ncbi.nlm.nih.gov/pubmed/16376634.

3. American Association of Pediatrics, "Breastfeeding"; accessed on January 12, 2013, from www.aap.org/healthtopics/breastfeeding.cfm.

4. World Health Organization, "Breastfeeding," accessed on January 12, 2013, from www.who.int/topics/breastfeeding/en/.

5. American Association of Pediatrics, "Toilet Training"; accessed on January 12, 2013, from www.aap.org/publiced/BR_ToiletTrain.htm.

6. *CNN*, "Spanking Detrimental to Children, Study Says," September 16, 2009; accessed on January 12, 2013, from www.cnn.com/2009/HEALTH/09/16/spanking.children.parenting/index.html?iref=allsearch.

7. Ibid.

8. Ibid.

9. Ibid.

10. Ibid.

11. J. Huttenlocher, "Language Input and Language Growth," *Preventive Medicine: An International Journal Devoted to Practice and Theory* 27, no. 2 (1998): 195–199.

12. P. Kuhl, "How Babies Acquire Building Blocks of Speech Affects Later Reading, Language Ability," July 2001; accessed on January 12, 2013, at www.sciencedaily.com/releases/2001/07/010730080042.htm.

13. Professionals and Researchers: Quick Reference and Fact Sheets. March of Dimes Birth Defects Foundation; accessed on January 12, 2013, at www.marchofdimes.com/professionals/14332_1206.asp.

14. *Time*, "TV for Babies: Does It Help or Hurt?", March 3, 2009; accessed on January 12, 2013, at www.time.com/time/health/article/0,8599,1882560,00.html?iid=sphere-inline-sidebar.

15. Ibid.

16. Eric H. Lenneberg, "The Biological Foundations of Language," in Mark Lester, ed., *Readings in Applied Transformational Grammar* (New York: Holt, Rinehart and Winston, 1970), 8.

17. Linda Acredolo and Susan Goodwyn, *Baby Signs: How to Talk with Your Baby Before Your Baby Can Talk* (Chicago: Contemporary Books, 1996).

18. T. R. Hart and B. Risley, *Meaningful Differences in the Everyday Experience of Young American Children* (Baltimore, MD: Paul H. Brookes Co., 1995).

19. E. L. Newport, "Mother, I'd Rather Do It Myself: Some Effects and Non-Effects on Maternal Speech Style," in C. E. Snow and C. A. Ferguson, eds., *Talking to Children* (Cambridge: Cambridge University Press, 1977), 112–129.

20. T. R. Hart and B. Risley, *Meaningful Differences in the Everyday Experience of Young American Children* (Baltimore, MD: Paul H. Brookes Co., 1995).

21. R. Brown, *A First Language* (Cambridge, MA: Harvard University Press, 1973), 281.

22. L. Bloom, *Language Development: Form and Function in Emerging Grammars* (Cambridge, MA: MIT Press, 1970).

23. J. Portner, "Two Studies Link High-Quality Day Care and Child Development," *Education Week* (April 19, 1995): 6.

24. Ibid.

25. TheFreeLibrary.com, "Parenting Predictors of Father-Child Attachment Security: Interactive Effects of Father Involvement and Fathering Quality"; accessed on January 12, 2013, from www.thefreelibrary.com/Parenting+predictors+of+father-child+attachment+security%3a+interactive...-a0172831835.

26. A. Thomas, S. Chess, and H. Birch, "The Origin of Personality," *Scientific American* (1970): 102–109.

27. Zero to Three, home page, http://zerotothree.org.

28. A. Mehrabian, "Communication Without Words," *Psychology Today* 2, no. 4 (1968), 53–56.

29. Bredekamp and Copple, *Developmentally Appropriate Practice,* 9. NAEYC.org. Permission granted to reproduce.

30. Ibid.

31. LSU Ag-Center, "Infants, Toddlers Need Welcoming, Responsive Environment," updated 2011; accessed on January 12, 2013, at http://www.lsuagcenter.com/en/family_home/family/childcare/be_child_care_aware/environments/Infants+Toddlers+Need+Welcoming+Responsive+Environment.htm.

32. Infant-Toddler Zone: Infant and Toddler Safety, *Infant and Toddler Safety Handbook*; accessed on January 12, 2013, at http://ncchildcare.dhhs.state.nc.us/pdf_forms/infant_toddler_traning_module.pdf

33. NAEYC, "Supportive Care for Infants and Toddlers"; accessed on January 12, 2013, at http://journal.naeyc.org/btj/200607/Huffman706BTJ.pdf.

34. I. Florez, "Developing Young Children's Self-Regulation Through Everyday Experiences," 2011; accessed on August 2, 2012, at www.parents.com/toddlers-www.naeyc.org/files/yc/.../Self-Regulation_Florez_OnlineJuly2011.pdf.

35. *Beyond the Journal*, Young Children on the Web; accessed on July 2006, at http://journal.naeyc.org/btj/200607/Gillespie709BTJ.pdf.

36. Ibid.

37. Ibid.

38. Ibid.

39. Ibid.

40. Ibid.

41. Ibid.

42. Ibid.

43. Parents as Teachers, "Helping Your Child Learn Self-Regulation Through Play," 2010; accessed on January 12, 2013, accessed on www.parentsasteachers.org/site/pp.asp?c=ekIRLcMZJxE&b=307151.

44. Ibid.

CHAPTER 10

1. New America Foundation, *Hillary Clinton, the 'Accelerator' and More,* June 17, 2013; accessed on June 17, 2013, at http://earlyed.newamerica.net/blogposts/2013/hillary_clinton_the_accelerator_and_more 86146.

2. America's Promise Alliance, *Letter Delivered to President Obama and Congressional Members,* May 29, 2013; accessed on June 17, 2013, at http://www.americaspromise.org/News-and-Events/News-and-Features/APB-2013/Vol-13/Ready Nation-Business-Letter-on-Early-Childhood.aspx.

3. New America Foundation, *Hillary Clinton, the 'Accelerator' and More,* 2013.

4. American Federation of Teachers—A Union of Professionals, *Welcome Early Childhood Educators and Child Care Providers,* 2009; accessed on June 22, 2009, at http://aft.org/early-childhood/index.htm.

5. W. T. Dickens, I. Sawhill, and J. Tebbs, *Policy Brief no. 153: The Effects of Investing in Early Childhood Education on Economic Growth* (Washington, DC: The Brookings Institution, April 2006), www.brookings.edu/comm/policybriefs/pb153.pdf.

6. Ibid.

7. California Department of Education, *Preschool for All: A First-Class Learning Initiative,* 2006, www.cde.ca.gov/eo/in/se/yr05preschoolwp.asp?print=yes.

8. L. J. Calman and L. Tarr-Whelan, *Early Childhood Education for All: A Wise Investment* (New York: Legal Momentum, 2005), http://web.mit.edu/workplacecenter/docs/Full%20Report.pdf.

9. Ibid.

10. HighScope, *Lifetime Effects: The HighScope Perry Preschool Study Through Age 40,* 2005; accessed at www.highscope.org/content.asp?contentid=219.

11. The Chicago Child–Parent Center Program, home page; www.waisman.wisc.edu/cls/Program.htm.

12. National Institute for Early Education Research. *The APPLES Blossom: Abbott Preschool Program Longitudinal Effects Study (APPLES) Preliminary Results Through 2nd Grade,* June 2009; accessed at http://nieer.org/pdf/apples_second_grade_results.pdf.

13. C. Rivera, "L.A. Study Affirms Benefits of Preschool," April 19, 2010. *Los Angeles Times*; www.latimes.com/news/local/la-me-0420-preschool-20100419,0,2289045.story.

14. Pew Center on the States, "Economy Threatens Impressive Expansion of State Pre-K Programs," April 8, 2009; accessed on June 17, 2013, at www.pewcenteronthestates.org/news_room_detail.aspx?id=50884.

15. B. Bowman, M. S. Donovan, and M. S. Burns, *Eager to Learn: Educating Our Preschoolers* (Washington, DC: National Academy Press, 2001), 25–28.

16. Montgomery County Public Schools, *PEP Program Description,*(2009; accessed on June 17, 2013, at www.montgomeryschoolsmd.org/curriculum/pep/description.shtm.

17. Ibid.

18. Healy Communications, Inc., *First-Ever National Preschool Teacher of the Year Award Winners Announced by Story Reader,* September 18, 2006; accessed on June 17, 2013, from www.pubint.com/about/dsp_pr_PTOTYWinnersReleaseFINAL.cfm.

19. Ibid.

20. Culver City Unified School District, News and Announcements, April 20, 2009; accessed on June 17, 2013, at http://ccusd.org/apps/news/show_news.jsp?REC_ID=93423&id=0.

21. "Early Childhood Highlights: A Review of School Readiness Practices in the States," *Child Trends* 1, no. 3 (2010); accessed on June 21, 2010, at www.childtrends.org/_docdisp_page.cfm?LID=70467B6D-CD19-491A-A0AFC6E4F9611771.

22. Florida Department of Education, Office of Early Learning, "Florida Voluntary Prekindergarten Education Standards," November 2011; accessed on June 4, 2013, at www.fldoe.org/earlylearning/perform.asp.

23. Basque Research, Behind a Child with Aggressive Behavior There Is a Negative Family Environment, *ScienceDaily*, March 17, 2010; Retrieved on August 5, 2010, from www.sciencedaily.com/releases/2010/03/100317101346.htm.

24. M. Boethel, *Readiness: School, Community, and Family Connections* (Austin, Texas: National Center for Family and Community Connections with Schools, 2004); www.sedl.org/connections/resources/readiness-synthesis.pdf.

25. Ibid.

26. Based on information constructed by Lesley Mandel Morrow, professor and coordinator of early childhood programs, Rutgers University.

27. M. Parten, "Social Participation Among Pre-School Children," *Journal of Abnormal and Social Psychology,* 27 (1933): 243–269.

28. The Grove School, 2010.

29. L. L. Flynn and J. Kieff, "Including *Everyone* in Outdoor Play," *Young Children* 57, no. 3, (2002): 20–26. Reprinted with

permission from the National Association for the Education of Young Children (NAEYC), www.naeyc.

30. S. Urahn and S. Watson, "A Movement Transformed," November 19, 2007; accessed at www.prospect.org/cs/articles?article=a_movement_transformed.

31. Children's Alliance, The Achievement Gap Starts Before Kindergarten, July 17, 2009; accessed on May 10, 2010, at www.childrensalliance.org/blog/achievement-gap-starts-kindergarten.

32. S. Urahn and S. Watson, "A Movement Transformed," November 19, 2007; accessed at www.prospect.org/cs/articles?article=a_movement_transformed.

33. California Department of Education, "Preschool for All"; accessed on October 24, 2007, at www.cde.ca.gov/eo/in/se/yr05preschoolwp.asp.

34. M. Martin, *Passion for Childcare Leads to Chain of 'Palaces'*, May 6, 2010; accessed on June 17, 2013. at http://lacrossetribune.com/couleenews/lifestyles/passion-for-child-care-leads-to-chain-of-palaces/article_3d22811d-12f8-5d35-b245-3f6b53ce54b0.html.

35. Love A Lot Preschool, home page, 2010; accessed at www.lovealotpreschool.com/program_pages/specialty.html.

36. Nobel Learning Communities, NLCI PE Program Keeps Preschoolers Active and Healthy, March 30, 2009; accessed at www.nobellearning.com/Default.aspx?DN=1699716d-d2db-42a8-8e87-6d147202631e.

37. C. J. McVicker, "Young Readers Respond: The Importance of Child Participation in Emerging Literacy," *Young Children* 62, no. 3 (2007), 18.

38. National Early Literacy Panel, *Developing Early Literacy: Report of the National Early Literacy Panel* (Washington, DC: National Institute for Literacy, 2008).

39. Ibid.

40. Ibid.

41. Ibid.

42. Ibid.

43. L. Indiana, "Vocabulary Activities," Teachers Net Gazette 4, no. 7 (2003); accessed at http://teachers.net/gazette/backissues.

44. K. Lowry, *Discourse Planning Skills* (London, Ontario: Thames Valley Children's Center, 1994).

45. Crawmer's Critterz Preschool, home page, 2010; http://bendpreschool.com/index.html.

46. Albany Children's Center, home page, 2010; http://acc-ausd.ca.schoolloop.com/cms/page_view?d=x&piid=&vpid=1225554129399.

47. L. Braunt and California Preschool Instructional Network, *Transitions: Preschool to Kindergarten and Beyond*, 2006; accessed on May 14, 2010, at www.cpin.us/docs/mod_transitionsfinal2.10.06.pdf.

48. Gertie Belle Rogers Elementary, Mrs. Christensen's Page, 2010; accessed on May 14, 2010, at http://ac069.k12.sd.us.

49. Kokomo Center Schools, Kindergarten Round-up 2010–2011; accessed at www.kokomo.k12.in.us.

CHAPTER 11

1. Wake County Public School System, "Fuller Elementary Teacher Is 2010 Wake County Teacher of the Year," May 13, 2010; accessed on June 13, 2013, at www.wcpss.net/news/2010_may13_toy.

2. Norm's Notes, "2010–2011 Teacher of the Year Finalist: Abby Lowe," April 16, 2010; accessed on June 13, 2013, at http://normsnotessps.blogspot.com/2010/04/2010-2011-teacher-of-year-finalist-abby.html.

3. NEA Education and Policy Practice Department, "Full Day Kindergarten Helps Close Achievement Gaps," 2008; accessed on June 13, 2013, at www.nea.org/assets/docs/HE/mf_PB12_FullDayK.pdf.

4. National Center of Education Statistics "Kindergarten Entry Status: On-Time, Delayed-Entry, and Repeating Kindergartners," 2010; accessed on June 13, 2013, at http://nces.ed.gov/programs/coe/indicator_tea.asp.

5. G. Yara, "Kyrene, Tempe School Districts to Maintain All-Day Kindergarten," AzCentral, February 5, 2010; accessed on June 13, 2013, at www.azcentral.com/community/tempe/articles/2010/02/05/20100205tr-all-day-kindergarten-06-ON.html.

6. Anne Arundel County Public Schools, "Kindergarten FAQs," 2009; accessed on June 13, 2013, at www.aacps.org/early-childhood/mdlaw.asp.

7. University of Virginia, Study: 'Redshirting' Kindergarteners Not as Common as Reported, April 25, 2013, accessed on June 18, 2013, at http://news.virginia.edu/content/study-redshirting-kindergarteners-not-common-reported.

8. Illinois Early Learning Project, What Are the Effects of Academic Redshirting?, April 2009; accessed on December 13, 2009, at http://illinoisearlylearning.org/faqs/redshirting.htm.

9. C. Copple and S. Bredekamp, eds., *Developmentally Appropriate Practice in Early Childhood Programs: Serving Children from Birth Through Age 8*, 3rd ed., (Washington, DC: NAEYC, 2009), 8.

10. Troy School District, "Developmental Kindergarten Program," 2010–2011, accessed on February 16, 2010, at www.troy.k12.mi.us/tsdnews/dkbrochure.pdf.

11. The Honor Roll School, Transition Kindergarten, n.d.; accessed on February 16, 2010, at www.thehonorrollschool.com/page.cfm?p=19548.

12. Children's Defense Fund, *The Facts about Full-Day Kindergarten*, 2012; accessed on July 1, 2013, at www.childrensdefense.org/child-research.../the-facts-about-full-day.pdf#sthash.3VBxlDeq.pdf.

13. NASP Center. *Kindergarten—Full Versus Half-Day: Information for Parents and Early Childhood Educators*, 2004; accessed on June 19, 2013, at http://www.naspcenter.org/assessment/kindergarten_ho.html.

14. C. Peck, "Multiage Classrooms Aid Both Students, Teachers," *Arizona Republic*, January 17, 2010; accessed on February 18, 2010, at www.azcentral.com/arizonarepublic/local/articles/2010/01/17/20100117edpeck0117.html.

15. Ibid.

16. N. Xia and S. Kirby, RAND Education, *Retaining Students in Grade: A Literature Review of the Effects of Retention on Students' Academic and Nonacademic Outcome*, 2009; accessed on April 29, 2010, at www.rand.org/pubs/technical_reports/2009/RAND_TR678.sum.pdf.

17. Council of Chief State School Officers, "Addressing the Challenges: A Safe, Supportive, and Healthy School Environment," January 27, 2009; accessed on January 27, 2009, at www.ccsso.org/Projects/school_health_project/addressing_the_challenges/6498.cfm.

18. G. Hopkins, "School Wide Handwashing Campaign Cut Germs, Absenteeism," *Education World*, April 30, 2009; accessed on January 13, 2010, at www.educationworld.com/a_admin/admin/admin431.shtml.

19. M. Story, K. Kaphingst, R. Robinson-O'Brien, and K. Glanz, "Creating Healthy Food and Eating Environments: Policy and Environmental Approaches," *Annual Review Public Health*, November 21, 2007; accessed on November 1, 2009, at http://publhealth.annualreviews.org.

20. D. Lau Whela, "With America's Kids in Danger of Becoming Obese, a Growing Number of Schools Are Thinking Outside the Lunchbox," June 1, 2008; accessed on January 21, 2010, at www.schoollibraryjournal.com/article/CA6565675.html.

21. D. Weaver, "Long Beach Island Schools Ban Treats with Birthday Celebrations," *Atlantic Press*, December 28, 2009; accessed on May 19, 2010, at www.pressofatlanticcity.com/news/press/ocean/article_a67b3bbd-868d-5ae3-9f62-4f2f648bd3bd.html.

22. Whela, "With America's Kids in Danger of Becoming Obese," 2008.

23. Mayo Clinic, Celiac Disease, accessed on June 18, 2013, at http://www.mayoclinic.com/health/celiac-disease/DS00319.

24. Chesterfield Public County School District, Gluten Free Lunch Menu, 2013; accessed on June 19, 2013, at http://mychesterfieldschools.com/about/food-and-nutrition-services/lunch-menus/.

25. Elizabeth Dawson, Casa dei Bambini Montessori, 2010; at www.SantaMariaPreschool.com.

26. Council of Chief State School Officers, "Addressing the Challenges: A Safe, Supportive, and Healthy School Environment," January 27, 2009; accessed on February 18, 2010, at www.ccsso.org/projects/School_Health_Project/Addressing_the_Challenges/6498.cfm.

27. Ibid.

28. Glenwood Elementary School, "Positive Behavior Support," 2008; accessed on June 18, 2013, at www2.chccs.k12.nc.us/education/components/scrapbook/default.php?sectiondetailid=77033&&PHPSESSID=33b10693c22fd87c63d5b8699b9a0c4a.

29. Arizona Educational Foundation, 2010 Ambassador of Excellence, accessed on February 2, 2010, at www.azedfoundation.org/10tingle.php.

30. University College of Education, *NAS Report: Adult Literacy a Factor in U.S. Economic, Health Crises*, November 7, 2011; accessed on June 19, 2013, at http://www.coe.uga.edu/news/2011/11/07/nas-report-adult-literacy-a-factor-in-u-s-economic-health-crises.

31. Reading Rockets, *NELP Report: Developing Early Literacy*, National Early Literacy Panel, 2009; accessed on June 18, 2013, at www.readingrockets.org/articles/31095.

32. "Increasing the Literacy Behaviors of Preschool Children Through Environmental Modification and Teacher Mediation," *Journal of Research in Childhood Education*, September 22, 2007; accessed on April 29, 2010, at http://goliath.ecnext.com/coms2/gi_0199-7222031/Increasing-the-literacy-behaviors-of.html.

33. Ibid.

34. J. Harmon, et al., "Interactive Word Walls: More Than Just Reading the Writing on the Walls," *Journal of Adolescent & Adult Literacy*, February 2009; accessed on February 16, 2010, at www.scribd.com/doc/16127639/Interactive-Word-Walls.

35. Dolch Sight Words, accessed on April 27, 2010, at http://dolchsightwords.org.

36. W. A. Hoover, "The Importance of Phonemic Awareness in Learning to Read," *SEDL Letter* 14, no. 3 (2003); accessed on June 19, 2013, at www.sedl.org/pubs/sedl-letter/v14n03/3.html.

37. Contributed by Lauren Gonzales, Denton Independent School District, Denton, Texas.

38. V. Spandel, *Creating Writers Through 6-Trait Writing Assessment and Instruction,* 4th ed. (Boston: Allyn and Bacon, 2004).

39. Timmons Times blog, "Readers Workshop," October 16, 2007; accessed on May 4, 2010, at http://timmonstimes.blogspot.com/2007/10/video-streaming-readers-workshop.html.

40. San Mateo-Foster City School District, "Mathematics Framework for California Public Schools, Kindergarten–Mathematics Content Standards," accessed on June 22, 2010, at www.smfc.k12.ca.us/standards/kmathstand.pdf.

41. Contributed by Lori Cadwaller, kindergarten teacher, Garrett Park Elementary, Garrett Park, Maryland.

42. National Council for Social Studies, "About NCSS," accessed on November 1, 2009, at www.socialstudies.org/about.

CHAPTER 12

1. Alabama Department of Education, 2012 Alabama Teacher of the Year, May 11, 2012; accessed on June 20, 2013, at http://www.media.alabama.gov/AgencyTemplates/education/alsde_pr.aspx?id=5068&t=1

2. Ibid.

3. F. L. Stanton Elementary School, Teacher of the Year, 2012, accessed on June 20, 2013, at http://www.atlanta.k12.ga.us/Page/32523.

4. Darcy Grimes, NC Teacher of the Year 2012–2013; accessed on June 20, 2013, at http://www.darcygrimes.com.

5. US Census Bureau, Newsroom: Facts for Features 2011," "Back to School: 2011–2012," April 2012; accessed on June 20, 2013, at http://www.census.gov/newsroom/releases/archives/facts_for_features_special_editions/cb11-ff15.html.

6. Ibid.

7. US Census Bureau, "Hispanic Americans by the Number," Infoplease.com, 2012; accessed on June 20, 2013, at http://www.infoplease.com/spot/hhmcensus1.html.

8. Tampa Bay Times, "Pine Grove Elementary School students write cookbook, Nature Coast Technical High culinary students cook their recipes," June 19, 2009; accessed on July 1, 2013, at http://www.tampabay.com/news/education/k12/pine-grove-elementary-school-students-write-cookbook-nature-coast/1006748.

9. National Telecommunications and Information Administration, *Exploring the Digital Nation: America's Emerging Online Experience*, 2013; accessed on July 1, 2013, at http://www.ntia.doc.gov/files/ntia/publications/exploring_the_digital_nation_americas_emerging_online_experience.pdf.

10. Kids Count Data Center, "Children in Poverty"; accessed on June 24, 2013, at http://datacenter.kidscount.org/data/tables/43-children-in-poverty#detailed/1/any/false/867,133,38,35,18/any/321,322.

11. KidsHealth, "Precocious Puberty," 2012; accessed on June 11, 2012, at http://kidshealth.org/parent/medical/sexual/precocious.html#.

12. Child Development Institute, Stages of Social-Emotional Development; accessed on June 24, 2013, at http://childdevelopmentinfo.com/child-development/erickson.

13. T. Strine, C. Okoro, L. McGuire, and L. Balluz, "The Associations Among Childhood Headaches, Emotional and Behavior Difficulties, and Health Care Use," *Pediatrics* 117, no. 5 (2006): 1728–1735.

14. M. Lu, *Children's Literature in a Time of National Tragedy* (ERIC Clearinghouse on Reading, English, and Communication Digest), December 2001; accessed on June 18, 2013, at http://permanent.access.gpo.gov/websites/eric.ed.gov/ERIC_Digests/ed457525.htm.

15. "Childhood Depression: Tips for Parents," *Mental Health America*, May 6, 2010, accessed on June 18, 2013, at www.nmha.org/index.cfm?objectid=C7DF9240-1372-4D20-C81D80B5B7C5957B.

16. National Institute of Mental Health, Depression in Children and Adolescents: Factsheet, April 25, 2011; accessed on June 24, 2013, at http://www.nimh.nih.gov/health/publications/depression-in-children-and-adolescents/index.shtml.

17. Mental Health in Illinois, "Ideas on Promoting Good Mental Health for Children," 2009; accessed on June 24, 2013, at http://www.mentalhealthillinois.org/childrens-health/promoting-childrens-mental-health.

18. National Association of School Psychologists, NASP Resources, "Supporting Children's Mental Health: Tips for Parents and Educators," 2009; accessed on June 24 2013, at http://www.nasponline.org/resources/mentalhealth/mhtips.aspx.

19. The Freedom Forum, "Character Education," in *Finding Common Ground: A Guide to Religious Liberty in Public Schools*; accessed on June 25, 2013, at http://www.freedomforum.org/publications/first/findingcommonground/B13.CharacterEd.pdf.

20. Gary Brookings Institution, "Class Size: What Research Says and What It Means for State Policy," May 11, 2011; accessed on June 24, 2013, at http://brookings.edu/papers/2011/0511_class_size_whitehurst_chingos.aspx.

21. Ibid.

22. Contributed by Gary W. Baird, principal, Lead Mine Elementary School, Raleigh, North Carolina.

23. National Center of Response to Intervention, home page; accessed on June 19, 2013, at www.rti4success.org/.

24. Ibid.

25. Ibid.

26. Ibid.

27. Ibid.

28. Mary Ann Zehr, "RTI Said to Pay Off in Gains for English Learners," *Edweek* 29, no. 19 (2013): 1,10; accessed on June 18, 2013, at www.edweek.org/ew/articles/2010/01/22/19rtiells_ep.h29.html?tkn=Wpercent5bYCLqVUfF0pqicVwkwTVkZdlSyTBmx7rRRb.

29. Ibid.

30. Division for Early Childhood of the Council for Exceptional Children, the National Association for the Education of Young Children, and the National Head Start Association, *Frameworks for Response to Intervention in Early Childhood*, (n.a.); accessed on June 24, 2013, at http://www.naeyc.org/files/naeyc/RTI%20in%20Early%20Childhood.pdf.

31. The Annie E. Casey Foundation, EARLY WARNING! Why Reading by the End of Third Grade Matters; accessed on June 18, 2013, at www.aecf.org.

32. Contributed by Candice M. Bookman, first grade teacher, Lawrence Elementary School, Mesquite Independent School District, Mesquite, Texas, 2010.

33. Ibid.

34. Ibid.

35. Ibid.

36. Ibid.

37. Ibid.

38. Ibid.

39. Ibid.

40. Ibid.

41. Christopher T. Cross, Taniesha A. Woods, and Heidi Schweingruber, eds., *Mathematics Learning in Early Childhood: Paths Toward Excellence and Equity* (Washington, DC: National Academies Press, 2009); accessed on June 18, 2013, at www.nap.edu.

42. Ibid.

43. S. Feeney and N. K. Freeman, *Ethics and the Early Childhood Educator: Using the NAEYC Code* (Washington, DC: National Association for the Education of Young Children, 2005).

44. Public Schools of North Carolina, K–12 Curriculum and Instruction/NC Standard Course of Study, accessed on June 18, 2013, at www.dpi.state.nc.us/curriculum/.

45. US Department of Education, "FDIC and NCUA Chairs Join Education Secretary to Announce Partnership to Promote Financial Education and Savings Programs," press release, 2010; accessed on July 1, 2013, at http://www.ed.gov/news/press-releases/fdic-and-ncua-chairs-join-education-secretary-announce-partnership-promote-finan.

46. MyCentralJersey, Green Brook Second-Graders Learn the Ups and Downs of Personal Banking, May 3, 2010; accessed on June 18, 2013, from www.mycentraljersey.com/article/20100503/NEWS/5030325/-1/newsfront/Green-Brook-second-graders-learn-the-ups-and-downs-of-personal-banking.

47. *Science Daily,* "School Bullying Affects Majority of Elementary Students," April 12, 2007; accessed on June 18, 2013, at www.sciencedaily.com/releases/2007/04/070412072345.htm.

48. Ibid.

49. Erica L. Green, "Bullying, Suicide Attempt Reported at Elementary School," *The Baltimore Sun*, April 27, 2010; accessed on June 18, 2013, at http://articles.baltimoresun.com/2010-04-27/news/bs-ci-school-bullying-20100427_1_bullying-suicide-attempt-gilmor-elementary.

50. CBS News, "Boy, 9, Found Hanged in Texas School," January 22, 2010; accessed on June 18, 2013, at www.cbsnews.com/stories/2010/01/22/national/main6130070.shtml.

51. Kamaron Institute, Bullying Prevention Program Results; accessed on June 18, 2013, at http://kamaron.org/KC3-Program-Results.

52. SmartBean, What Are 21st Century Skills?, November 15, 2009; accessed on June 18, 2013, at www.thesmartbean.com/magazine/21st-century-skills-magazine/what-are-21st-century-skills/.

53. SmartBean, What Are 21st Century Skills?, November 15, 2009.

54. Ibid.

55. Helen Fitzgerald, American Hospice Foundation, "Guidelines for Parents to Help Their Children Through Grief," November 2004; accessed on January 28, 2010, at http://americanhospice.org/grieving-children/articles/61-guidelines-for-parents-to-help-their-children-through-grief.

56. Ibid.

CHAPTER 13

1. iTeach with iPads, "Reflection on the Apple Distinguished Educator Institute," 2013; accessed on July 23, 2013, at http://iteachwithipads.net.

2. Carrie Jostmeyer, "Insights and Inspiration: Winning Teacher Essay," 2013; accessed on July 18, 2013, at http://www.friscoisd.org/news/2013/03/01/carrie-jostmeyer-essay.

3. American Academy of Pediatrics, "Media and Children"; accessed on July 18, 2013, at http://www.aap.org/en-us/advocacy-and-policy/aap-health-initiatives/Pages/Media-and-Children.aspx?nfstatus=401&nftoken=00000000-0000-0000-0000-000000000000&nfstatusdescription=ERROR%3a+No+local+token.

4. National Educational Technology Standards for Students (NETS•S), 2nd ed. © 2007 ISTE (International Society for Technology in Education), www.iste.org. All rights reserved.

5. Ibid.

6. Steve Fetzik, "District 15 Uses iPads to Help Kindergarten Students Grow," *ABC Newspapers*, March 11, 2013; accessed on July 24, 2013, at http://abcnewspapers.com/2013/03/11/district-15-uses-ipads-to-help-kindergarten-students-grow.

7. Erin Adler, "Lakeville Test Shows iPads Boosted Education in Many Classrooms." *Star Tribune*, South Metro section, June 29, 2013; accessed on July 24, 2013, at http://www.startribune.com/local/south/213709671.html.

8. Contributed by Kristi Meeuwse, kindergarten teacher, Drayton Hall Elementary School, Charleston County School District, Charleston, South Carolina.

9. Apple, "Accessibility Features," 2010; accessed on June 20, 2013, at www.apple.com/ipad/features/accessibility.html.

10. National Education for the Education of Young Children and The Fred Rogers Center for Early Learning and Children's Media at Saint Vincent College, *Technology and Interactive Media as Tools in Early Childhood Programs Serving Children from Birth through Age 8*, 2012; accessed on June 18, 2013, at http://www.naeyc.org/content/technology-and-young-children.

11. The Assistive Technology Act of 2004, Publ L 108-364, October 24, 2004; accessed on June 18, 2013, at http://www.gpo.gov/fdsys/pkg/STATUTE-118/pdf/STATUTE-118-Pg1707.pdf.

12. Access STEM, "Kindergarten Bridge Program in Early Integration of Assistive Technology," 2013; accessed on July 22, 2013, at http://www.washington.edu/accesscomputing/articles?453.

13. K. Ash, "Schools Test E-Readers with Dyslexic Students," October 15, 2010; accessed June 18, 2013, at http://www.edweek.org/dd/articles/2010/10/20/01dyslexia.h04.html.

14. Benjamin Herold, "Miami-Dade Approves $63 Million Plan to Give All Students Digital Devices," *Education Week*, 2013; accessed on July 22, 2013, at http://blogs.edweek.org/edweek/DigitalEducation/2013/06/miami-dade_schools_pass_63_mil.html.

15. J. Engler, "STEM Education Is the Key to the U.S.'s Economic Future," 2012; accessed on June 18, 2013, at http://www.usnews.com/opinion/articles/2012/06/15/stem-education-is-the-key-to-the-uss-economic-future.

16. U.S. Bureau of Labor Statistics, "Occupational Outlook Handbook," March 2012; accessed on June 18, 2013, at http://www.bls.gov/ooh/about/projections-overview.htm.

17. State Educational Technology Directors Association, *Science, Technology, Engineering and Mathematics*, 2008; accessed on June 20, 2013, at www.setda.org/c/document_library/get_file?folderId=270&name=DLFE-257.pdf.

18. Ibid.

19. eInstruction, CPS Pulse, Student Response Systems Web page; accessed September 3, 2012, at www.einstruction.com/products/assessment/pulse/index.html.

20. Entire section contributed by Karla Burkholder and Cathy Faris, director of technology and technology coach at Northwest I.S.D., Fort Worth, Texas.

21. Entire section contributed by Pamela Beard, ESL specialist, Forest Ridge Elementary, College Station, Texas.

22. Ibid.

23. Contributed by Jodi Conrad. Abraham Lincoln Elementary, Glen Ellyn, Illinois.

24. K. Cassidy, Mrs. Cassidy's Classroom Blog, September 6, 2012; accessed on June 20, 2013, at http://classblogmeister.com/blog.php?blogger_id=1337.

25. Contributed by Cheri Sherley, the University of Texas Health Science Center at Houston's Children's Learning Institute, Houston, Texas.

26. Madison Metropolitan School District, "Stephens Elementary," 2011–2012; accessed on June 20, 2013, at www.madison.k12.wi.us/032.htm and http://boeweb.madison.k12.wi.us/policies/3721.

27. Oxford Public Schools, "Computer and Internet Acceptable Use Policy," 2012–2013; accessed on June 20, 2013 at http://osd.amces.schoolfusion.us/modules/cms/pages.phtml?pageid=90800&sessionid=0feff2b7c442ccc731b01c4331a64a98&sessionid=0feff2b7c442ccc731b01c4331a64a98.

28. Federal Trade Commission, Children's Online Privacy Protection Act, www.coppa.org.

29. Polk County Public Schools, "District Technology Plan 2012–2014"; accessed on June 20, 2013, at http://www.polk-fl.net/districtinfo/departments/ist/documents/12-14DistrictTechPlan.pdf.

30. A. S. Bondy and L. A. Frost, "The Picture Exchange Communication System," *Focus on Autistic Behavior* 9, no. 3 (1994): 1–19.

CHAPTER 14

1. Learning Works For Kids, "Executive Functions"; accessed on July 19, 2013, at http://learningworksforkids.com/the-science-of-lwk/executive-functions.

2. P. Tough, "Can the Right Kinds of Play Teach Self-Control?," *New York Times*, September 25, 2009; accessed on June 29, 2013, at www.nytimes.com/2009/09/27/magazine/27tools-t.html?pagewanted=1&_r=1.

3. A. Duckworth and M. E. P. Seligman, "Self-Discipline Outdoes IQ Predicting Academic Performance of Adolescents," *Journal of Psychological Science* 16, no. 12 (2005): 939–944.

4. S. E. Rimm-Kaufman, R. C. Pianta, and M. J. Cox, "Teachers' Judgments of Problems in the Transition to Kindergarten," *Early Childhood Research Quarterly* 15, no. 2 (2000): 147–166.

5. P. Tough, "Can the Right Kinds of Play Teach Self-Control?".

6. M. Tilley, "Civility in America; Can't We All Just Get Along," Children's Theater Company, September 5, 2007; accessed on June 29, 2013, at www.associatedcontent.com/article/362551/civility_in_america_cant_we_all_just.html?cat=9.

7. S. Wolk, "Hearts and Minds," *Educational Leadership* 61, no. 1 (2003): 14–18; accessed on June 29, 2013, at www.ascd.org/publications/educational_leadership/sept03/vol61/num01/Hearts_and_Minds.aspx.

8. Greg Adomaitis, NJ.com, "Broad Street School Awards Students Caught Caring in Bridgeton," 2011; accessed on July 25, 2013, at http://www.nj.com/cumberland/index.ssf/2011/12/broad_street_school_awards_stu.html.

9. L. R. Roehler and D. J. Cantlon, *Scaffolding: A Powerful Tool in Social Constructivist Classrooms,* 1996; accessed on July 25, 2013, at http://ed-web3.educ.msu.edu/literacy/papers/paperlr2.html.

10. Temple of Kriya Yoga-Chicago, "Y Is for Yoga: First- and Third-Grade Yogis at Jefferson Elementary School, Berwyn," March–April 2007; www.yogachicago.com/mar07/jefferson.shtml.

11. National Sleep Foundation, "How Much Sleep Do We Really Need?," 2009; www.sleepfoundation.org/article/how-sleep-works/how-much-sleep-do-we-really-need.

12. B. J. Casey, et al., *PNAS Early Edition,* "Behavioral and Neural Correlates of Delay of Gratification 40 Years Later," 2011; accessed on June 25, 2012, at http://www.pnas.org/content/early/2011/08/19/1108561108.full.pdf+html.

13. Ibid.

14. B. K. Hamre and R. C. Pianta, "Early Teacher–Child Relationships and the Trajectory of Children's School Outcome Through Eighth Grade," *Child Development* 72 (2001): 625–638.

15. G. W. Ladd and K. B. Burgess, "Do Relational Risks and Protective Factors Moderate the Linkages Between Childhood Aggression and Early Psychological and School Adjustment?" *Child Development* 72 (2001): 1579–1601.

16. Ibid.

17. *Stanford News,* "Babies Whose Efforts Are Praised Become More Motivated Kids, say Stanford Researcher," 2013; accessed on July 25, 2013, at http://news.stanford.edu/news/2013/february/talking-to-baby-021213.html.

18. J. Hsueh and H. Yoshikawa, "Working on Standard Schedules and Variable Shifts in Low-Income Families: Associations with Parental Psychological Well-Being, Family Functioning, and Child Well-Being," *Developmental Psychology* 43, no. 3 (2007): 620–632; accessed on June 25, 2012, at http://steinhardt.nyu.edu/scmsAdmin/media/users/jr189/Working_Nonstandard_Schedules_and_Variable_Shifts.pdf.

19. S. Tavernise, "Soaring Poverty Casts Spotlight on 'Lost Decade'," *New York Times,* September 13, 2011; accessed on June 25, 2012, at http://www.nytimes.com/2011/09/14/us/14census.html?pagewanted=all.

20. Ibid.

21. E. E. Pinderhughes, et al., "Discipline Responses, Influences of Parents' Socioeconomic Status, Ethnicity, Beliefs About Parenting, Stress, and Cognitive-Emotional Processes," *Journal of Family Psychology* 14, no. 3 (2000): 380–400.

22. Ibid

23. Ibid.

24. Ibid.

25. Global Initiative to End All Corporal Punishment of Children, *Progress Towards Prohibiting All Corporal Punishment in North America,* November 2009; accessed on June 19, 2013 at www.endcorporalpunishment.org/pages/pdfs/charts/Chart-NorthAmerica.pdf.

26. American Academics of Pediatrics, *Where We Stand: Spanking,* 2010; accessed on June 19, 2013 at www.healthychildren.org/English/family-life/family-dynamics/communication-discipline/pages/Where-We-Stand-Spanking.aspx?nfstatus=401&nftoken=00000000-0000-0000-0000-000000000000&nfstatusdescription=ERROR%3a+No+local+token.

27. C. Taylor et al., "Mothers' Spanking of 3-Year-Old Children and Subsequent Risk of Children's Aggressive Behavior," *Pediatrics* 125, no. 5 (2010): e1057–e1065.

CHAPTER 15

1. U.S. Census Bureau, "U.S. Interim Projections by Age, Sex, Race, and Hispanic Origin," 2008; accessed on May 18, 2010, at www.census.gov.

2. Pew Social & Demographic Trends, *The Rise of Intermarriage,* 2012; accessed on August 26, 2013, at http://www.pewsocial-trends.org/2012/02/16/the-rise-of-intermarriage.

3. The Condition of Education, English Language Learners, 2013; accessed on August 26, 2013, at http://nces.ed.gov/programs/coe/indicator_cgf.asp.

4. Census.gov, "Most Children Younger Than Age 1 Are Minorities, Census Bureau Reports," 2012; accessed on August 28, 2013, at http://www.census.gov/newsroom/releases/archives/population/cb12-90.html.

5. Tony Castro, "Hispanics. Now Majority in Texas Public Schools, Districts Assess if They Are Ready for Change," *Huffington Post,* June 6, 2013; accessed on August 1, 2013, at http://www.huffingtonpost.com/2013/06/12/hispanics-majority-texas-schools_n_3427239.html.

6. The Minneapolis Foundation, *A New Age of Immigrants: Making Immigration Work for Minnesota* (St. Paul, MN: Wilder Research, 2010); accessed at http://www.minneapolisfoundation.org/Libraries/Publications/ImmigrationReportFinal.sflb.ashx.

7. CitiData.com, Top 101 Cities with the Most Residents born in Haiti, (n.d.); accessed on August 28, 2013, at http://www.city-data.com/top2/h136.html.

8. National Center for Cultural Competence, "Conceptual Frameworks/Models, Guiding Values and Principals" (n.d.); accessed on June 1, 2010, at http://nccc.georgetown.edu/foundations/frameworks.html.

9. National Association for Multi-Cultural Education, "Definitions of Multi-Cultural," 2010; accessed on June 2, 2010, at http://nameorg.org/names-mission/definition-of-multicultural-education/.

10. "Teaching Kids Cultural Awareness," February 21, 2010; accessed May 17, 2010, at www.news4jax.com/news/22624613/detail.html.

11. Bright Hub, "Preschool Lesson Plans," March 24, 2010; accessed on August 26, 2013, at www.brighthub.com/education/early-childhood/articles/66983.aspx.

12. J. Gonzales and D. Tobiassen, "Teaching Diversity: A Place to Begin," *Scholastic World,* (n.d.); accessed on August 26, 2013, at http://content.scholastic.com/browse/article.jsp?id=3499.

13. W. Tulinsky, "Baleros in the Classroom," (n.d.); accessed on August 26, 2013, at www.lessonplanspage.com/LASSPEMD-BalerosInTheClassroomK12.htm.

14. C. Read, "F Is for Flexibility," Carol Read's ABC of Teaching Children (blog), March 2, 2010; accessed June 7, 2010, at http://carolread.wordpress.com/2010/03/02/f-is-for-flexibility.

15. J. Miller, "Schools Matter," April 9, 2010; accessed June 3, 2010, at www.schoolsmatter.info/2010/04/teacher-in-florida.html.

16. "Student Led Conferences Successful in Elementary and Middle School Grades," October 1, 2009, *Education World*; accessed August 26, 2013, at www.educationworld.com/a_admin/admin/admin326.shtml.

17. C. Metzler, "Teaching Children about Diversity," PBS Parents, March 11, 2010; accessed on August 26, 2013, at www.pbs.org/parents/experts/archive/2009/02/teaching-children-about-divers.html.

18. The School District of Philadelphia, Alain Locke Elementary School, Our Vision; accessed on August 15, 2013, at http://webgui.phila.k12.pa.us/schools/l/locke/about-us.

19. J. Lardeni, "Getting to Know You with Toilet Paper," 2010; accessed on August 26, 2013, at www.lessonplanspage.com/OBeginSchoolGettingToKnowYouToiletPaperIdeaK12.htm.

20. H. Barrett, "Special Characteristics," 2010; accessed on August 26, 2013, at www.lessonplanspage.com/OGettingToKnowStudentSpecialCharacteristicsBeginSchoolIdeaP12.htm.

21. A. Bayer, "Kids Are Asked to Make Largest Mural Ever," November 24, 2009; accessed on June 8, 2010, at www.examiner.com/examiner/x-28900-Minneapolis-Homeschooling-Examiner~y2009m11d24-Kids-are-asked-to-help-make-the-worlds-longest-mural.

22. R. Houston, "All About Me Scrapbooks," 2010; accessed on August 26, 2013, at www.lessonplanspage.com/OBeginningOfSchoolAllAboutMcPhotoSymbolJournalExpectationsScrapbook512.htm.

23. K. Radel, "Ideas for Teaching about Different Countries and Cultures," 2010; accessed on June 8, 2010, at www.lessonplanspage.com/SSLAOCICountriesandCulturesIdeas18.htm.

24. P. Ammonds Newcomb, "ASFL Students Have ePals Around the World," *Huntsville Times*, May 24, 2010; accessed on June 9, 2010, at http://blog.al.com/breaking/2010/05/asfl_students_have_epals_aroun.html.

25. California State Board of Education, "English Language Arts Content Standards for California Public Schools," June 2009; accessed on June 7, 2010, at www.cde.ca.gov/be/st/ss.

26. Florida Department of Education, "Benchmark Standards," revised December 2008; accessed on June 7, 2010, at www.floridastandards.org/Standards/PublicPreviewBenchmark2936.aspx?kw=culture.

27. *Federal Register* (June 4, 1975), 24128.

28. Dr. M. H. Mason Elementary School, "School Activities," 2010; accessed on June 9, 2010, at www.gwinnett.k12.ga.us/schooldom/MasonES/gcps-schooltemplate.nsf/Pages/Students.

29. D. Baker, "Teaching for Gender Difference," 2010; accessed on June 3, 2010, at www.narst.org/publications/research/gender.cfm.

30. Based on N. Carlsson-Paige and D. Levin, *Before Push Comes to Shove: Building Conflict Resolution Skills with Children,* (St. Paul, MN: Red Leaf Press, 1998).

31. A. Clutter and A. Zubieta, "Understanding the Latino Culture," 2009; accessed on May 27, 2010, at http://ohioline.osu.edu/hyg-fact/5000/pdf/5237.pdf.

32. E. Olivos, "Collaboration with Latino Families: A Critical Perspective on Home–School Interactions," *Intervention in School & Clinic* 45, no. 2 (2009): 109.

33. M. Thao, "Parent Involvement in School," December 2009; accessed on May 27, 2010, at www.wilder.org/download.0.html?report=2262.

34. Monica Schnee's ESL Classroom (website); accessed on August 15, 2013, at http://eslschnee.weebly.com/home.html.

35. Arizona Department of Education, English Language Learners, 2012 ELL Teacher of the Year, Melanie Conger; accessed on August 26, 2013, at http://www.azed.gov/english-language-learners/conference/2011-ell-teacher-of-the-year.

36. "No Child Left Behind Act," *National Association for Bilingual Education*, 2010; accessed on May 26, 2010, at www.nabe.org/advocacy.html.

37. Text contributed by Stacey Larson-Everson, Director of State and Federal Programs, Fallbrook Union Elementary School District, Fallbrook, California.

38. Jennifer Cheeseman Day, *Population Projections of the United States by Age, Sex, Race, and Hispanic Origin: 1995 to 2050,* U.S. Bureau of the Census, Current Population Reports, P25-1130 (Washington, DC: U.S. Government Printing Office, 1996).

39. Kids Count Data Center, "Children in Immigrant Families (Percent)," 2010; accessed on July, 2, 2012, at http://datacenter.kidscount.org/data/acrossstates/Rankings.aspx?ind=115.

40. Kids Count Data Center, "Children Who Have Difficulty Speaking English by Children in Immigrant Families (Percent)," March 2010; accessed on June 21, 2012, at http://datacenter.kidscount.org/data/acrossstates/Rankings.aspx?ind=128.

41. The Urban Institute, "Immigration Trends," 2010; accessed on June 11, 2012, at www.urban.org/uploadedpdf/412203-young-children.pdf.

42. Ibid.

43. L. A. Karoly, G. C. Gonzalez, "Early Care and Education for Children in Immigrant Families," *The Future of Children* 21, no. 1 (2011); accessed on June 11, 2012, at http://futureofchildren.org/publications/journals/article/index.xml?journalid=74&articleid=541&sectionid=3728.

44. U.S. Department of Commerce, U.S. Census Bureau, Language Use, "American Community Survey Data on Language Use," January 3, 2012; accessed on June 11, 2012, from http://www.census.gov/hhes/socdemo/language/data/acs/index.html.

45. The Annie E. Casey Foundation, "Kids Count, Data Snap Shot," 2012; accessed on June 11, 2012, at http://www.aecf.org/~/media/Pubs/Initiatives/KIDS%20COUNT/D/DataSnapshoton-HighPovertyCommunities/KIDSCOUNTDataSnapshot_HighPovertyCommunities.pdf.

46. R. Linquanti, Schools Moving Up: WestEd., *Fostering Academic Success for English Language Learners: What Do We Know?*; accessed on June 28, 2012, at http://www.wested.org/policy/pubs/fostering.

47. Course Crafters, *The ELL Outlook*, "When an ELL Has Difficulty Learning, Is the Problem a Disability or the Second-Language Acquisition Process?," accessed on May 20, 2010, from www.coursecrafters.com/ELL-Outlook/2004/mar_apr/ELLOutlook-ITIArticle4.htm.

48. TEA Student Assessment Division, "ELL Update," accessed on June 7, 2010, athttp://ritter.tea.state.tx.us/student.assessment/resources/conferences/tac/2008/ell_assessment_update.pdf.

CHAPTER 16

1. U.S. Department of Education, Office of Special Education Programs, Data Analysis System (DANS), OMB no. 1820043, "Children with Disabilities Receiving Special Education Under of the Individuals with Disabilities Education Act," 1998–2007, updated July 15, 2008; accessed on May 21, 2013, from http://nichcy.org/laws/idea.

2. Public Law 105–17 (1997).

3. Individuals with Disabilities Education Act Amendments of 2004, P.L. 108–44, 20 U.S.C. §§ SEC. 602, 1401 et seq; accessed on May 21, 2013, from http://nichcy.org/laws.

4. National Dissemination Center for Children with Disabilities, Part of IDEA; accessed on June 10, 2013, from www.nichcy.org/Laws/IDEA/Pages/PartB.aspx.

5. Ibid.

6. Ed.gov; accessed on June 10, 2013, at http://www.ed.gov.

7. U.S. Department of Education, Office of Special Education and Rehabilitative Services, Office of Special Education Programs, *28th Annual Report to Congress on the Implementation of the Individuals with Disabilities Education Act, 2006,* vol. 1 (Washington, DC: U.S. Government Printing Office, 2009).

8. Ibid.

9. Ibid.

10. Baltimore County Public Schools, *Baltimore County Infants and Toddler's Program*; accessed on August 13, 2013, at http://www.bcps.org/offices/special_ed/infants-toddlers.html.

11. 2009 Clarissa Hug National Teacher of the Year; accessed on August 15, 2013, at http://www.docstoc.com/docs/44027807/Gayle-Solis-Zavala-2009-Clarissa-Hug-National-Teacher-of-the-Year.

12. Council for Exceptional Children, 1996; accessed on June 2, 2013, at www.cec.sped.org.

13. Material in this section on itinerant special educators contributed by Faith Haertig Sadler, M.Ed., itinerant special education teacher in Seattle, Washington.

14. Autism Speaks, Facts About Autism; accessed on August 12, 2013, at http://www.autismspeaks.org/what-autism/facts-about-autism.

15. Ibid.

16. J. J. Woods and A. M. Wetherby, "Early Identification of and Intervention for Infants and Toddlers Who Are at Risk for Autism Spectrum Disorder," *Language, Speech, and Hearing Services in Schools 34* (2003): 180–293.

17. Autism Science Foundation, "Autism Diagnosis," 2012; accessed on July 5, 2012, at http://autismsciencefoundation.org/what-is-autism/autism-diagnosis.

18. Ibid.

19. J. J. Woods and A. M. Wetherby, "Early Identification of and Intervention for Infants and Toddlers Who Are at Risk for Autism Spectrum Disorder," *Language, Speech, and Hearing Services in Schools 34* (2003): 180–293.

20. S. Mastrangelo, "Play and the Child with Autism Spectrum Disorder: From Possibilities to Practice," *International Journal of Play Therapy 18,* no. 1 (2009): 13–30.

21. Michelle Castillo, "Induced Labor May Increase Risk Autism in Offspring," Autism Awareness, CBS News, 2013; accessed on August 13, 2013, at http://www.cbsnews.com/8301-204_162-57598203/induced-labor-may-increase-risk-of-autism-in-offspring.

22. The National Human Genome Research Institute, Learning about Autism; accessed on July 26, 2013, from www.genome.gov/25522099.

23. The Associated Press, "Gene Clues from Mideast Suggest Autism Occurs When Brain Cannot Learn Properly from Early Life," *The International Herald Tribune*, July 11, 2008; accessed on June 10, 2013, from www.iht.com/bin/printfriendly.php?id=14407868.

24. K. L. Spittler, "New Evidence Supports Theory of an Environmental Trigger for Autism," *NeuroPsychiatry Reviews* (2009): 6.

25. The National Human Genome Research Institute, Learning about Autism; accessed on July 26, 2013, from www.genome.gov/25522099.

26. Centers for Disease Control and Prevention (2007-01-08), Mercury and Vaccines (Thimerosal); accessed on July 2, 2012.

27. Mastrangelo, "Play and the Child with Autism Spectrum Disorder."

28. T. Wigram and C. Gold, "Music Therapy in the Assessment and Treatment of Autistic Spectrum Disorder: Clinical Application and Research Evidence," *Child Care, Health and Development 32* no. 5 (2005): 535–542.

29. Centers for Disease Control and Prevention, Attention-Deficit/Hyperactivity Disorder, Facts about ADHD, May 25, 2010; accessed on July 26, 2013, from www.cdc.gov/ncbddd/adhd/facts.html.

30. Ibid.

31. Mental Health America, Fact Sheet, Adult AD/HD in the Work Place; accessed on June 10, 2010, from www.mentalhealthamerica.net/go/information/get-info/ad/hd/adult-ad/hd-in-the-workplace/adult-ad/hd-in-the-workplace.

32. Centers for Disease Control and Prevention, Attention Deficit/Hyperactivity Disorder, Facts about ADHD, May 25, 2010; accessed on July 26, 2013, from www.cdc.gov/ncbddd/adhd/facts.html.

33. Centers for Disease Control and Prevention, ADHD: Symptoms and Diagnosis; accessed on August 14, 2013, at http://www.cdc.gov/ncbddd/adhd/diagnosis.html.

34. Ibid.

35. Ibid.

36. Ibid.

37. B. Bloom, R. A. Cohen, and G. Freeman, "Summary Health Statistics for U.S. Children: National Health Interview Survey, 2008," National Center for Health Statistics, *Vital and Health Statistics 10*, no. 244 (2009).

38. C. Adams, "Girls and ADHD," *Instructor 116,* no. 6 (2007): 31–35.

39. National Institute of Mental Health, *Attention Deficit Hyperactivity Disorder*; accessed on August 13, 2013, at http://www.nimh.nih.gov/health/publications/attention-deficit-hyperactivity-disorder/index.shtml.

40. Ibid.

41. H. Kozima, "Children-Robot Interaction: A Pilot Study in Autism Therapy," *Progress in Brain Research 164* (2007): 385–400 (abstract online); accessed on June 27, 2012, at http://www.ncbi.nlm.nih.gov/pubmed/17920443.

42. C. Chandler, "Animal-Assisted Therapy in Counseling and School Settings," ERIC Clearinghouse on Counseling and

Student Services, Greensboro, NC, 2001; accessed on June 27, 2012, at http://www.ericdigests.org/2002-3/animal.htm.

43. Ibid.

44. U.S. Department of Education, What Works Clearinghouse, "WWC Review of the Report 'Enhancing the Effectiveness of Special Education Programming for Children with Attention Deficit Hyperactivity Disorder Using a Daily Report Card'"; accessed on July 2, 2013, at http://ies.ed.gov/ncee/wwc.

45. *Pittsburg Post-Gazette*; accessed on August 14, 2013, at www.portal.state.pa.us/portal/.../2013_accommodations_guidelines_pdf.

46. Jacob K. Javits Gifted and Talented Students Education Act of 1988; accessed on July 26, 2013, at www2.ed.gov/programs/javits/index.html.

47. Illinois Association for Gifted and Talented Children (IAGC); accessed on August 15, 2013, at http://www.iagcgifted.org.

48. NYSED, Curriculum and Instruction, Gifted and Talented, June 3, 2009; accessed on August 16, 2013, at http://www.p12.nysed.gov/ciai/gt.

49. Duke Tip, Research and Resources, State Definitions, Laws, and Resources; accessed on August 16, 2013, at http://www.tip.duke.edu/node/346#Kentucky.

50. Ibid.

51. Childhelp. National Child Abuse Statistics; accessed on August 14, 2013, at http://www.childhelp-usa.com/pages/statistics.

52. About.com, Pediatrics, Child Abuse Statistics; accessed on June 10, 2013, from http://pediatrics.about.com/od/childabuse/a/05_abuse_stats.htm.

53. U.S. Statutes at Large, vol. 88, pt. 1 (Washington, DC: U.S. Government Printing Office, 1976), 5.

54. National Children's Alliance, National Statistics on Child Abuse; accessed on August 14, 2013, at http://www.nationalchildrensalliance.org/NCANationalStatistics.

55. Ibid.

56. Be Free, Physical Abuse; accessed on August 14, 2013, from http://www.be-free.info/enparents/physicalAbuse.htm.

57. About.com, Pediatrics, "Child Abuse Statistics."

58. Darkness to Light, Statistics Surrounding Child Sexual Abuse; accessed on July 26, 2013, at www.darkness2light.org/KnowAbout/statistics_2.asp.

59. Ibid.

60. Ibid.

61. Ibid.

62. Ibid.

63. The National Center on Family Homelessness, Children; accessed on August 15, 2013, at http://www.familyhomelessness.org/children.php?p=ts.

64. The National Center on Family Homelessness; accessed on August 15, 2013 at http://www.familyhomelessness.org/index.php.

65. Public Law 100-77, McKinney–Vento Homeless Education Act, Title VII-Subtitle B-Education for Homeless Children and Youths, 2001.

66. The National Center on Family Homelessness, *America's Youngest Outcasts: State Report Card on Child Homelessness*, March 2009; accessed on July 26, 2013, from www.homeless-childrenamerica.org/pdf/rc_full_report.pdf.

67. Albuquerque School District, Homeless Project; accessed on August 15, 2013, at http://www.aps.edu/title-i/homeless-project/about-the-homeless-project.

68. K. Kingsbury, "Keeping Homeless Kids in School," *Time*, March 23, 2009, 42–43.

CHAPTER 17

1. A. T. Henderson and K. L. Mapp, *A New Wave of Evidence: The Impact of School, Family, and Community Connections on Student Achievement* Austin, Texas: National Center for Family and Community Connections with Schools, Southwest Educational Development Laboratory, 2002).

2. W. Bushaw and S. Lopez, "The 42nd Annual Phi Delta Kappa/Gallup Poll of the Public's Attitudes Toward the Public Schools," *Phi Delta Kappan,* September 2010; accessed on July 10, 2012, at http://www.gallup.com/poll/142661/phi-delta-kappa-gallup-poll-2010.aspx.

3. WCSD Parent University, Washoe County School District, 2013; accessed on September 3, 2013, at http://www.washoecountyschools.net/parent_university/userfiles/file/Elementary%20Packet(1).pdf.

4. Jason Schultz, "Elementary School's 'Parent University' Helps Adults to Inspire Their Children," *The Palm Beach Post*, November 11, 2011; accessed on September 3, 2013, at http://www.palmbeachpost.com/news/news/education/elementary-schools-parent-university-helps-adults-/nLzrH.

5. J. S. Solochek, "Program Empowers Parents to Get More Involved with Children's Lives," *St. Petersburg Times,* April 5, 2009; accessed on July 10, 2012, at http://www.tampabay.com/news/education/k12/article989668.ece.

6. A. T. Henderson, et al. *Beyond the Bake Sale: The Essential Guide to Family/School Partnerships* (New York: New Press, 2007).

7. H. T. Knopf and K. J. Swick, "Using Our Understanding of Families to Strengthen Family Involvement," *Early Childhood Education Journal* 35, no. 5 (2008): 419–427.

8. A. Gelber and A. Isen. "Children's Schooling and Parents' Behavior: Evidence from the Head Start Impact Study," March 2012; accessed on July 11, 2012, at http://www.nber.org/papers/w17704.

9. Ibid.

10. Kay S. Hymowitz, "The Single-Mom Catastrophe," *Los Angeles Tribune,* June 3, 2012; accessed on September 3, 2013, at http://articles.latimes.com/2012/jun/03/opinion/la-oe-hymowitz-unmarried-mothers-20120603.

11. U.S. Census Bureau, "Custodial Mothers and Fathers and Their Child Support," November 2009; accessed August 24, 2013, from http://singleparents.about.com/gi/o.htm?zi=1/XJ&zTi=1&sdn=singleparents&cdn=parenting&tm=62&gps=420_139_1657_867&f=20&su=p284.9.336.ip_p504.3.336.ip_&tt=11&bt=0&bts=0&zu=http%3A//www.census.gov/prod/2009pubs/p60-237.pdf.

12. Ibid.

13. J. S. Coleman, *Parental Involvement in Education* (Washington, DC: U.S. Department of Education, 1991), 7.

14. U.S. Census Bureau, "Custodial Mothers and Fathers."

15. S. Jayson, "Non-Resident, but Present," *USA Today,* June 16, 2010.

16. National Fatherhood Initiative, Overview: What Is School-Based Programming, 2013; www.fatherhood.org/Page.aspx?pid=654.

17. Jane Yolen, *My Father Knows the Names of Things* (New York: Simon & Schuster Books For Young Readers, 2010).

18. Joseph Bruchac, *My Father Is Taller Than a Tree,* (New York, Penguin Group USA, 2008); accessed July 26, 2013, at http://www.us.penguingroup.com/nf/Book/BookDisplay/0,,9780803731738,00.html?strSrchSql=my+father+is+taller+than+a+tree/My_Father_Is_Taller_than_a_Tree_Joseph_Bruchac.

19. Watch D.O.G.S., fathers.com; accessed on September 3, 2013, at http://www.fathers.com/content/index.php?option=com_content&task=view&id=21&Itemid=60.

20. Pew Research Center, "Millenials: Portraits of the Generation Next," February 2010; accessed July 26, 2013, at http://pewsocialtrends.org/assets/pdf/millennials-confident-connected-open-to-change.pdf.

21. Pew Research Center, "The Return of the Multi-Generational Family Household," March 8, 2010; accessed July 26, 2013, at http://pewsocialtrends.org/assets/pdf/752-multi-generational-families.pdf.

22. Paola Scommegna, "More U.S. Children Raised by Grandparents," Population Reference Bureau, 2013; accessed on September 10, 2013, at http://www.prb.org/Publications/Articles/2012/US-children-grandparents.aspx.

23. S. Plummer, "Future Cowboys," *Tulsa World,* June 11, 2010; www.tulsaworld.com/news/article.aspx?subjectid=11&articleid=20100611_11_A11_Veteri115080.

24. Centers for Disease Control and Prevention, "About Teen Pregnancy," March 12, 2012; accessed on July 10, 2012, at http://www.cdc.gov/TeenPregnancy/AboutTeenPreg.htm.

25. Centers for Disease Control and Prevention, "NCHS Data Brief," April 2012; accessed June 25, 2012, at http://www.cdc.gov/nchs/data/databriefs/db89.htm.

26. Huffinton Post, "Teen Pregnancy: Mississippi Has the Highest Teen Pregnancy Rate in the U.S.," April 10, 2012; accessed on July 10, 2012, at http://www.huffingtonpost.com/2012/04/10/teen-pregnancy-rates_n_1413820.html.

27. Centers for Disease Control and Prevention, "About Teen Pregnancy," updated March 12, 2012; accessed on July 10, 2012, at http://www.cdc.gov/TeenPregnancy/AboutTeenPreg.htm.

28. C. Bowers, "Teen Pregnancies End Decade-Long Decline," CBS Evening News, January 26, 2010; accessed on July 10, 2012, at www.cbsnews.com/stories/2010/01/26/eveningnews/main6144496.shtml.

29. A. Dizon, "Seven Local Moms Overcome Stats to Graduate from High School," *Lubbock-Avalanche Journal*, lubbockonline.com, May 25, 2010; accessed on July 10, 2012, at http://lubbockonline.com/education/2010-05-25/seven-local-moms-overcome-stats-graduate-high-school.

30. C. Kieffer, "Dropout Reduction Aim of New Programs," *Tupelo News*, June 7, 2010; accessed at http://nems360.com/view/full_story/7821316/article-Dropout-reduction-aim-of-new-programs?instance=news_special_coverage_right_column.

31. American Civil Liberties Union, LGBT Parenting; accessed on September 9, 2013, at https://www.aclu.org/lgbt-rights/lgbt-parenting.

32. Mackenzie Carpenter, "What Happens to Kids Raised by Gay Parents? Research Suggests that They Turn Out About the Same, No Better, No Worse and No More Likely to Be Gay than Other Kids," *Pittsburg Post-Gazette*, June 10, 2007; accessed July 26, 2013, from www.post-gazette.com/pg/07161/793042-51.stm#ixzz0qHEotsZP.

33. M. Park, "Kids of Lesbians Have Fewer Behavioral Problems, Study Suggests," CNN Health, Gay in America; accessed on September 9, 2013, at http://www.cnn.com/2010/HEALTH/06/07/lesbian.children.adjustment/index.html.

34. American Civil Liberties Union, LGBT Parenting.

35. Ibid.

36. Carpenter, "What Happens to Kids Raised by Gay Parents?".

37. The American Academy of Child and Adolescent Psychiatry (AACAP), Children with Gay, Lesbian, Bisexual or Transgender Parents, August 2013; accessed on September 9, 2013, at http://www.aacap.org/AACAP/Families_and_Youth/Facts_for_Families/Facts_for_Families_Pages/Children_with_Lesbian_Gay_Bisexual_and_Transgender_Parents_92.aspx.

38. America's Promise Alliance, U.S. Military Demographics, 2010; accessed on September 9, 2013, at http://www.americaspromise.org/Our-Work/Military-Families/Military-Families-by-the-Numbers.aspx.

39. Brian Ferry, "Youngsville Woman Starts Pennies for Postage to Help Get Packages to Service Personnel," *Times Observer*; accessed July 26, 2013, from www.timesobserver.com/page/content.detail/id/531862.html.

40. The Armed Services YMCA, Operation Hero; accessed on September 9, 2013, at http://www.asymca.org/programs/operation-hero4.

41. Bureau of Justice Statistics, "Correctional Populations in the United States"; accessed September 9, 2013, from http://www.bjs.gov/index.cfm?ty=pbdetail&iid=4537.

42. Pew Charitable Trusts, *Collateral Costs: Incarceration's Effect on Economic Mobility* (Washington, DC: Pew Charitable Trusts, 2010); accessed on September 9, 2013, at http://www.pewtrusts.org/uploadedFiles/wwwpewtrustsorg/Reports/Economic_Mobility/Collateral%20Costs%20FINAL.pdf?n=5996.

43. Ibid.

44. Ibid.

45. W. Drash, "The 'Silent Victims' of Incarceration: Coping with Parents in Prison," CNN World, CNN Heroes; accessed on September 9, 2013, at http://www.cnn.com/2012/11/26/world/cnnheroes-prison-children.

46. Get On the Bus, home page, 2009; accessed on September 3, 2013, at http://www.getonthebus.us.

47. Ibid.

48. Sesame Street, Little Children, Big Challenges: Incarceration; accessed on September 9, 2013, at http://www.sesameworkshop.org/press-room/incarceration.

49. D. Samfield, "When It Comes to Reading, LAW Students Go Above and Beyond," June 18, 2010; accessed July 26, 2013, at www.nashobapublishing.com/shirley_news/ci_15325076.

50. S. Riddell, "More Preschools Collaborating with Community Partners," Kentucky Teacher; accessed on July 11, 2012, at http://www.kentuckyteacher.org/features/2012/06/more-preschools-are-collaborating-with-community-partners.

51. Hills Elementary School Website, accessed on July 11, 2012, at http://www.iowa-city.k12.ia.us/Schools/Hills/Highlights/HillsHighlights.html.

52. Boston Public Schools, "School Councils," 2012; accessed on July 12, 2012, at http://www.bostonpublicschools.org/school-councils.

53. Ibid.

54. Y. Rammohan, "New Technology Empowers CPS Parents," *Chicago Tonight,* June 5, 2012; accessed on July 11, 2012, at http://chicagotonight.wttw.com/2012/06/05/new-technology-empowers-cps-parents.

55. National Civic League, "The Campaign for Grade Level Reading," accessed on July 11, 2012, at http://www.allamericacity award.com.

56. S. Riddell, "Encourage Staff Members to Share 'Parent Info,'" *Kentucky Teacher*; accessed on July 11, 2012, at http://www.kentuckyteacher.org/leadership-letter/2012/07/encourage-staff-members-to-share-parentinfo.

57. Samfield, "When It Comes to Reading."

58. "Teacher Visits Hit Home," *Education World,* updated July 14, 2010; accessed on July 10, 2012, at http://www.education-world.com/a_admin/admin/admin241.shtml.

59. Buder Elementary Schools, Teacher Home Visits, PowerPoint presentation; accessed on July 11, 2012, at http://slpses.schoolwires.net//site/Default.aspx?PageType=6&SiteID=276&SearchString=home%20visits.

60. O. C. Moles, ed., "Personal Contacts," *Reaching All Families: Creating Family-Friendly Schools,* (Washington, DC: U.S. Department of Education, Office of Educational Research and Improvement, August 1996), updated January 8, 2002; available online at http://www.ed.gov/pubs/ReachFam/index.html.

61. R. J. Stiggins, *Student-Centered Classroom Assessment,* 2nd ed. (Upper Saddle River, NJ: Merrill/Prentice Hall, 1997), 499.

62. M. McGowan, *Mrs. Marci McGowan's First Grade Website,* 2010; accessed on July 10, 2012, at http://www.mrsmcgowan.com/index.html.

63. The Teachers' Podcast, "Twitter Used to Develop Second Graders' Writing Skills"; accessed on July 10, 2012, at http://teacherspodcast.org/2009/03/31/ep-36-digital-catchup-and-21st-century-learning-debate.

64. Raymore-Peculiar School District. *"School Uses Skype for Parent-Teacher Conferences"*; accessed on September 9, 2013 at http://www.raypec.k12.mo.us/CivicAlerts.aspx?AID=410.

65. Contributed by Carrie Jostmeyer, first grade teacher, Sparks Elementary, Frisco ISD, Frisco, Texas.

66. C. Johnson, "Oakland Literacy Program Needs Your Help" *SFGate*; accessed on September 9, 2013, at http://www.sfgate.com/bayarea/johnson/article/Oakland-literacy-program-needs-your-help-3188442.php.

67. Ibid.

68. Education Commission of the States, "The Progress of Education Reform," February 2010; www.ecs.org/clearinghouse/84/20/8420.pdf.

69. NCCP, "A National Portrait of Chronic Absenteeism in the Early Grades"; accessed July 26, 2013, from www.nccp.org/publications/pub_771.html.

GLOSSARY

504 plan A provision under the Americans with Disabilities Act that specifies a child with a disability cannot be excluded from participating in federally funded free programs.

Absorbent mind The idea that the minds of young children are receptive to and capable of learning. The child learns unconsciously by taking in information from the environment.

Accommodation Changing or altering existing schemes or creating new ones in response to new information.

Achievement gaps The difference in performance between low-income and minority students, students of different genders, and students with different levels of maternal education, compared to that of their peers.

Active learning The view that children develop knowledge and learn by being physically and mentally engaged in learning activities.

Adaptation The process of building schemes through interaction with the environment. Consists of two complementary processes—assimilation and accommodation.

Adaptive education Modifications in any classroom, program, environment, or curriculum that help students achieve desired educational goals.

Adult–child discourse The talk between an adult and a child, which includes adult suggestions about behavior and problem solving.

Advocacy The act of engaging in strategies designed to improve the circumstances of children and families. Advocates move beyond their day-to-day professional responsibilities and work collaboratively to help others.

Alignment The arrangement of standards, curriculum, and tests so that they complement one another.

Alphabetic knowledge (AK) Knowledge of the names and sounds associated with printed letters.

Alternative certification Teacher certification through which an individual who already has at least a bachelor's degree can obtain certification to teach.

Anecdotal record A brief written recording of student behavior that includes only what a teacher sees or hears, not what he or she thinks or infers.

Applied behavior analysis (ABA) A technique based on the learning theory of behaviorism, which states that all behavior is motivated by a purpose and is learned through systematic reinforcement.

Approaches to learning How children react to and engage in learning and activities associated with school.

Assessment The process of collecting information about children's development, learning, behavior, academic progress, need for special services, and attainment of grade level goals in order to make decisions.

Assimilation The process of fitting new information into existing schemes.

Assistive technology Any device used to promote the learning of children with disabilities.

Asthma A chronic inflammatory disorder of the airways; one of the most prevalent childhood illnesses in the United States.

Atelier A special area or studio for creating projects.

Atelierista A teacher trained in the visual arts who works with teachers and children.

Attachment An emotional tie between a parent/caregiver and an infant that endures over time.

Attention-deficit hyperactivity disorder (ADHD) Difficulty with attention and self-control, which leads to problems with learning, social functioning, and behavior that occur in more than one situation and have been present for a significant length of time.

Autism A developmental disability that typically appears during the first three years of life and is the result of a neurological disorder that affects the normal functioning of the brain, impacting development in the areas of social interaction and communication skills.

Autism spectrum disorder A neurological developmental disorder characterized by a deficit in communication and social interactions, as well as by the presence of restricted and repetitive behaviors.

Auto-education The idea that children teach themselves through appropriate materials and activities.

Autonomy An Erikson concept that says as toddlers mature physically and mentally, they want to do things by themselves with no outside help.

Baby signing Teaching babies to use signs or gestures to communicate a need or emotion.

Behavior guidance The processes by which children are helped to identify appropriate behaviors and use them.

Behavioral learning theories Theories that explain how children learn cognitively, socially, and behaviorally that play down the roles of biology and maturation in learning.

Behaviorism A learning theory based on the idea that behaviors are learned through rewards and punishment; popular in early childhood education today.

Blank tablet The belief that at birth the mind is blank and that experiences create the mind.

Blog A Web publishing tool that allows you to self-publish commentary in a journal format, while adding artwork and links to other blogs or websites.

Bloom's taxonomy Refers to a classification of different objectives that educators set for students in three domains: affective, psychomotor, and cognitive. Within the taxonomy, learning at higher levels is dependent on having mastered foundational knowledge and skills at lower levels of skills.

Bonding   A parent's initial emotional tie to an infant.

Book and print concepts   Activities that show how books look and how they work.

Brown v. Board of Education   Court ruling that stated, "Segregation of children in public schools solely on the basis of race deprives children of the minority group of equal educational opportunities, even though the physical facilities and other 'tangible' factors may be equal. The 'separate but equal' doctrine adopted in *Plessy v. Ferguson* has no place in the field of public education."

Bullying   Teasing, slapping, hitting, pushing, unwanted touching, taking personal belongings, name-calling, and making sexual comments and insults about looks, behavior, or culture.

Celiac disease   An immune reaction to eating gluten, a protein found in wheat, barley, and rye.

Center-based child care   Child care and education provided in a facility other than a home.

Cephalocaudal development   The principle that development proceeds from the head to the toes.

Challenging environments   Those environments that provide achievable and "stretching" experiences for all children.

Checklists   Lists of behaviors identifying children's skills and knowledge.

Child as sinful   View that children are basically sinful, need supervision and control, and should be taught to be obedient.

Child care   Comprehensive care and education of young children outside their homes.

Child centered   Term meaning that every child is a unique and special individual; that all children have a right to an education that helps them grow and develop to their fullest; that children are active participants in their own education and development; and teachers should consider children's ideas, preferences, learning styles, and interests in planning for and implementing instructional practices.

Child development associate (CDA)   An individual who has successfully completed the CDA assessment process and has been awarded the CDA credential. CDAs are able to meet the specific needs of children and work with parents and other adults to nurture children's physical, social, emotional, and intellectual growth in a child development framework.

Child development   The stages of physical, social, mental, and linguistic growth that occur from birth through age eight years.

Child study team   The group of individuals who determine a child's eligibility for special education.

Childhood depression   A disorder affecting as many as 1 in 33 children that can negatively impact feelings, thoughts, and behavior and can manifest itself with physical symptoms of illness.

Children as blank tablets   View that presupposes no innate genetic code or inborn traits exist and that the sum of what a child becomes depends on the nature and quality of experience.

Children as growing plants   View of children popularized by Froebel, which equates children to plants and teachers and parents to gardeners.

Children as investments   View that investing in the care and education of children reaps future benefits for parents and society.

Children as miniature adults   Belief that children are similar to adults and should be treated as such.

Children as property   Belief that children are literally the property of their parents.

Children with disabilities   IDEA defines children with disabilities as those children with mental retardation, hearing impairments (including deafness), speech or language impairments, visual impairments (including blindness), serious emotional disturbance, orthopedic impairments, autism, developmental delays, traumatic brain injury, other health impairments, or specific learning disabilities, and who, by reason thereof, need special education and related services.

Children's House   Montessori's first school especially designed to implement her ideas.

The Children's Online Privacy Protection Act (COPPA)   Legislation designed to ensure the privacy rights of children and protect them from unscrupulous individuals and companies.

Chronic school absence   When children miss 10 percent of the school days in a school year.

Chronosystem   The environmental contexts and events that influence children over their lifetimes, such as living in a technological age.

Civil behavior   Acting in polite, courteous, and respectful ways.

Civil Rights Act of 1964   Legislation that prohibits discrimination on the basis of race, color, religion, sex, or national origin; includes a provision that protects the constitutional rights of individuals in public facilities, including public education.

Classical conditioning   Association of automatic responses with new stimuli.

Classification   Refers to putting like things together and naming the group, such as big bears, little bears; shiny shells, dull shells; round buttons, square buttons; or smooth rocks, rough rocks.

Collaboration   Working jointly and cooperatively with other professionals, parents, and administrators.

Collaborative planning   A type of planning used by groups of teachers at the grade levels or across grade levels to plan curriculum daily, weekly, and monthly. Also called *team planning*.

Common Core State Standards (CCSS)   National benchmarks in math and English created to have uniformity no matter where students attend public schools.

Concrete operations stage   The stage of cognitive development during which children's thought is logical and can organize concrete experiences.

Constructivism   Theory that emphasizes the active role of children in developing their understanding and learning.

Consultation   Seeking advice and information from colleagues.

Content knowledge   The content and subjects teachers plan to teach.

Continuity of care   The ongoing nurturing relationship between a child and his or her caregiver.

Conventional literacy skills   Skills such as decoding (turning written words into spoken words), oral reading fluency, reading comprehension, writing, and spelling.

Cooperative learning groups   A context that allows English language learners to converse about meaningful ideas.

Coteaching The collaboration of a regular classroom teacher and a special education teacher in teaching lessons and activities.

Cultural awareness The appreciation for and understanding of people's cultures, socioeconomic status, and gender; includes understanding one's own culture.

Cultural competence The ability and confidence to interact effectively with children, families, and colleagues of different cultures.

Culturally appropriate practice An approach to education based on the premise that all people in the United States should receive proportional attention in the curriculum.

Culture A group's way of life, including basic values, beliefs, religion, language, clothing, food, and various practices.

Curriculum alignment The process of making sure that the content of the curriculum matches what the standards say students should know and be able to do.

Cyberbullying The threat, stalking, harassment, torment, and humiliation of one child by another through cell phones, MySpace, Facebook, Twitter, chat rooms, blogs, texting, and picture messaging.

Data-driven instruction A type of teaching in which analysis of assessment data is used to make decisions about how to best meet the instructional needs of each child.

Developmental kindergarten (DK) A kindergarten designed to provide children with additional time for maturation and physical, social, emotional, and intellectual development.

Developmentally and culturally responsive practice (DCRP) Teaching based on the ability to respond appropriately to children's and families' developmental, cultural, and ethnic backgrounds and needs.

Developmentally appropriate practice (DAP) Practice based on how children grow and develop and on individual and cultural differences.

Diabetes A chronic condition that affects how the body metabolizes sugar; one of the most common childhood diseases.

Differentiate To teach in response to the diverse needs of students so that all students within a classroom can learn effectively regardless of differences in ability.

Differentiated instruction (DI) An approach that enables teachers to plan strategically to meet the needs of every student in order to teach to the needs of each child and allow for diversity in the classroom.

Digital literacy The ability to use digital media for speaking, listening, reading, and writing purposes.

Discourse skills Activities that encourage telling stories and explaining how the world works.

Documentation Records of children's work, including videos, photographs, art, work samples, projects, and drawings.

Early childhood education The growth, development, and education of children birth through age eight.

Early childhood professional An educator who successfully teaches all children, promotes high personal standards, and continually expands his or her skills and knowledge.

Early Head Start A federal program serving pregnant women, infants, toddlers, and their families.

Early intervention A process of providing services and opportunities for children and families.

Economic Opportunity Act of 1964 (EOA) Implemented several social programs to promote the health, education, and general welfare of people from low socioeconomic backgrounds.

Education of All Handicapped Children Act (EAHC) Mandated that in order to receive federal funds, states must develop and implement policies that assure a Free Appropriate Public Education (FAPE) for all children with disabilities.

Elementary and Secondary Education Act (ESEA) Federal legislation that funds mainly elementary and secondary education.

Embedded instruction Involves teaching skills and behaviors in the context of classroom routines and transitions.

Emergent literacy Children's communication skills are in an emerging state; in the process of developing.

Émile Jean-Jacques Rousseau's famous book that outlines his ideas about how children should be reared.

Encouraging classroom A classroom environment that rewards student accomplishment and independence.

English language learners (ELLs) Children who speak a language other than English in the home and who are not fully fluent in English.

Environmental education Enables children to explore environmental issues, engage in problem solving, and find solutions for environmental issues.

Environmentalism The theory that the environment, rather than heredity, exerts the primary influence on intellectual growth and cultural development.

Equilibrium A balance between existing and new schemes, developed through assimilation and accommodation of new information.

Ethical conduct Responsible behavior toward students and parents that allows you to be considered a professional.

Event sampling A form of assessment that systematically observes a specific behavior during a particular period of time that is based on the ABC model.

Executive function (EF) *See* **self-regulation**.

Exosystem Environment or setting in which children do not play an active role but that nonetheless influences their development.

Expanding horizons approach Also called the *expanding environments approach*, an approach to teaching social studies in which the student is at the center of the expanding horizons and initial units, and at each grade level is exposed to an ever-widening environment.

Family child care Home-based care and education provided by a non-relative outside the child's home; also known as *family care*.

Fantasy play Play involving unrealistic notions and superheroes.

Forest schools Programs with the belief that by participating in engaging, motivating, and achievable tasks and activities in a woodland environment, each child has an opportunity to develop intrinsic motivation and sound emotional and social skills.

Formative assessment The ongoing process of gathering data on students over the school year.

Free and appropriate public education (FAPE) A free education suited to children's age, maturity, condition of disability, past achievements, and parental expectations.

Froebel's gifts Ten sets of learning materials designed to help children learn through play and manipulation.

Full inclusion An approach whereby students with disabilities receive all instruction and support services in a general classroom.

Gift of time The practice of giving children more time in a program or at home to develop physically, emotionally, socially, and cognitively as preparation for kindergarten.

Gluten sensitivity A spectrum of disorders, including celiac disease and wheat allergy, in which gluten has an adverse effect on the body (also called *gluten intolerance*).

Goodness of fit How well a teacher recognizes and responds or adapts to a child's temperament—also affects the learning of self-regulation.

Grade-level and across-levels planning Planning occurs in grade-level teams and across grade levels, for example, K–1. This is also called horizontal planning (same grade level) and vertical planning (grades above and/or below).

Grandfamilies Children living with their grandparents.

Guidelines (standards) Preschool statements of what children should know and be able to do.

Head Start One of the longest-running programs in the United States to address systemic poverty and education for young children and their families.

Head Start Program Performance Standards Federal guidelines for Head Start and Early Head Start, designed to ensure that all children and families receive high-quality services.

Healthy environments Those environments that provide for children's physical and psychological health, safety, and sense of security.

Hierarchy of needs Maslow's theory that basic needs must be satisfied before higher-level needs can be satisfied.

HighScope educational model A program for young children based on Piaget's and Vygotsky's ideas.

High-stakes testing An assessment test used to either admit children into programs or promote them from one grade to the next.

Holophrases The single words children use to refer to what they see, hear, and feel (e.g., *up, doll*).

Horizontal planning Collaboratively planning with your grade-level colleagues.

Implementation Committing to a certain action based on interpretations of observational data.

Impulse control See *self-regulation*.

Inclusion Generally defined as educating typically developing students in the same classroom as students who have various disabilities.

Inclusive classroom A regular classroom in which children with disabilities are included.

Individual cultural identity Learning about the self.

Individualization of instruction Providing for students' specific needs, disabilities, and preferences.

Individualized education plan (IEP) A plan for meeting an exceptional learner's educational needs, specifying goals, objectives, services, and procedures for evaluating progress.

Individualized family service plan (IFSP) A plan designed to help families reach their goals for themselves and their children, with varied support services.

Individuals with Disabilities Education Act (IDEA) The current reauthorization of the Education of All Handicapped Children Act; provides for inclusion, universal design, response to instruction, and differentiated instruction.

Infancy The first year of life.

Infant/toddler mental health The overall health and well-being of young children in the context of family, school, and community relationships.

Informal (free) play Play in which children participate in activities of interest to them.

Inquiry learning Involvement of children in activities and processes that lead to learning.

Intentional teaching Developing plans, selecting instructional strategies, and teaching to promote learning.

Interactive word wall A collection of frequently used words in the classroom that children use to make sentences or use in other classroom literacy activities.

Interpretation Forming a conclusion based on observational and assessment data with the intent of planning and improving teaching and learning.

Interview A common way that observers and researchers engage children in discussion through questions to obtain information.

Invented spelling Children's attempts to use their best judgments about spelling.

Itinerant teachers Professionals who travel from school to school, providing assistance and teaching students.

Key developmental indicators (KDIs) Activities that foster developmentally important skills and abilities.

Kindergarten The name Friedrich Froebel gave to his system of education for children ages three through six; means "garden of children."

Knowledge of learners and learning Understanding students and how they learn (DAP); managing classroom environments and guiding children.

Learned helplessness A condition that can develop when children perceive that they are not doing as well as they could or as well as their peers, lose confidence in their abilities and achievement, and then attribute their failures to a lack of ability. These children are passive and have learned to feel they are helpless.

Learning centers Areas of the classroom set up to promote student-centered, hands-on, active learning, organized around student interests, themes, and academic subjects.

Learning communities Communities grounded in key foundational practices, including morning meetings, respect for children, character education, and teaching civility.

Learning disability A condition which causes a child to have difficulty learning and using certain skills.

Least restrictive environment (LRE) Placement that meets the needs of students who are disabled in as regular a setting as possible.

Linguistically diverse parents Individuals whose English proficiency is minimal and who lack a comprehensive knowledge of the norms and social systems in the United States.

Literacy circles Discussion groups in which children meet regularly to talk about books.

Literacy education Teaching that focuses on reading, writing, speaking, and listening.

Locus of control The source of control over personal behavior, either internal or external.

Looping A single-graded class of children staying with the same teacher for two or more years.

Macrosystem The broader culture in which children live (e.g., democracy, individual freedom, and religious freedom).

Mastery-oriented attributions Attributions that include effort (industriousness), paying attention, determination, and perseverance.

Mentoring The process in which an experienced and highly qualified teacher works with a novice or beginning teacher to help the new teacher be successful.

Mesosystem Links or interactions between microsystems.

Microsystem The environmental settings in which children spend a lot of their time (e.g., children in child care spend about thirty-three hours a week there).

Middle childhood Describes children in Erikson's industry versus inferiority stage of social-emotional development, ages six to nine years, during which time they gain confidence and ego satisfaction from completing demanding tasks.

Migrant and Seasonal Head Start A federal program designed to provide educational and other services to children and families who earn income in agricultural work.

Migrant family A family with school-aged children that moves from one geographic location to another to engage in agricultural work.

Mixed-age grouping Students in two or three grade levels combined in one classroom with one teacher.

Model early childhood program An exemplary approach to early childhood education that serves as a guide to best practices.

Modes of response The various ways children respond to books and conversations.

Montessori method A system of early childhood education founded on the ideas and practices of Maria Montessori.

Motherese (parentese) The way parents and others speak to young children in a slow, exaggerated way that includes short sentences and repetition of words and phrases.

Multicultural awareness Developing in all children an appreciation and understanding of other people's cultures, socioeconomic status, and gender, including their own.

Multicultural infusion Making multiculturalism an explicit part of curriculum and programs.

Multigenerational families Living arrangements in which three or more generations share a common housing unit.

National Defense Education Act (NDEA) Provided federal funding for science, technology, engineering, math (STEM), and foreign language education and is considered by many to be the beginning of federal standards in education.

Naturalism Education that follows the natural development of children and does not force the educational process on them.

Naturalistic teaching strategies Incorporating instruction into opportunities that occur naturally or routinely in the classroom.

Negative reinforcement Taking away something to promote or diminish a behavior, such as removing your attention from someone (ignoring them).

Neural shearing (pruning) The selective elimination of synapses.

No Child Left Behind Act (NCLB) Federal law passed in 2001 that has significantly influenced early childhood education.

No Child Left Behind The current reauthorization of ESEA; provides federal funding for schools that accrue high test scores and meet adequate yearly progress (AYP).

Nondiscriminatory evaluation A fair evaluation is required to determine whether a student has a disability and, if so, what the student's education should consist of.

Obesity A medical condition in which excess body fat has stored to the amount that it may have an adverse effect on health, leading to reduced life expectancy and/or increased health problems.

Object permanence The concept that people and objects have an independent existence beyond the child's perception of them.

Observation Observation is the intentional, systematic act of looking at the behavior of a child in a particular setting, program, or situation.

Occupations Materials designed to engage children in learning activities.

Open-air nursery school School established by the McMillan sisters, who believed in education where young children could explore their imaginations, develop their sensory and perceptual faculties, and care for gardens and pets.

Operant conditioning Learning in which voluntary behavior is strengthened or weakened by consequences or antecedents—events that precede an action.

Operation A reversible mental action.

Orbis Pictus (*The World in Pictures*) Considered the first picture book for children.

Parent University A specific parent-focused program designed to provide parents with specific skills so they can help their children, families, and schools.

Parent/family involvement The participation of parents and other family members in all areas of their children's education and development, based on the premise that parents are the primary influence in children's lives.

Parent–teacher conferences or **family–teacher conferences** Meetings between parents and early childhood professionals to inform the parents of the child's progress and allow them to actively participate in the educational process.

Partial inclusion An approach whereby students with disabilities receive some instruction in a general classroom and some in a specialized setting.

Pedagogical content knowledge   The teaching skills teachers need to help all children learn.

Pedagogical knowledge   The ability to apply pedagogical and content knowledge to develop meaningful learning experiences for children.

Peer coaching   A process whereby teachers agree to learn from each other through observation, interaction, and discussions.

Performance assessment   The ongoing process of gathering information about students during learning and teaching. Also called informal assessment, formative assessment, and authentic assessment.

Philosophy of education   A set of beliefs about how children develop and learn and what and how they should be taught.

Phonological awareness (PA)   The ability to detect, manipulate, or analyze the auditory aspects of spoken language (including the ability to distinguish or segment words, syllables, or phonemes), independent of meaning.

Phonological memory (PM)   The ability to remember spoken information for a short period of time.

Picture Exchange Communication System (PECS)   An augmentative/alternative communication system that allows children to learn to exchange a picture of a desired item to communicate.

Plan-do-review   A sequence in which children, with the help of the teacher, initiate plans for projects or activities, work in learning centers to implement their plans, and then review what they have done with the teacher and their fellow classmates.

Plastic   Capable of being molded or adapted to conditions.

Play therapy   The developmentally appropriate practice and model to incorporate social experiences and enjoyable interactions to enhance a child's pretend skills, joint attention, communication skills, and appropriate behavior.

Plessy v. Ferguson   Court ruling that established the "separate but equal" doctrine, which determined that as long as the opportunities and accommodations were equal for both races, that segregating people in public places, including schools, was lawful.

Portfolio   A compilation of children's work samples, products, and teacher observations collected over time.

Positive classroom   A classroom environment that promotes appropriate behavior and success.

Positive reinforcement   Adding something to promote or diminish a behavior, such as giving a high-five for a job well done.

Poverty   The condition of having insufficient income to support a minimum standard of living.

Practical life   Montessori activities that teach skills related to everyday living.

Pre-kindergarten   A class or program preceding kindergarten for children usually from three to four years old.

Preoperational stage   The stage of cognitive development in which young children are capable of mental representations.

Prepared environment   A classroom or other space that is arranged and organized to support learning in general and/or special knowledge and skills.

Preschool years   The period from three to five years of age, before children enter kindergarten and when many children attend preschool programs.

Primary circular reactions   Repetitive actions that are centered on the infant's own body.

Print-rich environment   An environment that enables children to interact with many forms of print.

Private speech   Self-directed speech that children use to plan and guide their behavior.

Process praise   Praising children for what they do: "Eddy you did a very good job of teaching Amanda how to write her story on the iPad!" Process praise praises the child and what they accomplished.

Professional development   A process of studying, learning, changing, and becoming more professional.

Professional dispositions   The values, commitments, and professional ethics that influence behaviors toward students, families, colleagues, and communities and affect student learning, motivation, and development, as well as the educator's own professional growth.

Professional learning community (PLC)   A team of early childhood professionals working collaboratively to improve teaching and learning.

Progressivism   Dewey's theory of education that emphasizes the importance of focusing on the needs and interests of children rather than teachers.

Project Approach   An in-depth investigation of a topic worth learning more about.

Proximodistal development   The principle that development proceeds from the center of the body outward.

Puberty   The period of profound physical and emotional developmental changes in the transition from childhood to adolescence.

Public policy   All the plans that local, state, and national governmental and nongovernmental organizations have for implementing their goals.

Rapid automatic naming (RAN) of letters or digits   The ability to rapidly name a sequence of random letters or digits.

Rapid automatic naming (RAN) of objects or colors   The ability to rapidly name a sequence of repeating random sets of pictures of objects (e.g., "car," "tree," "house," "man") or colors.

Rating scales   Usually numeric scales that contain a list of descriptors for a set of behaviors or goals.

Receptive language   An individual whose skills appear to be typical but who has difficulty expressing himself or herself; interactions with peers are often contentious or stilted because of the difficulty of diverting from his or her own plans or adapting to peers' perspective.

Redshirting   The practice of postponing the entrance into kindergarten of age-eligible children to allow extra time for social-emotional, intellectual, and physical growth.

Reflective practice   The active process of thinking before teaching, during teaching, and after teaching in order to make decisions about how to plan, assess, and teach.

Reggio Emilia approach   An approach to education based on the philosophy and practice that children are active constructors of their own knowledge.

Reinforcement theory The belief that consequences strengthen behavior.

Resource room A room where students work individually or in small groups with special education teachers.

Resource teachers Professionals who provide assistance with materials and planning for teachers of exceptional students.

Respectful environments Environments that show respect for each individual child and for their culture, home language, individual abilities or disabilities, family context, and community.

Response An observable reaction to a stimulus.

Response to intervention/response to instruction (RTI) A multitiered approach to the early identification and support of students with learning and behavior needs.

Responsive relationships The relationship that exists between yourself, children, and their families in which you are responsive to their needs and interests.

Rubric Scoring guide that differentiates among levels of performance.

Running record A detailed narrative of a child's behavior that focuses on a sequence of events that occur over a period of time. Includes both factual observations and teacher's inferences.

Scaffolding The process of providing various types of support, guidance, or direction during the course of an activity.

Schemes Organized units of knowledge.

School readiness When children have the knowledge and abilities necessary for success in kindergarten.

Screening A type of summative assessment that gives a broad picture of what children know and are able to do, as well as their physical health and emotional status.

Seasonal family A family with children who are engaged primarily in seasonal agricultural labor and who have not changed their residence to another geographic location in the preceding two-year period.

Secondary circular reactions Repetitive actions focused on the qualities of objects, such as their shapes, sizes, colors, and noises.

Self-actualization An inherent tendency to reach one's true potential.

Self-regulation (executive function) The ability to keep track of and control one's behavior.

Self-regulation The ability of preschool children to control their emotions and behaviors, to delay gratification, and to build positive social relations with each other.

Self-talk Speech directed to oneself that helps guide one's behavior.

Sensitive periods In the Montessori method, those relatively brief times during which learning is most likely to occur. Also called *critical periods*.

Sensitive periods Periods of developmental time during which certain things are learned more easily than at earlier or later times.

Sensorimotor stage The stage during which children learn through the senses and motor activities.

Sensory education Learning experiences involving the five senses: seeing, touching, hearing, tasting, and smelling.

Sensory materials Montessori learning materials designed to promote learning through the senses and to train the senses for learning.

Sexism Prejudice or discrimination based on sex.

Sexual harassment Unwelcome sexual behavior and talk.

Shared reading A collaborative, interactive reading process between teacher and children in which they read and share a book.

Skill deficit The term indicating that a child has not learned how to perform a particular skill or behavior.

Social constructivist approach Approaches to teaching that emphasize the social context of learning and behavior.

Social learning theory Developed by Albert Bandura to explain how children learn and gain new information by observing others.

Social play Play of children with others and in groups.

Social story A personalized, detailed, and simple script that breaks down behavior and provides rules and directions.

Sociodramatic play Play involving realistic activities and events.

Sputnik The world's first satellite.

Standards Statements of what students should know and be able to do.

STEM The areas of science, technology, engineering, and mathematics.

Stimulus An event that activates behavior.

Summative assessments Those assessments given periodically to determine at a particular point in time what students know and are able to do. Examples of summative assessments include state, end of year, and end of grading period assessments.

Supportive classroom Physical arrangement of the classroom so that it is conducive to the behaviors taught.

Supportive environments Environments in which teachers believe each child can learn and help children understand and make meaning of their experiences.

Sure Start A Department of Defense Education Activity (DoDEA) program based on the Head Start program model for command-sponsored children at overseas installations.

Symbolic play The ability of a young child to have an object stand for something else.

Symbolic representation The ability to use mental images to stand for something else.

Synaptogenesis The rapid development of neural connections.

Telegraphic speech Two-word sentences that express actions and relationships (e.g., "Milk gone").

Temperament A child's general style of behavior.

Tertiary circular reactions Modifications that infants make in their behavior to explore the effects of those modifications.

Theory A set of explanations of how children develop and learn.

Time sampling Authentic means to assess children that involves focusing on a particular behavior over a continuous period of time.

Title I Section of the Elementary and Secondary Education Act (ESEA) that provides monies to supplement the education of children from low-income families.

Title IX Amended the Constitution to state, "No person in the United States shall, on the basis of sex, be excluded from participation in, be denied the benefits of, or be subjected to discrimination under any program or activity receiving federal financial assistance."

Toddlerhood Children twelve to twenty-four months.

Tolerance The ability of children (and adults!) to recognize, accept, and respect the rights and beliefs of others.

Transdisciplinary team model Professionals from various disciplines working together to integrate instructional strategies and therapy and to evaluate the effectiveness of their individual roles.

Transition A passage from one learning setting, grade, or program to another.

Transition kindergarten (TK) A kindergarten designed to serve children who may be old enough to go to first grade but are not quite ready to handle all of its expectations.

Twice exceptional Students with dual exceptionalities.

Twitter An online social networking service and microblogging service that enables its users to send and read text-based messages.

Typically developing The majority of developmental milestones at the time at which most young children achieve them without deficits in social or communication areas.

Unfolding Process by which the nature of children—what they are to be—develops as a result of maturation according to their innate developmental schedules.

Universal design (UD) A broad-spectrum solution that helps assure that environment, curriculum, and instructional strategies are accessible to all students.

Utopian The belief that by controlling circumstances and consequent outcomes of child rearing, it is possible to build a new and more perfect society.

Vertical planning Collaboratively planning with teachers in grades below and above that which you teach.

Vocabulary knowledge Activities that emphasize words and their meanings.

Warmth Displaying or exhibiting kindness and genuine affection.

Whole-language approach Philosophy of literacy development that advocates the use of all dimensions of language, reading, writing, listening, and speaking, to help children become motivated to read and write.

Word wall Designed to promote literacy learning, collection of words displayed on a wall or another display place in the classroom.

Work sample, or student artifact An example of children's work that demonstrates what they know and are able to do. Such examples are used as evidence to assess student abilities. Work samples can be physical or electronic and come in many different forms.

Writing or writing name The ability to write letters in isolation on request or to write one's own name.

Zero reject The Individuals with Disabilities Education Act calls for educating all children and excluding none from an education. Before IDEA many children were excluded from educational programs or were denied an education.

Zone of proximal development (ZPD) The range of tasks that are too difficult to master alone but that can be learned with guidance and assistance.

INDEX

for early intervention, 275
equal opportunity and, 274
funding for, 309
goals of, 293–294, 297
guidelines (standards) of, 293
and highly educated workforce, 273–274
popularity of, 273–275
public support for, 273
as research based and cost effective, 274
resources on, 311
statistics on, 273
teachers for, 309
transition to kindergarten from, 306–308
universal preschool, 308
wellness and healthy living in, 297
working parents and, 273
Prevent Child Abuse America (PCA), 495
Primary circular reactions, 247
Primary grades (1–3). *See also* Primary grades (1–3) curriculum; Primary school children (grades 1–3)
changes in, 343–345
class size in, 356–357
contemporary schooling and, 343
data-driven instruction in, 358–359
differentiated instruction in, 361–362
diverse learners in, 343–344, 346, 347–348, 379–380
embedded instruction in, 360
English language learners (ELLs) in, 344, 361
grade-level and across-levels planning in, 344
green schools and, 379
intentional teaching in, 362
learning contexts of, 343–345
physical environment in, 355
and political and educational changes, 345
resources on, 381
Response to Instruction/Intervention (RTI) in, 359–361
social environment in, 355
teacher roles in, 344, 357–358
testing in, 344
Primary grades (1–3) curriculum. *See also* Primary grades (1–3); Primary school children (grades 1–3)
academics in generally, 344
alignment and curriculum alignment in, 358
arts in, 374
bullying education, 377–378
character education in, 353–354
common core state standards (CCSS) for, 357–361
contemporary topics in, 377–378
engineering in, 37
environmental education in, 378–379
fiscal education, 377
foreign languages in, 448–450

green curricula, 379
horticultural therapy in, 379
mathematics in, 358, 368–371
physical education in, 345
pro-social and conflict resolution education in, 355–356
reading and language arts in, 358, 362–367
science in, 372–373
social studies in, 374–376
teaching thinking, 376–377
technology use and integration in, 344–345, 376, 394
twenty-first century skills in, 378
writing skills in, 358
Primary school children (grades 1–3). *See also* Primary grades (1–3); Primary grades (1–3) curriculum
character education for, 353–354
cognitive development of, 347, 352
compared with children from earlier generations, 345–346
emotional development of, 347, 349–351
height and weight of, 346
mental health of, 350–351
moral development of, 352–354
motor development of, 346–348
physical development of, 346, 347
play and, 351
portraits of, 347
social development of, 347, 348–349, 355–356
Print awareness, 328
Print-rich environment, 331
Prison/incarcerated families, 507
Private speech (self-talk), 135, 412, 415
Problem solving, 402, 413–414, 415
Process praise, 428
Professional development. *See also* Early childhood professionals
advocacy and, 18–19
career pyramid for, 23, 24
checklist for, 28–29
for child care staff, 199
collaboration for, 18
Common Core State Standards (CCSS) and, 228–229
definition of, 17
education and certification for, 23–26, 62
ethical conduct and, 18
just in time professional development, 18
mentoring, 17
peer coaching, 17
professional learning community (PLC), 17–18
Professional Standards for Preparation of Special Education Teachers, 463
for working with families, 508
Professional dispositions, 20–21
Professional learning community (PLC), 17–18

Progressivism, 112
Project Approach, 159, 175–177, 181
Project BabyFACE, 119
Proprietary child care, 186, 191–192
Prosocial behavior, 355–356, 422–423
Proximodistal development, 243
Pruning (neural shearing), 241
Psychosocial development theory, 145–147
PTA. *See* National Parent Teacher Association (PTA)
Puberty, 348
Public policy. *See also* Federal government; Head Start
child care and, 184–185
definition of, 37, 38
for primary grades (1–3), 345
Punishment. *See* Discipline

QuickTalker12, 392

Race. *See* Cultural diversity; *and specific racial and ethnic group, such as* Hispanics
Raising Our Children's Children (ROCC), 502
RAN. *See* Rapid automatic naming (RAN) *headings*
Rapid automatic naming (RAN) of letters or digits, 298
Rapid automatic naming (RAN) of objects or colors, 298
Rating scales, 70, 75–76
Readiness. *See* School readiness
Reading. *See also* Literacy education
arts integrated in, 338
balanced approach to, 331
children's literature and, 365–367
Common Core State Standards (CCSS) for, 225
as conventional literacy skill, 298
goal of reading by entry into first grade, 314
guided reading, 363–364
home libraries and, 512, 515
instructional approaches to, 329–335
instructional strategies for struggling readers, 365
instructional terminology on, 328
in kindergarten, 329–335
language experience approach to, 330
literacy circles, 364–365, 366–367
phonics instruction for, 330
in primary grades (1–3), 358, 362–367
print-rich environment for, 331
read or fail policy in primary grades, 362–363
reader's workshop, 333, 335
SE Model of lesson planning for, 332–333
shared reading, 331–332
technology for, 330, 398
whole-language approach to, 330–331
whole-word approach to, 329

PHOTO CREDITS